"Byrd and Luke have created a meaningful text focused on strengths-based approaches with an emphasis on multicultural sensitivity and social justice. At the heart of this book is respect and admiration for child and adolescent clients and for reaching an often-underserved population."
—**Bradley T. Erford,** *PhD, professor in the Department of Human Development Counseling at Peabody College at Vanderbilt University and former president of the American Counseling Association*

"Master's level counselor education programs primarily prepare counselors to work with adults. In this comprehensive book, the experienced authors do a masterful job of teaching counselors how to use a strengths-based approach when counseling children and adolescents."
—**Theodore P. Remley, Jr,** *contributing faculty member in the PhD program in counselor education and supervision at Walden University and professor of counseling at the University of Holy Cross*

"This long-awaited textbook resonates with me. It imparts extensive wisdom and knowledge, sustains a strengths-based lens throughout its chapters, instills hopes, and promotes growth for child clinicians and clinicians to be."
—**Yumiko Ogawa,** *PhD, associate professor at the Department of Counselor Education at New Jersey City University*

Counseling Children and Adolescents

Counseling Children and Adolescents focuses on relationship building and creating a deep level of understanding of developmental, attachment, and brain-based information.

Chapters place a clear emphasis on building strengths and developing empathy, awareness, and skills. By going beyond theory, and offering a strengths-based, attachment, neuro- and trauma-informed perspective, this text offers real-world situations and tried and true techniques for working with children and adolescents. Grounded in research and multicultural competency, the book focuses on encouragement, recognizing resiliency, and empowerment.

This book is an ideal guide for counselors looking for developmentally appropriate strategies to empower children and adolescents.

Rebekah Byrd, PhD, LPC (TN), LCMHC (NC), NCC, RPT-S, ACS, is an associate professor of counseling and the clinical experiences coordinator at Sacred Heart University.

Chad Luke, PhD, LPC/MHSP (TN), NCC, ACS, MAC, is an associate professor of counseling at Tennessee Tech University.

Counseling Children and Adolescents
Cultivating Empathic Connection

Rebekah Byrd and Chad Luke

NEW YORK AND LONDON

First published 2021
by Routledge
52 Vanderbilt Avenue, New York, NY 10017

and by Routledge
2 Park Square, Milton Park, Abingdon, Oxon, OX14 4RN

Routledge is an imprint of the Taylor & Francis Group, an informa business

© 2021 Rebekah Byrd and Chad Luke

The right of Rebekah Byrd and Chad Luke to be identified as authors of this work has been asserted by them in accordance with sections 77 and 78 of the Copyright, Designs and Patents Act 1988.

All rights reserved. No part of this book may be reprinted or reproduced or utilised in any form or by any electronic, mechanical, or other means, now known or hereafter invented, including photocopying and recording, or in any information storage or retrieval system, without permission in writing from the publishers.

Trademark notice: Product or corporate names may be trademarks or registered trademarks, and are used only for identification and explanation without intent to infringe.

Library of Congress Cataloging-in-Publication Data
A catalog record for this book has been requested

ISBN: 978-0-8153-9580-5 (hbk)
ISBN: 978-0-8153-9581-2 (pbk)
ISBN: 978-1-351-13315-9 (ebk)

Typeset in Sabon
by Apex CoVantage, LLC

Visit the Support Material: https://www.routledge.com/9780815395812

This book is dedicated to my wonderful children. Thank you for giving me endless chances to do and be better. I love you more than life.

– Rebekah

To my darling daughter, who challenges me and encourages me every day to be more fully human. You are the "heart of my sunshine".

– "D"

Contents

List of Tables   xi
List of Figures   xii
Guest Contributors   xiii
Foreword   xvii
Preface   xix
Acknowledgments   xxi

PART I
Knowledge   1

1 Introduction and Recognition of the Privilege of Counseling Children and Adolescents   3
REBEKAH BYRD AND CHAD LUKE

2 Strategies and Interventions for Empathic Connection   16
REBEKAH BYRD AND CHAD LUKE

3 A Review of Theories as Related to Children and Adolescents   34
CHAD LUKE AND REBEKAH BYRD

4 Understanding Attachment and Development Aspects of Children and Adolescents   52
EMILY DONALD, CHAD LUKE, AND REBEKAH BYRD

PART II
Awareness   67

5 Legal and Ethical Implications for Working With Minors   69
THEODORE P. REMLEY, JR., REBEKAH BYRD, AND CHAD LUKE

6 Family Counseling   93
JAMES BITTER, REBEKAH BYRD, AND CHAD LUKE

7 Parents, Caregivers, and Supportive Adults   110
REBEKAH BYRD AND CHAD LUKE

8 Trauma and the Child and Adolescent Brain 123
CHAD LUKE AND REBEKAH BYRD

9 At-Promise Children and Adolescents 138
CHARMAYNE ADAMS, JILLIAN BLUEFORD, CHAD LUKE, AND REBEKAH BYRD

PART III
Specific Skills, Theories, and Techniques 163

10 Children and Adolescents With Myriad Presenting Concerns 165
REBEKAH BYRD, AMANDA LAGUARDIA, AND CHAD LUKE

11 Grief and Loss Issues in Children and Adolescents 196
REBEKAH BYRD AND CHAD LUKE

12 Working With Transgender and Gender-Expansive Children and Adolescents 210
REBEKAH BYRD, MICKEY WHITE, AND CHAD LUKE

13 LGB Children and Adolescents 226
REBEKAH BYRD, CHRISTIAN CHAN, AND CHAD LUKE

14 Celebrating Diversity 246
CHAD LUKE AND REBEKAH BYRD

15 Play Therapy 257
REBEKAH BYRD, TERESA CHRISTENSEN, AND CHAD LUKE

16 Sandtray Therapy 277
SONYA LORELLE, REBEKAH BYRD, AND CHAD LUKE

17 Mindfulness Techniques for Working With Children and Adolescents 293
REBEKAH BYRD, REBECCA MILNER, AND CHAD LUKE

18 Expressive and Experiential Techniques 318
REBEKAH BYRD, SYBIL SMITH, AND CHAD LUKE

Appendix: Empowering Our Youth Resource Guide 336
Index 340

Tables

1.1	Perceived Negative Trait vs. Perceived Positive Trait	4
1.2	Using the Following Scale, Rate the Areas Regarding Frequency	8
2.1	Personal Factors That Influence Change	19
2.2	Identifying the Mistaken Goals of Children's Misbehavior	24
3.1	Discerning What and Where It Hurts	37
3.2	Psychopathology Is Relational and Meaningful	43
3.3	Psychopathology Is Historical and Developmental	44
3.4	Psychopathology Is Behavioral	46
3.5	Constructivist/Postmodern Views	47
3.6	Applications of Theory	48
8.1	Eight Dimensions of Stress Applied to Child/Adolescent	128
10.1	Assessments for Screening and Treatment of Non-Suicidal Self-Injury	171
10.2	Approaches to Suicide Prevention in Youth	173
10.3	Examples of Children or Teenagers Who May Qualify for Special Health and/or Behavioral Accommodations and Support in a School Setting	181
10.4	MI Theory Summary Chart	184
11.1	Adolescent Loss, Grief, and Trauma Responses	199
14.1	Emergent Model of the Individual Client Experience	250
14.2	Considerations for Multicultural Competency Domains	251
15.1	Travel Play Therapy Kit Supplies	273
16.1	Categories and Example Figures	280
17.1	Benefits From Mindfulness-Based Interventions	302
17.2	Child and Adolescent Mindfulness Measure (CAMM)	303
18.1	Challenges That Wilderness Therapy Is Successful in Treating	320
18.2	Community and Mental Health Settings Where Drama Therapists Work	329

Figures

2.1	Wellness Wheel	29
3.1	8-Factor Meta Model	39
6.1	Genogram of Lana and Patrick's Family	97
11.1	Common Manifestations of Grief Among Children	200
11.2	Continuum of Three Primary Styles of Grieving	203
11.3	Stroebe and Schut Dual Process Model	204
14.1	Adaptation of Fouad and Kantamneni's Model of Cultural Dimensions	252
14.2	Client-Related Dimensions	253
15.1	Therapeutic Powers of Play	260
16.1	Elliot's Initial Sand Tray	289
16.2	Elliot's Final Sand Tray	289

Guest Contributors

Acknowledging that this book covers many topics discussed in many separate books and separate classes (see Preface), we wanted to invite some experts to assist in our writing process. We are grateful and feel extremely honored that so many wonderful, skilled, and dedicated professionals were willing to work with us and write chapters in collaboration with us. We wanted this to provide readers with many expert voices that we have hopefully presented in a uniform fashion. Thank you all for being willing to write chapters with us, exchange ideas, and work so collaboratively to provide such helpful information. We know this will impact the lives of so many children and adolescents (and counselors)! Thank you again for the work you do and keep doing! We are grateful for you!

Charmayne Adams, Ph.D., LIMHP, NCC (she/hers) is Assistant Professor in the Department of Counseling at the University of Nebraska Omaha, an Independently Licensed Mental Health Provider in the state of Nebraska, and a Nationally Certified Counselor (NCC). Her work has primarily been with individuals in crisis or with a history of trauma. Additionally, she currently teaches the crisis and trauma course for the Department of Counseling at UNO. She has published and presented locally, regionally, and nationally on the topics of trauma-informed crisis intervention services, supporting vulnerable populations in times of crisis, and emotionally focused therapy with individuals in residential treatment.

James Bitter, Ed.D., (he/him) is Professor of Counseling and Human Services at East Tennessee State University in Johnson City, TN. He is a diplomate in Adlerian psychology (NASAP, 2002), and the former Editor of the *Journal of Individual Psychology*. He is the past President of the North American Society of Adlerian Psychology (NASAP), a position he held from 2016–2018. James is the author or co-author of four books, including *Adlerian Group Counseling and Therapy: Step-by-Step* (2004, with Manford Sonstegard); *Contributions to Adlerian Psychology* (2011); and *The Theory and Practice of Family Therapy and Counseling* (3rd ed., 2020). He has also authored more than 70 journal articles, chapters, and videotapes. He is the featured master therapist on the video for Adlerian family therapy on the Psychotherapy.net series *Family Therapy with the Experts*.

Jillian Blueford, Ph.D., LPC-C, NCC (she/hers) is a clinical assistant professor for the online school counseling graduate program at the University of Denver. Her professional clinical background includes working alongside children, adolescents, adults, and families in a variety of settings and primarily through a grief and loss focus. She is a Licensed Professional Counselor Candidate (Colorado) and a National Certified Counselor. Dr. Blueford's research focuses primarily on professional counselor competency in grief counseling, developing systemic grief models for professional counselors, and children and adolescent grief.

xiv *Guest Contributors*

Christian Chan, Ph.D., NCC (he/him) is an assistant professor in the Department of Counseling and Educational Development at The University of North Carolina at Greensboro, President of the Association for Adult Development and Aging (AADA), and a proud queer person of color. As a scholar-activist, his interests revolve around intersectionality; multiculturalism in counseling practice, supervision, and counselor education; social justice and activism; career development; critical research methodologies; and couples, family, and group modalities with socialization/communication of culture and social identities. As a recent recipient of the AADA President's Outstanding Service Award and Association for Lesbian, Gay, Bisexual, and Transgender Issues in Counseling (ALGBTIC) Ned Farley Service Award, he has actively contributed to over 36 peer-reviewed publications in journals, books, and edited volumes and has conducted over 115 refereed presentations at the national, regional, and state levels.

Teresa M. Christensen, Ph.D., LPC, NCC, RPT-S (she/hers) received a B.A. in both psychology and sociology from Adams State University. She earned a master's in mental health counseling and a Ph.D. in counselor education and supervision from Idaho State University. Teresa is currently a professor of counseling at Regis University and serves as the coordinator for the Counseling Children and Adolescents Post-Graduate Certificate. She developed the Regis University Center for Counseling and Play Therapy, approved by the Association for Play Therapy; and has been a Licensed Professional Counselor in Colorado, Virginia, Louisiana, and Idaho. She is also a Nationally Certified Counselor (NCC) and a Registered Play Therapist-Supervisor (RPT-S) who has counseled children, adolescents, and families for over 27 years. Prior to teaching at Regis, Teresa was a professor of counseling at Old Dominion University in Virginia and the University of New Orleans. In 2010, she started the Italy Play Therapy Institute taking place in Tuscany every spring. Teresa is a member of various professional organizations, has published several articles and book chapters, and has presented at various national and international conferences.

Emily Donald, Ph.D., LPC-S (NC), NCC, ACS, RPT (she/hers) is a counselor educator, Registered Play Therapist, Approved Clinical Supervisor, National Certified Counselor, and Licensed Clinical Mental Health Supervisor. She has a master's in community counseling and a Ph.D. in counseling from the University of North Carolina at Charlotte, where her studies included a focus on multicultural issues in counseling. Prior to moving into the world of counselor education, Dr. Donald worked in an agency setting serving clients ages three and up. Dr. Donald focuses much of her work on supporting students learning to work with children, adolescents, and their caregivers, and this is evident in her teaching, research, and presentation history. Overall, her research interests include play therapy and work with caregivers of children, supervision and teaching, and multiculturalism and social justice.

Amanda LaGuardia, Ph.D., LPCC-S (she/hers) is an associate professor of mental health counseling at the University of Cincinnati and a Licensed Professional Clinical Counselor Supervisor in Ohio. She holds a Ph.D. in counseling from Old Dominion University and received her M.A. in marriage and family and community counseling from East Tennessee State University. She is an assistant editor for *Counselor Education and Supervision* and was president of Chi Sigma Iota International (2019–2020). She specializes in working with children and families, researching and treating concerns related to trauma, non-suicidal self-injury, collaborative care, and gender/women's issues.

Sonya Lorelle, Ph.D., LCPC, RPT-S (she/hers) is Clinical Training Director for the counseling program at the Family Institute at Northwestern University. She holds a Ph.D. in counselor education from Old Dominion University and received her M.S. in community agency counseling from Missouri State University. She is a Licensed Clinical Professional Counselor in Illinois. She has worked as the children's counselor at an agency that provides services to homeless families and is a Registered Play Therapist Supervisor. She is on the board of the Illinois Play Therapy Association. Dr. Lorelle also has interest in international counseling and has volunteered to provide counseling services and play therapy education in several countries in Asia.

Rebecca Milner Ph.D., LPC (VA), LPC-MHSP (TN) (she/hers) is Assistant Professor and Counseling Program Coordinator at East Tennessee State University. She has an M.A. in community counseling, educational specialist, and a Ph.D. in counseling and supervision from James Madison University. She is a Licensed Professional Counselor in Virginia and Tennessee. She has previously worked as a generalist at a university counseling center and in psychological and risk assessment in a hospital. She is trained in Intergroup Dialogue and is a Qualified Administrator of the Intercultural Development Inventory. She is passionate about counselor education, the use of creativity in counseling, multiculturalism, and social justice.

Theodore P. Remley, Jr. Ph.D., LPC, NCC (he/him) is a professor of counseling at the University of Holy Cross in New Orleans, Louisiana. Dr. Remley holds a Ph.D. in counselor education from the University of Florida and a law degree (JD) from Catholic University in Washington, D.C. He is a National Certified Counselor (NCC) and a member of the Chi Sigma Iota national scholarship honorary in counseling. He is licensed as a Professional Counselor (LPC) in Louisiana and Mississippi and is licensed to practice law in Virginia and Florida. Dr. Remley is the author and co-author of a number of articles, books, and book chapters related to legal and ethical issues in counseling. For more than 17 years, he has directed very popular counselor institutes in Italy and Ireland, and in cooperation with the National Board of Certified Counselors (NBCC), in Bhutan, France, Argentina, and Malawi. Since 2015, Dr. Remley has directed the annual national refereed Law and Ethics in Counseling Conference held each year in New Orleans. Dr. Remley has been a school counselor and a college counselor and practiced law for seven years.

Sybil Smith M.A., LPC/MHSP, MT-BC, FAMI (she/hers) is a psychotherapist, approved clinical supervisor, board certified music therapist, and an assistant trainer for The Bonny Method of Guided Imagery and Music (GIM), with a passion for creativity and education. She received her bachelors in music therapy from Tennessee Technological University and her master's in marriage and family therapy from East Tennessee State University, and has extended training in DARE, EMDR, MARI, and GIM. Her clinical work has ranged from pre-K children through geriatric populations, with a special interest in creativity in the healing process and the way trauma affects human development and attachment. She is the co-owner of a group practice, The Journey Center for Healing Arts, an experiential trauma-focused practice in Johnson City, Tennessee, and focuses on creativity in clinical supervision and teaching GIM.

Mickey White, Ph.D., NCC (he/him) is a counselor educator and National Certified Counselor at East Tennessee State University. He has a master's in clinical mental health counseling and a Ph.D. in counseling from the University of North Texas. His clinical experiences include work in hospitals and community settings with children, adolescents, and adults, with a focus on LGBTGEQIAP+ populations. His research and professional interests primarily center on intersectionality of identities for transgender and gender-expansive individuals, particularly transgender people of color.

Additional research interests include liberatory pedagogical approaches in counselor education, multiculturalism and social justice, and the process of identity disclosure in counseling.

We also want to thank the many experts and compassionate counselors who wrote clinician's corners for the chapters. We hope these help the material come alive and seem applicable!

Foreword

If you have ever taken a look at child and adolescent counseling textbooks, you have likely noticed one of three things: textbooks that fail to cover important topics, textbooks that try to be comprehensive but lack detail and depth, and textbooks that simply regurgitate adult concepts under the guise of developmentally appropriate adaptations. If you had a textbook from each of these categories, together, they might provide enough information to educate those seeking to be child and adolescent counselors.

If individuals surveyed all of the boards of licensure and educational requirements necessary to become a licensed counselor, you would also notice that few states require specific coursework about child and adolescent counseling in order to work with these populations. Unless you were studying to become a school counselor, you might never have to consider the needs of children and adolescents, other than through a human development course. Part of a single course is not enough to develop competent practitioners.

From this observation, one could deduce that child and adolescent counseling does not garner enough time and attention. In essence and in the end, child and adolescent treatment suffers.

In the realm of mental health, children and adolescents get the proverbial "short end of the stick". In most states, they do not have the ability to consent to treatment and their care is left up to caregivers, those within education, and health and mental health professionals. Other than being asked for details about a particular situation, their experiences do not play into the decided courses of action. Assuming that those entrusted with the care of children and adolescents gather comprehensive and appropriate information, all too often the course of action is based on adult research rather than child and adolescent research. Children and adolescents are not little adults!

We have ample information about child and adolescent physical, social, cognitive, emotional, and brain development; yet, in a fast-paced society, seldom is this given the consideration it is due. Too quickly we rush to conceptualize, and too infrequently do we give the time and attention needed to understand. A supervisor of mine once said, "Don't understand too quickly". When he said this, he did not preface this as only applicable to adults. He left the interpretation open, so that I would consider this for all individuals regardless of where each is in their lifespan.

Life and our experiences of it are complicated and those trusted with the care of children and adolescents should realize that a single glimpse is at best a cloudy picture. Add to an individual's day-to-day experiences adverse events, and the glimpse moves from cloudy to blurry to occluded. The mantra that should follow and become engrained in the minds of those entrusted with the care of children and adolescents is: "We need to do better".

What's needed is better, comprehensive education for counselors in training. Changing educational requirements takes time; so, in the meantime, what's needed is a textbook that focuses on developing a foundational set of skills and competencies that applies research-derived principles specifically to the needs of children and adolescents. As such, the book *Counseling Children and Adolescents: Cultivating Empathic Connection* makes the shift as it outlines a new foundation for helping children and adolescents. Its chapters focus on the core principles of helping relationships and diversity, and teach us how to be ethical and accountable for what we do to help children and adolescents. Through attachment and brain science research, the authors and guest contributors demonstrate that their coverage of topics is current and truly developmentally focused. The scope of this text covers individual and systems theories, a myriad of issues, and developmentally sensitive therapeutic applications.

With this text, and hopefully others that follow its lead, should come a realization that children and adolescents need to be treated with respect. One should come to understand that child and adolescent treatment should be a routine subject in all counselor training programs and in the educational requirements for licensure. Our codes of ethics include passages that cover competency to practice and accountability of actions. However, are these codes routinely applied to those, with little training, that end up working with children and adolescents? Why is this allowed, and who will say things must change?

Edward F. Hudspeth, PhD, NCC, LPC-S, ACS, RPT-S, RPh, CPC
Associate Professor and Program Director
Clinical Mental Health Counseling
Sacred Heart University

Preface

Purpose of Text

First of all, we would like to thank you for selecting this text. We want to acknowledge that this was a labor of love and grief. This text was born out of love for the children and adolescents we serve. We have the utmost adoration and respect for the children and adolescents that grace us with time in their lives. This text was also born out of a deep and profound grief for how children and adolescents are too often treated in our society. We have observed the persistent objectification and dehumanization of the youngest of our society, and this continues.

Our purpose with this text is to offer strengths-based approaches to working with children and adolescents. We also feel strongly that if counselors understand children and adolescents from an attachment, trauma-informed, neuro-informed perspective, the techniques you use will be that much more meaningful and successful. Whether you use play therapy, art, mindfulness, or other techniques in your work with children and adolescents, understanding the foundations of attachment, the impact of trauma, and the ways in which their brains work will make your work more meaningful, beneficial, and successful.

We have offered developmentally appropriate techniques, trauma-informed material, and practice-based approaches that take into consideration the person of the child and/or adolescent – instead of asking the child or adolescent to rely on talk therapy approaches. We have also empowered you – the counselor – and armed you with information to feel confident in your role and to advocate on behalf of your clients and yourselves.

We are aware that we cannot provide full coverage to all significant and imperative topics related to counseling children and adolescents. We have grappled all along the way to make a text that honors and empowers the unique person of each child, adolescent, and parent/caregiver with whom we have had the privilege to work. We also grieve the fact that little to no accreditation standards exist for training professionals to work with children and adolescents, and all too often the work is relegated to one class – often an elective. Often what is present in multiple separate classes normed on adult clients (theories, legal and ethical issues, diversity, trauma, etc.) is addressed in *a single class* on children and adolescents – making any text on the topic seem incomplete and certainly lacking in information; any of these topics for adults each have their own dedicated class and textbook.

We are excited to offer our list of chapters and topics we believe to be acutely important. We have attempted to acknowledge some topics that could not be fully addressed in this text by adding resources (this is located in the Appendix).

Content

What you will find in this text is an overview of many topics related to child and adolescent counseling. Research shows that counselors in training must understand knowledge and awareness before skills can be developed and strengthened. This text takes that approach to learning. The first four chapters focus on knowledge. Part I includes Chapter 1: *Introduction and Recognition of the Privilege of Counseling Children and Adolescents*; Chapter 2: *Strategies and Interventions for Empathic Connection*; Chapter 3: *A Review of Theories as Related to Children and Adolescents*; Chapter 4: *Understanding Attachment and Development Aspects of Children and Adolescents*.

Part II addresses awareness and includes Chapter 5: *Legal and Ethical Implications for Working With Minors;* Chapter 6: *Family Counseling*; Chapter 7: *Parents, Caregivers, and Supportive Adults*; Chapter 8: *Trauma and the Child and Adolescent Brain*; Chapter 9: *At-Promise Children and Adolescents*.

Part III is dedicated to specific skills, theories, and techniques. While this is not a theories text, we will address some theories as applied to child and adolescent counseling. We also understand that we addressed many techniques and approaches to working with children and adolescents that require additional training and expertise. We hope that by learning about these, you will feel inspired to learn more on your own as this is certainly not comprehensive. The chapters in this section include Chapter 10: *Children and Adolescents With Myriad Presenting Concerns*; Chapter 11: *Grief and Loss Issues in Children and Adolescents*; Chapter 12: *Working with Transgender and Gender-Expansive Children and Adolescents*; Chapter 13: *LGB Children and Adolescents*; Chapter 14: *Celebrating Diversity*; Chapter 15: *Play Therapy*; Chapter 16: *Sandtray Therapy*; Chapter 17: *Mindfulness Techniques for Working with Children and Adolescents*; Chapter 18: *Expressive and Experiential Techniques*.

Emphasis of the Text

This text aims to encourage and empower the child and adolescent through strengths-based approaches. We have observed all too often counselors feeling defeated and unprepared to work with children and adolescents. We have also observed the frustration that occurs on the part of both the counselor and the client when this happens. This text offers information and skills that address the needs of children and adolescents. We have emphasized numerous considerations and offer many approaches for working successfully with child and adolescent clients. We believe these approaches to be beneficial and believe these approaches assist the client in feeling valued and understood. It is also our mission to infuse social justice and multicultural awareness into everything we do as counselor educators. The book as a whole takes a social justice approach to teaching and learning. While we do have a chapter on celebrating diversity, you will discover that this is an emphasis woven throughout the text and in every encounter we have. It is imperative for counselors to advocate for our clients and for our society as a whole.

Pedagogical Elements in the Text

Included in each chapter are objectives and focus questions (self-awareness questions) for you to consider as you read. Summaries at the end of each chapter are also present for your use. Each chapter has a PowerPoint associated and resources are available in the Appendix for many important topics not covered in this first edition.

A special feature we are excited about is having a "Clinician's Corner" section where a clinician shares a few paragraphs about a specific technique that resonated with a client, a self-reflective "aha!" moment for them in training/counseling, a brief story about the power of counseling and the amazing qualities of children and adolescents, etc. We have included these in each chapter.

Acknowledgments

This book would not have been possible without first acknowledging all of the many children and adolescents who have taught us along the way. We thank them from the depths of our hearts. We would also like to thank our guest contributors – we have wonderful colleagues and experts to work with and we are so grateful you gave your time, energy, and expertise to assist us with this text. Thank you also to everyone to helped make the Clinician's Corners wonderful and engaging. To our group of guest contributors and Clinician's Corners authors – thank you for the work you do in our profession and for children and adolescents. You all are truly an amazing group of colleagues and friends. We also want to thank Abby Frantom and Alison Love for helping read chapters, provide feedback as graduate students (for whom this book was written) – and thank you Alison for doing an awesome job on almost all of the PowerPoints! We appreciate your support and encouragement along this long process as well. To my (Rebekah) wonderful creative two children – thank you for painting the picture on the front cover – keep producing art and expressing yourselves in your own creative and unique ways! Thank you to the many wonderful people at Routledge who believed in this text from the very beginning. Anna – you have been encouraging and supportive, and we thank you so much for that. Routledge – thank you for all you do. This book would not have been possible without you. Thank you to our families who are probably more excited that this book is complete than even we are – thank you for believing in this process even when we were too tired to do so ourselves. Thank you all so very much!

Part I
Knowledge

1 Introduction and Recognition of the Privilege of Counseling Children and Adolescents

Rebekah Byrd and Chad Luke

Objectives

- Describe and define many key terms from this chapter.
- Understand the importance of utilizing a strengths-based approach to working with children and adolescents.
- Analyze the benefits of the counseling relationship.
- Identify ways in which stress and distress manifest for you specifically.
- Examine techniques for self-care.
- Evaluate the importance of being one supportive adult.

Reflective Questions

- What brought me to the field of counseling children and adolescents? What will keep my passion for working with them (even in complex systems)?
- In what ways will I make sure my approach to working with children and adolescents is strengths-based? How will I help model this approach for others?
- What "Tenets for Relating to Children" do I need to pay more attention to?
- How can I start understanding stress, distress, burnout, and impairment while still in training?
- What are my current self-care practices?
- In what ways can I become more self-compassionate?
- How important do I believe the "power of one" can be in counseling?

The Heart and Passion for Counseling Children and Adolescents

We have seen, as we are sure many of you have, the passion that exists in many for counseling children and adolescents. While many are terrified to work with children and adolescents, there are those of us who couldn't imagine ourselves doing anything else. Since we were young ourselves, we were drawn to children and adolescents; their wonder, their curiosities, their imaginations, their ability to explore and play for hours on end. We enter graduate school and training programs with hearts for supporting and encouraging children and adolescents however we can. We progress through our programs and do just that. Then one day, we find ourselves in a system (community, agency, school, etc.) where we feel those passions are dwindling. We are overwhelmed with unmet needs, underserved populations, ignored diversity issues, and blatant racism, paperwork, and bureaucracy. The passion for working with children and adolescents seems not enough to sustain heavy caseloads and inadequate support and resources.

Hopefully, this book will assist in preparation and skill building on the front end so that the passion reaches the end of the day and the end of the (never-ending) caseloads and ever-present needs. Don't lose this passion! Remember why you wanted to do this work! When the days are never as long as the list of concerns, remember your love and heart for children and adolescents, and how it started in the first place.

Strengths-Based Approach

When many aspects of a child/adolescent's life may seem deficit and competition focused, it stands out for counselors to be focused on strengths. Counseling and treatment need not focus primarily on what is broken but instead need to cultivate and encourage what is positive and good within (Seligman, 1999). Understanding that all children and adolescents have strengths, it is the counselor's job to find these and build upon them – even when the child/adolescent cannot seem to see these strengths in themselves.

While focusing on strengths is certainly not a new concept, we need reminding. Counselors also serve as models for the other counselors around them, caseworkers, parents/caregivers, physicians, and entire treatment teams. Modeling a strengths-based approach is also an important part of advocating for that child and adolescent. You can turn most anything into a strength. Even something that may be troubling and/or annoying could have been (and most likely was) at some point a protective factor. Try to think of some more positive traits for each perceived negative trait listed in Table 1.1.

We have personally observed many times when working with children and adolescents the all too popular "I dunno" shoulder shrug when we have discussed positive self-characteristics. Sometimes we think this is because we teach people in our society not to "brag" or "boast", but more often we have found it is actually because they simply do not know. They do not know or cannot recognize one *single* positive characteristic within themselves. This breaks our hearts every time. It is the counselor's job to not only recognize these within them, but to work with them in hopes that they believe them and can start to recognize these within themselves. We must believe in our children and adolescents so that they can learn to believe in themselves.

Increasing research has focused on "at-risk" youth. However, it is also important to understand that at any given point in a child/adolescent's life, "even the most advantaged youth may be at risk for participating in or developing problematic behaviors" (Smith, 2006, p. 14). Strengths-base counseling theory is founded on multicultural counseling research and concepts and in prevention research literature (Smith, 2006). Understanding

Table 1.1 Perceived Negative Trait vs. Perceived Positive Trait

Perceived Negative Trait	*Perceived Positive Trait*
Stubborn	Determined
Bossy	Leadership skills
Shy	Observant
Tattletale	Honest/Ethical
Pleaser	Respectful
Loud	Excited
Rowdy	Energetic
Messy	Creative
Selfish	Protective
Arrogant	Confident
Sensitive	Empathic
Slow	Careful/Thorough

strengths can mean understanding the ways in which individuals cope with difficult situations. Further, strengths are ever evolving, changing, adapting, and growing traits rooted in the individual's culture (Smith, 2006). Smith describes strengths that can be: culturally bound (related to or found in one's culture), contextually based (developed or understood within a given or specific situation or context), developmental and lifespan oriented (age related, learned, and/or taught), adaptable and functional (ability to be adapted and/or applied in different situations), normed on society/culture/environment, transcendence (strengths assist in transcending life's hardships), and polarities (develop from polarities). Let's understand the information and research on "at-risk" youth, but let's change our lens to understanding the children and adolescents that are, instead, "at promise".

Empowering Children and Adolescents

It is estimated that a little over 74 million children and adolescents under the age of 18 reside in the United States and Puerto Rico (U.S. Census Bureau, 2018). In the United States, about 1 out of every 4–5 youth (ages 13–18) meets criteria for a mental health diagnosis with lasting impairment noted across their lifetime (Merikangas et al., 2010). Further, this same study noted ages of onset for major disorders such as "50% of disorders had their onset by age 6 for anxiety disorders, by age 11 for behavior disorders, and by age 13 for mood disorders and by age 15 for substance use disorders" (Merikangas et al., 2010, p. 987). A review of the literature reveals that only a minority of children and adolescents with mental health needs are able to access treatment (Reardon et al., 2017). Further, Twenge (2017) notes that even previous generations are still at substantial risk as we "are at the forefront of the worst mental health crisis in decades, with rates of teen depression and suicide skyrocketing since 2011" (p. 3).

These statistics point to the issue of children and adolescents needing help, and yet not receiving it. Counselors working in community agency settings are overloaded, and yet only see a small percentage of the child and adolescent population in need of these services. The children and adolescents who are still in need of services either seek help at school or do not receive the help they need. The National Association for College Admission Counseling (NACAC) and the American School Counselor Association (ASCA) conducted a 10-year report of national student-to-counselor ratios. This report noted that the national student-to-counselor ratio in the schools is an overwhelming 482 students to every *one* school counselor. It seems safe to say that children and adolescents are in need of services they are not receiving. As a note, the American School Counseling Association (2012) advocates for student-to-counselor ratios of 250:1. This is almost *half* of the current national average.

Counseling Children and Adolescents

It appears that most counseling programs teach classes based on adult populations. Students may have the choice of one or two classes specific to working with children and adolescents while the rest of their program of study is heavily reliant on skills, theory, techniques, and issues pertaining to an adult population. Transferring this knowledge and awareness to a child and adolescent population can be challenging without the proper tools. We hope that this book will provide you with some tools so that you feel confident and prepared to navigate this important work.

We will discuss the importance of the counseling relationship in the next section, but I ask you to keep the counseling relationship and yourself as a key component in that relationship, in mind as you read the following. Please ask yourself to what extent you believe the following – and be honest with your beliefs.

Tenets for Relating to Children

- **Children are not miniature adults.** The therapist does not respond to them as if they were.
- **Children are people.** They are capable of experiencing deep emotional pain and joy.
- **Children are unique and worthy of respect.** The therapist prizes the uniqueness of each child and respects the person the child is.
- **Children are resilient.** Children possess tremendous capacity to overcome obstacles and circumstances in their lives.
- **Children have an inherent tendency toward growth and maturity.** They possess an inner intuitive wisdom.
- **Children are capable of positive self-direction.** They are capable of dealing with their world in creative ways.
- **Children's natural language is play.** This is the medium of self-expression with which they are most comfortable.
- **Children have a right to remain silent.** The therapist respects a child's decision not to talk.
- **Children will take the therapeutic experience to where they need to be.** The therapist does not attempt to determine when or how a child should play.
- **Children's growth cannot be sped up.** The therapist recognizes this and is patient with the child's developmental process.

(Landreth, 2012, p. 46)

How did you do on that self-assessment? Can you recognize some areas in which you may be challenged? Can you recognize some areas in which you excel? You aren't expected to have this all figured out quite yet, but keep pondering over these tenets. This list is so important and serves as such a wonderful grounding technique that you will see this list again in Chapter 15 of this volume. We also recommend putting the list on your computer or your office wall as a constant reminder and foundation for the work we do with children/adolescents.

The Benefits of the Counseling Relationship

Rapport and the therapeutic alliance are of utmost importance. Researchers have noted that independent of the many approaches to counseling, treatment, and therapeutic measures, the client-counselor relationship is a predictor of positive clinical outcomes (Ardito & Rabellino, 2011; Horvath & Bedi, 2002; Norcross, 2002). Davidson and Scott (2009) note that "a therapist who lacks the ability and skill to form a strong collaborative relationship will be ineffective, no matter how many technical interventions they can perform, as alliance is necessary for engagement" (p. 122). Having a strong client-counselor alliance is imperative for growth and change to occur. Competence is also just as important. When the alliance is formed, and the client is motivated, the counselor must possess competence for working with that unique individual (Trepka, Rees, Shapiro, Hardy, & Barkham, 2004).

Stress, Distress, and Burnout

Stress is defined as:

> a physical, mental, or emotional factor that causes bodily or mental tension. Stresses can be external (from the environment, psychological, or social situations) or internal

(illness, or from a medical procedure). Stress can initiate the "fight or flight" response, a complex reaction of neurologic and endocrinologic systems.

(MedicineNet, 2016, para 1)

Counselors experience stress in many ways. Counselors are stressed about increasing caseloads, changing and growing paperwork, unmet needs, decreases in resources, client struggles, client trauma, community events, natural disasters, abuse, legal mandates, ethical dilemmas, managed care, and the list goes on and on. Counselors can be bombarded with client trauma, a need to lead at their agency/school, and growing demands on their time, empathy reserves, and energy. Counselors also struggle to manage the emotional, mental, and physical challenges of caring for clients (Osborn, 2004) that is unique to those in the helping profession.

When someone is stressed, each individual will handle that stress in his/her own unique way. It is important to understand how you personally respond to stress. When you are stressed, what do you do to cope? How do you feel? Where do you feel your stress in your body? Since this can manifest differently for everyone, it is important to recognize your unique signs. Understanding how you personally deal with stress is imperative to your being able to effectively manage stress so that it doesn't lead to distress, burnout, and/or impairment.

Stress is inherent to any job and is a normal part of life, but counselors and those in the helping profession often find stress related to working with individuals more difficult to resolve or cope with (Kirk-Brown & Wallace, 2004; Skovholt, Grier, & Hanson, 2001). Unmanaged stress leads to distress, which can look different for everyone. For example, some individuals may deal with distress by sleeping more, while some may find it difficult to sleep. Some may notice their appetite increases or they cope with stress by eating, while others may find they don't have much of an appetite at all. Another example of distress could be that some individuals may withdraw, while others may seek the company or companionship in others during a particularly stressful time. If the stress is manifesting in more problems such as inability to sleep and/or eat, increased anxiety, or inability to function as one used to, this is a sign of distress.

Stress and distress, over time, can lead to burnout. For counselors, burnout can be a slippery slope in that it is certainly not considered best practice but can also be deemed unethical. Burnout, as related to counselors, "is the result of a decreased ability to attach with the next client because of the emotional depletion accumulated over a period of caring for others" (Skovholt et al., 2001, p. 171). One of our ethical obligations as counselors is to understand our professional responsibility. Noted under "Section C: Professional Responsibility" of the American Counseling Association (ACA) Code of Ethics is the concept of self-care. The ACA Code of Ethics states that "counselors engage in self-care activities to maintain and promote their own emotional, physical, mental, and spiritual well-being to best meet their professional responsibilities" (2014, p. 8). Self-care is not only an ethical requirement, but it is also imperative to managing stress and distress that can lead to burnout and impairment. Counselor burnout may often go unnoticed (Lee et al., 2007), so it is of upmost importance that we are paying attention to this so that burnout does not negatively impact our clients or the work we do.

Self-Care and Self-Compassion

Self-care is something we do to take care of ourselves emotionally, mentally, and physically (Michael, 2016). As mentioned, self-care is an ethical responsibility. Further, the concept of self-care is also part of the accreditation standards for counselor training programs

(CACREP, 2015). However, little information is available on how to integrate this into the life of a counselor effectively. Self-care practices for counselors have received little attention in the field of research (Star, 2014). Additionally, due to being inundated with high expectations for a counselor's abilities, time, and resources (Osborn, 2004), self-care is often difficult or nearly impossible to fit in. We will speak more on wellness and mindfulness in chapters to come, but for now, take the following assessment to see where you stand with your current self-care practices.

Self-Care Assessment

This assessment tool (Table 1.2) offers a summary of approaches that are effective in promoting self-care. Please complete the full assessment and then choose one item from each main area that you will dedicate intention toward improving.

Table 1.2 Using the Following Scale, Rate the Areas Regarding Frequency

5 = Frequently
4 = Occasionally
3 = Rarely
2 = Never
1 = It never occurred to me

Physical Self-Care

___ Eat regularly (e.g., breakfast, lunch, and dinner)
___ Eat healthy, healing, and wholesome foods
___ Exercise/move body actively and intentionally
___ Seek regular medical/wellness care services for prevention (doctor, chiropractic care, acupuncture, etc.)
___ Seek care when needed for sickness or injury
___ Take time off/personal days when needed
___ Receive massages, chiropractic care, or acupuncture
___ Dance, swim, walk, run, hike, play sports, sing, or do some other physical activity that is fun and enjoyable
___ Take time to be sexual – with yourself, with a partner
___ Get enough sleep
___ Wear clothes that make you feel good, confident, and comfortable
___ Take vacations
___ Take day trips or mini-vacations
___ Make time away from phones, computers, and other devices
___ Other:

Psychological Self-Care

___ Make time for self-reflection and self-awareness
___ Have your own personal counseling/therapy
___ Write in a journal or meditate
___ Read literature that is unrelated to work
___ Do something at which you are not expert or in charge
___ Work to decrease stress in your life
___ Let others know different aspects of you
___ Notice your inner experience – take note of your thoughts, judgments, beliefs, attitudes, and feelings
___ Engage your intelligence in a new area, e.g., go to an art museum, history exhibit, sports event, auction, theater performance
___ Practice receiving from others
___ Be curious

_____ Say "no" or "not right now" to extra responsibilities
_____ Other:

Emotional Self-Care

_____ Spend time with others whose company you enjoy and who support and encourage you
_____ Stay in contact with important people in your life
_____ Give yourself affirmations, encourage yourself and be compassionate with yourself
_____ Love yourself
_____ Re-read favorite books, re-watch favorite movies or shows
_____ Identify comforting activities, objects, people, relationships, places, and seek them out often
_____ Allow yourself to feel your feelings and to cry
_____ Find things that make you laugh and smile
_____ Express your outrage in social justice and advocacy, letters and donations, marches, protests
_____ Play with children and animals
_____ Other:

Spiritual Self-Care

_____ Make time for reflection and self-awareness
_____ Spend time in and with nature
_____ Find a spiritual connection or community
_____ Be open to what inspires you
_____ Cherish your optimism and hope
_____ Be aware of nonmaterial aspects of life
_____ Try at times to not be in charge or the expert
_____ Be open to not knowing
_____ Identify what is meaningful to you and notice its place in your life
_____ Meditate
_____ Pray
_____ Sing
_____ Spend time with children and animals
_____ Have experiences of awe
_____ Contribute to causes in which you believe
_____ Read inspirational literature (podcasts, music, etc.)
_____ Other:

Workplace or Professional Self-Care

_____ Take a break during the work day (e.g., lunch)
_____ Take time to converse with co-workers
_____ Make quiet time to complete tasks
_____ Identify projects or tasks that are exciting or rewarding
_____ Set boundaries and limits with your clients and colleagues
_____ Balance your caseload so that no one or part of a day is "too much"
_____ Arrange your work space so it is comfortable, comforting, and feels restorative
_____ Get regular supervision or consultation
_____ Ask and negotiate for your needs (benefits, pay raise)
_____ Have a peer support group
_____ Develop a non-trauma area of professional interest
_____ Other:

Balance

_____ Strive for balance within your work life and work day
_____ Strive for balance among work, family, relationships, play, and rest

Source: Adapted from Saakvitne, K. W., & Pearlman, L. A. (1996)

How did you do on your self-care assessment? Were there some items that you recognize you are paying close attention to? Were there others that could use more energy? Knowing that this will likely change from moment to moment, how did this assessment help you become aware of self-care that you may have been neglecting?

Research in the helping profession is clear with regard to self-care; self-care is an essential component of counselor training, personal practice, and professional responsibility (Coaston, 2017; Mayorga, Devries, & Wardle, 2015). Recent research on self-care noted that lower levels of self-care served to actually increase stress levels among counselors in training (Mayorga et al., 2015). Counselors in training will do well to learn self-care practices while in graduate school to benefit from and integrate this as an essential part of the counselor's roles and responsibilities. A study conducted on Mindfulness-Based Stress Reduction (MBSR) practices and self-care states that

> compared to cohort controls, students in the MBSR program reported significant prepost course declines in perceived stress, negative affect, state and trait anxiety, and rumination, and significant increases in positive affect and self-compassion. These findings suggest that MBSR may not only lower stress and distress but also enhance the ability to regulate emotional states, as reflected in the declines in rumination.
> (Shapiro, Brown, & Biegel, 2007, p. 111)

Coaston (2017) and Nelson, Hall, Anderson, Birtles, and Hemming (2017) discussed the importance of incorporating self-compassion practices (which includes mindfulness) into our understanding of self-care. Neff (2003) conceptualizes that

> Self-compassion entails three main components: (a) self-kindness – being kind and understanding toward oneself in instances of pain or failure rather than being harshly self-critical, (b) common humanity – perceiving one's experiences as part of the larger human experience rather than seeing them as separating and isolating, and (c) mindfulness – holding painful thoughts and feelings in balanced awareness rather than over-identifying with them.
> (p. 85)

Self-compassion is important for counselors to understand and practice for our own wellness, but also so that we can model this for our clients to enhance their wellness. Additionally, "self-compassion is generally considered the foundation for compassion towards others" (Morgan, Morgan, & Germer, 2013, p. 87). Further, Skovholt et al. (2001) outlined six paths for counselor personal and professional self-care: (a) maximizing professional success; (b) creating and sustaining an active, individually designed development method; (c) increasing professional self-understanding; (d) creating a professional greenhouse at work; (e) minimizing ambiguous professional loss; and (f) focusing on one's own need for balanced wellness (p. 171).

Growing evidence suggests that self-compassion is a vital aspect of change in therapeutic work and is negatively correlated with both depression and anxiety (Barnard & Curry, 2011). Self-compassion can assist in reduction of psychopathology symptoms and increase mental and emotional well-being (Germer & Neff, 2013); counselors (as well as clients) can get focused on shame, self-criticism, and self-doubt. In these moments, we need the self-compassion that helps us understand how to be careful and kind to ourselves, even in the middle of the pain (Morgan et al., 2013). However, self-compassion takes practice. The following is an activity that can be used in individual, group, or large classroom counseling. Adapt the directions depending on the setting and how many participants.

Self-Compassion Exercise: Letter of Encouragement

Directions: Instruct participants to write an anonymous letter of encouragement to someone feeling self-doubt, down, inadequate, anxious about what's ahead (etc.). Be both general and specific. You can draw from your own needs for encouragement when writing this – what have you found particularly useful when feeling encouraged by others or yourself? What has helped you in the past?

Let participants know that this will be collected. As the facilitator, have a way to gather letters making note of who wrote what (either writing on the outside of the letter or envelope, or using a numbering system, etc.). Place them all into plain envelopes and hand them back after the letters are collected. It will appear as though you are handing them back randomly; however, everyone will get their own letter back. This has been a very powerful experience when participants are able to read, sit with, and decide to accept or not accept their very own words of encouragement. A discussion about this will follow.

- What was it like writing this in the beginning?
- What was it like to receive your own letter back?
- What did you notice when you read this back – your own words?
- You are the only expert on you. Knowing your innermost desires, wishes, dreams, was it harder to accept your own words of encouragement to yourself as opposed to someone else?
- How are you able to accept or not accept your own words of encouragement (and self-compassion)?
- How does this activity tie into self-compassion?
- What are ways you can learn to cultivate self-compassion?

I (Rebekah) have done this activity in many settings, including supervision. It is often that I will have supervisees contact me months and even years later and tell me they came across their letter at a time they really needed it. Reading those words was healing for them. Even counselors need to work on self-compassion.

Charge: Power of One

We have often heard seasoned counselors and counselors in training express beliefs associated with not *doing* enough for their clients. We can recall supervision after discussion after consultation in which a counselor stated "I just don't know if I did enough. I am not sure if I was doing much today in my session". After a brief discussion in which we determined that the counselor was actively present, paying attention, reflecting, being with, and using many counseling skills and not in fact sitting planning out their grocery list while uttering the occasional "uh-huh", we validate that while this is a common belief among caring clinicians, it is a belief we want examined and then extinguished. An ethical, active, clinician abiding by best practice is doing so much for their clients.

At a former university, we have a free community counseling clinic where we see individuals of all ages, couples, conduct groups, do play therapy, family therapy, and utilize expressive arts and creativity in counseling. We have had clients confide in their counselors that they have never spoken to anyone about their experience, how they feel, family secrets – you name it – that they have never told anyone. Ever. We have had adults in their 60s and 70s tell us this. We have also had clients tell us that our clinic and our counselors have saved their life. So when we hear a counselor say they didn't feel like they did much aside from listen, we can tell you that *listening is not to be taken for granted*. As supervisors watching these sessions live and on video, we can also tell you that they did much more than listen. They:

- were genuine and warm
- showed accurate empathy
- displayed non-judgmental positive regard
- communicated understanding and concern verbally and non-verbally
- validated experience and feelings
- paraphrased
- reflected feelings
- supportively challenged contradictions
- displayed cultural awareness and competencies
- understood and responded to the client's developmental level
- used silence as a therapeutic tool
- used immediacy
- self-disclosed when appropriate and to further discussion or therapeutic rapport
- utilized appropriate interventions
- discussed goal setting
- promoted wellness, self-care, and self-compassion

We could continue this list, but these are just some of the many skills noted through the years as we supervise counselors who report feeling as if they *weren't doing much*. Please don't discount the impact of the relationship and the power of counseling.

Research shows that having one supportive adult is a protective factor for children and adolescents, not just with normal developmental hurdles but those faced with grave adversities (Center on the Developing Child at Harvard University, 2015). Further, this study points to these supportive relationships as being the solitary most shared factor in resilience building. These relationships not only add in resilience development, but they also actively shield children from developmental disturbance.

Having a supportive adult present in the school is imperative for our LGBTGEQIAPT+ students. One supportive adult can provide a much-needed protective factor for LGBTGEQIAPT + youth (LGBTGEQIAP+ includes terms associated with clients identifying as lesbian; gay; bisexual; trans*, transgender and Two-Spirit [2S; Native Identity]; gender expansive; queer and questioning; intersex; agender, asexual and aromantic; pansexual, pan/polygender, and poly relationship systems; and other related identities) (McCabe & Rubinson, 2008; Pendragon, 2010). LGBTGEQIAPT+ students who felt that there was no supportive adult in the school that they could trust were more likely to have their safety threatened at school and to have attempted suicide *several* times in the preceding year (Goodenow, Szalacha, & Westheimer, 2006). Researchers Buote, Darwich, Humel, Waterhous, and Danbrook (2012) have highlighted several benefits to having a supportive adult: (a) increased likelihood of reaching out for support; (b) greater levels of comfort with sexuality; (c) better levels of coping; (d) lower levels of alcohol use; and (e) lower levels of harm.

Summary

Understanding your passion for working with children and adolescents will help you stay driven and compassionate in a complex and challenging profession. Having a strengths-based approach to the work that we do helps support children and adolescents from an empowering perspective instead of one focused on deficits. Literature supports that the counseling relationship is of utmost importance for client success. Students need to learn and incorporate a meaningful practice of self-care and self-compassion for mitigating negative effects of stress, distress, and burnout and for proper prevention of impairment. As a counselor, you may be the only supportive person in the child and adolescent's life. Making sure that you take care of yourself so that you can continue to be there for children and adolescents is vital.

Clinician's Corner

Working with children and adolescents is a privilege that I do not take lightly, and it should be viewed as such to all who work in educational or clinical settings. When I went to graduate school to obtain my master's in counseling, I did so because I knew that I wanted to work with people, but particularly the youth. As a child, I experienced a few traumatic events that affected me deeply, and I struggled from time to time. I didn't know how to express myself, and none of the adults in my life really understood how much of an impact those events had on me or my future development. Thankfully, I was resilient and able to thrive regardless of those events, but it gave me the motivation to want to help others the way I wanted to be helped as a child.

My experience in this field has ranged from working in both K–8 and 9–12 settings as a school counseling intern, where I worked with a range of students dealing with behavioral issues, academic stressors, anxiety, bullying, neglect, and suicidal thoughts, as well as abuse. I have also worked in higher education supporting students as a mentor and academic advisor. Currently, I work in the college access field supporting rural adolescents with their college-going process and career plans. We work with many low-income and first-generation students in our region, in the hopes of breaking the vicious cycle of generational poverty for them. The bottom line is that there are so many children and adolescents that are hurting or struggling with one or more issues, and they need clinicians in their corner to help them navigate their lives.

If I had to offer a piece of advice to a new clinician or clinician-in-training, it would be this: be intentional in your work with children and adolescents, and know the "why" for why you do the work that you do. Sadly, there are people who end up being therapists, counselors, etc., who don't have a heart for this career or who do it for the wrong reasons. A person must go into this field having a servant's heart and a willingness to make an impact on the individuals that need them. You have the chance to make a difference in so many lives of children and adolescents, and you can be the advocate for them that they may not have at home or at school. Believe me, they need us – they need *you*. Be the person for them that you may have needed at some point in your life.

Shawn Stewart, M.A.
Niswonger Foundation

References

American Counseling Association. (2014). *ACA code of ethics*. Alexandria, VA: Author.

American School Counselor Association. (2012). *The ASCA national model: A framework for school counseling programs* (3rd ed.). Alexandria, VA: Author.

Ardito, R. B., & Rabellino, D. (2011). Therapeutic alliance and outcome of psychotherapy: Historical excursus, measurements, and prospects for research. *Frontiers in Psychology, 2*, 270. http://doi.org/10.3389/fpsyg.2011.00270

Barnard, L. K., & Curry, J. F. (2011). Self-compassion: Conceptualizations, correlates, & interventions. *Review of General Psychology, 15*(4), 289–303. https://doi.org/10.1037/a0025754

Buote, D., Darwich, L., Humel, S., Waterhous, T., & Danbrook, M. (2012). *The health of LGBTQ youth: Risk and protective factors*. Health Canada. Retrieved from https://arboreducational.com/wp-content/uploads/2013/11/GLBTQ-Youth__May-2012__HC.pdf

Center on the Developing Child at Harvard University. (2015). *Supportive relationships and active skill-building strengthen the foundations of resilience: Working paper No. 13*. Retrieved from www.developingchild.harvard.edu

Coaston, S. C. (2017). Self-care through self-compassion: A balm for burnout. *The Professional Counselor, 7*(3), 285–297. https://doi.org/10.15241/scc.7.3.285

Council for Accreditation of Counseling and Related Education Programs. (2015). *2016 CACREP Standards*. Retrieved from www.cacrep.org/wp-content/uploads/2017/08/2016-Standards-with-citations.pdf

Davidson, K., & Scott, J. (2009). Does therapists' competence matter in delivering psychological therapy? *Psychiatric Bulletin, 33*, 121–123. https://doi.org/10.1192/pb.bp.108.020214

Germer, C. K., & Neff, K. D. (2013). Self-compassion in clinical practice. *Journal of Clinical Psychology: In Session, 69*(8), 856–867. https://doi.org/10.1002/jclp.22021

Goodenow, C., Szalacha, L., & Westheimer, K. (2006). School support groups, other school factors, and the safety of sexual minority adolescents. *Psychology in the Schools, 43*, 573–589.

Horvath, A. O., & Bedi, R. P. (2002). The alliance. In J. C. Norcross (Ed.), *Psychotherapy relationships that work: Therapist contributions and responsiveness to patients* (pp. 37–69). New York: Oxford University Press.

Kirk-Brown, A., & Wallace, D. (2004). Predicting burnout and job satisfaction in workplace counselors: The influence of role stressors, job challenge, and organizational knowledge. *Journal of Employment Counseling, 41*, 29–37. https://doi.org/10.1002/j.2161-1920.2004.tb00875.x

Landreth, G. (2012). *Play therapy: The art of the relationship* (3rd ed.). New York: Brunner-Routledge.

Lee, S. M., Baker, C. R., Cho, S. H., Heckathorn, D. E., Holland, M. W., Newgent, R. A., . . . Yu, K. (2007). Development and initial psychometrics of the Counselor Burnout Inventory. (Report). *Measurement and Evaluation in Counseling and Development, 40*(3), 142–154. https://doi.org/10.1017/jgc.2018.3

Mayorga, M., Devries, S. R., & Wardle, E. A. (2015). The practice of self-care among counseling students. *Journal on Educational Psychology, 8*(3), 21–28. https://doi.org/10.26634/jpsy.8.3.3101

McCabe, P. C., & Rubinson, F. (2008). Committing to social justice: The behavioral intention of school psychology and education trainees to advocate for lesbian, gay, bisexual and transgendered youth. *School Psychology Review, 37*(4), 469–486.

MedicineNet. (2016). *Medical definition of stress*. Retrieved from www.medicinenet.com/script/main/art.asp?articlekey=20104#stress_facts

Merikangas, K. R., He, J., Burstein, M., Swanson, S. A., Avenevoli, S., Cui, L., . . . Swendsen, J. (2010). Lifetime prevalence of mental disorders in US adolescents: Results from the National Comorbidity Study-Adolescent supplement (NCS-A). *Journal of the American Academy of Child and Adolescent Psychiatry, 49*(10), 980–989. http://doi.org/10.1016/j.jaac.2010.05.017

Michael, R. (2016). What self-care is – And what it isn't. *Psych Central*. Retrieved November 27, 2018, from https://psychcentral.com/blog/what-self-care-is-and-what-it-isnt-2/

Morgan, W. D., Morgan, S. T., & Germer, C. K. (2013). Cultivating attention and compassion. In C. K. Germer, R. D. Siegel, & P. R. Fulton (Eds.), *Mindfulness and psychotherapy* (2nd ed., pp. 76–93). New York: The Guilford Press.

Neff, K. (2003). Self-compassion: An alternative conceptualization of a healthy attitude toward oneself. *Self and Identity, 2*, 85–101. https://doi.org/10.1080/15298860309032

Nelson, J. R., Hall, B. S., Anderson, J. L., Birtles, C., & Hemming, L. (2017). Self–Compassion as self-care: A simple and effective tool for counselor educators and counseling students. *Journal of Creativity in Mental Health*. https://doi.org/10.1080/15401383.2017.1328292

Norcross, J. C. (2002). *Psychotherapy relationships that work: Therapist contributions and responsiveness to patients*. New York: Oxford University Press.

Osborn, C. (2004). Seven salutary suggestions for counselor stamina. *Journal of Counseling & Development, 82*(3), 319–328. https://doi.org/10.1002/j.1556-6678.2004.tb00317.x

Pendragon, K. K. (2010). Coping behaviors among sexual minority females. *Journal of Lesbian Studies*, *14*, 5–15.

Reardon, T., Harvey, K., Baranowska, M., O'Brien, D., Smith, L., & Creswell, C. (2017). What do parents perceive are the barriers and facilitators to accessing psychological treatment for mental health problems in children and adolescents? A systematic review of qualitative and quantitative studies. *European Child & Adolescent Psychiatry*, *26*(6), 623–647. http://doi.org/10.1007/s00787-016-0930-6

Saakvitne, K. W., & Pearlman, L. A. (1996). *Transforming the pain: A workbook on vicarious traumatization for helping professionals who work with traumatized clients.* New York: W.W. Norton & Company.

Seligman, M. E. (1999). Teaching positive psychology. *APA Monitor on Psychology*, *30*(7). Retrieved from www.apa.org

Shapiro, S. L., Brown, K. B., & Biegel, G. M. (2007). Teaching self-care to caregivers: Effects of mindfulness-based stress reduction on the mental health of therapists in training. *Training and Education in Professional Psychology*, *1*(2), 105–115. https://doi.org/10.1037/1931-3981.2.105

Skovholt, T. M., Grier, T. L., & Hanson, M. R. (2001). Career counseling for longevity: Self-care and burnout prevention strategies for counselor resilience. *Journal of Career Development*, *27*(3), 167–176. https://doi.org/10.1023/A:1007830908587

Smith, E. J. (2006). The strengths-based counseling model. *The Counseling Psychologist*, *34*(1), 13–79. https://doi.org/10.1177/0011000005277018

Star, K. L. (2014). *The relationship between self-care practices, burnout, compassion fatigue and compassion satisfaction among professional counselors and counselors-in-training*, Doctoral Dissertation. Retrieved from https://etd.ohiolink.edu/!etd.send_file?accession=kent1364220500&disposition=inline

Trepka, C., Rees, A., Shapiro, D. A., Hardy, G. E., & Barkham, M. (2004). Therapist competence and outcome of cognitive therapy for depression. *Cognitive Therapy and Research*, *28*(2), 143–157.

Twenge, J. M. (2017). *iGen: Why today's super-connected kids are growing up less rebellious, more tolerant, less happy – and completely unprepared for adulthood.* New York: Atria Books.

U.S. Census Bureau, Population Division. (2018). *Annual estimates of the resident population for selected age groups by sex for the United States, States, counties and Puerto Rico Commonwealth and municipios: April 1, 2010 to July 1, 2017.* Retrieved from https://factfinder.census.gov/faces/tableservices/jsf/pages/productview.xhtml?pid=PEP_2017_PEPAGESEX&prodType=table

2 Strategies and Interventions for Empathic Connection

Rebekah Byrd and Chad Luke

Objectives

- Contemplate your own thoughts about how individuals change.
- Understand the stages of change and how they are related to counseling.
- Evaluate developmentally appropriate techniques and interventions for working with children and adolescents.
- Examine wellness for yourself and think about how to integrate this into counseling children and adolescents.
- Identify ways to make sure your counseling is holistic.
- Understand the benefits to using encouragement versus praise.
- Understand that all counseling is multicultural.

Reflective Questions

- What are my current beliefs about how change occurs for an individual?
- What can help me recognize what state of change a client is in and adapt counseling interventions appropriately?
- What is my current level of wellness? How do I incorporate wellness practices in my own life, and how will I help my clients with this important concept?
- How will I make sure I am working with the whole child?
- In what ways can I seek to encourage instead of praise children and adolescents?
- How can I make sure I am seeking to be culturally sensitive in all my work with children and adolescents?

The approach to this text is a strength-based approach. Grounded in research and multicultural competency, this text will focus on encouragement, recognizing resiliency, and empowerment. This text will seek to empower children, adolescents, and clinicians for continued challenging work in a complex and often scary world. By going beyond theory, this text offers myriad tried and true techniques for working with children and adolescents. These techniques range from mindfulness to play therapy to wilderness therapy. Counselors in training will feel prepared to discuss developmentally appropriate strategies with parents and teachers involved, feel confident in the abilities of the child to change given the right therapeutic alliance, and empower all involved to work together for the better of the child at the child's pace. The rate of burnout in this area is not one to take lightly. With proper training, we can help alleviate stress and distress that leads to burnout among counselors. Children and adolescents are counting on well-trained, competent, compassionate adults. We need to be those adults – for them and for ourselves.

Beliefs About Human Nature

When thinking about their own beliefs about human nature, counselors must inspect their own beliefs about how individuals change. When we think about change, why people change, and why people don't change, there are many questions that arise. Kottler, who has been researching change for decades, noted eight questions that plead for greater conclusive answers (Kottler, 2018). These have been adapted as follows:

1. Why is it that even when people know change is absolutely imperative for their well-being, they will still avoid and resist these changes?
2. What makes people decide to change?
3. How can changes be incremental and also gradual? Why is it that they can also be both sudden and dramatic?
4. Why is it that some individuals will become debilitated and impaired when encountering disasters and trauma, while others seem to experience personal growth as an outcome to their hardship?
5. Within an individual, group, or even a large organization, what are the breaking points that seem to start a movement of incremental and perhaps cumulative changes?
6. Even when the results seem to be sustaining and beneficial, why is it that most changes don't seem to last?
7. How can we work to prevent relapse?
8. If common factors of successful change exist, how can we understand, design, and control those factors in an effort to encourage and support sustainable change?

Kottler goes on to say that the phenomena for understanding such questions about change are much too multifaceted and complex for unsophisticated explanations. In short, how people change is still much of a mystery. So then, how do we as counselors conceptualize this so as to help our clients heal, progress, and meet their goals?

How Individuals Change

What are your own ideas about how change takes place for an individual? How does an individual change? Is change easy? Have you ever tried to quit a behavior? How did you do this? What difficulties did you face to sustain this long-term? What about adopting a new routine or habit? How did you do with that? What are your beliefs associated with how quickly an individual can change and incorporate new techniques into her/his life? Think about an event, a circumstance, an experience, or even an insight in your life that changed you in a profound way – changed how you interact, operate, view the world and others, view yourself. What happened? What was that like for you? How did you change, and what exactly promoted that change for you?

These questions are difficult, at best, to answer – some would say almost impossible to explain or describe in a way that would make sense to someone else who didn't experience it. Many theories exist as to how people change. The Transtheoretical Model, also referred to as the stages of change, is a framework that has been well recognized, established, and validated in preventative medicine literature (Parker, Martin, Martines, Marsh, & Jackson, 2010). This model notes the stages of change as a process involving progression through a sequence of six stages (Prochaska & Velicer, 1997). These stages have been adapted as follows:

Precontemplation: In this stage, people are not planning to take action in the foreseeable future (next six months). People can be in this stage because they are unaware or uneducated about the consequences of their behavior. They may have tried to change in the past, but were unsuccessful and are unmotivated to change currently.

Contemplation: This stage is one in which people are planning to change within the next six months. They are aware of both the pros and cons to change – but perhaps more aware of the pros.

Preparation: In this stage, people are planning to take action in the immediate future, defined as the next month. These individuals have a plan and have likely taken some significant steps in the past year.

Action: In this stage, people have taken significant steps to change their behavior or lifestyle in the last six months and plan to continue moving forward with more healthy choices.

Maintenance: This stage is one in which people are working hard to prevent relapse, but may not be actively in the change process as they were in the action stage. In this stage, they are less likely to relapse and experience less temptation to do so. They have growing confidence to keep moving on a healthier path. This stage can last anywhere from six months to five years.

Termination: This stage is when individuals have absolutely no temptation to relapse. They also possess 100% self-efficacy. No matter what life throws at them, they are steadfast in their changes and will not revert back to unhealthy behaviors for coping.

It is important to note that in this model, relapse is not a stage of its own. Relapse is the return from the action of maintenance stage back to an earlier stage. Prochaska and Velicer (1997) further note that most people who relapse return to either the contemplation stage or the preparation stage.

Norcross, Krebs, and Prochaska (2011) conducted a meta-analysis of 39 studies which included 8,238 psychotherapy clients. In this study, they evaluated the stages of change and readiness measures of clients in order to predict psychotherapy results. The results support that using the stages of change are beneficial and useful in predicting significant treatment outcome measures such as the therapeutic alliance, symptom relief, and early dropping out behavior. Noted in this study were many therapist behaviors that improved treatment outcomes for clients. Following is an adapted version of the research-supported list of the behaviors that therapist need utilize (Norcross et al., 2011).

Evaluate the client's stage of change. It is important to understand the client's stage and preparation for change. Without understanding this, the treatment cannot be appropriately tailored to fit the client. It is suggested to ask "Would you say you are not ready to change in the next six months (precontemplation), thinking about changing in the next six months (contemplation), thinking about changing in the next month (preparation), or have you already made some progress (action)?" (p. 151). The stage that the client is in will likely be different for each specific issue or treatment goal so be prepared to assess this for each.

Do not treat all clients as if they are in the action stage. Often helping professionals may address client goals with action-oriented techniques and can become disappointed and discouraged when clients are unmotivated or stop attending therapy. Most clients are not currently in the action stage and should not be treated as such. If helping professionals treat all clients as if in the action phase, they risk a great disservice to most of the clients they encounter. It may be more helpful to think in terms of stages instead of action.

Set accurate and realistic goals by progressing one stage at a time. Of course, it is understood that setting accurate and realistic goals can be difficult in the age of managed care and time limits for services. If we understand change as a progression through stages that happens over time, then we understand that clients are changing when they are making progress. Therefore, it is important to help them when they get stuck in the precontemplation stage.

Treat clients in the precontemplation stage with care. It has been noted in the research that people in the precontemplation stage may be overly focused on the cons for changing and not give enough thought, attention, or worth to the pros of a given change. We need to be careful not to push or impose action upon individuals in the precontemplation stage so as not to misunderstand them, hurt the therapeutic alliance, and drive them away. Helping professionals also need to take care to not mistake a client in the precontemplation stage for being resistant. "When this occurs, we find that it is often the therapists who are not ready or motivated to match their relationship and methods to clients' needs, and are resistant to trying new approaches to retaining more clients" (Norcross et al., 2011, p. 152).

Tailor and fit the processes to the stages. Research has consistently noted that clients progress best by moving from precontemplation and contemplation into preparation by utilizing insight and awareness factors such as self-liberation, consciousness raising, and dramatic relief/emotional encouragement. Clients move best from the preparation stage to the action and maintenance stages by utilizing more action-based techniques such as "counterconditioning, stimulus control, and reinforcement management" (p. 152).

Avoid mismatching stages and processes. Understanding an individual's stage of change is necessary for understanding proper techniques to guide treatment (see Norcross et al., 2011).

Recommend stage-matched relationships of choice as well as treatments of choice. Researchers note that after establishing the client's current stage of change, then you can use the proper techniques to assist in moving forward to the next stage.

Practice integratively. Researchers have noted that helping professionals may use multiple (even dissimilar) theories and models for helping to assist clients in moving forward in the stages of change. This has been shown to be beneficial.

Anticipate recycling. It is very common for clients to cycle back through the stages multiple times before arriving at the maintenance phase long-term. Helping professionals should expect this to occur and be prepared to include information on relapse.

Counselors need to understand these behaviors and how they contribute to improved client outcomes and treatment goals. As mentioned previously, understanding when a client is in the precontemplative stage is essential so as not to label the client as "resistant". Clients can benefit from a counselor who understands how hard it can be to change and is supportive and encouraging instead of a counselor who believes clients to be resistant. Further, Kottler (2018, p. 32) identifies many personal factors that influence an individual's ability or capacity for change. These include (Table 2.1):

Table 2.1 Personal Factors That Influence Change

Past experiences	Previous trauma
Perceptual sensitivity	Cultural background
Cognitive deficits	Cognitive rigidity
Self-discipline	Emotional regulation
Tolerance for ambiguity	Willingness to explore unknown
Willingness to take risks	Interpersonal skills
Social support or isolation	Peer pressure and family dynamics
Impulsivity	Tendency to externalize blame
Openness to feedback	Resilience
Hardiness	Optimism versus pessimism
Debilitating emotional problems	Emotional volatility
Stress inoculation	Tolerance for pain and discomfort
Self-reflection	Capacity for insight

The Person of the Counselor

No matter what theoretical orientation or what skills or techniques you use in counseling, don't forget that you as the counselor are extremely important in the process. As noted in Chapter 1 of this volume, but bears repeating, the client-counselor relationship is a predictor of positive clinical outcomes aside from the techniques and theories used (Ardito & Rabellino, 2011; Horvath & Bedi, 2002). To explain this further, you may have the best techniques and interventions, but without a strong rapport and trusting therapeutic alliance, the counseling will be ineffective. Having a strong client-counselor alliance is imperative for development, healing, and success in counseling.

All Counseling Is Multicultural

Multicultural counseling can be understood as counseling that not only incorporates cultural characteristics and identities into the counseling relationship, but also seeks to understand the culture and its impact on the counseling relationship, therapeutic alliance, session progression, and outcome (Hays & Mcleod, 2018). "Culture consists of the shared values, practices, and social norms, and worldviews associated with a particular group. Cultural groups may be based on race, ethnicity, gender, sexual identity, socio-economic status, disability, age, and spirituality to name a few categories" (Hays & Mcleod, 2018, p. 5). Subcategories also exist within each of these cultural categories (Hays & Mcleod, 2018).

Strategies for Working With Children and Adolescents

Following are some tips for working with children and adolescents that can be incorporated into almost any therapeutic approach, technique, or intervention. Being careful with questions, using silence in a therapeutic way, avoiding power struggles, constantly using encouragement in everything we do, and using ourselves – the person of the counselor – are all essential strategies to effectively working with children and adolescents.

Careful With Questions

A misconception exists in which people believe that in order to effectively work with clients, often and especially children and adolescents, that the way to do this is to ask questions. This often reveals a tennis match (or table tennis, if you prefer) by going back and forth with question and then answer. Question, and then answer. Question, and then answer – or maybe just multiple shoulder shrugs. Have you ever seen this type of "session" before? Maybe you have been in one as a client or a counselor – what was that like for you?

Children and adolescents are used to adults interacting with them in this way and will often end up in our offices passively silent until we start the rapid-fire round of questions. It is important to *question* our use of questions in working with children and adolescents. There are counseling programs that have trained students to rarely if ever ask questions. I can think of one that never allowed questions at all. By starting off your session with a general statement of "tell me about yourself", often children and adolescents can get a sense that you really want to get to know them, that who they are matters, and that you care – especially when most of the time, a referral has been made by someone else telling you the child's or adolescent's problems. This can often set up distrust from the beginning as teachers, physicians, caregivers, and many others may have done the initial referral to check for fit, before you even meet with the child or adolescent. Often children may not understand this, however, adolescents seem well aware that people have been talking about them to you – and they mostly may not feel good about this.

Questions, often without meaning to, can seem shaming, judging, and blaming, and can focus on details that derail the client from their concerns or the point of their story. It is important to focus on feelings instead of content. Counselors who get caught up in details of a story, asking questions for their benefit, may not be using questions to further the session or add to their client's understanding of self or others in a meaningful way. When in session, it is beneficial to ask yourself if your questions are relevant and necessary. Often a statement on feelings can illicit further elaboration from the client to aid in more understanding than a question could. See the different examples as follows from a counselor and adolescent who have been working together for about three weeks. Before this session, the mom notifies the counselor that the adolescent has been having issues with feeling worried and anxious at school, although this has not previously come up in session.

Counselor: So Leilani, your mom tells me you have been feeling anxious and worried at school.
Adolescent: Oh she did? Well, yeah. I guess so.
Counselor: What do you think is making you feel anxious and worried?
Adolescent: I dunno.
Counselor: But you feel this way at school and not at home?
Adolescent: Yeah.
Counselor: So has this just recently started?
Adolescent: Yeah, I guess.

Where does the counselor go from here? Does the counselor keep asking questions to figure things out? How has the counselor set this up to not be a session in which the counselor is in charge and is the lead and asks questions that the adolescent then answers? Do you think the adolescent feels part of this process, or is the adolescent disengaged perhaps? You may think this example is simplistic, but I assure you, this happens time and time again. I have observed it more times than I would like to count. How might things go differently if the following were to occur:

Counselor: Hi, Leilani. I am glad you could make it today. Tell me a little bit about your week.
Adolescent: Ummm, I dunno. I went to school and I went to soccer and then that is about it. Just school and soccer mostly right now.
Counselor: Oh, yes, I can imagine having both school and being involved in a sport takes up so much of your time.
Adolescent: Yeah. I don't really have time for anything else.
Counselor: That must be hard during soccer season. I am sure you are tired.
Adolescent: Yeah. And I have been feeling really anxious lately at school. Like out of nowhere. Like really worried for no reason.
Counselor: That sounds like it is upsetting you and making your busy schedule even more difficult to manage. I am glad that you brought that up because in here, we can work on that, discuss what that is like for you, and come up with some ways together, that will hopefully help.

How did those two excerpts feel different for you? Understanding how to make statements is important so as not to constantly rely on asking questions. This is certainly a skill that takes practice. Following are some examples of statements that can be used in the place of questions. As you read the client's response, note what comes to mind for you that you would say if you were trying not to ask questions.

Client:	I am so pissed. My parents won't let me go to the dance this week because I lied about my homework.
Counselor Question:	Why did you lie about your homework? (This seems like a normal and natural response, right? However, natural or normal does not mean therapeutic.)
Counselor Statement:	Oh, no! I can see how upset you are. You have been looking forward to that dance for a while now.
Client:	I can't go back to that class. I hate history and the kids in there make fun of me. I would rather fail than go back there.
Counselor Question:	What happened? What are the kids doing to make fun of you?
Counselor Statement:	Sounds like you are completely over having to be in that class. And you are feeling so helpless and hopeless that failing the class seems like a better option for you right now than ever having to go back.
Client:	I made the football team!!!! I can't believe it! I made the team!
Counselor Question:	Oh, my! When did you find out?
Counselor Statement:	Wow! You worked so hard to prepare the semester before and you were so dedicated to your routine. It really paid off. I can see how proud you are of yourself. You really put the time in and accomplished your goal!
Client:	My best friend won't talk to me. (Client starts to cry.)
Counselor Question:	Did something happen? Why won't he/she talk to you?
Counselor Statement:	You are feeling really sad, hurt, and confused right now.

Which response do you think helps the client feel heard and understood? The questions listed, for the most part, seemed like natural responses; one you might ask as a friend – and one the client, I am sure, has been asked several times by friend and adults (likely by caregivers or teachers) and is not surprised to hear again. Which response furthers discussion? Which response builds trust and rapport? Which response helps the client acknowledge and understand feelings?

Of course, there are times to ask questions in counseling, and this is a skill – but it is not the only skill and it is not a skill to default to constantly. When it is necessary to ask questions, make sure you are asking questions in an open-ended fashion. Open-ended questions are helpful in that they require more than a one-word response to answer. Open-ended questions can't be answered by simply responding with a "yes" or a "no". Following are a few examples.

What is your favorite thing about school?
When have you felt so excited you couldn't stand it?
What do you like most about being in middle school?
What do you want to have accomplished in the next three years?
What are your goals for this week?
How have you noticed yourself reacting now that is different from before?

Therapeutic Silence

We feel like there should be scary music playing when someone says *therapeutic silence*. It is often a scary concept for many. We really hope that this section can assist in making it not so scary.

Silence is a skill, and like other counseling skills, using silence needs practice. Counselors also need to understand how and when to use silence based on client needs and depending on how and when it is used (Hill, Thompson, & Ladany, 2003). Beginning counselors and seasoned counselors alike can often feel pressure to constantly be talking or "doing something" or having the client talking or doing something. I ask that you challenge your thinking that assumes silence isn't still very active. I have seen what seemed to be a clear pause or a moment of reflection turn into the counselor feeling anxious and pressured to fill the silence with words – which often ends up in the counselor doing what? You guessed it – asking a question. We need to be comfortable with these pauses. We need to be comfortable with therapeutic silence and give our clients this space to think, reflect, and contemplate. This may be the first time the client has ever talked about something, and allowing reverent reflection is imperative and honestly it is just respectful. Have you ever been trying to thoughtfully approach a difficult topic and describe your feelings associated with it to have someone interrupt and ask questions that weren't even really related to what you were trying to discuss? Often the person doesn't even know they are doing this because they are trying to understand, but if they just listened instead of asking questions, you could get to the point you were trying to make.

Often people need a safe space to do this, and often they need a quiet space to do this. The counseling session may be the only moment of quiet in the client's life, so please allow this and don't seek to fill the space with words because you (the counselor) are uncomfortable. If this occurs, it behooves you to seek to understand why you are uncomfortable with silence. Are there strong feelings the client has brought up that feel uncomfortable to you? Are there strong feelings being brought up for you that you may need to do your own work in processing? Be aware of this as you move forward in your training.

In a qualitative study examining the use of silence in therapy, researchers (Ladany, Hill, Thompson, & O'Brien, 2004) found that therapists used silence to support and respect the client (provide a space to explore, and encourage and support the client in being themself, and honor what the client discussed) and to communicate empathy. Silence was also used to convey understanding and to build upon therapeutic work. Researchers further noted that therapists would use this skill as a way to assist clients in their own reflection, to help in revealing feelings, and to return responsibility. Therapists also noted that at times they have used silence to give themselves time and space to gather their thoughts so as to respond to their clients appropriately and in the best therapeutic manner. It is important to remember that rapport needs to be built for silence to feel supportive and therapeutic. It is also recommended to use silence carefully and cautiously so that clients don't feel intimidated. Further, therapists in this study reported not using silence with clients who were psychotic, highly suspicious, anxious or paranoid, those a danger to themselves or others, or those new to therapy. Generally speaking, clinicals have reported silence has had a positive impact with their clients (Hill et al., 2003).

Power Struggles

Just the phrase "power struggles" makes me cringe a little, if I am honest. What is a power struggle? In short, it is when two people are struggling for control. Children and adolescents are developmentally supposed to strive for control and autonomy. Caregivers and other adults are constantly getting into power struggles in an effort to make children and adolescents comply – whether it be getting a child to do his/her homework, eat his/her vegetables, go to class, you name it. A power struggle can occur and progress when children or adolescents don't follow rules and expectations, are unaccepting to a consequence, or even when they do follow rules and expectations or accept a consequence but they have a bad attitude while doing so (Mendler & Mendler, 2012). This can happen pretty much anytime a child or adolescent is asked to do something, and he/she refuses. Adults have the choice of how they respond so as not to get into a struggle over said power. Power struggles are everywhere.

Power struggles – don't get into them. Don't engage. Just don't do it. No one wins in a power struggle with a child or adolescent. Congratulations – you are an adult. You are bigger, stronger, and you have power that you can exert over a child or adolescent. But don't do it. It is certainly not therapeutic, and it certainly won't build rapport or help the child feel heard or understood. It *will* certainly make the child not trust you, not feel supported by you, and not see you as an ally. Even if you do get a child or adolescent to comply, let's be clear: you didn't win the power struggle. You still lost – and you perhaps also lost the child or adolescent in the process. It is important to recognize when power struggles are occurring and what you can do about them.

Many individuals have ideas as to why children misbehave. One of the most widely recognized concepts comes from Alfred Adler's work, expanded on by Dreikurs, Grunwald, and Pepper (1982), and notes the goals of children and what their behavior is actually telling us. Table 2.2 is a chart on these mistaken goals.

Encouragement (vs. Praise)

There could be an entire chapter on encouragement versus praise. This is such an important consideration when working with children and adolescents. Encouragement focuses on the

Table 2.2 Identifying the Mistaken Goals of Children's Misbehavior*

Mistaken Goals	Observed Behavior	Adult Response	What the Child Does When Corrected
Attention Getting	Model child Cute and charming Pest and nuisance Lazy	Irritated Annoyed Frustrated	Stops for a short while when corrected – even just a few moments or minutes
Power struggle	Rebellious Argues and fights Stubborn Passive-aggressive	Angry Challenged Defeated	Keeps going even when told to stop and may even intensify the misbehavior
Revenge	Vicious or violent Vandalism Meanness Violent Passivity	Hurt	Intensifies the misbehavior and the misbehavior becomes mean
Assumed disability	Acts hopeless Gives up Is discouraged Acts incompetent	Despair Helplessness	Limited or no interaction – adults start to give up, too; won't try

* Adapted from Dreikurs, Grunwald, and Pepper (1982)

process, while praise focuses on the product. Think about a child who draws a picture, finishes a project, learns to ride a bike – the praise is focused on what they did; often the finished product. Praise often misses the effort, dedication, and hard work involved in completing something. What happens when the child doesn't finish the picture, can't complete the project, or gets frustrated while learning to ride a bike and quits? If we have only been praising the end result or finished product, this child could feel very discouraged and disheartened. Children and adolescents need to realize that they can do hard things and that their effort, determination, and perseverance is important, that the characteristics of their personality are important and mostly that *they* are important; not the product or end result of what they do. Praise is also coming from someone else. We want children and adolescents to rely and trust themselves. You can certainly read more about this, but here are a few examples.

Praise: That picture is beautiful!
Encouragement: You worked really hard on that!
Praise: I'm proud of you!
Encouragement: You seem proud of yourself!
Praise: Good job! (This is so general, and kids are used to hearing this all the time – but what does it really mean?)
Encouragement: You were able to get those blocks just how you wanted them! or You put all the cards back in order! (Be specific instead of general.)
Praise: You are so smart!
Encouragement: You kept working and didn't give up, even when it was hard!

Can you see the difference in these statements? In Jane Nelsen's (2006) book on positive discipline, she discusses that praise can often rob the child of ownership over an accomplished task or an achievement, while encouragement provides an opportunity for the child to be responsible for and take ownership for themselves and their effort. Isn't that what we want children and adolescents to do? We don't want to create beings that feed off of praise; we want children and adolescents to be self-motivated, and have a sense of inner direction as opposed to always seeking the approval of others. Nelsen also discusses that encouragement promotes self-reliance, self-confidence, and autonomy, while praise promotes a dependence on others.

Developmentally Appropriate Interventions and Techniques

In this section, we will introduce developmentally appropriate interventions and techniques. Chapters addressing these specific techniques in greater detail will follow later in this text. This introduction asks you to examine your ideas about a one-size-fits-all model of counseling and instead understand techniques from a developmental and individualized perspective. We will talk in depth about each of these interventions in later chapters, but here are some interventions and techniques to start to consider.

Family Counseling

Children are born into a group, and many of them will never actually live outside of a group. That initial group, the family, regardless of how it is structured, will serve as a foundation for the child's development and as a model for how to live and function in the larger systems of society. Within the family, children learn to act and interact; to speak and to communicate; to walk and move – and to manipulate the environment; to experience the joys and limits of freedom and the value of safety. Starting with nothing more than temperament and a striving for growth, they gain increasing access to the world and cobble together a sense of self and personhood, an understanding of and relationship with others. They also draw conclusions about self, others, life and the world. Everything they learn and experience, they do relationally. Even their sense of self is a self-in-relationship.

Child and adolescent counselors should take classes in family counseling, even if not present in the core program of study. Family counseling is an essential aspect of working with children and adolescents. The family is the foundation for the lives that children lead even when they are involved in the larger macro-systems of society, like school or sports or religion.

Play Therapy

Play therapy is a type of counseling in which play is used to communicate instead of relying on talk in traditional therapy modalities. Play therapy is an evidenced-based practice and is shown to be effective with children with varying presenting problems and concerns, and also as a tool for wellness and prevention (Ray & McCullough, 2016). In play therapy, there is a playroom where the child is able to play out their thoughts, feelings, and situations by using toys, art, and other play media tools. Using a child's language of play is important since children under the age of 12 generally have limited ability to discuss their thoughts and feelings, and also lack the ability to use abstract verbal reasoning (Kottman, 2011). Whole parts of the brain are involved when a child is playing which develops critical connections leading to positive development and growth of the child (Mellenthin, 2018).

Play therapy is powerful! We have witnessed this time and time again and have seen the change this has made in the lives of many children, adults, and families throughout the years. Play is a child's natural form of communication. Instead of adults trying to get kids to talk, play therapy lets the child communicate through play. Children are *always* communicating with us. They may not always be talking, but they are always communicating. It is our job as counselors to learn and respect their form of communication and to pay attention. As Landreth (2012) noted, play is the child's language and toys are, in a sense, their words. It is hoped that by introducing you to this amazing type of counseling, you will seek out further training, as it requires specialized training, education, and supervised experience to become a registered play therapist.

Sandtray Therapy

Sandtray Therapy is supported as an effective intervention for children and adolescents with varying presenting issues. Homeyer and Sweeney define sandtray as:

> An expressive and projective mode of psychotherapy involving the unfolding and processing of intra- and inter-personal issues through the use of specific sandtray materials as a nonverbal medium of communication, led by the client(s) and facilitated by a trained therapist. It is a process that seeks to promote safety and control for the client so that emotionally charged issues can be addressed through the medium.
>
> (2011, p. 4)

A sandtray is a container holding sand that the child or adolescent places selected items into. These trays can be of varying shapes and sizes and can be made out of wood or plastic. Miniature items are placed in the trays according to the creator's preferences. Many items can be used as sandtray miniatures. There are sandtray rooms with shelves upon shelves of miniatures, and there are portable sandtrays.

Further, sandtray provides clients with therapeutic means to use their senses in a way that encourages release, healing, and relaxation (Oaklander, 2007; Gil, 2006). Other authors note the sensory experience in sandtray as well by discussing how sand offers "a contrasting tactile experience where they may reconnect with their own body and experience positive and pleasurable sensations that promote physical and psychological wellbeing" (Tornero & Capella, 2017, p. 10). Sandtray can be useful in many types of clinical work, with multiple populations and ages of individuals. Sandtray has been useful in individual work, group processes, family therapy, and couples counseling, and has been used in clinical supervision.

Mindfulness Techniques

Mindfulness can be understood as paying total attention to the present moment with a nonjudgmental awareness of the internal and external experience as it changes from moment to moment (Kabat-Zinn, 2003). In short, it can be described as "paying attention in a particular way: on purpose, in the present moment, and nonjudgmentally" (Kabat-Zinn, 1994, p. 4). Further, mindfulness is not focused on pathology and is instead a strengths-based intervention (Remple, 2012).

Current research on the benefits of mindfulness with children and adolescents is growing. Researchers have noted that mindfulness increases consideration for others and also increases levels of empathy (Abid, Irfan, & Naeem, 2017). Researchers suggest that mindfulness teaches children a way in which to manage or cope with stress, and "mindfulness training may also change brain structure and function in a manner that helps to buffer against dysregulated stress reactivity" (Brown, 2015, p. 302). Hilt and Pollak (2012) discussed how mindfulness training can help children and adolescents out of a ruminative state. Mindfulness is also noted to have a negative association with bullying behaviors (Abid et al., 2017). Further,

> the currently available studies support the conclusion that mindfulness training is efficacious for some neurocognitive, psychosocial, and psychobiological outcomes, and that this training approach is feasible and acceptable for diverse groups of youth, with no published reports of treatment contraindications.
>
> (Brown, 2015, p. 303)

Counselors working with children and adolescents can use mindfulness techniques to increase impulse control and self-awareness and to reduce emotional reactivity to problematic and stressful events (Thomas & Gauntlet-Gilbert, 2008).

Expressive and Experiential Techniques

Many expressive and experiential techniques work well with children and adolescents (and adults!!). We are not able to cover all of them in this text; however, we do discuss adventure/wilderness/outdoor therapy and uses for such with children and adolescents. We discuss ways in which counselors can use music, yoga, dance, art, and drama in the work they do. We give information about becoming specialized in these areas, and also information about using techniques to assist clients. Many complementary, alternative, and other healing modalities exist, as well. We will briefly cover a few of these in this text. It is important to get creative and seek to match your techniques with the needs of your client instead of using a one-size-fits-all approach to clinical work.

Counseling the Whole Child

When we hear the term holistic, what comes to mind? Counseling the whole child is referring to an approach to working with children and adolescents. When considering the person as a whole, counselors are taking into account every part of the individual that makes up a whole – physical, emotional/mental, and spiritual selves – thus seeking to understand body, mind, and spirit. As opposed to a problem-based, symptoms approach that often focuses on parts of a whole instead of taking the whole person into consideration, counseling the whole child is a way to understand each individual's culture, emotional and mental well-being, physical attributes, spiritual needs – and the connections and overlaps of the aspects that make up each individual person. For example, when a child is repeatedly asking to leave school due to a stomachache, we could simply treat symptoms, or we could seek to understand a mind-body connection and how symptoms can manifest in myriad ways – physical, emotional/mental, and spiritual. Understanding that feelings of anxiety and depression often manifest in bodily discomfort, we take into account the emotional/mental aspects, as well as the physical. Of course, sometimes a stomachache is just a stomachache. When we seek to treat the individual as a whole, counselors understand that "mind and body are intimately connected chemically and share a vital energetic force that cannot be separated into parts. It is this energy, this circulation of emotional information throughout the body and mind, that supports health and well-being" (Latorre, 2000, p. 67). Thus, it is important to understand that we are not working with a collection of symptoms or a checklist approach to diagnosis and treatment; we are working with people, individuals, and systems that are complex and multifaceted.

Wellness-Based Approach

As counselors, we take a holistic and wellness-based approach to working with clients, and we view issues, presenting concerns, and live stressors as a part of a whole. The wellness-based approach of counseling is the foundation for our field. Having a wellness, holistic, and developmental approach to working with children and adolescents is often what sets us apart from other helping professional foundational concepts. Myers, Sweeney, and Witmer (2000) defined wellness as "a way of life oriented toward optimal health and well-being, in which body, mind, and spirit are integrated by the individual to live life more fully within the human and natural community" (p. 252).

Wellness Wheel

Figure 2.1 is one example of a wellness wheel. This is an example of an informal evaluation tool easily accessible for use in counseling. Many examples exist in literature and on the internet. After examining the wheel, what areas might you need to pay attention to? What areas might you be doing well in?

Based on Individual Psychology and the work of Alfred Adler, Sweeney and Witmer (1991) and Witmer and Sweeney (1992) developed the Wheel of Wellness for use in counseling. Their Wheel of Wellness has been used in classes, workshops, and trainings

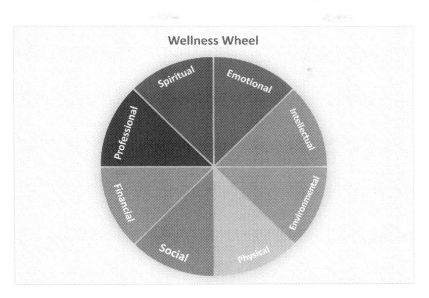

Figure 2.1 Wellness Wheel

with counselors in training, counselors, clinicians, other professionals, and with clients in individual, group, and couples settings in primarily adult populations (Myers et al., 2000). The authors suggest using the Wheel of Wellness in counseling in a four-phase approach:

> (1) introduction of the Wheel of Wellness model, including a lifespan focus; (2) formal or informal assessment, or both, based on the model; (3) intentional interventions to enhance wellness in selected areas of the Wheel; and (4) evaluation, follow-up, and continuation of Steps 2 through 4.
>
> (p. 257)

While this book does not serve as counseling, or self-help per se, it is certainly important for you as a counselor to constantly be doing your own work. Have you ever assessed your own level of wellness and thought about what that might mean for you? What follows are a few questions adapted from the Wellness Evaluation of Lifestyle assessment (WEL; Myers, 1998; Myers, Witmer, & Sweeney, 1996), a more formal evaluation tool for use in counseling and originally developed to evaluate every factor present in the Wheel of Wellness (Sweeney & Witmer, 1991; Witmer & Sweeney, 1992). It has over 100 statements for individuals to evaluate honestly. There are full versions available in the literature and online with information for scoring and use in counseling. As an introduction to this assessment, when examining these adapted statements, take into consideration if you strongly agree, agree, disagree, or strongly disagree with each. Answer honestly and as you are most of the time in your life. Please don't answer as you wish yourself to be.

I enjoy leisure activities that feel fulfilling to me.
Generally speaking, I find a way to cope with stress in healthy ways.
I truly value the person I am.
I have friends who truly value the person I am.
When difficult situations arise, I am able to work through them.

I am supported as an individual within my culture and community.
I try to take care of myself by eating well.
I set goals for myself and seek to follow through.
Generally speaking, I enjoy the work I do.

What are your thoughts on these statements? By utilizing wellness wheels and formal and informal evaluations to wellness, we can build rapport, develop goals with our clients, and seek to work toward healing. This is all a part of a strengths-based and holistic approach, and can be beneficial if you have done work yourself in these areas, especially since the wellness approach is foundational for our field of counseling.

Multicultural Implications and Advocacy

Understanding that all counseling is multicultural is important. Much consideration needs to be given to the person of the client and that every single child and adolescent has a different and complex culture. While there are entire books written on multicultural competence, this book hopes to bring in culturally sensitive techniques and information into each chapter, along with having a chapter dedicated to specific multicultural information.

In introducing cultural competence information, it is imperative that we start with counselor self-awareness. Understanding your own level or knowledge, awareness, and skills for working with a diverse group of children and adolescents is essential. Knowledge, awareness, and skills are the foundational building blocks for all work as clinicians and certainly for building cultural competence. As we understand it is impossible to ever fully be culturally competent, we seek to always be culturally sensitive and acknowledge that we will be seeking cultural competence during our professional careers and hopefully throughout our lifetimes. It is also important to understand that cultural competence is not just an ethical imperative – it is really a lifestyle. In Sue and Sue's *Counseling the Culturally Diverse* text, they offer an essential place to start for understanding culture.

1. Listen and be open to stories of those most disempowered in this society. Counseling has always been about listening to our clients. Don't allow your emotional reactions to negate their voices because you become defensive.
2. Know that although you were not born wanting to be racist, sexist, or heterosexist, or to be prejudiced against any other group, your cultural conditioning has imbued certain biases and prejudices in you. No person or group is free from inheriting the biases of this society.
3. Understand and acknowledge your intense emotions and what they mean for you. *CCD* [*Counseling the Culturally Diverse*] speaks about unfairness, racism, sexism, and prejudice, making some feel accused and blamed. The "isms" of our society are not pleasant topics, and we often feel unfairly accused.
4. It is important that helping professionals understand how they may still benefit from the past actions of their predecessors and continue to reap the benefits of the present social/educational arrangements.
5. Understand that multicultural training requires more than book learning. In your journey to *cultural competence*, it is necessary to supplement your intellectual development with experiential reality.
6. Don't be afraid to explore yourself as a racial/cultural being. An overwhelming number of mental health practitioners believe they are good, decent, and moral people. Because most of us would not intentionally discriminate, we often find great difficulty in realizing that our belief systems and actions may have oppressed others.

7. Open dialogue – to discuss and work through differences in thoughts, beliefs, and values – is crucial to becoming culturally competent. It is healthy when we are allowed to engage in free dialogue with one another. To a large extent, unspoken thoughts and feelings serve as barriers to open and honest dialogue about the pain of discrimination and how each and every one of us perpetuates bias through our silence or obliviousness.
8. Finally, continue to use these suggestions in reading throughout the text. What emotions or feelings are you experiencing? Where are they coming from? Are they blocking your understanding of the material? What do these reactions mean for your personal and as a helping professional?

(2015, pp. 31–32)

While it can be challenging to humbly and honestly approach these topics while being self-aware and open to the work we need to do on ourselves, the work is rewarding and certainly worthwhile. We will visit cultural considerations in each chapter and have a chapter dedicated to our continued striving for competence and celebration of diversity.

Summary

This chapter has asked you to think about your own beliefs about human nature and how individuals change. No doubt you will continue to formulate your own ideas about this and incorporate that into your counseling work. Understanding the stages of change can be beneficial for work with children and adolescents.

Developmentally appropriate interventions and techniques were introduced, with complete chapters on specific techniques following later in this text. As you began to think about specific techniques for working with children and adolescents, you started to examine your ideas about a one-size-fits-all model of counseling and understand techniques from a developmental and individualized perspective. A section on counseling the whole child addressed a holistic approach instead of a symptoms-based model focused on pathology. The wellness-based approach of counseling as a foundation for our field was presented as you assessed your current level of wellness.

Specific strategies for working with children and adolescents were offered. Such strategies include being careful with questions, using silence in a therapeutic way, avoiding power struggles, constantly using encouragement in everything we do, and using ourselves – the person of the counselor to benefit the therapeutic alliance and the counseling process as it relates to children and adolescents. The chapter closes with an introduction and challenge to approach all counseling as multicultural. This started our conversation about continued striving for cultural sensitivity.

Clinician's Corner

During my professional journey as an educator, I have encountered many students who shy away from counseling children and adolescents. I am always curious to the reasoning behind their decision, as I enjoy working with children and adolescents, with adolescents being my favorite population.

One of the hardest things I have experienced in working with children and adolescents is that you have to have a foundation in human development. Lifespan development and developmental theories provide helpful information about children and adolescent development. When you understand development during periods of time, counselors are better able to tailor interventions in addressing those developmental issues and milestones. Also, counselors are able to make clinical decisions on whether behaviors are developmentally appropriate or developmentally inappropriate.

Additionally, even when they have a foundation in human development, counselors should be culturally sensitive to the needs of children and adolescents. For example, issues related to race/ethnicity, ability, gender identity, sexual/affectional orientation, etc., are complex issues that can compound the developmental experience for children and adolescents. Being sensitive to these issues will help ensure that you are providing culturally sensitive care to children and adolescents.

Finally, some children and adolescents are experiencing trauma or being exposed to traumatic events throughout their development. This, too, adds more complexity to the care that counselors provide. It is also beneficial to have a foundation and/or expertise in trauma-informed care with children and adolescents.

Although most of my time now is spent as an educator with limited time providing clinical services, I continue to educate myself about work with children and adolescents by attending professional development workshops and conferences.

Tamekia Bell, Ph.D., LCPC(IL), NCC
Governors State University

References

Abid, M., Irfan, M., & Naeem, F. (2017). Relationship between mindfulness and bullying behavior among school children: An exploratory study from Pakistan. *Journal of Postgraduate Medical Institute, 31*(1), 256–259.

Ardito, R. B., & Rabellino, D. (2011). Therapeutic alliance and outcome of psychotherapy: Historical excursus, measurements, and prospects for research. *Frontiers in Psychology, 2*, 270. http://doi.org/10.3389/fpsyg.2011.00270

Brown, D. S. (2015). Mindfulness training for children and adolescents: A state-of-the-science review. In K. W. Brown, J. D. Creswell, & R. M. Ryan (Eds.), *Handbook of mindfulness: Theory, research and practice*. New York: Guilford Press.

Dreikurs, R., Grunwald, B. B., & Pepper, F. C. (1982). *Maintaining sanity in the classroom: Classroom management techniques* (2nd ed.). Harper & Row.

Gil, E. (2006). *Helping abused and traumatized children: Integrating directive and nondirective approaches*. New York: The Guilford Press.

Hays, D. G., & Mcleod, A. L. (2018). The culturally competent counselor. In D. G. Hays & B. T. Erford (Eds.), *Developing multicultural competence: A systems approach* (3rd ed., pp. 2–36). New York: Pearson.

Hill, C. E., Thompson, B. J., & Ladany, N. (2003). Therapists use of silence in therapy: A survey. *Journal of Clinical Psychology, 59*(4), 513–524. https://doi.org/10.1002/jclp.1015

Hilt, L. M., & Pollak, S. D. (2012). Getting out of rumination: Comparison of three brief interventions in a sample of youth. *Journal of Abnormal Child Psychology, 40*(7), 1157–1165. https://doi.org/10.1007/s10802-012-9638-3

Homeyer, L. E., & Sweeney, D. S. (2011). *Sandtray therapy: A practical manual* (2nd ed.). New York: Routledge.

Horvath, A. O., & Bedi, R. P. (2002). The alliance. In J. C. Norcross (Ed.), *Psychotherapy relationships that work: Therapist contributions and responsiveness to patients* (pp. 37–69). New York: Oxford University Press.

Kabat-Zinn, J. (1994). *Wherever you go, there you are: Mindfulness meditation in everyday life*. New York: Hyperion.

Kabat-Zinn, J. (2003). Mindfulness-based interventions in context: Past, present, and future. *Clinical Psychology: Science and Practice, 10*(2), 144–156. https://doi.org/10.1093/clipsy/bpg016

Kottler, J. (2018). *Change: What really leads to lasting personal transformation*. New York: Oxford University Press.

Kottman, T. (2011). *Play therapy: Basics and beyond* (2nd ed.). Alexandria, VA: American Counseling Association.

Ladany, N., Hill, C. E., Thompson, B. J., & O'Brien, K. M. (2004). Therapist perspectives on using silence in therapy: A qualitative study. *Counseling and Psychotherapy Research, 4*(1), 80–89. https://doi.org/10.1080/14733140412331384088

Landreth, G. (2012). *Play therapy: The art of the relationship* (3rd ed.). New York: Brunner-Routledge.

Latorre, M. A. (2000). A holistic view of psychotherapy: Connecting mind, body, and spirit. *Perspectives in Psychiatric Care, 36*(2), 67–68. https://doi.org/10.1111/j.1744-6163.2000.tb00693.x

Mellenthin, C. (2018). *Play therapy: Engaging and powerful techniques for the treatment of childhood disorders*. Eau Claire, WI: PESI Publishing & Media.

Mendler, A. N., & Mendler, B. D. (2012). *Power struggles: Successful techniques for educators* (2nd ed.). Bloomington, IN: Solution Tree Press.

Myers, J. E. (1998). *Manual for the wellness evaluation of lifestyle*. Palo Alto, CA: MindGarden.

Myers, J. E., Sweeney, T. J., & Witmer, J. M. (2000). The wheel of wellness counseling for wellness: A holistic model for treatment planning. *Journal of Counseling & Development, 78*, 251–266. https://doi.org/10.1002/j/1556-6676.2000.tb01906.x

Myers, J. E., Witmer, J. M., & Sweeney, T. J. (1996). *The wellness evaluation of lifestyle*. Palo Alto, CA: MindGarden, Inc.

Nelsen, J. (2006). *Positive discipline*. New York: Random House Inc.

Norcross, J. C., Krebs, P. M., & Prochaska, J. O. (2011). Stages of change. *Journal of Clinical Psychology, 67*(2), 143–154. https://doi.org/10.1002/jclp.20758

Oaklander, V. (2007). *Windows to our children: A gestalt therapy approach to children and adolescents*. Gouldsboro, ME: The Gestalt Journal Press.

Parker, P. D., Martin, A. J., Martines, C., Marsh, H. W., & Jackson, S. A. (2010). Stages of change in physical activity: A validation study in late adolescences. *Health Education & Behavior, 37*(2), 318–329. https://doi.org/10.1177/1090198109333281

Prochaska, J. O., & Velicer, W. F. (1997). The transtheoretical model of health behavior change. *American Journal of Health Promotion, 12*(1), 38–48. https://doi.org/10.4278/0890-1171-12.1.38

Ray, D. C., & McCullough, R. (2015; revised 2016). *Evidence-based practice statement: Play therapy*. Research Report. Retrieved from Association for Play Therapy website: www.a4pt.org/?page=EvidenceBased

Remple, K. D. (2012). Mindfulness for children and youth: A review of the literature with an argument for school-based implementation. *Canadian Journal of Counselling and Psychotherapy, 46*(3), 201–220.

Sue, D. W., & Sue, D. (2015). *Counseling the culturally diverse: Theory and practice* (7th ed.). Hoboken, NJ: John Wiley & Sons, Inc.

Sweeney, T. J., & Witmer, J. M. (1991). Beyond social interest: Striving toward optimum health and wellness. *Individual Psychology, 47*, 527–540.

Thomas, M., & Gauntlet-Gilbert, J. (2008). Mindfulness with children and adolescents: Effective clinical application. *Clinical Child Psychology and Psychiatry, 13*(3), 395–407. https://doi.org/10.1177/1359104508090603

Tornero, M. D. L. A., & Capella, C. (2017). Change during psychotherapy through sand play tray in children that have been sexually abused. *Frontiers in Psychology, 8*, 1–12. https://doi.org/10.3389/fpsyg.2017.00617

Witmer, J. M., & Sweeney, T. J. (1992). A holistic model for wellness and prevention over the lifespan. *Journal of Counseling and Development, 71*, 140–148. https://doi.org/10.1002/j.1556-6676.1992.tb02189.x

3 A Review of Theories as Related to Children and Adolescents

Chad Luke and Rebekah Byrd

Objectives

- Understand your own views regarding normative development.
- Examine your own views of how development goes awry.
- Understand the role of counseling theory in addressing both normative and non-normative development.
- Reintroduce counseling theories.
- Apply counseling theory to both children and adolescents.
- Differentiate use of theory base of presenting problem.
- Identify eight dimensions of human experience to factor in while working with children and adolescents.

Reflective Questions

- Which of the theories that I've learned about up to this point resonate most strongly with me?
- What differences, if any, are there between theories when applied to adults and when applied to children and adolescents?
- How can I use information about counseling theories to better inform my own development?
- How can I use information about counseling theories to better inform my practice?
- What are some ways I can use theory to better understand when development runs off course?

This is not a theories text. Counselors in training have an entire class (and sometimes more) dedicated to just theories. However, most of the time these theories are only presented in regards to working with adults. Children and adolescents can be left out of the theories classes, which is an issue raised by many in Council for Accreditation of Counseling and Related Education Programs (CACREP) programs. While this text is not a theories text, it is vital to the work counselors do with children and adolescents to understand specific theories and how they apply to working with this population. Some theories lend themselves better and other theories are missing from theories classes all together. This chapter will focus on those theories. Theories that are especially helpful when working with children and adolescents include Adlerian, solution-focused brief counseling, Rational Emotive Behavior Therapy, group counseling, child-centered counseling, narrative counseling, Gestalt, reality and choice therapy, and Cognitive Behavioral Therapy. Other important theories for working with children and adolescents and ones often left out of theories classes altogether include relational cultural theory, feminist therapy, dialectical behavioral therapy, humanistic therapy, the holistic and integrative therapy approach, and creativity in counseling. Of major importance in this chapter is a focus on "what" more than "why" in counseling children and adolescents. Rather than using theory to try to tell us *why* a child or adolescent is behaving in a certain way, this chapter will use theory to describe *what* is happening with the child or adolescent and to direct *what* to do next. Multicultural implications, summary, and references are presented at the end of this chapter.

In this chapter, we begin by returning to the core maxims in working with children and with adolescents, some of which are extensions of the work of others (see Landreth, 2012).

- Children are not diminutive (young, small) adults, and thus cannot be expected to have the same emotional regulatory capabilities as adults, nor do they have the cognitive development needed to engage in particular types of talk therapy.
- At the same time, children are not somehow less than human, so they cannot be treated as objects incapable of experiencing and understanding complex emotions.
- Therefore, children need therapeutic approaches that honor their primary language – play – but also recognize the limits of experience, mentalizing, and regulation.
- Adolescents, too, have unique characteristics that affect their ability to benefit from various therapeutic approaches. Cognitive capacities are often swamped by hormonal changes and egocentrism; therefore, counseling, regardless of the theoretical underpinnings, may take a different tack.

First, we describe the more common factors that all therapeutic approaches share.

Common Factors: What Works in Counseling With Children and Adolescents

Before looking at the ways specific counseling theories inform our work with children, adolescents, and their families or caregivers, it helps to first note what most theories share in common. The client's current explanation for what is wrong may not actually lead to problem resolution (Wampold & Ulvenes, 2019).

The common factors (CF) approach, first named in Frank and Frank (1993) and expanded upon by Wampold (2001), seeks to understand the effects of psychotherapies by what they have in common, not what makes each unique. The approach may best be understood as consisting of five factors, though there are various versions that exist. Laska, Gurman, and Wampold (2014) describe them this way:

(a) an emotionally charged bond between the therapist and patient,
(b) a confiding healing setting in which therapy takes place,
(c) a therapist who provides a psychologically derived and culturally embedded explanation for emotional distress,
(d) an explanation that is adaptive (i.e., provides viable and believable options for overcoming specific difficulties) and is accepted by the patient, and
(e) a set of procedures or rituals engaged by the patient and therapist that leads the patient to enact something that is positive, helpful, or adaptive.

(p. 469)

The common factors view is contrasted by treatment *specific factors* approaches, like Cognitive Behavioral Therapy (CBT), for example, wherein the specific factor is cognitive restructuring. Nevertheless, the CBT community has evolved to recognize the role of so-called common factors in making treatment more effective. The current state of the research is that beyond the dichotomies (common versus specific factors), both are needed in concert for counseling to be effective (Norcross & Wampold, 2019). Norcross and Wampold (2019) challenge the interpretation of common factors approaches that all that is needed is a warm, earnest, and sincere relationship for counseling to be effective. It is this relationship plus intentionality, often demonstrated through a well-reasoned theoretical approach and intervention. But for now, back to CF.

As you review the preceding list, consider a recent relationship you have had with a professional, like a physician. You entered into the relationship with this person to address something that mattered to you – there was something at *stake* (a). You may have extended a measure of trust in the *place* of the physician building and office – a place where things that matter are addressed (b). As you discuss your concerns with your physician, you may find yourself looking for an explanation of your experience that makes sense to you and is appropriate to your cultural identity and social norms (c). You then likely listen for the explanation that brings with it hope for some adaptation within your experience (d). Finally, with these conditions met, you will receive and follow a set of treatment recommendations (e). While your engagement in the treatment remains somewhat unpredictable, these five factors increase the likelihood that you will experience success. And while this parallel and others like it (e.g., attorney, priest, accountant, etc.) are limited, we can see that there are common conditions that seem to promote a sense of hope or well-being. Thus is the case with CF in counseling.

As you consider counseling with children and adolescents, keep in mind what it might take to form this therapeutic relationship with a young individual, then how you might use the material in this chapter to guide your thinking about how to intervene.

Theories: What and Where It Hurts

As depicted in Table 3.1, discerning where the hurt is – or in other terms, where the problem is – takes time and patience using warm attending and gentle questioning. Even with this approach, it can be challenging to identify where the hurt is. Even caregivers who observe the child or adolescent daily over long periods of time may struggle to determine where the hurt is. It is not easy to know where it hurts; it can be even more challenging to determine where to begin in addressing the hurt. One tool that all counselors have at their disposal to aid in this work are counseling theories. These theories can provide awareness of how to address hurts by providing a window into the mechanisms of hurt and trajectories of helping. Theories are ways of viewing client symptoms and disorders; they also provide a map to create a plan for treatment. It is important to remember that theories are lenses or filters for reality, they are not necessarily reality themselves. They represent our best ways (currently) of understanding human cognition, emotion, and behavior.

As you think about how people communicate hurts and how they try to make the hurt go away, it can be useful to take a broader perspective first. Luke (2017, 2020) describes an eight-factor meta-model for understanding counseling theory. It describes eight dimensions of experience, depicted in Figure 3.1. As you consider each dimension, it may be helpful to reflect on where theories locate the hurt and how they set about to address them.

Table 3.1 Discerning What and Where It Hurts

Child: My belly hurts	Caregiver: Are you OK?	Counselor: What brings you to counseling?
Caregiver: Where does it hurt?	Adolescent: (shrugs)	
Child: Here (pointing)	Caregiver: Does something hurt?	Caregiver: (pointing to adolescent) Their attitude. (adolescent rolls their eyes)
Caregiver: What does it feel like?	Adolescent: I don't know.	Counselor: Would you say more?
Child: It hurts.	Caregiver: Can I do something for you?	Caregiver: They are just negative.
Caregiver: What do you need?	Adolescent: (shrugs)	Counselor: So a negative attitude, then?
Child: Make it stop hurting.		Caregiver: Yes!

A Lens to View Dimensions of the Human Experience: Looking at the Component Parts

The eight-factor model (Luke, 2017, 2020) is a holistic model identifying eight components that every counselor must consider when working with clients, and includes: thinking, feelings, behaviors, environments, experiences, biology and genetics, relationships, and the socio-cultural context in which the client lives. Each domain is supported by underlying neurobiological mechanisms.

Relationships form the central feature of human experience – individual brains are best understood in the context of social relationships in terms of functioning (Kleinbub, 2017), in that brains are organized for complex socio-cognitive functioning (Clark-Polner & Clark, 2014). Counselors and clients exert a reciprocal influence on neurobiological functioning (Beckes, Ijzerman, & Tops, 2015), which has implications for counselors' intentionality in their ways of being and acting in session (Luke, 2020). It also has implications for how counselors care for themselves even while in session, as their brain is exposed to the client's (Palmieri et al., 2018).

Relationships

Research has long supported the view that humans are nothing if not social, and therefore require healthy relationships to develop and function effectively. Attachment studies and theorists have increased our awareness of this for children's development (e.g., Ainsworth, 1978), and now neuroscience has lent even greater weight to early relationships and their role in healthy development (see Luke, 2020). For example, early attachment (relationship with caregiver) plays a significant role in neural development, from cognition to stress management (Clark-Polner & Clark, 2014; Gennaro, Kleinbub, Mannarini, Salvatore, & Palmieri, 2019; Kleinbub, 2017). It is for these reasons that relationships are viewed as the core of the model and foundational to all theory. In other words, development begins with relationship, and individuals are best understood in relational context (Kleinbub, 2017).

Socio-Cultural Milieu

Humans exist in layer upon layer of contexts (Bronfenbrenner, 1979). These contexts shape individual behaviors, and really all other components of this model. From the perspective of this text, children represent a distinct cultural group, as do adolescents. And their developmental culture interacts with multiple other groups, such as family, friends, school, neighborhoods, places of worship, and society as a whole. What this means for counselors is that the client we see before us is but a glimpse into multiple facets of social and cultural characteristics that impact their perceptions and responses to both internal and external factors. Because of these layers, is it important to understand individual characteristics, or as MacDonald (1997) describes it, the "subjective individual culture of one's life experience" (p. 199). We describe six of these in the remainder of the model.

Biology/Genetics

Biology/genetics are always "in the room" in counseling, as all that is human arises from neurobiological processes (Kalat, 2019). The nature/nurture debate is well settled in neuroscience, at least as far as the interdependence between the two has been established (Kalat, 2019). The biological facet of these dimensions involves biological functions, including sleep, diet/nutrition, exercise, and overall physical health, to name a few. It is a vital part of assessment in counseling to address biological dimensions of functioning. The second facet involves genetics, or the material coded in an individual's DNA and passed down from previous generations. Given the building evidence of experience-dependent plasticity – the turning on of genes based on experiences and behaviors – it is important to recognize family history in the role heredity plays in functioning.

Environment

Environment includes both previous and current living situations and can be physical and/or emotional. Early environments shape the development of all humans, facilitating or blocking growth in core domains of experience like cognition, emotion, relationships, and behavior (Suleiman & Dahl, 2017). Environments earlier (than the present but after childhood) can reinforce, dispute, or alter the effects of previous environments. Current environments are perhaps the most readily apparent environments in working with clients. What is less apparent are the implicit environmental cues that evoke responses from individuals (Farah, 2018). For example, a client describes a certain pattern of behavior that is uncharacteristic of them generally when entering a certain environment (like childhood home). Unbeknownst to them, the myriad environmental cues (sights, smells, sounds, emotion, etc.) are activating memory systems that result in reactions.

Experience

Experience can be both proximal and distal, and as the wealth of lab and practice-based research show, can shape how our brain develops. Often referred to as experience-dependent plasticity (Sweatt, 2016), experiences in cognition, emotion, behavior, and environment can directly impact the structure and function of neural networks in the brain (Sweatt, 2016). In other words, experiences can be long lasting, even extending across generations, so the common expectation expressed in society that individuals "move on" from their experience may be easier said than done from a neurobiological perspective.

Cognition, Affect, and Behavior

Cognition, affect, and behavior are considered together here, as they often are in many theories of counseling, and because their interactions with each other are often the content of theory. Cognition, or thinking, is a type of behavior, but is a distinct phenomenon, as well. It encompasses language, perception, attention, memory, and other facets, as well (Pulvermüller, Garagnani, & Wennekers, 2014, as cited in Luke, 2020). Affect, emotion, and feelings have a long history of investigation in the fields of psychology and counseling. Often, emotions have been viewed as subordinate reactions to cognition or environmental cues, whereas more recent conceptions view them as fundamental to human functioning (Panksepp & Biven, 2012). Expanding on this latter view, Hansen (2012) and Luke (2020) view emotion as a separate, equally valid way of knowing truth, which must be attended to with care. Luke (2020) contends that it may be that neuroscience may one day find that cognition and emotion are more similar processes than dissimilar (see Panksepp, Lane, Solms, & Smith, 2017). Behavior, on the other hand, is a feature of human experience that is often the target in counseling, both as a referent for therapy and as a goal. Behavior is neurobiologically derived, though Skinner took issue with the field of neurobiology as is related to behavior (Bonnert et al., 2018). Luke (2020) asserts,

> The question for counselors concerns whether one believes that behavior is primarily a response to a stimulus (behaviorism) or if it is a psychological phenomenon in which some mediating variable (e.g., will, cognitive) affects the outcome of a given stimulus.
> (p. 22)

Each of these eight areas (Figure 3.1 Luke, 2017; 2020) have their neurobiological underpinnings, as well as effects. Enhancing our understanding of this reciprocal relationship, both between and among the eight factors, as well as the neurobiological cause and effect, will guide counselors into a richer appreciation for the client's inner and outer world. We contend that this will improve the therapeutic bond, and also serve as both a common factor and specific factor of therapeutic value (see Norcross & Wampold, 2019 for extended discussion of the need for both a common factors and specific factors approach to producing positive clinical outcomes).

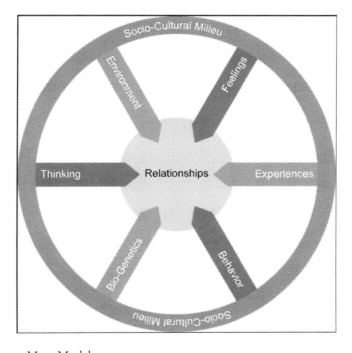

Figure 3.1 8-Factor Meta Model

Summary of Theory

It is far beyond the space and intent of this chapter to provide a comprehensive picture of each theory, much less survey the over 400 theoretical approaches out there (Norcross & Wampold, 2019). It is, however, useful to briefly summarize and highlight primary features of dominant approaches.

Humanistic-Existential Perspectives

In our view, humanistic-type therapies are essentially relationship-based approaches. One of the keys to working successfully with children and adolescents lies in relationship formation and maintenance. Children and adolescents have something of a sixth sense when it comes to sensing inauthentic people and responses. This requires counselors to invest in their own growth and self-awareness, leading to a crucial factor in working with this population: laying aside the pressure and natural tendency to act as a parental figure or teacher. Relationship-based approaches, namely person-centered or child-centered, require the counselor to actively promote an environment of Rogers' (1957) core conditions: genuineness or authenticity (sometimes called congruence), empathy or deep understanding of the client's experience, and unconditional positive regard or acceptance. A narrow view of these three core conditions interprets them as passive, when, in fact, they are very active processes (Luke, Miller, & McAuliffe, 2019). Let's look at each a little more closely.

Empathy is the process of entering another person's world and viewing the world through their eyes. It is from this core condition that we see the difficulty of this process. Often, counselors in training and counselors alike forget what childhood and adolescence is like. This happens through maturation and the demands of (emerging) adulthood. It happens through repression when a counselor's own childhood or adolescence involved overwhelmingly negative experiences. And it happens when a counselor's childhood was very positive, creating distance in their understanding of developmental difficulties of clients. In place of accurate, active empathy, counselors may default to projective sympathy (Luke, Redekop, & Moralejo, 2020), wherein they imagine what they would feel like (sympathy) if they were the child or adolescent, and then assume (project) that is what the child or adolescent is feeling. This represents a critical breakdown of empathy. Instead, the counselor must reflect on their own limitations in understanding a child's or adolescent's experience, and work diligently to gain that understanding.

In order to gain this depth of understanding, it is vital that the counselor learn the "language" of the client. Children speak a very different language than adults, and this language barrier requires counselors to relearn this language (Sommers-Flanagan & Sommers-Flanagan, 2007). Children's primary language is play (Landreth, 2012). This does not require that all counselors working with children become play therapists or learn to interpret play according to some interpretive tool. It merely requires that counselors engage in some form of play with their young clients. Not only do children "talk" *through* play, most talk *during* play, and this can be a terrific invitation into the client's world and worldview (see Axline, 1969). More will be said about play in Chapter 15 of this volume, but it is important to remember two dimensions of using play to learn about the child: first, play has to be defined by the child, not the counselor, so imposing an adult-oriented or even therapy-oriented play is less productive or even counterproductive; second, play must be used with intentionality. This means that the counselor must be more active that just spending 45 minutes playing "Crazy Eights" (except in very specific cases or circumstances).

If play is the language of children and learning that language is the path to empathy, what, you may ask, is the language of adolescence? Learning the language of adolescents is a little like trying to hit a moving target. Depending on the age and experiences of the individual, adolescence is a bridge between childhood and emerging adulthood, so the language tends to oscillate between childlike play and adult-like speech. This can make interacting with adolescents challenging, but also thrilling! You rarely know what to expect – a surprise childlike response or a precocious adult-like response. Adaptability on the part of counselors is key here. We have had 17-year-old clients who wanted to play very childlike games in session, and we have had 13-year-olds who wanted to spend time in session reflecting on the meaning of life. Thrilling! Adolescents still need play, and may best communicate through play. This can mean reintroducing childlike play as needed, or investing in adolescent play. This might involve listening with them to their current favorite song, watching them play a videogame, or viewing with them a favorite YouTuber. The point of this all is to gain a better sense of the individual sitting with you, so that your understanding of their experience is more complete.

Empathy really sets the stage to implement the other two core factors, congruence and acceptance. We describe implementation of these because they are not static features of humanistic characteristics. Just as empathy is active – experiencing and then expressing – so too are the others. Congruence, genuineness, or authenticity is really about the inside of the counselor matching the outside. It entails an awareness of one's experience of another person and strives to both modify a negative feeling toward a client, while also being true to that initial feeling. In other words, if I feel negatively toward my client, I must not try to push that out of my awareness, as that will certainly "leak" into the relationship (Luke, 2020); instead, I work to understand my feelings toward my client and use them to: (a) understand myself better; and (b) understand others' experiences of my client. In session, this does not mean that I tell my client all my thoughts and feelings toward them (Rogers, 1942), especially since some of my experience might say more about me than it does them. Instead, I might offer a reflection of my feelings with my client for the purpose of providing my client with genuine feedback. For example, "when you describe some of the behaviors you engage in with your peers at school, I find myself feeling concerned about you and them". This can lead to a discussion of the ways off-putting behaviors may be in conflict with their values, as aligning behaviors with values is a hallmark of a person-centered approach (Rogers, 1942). This only works, however, when a counselor has invested in experiencing and expressing empathy, along with the next feature, acceptance.

Unconditional positive regard, or acceptance, involves looking inside oneself to find what truly matters. This enables the counselor to move beyond mere performance expectations that can be inadvertently imposed on clients. I hasten to add that this is not acceptance of negative or destructive behavior; it is acceptance of the person behind the behavior. One way to say this is,

> It is generally safe to assume that clients enter counseling in some degree of fear or uncertainty that their cognitive and emotional experiences will be [viewed] as intolerable to the counselor as they have been to both themselves and to others who matter to them. For this reason, Rogers (1942) asserts that it is essential to habituate to accepting clients' negative and positive expressions, to avoid the dangers of coming across as judging either.
> (Luke, 2020, p. 122)

For many clients, whether child, adolescent, or adult, this will be the first, or one of the very few, times that another person worked so hard to understand their experience, and once understood, withheld judgment, and even responded with warmth and caring. This is vital to grasp, as one of the chief criticisms students and new counselors have of this approach is that it is not active, that it does not feel like the counselor is *doing* anything. This is fair to a certain extent, but adopting these characteristics in practice is both harder than it seems, and is a prerequisite for trying to introduce some change in the client. Implementing these characteristics, as any counselor who has tried this can tell you, is anything but passive; it is difficult and takes a lot of work! It is important to recall at this point, that for Rogers (e.g., 1995), humans are made to develop, adapt, and fully become, such that the role of counseling is to help remove barriers to this natural growth process.

Motivational Interviewing

Once it is time to move further into more explicit action (recognizing that the core conditions are very active and hard work, too), one way is to move toward motivational interviewing (MI), an approach that is a direct outgrowth of person-centered counseling. MI begins with the assumption that *most* people are *mostly* ambivalent about *most* change (Luke, 2020). The role of the counselor, then, is not to try to convince the child or adolescent – or even the caregivers – that they must change, but to walk with them through their ambivalence. The reason is that most children and adolescents have a sense of what is not working, or at least that something is wrong, and except in very rare cases or when working with very young children, clients know why they are in counseling. It is interesting to observe from our combined decades of clinical practice with children and adolescents how these individuals will expect counseling to be another adult telling them what they need to fix (see Vernon & Schimmel, 2019). MI challenges this assumption right away, and is often a surprise for clients and their families.

MI is particularly important when dealing with the parent or caregiver of the client, as many sessions may start with a parent or caregiver providing a behavior report card, detailing what the client has done wrong since the previous session. While allowing a parent or caregiver to vent about their frustrations, it is important that this not happen in front of the child/adolescent, and that the venting be closely limited. This type of venting can and often does lead to the family believing that: (a) the client is more problem than person; and (b) that this information is to be taken as the counselor's responsibility to fix the client.

Four steps involved in MI are: (a) Communicating Empathy; (b) Developing Discrepancies of Ambivalence; (c) Rolling with Resistance; and (d) Evoking Self-Efficacy (Miller & Rollnick, 2012). Luke (2020) summarizes the steps this way:

Communicating Empathy: This first level has been addressed thoroughly in this chapter, but it bears repeating: when a counselor works hard to understand a client's cognitive and affective experience, and communicates through body and words, clients know it and are likely to be more committed to the relationship and therapeutic process, not to mention to apply this orientation toward their lives.

Ambivalence and Discrepancy: Think about the last time you wanted to or tried to change a thought, feeling, or behavior that was problematic for you. Would you describe your orientation toward change, in terms of your thinking, feeling, and behavior, as 100%? It's possible, of course, but not highly likely, given human motivation. Instead, we are often at war with ourselves over change, and we tend to play games with ourselves to stay stuck. One of the ways ambivalence emerges in clients is through the discrepancies in their communication. When counselors recognize this in themselves, it assists them in accepting it in their clients.

Rolling With Resistance: Although one of the core concepts in motivational interviewing involves managing resistance, we find it far more effective in cultivating empathy, genuineness, and unconditional positive regard (UPR) to refer to reluctance or the ambivalence described earlier. Our orientation toward clients shifts just by changing the language we use to describe them. In the first instance, "resistant" can evoke thoughts of active defiance in response to therapeutic endeavor and work. On the other hand, reluctance or ambivalence evokes reticence, or a sense that a client is not quite there yet. "Resist" feels like the client is not even willing to move in a healing direction. Nevertheless, regardless of the name given to it, rolling with the resistance keeps the counselor allied with the client, not blindly and passively following the client's lead, but choosing moments to motivate rather than resist the resistance. This is a powerful force in counseling and can create dissonance for the client, as many are unused to this in relationships.

Evoking Self-Efficacy: The process of drawing out client strengths and harnessing it toward building up clients' beliefs in their own ability to make healthy, meaningful decisions is the real goal of motivational interviewing. The other three steps set the stage for building this awareness of strength and willingness to exercise it on a daily basis. Self-efficacy is a well-researched construct leading to positive outcomes, in terms of both level of effort applied and duration of effort in the presence of obstacles. Table 3.2 presents a summary of humanistic perspectives adapted from Luke (2020).

Psychoanalytic/Psychodynamic Perspectives

Psychoanalytic/psychodynamic approaches are, from our perspective, essentially developmental approaches – those that deal with clients in relation to key moments over the course of natural development. These typically are stage-based theories, highlighting that stages of development are made up of tasks, the completion or successful resolution of which enables individuals to advance to the subsequent stage and begin to address the tasks therein. Most notable, perhaps, is psychoanalytic theory, which, once sexuality-is-all has been removed, provides a description of critical periods in development around early caregivers that form the foundation for sense of self and template for future relationships. This stage-based approach is also seen in Erikson's (1968) psychosocial stages of development. The stages have been updated and revised (Newman & Newman, 2015) to reflect a longer modern lifespan and additional stages, including prenatal development and emerging adulthood. At each stage, successful navigating of tasks results in an ego adaptation that promotes healthy development and movement to the next stage, whereas lack of success leads to a core pathology that inhibits growth to the next stage, making the individual vulnerable to compounding difficulties in subsequent stages. The first of two things to note about this

Table 3.2 Psychopathology Is Relational and Meaningful

Psychopathology Is Relational and Meaningful		
Foundational Concept	Humanistic Component	Therapeutic Value
Humans are made to be growth oriented, as long as conditions of worth are not externally imposed, leading to internalized limitations	Person-centered therapy (PCT) Empathy, genuineness, unconditional positive regard (UPR)	Anticipation and perception of acceptance/rejection at the neural level
Meaning and intentionality are essential for acting in goal-directed ways	Existential counseling: phenomenology	Inherent power in freedom and responsibility, Socratic questioning
Difficulties in living come from trying to live in fractured states, wherein we fail to accept aspects of ourselves	Gestalt: holism, here-and-now experiencing, experimentation	Counseling that activates multiple systems can be most effective, reconciling hated "parts" as essential to well-being

model is that success in a stage does not mean permanent success. For example, establishment of basic trust in the first 18 months does not ensure that trust won't be damaged or even undone by future trauma. Second, lack of success in a task or difficulty at a given stage is not permanent. Individuals can recover some degree of functioning associated with a developmental stage. The third developmental model of note is Individual Psychology or Adlerian Therapy, wherein early relationships once again form the foundation of healthy development leading to social interest. Adler's model has been the most operationalized therapeutically, in terms of stages of treatment and specific interventions. Many of Adler's theory shows up in other systems of psychotherapy, at times recognized as such, and other times incorporated without attribution. The essence of Adler's work is that early recollections – or, more accurately, our perceptions of those early recollections – shape our understanding of ourselves and our place in the world. Typically, these recollections are of relationships or are formed in the context of relationships. These relationships begin to define our sense of self, and the degree to which we are inwardly oriented (inferiority) or externally oriented (social interest). As applied to children, Adlerian theory has been applied to understanding motivation for behavior. Rudolf Dreikurs, a well-known successor, described problem behaviors (discouragement) in terms of four mistaken goals that are indispensable to counselors working with children, adolescents, and in particular, caregivers (see Dreikurs & Soltz, 1968). Mistaken goals come in four varieties: seeking attention, seeking power, seeking revenge, and seeking to prove inadequacy. Rather than viewing children or adolescents' behaviors as annoying or malicious, or character based, Dreikurs reframes these behaviors as ineffective ways of meeting legitimate needs. Table 3.3 presents a summary of psychodynamic perspectives adapted from Luke (2020).

Table 3.3 Psychopathology Is Historical and Developmental

Psychopathology Is Historical and Developmental

Foundational Concept	Psychodynamic Component	Therapeutic Value
Early relationships and brain development: The brain develops in the context of relationship; Beckes et al., "radically embodied theory of attachment and relationships" (2015)	Early relationships: Over the years, there has been a concerted analytic effort to identify in greater detail how early relationships form, how these early relationships affect later relationships, and how these relationships can be positively affected by contemporary clinicians – essentially, which relational acts can help to repair the damage caused by inadequate or abusive parenting (Redekop, Luke, & Malone, 2017, p. 104)	Illuminates the need for and power of interpersonal relationships at a neurological level
Consciousness: The brain processes operate at varying levels of awareness (consciousness) for adaptive reasons (although these can become problematic, as well)	"Less-than-conscious": The notion that instinctual drives operate outside of awareness and direct thinking and behavior; this applies to relational patterns, as well	Helps challenge how aware we *think* we are versus how unaware we *think* we are
Memory systems: This refers to how the brain encodes, stores, and retrieves information, especially the encoding of early memories compared with their retrieval later in life	Early memories: Whether repressed or not, early experiences, and the perceptions of those events, shape current functioning	Challenges how memories actually work, relative to perception and memory limitations

Cognitive- and Behavior-Based Perspectives

In this section, we briefly cover cognitive and behavioral strategies used in counseling children and adolescents. This section serves as a refresher, as it points the way to additional resources. When considering which approach to use in general, and with cognitive and behavioral strategies specifically, first identify whether the issue is related more to mood or to behavior. In addition to this, consider the age and developmental level of the child or adolescent.

Cognitive therapies, such as Aaron Beck's Cognitive Therapy (CT) and Albert Ellis's Rational Emotive Behavior Therapy (REBT), employ strategies that address the individual's thinking patterns that are self-defeating or dysfunctional, that lead to negative feels, and then to ineffective behaviors. Let's look at this a little more closely. For CT, CBT, and REBT, it is not the situation itself that results in emotional distress and behavioral dysregulation; instead, it is what we believe or tell ourselves about the situation that determines our feelings and subsequent behavior. Beck identified at least a dozen dysfunctional thoughts that most are familiar with, so for the sake of space, we have included a link to a website that summarizes these nicely. Ellis also identified a list of 12 irrational beliefs stemming from three core irrational philosophies of life. These automatic thoughts, core beliefs, and irrational philosophies undermine our ability to feel and act in productive ways. However, feelings and behaviors can be modified through the challenging and confronting of these dysfunctional thoughts and irrational beliefs. Clients can be guided through the process of keeping a thought journal in which they identify: (a) a challenging (**A**ctivating) event; (b) their **B**elief about that event; and (c) the emotional or behavioral **C**onsequences of that belief. After these patterns are discerned, the counselor works to help clients **D**ispute or challenge their thoughts or beliefs by identifying the "stinking thinking" or core irrational beliefs, then looking for evidence for this belief and seeking alternative explanations for their belief. Finally, clients are guided to **E**valuate their feelings after challenging these thoughts and beliefs.

Here is an important caveat to these approaches: counseling from these models does not mean that counselors help clients turn negative thoughts into positive thoughts. This misapplication of the model causes more harm than good, as it oversimplifies the client's struggles. Cognitive approaches are not positive thinking approaches and must not be treated as such; they are functional and rational thinking approaches that empower clients to control what they can control in a situation. One of the strengths of these approaches is that, if properly implemented in families, there can be quick gains, but these gains can be short-lived or superficial if additional, relational factors are not incorporated. Table 3.4 presents a summary of behavioral perspectives adapted from Luke (2020).

Constructivist/Postmodern Perspectives

The idea that reality is constructed is a challenging one to grasp. Reality is constructed in a number of ways, most of them outside our awareness. Often, comments and behaviors, and even a *DSM* (*Diagnostic and Statistical Manual of Mental Disorders*) diagnosis, is the only way to observe a child's or adolescent's reality. What's more, realty is a social construction, so working with a child or adolescent requires an understanding of how reality was constructed in the family system. A child who plays too loudly in the home is told to be quiet and even punished or banished (sent to their room). The socially constructed reality in that system may be children should be seen and not heard (Transactional Analysis refers to this as an injunction: don't be a child). Because the child is part of the system, and

Table 3.4 Psychopathology Is Behavioral

Psychopathology Is Behavioral

Neuro-Concept	Behavioral Component	Therapeutic Value
Hebb's rule as a specific form of neuroplasticity: "Neurons that fire together wire together"	Classical conditioning: Associative learning (paired condition and stimulus) entrenched behaviors that can be self-defeating and resistant to change	Explains how we get stuck in maladaptive behavioral patterns by making associations when there is limited value or even evidence
Biochemical changes in the brain in response to learning	Operant conditioning and social cognitive therapy: Instrumental learning and relearning new ways to behave by managing antecedents and consequents	Change is possible at the neurological level through the examination of what proceeds and what follows a behavior
Left- and right-brain processing: Logic (rationality) versus creativity (emotion)	Rational Emotive Behavior Therapy: What informs your decision making?	Emotions are real, but they do not necessarily represent reality; it is important to honor clients' perspectives while inviting them to challenge them
Mirror neurons/mirror system	SLT: (Bandura, 1982) often presented as the neural basis of empathy, most clearly the neural basis of mimicry and social modeling	Humans learn through observation, so this raises questions about incidental versus intentional learning
Language and attention in the brain: Movement of memory and awareness from implicit to explicit	Mindfulness and acceptance: Being aware of uncomfortable affective experiences without trying to change them	Behavior must be brought into awareness before it is able to be consciously changed (a shift from radical behaviorism)
	Reality therapy's WDEP: Wants, doing, evaluation, and planning	How does what you are *doing* reveal what you actually want?

depending on other support factors, the child may interpret this reality in terms of their own reality: it's not okay to be me. While simplistic, this example highlights how children and adolescents create their own reality based in part on their perception of the socially constructed realities of the systems in which they live (e.g., home, school, community).

One way of understanding the child's or adolescent's constructed reality, and in which a path to intervention unfolds, is through observation. Often described as the Hawthorne Effect, merely observing a phenomenon yields power to make changes. Counselors model in session by merely reflecting on an observation during a session. This can lead to family members making observations – while suspending judgment – of the child or adolescent. Perhaps most importantly, the child or adolescent can observe themselves in a thought, feeling, or behavior.

Once observation is practiced, the way to change or challenge reality is to observe and manage expectations related to the observation. This Pygmalion Effect, as it is called, highlights how expectation shapes perception. The classic study (Rosenthal & Jacobson, 1968) showed how teachers perceived and then treated differently, two halves of a class, based on made-up information about which students had high potential and which had low. In these studies, all the students were roughly equal, but the high potential students outperformed the low potential ones, based almost solely on the teacher's perception. Table 3.5 presents a summary of constructivist/postmodern perspectives adapted from Luke (2020).

Table 3.5 Constructivist/Postmodern Views

Constructivist/Postmodern Views: Psychopathology Is Constructed

Constructivist Component	Neuro-concept	Therapeutic Value
Therapeutic relationship	Right-mode processing and the brain	Brain-based ability to connect to clients where they are
Hawthorne Effect	Attention and attending/mindfulness	Observation changes behavior!
Narrative: Making meaning, positive expectations	Mind-brain problem/visual blind spot	Addresses the thought experiment, "Who or what does your thinking for you? What makes the brain do what it does?"; "shoot where you are aiming" allows clients to recalibrate their personal trajectory
Solution-focused therapy (SFT)/counseling	Orientation toward finding solutions unless sympathetic nervous system is overwhelmed	Solutions are readily apparent for the human brain, which is built to be resilient. However, it can be deceived and distracted when attention is channeled toward problems and flooded. Counseling offers a space for safe reflection and reorientation

Applications of Theory

Table 3.6 presents a summary of applications of theory adapted from Luke (2020).

Multicultural Implications and Advocacy

It is of critical importance in the ethical, effective application of theory that theory be used with an understanding of childhood and adolescence, each as their own culture. Just as we are responsible to adapt theory and techniques to clients of various cultural backgrounds, we must adapt theory to children and adolescents. We must modify our language to be accessible without being condescending, and in ways that honor the lived experiences of children and adolescents. This is amplified as we work with children and adolescents representing differences in race, ethnicity, gender identity, religion, etc. Our applications of theories via techniques must recognize the intersectionality with each client.

Summary

As we hope you have seen in this chapter, the person of the counselor, their orientation toward the culture of childhood and adolescents, and theory must come together in order to increase the likelihood of positive outcomes. Theory assists in forming a rationale for understanding clients and intervening appropriately, especially as it exists in a common factors context. Therefore, selecting a theory that resonates with you and your client (and their parent/caregiver) can provide support, structure, and confidence in all parties. We hope you will embrace the process of theory exploration, even as you cultivate the factors that matter across theories.

Clinician's Corner

One of the important aspects of working with adolescents is developing a "real" therapeutic relationship. What I mean by that is that the counselor needs to be comfortable with displaying some level of vulnerability in order for the adolescent to connect with you. You

Table 3.6 Applications of Theory

Theory	Aphorism	Branch	Depression	Anxiety	Stress and Trauma
Psychoanalytic views	Psychopathology is historical, developmental	Freudian	Melancholia and loss	Love unrequited; or death	Attachment in early childhood sets the stage for stress tolerance
		Adlerian	Inferiority	Inferiority, vis-à-vis perception of self, by self and others	
Cognitive behavioral views	Psychopathology is behavioral	Cognitive	Distorted thinking leads to distorted emotion and then to distorted behavior	Results from distorted thinking	Avoidance leads to contraction and rigidity versus stress inoculation
		Behavioral	Avoidance leads to reinforcement of avoidance	Anxiety is natural; avoidance is what leads to problems	A historical approach to managing challenges (memories of successes are filtered out)
		Mindfulness-based adaptations	Emotion as real leading to emotion as reality	Meta-anxiety is the problem	
Humanistic-existential views	Psychopathology is relational	Person-centered	Represents a lack of supportive environment in which to flourish	Isolation	Non-supportive environment/ relationships lead to perceived threats to sense of self or even existence
		Existential	Freedom to choose but abdication of choice	Life and death	
		Gestalt	Division of self: Self as what is said versus what is done	Anxiety is enacted	
Constructivist views	Psychopathology is constructed	Narrative, solution-focused	Results from a problem-saturated narrative of one's own design	"Management versus elimination" (Quick, 2013)	A historical approach to managing challenges (memories of successes are filtered out)

need to be ready to reveal some benign aspect of your life to your adolescent client, like your favorite TV show or what kind of student you were in high school. You do need to respect professional boundaries, but you have to be willing to connect with them on that level. Once I establish that therapeutic relationship, I like to use a timeline technique. I really do not have a name for it, but I use it with all of my adolescent clients, especially clients in the foster care system. I just ask them to draw a line and label the line with significant life events. Then, I use a combination of Rational Emotive Behavioral Therapy (REBT) and family systems to process an individual event. It helps me understand the client on a deeper level and allows the client to construct their story. My interaction with them is focused on ways in which the event affected them emotionally, physically, and psychologically, and also on the role a family member may have had during that event. Adolescents do not like to admit that family influences their behaviors, so this is a technique that allows them to admit this on their own terms.

Dr. Shawn L. Spurgeon, LPC-MHSP, NCC, ACS
The University of Tennessee, Knoxville

References

Ainsworth, M. D. S. (1978). The Bowlby-Ainsworth attachment theory. *Behavioral and Brain Sciences, 1*(3), 436–438. https://doi.org/10.1017/S0140525X00075828

Axline, V. M. (1969). *Play therapy*. Ballantine Books.

Bandura, A. (1982). Self-efficacy mechanism in human agency. *American Psychologist, 37*(2), 122. https://psycnet.apa.org/doi/10.1037/0003-066X.37.2.122

Beckes, L., Ijzerman, H., & Tops, M. (2015). Toward a radically embodied neuroscience of attachment and relationships. *Frontiers in Human Neuroscience, 9*, 266. Retrieved from www.frontiersin.org/articles/10.3389/fnhum.2015.00266/full

Bonnert, M., Olén, O., Bjureberg, J., Lalouni, M., Hedman-Lagerlöf, E., Serlachius, E., & Ljótsson, B. (2018). The role of avoidance behavior in the treatment of adolescents with irritable bowel syndrome: A mediation analysis. *Behaviour Research and Therapy, 105*, 27–35. https://doi.org/10.1016/j.brat.2018.03.006

Bronfenbrenner, U. (1979). *The ecology of human development*. Cambridge, MA: Harvard University Press.

Clark-Polner, E., & Clark, M. S. (2014). Understanding and accounting for relational context is critical for social neuroscience. *Frontiers in Human Neuroscience, 8*. Retrieved from www.frontiersin.org/articles/10.3389/fnhum.2014.00127/full

Dreikurs, R., & Soltz, V. (1968). *Children: The challenge*. Meredith Press.

Erikson, E. H. (1968). *Identity: Youth and crisis*. W.W. Norton & Company.

Farah, M. J. (2018). Socioeconomic status and the brain: Prospects for neuroscience-informed policy. *Nature Reviews Neuroscience, 19*(7), 428–438. https://doi.org/10.1038/s41583-018-0023-2

Frank, J. D., & Frank, J. B. (1993). *Persuasion and healing: A comparative study of psychotherapy* (3rd ed.). Johns Hopkins University Press.

Gennaro, A., Kleinbub, J. R., Mannarini, S., Salvatore, S., & Palmieri, A. (2019). Training in psychotherapy: A call for embodied and psychophysiological approaches. *Research in Psychotherapy: Psychopathology, Process and Outcome, 22*(3). https://doi.org/10.4081/ripppo.2019.395

Hansen, J. T. (2012). Extending the humanistic vision: Toward a humanities foundation for the counseling profession. *The Journal of Humanistic Counseling, 51*(2), 133–144. https://doi.org/10.1002/j.2161-1939.2012.00011.x

Kalat, J. W. (2019). *Biological psychology*. Cengage.

Kleinbub, J. R. (2017). State of the art of interpersonal physiology in psychotherapy: A systematic review. *Frontiers in psychology, 8*, 2053. https://doi.org/10.3389/fpsyg.2017.02053

Landreth, G. L. (2012). *Play therapy: The art of the relationship* (3rd ed.). Routledge.

Laska, K. M., Gurman, A. S., & Wampold, B. E. (2014). Expanding the lens of evidence-based practice in psychotherapy: A common factors perspective. *Psychotherapy*, *51*(4), 467–481. https://psycnet.apa.org/doi/10.1037/a0034332

Luke, C. (2017). Learner-centered counseling theory: An innovative perspective. *Journal of Creativity in Mental Health*, *12*(3) 305–319. https://doi.org/10.1080/15401383.2016.1249445

Luke, C. (2020). *Neuroscience for counselors and therapists: Integrating the sciences of mind and brain* (2nd ed.). Cognella.

Luke, C., Miller, R., & McAuliffe, G. (2019). Neuro-informed mental health counseling: A person-first perspective. *Journal of Mental Health Counseling*, *41*(1). https://doi.org/10.17744/mehc.41.1.06

Luke, C., Redekop, F., & Moralejo, J. (2020). From microaggressions to neural aggressions: A neuro-informed counseling perspective. *Journal of Multicultural Counseling and Development*, *48*(2), 120–129. https://doi.org/10.1002/jmcd.12170

MacDonald, G. (1997). Issues in multi-cultural counseling supervision. In *Caring in an Age of Technology*. Proceedings of the International Conference on Counseling in the 21st Century, 6th, Beijing, China, May 29–30, 1997.

Miller, W. R., & Rollnick, S. (2012). *Motivational interviewing: Helping people change*. Guilford Press.

Newman, B. M., & Newman, P. R. (2015). *Development through life: A psychosocial approach* (12th ed.). Cengage Learning. Of mind and brain (2nd ed.). San Diego, CA: Cognella Academic Press.

Norcross, J. C., & Wampold, B. E. (2019). *Psychotherapy relationships that work: Volume 2: Evidence-based therapist responsiveness*. Oxford: Oxford University Press.

Palmieri, A., Kleinbub, J. R., Calvo, V., Benelli, E., Messina, I., Sambin, M., & Voci, A. (2018). Attachment-security prime effect on skin-conductance synchronization in psychotherapists: An empirical study. *Journal of Counseling Psychology*, *65*(4), 490–499. https://doi.org/doi/10.1037/cou0000273

Panksepp, J., & Biven, L. (2012). *The archaeology of mind: Neuroevolutionary origins of human emotions*. W.W. Norton & Company.

Panksepp, J., Lane, R. D., Solms, M., & Smith, R. (2017). Reconciling cognitive and affective neuroscience perspectives on the brain basis of emotional experience. *Neuroscience & Biobehavioral Reviews*, *76*, 187–215. https://doi.org/10.1016/j.neubiorev.2016.09.010

Pulvermüller, F., Garagnani, M., & Wennekers, T. (2014). Thinking in circuits: Toward neurobiological explanation in cognitive neuroscience. *Biological Cybernetics*, *108*(5), 573–593. https://doi.org/10.1007/s00422-014-0603-9

Quick, E. K. (2013). *Solution focused anxiety management: A treatment and training manual*. Academic Press.

Redekop, F., Luke, C., & Malone, F. (2017). From the couch to the chair: Applying psychoanalytic theory and practice in counseling. *Journal of Counseling & Development*, *95*(1), 100–109. https://doi.org/10.1002/jcad.12121

Rogers, C. R. (1942). *Counseling and psychotherapy: Newer concepts in practice*. Houghton Mifflin.

Rogers, C. R. (1957). The necessary and sufficient conditions of therapeutic personality change. *Journal of Consulting Psychology*, *21*, 95–103. https://doi.org/10.1037/h0045357

Rogers, C. R. (1995). *A way of being*. Houghton Mifflin Harcourt.

Rosenthal, R., & Jacobson, L. (1968). Pygmalion in the classroom. *The Urban Review*, *3*(1), 16–20. https://link.springer.com/content/pdf/10.1007/BF02322211.pdf

Sommers-Flanagan, J., & Sommers-Flanagan, R. (2007). *Tough kids, cool counseling* (2nd ed.). American Counseling Association.

Suleiman, A. B., & Dahl, R. E. (2017). Leveraging neuroscience to inform adolescent health: The need for an innovative transdisciplinary developmental science of adolescence. *Journal of Adolescent Health*, *60*(3), 240–248. https://doi.org/10.1016/j.jadohealth.2016.12.010

Sweatt, J. D. (2016). Neural plasticity and behavior – Sixty years of conceptual advances. *Journal of Neurochemistry*, *139*, 179–199. https://doi.org/10.1111/jnc.13580

Vernon, A., & Schimmel, C. J. (2019). *Counseling children and adolescents* (4th ed.). Cognella.

Wampold, B. E. (2001). Contextualizing psychotherapy as a healing practice: Culture, history, and methods. *Applied and Preventive Psychology*, *10*(2), 69–86. https://doi.org/10.1017/S0962-1849(02)01001-6

Wampold, B. E., & Ulvenes, P. G. (2019). Integration of common factors and specific ingredients. In J. C. Norcross & M. R. Golfried (Eds.), *Handbook of psychotherapy integration* (3rd ed., pp. 69–87). Oxford: Oxford University Press.

4 Understanding Attachment and Development Aspects of Children and Adolescents

Emily Donald, Chad Luke, and Rebekah Byrd

Emily Donald as guest contributor

Objectives

- Gain a basic understanding of attachment theory.
- Recognize the signs of different types of attachment between child and parent/caregiver.
- Understand and apply the developmental and therapeutic links between attachment theory and cognitive and psychosocial development, respectively.
- Explore attachment dynamics across infancy, childhood, and adolescence.
- Recognize patterns and implications of caregiver attachment characteristics.

Reflective Questions

- What are the first words that come to mind when you think of your childhood relationship with a primary caregiver?
- How do you think your relationship (attachment) with your early primary caregiver shaped the way you experience the world? Can you think of specific examples?
- As you approach adult relationships, are there behaviors you have in those contexts that surprise you?
- What characteristics of your early relationship with parents/caregivers do you value and want to pass on to possible offspring?
- What characteristics of your early relationship with parents/caregivers concern you and are not ones that you would want to pass on to possible offspring?

Attachment is the "strong disposition to seek proximity to and contact with a specific figure and to do so in certain situations, notably when frightened, tired or ill" (Bowlby, 1969/1982, p. 371). Attachment theory is the initial work of John Bowlby, and later Mary Ainsworth, which came about when Bowlby integrated the fields of evolutionary biology, ethology, developmental psychology, cognitive science, and control systems theory to explain children's ties to their mothers. With the advent of this new theory, infant attachment to the mother could be explained by means other than secondary drives (e.g., association of the mother with reduction of hunger), which had been the prevailing theory up until Bowlby's introduction of attachment theory. With the introduction of attachment theory, a comprehensive theory based on natural selection and species survival entered the realm of psychology. In this chapter, counselors working with young people will be introduced to the basic concepts of attachment theory, the developmental progression of attachment, and a primer on attachment-based interventions. Although the attachment literature is far too broad for a complete summary, as complete texts are written about the theory alone (see Simpson & Rholes, 2015 and Cassidy & Shaver, 2016), the goal of this chapter is to introduce counselors in training to this important theory and provide resources for further learning.

Attachment Theory Overview

Attachment theory posits that the safety and security provided by close proximity to a caregiver affords the young of a particular species a higher chance of survival. As those who are inclined to seek safety have higher rates of survival, these traits are passed on generation to generation, leading to the evolution of caregiver proximity seeking in times of fear or insecurity. Human infants emerge from their first attachment bond in the womb into a world of uncertainty, wherein they will hopefully attach psychologically and socially to a primary caregiver, and as outlined later in the chapter, this attachment evolves over time in an interaction between the infant's behavior and the caregiver's responses. Around the end of their first year, children develop selective attachments to specific caregivers to whom they turn to meet their attachment needs. They use that caregiver as a secure base (Ainsworth, 1963) from which to explore their world and a safe haven to whom they can retreat in times of distress.

To better understand these concepts, it helps to understand the five behavioral systems proposed by Bowlby and Ainsworth. These systems interact in a variety of ways that allow for infants/children/adolescents to explore their world, while maintaining safety. The first of these systems is the attachment behavioral system. The attachment behavioral system consists of attachment behaviors designed to maintain a desired distance from the mother while accounting for context (e.g., closer when afraid, farther when exploring and feeling safe; Bowlby, 1969/1982). The exploratory behavioral system consists of behaviors the child uses to learn about their environment and gain knowledge of the environment necessary for survival. The fear/wariness system is activated when the child is presented with frightening or novel and unfamiliar stimuli (e.g., a new person during certain developmental phases). The sociable system represents behaviors associated with the tendency to connect with others (Ainsworth, 1989). This is different from the attachment system in which the behaviors are directed at a caregiver; the sociable system is behaviors connected to those who are not attachment figures (e.g., friends, acquaintances, other new people). Finally, the caregiving system is the system of parenting behaviors. These systems interact in a variety of ways that change over the course of development. For example, when the fear/wariness system is active, the exploratory system is inhibited, and the attachment system becomes active. This might look like a child wandering off from their attachment figure (exploratory system), realizing they have come in contact with an unfamiliar person and feeling afraid (fear/wariness system), and running back to close proximity with the caregiver (attachment system). The caregiver may then respond with soothing verbalizations and physical touch (caregiving system).

When repeated over time, these interactions lead to the formation of internal working models (IWMs) about self, others, and relationships. IWMs are the beliefs and representations that one internalizes for how things work. For example, a securely attached person likely has IWMs that represent the self as lovable and deserving of care, others as generally trustworthy and safe, and relationships as safe places to seek care and connection. An insecurely attached person may have IWMs that suggest that the self is unlovable, others are not safe and trustworthy, and close relationships lead to unpleasant outcomes. These models form the basis for attachment style and influence the way people engage in relationships of all types.

There are two models regarding attachment stability over time (Fraley, 2002). The revisionist model posits that ongoing experiences directly affect these IWMs and attachment representations are updated over time. Alternatively, the prototype model suggests that there is an underlying factor that influences attachment style; this underlying factor was formed early and remains mostly stable. The prototype model does not suggest that IWMs and attachment representations cannot be updated based on new experiences. Instead, the hypothesis is that they are influenced by this underlying model in ways that keep attachment largely stable over the lifetime. Much of the evidence from the vast attachment literature supports the notion of the protype model, suggesting that early attachment experiences consolidate to form a basic prototype that underlies attachment style (e.g., Fraley, Vicary, Brumbaugh, & Roisman, 2011).

Another component of attachment theory is the measurement and classification of attachment style or category. Ainsworth, Blehar, Waters, and Wall (1978) designed the Strange Situation Procedure (SSP) to identify patterns in infant-parent attachment. The SSP is used to classify infant attachment following observation of an infant's attachment and exploratory behaviors, particularly following a period of brief separation from the parent. The original use of the SSP resulted in three categories of attachment: secure, avoidant, or ambivalent/resistant. Following additional research, Main and Solomon (1990) added disorganized/disoriented, resulting in four total classifications. Secure infants protest separation, seek their caregiver upon the caregiver's return, and resume their exploratory activities once soothed by the caregiver. Resistant infants express more intense reactions to separation than do securely attached infants; their comfort seeking is minimal; they remain upset when reunited; and they resist the caregiver's attempts to settle them. Avoidant infants do not really respond to separation, and they mostly ignore their caregiver when reunited. Finally, disorganized infants have no clear pattern and seem to be unable to use their caregiver as an attachment figure. They may even show fear of the caregiver. This style is the most problematic, as it results in a bind for the attachment-seeking infant; the person who activates the attachment system and is supposed to provide caregiving is also the one who activates the fear/wariness system. There is no clear resolution to this attachment-based dilemma.

Although the SSP is used to classify attachment in infants up to 20 months of age, a modified version may be used to classify preschool children's attachment into similar categories (Cassidy, Marvin, & The MacArthur Working Group on Attachment, 1992). Adolescents' and adults' attachment is often classified in the literature in one of two ways, in the tradition of the developmental psychologists using the Adult Attachment Interview (AAI; George, Kaplan, & Main, 1996) or in the tradition of the social psychologists using a self-report measure such as the Experiences in Close Relationships Scale (ECR; Brennan, Clark, & Shaver, 1998). The AAI results in a classification of secure, dismissing, or preoccupied based on the person's narrative of early attachment experiences. The social psychology tradition assigns attachment styles, which are dimensional and include attachment anxiety and avoidance. Persons low on both are more secure, while being high on one of the dimensions represents insecurity. Those high in avoidance tend to deactivate the attachment behavioral system and feel rejecting of intimacy and closeness in relationships, and those high in the anxiety dimension tend to overactivate the attachment behavioral system and desire closeness, while fearing separation. Understanding adult classifications is important, even for those who are working with children only, as these classifications are important when considering caregiver behavioral systems and how those might be affected by the caregiver's own attachment behavioral system.

Child Development and Attachment

Attachment theory can also be considered in the context of child development theories. Cognitive, language, and social development interact to influence the development of attachment. In what follows, we highlight several theories and relate them to attachment theory.

Piaget's Cognitive Development Theory

Jean Piaget's (1952) cognitive developmental theory is widely known and influential in the education and psychology related to children. Piaget posits that children learn through interactions with their world and the things in it. As they interact in the world, children develop schemas (i.e., beliefs about the nature of things in their world). Learning is a process of reestablishing equilibrium in the face of new experiences (Waite-Stupiansky, 2017). As such, intelligence develops through a process of assimilation (an integration of new information into existing schemas) or accommodation (when schemas are modified to fit what is being observed in the environment; Kohler, 2008). "Intelligence, therefore, consists of changeable schemata, structure and contents, as well as of the unchangeable functions assimilation and accommodation" (Kohler, 2008, p. 164). When considering the context of attachment theory, this aligns with the concept of IWMs and how IWMs are developed over time. Information is assimilated into the beliefs about self, others, and relationships in order to form attachment representations and those are accommodated for information that differs. The debate in attachment literature is whether or not this is ongoing (e.g., prototype versus revisionist models).

Piaget's model consists of four stages that proceed predictably, but not necessarily linearly (Waite-Stupiansky, 2017). These stages are defined by shifts in how children learn and the "underlying cognitive organization or deep structure that determines what insights and skills can be acquired" (Kohler, 2008, p. 168). The stages are: sensorimotor, occurring from birth to approximately 1.5 or 2 years of age; pre-operational, occurring from 2–7 years of age; concrete operational, occurring from 7–10/11 years of age; and formal operational, occurring from 11–15/16 years of age (Kohler, 2008). During the sensorimotor stage, children's learning comes from direct interaction with their world via their senses. At first, movement is wholly uncoordinated, but as children develop and gain more control over their movements, they learn that things they do can affect their environment (e.g., dropping the rattle leads to a caregiver picking it up). During this time, attachment behaviors are first less directed by the infant, as they have little control over their movement, but as control develops, so too do specific attachment behaviors (see discussion later in this chapter). Also during the sensorimotor stage, children learn object permanence, which from an attachment perspective allows the child to understand that the attachment figure still exists, even when out of sight. With the development of language comes the development of symbolic thought, and during the pre-operational stage, children know that objects can be represented by symbols. They remain very concrete in thinking and egocentric in their perspective, but their sense of logic is developing. Concrete operations are characterized by increased ability to use logic and a reduction in egocentrism. This development begins to allow the child to take others' perspectives and adjust attachment behaviors accordingly. Children's thinking during this stage remains very concrete. Finally, with the advent of abstract thought, comes formal operations. Children in this stage can reason without the need for concrete representations. During this time, children are moving into adolescence and the use of the secure base and safe havens of the attachment relationship align with this ability to be more abstract. Connections may be via phone, rather than physical proximity, as they do not need the concrete interaction.

The Erikson Psychosocial Development Model

The Erikson (1968) psychosocial developmental model consists of eight stages, during which fundamental aspects of identity are explored and resolved. The first of these stages, Trust/Mistrust, aligns with infancy or birth to around 18 months (Jones & Waite-Stupiansky,

2017). During this stage, infants develop trust when their needs are consistently met by caregivers; they learn that they can rely on others to get their needs met. However, mistrust can develop when needs are not met. Healthy tension between these two poles is maintained when infants also demonstrate mistrust of strangers. It is fairly easy to see the connection between this stage and attachment theory, as it reflects the interaction of the attachment, caregiving, and fear/wariness system. The learning that takes place in this stage parallels the development of IWMs of self, others, and relationships. The second of the Erikson stages occurs around when infants become toddlers to around preschool age (18 months to 3 years of age). In this stage, Autonomy/Shame and Doubt, the struggle to achieve autonomy is evident in the toddler's assertion of their needs with great conviction, as well as their desire to do things without help. With this phase, in typical development, comes mobility via walking, and the toddler can explore their environment. With support from caregivers, toddlers can learn that they are able to do things themselves, which suggests caregiver support of the exploratory system in attachment theory. Once toddlerhood passes, children enter the preschool period (about 3–5 years of age) and the stage Initiative/Guilt. During this phase, children are highly motivated to learn and try new things and they explore the process of relating to others during this highly play-based phase of development. When these explorations are successful, initiative develops. This stage highlights the role of, again, the exploratory system and caregiver support thereof, as well as the entry of the sociability system where children start making social connections. Once children enter school age (5–12 years of age), the tasks are Industry/Inferiority. With school, children begin to take some responsibility for self; they learn, and successes lead to confidence. Failure, while in too great of quantities can lead to the inferiority pole, can help balance confidence to achieve realistic expectations.

During adolescence, from 12–18 years of age, the primary task is that of identity development (Adler-Tapia, 2012). This stage is Identity/Role Confusion. During adolescence, the role of social relationships becomes front and center for the young person. They explore different aspects of their identity and their relationships with peers. At the same time, the young person prepares for the roles of adulthood. As is discussed later in the chapter, this can be a challenging phase. Caregiver support of the exploratory system in adolescence is important, as the adolescent learns social behavior that is necessary for independence and begins to transfer attachments to people other than parents. Although it is not a stage of childhood or adolescence, Intimacy/Isolation is relevant here with regard to understanding what caregivers might be experiencing during the time their child is progressing through developmental stages. During this stage (18–40 years of age), people form close relationships and develop long-term commitments with partners or friends, representing the transference of attachments to long-term friends or romantic partners. Erikson's other stages include Generativity/Stagnation and Ego Integrity/Despair. However, as these are not directly relevant to caregiving for children and adolescents, they will not be covered in detail.

Developmental Progression of Attachment

Counselors working with children and adolescents need to understand how attachment develops. This helps to explain behaviors, as well as conceptualize treatment. For example, counselors who understand how the attachment needs of a child in middle childhood vary from those of one in infancy and early childhood can help parents cope with and adapt to changes in needs. They can help teachers better understand student behavior and provide much-needed context for how a given student may be behaving in class as related to their attachment style, attachment-related experiences, and the way they see self, others, and relationships. Counselors who understand attachment can conceptualize the counseling relationship as a potential attachment relationship wherein the child acquires new information to counteract the effects of attachment insecurity. But in order to do this, the counselor must understand how attachment develops over time and what the needed caregiver adjustments are based on developmental phases.

Attachment During Infancy and Early Childhood

Attachment begins early in the caregiver-child relationship. Infants come preprogrammed with behaviors that are especially effective at helping to build attachments with their primary caregiver. They are drawn to human faces; they tend to quiet to the sound of human voices; they have faces that are attractive to adults. Babies are uniquely positioned to engage capable adults in the caregiving that is required for them to survive, a concept that is at the core of Bowlby's attachment theory.

> The biological function of attachment behavior, and of wary behavior, is protection of the youngster from a wide range of dangers. The biological function of exploratory and sociable behavior is that of learning the skills necessary for more self-reliant survival, both in terms of individual skills and smooth integration into the social group.
> (Marvin, Britner, & Russell, 2016, p. 275)

Bowlby (1969/1982) conceptualized the developmental process of early attachment as consisting of four phases. In Phase I, which ends around 8–12 weeks old, infants do not particularly discriminate among caregivers. With a lack of ability to get around on their own, the very young infant's primary behaviors are attachment and wary behaviors. Initial attachment behaviors are very simple. They consist of patterns like crying which elicits caregiver comfort, which alleviates whatever is causing the crying and thus terminates the crying behavior.

The development of the infant's sensory and motor systems allows the infant to take more control in the attachment interactions; thus, Phase II begins. What were originally simple interactions as previously described can now become more complex due to the infant's developing motor control. As development continues, infants become more and more active in the attachment-based interactions. For example, an older infant may smile at a caregiver to initiate interaction, whereas the infant in Phase I simply cried due to discomfort and incidentally received care. Also during Phase II, as the infant is better able to differentiate between caregivers, attachment behavior becomes more coordinated and directed at specific caregivers who are the most present and familiar.

Around 6–9 months of age, Phase III begins. During Phase III, infants become mobile and rapidly develop. The child is at this point able to be goal-directed in their use of attachment behaviors, using behaviors to achieve a visualized goal. For example, a child wanting to have their mother's attention may crawl to her and pull up on her knee. In Phase III, the interaction of the four behavioral systems of attachment (wariness/fear, attachment, sociability, and exploration) emerges in a much clearer way. The sociability system may be engaged as the infant/child comes across new people. However, they experience wariness of strangers, especially as they get older and more mobile, and thus the wariness system may be engaged and attachment behaviors such as clinging to the caregiver or returning to the caregiver are employed. The ability to get around and further cognitive development mean that the child is more motivated and better able to explore their environment, which means that the child can potentially come in contact with real danger. For example, a child who is mobile may stray a bit far from the caregiver and notice that they are uncertain of their surroundings. This leads to the activation of the fear/wariness system and in turn the attachment system, as the infant explores using the caregiver as a secure base. These systems are all interrelated, with the exploration system being inactivated when the wariness system is activated and the child seeks the safety of the caregiver (activation of the attachment system).

These early months of attachment represented by Phases I–III are especially important, as the evidence suggests that as early as the first three months of life, infants' interactions with their caregiver develop into behaviors that influence their later attachment styles (Marvin et al., 2016). As such, counselors working with parents and very young children should be informed about infant mental health (IMH). "Grounded in attachment theory, infant mental health is the shared attention to the infant, the parent, and the early developing attachment relationship" (Weatherston & Browne, 2016, p. 260). Different from an individual approach, IMH specialists ask about the baby, the parent, their relationship, and challenges. They are keen observers of interactions between caregivers and infants, as well as educators who teach caregivers skills and call attention to the effect the caregiver has on the infant. The goal of IMH is preventative, as the focus is to promote healthy development and a healthy caregiver-child relationship. It is provided pre- and postnatally, and is flexible in length of delivery, as well as location of service delivery. As a detailed review of IMH is not within the goals of this text, counselors looking to learn more about IMH are encouraged to access the literature and trainings pertaining to it. However, all child and adolescent counselors are encouraged to be aware of IMH, as via their work they may come into contact with caregivers of young children (e.g., younger siblings or adolescents who become parents and need support).

The final phase, Phase IV, begins around age 4. At this time, children are more comfortable with straying from their primary attachment figure(s), unlike when they were younger (1–2-year-olds) and showed great concern at being separated from those figures. This reduction in fear of separation and decreasing association between the wariness and attachment systems in the presence of strangers sets the stage for future social relationships, as the sociability system and the wariness system begin to function together more. By Phase IV, children have developed physical skills that allow them to control contact with their caregiver, as well as communication skills that allow them to communicate to their caregiver clearly in order to shift the caregiver's behaviors. Before, this was accomplished with physical intervention (e.g., grabbing the mother's face and turning it). In summarizing research, Marvin et al. (2016) state that by Phase IV (approximately 4 years old), children have developed the cognitive ability to understand that others have different perspectives from them and to consider those perspectives in choosing behaviors. Although the child in Phase IV still seeks their caregiver when upset,

> this older preschooler has come to organize attachment behavior in a new way: one that enables the child to realize that he or she and the attachment figure have a continuing relationship whether or not they are in close proximity.
>
> (Marvin et al., 2016, p. 287)

Attachment During Middle Childhood

As the child ages, attachment evolves. Four characteristics separate middle childhood attachment from early childhood attachment (Marvin et al., 2016). First, the younger child is concerned with being physically close to the attachment figure. Separation, for most children, causes distress when it is not chosen by the child. However, in middle childhood, the need for physical proximity decreases and the goal is availability of that figure; in other words, the attachment figure is accessible if needed. Second, although some shifts occur in adolescence, for the older child, the parents remain the primary attachment figures with no development of other attachment figure connections. Third, during this time, the attachment figure and child begin to move toward a more collaborative partnership. The child takes on more responsibility and the parent becomes more of a resource. Finally, attachment figures continue to function as a safe haven and secure base. Children at this age still retreat to attachment figures when upset and those figures still operate as a secure base for exploration. However, at this age, that function looks different. At this point, secure base functions may include behaviors like encouraging the child to try out for a play, attend a social gathering, or take on a new challenge. These express belief in the child and encourage the exploratory system. This new phase of development requires of the attachment figure the same ongoing sensitive and responsive caregiving, but also includes support for exploration behaviors and increased autonomy of the child.

Attachment During Adolescence

During adolescence, the need for flexibility continues. While adolescents maintain attachment to their primary caregivers and still turn to them in times of distress, attachment relationships begin to expand to include peers and romantic partners. Like getting basic care in infancy, this is an important part of survival, as humans are a social species and must group together. Thus, the focus of attachment during adolescence is more on transferring those needs from the parent/caregiver to peers and romantic partners. Although this is a normal part of the developmental process, as adolescents prepare to be responsible for themselves and getting their own attachment needs met, it can provide challenges, even in the context of a secure caregiver-child relationship.

> For a secure partnership to be maintained, two key ingredients are required: a strong capacity to communicate across the increasingly divergent perspectives and needs of the parent and teen, and a willingness on both sides to manage conflict in a way that allows the adolescent to seek autonomy while maintaining the parent-teen relationship.
> (Allen & Tan, 2016, p. 404)

This is critical understanding for counselors who work with adolescents and their parents/caregivers, as this is often a very difficult time for caregivers, and support in adapting their caregiving approach may be critical in maintaining the relationship.

Developmentally speaking, the adolescent has acquired the skills to take perspectives outside of themselves and negotiate with caregivers, maintaining the attachment relationship while also establishing autonomy. Peers become increasingly important, but may not always serve as full attachment figures with the safe haven and secure base characteristics of the parent/caregiver attachment relationship. For example, the adolescent may go to a peer for support and discussion of problems, but not when they are feeling deeply scared and needing security. Access to the parent, which used to be primarily a physical construct, transitions to a more symbolic representation (e.g., texting or phoning a parent). Further, exploration, which also used to be primarily a physical experience, expands to include the adolescent's own beliefs and ways of seeing things, as well as the exploration of new relationships (Dubois-Comtois, Cyr, Pascuzzo, Lessard, & Poulin, 2013). While all of these changes are happening during adolescence, it actually remains a period of stability in attachment, supporting the notion that there is an underlying prototype that remains stable and influences IWMs (Jones et al., 2018).

Another reason why attachment remains important for counselors working with adolescents to understand is that it has close links to mental health. Meta-analyses suggest that insecure attachment is related to adolescent anxiety (e.g., Colonnesi et al., 2011; Kerns & Brumariu, 2014), though the development of a clinically diagnosable disorder may be related also to the presence of other risk factors (Kerns & Brumariu, 2014), and the relationship between insecure attachment and anxiety may be affected by other factors associated with insecurity, such as lack of competence in social interaction. Further, adolescent depression is associated with attachment insecurity, though the link needs to be studied more closely (Brumariu & Kerns, 2010). According to Allen and Tan's (2016) summary, adolescent attachment security is also linked to management of conflict with parents, competence in friendships and relationships, communication with parents, agreement with parents more on perceptions, and mental health, with attachment security influencing all of these variables positively. Given the vast links to mental health and relationship health, it is important for counselors working with this age to understand the possible effects of attachment status on adolescents' health and conceptualize problems accordingly.

In their recommendations for working with adolescents from an attachment perspective, Dubois-Comtois et al. (2013) recommend either individual or parent-adolescent therapy approaches. With individual therapy, the therapist serves as the attachment figure for the adolescent, helping them to explore thoughts, feelings, and behaviors and learn new relationship-based behaviors. Using an attachment lens, the therapist can evaluate the adolescent's attachment style and design appropriate interventions. Adolescents who demonstrate attachment insecurity will likely need more time to develop trust. In parent-adolescent therapy, therapists are able to observe parental attachment style and how that affects associated caregiving behaviors. The attachment-informed counselor can then use interventions to help the parent become a more effective caregiver. This requires establishing a strong therapeutic alliance with the caregiver, as well as the adolescent. As new patterns of interaction are established, shifts happen within the parent-adolescent relationship.

Caregivers and Attachment

It is important that counselors working with children also understand the role of attachment in caregiving, as they are likely to either work with parents directly or have the opportunity to provide attachment-informed resources and interventions aimed at parents. This involvement with caregivers transcends setting for counselors. Those in clinical settings are more likely to have direct involvement with parents, while those in school settings may only have indirect involvement and the opportunity to better understand their students in the context of understanding attachment in caregiving. However, those based in schools are advised to use their understanding of attachment and its influences on child development to inform systemic interventions. Such interventions can even be aimed at teachers, who may also have their interactions with students affected by their own attachment-based models of caregiving. Although it is not ethical for school counselors to enter into therapeutic relationships with the teachers or parents in a school, they can provide attachment-informed psychoeducational materials that may increase caregiver awareness.

Literature supports the notion that the parent or caregiver's attachment style has an effect on their ability to provide sensitive and responsive caregiving that is critical to healthy child development (e.g., helping infants learn to self-regulate, a skill that carries through into childhood [Lecuyer & Houck, 2006]). According to their review of the literature on attachment and caregiving, Jones et al. (2015) report that self-reported parental attachment insecurity is linked to less sensitive, supportive, and responsive parenting, as well as other behaviors, emotions, and cognitions that are not helpful for parenting. Counselors hoping to support healthy development of attachment by supporting parents and caregivers gain much from understanding how attachment styles of parents and caregivers influence their behavior, emotions, and cognitions related to parenting.

Specifically, behaviors associated with attachment insecurity include decreased consistency, increased use of authoritarian and permissive parenting styles, decreased caring behaviors, and decreased involvement (Jones, Cassidy, & Shaver, 2015b). Further, attachment insecurity is associated with higher risk of child abuse and possibly increased use of corporal punishment, two outcomes with which counselors working with children and adolescents should be concerned given the risks they pose for children. Finally, Jones et al. (2015b) noted that the literature suggests that insecure parental attachment may be related to parents being unable to engage in constructive behavior when in conflict with children. This is especially relevant in a counseling context, as conflict is bound to arise in the parent-child relationship, particularly as the child moves into and through adolescence. Counselors can assist parents in skill building, as well as understanding the ways their own attachment status may be interfering with their ability to communicate effectively.

Parents who identify as insecurely attached may also feel less close to their child, feel less satisfied as a parent, and feel more parental stress (Jones, Cassidy, & Shaver, 2015a). Finally, attachment insecurity is associated with several beliefs about parenting. Parents who self-report insecurity have a more negative view of themselves as a parent, as well as of the parent-child relationship (Jones et al., 2015a). They may perceive their child's behaviors more negatively, though this is inconsistently supported in the attachment literature. Finally, avoidance in particular is associated with unhelpful beliefs about infant distress, including misattributing the stress to the infant themselves versus situational factors. Empathy, as both a cognitive and emotional construct, is also affected by parental attachment, with avoidance being associated with less empathy (Stern, Borelli, & Smiley, 2015). Further, empathy by a parent is experienced by children as parental warmth, suggesting that the empathy felt and thought by a parent translates into behaviors that increase experiences of parental warmth. Empathy has been found to be associated with secure attachment. This suggests that "parents' capacity to hold a coherent model of the child's mind and to reflect on the thoughts and emotions underlying behavior is central to the development of attachment" (Stern et al., 2015, p. 15). Not related to individual parental characteristics, but still important for counselors to understand, is that attachment insecurity can also cause challenges in a co-parenting relationship (Talbot, Baker, & McHale, 2009).

Another way to understand how parent attachment influences the parent-child relationship is to consider it in the context of the two behavioral systems involved. The parent has a set of caregiving behaviors, and the child a set of attachment behaviors (Bowlby, 1969/1982, 1988). Ideally, when the child's need for a safe haven is activated, the parent's ability to respond sensitively in caregiving is as well. In concert, ideally when the child needs a secure base from which they can explore, the parent is able to respond with caregiving that is encouraging and supportive. However, the caregiver's own attachment system may be activated by the child's attachment behaviors. As such,

> it may be best to think of child behavior not as increasing activation of the parent's own attachment system, but of child behavior as increasing activation of a caregiving system operating within the context of threat assessment that is influenced by the parent's attachment system.
>
> (Jones et al., 2015b, p. 46)

This is evident in the reactions of both anxious and avoidant mothers to infant distress. For example, consider a situation in which a parent's own attachment system suggests that closeness is to be avoided and is not safe. When the infant's attachment behavior is designed to achieve closeness (e.g., a distressed infant who wants to be picked up), this may trigger the parent's own perception of threat related to being needed and end in a mismatch in parental behavior with child needs. Insecurity in terms of avoidance may lead to that parent not picking up the child and comforting them, with the child learning that the caregiver cannot be relied upon for soothing. A parent with attachment anxiety may also miss the mark in aligning with the child's needs. For example, their own anxiety-based behavior of keeping the child close may cause a mismatch when the child is motivated to go and explore. Overall, attachment insecurity in parents can interfere with the safe base and secure haven that children need to be able to feel secure and explore their world (Bowlby, 1988).

Counseling Interventions

There are several interventions that counselors working with children can consider. Dozier and Roben (2015) highlight themes of attachment-based interventions. These themes are not applicable to all of the following recommendations, but represent a summary of issues addressed by attachment-based intervention strategies. Intervention themes include: a focus on parents, early intervention, intervention in homes, addressing the most important parental behaviors (e.g., those that are associated with sensitive and responsive caregiving), nurturing behavior by parents, attunement, parental delight, nonfrightening behavior, and parental trauma and attachment. First, Filial Therapy, an intervention that focuses on the parent-child relationship, can be effective for working with parents and caregivers to be more responsive and sensitive in their parenting. In particular, Child-Parent Relationship Therapy (CPRT; Landreth & Bratton, 2020) is one approach to Filial Therapy with a solid evidence base of effectiveness. During this 10-week model, parents participate in a group and practice skills in weekly play sessions with their child. Toward the end of the group, parents are encouraged to generalize these skills outside of the play sessions. Parents are taught specific skills that allow them to tune into the child's emotions and respond with empathy. Additionally, they learn skills of letting the child lead (which aligns well with supporting the exploratory system) and setting limits around safety (which aligns well with being a source of safety). There is evidence that this intervention can also work with other caregiving populations, including teachers (e.g., Morrison, 2006). This is also discussed briefly in Chapter 15 of this volume.

Zeanah, Berlin, and Boris (2011) also recommend several interventions. Video-based Intervention to Promote Positive Parenting (VIPP) is one that is designed for parents and infants under 1 year of age (Juffer, Bakermans-Kranenburg, & van Ijzendoorn, 2007). It has research supporting suggested positive effects on attachment-related dimensions and has advantages that include being delivered at home and requiring only four home visits. Zeanah et al. also recommend the Circle of Security intervention (COS; Marvin, Cooper, Hoffman, & Powell, 2002). Like CPRT, this is designed to be a group intervention, but can be adapted to working with a single caregiver. A combination of video review and educating parents about attachment, COS is based in the work of many prominent attachment researchers. When educating parents about secure base and safe haven using a circular image wherein the child is depicted exploring and seeking safety, the hope is that parents will learn to be more responsive to the child's cues. Finally, Attachment and Biobehavioral Catch-up (ABC; Dozier, Lindheim, & Ackerman, 2005) is a 10-session intervention developed for work with foster parents. It consists of treatment modules and uses live interaction for feedback.

Multicultural Implications and Advocacy

Attachment theory has held sway over developmental psychology for more than 50 years. However, its ascent to the top of the socio-developmental hierarchy has not been without challenge. Recently, Keller (2018) has called into question the claims of universality of attachment theory, calling it the WEIRDest theory, wherein it is "the psychology of Western, educated, industrialized, rich and democratic (WEIRD) people" (p. 11414). She writes that families around the world care for their children, but that this care looks different in different cultures. We echo this and caution counselors against using only a WEIRD lens through which to view attachment, especially of those poorest and most historically marginalized groups among us. Morelli et al. (2018) challenge the notion of Western individualism in consideration of attachment. For instance, Keller notes that children's rights may be elevated over parental rights in Western cultures, whereas many parts of the world would view these as artificial divisions of the family unit. What this means for counselors is that we must be cautious in assigning values or judgments about certain interaction patterns in the families we serve. Marginalized, underrepresented, and generationally impoverished families view attachment in different ways, so it is vital that counselors seek to learn about their culture.

Summary

In summary, the collective literature on attachment and parenting suggests that parental attachment security is associated with more desirable parenting cognitions, emotions, and behaviors. Counselors who work with young people can approach parents and caregivers from a more informed place if they understand that the caregiver's own attachment may be influencing their reactions to their child. In particular, it is important to understand the link between sensitive and responsive caregiving, as it is linked to secure infant attachment (e.g., De Wolff & Van Ijzendoorn, 1997; Lucassen et al., 2011) and other positive outcomes. Supporting parents and caregivers in developing sensitive and responsive caregiving behaviors is crucial for young people, and counselors can play a significant role. Taken together, all of this information helps counselors better understand the context in which the child or adolescent is functioning, better support parents and caregivers, and design interventions that affect not only the individual student or child, but the whole system of caregiving.

Clinician's Corner

I often explain to caregivers that play therapy is not "just" meaningless play. For children, play is essential for exploring the world, mastering new skills, and learning about self. It is a way that children express their internal states, then make them visible on the outside. As a play therapist, I am present to support children in their healing of anxiety, trauma, and feelings of abandonment. As the brain's prefrontal cortex developed along with the physical body, perhaps we forgot an essential truth of childhood: as we played, therefore we worked hard, we processed, and we experienced the world with our whole beings. Children often need a trusted adult or a knowledgeable therapist to witness the process along the way and to assist with co-regulation of emotions resulting from trauma and adverse experiences.

From the classic study of adverse childhood experiences (ACE), we have learned how critical "serve and return" is for a young, developing brain. "Serve and return" means that when children communicate with us, we respond to them with a language they understand. We coo along with babies and we play simple games with preschoolers, all of which demonstrates we are attuned to their ways of interacting with the world.

I engage parents in activities that help them understand the importance of meeting children on children's level of development. These insights help parents understand play therapy better and eliminate the expectations that children sit in my sessions and listen to me lecture them about good behaviors. A few simple examples of "serve and return" activities in my sessions include tic-tac-toe, making a special handshake, having a staring contest, telling knock-knock jokes, or singing a song about a friend. I invite the caregivers to play these games in our sessions with the children to strengthen the caregiver-child bond. I listen to the children's laughter and watch them get engaged with their caregivers with joy and enthusiasm. This reciprocity assists with building resilience against adverse childhood experiences and past traumas.

Sometimes parents struggle to play and interact with their children in our sessions, as it has been a while for them since they related to anyone through play. I often highlight parental strengths that are already evident to build confidence of these caregivers. I provide gentle psychoeducation on the importance of "serve and return" and the role it plays in fostering children's resilience. Children learn by observation and by watching a trusted caregiver interact with them in ways children understand. I also guide caregivers in the use of deep breathing to model for children how to soothe their dysregulated nervous systems. Children only have one childhood. They need our breath, our attention, and our understanding that the hardest work of childhood is not "just" meaningless play.

Jana Dobesova, LPC-MHSP, RPT
Camelot Care Centers

References

Adler-Tapia, R. (2012). *Child psychotherapy: Integrating developmental theory into clinical practice*. New York: Springer.

Ainsworth, M. D. S. (1963). The development of infant-mother interaction among the Ganda. In B. M. Foss (Ed.), *Determinants of infant behavior* (Vol. 2, pp. 67–112). New York: Wiley.

Ainsworth, M. D. S. (1989). Attachments beyond infancy. *American Psychologist, 44*, 709–716.

Ainsworth, M. D. S., Blehar, M. C., Waters, E., & Wall, S. (1978). *Patterns of attachment: A psychological study of the Strange Situation*. Hillsdale, NJ: Erlbaum.

Allen, J. P., & Tan, J. S. (2016). The multiple facets of attachment in adolescence. In J. Cassidy & P. R. Shaver (Eds.), *Handbook of attachment: Theory, research, and clinical applications* (3rd ed., pp. 399–415). Guilford.

Bowlby, J. (1969/1982). *Attachment and loss: Volume 1. Attachment*. New York: Basic Books (Original work published 1969).

Bowlby, J. (1988). *A secure base: Parent-child attachment and healthy human development*. London: Routledge.

Brennan, K. A., Clark, C. L., & Shaver, P. R. (1998). Self-report measurement of adult romantic attachment: An integrative overview. In J. A. Simpson & W. S. Rholes (Eds.), *Attachment theory and close relationships* (pp. 46–76). New York: Guilford.

Brumariu, L. E., & Kerns, K. A. (2010). Parent-child attachment and internalizing symptoms in childhood and adolescence: A review of empirical findings and future directions. *Development and Psychopathology, 22*, 177–203. https://doi.org/10.1017/S0954579409990344

Cassidy, J., Marvin, R. S., & The MacArthur Working Group on Attachment. (1992). *Attachment organization in preschool children: Coding guidelines* (4th ed.). Unpublished manuscript, University of Virginia.

Cassidy, J., & Shaver, P. R. (Eds.). (2016). *Handbook of attachment: Theory, research, and clinical applications* (3rd ed.). New York: The Guilford Press.

Colonnesi, C., Draijer, E. M., Stams, G. J. J. M., Van der Bruggen, C. O., Bögels, S. M., & Noom, M. J. (2011). The relation between insecure attachment and child anxiety: A meta-analytic review.

Journal of Clinical Child & Adolescent Psychology, 40, 630–645. https://doi.org/10.1080/15374 416.2011.581623

De Wolff, M., & Van Ijzendoorn, M. (1997). Sensitivity and attachment: A meta-analysis on parental antecedents of infant attachment. *Child Development, 68,* 571–591.

Dozier, M., Lindheim, O., & Ackerman, J. (2005). Attachment and biobehavioral catch-up. In L. Berlin, Y. Ziv, L. Amaya-Jackson, & M. T. Greenberg (Eds.), *Enhancing early attachments* (pp. 178–194). New York: Guilford Press.

Dozier, M., & Roben, C. K. P. (2015). Attachment-related preventative interventions. In J. A. Simpson & W. S. Rholes (Eds.), *Attachment theory and research: New directions and emerging themes* (pp. 234–260). New York: The Guilford Press.

Dubois-Comtois, K., Cyr, C., Pascuzzo, K., Lessard, M., & Poulin, C. (2013). Attachment theory in clinical work with adolescents. *Journal of Child & Adolescent Behavior, 1*(3), 1–8. https://doi.org/10.4172/2375-4494.1000111

Erikson, E. H. (1968). *Identity: Youth and crisis.* New York: W.W. Norton & Company.

Fraley, R. C. (2002). Attachment stability from infancy to adulthood: Meta-analysis and dynamic modeling of developmental mechanisms. *Personality and Social Psychology Review, 6,* 123–151. http://doi.org/10.1207/S15327957PSPR0602_03

Fraley, R. C., Vicary, A. M., Brumbaugh, C. C., & Roisman, G. I. (2011). Patterns of stability in adult attachment: An empirical test of two models of continuity and change. *Journal of Personality and Social Psychology, 101,* 974–992. https://doi.org/10.1037/a0024150

George, C., Kaplan, N., & Main, M. (1996). *Adult Attachment Interview protocol* (3rd ed.). Unpublished manuscript, University of California at Berkley.

Jones, E., & Waite-Stupiansky, S. (2017). The Eriksons' psychosocial development theory. In L. E. Cohen & S. Waite-Stupiansky (Eds.), *Theories of early childhood education: Developmental, behaviorist, and critical* (pp. 3–17). New York: Routledge.

Jones, J. D., Cassidy, J., & Shaver, P. R. (2015a). Adult attachment style and parenting. In J. A. Simpson & W. S. Rholes (Eds.), *Attachment theory and research: New directions and emerging themes* (pp. 234–260). New York: The Guilford Press.

Jones, J. D., Cassidy, J., & Shaver, P. R. (2015b). Parents' self-reported attachment styles: A review of links with parenting behaviors, emotions, and cognitions. *Personality and Social Psychology Review, 19,* 44–76. https://doi.org/10.1177/1088868314541858

Jones, J. D., Fraley, R. C., Ehrlich, K. B., Stern, J. A., Lejuez, C. W., Shaver, P. R., & Cassidy, J. (2018). Stability of attachment style in adolescence: An empirical test of alternative developmental processes. *Child Development, 89,* 871–880. https://doi.org/10.1111/cdev.12775

Juffer, F., Bakermans-Kranenburg, M. J., & van Ijzendoorn, M. H. (2007). *Promoting positive parenting: An attachment-based intervention.* Mahwah, NJ: Lawrence Erlbaum.

Keller, H. (2018). Universality claim of attachment theory: Children's socioemotional development across cultures. *Proceedings of the National Academy of Sciences, 115*(45), 11414–11419. https://doi.org/10.1073/pnas.1720325115

Kerns, K. A., & Brumariu, L. E. (2014). Is insecure parent-child attachment a risk factor for the development of anxiety in childhood or adolescence? *Child Development Perspectives, 8,* 12–17. https://doi.org/10.1111/cdep.12054

Kohler, R. (2008). *Jean Piaget.* London: Bloomsbury Academic.

Landreth, G. L., & Bratton, S. C. (2020). *Child-parent relationship therapy (CPRT): An evidence based 10-session filial therapy model.* New York: Routledge.

Lecuyer, E., & Houck, G. M. (2006). Maternal limit-setting in toddlerhood: Socialization strategies for the development of self-regulation. *Infant Mental Health Journal, 27,* 344–370.

Lucassen, N., Tharner, A., Van Ijzendoorn, M. H., Bakermans-Kranenburg, M. J., Volling, B. L., Verhulst, F. C., . . . Tiemeier, H. (2011). The association between paternal sensitivity and infant-father attachment security: A meta-analysis of three decades of research. *Journal of Family Psychology, 25,* 986–992.

Main, M., & Solomon, J. (1990). Procedures for identifying infants as disorganized/disoriented during the Ainsworth Strange Situation. In M. T. Greenberg, D. Cicchetti, & E. M. Cummings (Eds.), *Attachment in the preschool years: Theory, research and intervention* (pp. 121–160). Chicago, IL: University of Chicago Press.

Marvin, R. S., Britner, P. A., & Russell, B. S. (2016). Normative development: The ontogeny of attachment in childhood. In J. Cassidy & P. R. Shaver (Eds.), *Handbook of attachment: Theory, research, and clinical applications* (3rd ed., pp. 273–291). Guilford.

Marvin, R. S., Cooper, G., Hoffman, K., & Powell, B. (2002). The Circle of Security project: Attachment-based intervention with caregiver – Preschool child dyads. *Attachment and Human Development, 4,* 107–124.

Morelli, G., Quinn, N., Chaudhary, N., Vicedo, M., Rosabal-Coto, M., Keller, H., . . . Takada, A. (2018). Ethical challenges of parenting interventions in low to middle-income countries. *Journal of Cross-Cultural Psychology, 49*(1), 5–24. https://doi.org/10.1177%2F0022022117746241

Morrison, M. (2006). *An early mental health intervention for disadvantaged preschool children with behavior problems: The effectiveness of training Head Start teachers in child teacher relationship training (CTRT)*, Doctoral Dissertation. ProQuest Dissertations & Theses (UMI Number 3227022). Retrieved from http://citeseerx.ist.psu.edu/viewdoc/download?doi=10.1.1.869.2787&rep=rep1&type=pdf

Piaget, J. (1952). *The origins of intelligence in children.* New York: International Universities Press.

Simpson, J. A., & Rholes, W. S. (Eds.). (2015). *Attachment theory and research: New directions and emerging themes.* New York: The Guilford Press.

Stern, J. A., Borelli, J. L., & Smiley, P. A. (2015). Assessing parental empathy: A role for empathy in child attachment. *Attachment & Human Development, 17,* 1–22. https://doi.org/10.1080/14616734.2014.969749

Talbot, J. A., Baker, J. K., & McHale, J. P. (2009). Sharing the love: Prebirth adult attachment status and coparenting adjustment during early infancy. *Parenting: Science and Practice, 9,* 56–77.

Waite-Stupiansky, S. (2017). Jean Piaget's constructivist theory of learning. In L. E. Cohen & S. Waite-Stupiansky (Eds.), *Theories of early childhood education: Developmental, behaviorist, and critical* (pp. 3–17). New York: Routledge.

Weatherston, S. J., & Browne, J. V. (2016). What is infant mental health and why is it important for high-risk infants and their families? *Newborn & Infant Nursing Reviews, 16,* 259–263. https://doi.org/10.1053/j.nainr.2016.09.026

Zeanah, C. H., Berlin, L. J., & Boris, N. W. (2011). Practitioner review: Clinical applications of attachment theory and research for infants and young children. *The Journal of Child Psychology and Psychiatry, 52,* 819–833. https://doi.org/10.1111/j.1469-7610.2011.02399.x

Part II
Awareness

5 Legal and Ethical Implications for Working With Minors

Theodore P. Remley, Jr., Rebekah Byrd, and Chad Luke

Theodore P. Remley, Jr. as guest contributor

Objectives

- Describe and define many key terms from this chapter as associated with legal and ethical concepts.
- Understand, in depth, the importance of beneficence and its far-reaching imperatives.
- Recognize the difference between legal and ethical issues, and when to contact a lawyer.
- Identify ways in which codes of ethics guide our ethical practice as counselors.
- Compare and contrast codes of ethics of organizations to which you belong.
- Examine information related to working with minors, upholding confidentiality, and understanding privileged communication.
- Apply aspects of ethical decision making to an ethical dilemma.
- Examine advocacy competencies and understand ways in which culture impacts ethical decision making.

Reflective Questions

- What are my current ideas about legal and ethical issues in counseling?
- What are my current conceptualizations about using ethical codes and ethical decision making processes to guide my practice?
- How might legal and ethical issues differ for minors and adults?
- How do I understand my own values, beliefs, and culture as a counselor, and how is understanding this essential for understanding others?
- What cultural implications for ethical practice am I currently aware of?

It is a difficult concept to grasp that ethically, the child or adolescent is the client, but legally, a counselor's responsibility is to the parents/caregivers. Counselors and supervisors struggle with this concept when working with minors. This is foundational to working with minors and must be understood. When considering ethical, legal, and best practice implications, critical thinking is needed to engage in and thoughtfully process complex ethical dilemmas.

This chapter will urge you to take this information seriously and cautiously – but not become fearful about the services you provide. Often, counselors become scared about legal implications and talk of lawsuits. This chapter seeks to equip you with the information, resources, and critical thinking skills necessary to feel confident in your ability to move through complex situations for the betterment of clients. This chapter recognizes that training programs often have an entire class on legal and ethical issues in counseling. However, too often, work with minors is barely a focus – if it is taught at all. This chapter seeks to bridge that gap and provide you with the necessary information for protecting clients and practicing ethically – as that is our obligation.

Kitchener and Anderson (2011) state that

> ethics is a branch of philosophy that addresses questions of how people ought to act toward each other, that pronounces judgments of value about actions (e.g., whether someone ought to be praised or blamed for those actions), and that develops rules of ethical justifications (e.g., how we can justify holding one set of values over another).
>
> (p. 25)

Because people hold different beliefs and values that influence actions, many professional organizations have developed ethical codes to unify professions and provide a framework from which to practice. We will discuss the American Counseling Association (ACA) Code of Ethics and note other ethical codes for practice, but before we move into that, it is important to understand our guiding principles for ethical counseling practice.

Guiding Principles

The foundation of our ethical obligations lies in understanding five guiding principles. These principles are pivotal in providing ethical and best practice services. Beauchamp and Childress (1979) outlined four of those principles that are central to our counseling profession. Those are beneficence, non-maleficence, autonomy, and justice. The fifth guiding principle, fidelity, was added later by Kitchener (1984). Kitchener and Anderson (2011) wrote

> we argue that the principles of beneficence, nonmaleficence, autonomy, justice, and fidelity suggest that each person and each problem ought to be considered from a perspective that would offer the appropriate respect for people's rights and dignity, including their privacy, confidentiality, and autonomy.
>
> (p. 45)

Beneficence

Beneficence means simply to do good. Counselors must approach ethical practice with the intentions and skills necessary to do good and promote well-being for the client. This bears repeating: counselors must approach ethical practice with the intentions and skills necessary to do good and promote well-being for the client – not what *you* think the client should do. Further, the ACA Code of Ethics (2014) preamble notes that beneficence also includes working for the good of not just the client, but also society. Kitchener and Anderson (2011) also discuss that "beneficence suggests there are positive obligations like helping others and maintaining confidentiality to the greatest extent ethically and legally possible" (p. 40). What follows is an ABCDE (Sileo & Kopala, 1993, pp. 94–95) guide to promoting beneficence when working with clients.

A = Assessment

1. What is the client's mental state?
    a. What are his/her strengths, support systems, weaknesses?
    b. Is a psychiatric/medical consult necessary?
2. How serious is the client's disclosure? Is someone at risk for physical harm?
3. Are there cultural values and beliefs which should be considered while assessing the client?
4. What are my values, feelings, and reactions to the client's disclosure?

B = Benefit

1. How will the client benefit by my action?
2. How will the therapeutic relationship benefit?
3. How will others benefit?
4. Which action will benefit the most individuals?

C = Consequences and Consultation

1. What will the ethical, legal, emotional, and therapeutic consequences be for:

   a. The client?
   b. The counselor?
   c. Potential clients?

2. Have I consulted with colleagues, supervisors, agency administrators, legal counsel, professional ethics boards, or professional organizations?

D = Duty

1. To whom do I have a duty?

   a. My client?
   b. The client's family?
   c. A significant other?
   d. The counseling profession?
   e. My place of employment?
   f. The legal system?
   g. Society?

E = Education

1. Do I know and understand what the ethical principles and codes say regarding this issue?
2. Have I consulted the ethical casebooks?
3. Have I recently reviewed the laws that govern counseling practice?
4. Have I been continuing my education through journals, seminars, workshops, conferences, or course work?

As you can see, this is a complex issue that requires critical thinking skills in many areas, and this is just one of our foundational principles! Often students in legal and ethical classes have said: "*Just tell me what to do! What is the right answer?!*" and in counseling, often the answer is "*it depends*". Understanding how to thoughtfully process through ethical issues is imperative. As you can see from the preceding assessment, it depends on many factors that are specific to each client and each case. As you work your way through ethical decision making, use this information to inform your work and your approach.

Non-Maleficence

Non-maleficence means to do no harm. Non-maleficence also includes avoiding actions and practices that have the potential to cause harm (ACA, 2014; Jiggins & Asempapa, 2016). Counselors are beseeched to not only promote the welfare and mental health of their clients by doing good, we are also charged with making sure our actions or practices cannot in any way cause harm. Beneficence and non-maleficence are model ethical standards that guide the counselor and work in harmony to protect the clients we serve (Jiggins & Asempapa, 2016). Further, Forester-Miller and Davis (2016) note that "weighing potential harm against potential benefits is important in a counselor's efforts toward ensuring 'no harm'" (p. 2). When weighing ethical obligations in the face of an ethical dilemma, counselors understand that non-maleficence is foundational to promoting welfare. If, in the course of ethical decision making, a counselor must choose between beneficence and non-maleficence, "the stronger obligation could be summarized as 'in trying to help others, at least do not harm them'" (Kitchener & Anderson, 2011, p. 48).

Autonomy refers to respecting the rights and wishes of your client. Autonomy means that the counselor seeks to understand that which the client wants, believes, and values while offering the freedom for the client to control their own outcomes and purpose. It is important for counselors to understand where the counselor ends and where the client begins, meaning that it is essential for counselors to understand the differences between their values, beliefs, and desires, and those of their clients. Ethical counselors will work to promote the autonomy of their clients based on the clients' freedom and decision making, certainly not based on that which the counselor believes and/or would choose for her/himself. We try to explain this in class to counselors by stating that if you find yourself conflicted about something your client is doing that you don't agree with, there is a place you get to go to discuss your own ideas and beliefs – your own counseling! The client's session is not based on the beliefs and perspectives of the counselor – it is based on the beliefs and perspectives of the client. Barring any legal mandate, at any point if you find yourself in a situation in which you believe your client's actions or desires to be challenging to your own, you must seek supervision and/or counseling to discuss this, as the counseling session is about your client. Supervision and personal counseling about these matters will help to ensure that your counseling remains non-judgmental and safe for your client to explore options and exert autonomy.

Justice

Justice refers to fairness or rightness. The ACA Code of Ethics (2014) defines justice as "treating individuals equitably and fostering fairness and equality" (p. 3). Treating individuals equitably and fairly does not mean that a counselor treats every client the same. Kitchener (1984) noted that justice is about "treating equals equally and unequals unequally but in proportion to their relevant differences" (p. 49). For example, when working with a client for whom we use a translator, we would treat the client the same as every other client in other capacities. If we were to only consider fairness and treat every client the same, would we then need a translator for every client we see? Therefore, to apply the concept of justice, we must understand equity. In assessing ethical decision making, we must consider whether our actions treat all clients equally – and if the answer is no, then we must be able to justify that the variance in treatment is applicable to the specific situation at hand (Velasquez, Andre, Shanks, & Meyer, 2018).

Fidelity

Fidelity is about doing what you say you will do. Fidelity involves being true to your word, and being trustworthy and dependable. The ACA Code of Ethics (2014) states that fidelity "or honoring commitments and keeping promises, including fulfilling one's responsibilities of trust in professional relationships" (p. 3). Fidelity is crucial to the therapeutic alliance. Since relationships are based on trust, it is vital that counselors honor this agreement between the counselor and the client (Kitchener & Anderson, 2011).

Codes of Ethics

Counselors use codes of ethics to guide and support ethical decision making in the field. Ethical codes came about to uphold best practice within the profession, set by those in the profession. Unlike laws that were set by the community for the community, ethical codes go above and beyond to outline what the profession says is acceptable – in order to protect others from impaired professionals, and also to provide best practice guidelines for those within the field. Our ethical codes provide counselors with an understanding of our collective identity and standards from which we practice (Jungers & Gregoire, 2013).

ACA Code of Ethics

The American Counseling Association Code of Ethics is the primary code of ethics for counselors. Since ethical codes endure revisions as needed, counselors understand that the code is a "living document" (Corey, Corey, & Corey, 2019, p. 9). The most recent revision of the Code of Ethics was released in 2014, making this the seventh version established by ACA (Remley & Herlihy, 2016). Counselors must stay updated and aware of the changes made to the profession's ethical codes. As new information, advocacy efforts, and ethical issues come to light, codes are revised to reflect best practice and provide guiding principles for counselors. For example, one of the recent revisions to the code outlined information pertaining to distance counseling, technology, and social media – information not pertinent to earlier revisions. Counselors must have an understanding of the codes of ethics which they follow and stay updated as these codes shift in order to best serve and protect our clients.

Specialization Codes

As a counselor, you may hold multiple licensures or certificates, and must be aware of the multiple codes of ethics to which you are beholden. For example, the authors of this chapter are members of ACA, have licenses in different states (Tennessee, North Carolina, and Louisiana) and are members of multiple ACA divisions, while holding credentials as NCC (National Certified Counselor), RPT-S (Registered Play Therapist Supervisor), and ACS (Approved Clinical Supervisor). Associations, specialty groups, and other certification groups have also established codes of ethics for those members. For example, the American School Counseling Association (ASCA) has a code of ethics and many position statements addressing best practices and ethical obligations for school counselors (2016). The American Mental Health Counseling Association also has a code of ethics (AMHCA, 2015).

State Licensure Codes

Most states require counselors to apply for a license in order to practice counseling in that particular state. Most states also have a code of ethics guiding counselor practice. While some states have their own code (e.g., Alabama, Florida, Kentucky), other states subscribe to the ACA Code of Ethics as their guidelines (e.g., North Carolina, Tennessee, Louisiana). According to ACA (2016), this means that

> ACA's standards shall be used as aids in resolving ambiguities which may arise in interpretation of the rules of professional ethics and conduct, except that the board's rules of standards of ethical practice and professional conduct shall prevail whenever any conflict exists between these rules and ACA's standards.
>
> (p. 127)

This means that when the state code and the ACA code may be in disagreement, the ACA code will serve as the code to uphold. ACA (2016) notes that 18 jurisdictions out of 52 have adopted the ACA Code of Ethics as of that year.

Certification Codes

The National Board for Certified Counselors (NBCC) is a national certification that is voluntary and not based on state licensure. The NBCC has a code of ethics that all nationally certified counselors must follow (2016). Another example of a certification code is the American Association for Marriage and Family Therapy. This association also has an established code of ethics to guide clinical practice (2015). As you can see, there are many codes of ethics to guide our practice.

Further, there are also associations with guidelines (not codes, per se) for members and those credentialed to know and understand but refer to the members' primary licensing board as authority. The Association for Play Therapy has established *Play Therapy Best Practices: Clinical, Professional, and Ethical Issues* for registered play therapists and members of their association (2016), but makes it clear that the guidelines do not "replace or substitute any laws, standards, guidelines, rules or regulations promulgated by a practitioner's primary licensure or certification authority" (p. 18). As counselors, we have to understand the multiple codes and best practice information that guide our work.

Counseling Minors

Because counselors of minors have legal obligations to the parents or guardians of the children they counsel, and at the same time have ethical obligations to their minor clients and a different set of ethical obligations to the parents or guardians of the minors, there are times when the legal and ethical obligations of counselors of children collide (Lazovsky, 2008; Orton, 1997; Salo, 2015). In most situations in counseling practice, legal and ethical obligations are parallel and complementary, but because minors have only limited legal rights in our society (Davis & Mickelson, 1994; Kramer, 1994), there are times when counselors of minors must seek legal advice to ensure they are not violating the rights of children or their parents or guardians. Counselors must understand both legal and ethical duties to working with minor clients.

Obtaining Legal Advice

When counselors are faced with ethical or legal dilemmas, the process for resolving the two are much different. Consulting ethical standards that are reviewed above is an important part of ethical decision making, and consulting with peers and experts is critical. Ethical decision-making models are reviewed later in this chapter. On the other hand, resolving legal questions often requires that counselors seek legal advice.

There are circumstances in which counselors in all settings have to seek legal advice. Some situations that require counselors to seek legal advice include the following: (a) a counselor receives a subpoena for records or for testimony and is unsure whether the information is privileged; (b) a complaint is filed with a licensure board or certifying agency regarding the actions of a counselor claiming unethical conduct; (c) a parent or guardian of a minor asks a counselor to come and testify at a child custody hearing that will determine who is awarded custody of the child; (d) a counselor is asked to give information to an investigator after filing a suspected child abuse report; (e) the parent of a minor client who attempted suicide sends a letter to the counselor alleging that the counselor is incompetent and threatening to sue the counselor for malpractice; or (f) a minor client accuses a counselor of inappropriate touching during a counseling session and alleges sexual assault.

Sometimes it is difficult for counselors to determine whether they need legal advice. Generally, counselors are well-advised to seek advice from an attorney if clients are involved in legal proceedings and client records have been subpoenaed or counselors have been subpoenaed to appear at a deposition, hearing, or trial; if lawyers for clients or parents or guardians of clients have contacted counselors about the services they are providing; or if someone is accusing counselors of misconduct. In short, if you have been contacted by a client's lawyer, it is a good idea to contact one on your behalf to assist in navigating legal terrain.

Counselors of children or adolescents who have an independent private practice need to establish a relationship with an attorney so that they can pay for legal advice when it is needed. Private practitioners sometimes retain lawyers to help them set up their businesses and to advise them regarding practice contracts they might sign such as leases or contracts to deliver services to agencies. When counselors in private practice are seeking an attorney to hire for practice-related legal services, it often would be wise to ask other counselors or mental health practitioners in the community which attorney provides them with legal advice. Mental health services may not be understood by all lawyers, so it is beneficial to counselors to find attorneys who understand mental health and legal issues faced by counselors.

Counselors who counsel children and adolescents and who work in schools, agencies, hospitals, or are employed by some other entity have legal advice available to them as a result of their employment. When employed counselors have legal questions, they should inform their direct supervisors and request legal advice. Usually, employed counselors do not have direct access to attorneys who advise their employers, but supervisors have an obligation to obtain legal advice for counselors who request it and to pass the legal advice to their employees who are counselors. Sometimes employers will provide counselors with direct consultation with attorneys who are paid by the employer, but that is rare because of the high cost of legal services. Employed counselors who request legal advice should follow the advice they are given.

Rights of Parents and Guardians

An initial right of parents or guardians of children and adolescents is the decision as to whether to seek counseling for their child. When there is more than one parent or legal guardian, the permission of one is all that is required to initiate counseling, unless a court order specifies otherwise, as in a joint parenting decree. On the other hand, a second parent or guardian has a right to demand that counseling cease after it has been initiated. Counselors may accept a child for counseling with the permission of one parent or guardian but should terminate counseling if another parent or guardian objects. A parent or guardian who wants a child counseled over the objection of another parent or guardian could choose to seek a court order.

If a parent or guardian demands that counselors disclose information given to them in sessions with children or adolescents, a first step would be for counselors to attempt to win the trust of the parents or guardians by assuring them they would inform the parents or guardians of anything they need to know about their children to keep them safe. Children vary in their desire for privacy in counseling situations. Counselors should not assume that all of their clients who are children or adolescents do not want their parents or guardians to know what they have discussed in counseling sessions. Trice-Black, Riechel, and Shillingford (2013) have suggested that inquiries about counseling information should be responded to differently depending on the age of the child and the setting in which the counseling is taking place. Certainly, children should be consulted regarding their preferences regarding private information. Younger children seldom express an interest in privacy, whereas privacy may be of extreme importance to adolescent clients (Corr & Balk, 2010; Huey, 1996; Isaacs & Stone, 1999). Generally, school counselors, especially those at the elementary level, tend to favor giving parents and guardians information about their child's counseling sessions, whereas community mental health counselors tend to believe that clients who are children or adolescents should have the same privacy rights as adult clients have (Hendrix, 1991).

Utmost Importance of Confidentiality

I (Rebekah) have often worked with children and adolescents who have told me that they refuse to talk. I can imagine this might make any beginning counselor and even some seasoned counselors nervous, but I tend to trust that the client has a very good reason for refusing to talk to me and I respect that. It is important for counselors working with children and adolescents to check your power (and ego) at the door. I have often seen counselors get into power struggles with children and adolescents over their decision to stay silent in a session. I will not try to coax a child or adolescent into talking, and I will certainly never guilt a child or adolescent into speaking with me. This does not promote the dignity of the client and certainly does not build a strong therapeutic alliance honoring safety, autonomy, and trust. In this text, we will discuss many techniques for working with children and adolescents that don't rely on talk as the main form of communication. We hope that these skills will help you feel confident to navigate a situation such as this.

It has been in many similar counseling experiences where a client refuses to talk that sometimes they reveal why – in many instances, a client has said that it is because their last counselor went and told their parent, teacher, coach (fill in the blank) exactly what they said, so why should they trust another counselor? I (Rebekah) have seen this myself in the school setting, the community agency setting, and in inpatient settings. I have often wondered why this is the case. Do trained clinicians forget confidentiality? Do counselors get scared when working with minors and reveal confidential information, even when unnecessary? Whatever the reason, it is imperative to understand confidentiality as it pertains to minors.

It is widely accepted and generally understood by counselors, ethical codes, and laws that confidentiality is to be broken when a counselor suspects child abuse or neglect, when a client is a harm to self, and also in instances when the client indicates harm to others in imminent danger (Mitchell, Disque, & Robertson, 2002). The ACA Code of Ethics (2014) discusses trust as a cornerstone of the therapeutic relationship. Further, confidentiality "should be guarded at extreme costs, lest the profession redefine itself" (Mitchell et al., 2002, p. 158). Additionally, school counselors and other counselors working in school and inpatient settings have to also consider other adults involved (e.g., case managers, school social workers, teachers, members of the treatment team) when making decisions of breaching confidentiality. The ASCA Code of Ethics (2016) defines confidentiality as "the ethical duty of school counselors to responsibly protect a student's private communications shared in counseling" (p. 9). The ASCA Code also states that

> privacy that should be honored to the greatest extent possible, while balancing other competing interests (e.g., best interests of students, safety of others, parental rights) and adhering to laws, policies and ethical standards pertaining to confidentiality and disclosure in the school setting.
>
> (p. 1)

This can often be confusing for counselors and school counselors working with minors – the work of seeking a collaborative relationship with parents while also maintaining the therapeutic alliance, rapport, and confidentiality of the minor involved (Lazovsky, 2008). A delicate balance exists between working with parents and minors. We need parent/caregiver involvement. If possible, we want to strengthen the relationship with the client and their parents. This serves as such an important protective factor and adds to the long-term success of the client. Of course, there are situations in which this might not be healthy, or even safe, but having parents/guardians involved in the life of their child or adolescent can serve many beneficial roles.

Confidentiality and Privileged Communication

Counselors who provide services to all ages of clients find ethical and legal dilemmas related to confidentiality to occur frequently and be the most difficult to resolve (Fisher, 2008, 2016). Confidentiality is an ethical principle and is related to the obligation of counselors to respect the privacy of clients and not to reveal private information they know about clients without their consent. Privileged communication is a legal concept.

In order for privileged communication to exist, there must be a state or federal statute that grants privilege to categories of counselors (for example, those licensed by a state) and their clients. If a privileged communication statute does exist, then clients are protected by law from having confidential communications with their counselors disclosed in a court of law without their permission (Garner, 2014). All 50 states have enacted some type of privileged communication statute for clients of mental health professionals (Remley, Herlihy, & Herlihy, 1997; *Jaffee v. Redmond et al.*, 1996). Because statutes are regularly changed, it is impossible to list all of the states that have privileged communication statutes that protect the clients of various types of counselors. In most states, clients of counselors who are licensed by the state have privilege with their counselors (Glosoff, Herlihy, Herlihy, & Spence, 1997; Glosoff, Herlihy, Herlihy, & Spence, 2000), and in a few states, clients of school counselors have privilege with the counselors. Some federal statutes grant privilege to clients of counselors who provide services in some substance abuse rehabilitation programs. It is important for counselors of children and adolescents to investigate their state and federal laws and to know whether their counseling relationships with their clients are privileged by statute.

One issue that concerns counselors of minors occurs when parents or guardians seek information about a minor client's counseling sessions and the minor client objects to providing the information to their parents or guardians. While many counselors who provide services to minors report seldom being faced with children objecting to their parents or guardians being given information about their counseling sessions, others report that it has been a problem for them (Mitchell et al., 2002). A method to address such situations has been suggested by Remley and Herlihy (2016) and basically involves keeping in mind that parents and guardians generally have a legal right to know the information, and attempting to resolve the conflict between the child and their parents or guardians.

Informed Consent and Assent

The foundation for the counseling relationship is trust. Informed consent is one of the first steps to establishing a relationship founded on trust and well-being. Simply stated, informed consent refers to the client's right to understand and have autonomy in selecting the counseling they will participate in. Informed consent means that the client has the information needed to make knowledgeable choices about their participation in counseling services. Often, this information is noted in the counselor's Professional Disclosure Statement. It is the counselor's responsibility to provide adequate and updated information about the services provided and to discuss these with the client throughout the counseling relationship. The ACA Code of Ethics (2014, p. 4) states:

> Clients have the freedom to choose whether to enter into or remain in a counseling relationship and need adequate information about the counseling process and the counselor. Counselors have an obligation to review in writing and verbally with clients the rights and responsibilities of both counselors and clients. Informed consent is an ongoing part of the counseling process, and counselors appropriately document discussions of informed consent throughout the counseling relationship.

When working with minors, parents and guardians must sign the informed consent document in order for the counselor to be able to provide services. However, children and adolescents also have the right to understand the counseling relationship, what is involved/expected, and to have autonomy in selecting the counseling in which they will participate. Assent refers to the process of involving the child and adolescent in decision making about counseling services provided. While legally, the parent or guardian must give permission for services, it is ethical and considered best practice to explain the process to the child or adolescent, and involve them in decision making as much as developmentally appropriate. It is also suggested to include a signature line on documentation for the child or adolescent, along with the signature for parents and guardians.

Recordkeeping

The types of records counselors keep who provide services to children and adolescents depend on the settings in which the counselors practice. For example, school counselors typically keep minimal records on the students they counsel because of the volume of their caseloads that are compliant with the Family Educational Rights and Privacy Act (FERPA); counselors in hospitals or other healthcare settings usually keep extensive records that are compliant with the Health Insurance Portability and Accountability Act (HIPAA) and are similar to records kept by the other healthcare professionals in those settings; counselors in colleges and universities might keep extensive records that are both FERPA- and HIPAA-compliant; counselors in community mental health, substance abuse, rehabilitation, or juvenile treatment agencies keep records that are dictated by their employer that could range from few to extensive records; and counselors who have independent private practices usually keep both business and clinical records for their clients. Much of recordkeeping is dependent on whether a third party is reimbursing clients for the counseling services they received. Health insurance payors usually require that clients receive a diagnosis and that a treatment plan is created. In addition, insurance companies usually require that progress notes are kept that chart the progress of clients toward reaching their treatment plan goals. Counseling recordkeeping varies widely from setting to setting, and agency to agency. Employed counselors should always follow recordkeeping practices required by their employers.

It is important to keep records. When I (Rebekah) was working in the school setting, I kept brief records because I saw so many students a day – sometimes for only 15 minutes or so. There was an instance when a student was said to be involved in an encounter off campus during the school day. The student said he was not off campus, but was in fact with me. If I had not been keeping proper records, I would not have been able to substantiate the time when the student was with me. Aside from the importance of school counselors or school-based counselors using records to support data-driven initiatives, records protect you and the client.

Since the parents or guardians of clients who are children or adolescents are the legal clients of counselors, parents and guardians have a right to access the counseling records of the minors. Custody orders, suspected abuse situations, or state or federal statutes might alter the general rights that parents and guardians have to their children's counseling records, so legal advice should be sought when counselors are unsure whether parents or guardians should have copies of the counseling records of minors. Whether minor clients should be given access to their counseling records would depend on the evaluation of counselors whether the minors have the maturity to understand the records and have a legitimate reason for wanting to see the records. It is suggested that the counselor talk to parents, caregivers, and guardians about the issues with just handing over notes. In most cases, counselors can discuss with the child and adolescent what updates they can provide parents, discuss the importance of trust and the therapeutic alliance with parents, and acknowledge the parents' worries and concerns for their child or adolescent.

A very important part of recordkeeping for counselors who provide services to children and adolescents is documenting steps taken by counselors under difficult circumstances (Wiger, 1999). It is vital that counselors write details of actions they took in situations in which suicide or violence may be suspected, a suspected abuse report must be filed, or when clients, parents, or guardians complain about the services rendered by counselors. Despite the need for documentation in crisis situations, counselors must be careful to avoid routinely creating massive amounts of records, especially when the quality of counseling services rendered suffers due to time spent in recordkeeping (Kennedy, 2003; Remley & Herlihy, 2016).

Audio and video recordings of client sessions for the purpose of supervision are considered records. Students earning counseling degrees must record counseling sessions that will be watched or listened to by their clinical supervisors. In addition, after receiving their master's degrees, counselors must practice under supervision for a minimum of two years (and sometimes longer) before being eligible to obtain a state counseling license. Minor clients must know their counseling sessions are being recorded and must agree to the process. In addition, permission for recording must be obtained from a parent or guardian. Best practice suggests that permission from minor clients, a parent, or a guardian be obtained in writing.

All records kept by counselors must be kept confidential. Counselors must take reasonable steps to ensure that written or recorded records are kept in a way that unauthorized individuals do not have access to them. Written records should be kept in locked places and electronic records must be password protected. When records are transmitted electronically, the best method for privacy of clients is to encrypt the records so that they cannot be intercepted and read by any individuals who are not the intended recipients.

Managing Custody Disputes

It is not unusual for counselors of minors to find themselves caught in the middle of legal proceedings of parents or guardians who are involved in litigation regarding the custody of the counselors' clients. Counselors of minors should always focus on their role as counselors to children in such situations and should refuse to become an advocate for any one parent or guardian when custody is being disputed. When counselors are asked to provide letters of support or to attend court proceedings related to child custody, they should decline and explain that becoming an advocate would conflict with their responsibilities to be the child's counselor.

Minor clients are not well served if their counselors become an advocate for one of their parents or guardians in legal battles for child custody. Counselors must be able to maintain working relationships with all parents and guardians when a separation or divorce occurs. In addition, counselors of minors have very little information about the home circumstances of the children they counsel, so they are not in a position to be recommending custody by one parent over another one.

Even after refusing to attend child custody legal proceedings voluntarily, counselors of minors may receive a subpoena that requires them to be present. Responding to subpoenas generally is discussed in the following section, and legal advice should be sought. If counselors are forced through subpoenas to attend child custody hearings, they should maintain their neutrality and should refuse to give a professional opinion about child custody awards because they do not have adequate information to form judgments about who is the better parent or guardian. Even though counselors of children may have personal opinions based on their interactions with their child clients and the client's parents or guardians, a professional opinion would require that counselors have much more information than they possess. Professional child custody evaluators are given expert witness status in child custody legal proceedings, but before they render an opinion, the evaluators interview all of the parties individually, observe parents and guardians interacting with children, visit the homes of the parents or guardians, administer personality tests to all parties, and gather other information prior to making custody recommendations to a judge.

Responding to Subpoenas

When counselors receive subpoenas for records or to testify, they must obtain legal advice to ensure they do not respond when doing so would violate a client's privacy or fail to respond when they are legally required to do so (Borkosky, 2016; Gutheil & Drogin, 2013). The legal documents known as subpoenas require counselors to produce copies of records; appear at a deposition, court hearing, or trial; or bring their records with them when they appear in court (Barsky & Gould, 2002; Bowerbank, 2006; Childress-Beatty & Koocher, 2013; Cottone & Tarvydas, 2007; Levy, Galambos, & Skarbek, 2014; Palusci, Hicks, & Vandervort, 2001).

In some instances, the information counselors of minors have in their records or know of from sessions may be legally privileged, in which cases counselors are not allowed to provide information and subpoenas issued requesting information can be legally challenged. In other circumstances, the information may be legally available to the person who has caused the subpoena to be issued (Woody, 1988). Even when information is privileged, the person holding the privilege can waive it, or there are exceptions to privilege statutes that might be present. The only way to determine whether to comply with a subpoena is to obtain legal advice. The attorney you consult will tell you whether or not you are legally obligated to produce records or appear. The attorney you consult could request that the attorney who issued the subpoena withdraw it, might advise your client's parents or guardians to file a motion to quash the subpoena, or might advise you to comply with the subpoena.

Reporting Child Abuse

Child abuse and neglect are serious issues impacting many. The U.S. Department of Health and Human Services reported that there were 4.1 million referrals including 7.4 million children in 2016 (USDHHS, 2018). However, most of the child abuse and neglect victims are not determined (Bryant, 2009). This USDHHS report also noted that the child protective services (CPS) investigation response or alternate response increased from 2012–2016 at a rate of 9.5 percent (2016). Further, in 2016, an estimated 1,750 children died due to abuse and neglect (USDHHS, 2018). It is also shocking to note that research examining the agreement between reports of abuse and CPS determinations suggests that rates of abuse were actually 4–6 times higher than stated in CPS official records (Everson et al., 2008).

Counselors are legally mandated to report suspicion of abuse and neglect. In all 50 states and U.S. territories including the District of Columbia, there exist laws that mandate child abuse and neglect reporting (USDHHS, 2018). Counselors should understand specific requirements and reporting procedures in their state. Statues vary from state to state, and laws are changing continuously (Remley & Herlihy, 2016). Past abuse, current abuse, who must report, who is doing the abuse (caretaker, parent, sibling, etc.), and what is necessary to report are all factors to consider when reporting. Consulting state laws is imperative to understanding legal obligations in your state of practice (Remley & Herlihy, 2016).

Remley and Herlihy (2016) discuss four main reasons that counselors may be reluctant to report suspected abuse or neglect:

> desire to avoid betraying the child's trust, fear that a child protective services investigation will be poorly handled, fear of retaliation from the alleged perpetrator, or hope of maintaining the counseling relationship with the family so that the abusing adults can be helped to learn more appropriate parenting skills.
>
> (p. 273)

Important to note are protective clauses of mandatory reporting. These laws protect counselors who report child abuse and/or neglect in good faith. This means that if the counselor believes that the child abuse or neglect was occurring or previously occurred, they will be protected against potential lawsuits against them from those who were reported (Remley & Herlihy, 2016).

Duty to Protect and Warn

If counselors who provide services to minors determine that a client may be at risk of harm to self or others, the counselors must take any action necessary to prevent harm to their clients or to other parties. When unsure of whether a particular child or adolescent may be at risk for suicide or violence, counselors always are advised to consult with supervisors or colleagues (Sommers-Flanagan, Sommers-Flanagan, & Lynch, 2001). The privacy which counselors generally owe to minor clients and their parents or guardians does not apply when counselors believe clients may be at risk of harming themselves or other people, but only the minimum of confidential information that is necessary should be revealed. Dealing with clients who may be at risk for suicide or for harming another person is probably one of the most difficult situations counselors of children and adolescents will face (Corey et al., 2019; Miller, McGlothlin, & West, 2013).

Counselors who conduct an assessment and determine that clients may be at risk for suicide or violence do not have to determine whether clients really are at risk. Instead, counselors must work to have clients who may be at risk evaluated by a physician or another health professional who has the ability to hospitalize the client, even against their will, if necessary. It is impossible to predict whether a particular client will attempt suicide or will actually harm another person, but counselors must ask questions that will help them to determine whether a client may be at risk (Capuzzi, 2002; Jacobs, Brewer, & Klein-Benheim, 1999; Laux, 2002; Myer, 2001; Rogers, 2001; Rogers, Lewis, & Subich, 2002; Schwartz, 2000; Schwartz & Cohen, 2001; Stanard, 2000). Although counselors do not have a duty to determine whether a client is at risk for suicide or violence, they do have a duty to assess the client to determine whether the client may be at risk (Bursztajn, Gutheil, Hamm, & Brodsky, 1983; Drukteinis, 1985; Perr, 1985). There are accepted methods of performing such risk assessments that counselors of children and adolescents must know (Allen et al., 2002; McGlothlin, Rainey, & Kindsvatter, 2005; Morris & Minton, 2012; Shannonhouse, Lin, Shaw, & Porter, 2017). Counselors who did not learn how to assess for risk of suicide or violence in their graduate preparation programs must educate themselves through continuing education or readings (Daniel & Goldston, 2012; Linehan, Comtois, & Ward-Ciesielski, 2012; Meneese & Yutrzenka, 1990; Sapyta et al., 2012).

Literature is emerging on how counselors of children and adolescents should respond when they determine that a client is engaging in self-harm activities such as cutting, burning, self-bruising, etc. While some such activities are thought to be non-suicidal (Jagger & Sterner, 2016; Ross & Heath, 2002; Walsh, 2006; Zetterqvist, 2015), counselors of minors must assess the activities to determine whether their clients may be suicidal (Brausch & Gutierrez, 2010; Buser, Buser, & Rutt, 2017; Kakhnovets, Young, Purnell, Huebner, & Bishop, 2010; Nock, Holmberg, Photos, & Michel, 2007; Nock, Prinstein, & Sterba, 2010; Toprak, Cetin, Guven, Can, & Demircan, 2011; Wester, Ivers, Villalba, Trepal, & Henson, 2016; Wester & McKibben, 2016; Whisenhunt et al., 2014). Assessments for self-injurious behavior (Buser, Peterson, & Hill, 2016) and risk of suicide (Erickson & Abel, 2013; Lotito & Cook, 2015; McGlothlin, Page, & Jager, 2016) are available for counselors of children and adolescents. We will discuss this more in a later chapter.

Employed counselors should consult with their supervisors and must always follow any established policies or procedures when they determine that a child or adolescent client may be at risk for suicide or violence. Counselors in private practice should make sure that a parent or guardian of a minor who the counselor believes may be at risk for suicide or violence understands the counselor's concerns, agrees to take responsibility for the safety of the client, and agrees to submit the minor to a physician or qualified healthcare professional to be evaluated.

For self-protection, counselors of children and adolescents should always thoroughly document in their notes each time they assess a client to determine whether the client may be at risk for suicide or violence (Boughner & Logan, 1999; Gutheil, 1999). The reasons for deciding that either the client might be at risk, or probably was not at risk at that time, should be included in the documentation. When clients are minors, each time an assessment for suicide or violence is conducted by counselors, whether or not the assessment leads to a conclusion the clients are at risk, parents or guardians of the clients should be informed (Capuzzi, 2002).

If a counselor of children or adolescents determines that a client may be at risk of harming an identifiable person, then the ethical standards for counselors (American Counseling Association, 2014) plus the law in all states except Texas (*Thapar v.* Zezulka, 1999) require that counselor make efforts to notify the intended victim (Burkemper, 2002; *Tarasoff v. Regents of University of California*, 1976). If counselors believe they need to warn intended victims, they should consult with an attorney to determine what the law in their state requires, and should always involve supervisors when the counselors are employed.

Issues in the School

School counselors take on the role of parent substitute when they counsel children and adolescents in school settings. When parents and guardians send their children to schools, they expect the professionals in the schools to make sure their children are not harmed.

As a result, the duties of school counselors to parents and guardians are stronger than the duties of counselors in other settings.

School counselors consult often about students with other school personnel including principals, other administrators, teachers, social workers, and nurses. School counselors have to balance the privacy rights of their student clients and the parents and guardians of their students with the need of other school professionals to know information about the students in the school. Student clients and their parents and guardians should know when information is being shared with others, and what type of information it is. School counselors must adhere to FERPA regulations regarding private information.

Issues in Agencies and Private Practices

Counselors who provide counseling services to children and adolescents in settings other than schools have special concerns with which they must deal. Almost all non-school settings must follow HIPAA privacy rules and regulations. Counselors must secure permission to counsel minors, must provide information regarding the counseling to parents and guardians when they request it, and must discontinue counseling when requested. Counselors of minors in agencies and private practices often consult with others who provide services to their clients such as social workers, physicians, psychologists, and others. Shared information must be protected, and permission must be obtained from parents and guardians prior to consultations taking place.

Making Informed Decisions

Counselors are often faced with difficult situations involving ethics. It is imperative that counselors know how to critically think through situations and consider options for best practice. You will certainly encounter situations in which a decision is required, and you have multiple outcomes to choose from. How do you make the best choice possible? First, remember to consider the foundation of our ethical obligations, the five guiding principles discussed earlier: beneficence, non-maleficence, autonomy, justice, and fidelity. Consider each guiding principle in depth and in relation to the situation at hand. Next, it is critical to work through a model for decision making. This is not merely a suggestion for decision making, this is an ethical imperative. The ACA Code of Ethics (2014) is clear:

> *I.1.b. Ethical Decision Making*
>
> When counselors are faced with an ethical dilemma, they use and document, as appropriate, an ethical decision making model that may include, but is not limited to, consultation; consideration of relevant ethical standards, principles, and laws; generation of potential courses of action; deliberation of risks and benefits; and selection of an objective decision based on the circumstances and welfare of all involved.
>
> (p. 19)

Model for Decision Making

Many models for decision making exist. The ACA Code of Ethics (2014) includes aspects of an ethical decision-making model for consideration by counselors. The ACA further does not endorse one specific decision-making model, but encourages counselors to utilize a model that is both reliable and can withstand public investigation (2014). You are encouraged to think through ethical decision making in a meaningful and critical way. The following is not a particular model per se, but will present aspects common in many

84   *Theodore P. Remley et al.*

available models. Present in the following is a consideration for foundational principles, feminist approaches to decision making, multicultural considerations and ethics, social constructivism, and other specialty models (Remley & Herlihy, 2016).

Remley and Herlihy (2016) list the following items for inclusion in many ethical decision-making models. The items that follow are to be considered as a continuing process, and not a step-by-step model. Added to Remley and Herlihy's list is information from the Transcultural Integrative Model (Garcia, Cartwright, Winston, & Borzuchowska, 2003). This model was based on the initial work of Tarvydas (1998) and added to by Garcia et al. in 2003. This model is rooted in virtue ethics, principle ethics, relational method, and social constructivism techniques. What follows is not a complete or comprehensive discussion of this model. However, aspects of the Transcultural Integrative Model have been added to the concepts.

Identify and define the problem. Think about all aspects of the situation and gather more information as needed. It is important to decipher what is a legal issue and needs legal attention, and what is an ethical issue. Take your time, as permitted, to consider and define the situation at hand. You must also consider your attitudes and reactions to culture. What is your knowledge of the client's culture? What is your awareness of your own and the client's cultural identity? What is your awareness of cultural competency skills in this case?

Involve your client in the decision-making process. A collaborative, more holistic, and mutual approach to decision making involves the client, except in extenuating circumstances which are very rare. Counselors need to understand that involving the client is a part of the process throughout counseling and decision making. Walden (2015) discusses the importance of making decisions with clients:

> Because of the potential for harm to clients, more attention must be given to understanding the client's perspective and to educating and empowering clients. Inclusion of the client in ethical considerations is not an attempt to "victim blame" or to shift the responsibility for ethical practice onto the client – the professional always bears the onus for maintaining professionalism and ethical practice – rather, inclusion of the client can be a strong asset to the counselor in resolving ethical dilemmas and can be a course of empowerment for the client.
>
> (p. 63)

Review relevant codes of ethics and the professional literature. Although you must continuously be aware of the code of ethics which apply, a thorough and detailed examination is necessary when faced with ethical issues. As we discussed earlier, there may be multiple codes of ethics you need to review depending on your professional memberships, certifications, and licenses. It is not realistic to expect that you would have this information memorized. Understanding which codes apply to the situation at hand will assist you in thinking about the options available. Just as understanding and applying the codes is important, it is also important to understand relevant and recent literature. The Transcultural Integrative Model (Garcia et al., 2003) suggests making sure that relevant codes contain diversity standards. It is also important to examine laws, policies, and procedures that could be discriminatory in nature. Additionally, if conflicts between laws and ethics exists, it is necessary to determine whether these are a result of a cultural perspective.

Consider the principles and virtues. Counselors need to consider how moral principles can be applied to the particular ethical dilemma at hand. Considering both principle and virtue ethics assists in decision making and also in understanding what principles may conflict. Remley and Herlihy (2016) suggest ranking these in order of what is priority in each specific case, as these will certainly be different for each scenario.

Tune into your feelings. As counselors, we understand the importance of self-awareness. Being aware of your own feelings as related to the situation at hand can assist in understanding your decision-making process. Are your feelings influencing your process? Are your feelings related to your values and beliefs? "To what extent are you being influenced, for instance, by emotions such as fear, self-doubt, of an overwhelming sense of responsibility?" (Remley & Herlihy, 2016, p. 16). Acknowledging and being aware of your own feelings is an important step in ethical decision making.

Consult with colleagues or experts. Consulting is essential. We do not practice counseling in a vacuum, and we do not just make a decision rapidly, move on, and hope for the best. Consultation is not a suggestion; it is an ethical imperative. Consultation assists in helping us see aspects we may not have considered because we are an active member of the counseling relationship and therefore not objective. Consultation is a necessary step in decision making, supported by multiple codes of ethics, and important if your decisions are challenged in court (Wheeler & Bertram, 2012). Important in all consultation, as is outlined by the Transcultural Integrative Model (Garcia et al., 2003), is making sure that your consultation reflects professionals and supervisors in the field with relevant multicultural competencies and expertise.

Consider the context. Each counseling session and relationship is unique. Even in similar circumstances, not two situations are exactly alike. Considering the context specific to each case is necessary in ethical decision making. Your beliefs, values, and culture certainly play a role in how you understand the dilemma at hand, and the same is true for your client who has their own beliefs, values and culture that likely differ from yours (Remley & Herlihy, 2016). Counselors also need to reflect on consequences of decision making that involve not only the client, but the client's family, community, and other professionals (Remley & Herlihy, 2016). Additionally, the Transcultural Integrative Model (Garcia et al., 2003) suggests gathering cultural information as it applies to the case (e.g., immigration information, family, community, and cultural values) and making sure this information is considered when analyzing the dilemma.

Identify desired outcomes and consider possible actions to achieve the outcomes. Often in the case of ethical dilemmas, many actions can be chosen, with many outcomes possible. You should carefully consider each action with the accompanying outcomes associated. Remley and Herlihy (2016) note that there could even be a number of desired outcomes, and counselors may need to prioritize these possibly having to make a choice for one over another. Further, the Transcultural Integrative Model (Garcia et al., 2003) of ethical decision making asks counselors to distinguish the worldviews involved in the identified outcomes. Do these reflect the worldview of the client, the worldview of the counselor, or the worldview of both? Ensure that the possible actions and outcomes mirror the culture of those involved, while considering both positive and negative consequences of each possible action or outcome.

Choose and act on your choice. After thoughtful consideration involving steps listed previously and more aspects of decision making, you eventually must decide what to do – and then you must do it. Remley and Herlihy (2016) suggest that counselors check their action (or series of actions) to see if they are congruent with their moral principles. Ethical decision making is not easy and involves many aspects important for consideration. Counselors should make sure their course of action and outcome reflects an agreement among the cultural worldview of the client and others involved in the dilemma, as discussed in the Transcultural Integrative Model. Further, when implementing a plan, counselors must also identify relevant cultural strategies and resources (Garcia et al., 2003).

After the decision is made, Stadler (1986) suggests that the counselor use the following self-tests. In considering justice, would you treat other clients the same in this situation?

In considering universality, would you recommend this same course of action to other counselors? In terms of publicity, would you stand by your actions and be willing to have them known by others/reported publicly?

As you can see, ethical decision making is not about telling counselors what to do, or telling them the "right" answer. Ethical decision making is about thinking critically about a complex issue and being able to consider many factors for ethical decision making. You must have a process by which you think through dilemmas. It is recommended that you consider the aspects presented in this chapter and apply them to your own development.

Multicultural Implications and Advocacy

As stated earlier, your beliefs, values, and culture certainly play a role in how you understand ethical issues. Culture impacts the ways in which counselors approach ethical decision making and critical thinking about ethical dilemmas (Pack-Brown, Thomas, & Seymour, 2008). As a profession, counseling is dedicated and deeply committed to multicultural competency, social justice, and advocacy efforts. This is a mission that extends to every facet of counseling and professional service.

The Transcultural Integrative Model (Garcia et al., 2003) of ethical dilemma resolution discusses that counselors should "anticipate cultural barriers such as biases, discrimination, stereotypes, and prejudices. Develop effective and relevant cultural-specific counter measures, for instance, culturally sensitive conflict resolution and support" (p. 273). The ACA Code of Ethics has been edited multiple times throughout our profession's history to include and address issues of multiculturalism, advocacy, and ethical standards and it will continue to be edited as our profession develops. The 2014 Code of Ethics states that "honoring diversity and embracing a multicultural approach in support of the worth, dignity, potential, and uniqueness of people within their social and cultural contexts" (ACA Code of Ethics, 2014, p. 2) is a core professional value. The Code of Ethics also makes clear the ethical imperative of counselors to advocate on behalf of our clients not just on the individual level, but as a group, institution, and society to address barriers and obstacles that hinder client access, progress, and development. Further, advocacy competencies were developed to assist counselors in advocacy efforts in many domains (Lewis, Arnold, House, & Toporek, 2003). We discuss multicultural competencies and advocacy throughout this text. It is up to you to continue on the journey of self-awareness and to always seek to address culture and advocacy throughout your life as a counselor.

Summary

Understanding the differences involved in working with minors as opposed to adults is essential for ethical practice. Counselors need critical thinking skills to engage in and think through complex ethical dilemmas. This chapter urges counselors to take this information seriously and cautiously – but not become fearful about the services provided. With updated information and resources, counselors can feel equipped and confident in their abilities to move through complex situations for the betterment of their clients. Much like in Chapter 3 of this volume, this chapter recognizes that counselors in training receive an entire class on legal and ethical issues in counseling. However, too often, work with minors is barely a focus – if it is taught at all. This chapter provided counselors with the necessary information for protecting their clients and practicing ethically.

Essential aspects of practice such as ethical obligations with discussions on multiple ethical codes was discussed. Understanding how to use multiple codes of ethics to the benefit of the client to promote beneficence is crucial. The importance of confidentiality, privileged communication, and aspects related to working with minors were discussed. Informed consent and assent specific to working with minors was addressed. Record keeping and the importance of documentation followed. Counselors must be aware of child abuse reporting laws in their states, and abide by such laws while keeping with their ethical responsibilities. Importance is placed on assisting counselors in training in making sound, informed, and ethical decisions. Factors included in models for ethical decision making were presented. Multicultural understandings and advocacy efforts through ethical practice were also addressed.

Clinician's Corner

I am a fairly well-known counselor educator in the region in which I live and work. My wife and I have a wonderful daughter who suffers from a psychiatric disorder that at times has included hallucinations and delusions. These started when she was 13 years old, and in the eighth grade, she overdosed on Darvon because the inside of her was just too much to bear. After that, she saw a psychiatrist for a while who also met with my wife and me, but he was scrupulous in maintaining confidentiality. My daughter has had one other psychiatrist, and he, too, was scrupulous about maintaining confidentiality. I wish I could say the same for the school counselor who occasionally met with my daughter, the social worker who met with my daughter, and the child psychologist, who was the worst in terms of breaking confidentiality. Indeed, the psychologist was supposed to be the best in our area, and he never missed a chance to talk to my wife or me about things he and my daughter discussed. The social worker was a little better, but when she began to feel that our daughter was too much for her, she, too, met with us to discuss confidential information. By far, the school counselor leaked the most. She not only talked to us, but also to one or more of our daughter's teachers and to at least one administrator. I had my daughter stop seeing her within two weeks.
Parent and Counselor Educator

Answering Clients' Legal and Ethical Questions

I work in an Intensive Outpatient Program (IOP) environment with adolescents who have substance use disorder diagnoses. Many of them present to treatment at the recommendation of their probation officer ("P.O.") or their DCS (Department of Children's Services) worker, and they will often let me know early on in treatment that they are there "to get out of trouble" and they don't especially want to change the way they think about drugs or alcohol. During this initial period in treatment, the clients try not to say too much because they are worried about getting into more trouble. Clients who talk about still spending time with their risky peers, for instance, will recognize that perhaps they have said too much and will ask, "So you're gonna tell my caseworker/P.O. about this, aren't you?"

This is where real, therapeutic work can begin to unfold! I will often reflect that the client is asking a basic information-seeking question, and so I give them a factual answer. This invariably leads to other group members chipping in "what if" questions, testing the limits of confidentiality. After fielding fact-seeking questions for a few minutes, I will generally offer a reflection and say something like: "We spend a great deal of time together, and you all want to know whether or not you can trust me. It makes sense that you're concerned about me telling your referral sources everything you're doing, but that's not my job. My job is to be with you and keep what you say in confidence, so long as you aren't suicidal or homicidal and you aren't telling me about child or elder abuse".

In the spirit of transparency, I then tell my clients that if I think something warrants talking with their referral sources, we can talk with them together. In giving them the information they ask for, reflecting their need for trust and safety, describing my commitment to confidentiality while defining boundaries, and giving them the opportunity to work together, I find that the group experience tends to become more therapeutic and clients are more willing to engage in the therapy process.

Nathan Strickland LPC/MHSP-temp
Bradford Health Services

References

Allen, M., Burt, K., Bryan, E., Carter, D., Orsi, R., & Durkan, L. (2002). School counselors' preparation for and participation in crisis intervention. *Professional School Counseling, 6,* 96–102.

American Association for Marriage and Family Therapy. (2015). *AAMFT code of ethics.* Alexandria, VA: Author.

American Counseling Association. (2014). *ACA code of ethics.* Alexandria, VA: Author.

American Counseling Association. (2016). *Licensure requirements for professional counselors: A state-by-state report.* Alexandria, VA: Author.

American Mental Health Counselors Association. (2015). *AMHCA code of ethics.* Alexandria, VA: Author.

American School Counseling Association. (2016). *ASCA ethical standards for school counselors.* Alexandria, VA: Author.

Association for Play Therapy. (2016). *Play therapy best practices: Clinical, professional, and ethical issues.* Clovis, CA: Author.

Barsky, A. E., & Gould, J. W. (2002). *Clinicians in court: A guide to subpoenas, depositions, testifying, and everything else you need to know.* New York: Guilford Press.

Beauchamp, T., & Childress, J. F. (1979). *Principles of biomedical ethics.* New York: Oxford University Press.

Borkosky, B. G. (2016). "Coping with subpoenas": No longer consistent with law, ethics, or social policy. *Professional Psychology: Research and Practice, 47,* 250–251. https://doi.org/10.1037/pro0000091

Boughner, S. R., & Logan, J. P. (1999). Robert H. Woody: Legal issues in couple and family counseling. *The Family Journal, 7,* 302–310.

Bowerbank, J. E. (2006). Do's and don'ts about a nonparty's response to federal and state court deposition subpoenas involving civil litigation. *Orange County Lawyer, 48,* 38–41.

Brausch, A. M., & Gutierrez, P. M. (2010). Differences in nonsuicidal suicide and self-injury attempts in adolescents. *Youth Adolescence, 39,* 233–242. https://doi.org/10.1007/s10964-009-9482-0

Bryant, J. (2009). School counselors and child abuse reporting: A national survey. *Professional School Counseling, 12*(5), 333–342. https://doi.org/10.5330/PSC.n.2010-12.333

Burkemper, E. M. (2002). Family therapists' ethical decision-making processes in two duty-to-warn situations. *Journal of Marital and Family Therapy, 28,* 203–211.

Bursztajn, H., Gutheil, T. G., Hamm, R. M., & Brodsky, A. (1983). Subjective data and suicide assessment in the light of recent legal developments. Part II: Clinical uses of legal standards in the interpretation of subjective data. *International Journal of Law and Psychiatry, 6,* 331–350.

Buser, T. J., Buser, J. K., & Rutt, C. C. (2017). Predictors of unintentionally severe harm during nonsuicidal self-injury. *Journal of Counseling and Development, 95,* 2–17. https://doi.org/10.1002/jcad.12113

Buser, T. J., Peterson, C. H., & Hill, T. M. (2016). Brief severity index for nonsuicidal self-injury: Initial validation of a self-report measure. *Journal of Mental Health Counseling, 38,* 28–46. https://doi.org/10.17744/mehc.38.1.03

Capuzzi, D. (2002). Legal and ethical challenges in counseling suicidal students. *Professional School Counseling, 6,* 36–45.

Childress-Beatty, L., & Koocher, G. P. (2013). Dealing with subpoenas. In G. P. Koocher, J. C. Norcross, & B. A. Greene (Eds.), *Psychologists' desk reference* (3rd ed., pp. 564–567). New York: Oxford University Press.

Corey, G., Corey, M. S., & Corey, C. (2019). *Issues and ethics in the helping professions* (10th ed.). Boston, MA: Cengage Learning.

Corr, C. A., & Balk, D. E. (2010). *Children's encounters with death, bereavement, and coping.* New York: Springer.

Cottone, R. R., & Tarvydas, V. M. (2007). *Counseling ethics and decision making* (3rd ed.). Upper Saddle River, NJ: Pearson Merrill Prentice-Hall.

Daniel, S. S., & Goldston, D. B. (2012). Hopelessness and lack of connectedness to others as risk factors for suicidal behavior across the lifespan: Implications for cognitive-behavioral treatment. *Cognitive and Behavioral Practice, 19,* 288–300. https://doi.org/10.1016/j.cbpra.2011.05.003

Davis, J. L., & Mickelson, D. J. (1994). School counselors: Are you aware of ethical and legal aspects of counseling? *The School Counselor, 42,* 5–13.

Drukteinis, A. M. (1985). Psychiatric perspectives on civil liability for suicide. *Bulletin of American Academy of Psychiatry Law, 13,* 71–83.

Erickson, A., & Abel, N. (2013). A high school counselor's leadership in providing school-wide screenings for depression and enhancing suicide awareness. *Professional School Counseling, 16,* 283–289. https://doi.org/10.5330/PSC.n.2013-16.283

Everson, M. D., Smith, J. B., Hussey, J. M., English, D., Litrownik, A. J., Dubowitz, H., . . . Runyan, D. K. (2008). Concordance between adolescent reports of childhood abuse and Child Protective Service determinations in an at-risk sample of young adolescents. *Child Maltreatment, 13*(1), 14–26. https://doi.org/10.1177/1077559507307837

Fisher, M. A. (2008). Protecting confidentiality rights: The need for an ethical practice model. *American Psychologist, 63,* 1–13.

Fisher, M. A. (2016). *Confidentiality limits in psychotherapy: Ethics checklists for mental health professionals.* Washington, DC: American Psychological Association.

Forester-Miller, H., & Davis, T. E. (2016). *Practitioner's guide to ethical decision making* (Rev. ed.). Retrieved from www.counseling.org/docs/default-source/ethics/practitioner's-guide-toethical-decision-making.pdf

Garcia, J. G., Cartwright, B., Winston, S. M., & Borzuchowska, B. (2003). A transcultural integrative model for ethical decision making in counseling. *Journal of Counseling and Development, 81,* 268–277.

Garner, B. A. (Ed.). (2014). *Black's law dictionary* (10th ed.). New York: Thomson West.

Glosoff, H. L., Herlihy, B., & Spence, B. (2000). Privileged communication in the counselor – Client relationship. *Journal of Counseling & Development, 78,* 454–462. Retrieved from http://onlinelibrary.wiley.com/doi/10.1002/j.1556-6676.2000.tb01929.x/abstract

Glosoff, H. L., Herlihy, S., Herlihy, B., & Spence, B. (1997). Privileged communication in the psychologist – Client relationship. *Professional Psychology: Research and Practice, 28,* 573–581.

Gutheil, T. G. (1999). Liability issues and liability prevention in suicide. In D. G. Jacobs (Ed.), *The Harvard Medical School guide to suicide assessment and intervention* (pp. 561–578). San Francisco, CA: Jossey-Bass.

Gutheil, T. G., & Drogin, E. Y. (2013). *The mental health professional in court.* Arlington, VA: American Psychiatric Association.

Hendrix, D. H. (1991). Ethics and intrafamily confidentiality in counseling with children. *Journal of Mental Health Counseling, 13,* 323–333.

Huey, W. C. (1996). Counseling minor clients. In B. Herlihy & G. Corey (Eds.), *ACA ethical standards casebook* (5th ed., pp. 241–245). Alexandria, VA: American Counseling Association.

Isaacs, M. L., & Stone, C. (1999). School counselors and confidentiality: Factors affecting professional choices. *Professional School Counseling, 2,* 258–266.

Jacobs, D. G., Brewer, M., & Klein-Benheim, M. (1999). Suicide assessment: An overview and recommended protocol. In D. G. Jacobs (Ed.), *The Harvard Medical School guide to suicide assessment and intervention* (pp. 3–39). San Francisco, CA: Jossey-Bass.

Jaffee v. Redmond et al., 1996 WL 314841 (U.S. June 13, 1996).

Jagger, G. E., & Sterner, W. R. (2016). Excoriation: What counselors need to know about skin picking disorder. *Journal of Mental Health Counseling, 38,* 281–297. https://doi.org/10.17744/mehc.38.4.01

Jiggins, K. C., & Asempapa, B. (2016). Values in the counseling profession: Unethical vs. non-maleficence. In *VISTAS 2016* (pp. 1–10). Retrieved from www.counseling.org/docs/default-source/vistas/articl e_3452fd25f16116603abcacff0000bee5e7.pdf?sfvrsn=cceb452c_4

Jungers, C. M., & Gregoire, J. (2013). *Counseling ethics: Philosophical and professional foundations*. New York: Springer Publishing Company, LLC.

Kakhnovets, R., Young, H. L., Purnell, A. L., Huebner, E., & Bishop, C. (2010). Self-reported experience of self-injurious behavior in college students. *Journal of Mental Health Counseling, 32*, 309–323.

Kennedy, J. A. (2003). *Psychiatric treatment planning* (2nd ed.). Arlington, VA: American Psychiatric Publishing.

Kitchener, K. S. (1984). Intuition, critical evaluation and ethical principles: The foundation for ethical decisions in counseling psychology. *Counseling Psychologist, 12*, 43–55.

Kitchener, K. S., & Anderson, S. K. (2011). *Foundations of ethical practice, research, and teaching in psychology and counseling* (2nd ed.). New York: Routledge.

Kramer, D. T. (1994). *Legal rights of children* (2nd ed.). New York: McGraw-Hill.

Laux, J. M. (2002). A primer on suicidology: Implications for counselors. *Journal of Counseling & Development, 80*, 380–383.

Lazovsky, R. (2008). Maintaining confidentiality with minors: Dilemmas of school counselors. *Professional School Counseling, 11*(5), 335–346. https://doi.org/10.1177/2156759X0801100507

Levy, J., Galambos, G., & Skarbek, Y. (2014). The erosion of psychiatrist-patient confidentiality by subpoenas. *Australasian Psychiatry, 22*, 332–336. https://doi.org/10.1177/1039856214536241

Lewis, J. A., Arnold, M. S., House, R., & Toporek, R. L. (2003). *ACA advocacy competencies*. Retrieved February 5, 2019, from www.counseling.org/resources/competencies/advocacy_competencies.pdf

Linehan, M. M., Comtois, K. A., & Ward-Ciesielski, E. F. (2012). Assessing and managing risk with suicidal individuals. *Cognitive and Behavorial Practice, 19*, 218–232. https://doi.org/10.1016/j.cbpra.2010.11.008

Lotito, M., & Cook, E. (2015). A review of suicide risk assessment instruments and approaches. *Suicidality and Self-Injurious Behavior, 5*(5), 216–223. https://doi.org/10.9740/mhc.2015.09.216

McGlothlin, J. M., Page, B., & Jager, K. (2016). Validation of the SIMPLE STEPS model of suicide assessment. *Journal of Mental Health Counseling, 38*, 298–307. https://doi.org/10.17744/mehc.38.4.02

McGlothlin, J. M., Rainey, S., & Kindsvatter, A. (2005). Suicidal clients and supervisees: A model for considering supervisor roles. *Counselor Education and Supervision, 45*, 135–146.

Meneese, W. B., & Yutrzenka, B. A. (1990). Correlates of suicidal ideation among rural adolescents. *Suicide and Life-Threatening Behavior, 20*, 206–212.

Miller, L. G., McGlothlin, J. M., & West, J. D. (2013). Taking the fear out of suicide assessment and intervention: A pedagogical and humanistic practice. *The Journal of Humanistic Counseling, 52*, 106–121. https://doi.org/10.1002/j.2161-1939.2013.00036.x

Mitchell, C. W., Disque, G., & Robertson, P. (2002). When parents want to know: Responding to parental demands for confidential information. *Professional School Counseling, 6*(2), 156–161.

Morris, C. A. W., & Minton, C. A. B. (2012). Crisis in the curriculum? New counselors' crisis preparation, experiences, and self-efficacy. *Counselor Education and Supervision, 51*, 256–269. https://doi.org/10.1002/j.1556-6978.2012.00019.x

Myer, R. A. (2001). *Assessment for crisis intervention: A triage assessment model*. Belmont, CA: Brooks/Cole.

National Board for Certified Counselors, Inc. and Affiliates (NBCC). (2016). *National board for certified counselors code of ethics*. Greensboro, NC: Author.

Nock, M. K., Holmberg, E. B., Photos, V. I., & Michel, B. D. (2007). Self-injurious thoughts and behaviors interview: Development, reliability, and validity in an adolescent sample. *Psychological Assessment, 19*, 309–317. https://doi.org/10.1037/1040-3590.19.3.309

Nock, M. K., Prinstein, M. J., & Sterba, S. K. (2010). Revealing the form and function of selfinjurious thoughts and behaviors: A real-time ecological assessment study among adolescents and young adults. *Psychology of Violence, 1*, 36–52. https://doi.org/10.1037/2152-0828.1.S.36

Orton, G. L. (1997). *Strategies for counseling with children and their parents*. Pacific Grove, CA: Brooks/Cole.

Pack-Brown, S. P., Thomas, T. L., & Seymour, J. M. (2008). Infusing professional ethics into counselor education programs: A multicultural/social justice perspective. *Journal of Counseling and Development, 86*(3), 296–302.

Palusci, V. J., Hicks, R. A., & Vandervort, F. E. (2001). "You are hereby commanded to appear": Pediatrician subpoena and court appearance in child maltreatment. *Pediatrics, 107,* 1427–1430.

Perr, I. N. (1985). Suicide litigation and risk management: A review of 32 cases. *The Bulletin of the American Academy of Psychiatry and the Law, 13,* 209–219.

Remley, T. P., Jr., & Herlihy, B. (2016). *Ethical, legal, and professional issues in counseling* (5th ed.). Boston, MA: Pearson.

Remley, T. P., Jr., Herlihy, B., & Herlihy, S. (1997). The U.S. Supreme Court decision in *Jaffee v. Redmond*: Implications for counselors. *Journal of Counseling & Development, 75,* 213–218.

Rogers, J. R. (2001). Suicide risk assessment. In E. R. Welfel & R. E. Ingersoll (Eds.), *The mental health desk reference* (pp. 259–264). New York: Wiley.

Rogers, J. R., Lewis, M. M., & Subich, L. M. (2002). Validity of the suicide assessment checklist in an emergency crisis center. *Journal of Counseling & Development, 80,* 493–502.

Ross, S., & Heath, N. (2002). A study of the frequency of selfmutilation in a community sample of adolescents. *Journal of Youth and Adolescence, 31,* 67–77.

Salo, M. (2015). Counseling minor clients. In B. Herlihy & G. Corey (Eds.), *ACA ethical standards casebook* (7th ed., pp. 205–207). Alexandria, VA: American Counseling Association.

Sapyta, J., Goldston, D. B., Erkanli, A., Daniel, S. S., Heilbron, N., Mayfield, A., & Treadway, S. L. (2012). Evaluating the predictive validity of suicidal intent and medical lethality in youth. *Journal of Consulting and Clinical Psychology, 80,* 222–231. https://doi.org/10.1037/a0026870

Schwartz, R. C. (2000). Suicidality in schizophrenia: Implications for the counseling profession. *Journal of Counseling & Development, 78,* 496–499.

Schwartz, R. C., & Cohen, B. N. (2001). Risk factors for suicidality among clients with schizophrenia. *Journal of Counseling & Development, 79,* 314–319.

Shannonhouse, L., Lin, Y. D., Shaw, K., & Porter, M. (2017). Suicide intervention training for K-12 schools: A quasi-experimental study on ASIST. *Journal of Counseling and Development, 95,* 3–13. https://doi.org/10.1002/jcad.12112

Sileo, F. J., & Kopala, M. (1993). An A-B-C-D-E work sheet for promoting beneficence when considering ethical issues. *Counseling and Values, 37,* 89–95. https://doi.org/10.1002/j.2161-007X.1993.tb00800.x

Sommers-Flanagan, R., Sommers-Flanagan, J., & Lynch, K. L. (2001). Counseling interventions with suicidal clients. In E. R. Welfel & R. E. Ingersoll (Eds.), *The mental health desk reference* (pp. 264–270). New York: Wiley.

Stadler, H. A. (1986). Making hard choices: Clarifying controversial ethical issues. *Counseling and Human Development, 19,* 1–10.

Stanard, R. P. (2000). Assessment and treatment of adolescent depression and suicidality. *Journal of Mental Health Counseling, 22,* 204–217.

Tarasoff v. Regents of University of California, 529 P. 2d 553, 118 Cal. Rptr. 129 (1974), vacated, 17 Cal. 3d 425, 551 P. 2d 334, 131 Cal. Rptr. 14 (1976).

Tarvydas, V. M. (1998). Ethical decision-making processes. In R. R. Cottone & V. M. Tarvydas (Eds.), *Ethical and professional issues in counseling* (pp. 144–154). Upper Saddle River, NJ: Prentice Hall.

Thapar v. Zezulka, 994 S.W.2d 635 (Tex. 1999).

Toprak, S., Cetin, I., Guven, T., Can, G., & Demircan, C. (2011). Self-harm, suicidal ideation and suicide attempts among college students. *Psychiatric Research, 187,* 140–144.

Trice-Black, S., Riechel, M. E. K., & Shillingford, M. A. (2013). School counselors' constructions of student confidentiality. *Journal of School Counseling, 11*(12). Retrieved from www.jsc.montana.edu/articles/v11n12.pdf

U.S. Department of Health & Human Services, Administration for Children and Families, Administration on Children, Youth and Families, Children's Bureau. (2018). *Child maltreatment 2016.* Retrieved from www.acf.hhs.gov/cb/research-data-technology/statistics-research/child-maltreatment

Velasquez, M., Andre, C., Shanks, T., & Meyer, M. J. (2018). *Justice and fairness.* Retrieved from www.scu.edu/ethics/ethics-resources/ethical-decision-making/justice-and-fairness/

Walden, S. L. (2015). Inclusion of the clients' voice in ethical practice. In B. Herlihy & G. Corey (Eds.), *Boundary issues in counseling: Multiple roles and responsibilities* (3rd ed., pp. 59–62). Alexandria, VA: American Counseling Association.

Walsh, B. W. (2006). *Treating self-injury: A practical guide*. New York: Guilford Press.

Wester, K. L., Ivers, N., Villalba, J. A., Trepal, H. C., & Henson, R. (2016). The relationship between nonsuicidal self-injury and suicidal ideation. *Journal of Counseling and Development, 94*, 3–12. https://doi.org/10.1002/jcad.12057

Wester, K. L., & McKibben, B. (2016). Participants' experiences of non-suicidal self-injury: Supporting existing therapy and emerging conceptual pathways. *Journal of Mental Health Counseling, 38*(1), 12–27. https://doi.org/10.17744/mehc.38.1.02

Wheeler, A. M., & Bertram, B. (2012). *The counselor and the law* (6th ed.). Alexandria, VA: American Counseling Association.

Whisenhunt, J., Chang, C., Brack, G., Orr, J., Adams, L., Paige, M., . . . O'Hara, C. (2014). Professional counselors' conceptualizations of the relationship between suicide and self-injury. *Journal of Mental Health Counseling, 36*, 263–282. https://doi.org/10.17744/mehc.36.3.gu744380310581u5

Wiger, D. E. (1999). *The clinical documentation sourcebook* (2nd ed.). New York: Wiley.

Woody, R. H. (1988). *Fifty ways to avoid malpractice*. Sarasota, FL: Professional Resource Exchange.

Zetterqvist, M. (2015). The DSM-5 diagnosis of nonsuicidal self-injury disorder: A review of the empirical literature. *Child & Adolescent Psychiatry & Mental Health, 9*(31). https://doi.org/10.1186/s13034-015-0062-7

6 Family Counseling

James Bitter, Rebekah Byrd, and Chad Luke
James Bitter as guest contributor

Objectives

- Describe and define many key terms from this chapter.
- Understand the importance of using family counseling approaches in multiple settings.
- Analyze the four models presented in the integrated approach.
- Evaluate the basic skills necessary for family counseling.
- Examine techniques for use in family counseling.
- Evaluate the importance of supporting caregivers and families.
- Understand multicultural considerations for family counseling.

Reflective Questions

- How prepared and willing am I to work with families?
- What is my current understanding of systems and family work in counseling?
- In what ways will I adopt an integrative approach to family work?
- What basic skills for family counseling do I need more practice in?
- How can I start understanding all family counseling as multicultural?
- How important do I believe caregivers and families are in the treatment of children and adolescents?

What Is Family Counseling?

The aim of this chapter is not to outline the history of family therapy, discuss theories in depth, or be used in place of training and coursework in that imperative area. This chapter will outline helpful information and provide assistance to counselors working with children and adolescents. We suggest that child and adolescent counselors take classes in family counseling even if not present in the core program of study. Child and adolescent counselors need training in this area in graduate coursework (core or elective classes), continuing education, and in an ongoing format.

Multiple types of family counseling exist. As opposed to individual or couples work, family counseling usually has other members of the family present and is systems-focused. Whole Family Therapy (WFT) discusses treatment with the whole family involved including parents/caregivers, children, and any siblings and can also include grandparents, friends, community members or extended relationships considered significant in the family system (Breunlin & Jacobsen, 2014). Relational Family Therapy discusses working with some subsystem of the family or even an individual family member, and can include working with the father and child in a larger family system (Breunlin & Jacobsen, 2014).

Children are born into a group, and many of them will never actually live outside of a group. That initial group, the family, regardless of how it is structured, will serve as a foundation for the child's development and as a model for how to live and function in the larger systems of society. Within the family, children learn to act and interact; to speak and to communicate; to walk and move – and to manipulate the environment; and to experience the joys and limits of freedom and the value of safety. Starting with nothing more than temperament and a striving for growth, they gain increasing access to the world and cobble together a sense of self and personhood, an understanding of and relationship with others. They also draw conclusions about self, others, life, and the world. Everything they learn and experience, they do relationally. Even their sense of self is a self-in-relationship.

Of course, none of this happens quickly. We now know that the adolescent brain is growing into young adulthood, at least until the mid-twenties (Arain et al., 2013). The quality of family life during these several decades is highly predictive of how these children and adolescents will develop, the opportunities they will have, and the trajectory of their adult lives.

Given this important information, what are the essential qualities of constructive families and how do they operate? What is the demarcation line between functional and dysfunctional? When children and adolescents are exhibiting problem behaviors or physical, emotional, or mental illnesses, how can interventions in families turn the tide, make a difference – and ensure that the difference made is a difference that matters?

The field of family counseling starts with the systemic perspectives that Alfred Adler applied to working with children, their families, and the schools that served them (Bitter & Byrd, 2017). In the 1920s, Adler and his associates started more than 30 child guidance centers in Vienna, Austria, in which they would conduct open-forum family counseling sessions in front of a community audience. By 1934, all of these centers had been closed by the Nazis.

Today, there are dozens of models and many hundreds of approaches to systemic family counseling and therapy (Bitter, 2020). Some of the most prominent are Bowen's multigenerational approach (Kerr, 2019; Titelman, 2008), Satir's human validation process model (Satir, Banmen, Gerber, & Gomori, 1991), Whitaker's symbolic-experiential therapy (Keith, 2014), structural family therapy (Minuchin, Reiter, & Borda, 2014), strategic therapy (Haley & Richeport-Haley, 2003), solution-focused/solution-oriented brief therapy (Ratner et al., 2012), and the postmodern, social constructionist approaches like narrative therapy (White & Epston, 1990), linguistic therapy (Anderson & Jensen, 2018), and reflecting teams (Andersen, 1991). There are cultural forms of family interventions, like NTU psychotherapy (Phillips, 1990), and there are feminist models of family counseling, too (Silverstein & Goodrich, 2003). Some models that started with a focus on the individual later developed more systemic approaches, including object-relations family therapy and cognitive behavioral family therapy. Like the field of psychotherapy in general, there are core factors across these models that account for success in therapy with the most important one under the control of the counselor being the quality of the relationship that the therapist forms with the family and its members (Sprenkle, Davis, & Lebow, 2009).

For the rest of this chapter, we are going to focus on parts of the theories and practices used in four models of family counseling, and we are going to use these models as a way to propose an integrative model to family counseling involving children and adolescents. The four models are: object-relations family therapy with its focus on attachment theory; Adlerian family therapy with its focus on teleology and the interactive nature of goals in family interactions; Satir's human validation process model with its emphasis on self-esteem, communication, and the transformation of family rules; and McGoldrick's (2016) use of genograms in mapping the influences of multiple generations on children. We will also make use of a slight adaptation of metaframeworks (Breunlin, Schwartz, & MacKune-Karrer, 2001; Pinsoff et al., 2018) to look at systemic, developmental, cultural, and gender factors across models.

Basic Skills

For the purpose of presenting an integrative approach to family counseling involving children, the process is somewhat artificially broken down into four stages: (a) forming a relationship; (b) conducting an assessment; (c) creating shared meaning and goal setting; and (d) implementing change. The therapeutic relationships that are most effective are collaborative, and they are built on mutual respect and many of the qualities already addressed in this chapter. There are almost as many assessments as there are models of therapy, but here, assessment will focus on genograms (McGoldrick, 2016), mistaken goals, communication styles, and perspectives offered within metaframeworks (Breunlin et al., 2001). Shared meaning and goal setting require collaboration and reaching a mutual clarity about what is occurring, what is motivating it, and what needs to change. Such goal setting flows directly from a successful assessment, and both lay the foundation for the effective implementation of change.

Forming a Relationship

In systems therapy, forming a relationship is sometimes called *joining* (Minuchin et al., 2014), and in other models, it is the creation of *a holding space* (Scharff & Scharff, 2011). Successful therapeutic relationships rely first of all on empathy (emotional attunement) and careful listening. Caring about one's clients is ultimately a goal, but caring is not the first thing that occurs. Beginning sessions rely on the counselor's curiosity, interest, sometimes fascination, and a willingness to enter the system as a participant-observer. It is in the initial sessions that *presence* and focus are offered to the family and its members. Satir et al. (1991) call the first stage of family counseling *making contact*. It involves bring all of one's senses into the present moment, into the here and now, and to be able to sense not only the emotions but also the dynamics of the family. Such emotional attunement may even involve emotion coaching (Gottman & Gottman, 2018), or the process of helping parents and children gain access to what they are experiencing with each other.

The process and structure of family therapy are the responsibility of the counselor. From meeting the individual members and welcoming them into the therapeutic process to observing and intervening in family patterns and interactions, the counselor sets the tone, rhythm, and pace of therapy. Engagement, warmth, friendliness, and concern provide the first experiences of a holding space. Transition statements ("We will be moving from this waiting room two doors down to our consultation room") ground family members and give them control over initial movements. Very early in the first session, the counselor is observant, noting who sits where; who talks to whom about what – and in what tone; if the family is in immediate crisis or if there is time to get to know them; if there are alliances or isolations occurring in real time; and even who speaks first and what emotional experiences and needs are present. From the very beginning, the counselor is both engaged and ready to begin an assessment.

Conducting an Assessment

Many of the early pioneers in family therapy relied on family maps to keep the family members straight and to depict the relationships between them. In 1985, McGoldrick and Gerson brought the various mapping processes together in their creation of *genograms* (McGoldrick, Gerson, & Petry, 2020). While the process is too long to fully delineate here, a full genogram presents a multigenerational map of the family, including a marking of emotional and relational connections; the movement of the family through time and challenges, births to deaths and everything in between; and considerations of the impact of race, ethnicity, culture, religion, gender, affectional orientation, ability, age, and socioeconomic status. In this sense, the genogram is an emotional/structural picture that leads into the stories of the family's life.

At a very basic level, men are represented in a genogram by squares, and circles represent women. The focus person in the family – the one about whom the family has come for help or the one experiencing problems – is called the Index Person or IP. This person is indicated in the genogram by either a double square or a double circle. Solid lines indicate a formal relationship while dashed lines note informal relationships. An initial start to an intake genogram is presented in Figure 6.1 for the family in the case study. A more complete genogram would evolve over several sessions, but most family counselors will start the genogram early in the first session.

Genograms also act as a foundation for investigating the perspectives offered in *metaframeworks*: Breunlin et al. (2001) developed six lenses that focus assessment from different perspectives – perspectives that would often be lost or overlooked if not specifically investigated. These lenses are called internal family systems; sequences; the organizational lens; the developmental lens; the multicultural (race, ethnicity, and culture) lens; and the gender lens.

Six Lenses

The internal family systems lens looks at each family member as a system of parts, some of which are relied on often, some of which are available but seldom used, and some of which are discarded or set aside. This first lens allows the counselor to consider what parts are present at any given time and how they interact with the parts of others in the family.

The sequence lens helps the counselor to track patterns of interaction among family members at four levels. Level 1 sequences are face-to-face interactions that occur between two or more family members. This is the level at which triangulation can be observed. Level 2 sequences are routines that family members use to support daily activity, while Level 3 sequences are broader processes that occur during the ebbs and flows of life. And finally, Level 4 sequences are transgenerational and often involve values and ways of behaving across time. Cultural sequences are Level 4 sequences.

Level 1 sequences are where the counselor can also consider the goals of children's misbehavior, because most of the time, misbehavior takes place in a face-to-face interaction. Young children who seek attention almost always seek that attention from a significant adult, parent, teacher, or childcare person in their lives. Dreikurs (1950) looks at both interactions and adult feelings to understand children's goals of misbehavior. When the goal is attention, *the child will often stop for a while* after being corrected, and in the midst of the misbehavior, the adult will feel *irritated, annoyed*, or *frustrated*. When the goal is a power struggle, *the mistaken interaction will continue* and may even intensify. The adult will feel *angry, challenged*, or *defeated*. When revenge is the goal,

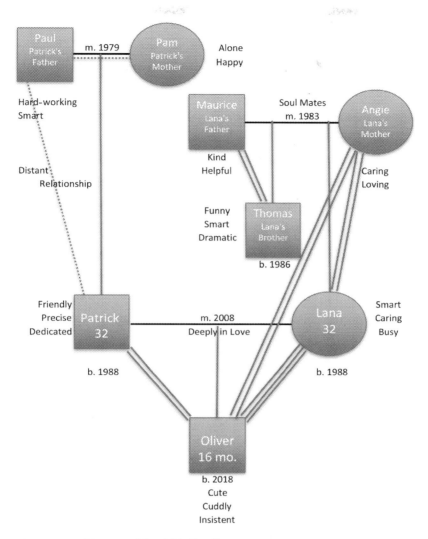

Figure 6.1 Genogram of Lana and Patrick's Family

the interaction may be intense and direct or indirect and vicious, all in an attempt to get even. The adult feeling is usually *hurt*. Dreikurs' fourth goal is indicated when *both the adult and the child seek to be left alone*, when they give up on each other. Both the adult and child will feel *despair*.

A simple interviewing sequence can often reveal the mistaken goals of both adults and children in negative interactions.

Counselor:	Tell me the last time that the problem happened. *What did the child do?*
Adult:	(The adult describes the child's misbehavior.)
Counselor:	*And then what did you do* – and what did the child do in response to you?
Adult:	(The adult gives a full description of the interaction.)
Counselor:	And when you were in the middle of this sequence, how were you *feeling*?

It is while negative interactions (sequences) are being reported or demonstrated that the counselor can also listen for the communication stances that the various family members assume. Each of Satir's (1988) dysfunctional stances may be used singularly or escalate into sequence of different stances as distress increases. Dysfunctional communication stances always indicate that emotion coaching is needed, that congruence and I-messages need to be reinstituted and practiced, and that non-violent language will be a foundation for change and family leadership

An organizational lens starts with the perspective that parents should be the leaders of the family, not the children. There are roles and responsibilities that exist in families and that facilitate family functions. It is the organizational lens that addresses the family subsystems and boundaries. The spousal subsystem contains the functions of the adult couple, often the marriage, and does not include a child. A parental subsystem may include more than one parent in interaction with a child or children, but it also includes the interaction at any given time between one adult and one child. Siblings, too, are their own subsystem with roles and activities that belong only to them.

The developmental lens functions at two levels. Each family member is in the process of individual development at the same time that the family as a whole is progressing through the family life cycle. The dual perspective of this lens helps the counselor to assess how members of the family are handling the challenges of change. Change, of course, is inevitable; indeed, change is life. That does not mean, however, that change is easy. This lens lets the counselor assess whether the individuals are able to develop effectively and whether the family is appropriately supporting growth and development. It also helps the family members to see how they are using their resources in relation to the challenges they all face together.

No individual (nor any family, for that matter) is culture-free. Even though members of the dominant culture often adopt the privilege of not having to pay attention to their own cultural background, those in marginalized cultures are usually quite clear about the impact of race, ethnicity, and culture in their lives. Again, Monica McGoldrick and her colleagues have led the way in the integration of this lens into family therapy (see McGoldrick, Giordano, & Garcia Preto, 2005). This is a very broad lens that considers immigration and acculturation, economic privilege or poverty, education, ethnicity, race, religion, culture, age, health and ability, regional background, and discrimination and oppression.

Because patriarchy affects all people in all cultures across the world and across time and history, gender needs its own lens. Over time, gender has become specified in roles and expectations that have been absorbed by families and individuals – often below awareness. Most of these roles and expectations have favored men and have too often had a negative and often dangerous effect on the lives of women. These roles and expectations evolve sometimes faster than either the individual or the family can handle the change, but noting where the family and its members are is part of this lens. What gender role is each family member assuming? What effect is patriarchy having on the family and its members? What ideas about gender need to be affirmed or challenged? What impact will the gender of the counselor have on the family? It is through this lens that the counselor also considers issues related to affectional orientation and discrimination experienced by families and members of the LGBTGEQIAP+ community.

Not all of these lenses are used with every single family. As you learn about the family, formulate a genogram, listen to the narrative of the family's life, some lenses will be more prominent than others, and some will not seem useful at all. Having these six lenses, however, provides an initial framework for investigation.

Shared Meaning and Goal Setting

None of the discussed assessments make a difference if they cannot be shared in a meaningful way with the family. The endpoint of assessment is always to help the family members understand where they are and to point toward a solution to their concerns or problems. Effective counselors share their new understanding tentatively, inviting the family members to consider possibilities without imposing or insisting on them. Adler (1931) noted:

> Treatment itself is an exercise in cooperation and a test of cooperation. We can succeed only if we are genuinely interested in the other. . . . Even if we felt we had understood [them], we should have no witness that we were right unless [they] also understood. A tactless truth can never be the whole truth; it shows that our understanding was not sufficient.
>
> (p. 72)

Some shared meaning will be offered in an attempt to help the family members gain a new perspective on how their family is working: what parts the family members are using often; how they interact and communicate; what their goals as individuals and as a family seem to be; how the family structure is working for or against them; and developmental, cultural, or gender issues that may be present. However the counselor enters into a sharing of meaning, this collaboration will be the foundation for choosing the goals for the family.

Especially with children, the disclosure of mistaken goals must be approached from a kind curiosity and a tentative guess. For example, with children who are constantly fighting, resulting in the parent telling them to stop multiple times, the goal disclosure might go like this.

Counselor: Do you know why the two of you fight with each other?
Child #1: Because he bothers me.
Child #2: No, I don't.
Counselor: That could be, but I have another idea. Would you like to hear it?
Child #1: Yes, okay.
Counselor: Could it be that you fight to see how many times you can get your father to tell you to stop?

Dreikurs (1950) suggested that when a tentative goal disclosure like this is used with young children (pre-adolescence), the most likely result will be what he called a *recognition reflex* or a little smile on the face and twinkle in the eyes. It is the look a child gets when knowing that you know what the child is seeking.

Just as the goal of attention-getting must be shared with children in concrete terms, so too must the goals of power, revenge, or assumed disability. The goal of a power struggle might be suggested as, "Could it be that you want to show them you are the boss?" or "Could it be that you don't want to do anything they want you to do?" The goal of revenge can be disclosed by asking, "Could it be that you feel oh so hurt, and you want to hurt them back, to get even?" And Dreikurs' last goal might be revealed in a question like, "Could it be that you just want to give up and be left alone?"

Implementing Change: Treatment for Families

Coming to an agreement about what is happening with the family and its members allows everyone to decide what they would like to change. Effective change is more than merely eliminating the presenting problem. It is change that seeks a preferred way of living, that invites connection and harmony, and that uses the best talents of everyone involved in meeting the challenges that the family faces. Broad goals like this need to be translated into concrete actions, but the ultimate end is to increase effective living for everyone involved.

Counselors know that nurturing families start with encouragement for the caregivers, helping each adult to feel like a leader or part of a leadership team and working in cooperative partnerships. This is certainly essential for school counselors, as having caregivers, families, and even communities involved in the schools can make a huge impact on a child's or adolescent's success in school and academic achievement (Van Roekel, 2008). Young children especially need presence, emotional attunement, and attachment from their caregivers, and emotion coaching, non-violent language, and congruent interactions may all have to be taught as part of therapy. Effective parenting is often different from the ways in which the adults were raised. In such cases, parent education may also be necessary (see Bitter, 2017).

When working with families, focusing on strengths and family resources builds a sense of resilience within the system. Change in small steps tends to be more easily accepted and enacted than large efforts. No matter how well a family implements change, there will be lapses and relapses. Gently predicting relapses can normalize them and help the family prepare to rebound again.

Counseling Session Using a Genogram

Lana is a 32-year-old psychologist who works in a counseling center at a college near her home. She is married to Patrick, and they have been married for 11½ years. Patrick is a baseball coach at Lana's college, and he is gone a lot at odd hours during the season and also when he is recruiting. After getting her bachelor's degree at the university where she met Patrick, Lana completed her graduate work in counseling psychology. They have a 16-month-old child, named Oliver. Most of the time, she feels content with the life they are building together.

An initial genogram of her nuclear family would look like Figure 6.1.

For the initial session, Oliver is in a play therapy room with a counseling intern who is staying emotionally attuned to him and is tracking his play and process. Lana is meeting with Jim, her counselor; Patrick was unable to attend the first session due to a conflict in his work schedule. After introductions, Jim and Lana create and initial genogram; he then asks her what she likes most about her life.

Jim (J): What do you like most about your life?
Lana (L): The balance.
J: The balance.
L: Yes. Enjoying my son greatly, and working part time, and then enjoying my professional life as well.
J: That's quite amazing, really. There are hundreds of people, including my own family, who would love to have balance, and have never seen it.
L: Well, some weeks, I don't. Many weeks, I do.

J:	If there's anything in your life you would like to see going better, what would that be?
L:	I would like to work on parenting. That is one thing I would like to see going better.
J:	So give me an example.
L:	My son has just begun to get into the stage of tantrum throwing. I'm a psychologist, and I have a lot of book information. But when he starts to tantrum, I feel like I'm at a loss.
J:	Okay.
L:	Translating that into actual parenting and doing that effectively . . . . Again, I'm at a loss.
J:	Yes. You know, a tantrum is really an elegant thing. Most children I know don't want to waste them: I've never seen, for instance, a child all by himself, alone in his room, throwing a tantrum. (laughter) They almost always need something. What does he need?
L:	Lately, it's something that he wants that I won't allow him to have. It might be that he wants the TV on at that moment, and we don't watch TV in the evenings. Or he wants the remote control or he wants something that's breakable, and he wants it right now. I don't give it to him, or I won't allow him to have it. That's when it's the throwing back his head, the lying on the floor, the screaming: I mean all of it.
J:	Okay, cool! (smiling)
L:	(laughing too). Well, that's a nice way to put it.
J:	You don't feel like it's so *cool* sometimes.
L:	No. I get more alarmed. I think I've done something wrong (throwing up hands). I go more that way, but I never thought of it as a good thing.
J:	When you do this (throws up hands), how does it feel?
L:	Just at a loss.
J:	Yes. Like "Oh my God . . . "
L:	Yes, exactly.
J:	Now, has he gotten to the point where he's realized the terrific advantage of Walmart?
L:	No (she laughs). I don't know.
J:	Really great tantrums are even better in public – especially if *you're* wearing a T-shirt that says, "By the way, I'm a child psychologist".
L:	(laughter) Yeah.
J:	When did he first learn that you were a psychologist?
L:	I don't know if he yet knows.
J:	Oh, yes. He knows. There are three professions in which children can smell it. They come out of the womb [knowing]: psychologist/counselor is way up there, not quite as high as minister. But it's way up there. And then, of course, if you happen to be a teacher or an educator. Anything that requires a public life of perfection. Are you any good at perfection?
L:	Yes. I've been known to . . .
J:	So what's your best stuff? How would you do *perfect* if you were a perfect parent?
L:	Somehow, in my head, really I think if I were a perfect parent, my child wouldn't throw fits. Or he would sleep through the night. That would be a big one, or he would eat all of his meals. Those are the kinds of things I start to question myself about whether I'm doing a good job.

J: So tell me the last time that he threw a temper tantrum and what you did.
L: Okay. The day before yesterday. He does go to a friend of mine's house two and half days a week, because I work part time. So lately, when I have been going to the house, the transition has been tough for him. So I walk in, and he asked me for something, of course non-verbally. I was writing a check to her for a week. And he wanted my pen, and he wanted my wallet. And I probably said, "No, I'm using these", and he threw himself back, and he started to scream.
J: Okay, and what did you do?
L: Kept writing the check, and of course, it took me longer, because he was grabbing at the pen. My friend, Marcie, brought him into the kitchen to get him a cup of water, because he was still screaming. When I was done, I held him in my lap, and I embraced him, and he calmed down, and he then just sat with me for about five minutes. And it really amazed me, because he wanted to be with me. At first when he came in, he didn't. Then, he threw the tantrum, and then he just sat in my lap. And I did give him a pacifier as well, those two things.
J: Okay, so how did that go for you?
L: Two parts to it. The first part where I kept writing the check and didn't stop: I doubted myself. I thought maybe there's a better intervention. I was a little embarrassed, because it was in front of another adult, so that part was hard. But when I finished writing the check and took him in my lap, then that part seemed really good. I enjoyed him, and I enjoyed that time. So the first part, I questioned myself. Should I stop? Should I keep going? What's the best thing to do here? That's where I'd get anxious. (Jim: Un-hum.) When I'd start to say: "What's the perfect thing? What's the best way? Is there a best way, and I'm not doing it?" But the second part was really good.
J: Okay, so the part of you that reached out to him, picked him up, held him – that part made you feel like you were competent.
L: Yes.
J: Caring.
L: Yes.
J: Loving.
L: Exactly.
J: Now, when did you get the idea that you could control other people? [checking on a mistaken goal that may be affecting her parenting approach]
L: Umm, that's a good question.
J: Thank you.
L: I think for a very long time.
J: Yes. So the hardest part you are going to have to get over is that. Because even though I will tell you the truth, you're not going to believe it. (Lana: Okay.) The truth is this – and you already know it – there's only one person you can control and that's . . .
L: Me.
J: That's right. You can choose you, and you can choose what you are going to do for you, but that's it.
L: Okay.
J: Now, let's just think this through. I'm going to make this up. Are you ready?
L: Yes.

J:	I like to put my name on things, so this is Jim's law of paradox. I don't actually believe much in paradoxical interventions, but I think life is paradoxical. So here it goes. Super responsible mothers are always surrounded by irresponsible children. (Lana: Umm.) Okay, here's another one. Mothers who want to make everything just so (who are neat and are careful) always have messy children. (pause) I say mothers because I am talking to you, but it goes for fathers, too. This is really neat about children: They can be one way with one parent, and another way with the other one. And some of them are so good that they can design one behavior that will irritate both parents in a different way.
L:	Uh-huh.
J:	Here's what I think your paradoxical position might be: a person who is devoted to balance always has a child who is out of balance.
L:	Um-hum.
J:	So what sends you into worry is when he starts to show himself to be out of balance. (pause) You would like [him to be like] my oldest daughter. You would like him to walk through life calm, serene, just slightly less comatose than Ghandi. (laughs)
L:	Yes. I mean I don't, but emotionally, I probably do.
J:	We don't have a lot of time. So based on what we have talked about so far, how are you feeling about all of this?
L:	It makes sense to me. [shared meaning; time to play]
J:	Oh, that's the worst. People never do anything that makes sense to them.
L:	No, it challenges me.
J:	Really? What could you imagine doing?
L:	Well, the words *laid back* comes to mind, and really trying to just let him be who he is.
J:	Okay. You really mean that?
L:	I really mean it. Yes. I really mean that's what I would want.
J:	Because boys, you know, come with testosterone.
L:	See, then I think of balance again, because that's what I come back to. He can be what he wants, and still I'm his parent. I have a big role in his life right now, and how to balance that: how to let him be who he is and provide some structure for him.
J:	Sure. Now, how are you feeling as you are saying that?
L:	More heady.
J:	What's happening in your stomach?
L:	Tightness.
J:	Yes. Just breathe into that. Let's go to your strength. So just imagine yourself being in a place where you feel really calm. (pause) When you go there, everything about you looks serene. When you talk about your son and his tantrums, everything looks and feels tight. So what would it take for you to stay in your calm place even while you are imagining your son throwing the world's greatest temper tantrum? (pause) What are you doing with your body when you do that?
L:	Breathing. Concentrating on Oliver; picturing him throwing himself to the floor.
J:	When you picture him throwing himself to the floor, what do you need at that moment in time?
L:	Just a warm hand on my shoulder, and a kind word. Yes, a kind word.

J: What would the word be? What would be said?
L: It's okay.
L: It's okay. Your partner (Lana: Patrick). Yes, Patrick. Can you feel his hand? [seeking to strengthen the partnership]
L: Yes. That's who I would want.
J: Yes. And you might even practice that for a while. Something where he puts his hand on your shoulder, and says, "Look, it's okay". Now, how does he do with your son's tantrums?
L: We tend to both get anxious and uptight about it.
J: You know, there is nothing better at a time like that than to have something to do, so it might help him to be able to put his hand on your shoulder and say "It's going to be okay".
L: Yes.
J: Now, what would your arms naturally do with a child who had calmed down?
L: I would naturally embrace.
J: So you have two things you can do. Is that right?
L: Both have a hand on my shoulder and embrace? Yes, I can do that.
J: So you would know what to do. How does that make you feel in terms of your own competence?
L: Umm. (pause) I think positive. Yes. It's hard to know how to translate what I know to do into behavior.
J: The reason it's hard is that very often when you are thinking about it, you are thinking about doing something to get your child to change. That, you can't do. But there is one person you can change, and that's you.
L: Yes.
J: Yes. It doesn't even matter what your child does. All you have to do is have an agreement with your spouse and partner.
L: That's great.
J: It is great.
L: That's actually helpful.
J: Now, I am going to tell you exactly when your son is going to give up throwing temper tantrums.
L: Okay. (laughs)
J: He will never throw another temper tantrum ever as soon as it no longer bothers you or your husband. (Lana: Umm.) He will only bring it out on grandma, and why not? She deserves it. (Both laugh.)
L: Yes. That's right.
J: Now, I am going to give you one other thing to do when you are all alone with him. One of the biggest mistakes that we make when we are with a child who is throwing a tantrum is that we talk.
L: That's the biggest mistake? That we talk.
J: Yes, because we can't talk without sounding upset. What do you think the purpose or goal of a tantrum is? [addressing mistaken goals]
L: In some ways, it just looks like he wants to explore the fullness of himself?
J: If that were true, he would be out in the middle of the yard screaming.
L: Yeah. (laughs)
J: He's not. He's screaming *with you*.
L: I don't know. To get his way? To get what he wants?

J:	Yes, it looks like this (Jim pounds on his chest). It's a very powerful stance, isn't it?
L:	Yes.
J:	You will do what I want or . . .
L:	Yeah.
J:	Power often hooks up with a parent's need to control. The fastest way to take you out of that equation is to get you to walk away. No one throws a tantrum without an audience. So where could you go?
L:	Oh, easily to another room, to a different part of the house.
J:	And he would be safe? (Lana: Yes.) And what will he do when you take off?
L:	Come after me? (laughs)
J:	Sure. So where can you go so he can't get to you until he's done?
L:	In my bedroom.
J:	Does it lock?
L:	Well, we're re-doing it so it doesn't have a doorknob, but it will.
J:	Okay.
L:	The bathroom would be another place.
J:	And when would you come out?
L:	When he's done. When he's finished.
J:	And what would you do when you come out?
L:	I would just reassure him that I love him.
J:	And what would you say?
L:	I love you . . . (she moves her arms almost like she would reach for him)
J:	What would your arms do?
L:	I think I would embrace him.
J:	Sure. So could you do that without talking? (pause) Here's what's going to happen if you talk. You are going to take him in your arms and you'll say, "Oliver, mama loves you", and then there will be in your voice even if you don't say it, "but . . . ."
L:	Okay. Okay.
J:	But I need you to stop your tantrums or something else like that.
L:	Yes.
J:	So you are just gone, and you've had some time by yourself. You haven't done anything terrible. You come out. You embrace him for a short while, and you get on with the rest of your day. (pause) Now, do you think his tantrums will stop then?
L:	Not right away.
J:	Not right away. It will get a little worse before it gets better. And that's when I want you to feel a hand on your shoulder and hear the words: "It'll be okay". This is about taking care of you, deciding what you will do, not what he will do. And right now, you are looking like this is something you feel you can do. [looking for commitment to change]
L:	Yes, this is good.
J:	Okay.
L:	Thank you.
J:	You're welcome.

The second session with Jim was not until a month later. During the intervening time, Oliver continued to meet with the play therapist intern who also worked with Lana on empathic responding to Oliver while he played (Filial Therapy). When next Jim met with

Lana, the temper tantrums had greatly reduced – maybe once or twice during the month, "maybe when he's tired", Lana suggested.

Family Counseling in the School Setting

We believe that school counselors are uniquely suited to conduct meaningful family work in the school setting and in the home setting when the school counselor conducts home visits. Often, counselors come to their work with children and adolescents while claiming a lack of desire to work with adults. We have heard this many times from students in training and caution counselors from adopting this viewpoint, as child and adolescent counselors must be trained in and have a desire to work with adults, as well. "The first and most essential support system for a child is his or her family" (Paylo, 2011, p. 140). Supporting the families of the children and adolescents with whom you work is essential and necessary for success and provides a protective factor for children and adolescents.

School counselors or school-based counselors can assist families in meaningful ways. The ASCA Ethical Standards for School Counselors (2016) discusses the importance of supporting families and further recognizes the significant role of parents/caregivers and families. Further ASCA School Counselor Professional Standards and Competencies (2019) address work with families as a part of the mindsets and behaviors of professional and competent school counselors. Yet many school counselors never received training in family systems or family counseling work (Perusse, Goodnough, & Noel, 2001). We believe child and adolescent counselors can design their programs of study to include family counseling and systems training if it is not a requirement. When we have worked in schools, we have noted countless times when caregivers did not feel free or encouraged to be involved in the schools on behalf of their children. Throughout the years, caregivers have expressed their beliefs about only being contacted by the school when something was wrong or something was needed from them. We have made it a point to contact parents for many reasons (notifying of success, achievements, opportunities, and general appreciation) so that we can start to change how parents view the school, their child, and their involvement. Parents may feel hesitant to be involved in the school, whether it is a result of cultural implications, language barriers, or their own experiences with a school system (Van Roekel, 2008). It is imperative for school counselors and school-based counselors to work with families in supporting the academic, social, and emotional development of each student.

Home-Based Family Counseling

Home-based family counseling (HBFC) services have been growing over the last few decades. It started as a response to assisting in crisis situations and with at-promise youth as a possible option or alternative to placements made outside of the home (Macchi & O'Conner, 2010). It seems to be expanding beyond this, as more agencies are providing these services and giving opportunities for families to be helped in their homes instead of expecting families to come into an (often) artificial office setting. When providing in-home services, it is often such a rich, organic, holistic, and realistic view of the family's real daily life and has provided an opportunity at times to get into deeper issues quicker than in the sterile, contrived office setting. After all, the home is where this family lives, grows, develops, argues, and functions on a daily basis. Family members are able to be their real selves in their daily environment in a way we can't replicate in a clinical mental health setting.

By being in a family's home, counselors are also a part of their world and observing their behaviors in ways we never get to do in an office. By being in a home-based setting, however, there are often other considerations counselors need or need elaborated on for this type of work. Examples of those are family intake training, advanced culturally sensitive interventions for in-home work, and assessment skills in both trauma and crisis (Hammond & Czyszczon, 2014). Counselors considering working in clients' homes should seek additional training in this area. Graduate programs and professional organizations need to address the increase in counselors working in home settings and include training opportunities (Bowen & Caron, 2016), as there are currently no professional guidelines for HBFC services (Hammond & Czyszczon, 2014).

Multicultural Implications and Advocacy

As noted, no family is culture-free. Therefore, all counseling is multicultural and all family counseling is multicultural. When working to involve families in counseling in myriad settings as discussed in this chapter, counselors need to understand and address the influence of culture in a family system. It is also important for counselors to consider ways in which families from non-dominant groups may be obligated or required in some ways to modify their lives, and what seems natural to them, when interacting with dominant culture (Hendrick, Bradley, & Robertson, 2015). Multicultural family counseling includes training in knowledge, awareness, and skills of multiculturally competent counseling, as counseling graduate trainings programs employ. Multicultural family work also consists of gaining skills and self-awareness of how to build rapport with families in the context of both the family's and the counselor's multidimensional reality while understanding privileged identities, as well (Thomas & Rastogi, 2009).

Summary

Family counseling is imperative for working with children and adolescents in multiple settings. This chapter focused on family therapy with children and adolescents. Counselors seeking to work with children and adolescents must understand a systems perspective and how it is necessary for family work. An integrative approach to family counseling involving children was presented in four stages: (a) forming a relationship; (b) conducting an assessment; (c) creating shared meaning and goal setting; and (d) implementing change. Assessment focused on genograms (McGoldrick, 2016), mistaken goals, communication styles, and perspectives offered within metaframeworks (Breunlin et al., 2001). Utilizing Adlerian family counseling and the focus on the goals and purposes of family interactions and Virginia Satir's human validation process model to focus on effective communication in families, an integrative model for effective interventions in families was discussed, along with basic family counseling skills across models. A multiple-lens model was proposed as part of assessment to ensure consideration of issues related to gender, affectional orientation, race, ethnicity, culture, age/development, ability, physical/mental health, and socioeconomic status. Counselors are encouraged to seek training and integrate continuing education in multicultural family therapy so as to best serve clients in multiple settings. Understanding how to engage families in counseling is important for the success of children and adolescents.

Clinician's Corner

I tell this story that I heard because parents often show up objectifying their child and want them to change their behavior and talk about them as if they aren't even there.

A mother and father go into a restaurant with their child and a waitress asks the child what they would like to eat. The child says a milkshake, some fries, and a piece of pie. One of the parents says, "No. Bring them a glass of milk, a grilled chicken sandwich, and a piece of fruit". The waitress comes back with the food and serves the child the milkshake, fries, and pie. The child pauses, looks at the waitress, then back at the parents and says with surprise, "she thinks I'm a real person".

Sometimes people come in with a concern that can be handled with just a strategic intervention.

A father came to see me with his daughter saying that she had seen a couple of counselors and nothing seemed to be helping her. She was waking up with a repeating nightmare and wasn't able to go back to sleep unless he spent the rest of the night in the bed with her. I got the details from the daughter about how there was a scary monster that would show up and then she had to yell out for her dad until he would come into her room and spend the night. When I asked why the monster left her alone for the rest of the night when her dad was there, she said the monster looks in the window and sees him there wearing his football jersey. The monster then just keeps on going and doesn't try to come. I ask if she would be willing to trick the monster. She likes this idea and agrees that she will start wearing her dad's football jersey to bed and the monster will think that it is her dad and just keep moving on. The dad called and told me his daughter had slept with no problems in his jersey every night for the last week.

Graham Disque, Ph.D., MFT
East Tennessee State University

References

Adler, A. (1931). *What life should mean to you*. Gossett and Dunlap.
American School Counselor Association. (2016). *ASCA ethical standards for school counselors*. Alexandria, VA: Author.
American School Counselor Association. (2019). *ASCA school counselor professional standards & competencies*. Alexandria, VA: Author.
Andersen, T. (1991). *The reflecting team: Dialogues and dialogues about the dialogues*. W.W. Norton & Company.
Anderson, H., & Jensen, P. (Eds.). (2018). *Innovations in the reflecting process*. Routledge.
Arain, M., Haque, M., Johal, L., Mathur, P., Nel, W., Rais, A., . . . Sharma, S. (2013). Maturation of the adolescent brain. *Neuropsychiatric Disease and Treatment*, 9, 449–461. https://doi.org/10.2147%2FNDT.S39776
Bitter, J. R. (2017). Parent study groups. In J. Carlson & S. B. Dermer (Eds.), *The sage encyclopedia of marriage, family, and couples counseling* (Vol. 3, pp. 1208–1210). Sage.
Bitter, J. R. (2020). *The theory and practice of couples & family counseling* (3rd ed.). American Counseling Association.
Bitter, J. R., & Byrd, R. (2017). Adlerian open-forum family counseling. In J. Carlson & S. B. Dermer (Eds.), *The sage encyclopedia of marriage, family, and couples counseling* (Vol. 1, pp. 20–23). Sage.
Bowen, J. M., & Caron, S. L. (2016). A qualitative analysis of home-based counselors' experiences in a rural setting. *Journal of Counseling and Development*, 94, 129–140. https://doi.org/10.1002/jcad.12070
Breunlin, D. C., & Jacobsen, E. (2014). Putting the "family" back into family therapy. *Family Process*, 53(3), 462–475. https://doi.org/10.1111/famp.12083
Breunlin, D. C., Schwartz, R. C., & MacKune-Karrer, B. (2001). *Metaframeworks: Transcending the models of family therapy* (Rev. ed.). Jossey-Bass.
Dreikurs, R. (1950). The immediate purpose of children's misbehavior, its recognition and correction. *Internationale Zeitschrift für Individual-Psychologie*, 19, 70–87.
Gottman, J. M., & Gottman, J. S. (2018). *The science of couples and family therapy*. W.W. Norton & Company.
Haley, J., & Richeport-Haley, M. (2003). *The art of strategic therapy*. Brunner-Routledge.

Hammond, C., & Czyszczon, G. (2014). Home-based family counseling: An emerging field in need of professionalization. *The Family Journal: Counseling and Therapy for Couples and Families*, 22(1), 56–61. https://doi.org/10.1177/1066480713505055

Hendrick, C. B., Bradley, L. J., & Robertson, D. L. (2015). Implementing multicultural ethics: Issues for family counselors. *The Family Journal: Counseling and Therapy for Couples and Families*, 23(2), 190–193. https://doi.org/10.1177/1066480715573251

Keith, D. (2014). *Continuing the experiential approach of Carl Whitaker: Process, practice, and magic*. Zeig, Tucker, & Theisen.

Kerr, M. D. (2019). *Bowen theory's secrets: Revealing the hidden life of families*. W.W. Norton & Company.

Macchi, C. R., & O'Conner, N. (2010). Common components of home-based family therapy models: The HBFT partnership in Kansas. *Contemporary Family Therapy*, 32, 444–458.

McGoldrick, M. (2016). *The genogram casebook: A clinical companion to Genograms: Assessment and intervention*. W.W. Norton & Company.

McGoldrick, M., Gerson, R., & Petry, S. (2020). *Genograms: Assessment and intervention* (4th ed.). W.W. Norton & Company.

McGoldrick, M., Giordano, J., & Garcia Preto, N. (Eds.). (2005). *Ethnicity and family therapy* (3rd ed.). Guilford.

Minuchin, S., Reiter, M. D., & Borda, C. (2014). *The craft of family therapy: Challenging certainties*. Routledge.

Paylo, M. J. (2011). Preparing school counseling students to aid families: Integrating a family systems perspective. *The Family Journal: Counseling and Therapy for Couples and Families*, 192(2), 140–146. https://doi.org/10.1177/1066480710397130

Perusse, R., Goodnough, G. E., & Noel, C. J. (2001). A national survey of school counselor preparation programs: Screening methods, faculty experiences, curricular content, and fieldwork requirements. *Counselor Education and Supervision*, 40(4), 252–262.

Phillips, F. B. (1990). *NTU psychotherapy: An Afrocentric approach*. Progressive Life Center.

Pinsoff, W. M., Breunlin, D. C., Russell, W. P., Lebow, J. L., Rampage, C., & Chambers, A. L. (2018). *Integrative systemic therapy: Metaframeworks for problem solving with individuals, couples, and families*. American Psychological Association.

Ratner, H., George, E., & Iveson, C. (2012). *Solution focused brief therapy*. Routledge.

Satir, V. (1988). *The new peoplemaking*. Science and Behavior Books.

Satir, V., Banmen, J., Gerber, J., & Gomori, M. (1991). *The Satir model: Family therapy and beyond*. Science and Behavior Books.

Scharff, D., & Scharff, J. S. (Speakers). (2011). *Object relations family therapy: Family therapy with the experts* (Moderators: J. Carlson & D. Kjos). Psychotherapy.net. (Original work published 1998).

Silverstein, L. B., & Goodrich, T. J. (Eds.). (2003). *Feminist family therapy: Empowerment in social context*. American Psychological Association.

Sprenkle, D. H., Davis, S. D., & Lebow, J. L. (2009). *Common factors in couple and family therapy: The overlooked foundation for effective practice*. Guilford.

Thomas, V., & Rastogi, M. (2009). *Multicultural couple therapy*. Sage.

Titelman, P. (Ed.). (2008). *Triangles: Bowen family systems theory perspectives*. Haworth.

Van Roekel, N. P. D. (2008). *Parent, family, community involvement in education*. Policy Brief. National Education Association.

White, M., & Epston, D. (1990). *Narrative means to therapeutic ends*. W.W. Norton & Company.

7 Parents, Caregivers, and Supportive Adults

Rebekah Byrd and Chad Luke

Objectives

- Recognize the different parenting styles and their impact on child/adolescent wellness.
- Identify parent/caregiver involvement in schools.
- Describe the U.S. Centers for Disease Control and Prevention (CDC) recommendations for connecting parents/caregivers with schools.
- Identify patterns of engagement of parents/caregivers with agencies.
- Learn to engage both child/adolescent and their parent/caregiver in understanding while respecting confidentiality.
- Describe the limits of confidentiality effectively in ways that keep children/adolescents and parents/caregivers engaged.
- Identify resources for helping empower parents/caregivers.
- Explore resources for supporting parents/caregivers in managing their relationship with the child/adolescent more effectively.

Reflective Questions

- What are my own beliefs about parenting?
- What parenting style did my parents/caregivers exhibit? How might this affect my attitudes toward the parents of my clients?
- How might I balance my allegiance to my client – child/adolescent – with the need to keep parents/caregivers engaged?
- What were my parents'/caregivers' interactions with my schools like?
- How might I support increasing the quality or quantity of my client's parents/caregivers in school?
- What barriers do I anticipate in engaging parents in the therapeutic process, especially if I am young, do not have a child, or have limited experience?
- How can I engage with parents in ways that build trust and confidence?
- What tools will keep handy to help empower parents/caregivers?

Importance of the Parent/Caregiver Relationship

As discussed in Chapter 4 on attachment and developmental aspects, the parent/caregiver-child relationship is extremely important in healthy development. To reiterate, the relationship with a primary caregiver lays down a neural template for adaptive skills, like emotion regulation, problem-solving, and healthy attachment. Having a healthy and positive parent/caregiver–child relationship is important for many reasons. Some of these include:

- Young children who grow with a secure and healthy attachment to their parents stand a better chance of developing happy and content relationships with others in their life.
- A child who has a secure relationship with his or her parents learns to regulate emotions under stress and in difficult situations.
- Promotes the child's mental, linguistic, and emotional development.
- Helps the child exhibit optimistic and confident social behaviors.
- Healthy parent involvement and intervention in the child's day-to-day life lay the foundation for better social and academic skills.
- A secure attachment leads to a healthy social, emotional, cognitive, and motivational development. Children also gain strong problem-solving skills when they have a positive relationship with their parents.

(Parenting NI, 2018, para 3)

We have to admit that as parents, we often feel confused, overwhelmed, and unprepared for parenting even though we both have doctoral degrees in counselor education and we are child and adolescent counselors (Rebekah is a play therapist, as well). Additionally, I (Rebekah) have been working with children in varying capacities (on my own) since I was around the age of 10/11. I think about that now and it scares me that anyone ever left a me – a 10-year-old – alone with their children. However, I was very responsible (everyone says that, right?) and it was a long time ago (not that long, though!). Now as a parent I read book after book on parenting (for my personal benefit and to assist my clients in finding resources they connect and identify with), and sometimes I want to throw my hands up in despair and futility.

Parenting Styles

In today's world, parents/caregivers are inundated with information (often conflicting) on how to raise children. Parents/caregivers are told the best ways to communicate with their children to get them to listen. Parents/caregivers are told what foods are good and what are bad. We are told what car seats are safe and which ones we should buy. We are told not to hover, or we are called helicopter parents. We are told not to give our children too much freedom, or we are called free-range parents. We are told how to put our children to bed and how often they should sleep and what to do about . . . *Every. Little. Thing.* One popular blog about parenting/caregiving discussed the mixed messages parents – specifically mothers – receive:

Give your kids limits, but let them make their own choices. Teach them independence, but make sure they know you're in charge. Meet your kids' emotional needs, but don't coddle them. Be your child's advocate, but don't fight their battles for them. Make sure your kids feel confident in their abilities and comfortable in their own skin, but don't praise them unless you praise them in exactly the right way using exactly the right words at exactly the right time.

(Reneau, 2019, para 13)

Often mothers specifically are blamed for errors in child rearing leading to shame, self-doubt, feelings of inadequacy, and more. Further blaming mothers/women in these contexts "deflects attention from social solutions for ensuring the well-being of children" (Garey & Arendell, 1999, p. 2). Even though we are overwhelmed with the information and messages coming at us constantly, what parents/caregivers often have very little of, is support and encouragement. Counselors may be the only people to provide parents/caregivers with this important assistance.

Parenting/caregiving styles have been discussed in the literature and research for decades. These styles have been found in research to even predict well-being in many areas (i.e., academic achievement, degree of problematic behavior, and social skills) among children and adolescents (Rosenthal & Fetherling, 2006). Many are aware of the four general types of parenting styles. They are generally referred to as authoritarian, authoritative, permissive, and uninvolved.

Authoritarian

Rosenthal and Fetherling (2006) discuss authoritarian parents/caregivers as being very controlling, firm, and strict. These are parents/caregivers who believe in rules, justice, obedience, and punishment (Rosenthal & Fetherling, 2006). These authors also note that authoritarian parents/caregivers are not very responsive to their children, but they are highly demanding of them. Further, they discuss that children of authoritarian parents/caregivers may have higher anxiety, lower self-esteem, poorer social skills, and higher levels of depression. While the results of authoritarian parenting may be effective in the short term, long-term effects on youth are troublesome, including depression (King, Vidourek, & Merianos, 2016)

Authoritative

Authoritative parents/caregivers are not too strict (like authoritarian) or too lenient (like permissive) – this style is just right and focuses on positive reinforcement and building upon capabilities and characteristics of the child (Jadon & Tripathi, 2017). Rosenthal and Fetherling (2006) discuss that while authoritative parents/caregivers do uphold a degree of control and authority, they are not controlling and strict like authoritarian parents, and they are warmer and seek to communicate with their children – they are both responsive and demanding. These authors further discuss that authoritative parents/caregivers strive for balance between their child's/adolescent's wish for autonomy, independence, and freedom to express themselves, and the parents'/caregivers' needs to be heard and understood. Additionally, authoritative parenting/caregiving is "one of the most consistence predictors of social competence" (Rosenthal & Fetherling, 2006, p. 24).

Permissive

Permissive parents are lenient, make few demands, and avoid conflict (Rosenthal & Fetherling, 2006). Children of parents/caregivers who are permissive may end up feeling entitled, use substances, be more likely to have problem behavior, experience lower success/performance in school (Rosenthal & Fetherling, 2006), and display increased impulsivity and lack discipline (Jadon & Tripathi, 2017). Further, permissive parenting has been linked with various forms of high-risk behavior (Jinnah & Stoneman, 2016), high delinquency, and having deviant peers (Mann, Kretsch, Tacket, Harden, & Tucker-Drob, 2015).

Uninvolved

Rosenthal and Fetherling (2006) note that an uninvolved parenting style is "low in both demandingness and responsiveness. At worst, it can verge into neglect" (p. 23). It is also said to be low in sensitivity and emotional warmth (Konopka, Rek-Owodzin, Pelka-Wysiecka, & Samochowiec, 2018). Uninvolved parents do not seem to exhibit unprompted interest or pay unsolicited attention to a child – instead they respond only when attention is demanded or when it is the expectation to respond (Konopka et al., 2018). These researchers also noted that "Among risk the factors predisposing the child to depression are the following: negative parental attitudes such as emotional coldness, rejection, distance and lack of parental support as well as excessive criticism, over controlling and uninvolved parental style" (p. 927). Counselors can assist parents/caregivers in adopting new ways of being with their child/adolescent. Counselors can provide support for challenging behavior, discuss developmental considerations, and normalize parental/caregiver struggles. Parents/caregivers who feel understood and supported are more likely to be those things for their children/adolescents.

Parent/Caregiver Engagement in Schools

The U.S. Department of Education (2019) notes that in 2019, there were 56.6 million children and adolescents in the United States who attended elementary, middle, and high schools. Estimates from the U.S. Department of Education (2004) suggest that children and adolescents spend roughly 6.7 hours at school per weekday and on average around 180 days per year at school. It is important for those working in the school setting to consider the impact of parental involvement on the lives of children and adolescents spending so much time away from parents/caregivers.

Parental/caregiver engagement in the school life of their child or adolescent is seen as an encouraging, promising, and reassuring protective factor (CDC, 2012). Many benefits exist for parental/caregiver involvement. Having engaged parents/caregivers has been shown to decrease the likelihood that children and adolescents will participate in activities such as tobacco use (Guilamo-Ramos et al., 2010) and substance use (Hayakawa, Giovanelli, Englund, & Reynolds, 2016). Myriad research has noted that having parental/caregiver engagement in the school is highly linked to successful student behavior, including improved social skills (El Nokali, Bachman, & Votruba-Drzal, 2010). Further, when parents/caregivers are involved, children and adolescents also exhibit higher academic performance and achievement (Jeynes, 2007). Counselors are in a strong position to advocate for ways to involve parents/caregivers.

The U.S. Centers for Disease Control and Prevention (CDC, 2012) recommended three main ways to be involved and continue to engage parents/caregivers in the school lives of their child or adolescent: connect, engage, and sustain. The CDC (2012) offered that connection is an essential place to start before schools can start to engage parents in offered programs or activities. If parents/caregivers feel uncomfortable, unwelcome, or otherwise disconnected, it will be difficult or even impossible to promote engagement. What follows is a sample of a few of the ideas for connection with parents/caregivers offered by the CDC (2012). These were slightly modified, and counselors can take note of these ideas to apply to school, community, or other work settings.

- Does the school mission reflect the importance of parent engagement and establish a foundation for parent engagement in schools?
- Does the school have a well-planned program for parent engagement?
- Are policies and procedures in place to maximize parent engagement in the school's activities, services, and programs?
- Does the school have a friendly, welcoming environment for parents?
- Does the school welcome parents to participate in and contribute to the school's activities, services, and programs?

- Is there a district-level parent involvement and engagement plan that can guide the development of a school plan for involving parents in school health activities?
- Does the school have a dedicated committee of teachers, administrators, and parents (such as an Action Team for Partnerships) that helps the school plan, implement, evaluate, and continually improve its outreach to parents and the quality of parent engagement activities?
- Are school staff members provided with opportunities to learn how to increase parent engagement in school, including in health activities?
- What simple changes or modifications would make the school's physical environment more pleasant, accessible, and safe for parents and community members?

(p. 10–11)

The CDC explained that connection is the first essential step and next suggested ideas for types of involvement, expanded from researchers Epstein et al. (2009), that schools (or other settings) can offer as ways to engage parents/caregivers.

1. Providing parenting support.
2. Communicating with parents.
3. Providing a variety of volunteer opportunities.
4. Supporting learning at home.
5. Encouraging parents to be part of decision making in schools.
6. Collaborating with the community.

(2012, p. 12)

Finally, the CDC (2012) noted the importance of continued parental/caregiver engagement from the beginning and how this will likely result in continued engagement and sustainment. The CDC has outlined some ideas to assist in solving common barriers to sustained engagement (this is not a comprehensive list). These ideas can be utilized in a variety of settings.

- Schedule meetings and activities to match varying parent schedules.
- Provide incentives to encourage parents to attend at-school meetings and events.
- Provide alternative ways for parents to access information and communicate with school staff, aside from attending meetings and activities on school grounds.
- Provide transportation.
- Hold events off site or online.
- Provide opportunities for parents to get to know about the school and school staff in nonthreatening ways.
- Implement programs that are culturally sensitive and that reflect the social and environmental aspects of a community influenced by race/ethnicity, socio-economic status, locale (rural, suburban, urban), and culture.
- Provide translation services for non-English-speaking parents.
- Reduce barriers to understanding information.
- Provide professional development opportunities for school staff that focus on strengthening parent engagement.
- Develop strategies for working through staff resistance to change, turf issues, and power struggles that might hinder [staff]-parent interactions.

(2012, pp. 20–23)

Counselors can modify, add to, and adjust the previous suggestions to match their specific site and population needs. These are excellent recommendations for parent/

caregiver involvement that promote the success and welfare of our children and adolescents.

Parent/Caregiver Engagement in Agencies

A review of the literature reveals that only a minority of children and adolescents with mental health needs are able to access treatment (Reardon et al., 2017). We should be doing everything we can to support parents/caregivers so as to promote engagement with treatment. From working in schools and agencies over the years, I have observed that when the parent/caregiver is disrespected or feels disrespected, they often discontinue treatment. Kerkorian, McKay, and Bannon (2006) found that parents were roughly six times more likely to doubt the usefulness of treatment as a barrier to future services if they had experienced feeling disrespected by their child's previous mental health clinician. As it is, many barriers to treatment exist already without our agencies being unwelcoming or unsupportive. If parents are protective factors in school life, it makes sense then that they are essential to the process of treatment in agencies, as well. One study found that "the quality of the therapeutic alliance with parents and children, as well as parents' etiological beliefs regarding their children's mental health difficulties, also influence child mental health treatment engagement" (Gopalan et al., 2010, p. 191). Since parents/caregivers are often "key gatekeepers to treatment access" (Reardon et al., 2017, p. 623), counselors need to understand and work to address these barriers so that parents/caregivers can be engaged and work to support their child/adolescent.

Reardon et al. (2017) conducted a meta-analysis to examine the barriers parents experience when seeking mental health services. Their study revealed barriers such as "(1) systemic/structural issues, (2) views and attitudes toward services and treatment, (3) knowledge and understanding of mental health problems and the help-seeking process; and (4) family circumstances" (p. 623). These main four barriers included many themes and subheadings. These are worth considering, but are not a conclusive list. Systemic/structural issues included factors like services costs and financial considerations, waiting times for appointments, access to services including location and space, and availability of appointments. Views and attitudes toward services and treatment included barriers such as whether the professionals were supportive or dismissive, social stigma, and fear of diagnosis, labeling, or hospitalization. The main theme of knowledge and understanding of mental health programs and the help-seeking process revealed that the parent's understanding of the child's issue, acuity level, and knowledge about the help-seeking process were some of the issues related to this barrier. The last main barrier, family circumstance, included considerations for the family and its support network, and also understanding other demands and responsibilities which families must juggle. These factors are imperative for any counselor to consider when working with parents/caregivers.

Working With Parents/Caregivers in Counseling

Many counselors in training, both in school and mental health, planning to work with children and/or adolescents may be drawn to these populations – at least in part – due to an aversion or general lack of desire to work with adults. The reality, of course, is that most children and adolescents are tethered to an adult – at least one, and often more. Like many of you reading this, we really enjoy our time working with children and adolescents, and at times struggle more to connect and empathize with the parents/caregivers than with our client. However, all our clients who happen to be children/adolescents are part of a family system. Our work with them is 1 hour per week – if we're lucky – out of 168. If we want to see the advances in counseling continue, we must engage with parents/caregivers. Often, the child/adolescent is a symptom of system struggles, so change in the child/adolescent will be short-lived without also engaging the system at some level.

One way to approach working with parents/caregivers in counseling is to know the population. John and Rita Sommers-Flanagan (2011) offer a practical way to think of parents as a unique clinical population. They advise counselors recognize at least four characteristics of parents: first, they are adults looking for counseling to address non-adults; second, typically, parents are seeking advice or solutions or practical tips, so having resources on hand may be important; third, they may be skeptical of inexperienced counselors or of solutions they have already heard from other parents/teachers; and fourth, acknowledging the need for and then seeking help is difficult for parents/caregivers, which makes them feel vulnerable, yet defensive. These four observations can lead counselors of all experience levels to better empathize with parents/caregivers, leading to greater trust and more investment in the process.

There are myriad presenting problems in counseling, and even more strategies for addressing these problems. Therefore, we have assembled a sampling of the resources available online for counselors to use in working with parents, and also to share with parents to help them help their child or adolescent. It is important to communicate the legal status of confidential (privileged) communication, as well as the ethics of the profession.

Including Parents/Caregivers While Maintaining Confidentiality

We have said it before, but it bears repeating: whether or not you are a parent yourself, it is not possible for the counselor to be as hooked in to the child or adolescent client as a parent or caregiver. What this means in practice is that these parents/caregivers are very invested (there are exceptions, of course) and want to know what is happening in the counseling room. This may range from an inquisitive look to an assertive statement about expecting you to report what is said in counseling. These are anxiety-provoking situations for counselors in training and even at times for seasoned counselors. Legally, parents have rights to their children's records (this will vary by age of the child or adolescent by state, so please consult your state's laws regarding parents' rights). We think many of these potential conflicts can be addressed before they even arise by meeting with the parents and the child/adolescent for part of the first session. One of the most practical resources we have seen is from John and Rita Sommers-Flanagan (2007), in the second edition of their excellent text, *Tough Kids, Cool Counseling*. In it, they offer a sample of how counselors might approach the topic of confidentiality with parents/caregivers and children/adolescents. Here is an excerpt:

> I won't talk about what either of you say to me outside of here, except in a few rare situations where I legally or ethically have to speak with someone outside this office. For example, if any of you are a danger to yourself, or to anyone else, I won't keep that information private, Also, if I find out about child abuse or neglect that has happened or is happening, I'll work with you to get the best help possible . . .
>
> Now (the counselor looks at the child/adolescent), one of the trickiest situations is whether I should tell your mom and dad about what we talk about in here. Let me tell all of you how I like to work and see if it's okay with you. (Looks back at parents) I believe your son (daughter) needs to be able to trust me. So, I'd like you to agree that information I give you about my private conversations with him (her) be limited to general progress reports. In other words, aside from general progress reports, I won't inform you of details of what your child tells me. Of course, if your child is planning or

doing something that might be very dangerous or self-destructive, I will tell your child (turn and look to child) that he (she) is planning something I feel very uncomfortable with and then we'll have everyone (turn back to parents) come in for an appointment so we can talk directly about whatever dangerous thing has come up. Is this arrangement okay with all of you?

(pp. 30–31)

Approaching the topic of privacy keeps counselors out of the role of secret-keepers. Secrets are things you know you should share but feel pressure not to. Privacy, on the other hand, is the dignity-respecting dimension of building trust, and as such, it is vital to build with both the child/adolescent and with the parent/caregiver. Depending on the age of the child and the setting in which you work, it is often appropriate to meet with the parents/caregivers without the child or adolescent present to do intake, ask questions, and discuss the counseling relationship. The previous conversation about confidentiality can occur at the first meeting, with the child or adolescent present.

Empowering and Encouraging Parents/Caregivers

There are many considerations to keep in mind when working with children/adolescents. Whole books have been written about teaching parenting techniques, teaching positive discipline, and teaching parents/caregivers how to encourage rather than use empty praise. In addition, there are also many resources on supportive adults, consultation, and collaboration. We have assembled a list of resources to enable readers to find the one that suits the clinical situation, rather than trying to say everything in a few short pages. Readers are encouraged to peruse these sites and to make notes, use bookmarks in their browser, or otherwise take ownership of these resources, including adding your own to the list. This way, the resources will be available to you during a session, and you can pull one up without the pressure of remembering the site or its content.

Sample Resources

www.parenttoolkit.com

From the website:

> Parent Toolkit is a one-stop resource developed with parents in mind. It's produced by NBC News Learn and supported by Pearson and includes information about almost every aspect of your child's development, because they're all connected. Healthy, successful children can excel in many areas – in the classroom, on the court, and in their relationships with peers and adults. Our advice also covers important topics for navigating life after high school.

www2.ed.gov/parents/landing.jhtml

From the U.S. Department of Education, resources on education-related topics: reading, learning, disability, school success, and college preparation.

http://parents.nea.org

The National Education Association's parents/guardians page, a one-stop shop for parents/caregivers on topics like keeping kids curious, providing emotional support, parent & educator partnerships, and education innovation and policy.

www.childcareaware.org/families/

Recourses for parents/caregivers related to childcare. Resource categories include types of childcare, selecting childcare, regulations, costs, engagement for families, and fee assistance and respite.

www.pbs.org/parents/

Resources for education, engagement, social/emotional ideas, and activities for parents/caregivers to children of all ages.

www.sleephelp.org/childrens-sleep-guide/

Guide to all things sleep-related to aid parents/caregivers in knowing the sleep needs of their child/adolescent, and providing for them.

www.childwelfare.gov/topics/preventing/prevention-programs/parented/education-resource/

Comprehensive guide to parent education, including national parent helpline. Examples of resources include links to:

https://centerforparentingeducation.org

Includes resource list of books on parenting, list of articles covering many parenting-related issues, and a rich resource directory of curated sites for a host of parenting topics.

www.changingchildrensworlds.org

Information on and resources for parents/caregiver training model, International Child/Parent Development Program (ICDP)

https://childdevelopmentinfo.com/#gs.5mou11

From the website:

> The mission of Child Development Institute is to become the "go to" site for parents for information, products and services related to child development, psychology, health, parenting, learning, media, entertainment, family activities as well as to connect with other parents, professional experts organizations and other useful websites.

It contains thousands of links to resources for parents/caregivers on most topics of concern related to effective parenting.

www.cdc.gov/ncbddd/actearly/index.html

The U.S. Centers for Disease Control and Prevention site, designed to help parents and caregivers identify and track milestones, and resources for how to intervene if they are not on track.

http://the-parenting-center.com/support-advice/

The National Parenting Center's resource page of support and advice that ranges from pregnancy to adolescence.

https://npen.org/members-books-and-publications/

Book list for parents/caregivers from the National Parenting Education Network that covers everything from discipline strategies (that do not include spanking, time-outs, or bribery) to parenting in the media age.

http://parentsanonymous.org

Parents Anonymous is a national organization building healthy parent-child relationships, in part through support groups, as well as countless online resources to support parents/caregivers through the challenges of parenthood.

www.nationalparenthelpline.org

National Parent Helpline offers advocacy and support to parents. From the website:

> A trained National Parent Helpline® Advocate is ready to: listen to you, offer emotional support, help you problem-solve, support you in creating your own solutions, encourage you to take care of yourself, work with you to get connected to local services, explore new resources for your family, and help you build on your own strengths and continue to be a great parent!

www.childwelfare.gov/catalog/serieslist/?CWIGFunctionsaction=publicationCatalog;^$ain.dspSeriesDetail&publicationSeriesID=2

Links to 30 fact sheets for practitioners to guide their work and also to share with parents/caregivers to support effective parenting.

www.nationalcac.org/for-parents/

The National Children's Advocacy Center website, with myriad resources for parents/caregivers and practitioners to use in supporting safe and healthy environments for children.

www.childhelp.org/resources-parents/

ChildHelp website with downloadable parenting resources with practical tips for dealing with difficult behaviors, as well as for promoting health parent-child relationships. Includes a "Helpful Links" page for parents: www.childhelp.org/story-resource-center/helpful-links/

www.attachmentparenting.org/aboutus/whatwedo

Whether a parent or counselor agrees with this specific model, it is filled with useful resources for parents/caregivers and counselors. From the website:

> Attachment Parenting is an application of sensitive responsive parenting. Attachment Parenting is based in the practice of nurturing parenting methods that create strong emotional bonds, also known as secure attachment, between children and their parent(s). This style of parenting encourages responsiveness to children's emotional needs, enabling children to develop trust that their needs will be met. As a result, this strong attachment helps children develop the capacity for secure, empathic, peaceful, and enduring relationships that follow them into adulthood.

Multicultural Implications and Advocacy

All counseling is multicultural. Working with parents, caregivers, and supportive adults is no different. Counselors must remember to also have a strengths-based approach in the work we do with the important adults in the lives of the child or adolescent. Every family has its own unique culture, and many families have other diversity and cultural influences to consider when providing competent, supportive, and best practice care.

Data have substantiated that the mental health profession is failing to provide proper care for children, adolescents, and families of diverse backgrounds (Alegria, Atkins, Farmer, Slaton, & Stelk, 2010). The American Academy of Child and Adolescent Psychiatry noted the importance of cultural competency stating that the following are important for consideration in family life:

- Behaviors that are common and "normal" in one culture even when they are not in others
- Ways to manage everyday problems that can occur between a child and parents or others
- Religious beliefs, practices and events
- Family customs and traditions
- Conflicts that arise between parents and children if the child is spending more time with friends than with family
- Different ways of expressing emotions and problems

(AACAP 2019, para 3)

Further, AACAP (2019) discussed that mental health professionals can do many things to provide culturally competent care such as working with cultural, religious, or community organizations of families from different cultures if the family permits, including important family members who may not be blood related but are important nonetheless, in treatment if requested by the child, adolescent, or family to do so. The counselor must also understand which techniques and theories work best with different cultures. Counselors must also recognize their own biases and how this can impact treatment and the therapeutic alliance for all involved.

Summary

The role of parents, caregivers, and supportive adults in the child's or adolescent's life is not to be understated. The chapter discussed parenting styles and included information on how to assist parents/caregivers in the school setting and in agency settings. The onus is on the counselor and other staff to make sure these places are not only supportive and safe for our clients, but multiculturally sensitive. The chapter discussed ways in which counselors in training can empower and encourage parents/caregivers, as it is critical to remember that when parents/caregivers are unsupported and feel devalued, they often struggle to assist their children. This chapter discussed and provided resources for many techniques to teach parents and caregivers positive discipline and support them in meaningful ways. Multicultural implications and advocacy work are essential to address barriers to mental health services.

Clinician's Corner

I used to emphatically say that I would not go back through childhood and adolescence, even if you paid me millions of dollars. And for a long time, I was satisfied with this dogma. Then, my wife and I had our daughter. It turns out, as nature and a trickster universe would have it, I am going back through childhood and adolescence for free . . . I wish I had taken the millions! I think one of the hardest things for new counselors is getting "the question": "Do you have kids?" This is always a trap of sorts because there really is no right answer (except the truth, of course). The counselors I train and supervise often struggle with saying: "No, I don't have kids". The fear caregivers have is that there is no way this childless

20-something could understand how difficult parenting can be. So, I offer a description or parenthood based on my experience:

Take everything that is valuable to you: sense of safety, security, confidence, money, love, your heart, your brain, etc., and place these things into a container that is completely unaware of its contents. Then, watch as this juggernaut of a container does its best to wreck these treasures, precariously holding your treasures, all completely unselfconsciously. Oh, and while you're at it, stop sleeping, stop doing what you want when you want, and embrace fear as a lifestyle. Oh, and recognize that you would not trade it for the world.

In my early days of working with parents (before being wracked with the terror and guilt of parenthood), parents seemed to cut me slack if I sought to understand their experience. Eventually, they stopped asking me if I was a parent because I think they didn't need that information to be able to trust my investment in them, not just their child or adolescent.

Chad Luke, PhD, LPC-MHSP, NCC, ACS, MAC
Tennessee Tech University

References

Alegria, M., Atkins, M., Farmer, E., Slaton, E., & Stelk, W. (2010). One size does not fit all: Taking diversity, culture and context seriously. *Administration and Policy in Mental Health*, 37(1–2), 48–60. https://doi.org/10.1007/s10488-010-0283-2

American Academy of Child and Adolescent Psychiatry. (2019). *Diversity and culture in child mental health care*. Retrieved from www.aacap.org/AACAP/Families_and_Youth/Facts_for_Families/FFF-Guide/Diversity_and_Culture_in_Child_Mental_Health_Care-118.aspx

Centers for Disease Control and Prevention. (2012). *Parent engagement: Strategies for involving parents in school health*. Atlanta, GA: U.S. Department of Health and Human Services.

El Nokali, N. E., Bachman, H. J., & Votruba-Drzal, L. E. (2010). Parent involvement and children's academic and social development in elementary school. *Child Development*, 81(3), 988–1005.

Epstein, J. L., Sanders, M. G., Simon, B. S., Salinas, K. C., Jansorn, N. R., & Van Voorhis, R. L. (2009). *School, family, and community partnerships: Your handbook for action* (3rd ed.). Thousand Oaks, CA: Corwin Press.

Garey, A. L., & Arendell, T. (1999). *Children, work and family: Some thoughts on "Mother Blame"*. Center for Working Families, University of California, Berkeley. Retrieved from http://hdl.handle.net/2345/4099

Gopalan, G., Goldstein, L., Klingenstein, K., Sicher, C., Blake, C., & McKay, M. M. (2010). Engaging families into child mental health treatment: Updates and special considerations. *Journal of the Canadian Academy of Child and Adolescent Psychiatry*, 19(3), 182–196.

Guilamo-Ramos, V., Jaccard, J., Dittus, P., Gonzalez, B., Bouris, A., & Banspach, S. (2010). The Linking Lives health education program: A randomized clinical trial of a parent-based tobacco use prevention program for African American and Latino Youths. *American Journal of Public Health*, 100(9), 1641–1647.

Hayakawa, M., Giovanelli, A., Englund, M. M., & Reynolds, A. J. (2016). Not just academics: Paths of longitudinal effects from parent involvement to substance abuse in emerging adulthood. *The Journal of Adolescent Health: Official Publication of the Society for Adolescent Medicine*, 58(4), 433–439. https://doi.org/10.1016/j.jadohealth.2015.11.007

Jadon, P. S., & Tripathi, S. (2017). Effect of authoritarian parenting style on self esteem of the child: A systematic review. *International Journal of Advance Research and Innovative Ideas in Education*, 3(3), 909–913.

Jeynes, W. H. (2007). The relationship between parental involvement and urban secondary school student academic achievement: A meta-analysis. *Urban Education*, 42, 82–110.

Jinnah, H. A., & Stoneman, Z. (2016). Influence of permissive parenting on youth farm risk behaviors. *Journal of Agromedicine*, 21(3), 244–252. https://doi.org/10.1080/1059924X.2016.1179610

Kerkorian, D., McKay, M., & Bannon, W. M., Jr. (2006). Seeking help a second time: Parents'/caregivers' characterizations of previous experiences with mental health services for their children and perceptions of barriers to future use. *American Journal of Orthopsychiatry, 76*(2), 161–166. https://doi.org/10.1037/00002-9432.76.2.16

King, K. A., Vidourek, R. A., & Merianos, A. L. (2016). Authoritarian parenting and youth depression: Results from a national study. *Journal of Prevention & Intervention in the Community, 44*(2), 130–139. https://doi.org/10.1080/10852352.2016.1132870

Konopka, A., Rek-Owodzin, K., Pelka-Wysiecka, J., & Samochowiec, J. (2018). Parenting style in family and the risk of psychopathology. *Postępy Higieny i Medycyny Doświadczalnej, 72*, 924–931. https://doi.org/10.5604/01.3001.0012.7026

Mann, F. D., Kretsch, N., Tacket, J. L., Harden, K. P., & Tucker-Drob, E. M. (2015). Person x environment interactions on adolescent delinquency: Sensation seeking, peer deviance and parental monitoring. *Personality and Individual Differences, 76*, 129–134. https://doi.org/10.1016/j.paid.2014.11.055

Parenting NI. (2018). *Parent-child relationship-why it's important*. Retrieved from www.parentingni.org/blog/parent-child-relationship-why-its-important/#targetText=Promotes%20the%20child's%20mental%2C%20linguistic,better%20social%20and%20academic%20skills

Reardon, T., Harvey, K., Baranowska, M., O'Brien, D., Smith, L., & Creswell, C. (2017). What do parents perceive are the barriers and facilitators to accessing psychological treatment for mental health problems in children and adolescents? A systematic review of qualitative and quantitative studies. *European Child & Adolescent Psychiatry, 26*(6), 623–647. http://doi.org/10.1007/s00787-016-0930-6

Reneau, A. (2019). *The maddening mixed messages we give moms*. Retrieved from www.scarymommy.com/mixed-messages-parenting-advice/

Rosenthal, M., & Fetherling, D. (2006). *Be a parent, not a pushover, a guide to raising happy, emotionally healthy teens*. Nashville, TN: Thomas Nelson, Inc.

Sommers-Flanagan, J., & Sommers-Flanagan, R. (2007). *Tough kids, cool counseling: User-friendly approaches for challenging youth* (2nd ed.). American Counseling Association.

Sommers-Flanagan, J., & Sommers-Flanagan, R. (2011). *How to listen so parents will talk and talk so parents will listen*. Wiley.

U.S. Department of Education, Institute of Educations Sciences, National Center for Education Statistics. (2019). *Fast facts: Back to school statistics*. Washington, DC.

U.S. Department of Education, National Center for Education Statistics. (2004). *Private school universe survey*. Washington, DC.

8 Trauma and the Child and Adolescent Brain

Chad Luke and Rebekah Byrd

Objectives

- Learn about the general structure, systems, and functions of the human brain.
- Begin to differentiate stress from trauma and how the distinctions are more academic than actual.
- Be able to apply the eight-factor model of human phenomena to stress and trauma.
- Identify neuroscience axioms for working with trauma in children and adolescents.
- Become familiar with the neuroscience of adverse childhood experiences (ACEs).

Reflective Questions

- What are my beliefs about trauma in childhood and adolescence?
- What biases might I hold about someone who has experienced trauma?
- Where is trauma in the brain, and how can this inform my work with children and adolescents?
- How can an enhanced understanding of the brain and trauma assist me in my own personal growth and development?

Summarize Structures, Systems, and Functions of the Brain

The content in this section is modeled after Chapter 2 from *Neuroscience for Counselors and Therapists* (2nd ed) (Luke, 2020) because there is a lot to learn about the brain and nervous system, but it has been described numerous times and in multiple ways. One way to conceptualize neuroanatomy (structure) and physiology (function) is a 1-2-3-4-5 heuristic, which is intended to provide counselors with a quick way to conceptualize structures, systems, and functions of the brain, and in a way that can be safely shared with parents and other caregivers. This material provides a basic foundation for further understanding the brain and trauma, but for a more in-depth exposition, readers might consult Field, Jones, and Russell-Chapin (2017).

1. Brain

First and foremost, the brain is best understood as a whole unit rather than a collection of independent regions or structures, and this holistic view is most usefully viewed in the brain's connection with others. So just as the whole brain must be understood as an integrated system of systems, an individual brain is also best understood as one part of a larger system in relation to other brains (human relationships). For example, while the amygdala is thought of as the center of fear and emotion, is merely plays its role in larger systems, like the limbic system, which connects the hindbrain to the midbrain, but also has a direct connection to the forebrain. While it is true that the amygdala plays a specific role, it is its relationship to other structures and systems (or lack thereof) that defines its identify and purpose. Likewise, an individual client is part of a series of systems – broken, damaged, or nonexistent as they may be – which helps us understand the function and purpose of the individual. Without an understanding of the whole individual, who is part of larger systems, we can only ever have an incomplete picture of that child or adolescent. Researchers have identified previous limitations of brain research in the study of a brain in isolation, one at a time, when the most meaningful data on brain function can come from studies of a brain in relationship to others. Likewise, working with a child or adolescent as if that person were an isolated being misses the larger picture of what functioning can look like. This matters whether the relational context for the child/adolescent (and their brain) is explored in terms of rupture or of repair.

2. Hemispheres

There are so many parallels to therapy in general, and with children and adolescents in particular that come from an understanding of the two hemispheres of the brain, that this section will barely scratch the surface. To start, it is helpful to clear up some confusion regarding brain hemispheric function. It would be inaccurate to describe a person as left-brained or right-brained. While it is true that each hemisphere has its own specialization, because the majority of structures in the forebrain, midbrain, and limbic system are bilateral (structures in one hemisphere are mirrored in the other hemisphere), both hemispheres are necessary for healthy functioning. It is accurate to understand the specialization of each hemisphere, and equally so to understand the way the two hemispheres communicate with one another. The left hemisphere can be understood through what Siegel (2012) calls the four Ls: language, linearity, literalness, and logic. In contrast, the right hemisphere directs emotion, creativity, and relationship. Here is a sample application with an adolescent named Jemma who has a history of trauma and struggles with anxiety and anger: the work of the counselor is to assist Jemma to integrate these two hemispheres. Because of the bilateral nature of the brain's structures, Jemma's amygdala and hippocampus exist in each hemisphere, but because the two hemispheres process information and experiences differently, Jemma's anxiety does not make her left- or right-brained. Instead, how she experiences and then expresses her anxiety may vary depending upon the mode through which she is processing (Siegel [2015] calls this left-mode and right-mode processing). In other words, at times, Jemma's anxiety may be expressed verbally and at other times emotionally. Neither are right; neither are wrong. However, the ability to choose one's mode of processing may be critical for post-traumatic growth. For example, we may use left-mode processing to verbalize a concept like anxiety, but for someone who has never experienced severe anxiety, this word may have very limited meaning. Or, in Jemma's case, feelings were not allowed to be openly expressed by the children in the home, so talking about feelings (left-mode processing) is not only foreign but triggering. Instead, Jemma stays emotionally activated as an expression of her past and present anxiety (right-mode processing) so she never feels as if she can manage those emotions. Jemma's trauma keeps her feeling overwhelmed due to limited access of left-mode processing (in essence, thinking logically, in a linear fashion about her trauma). This is not the same as trying to use cognitive therapy to bring her emotions under the control of rational cognitions; it is about harmonizing between the hemispheres to allow for a complete experiencing and processing of the past trauma and current anxiety. In the brain, the structure responsible for this harmonizing, or horizontal integration, as Seigel puts it, is the corpus callosum. This high-density nerve bundle works to unite and integrate the processing of each hemisphere. In counseling, the therapist is the equivalent of the corpus callosum, bringing together into unified experience, the intolerable facets, as well as the strengths, of a client's existence.

3. Levels of Functional Governance

In 1990, Paul MacLean proposed the triune brain, an understanding of the brain based on its evolutionary development, from the inside out, across three layers: the reptilian, paleomammalian, and neomammalian brain. The reptilian, or lizard, brain is a primal layer that houses basic life functions and evolved to react to the environmental stimuli in order to survive. It is purely stimulus-response in nature. Luke (2020) refers to this as *survival of the individual*. Next in the evolutionary-developmental sequence was the development of the paleomammalian, or rat, brain. This includes the limbic region which connects the midbrain with the cortex neocortex. This stage of evolutionary brain development involves what Luke refers to as *survival in community*. Last to develop was the mammalian, or monkey, brain and is the part of the brain – the neocortex – with a large percentage devoted to social functioning (Purves et al., 2018). It is in this functional level that allows survival in a relational context or *survival and connection* (Luke, 2020). The nature of evolutionary development is that organs or parts of organs and systems remain long after other faculties have emerged. For counselors, this is important in assessing the functioning of the child or adolescent in order to understand how they are moving through their world: lizard, rat, or monkey. Likewise, from a systems perspective, the family unit from and in which the child lives can also be said to function at one of these three levels. It is not difficult to imagine a reptilian type of family system wherein all members are merely reacting to environmental stimuli, while others in the paleomammalian type system are emotion-driven, or in the neomammalian type family system in which connection and relationship are more probable. It is also, therefore, easier to understand which type of system might promote resilience and post-traumatic growth in a brain that has experienced trauma, and the ones that do not.

> Clients can be invited to set their goals for counseling related to living based on survival of the individual (reptilian), survival in community (paleomammalian), or survival and connection (neomammalian). In other words, would clients prefer to live by reflex alone, instinct, or relationship?
>
> (Luke, 2020, p. 44)

4. Cortical Lobes

Many of us may be familiar with the four main lobes of the cortex: the frontal, temporal, parietal, and occipital lobes. These lobes represent relatively discrete areas of functioning. For instance, the occipital lobe is the primary visual cortex and governs seeing, as well as meaning-making of sight. For example, Erik Wiehenmeyer is the first blind person to summit Mount Everest. He demonstrated the use of a device called brainport that uses a camera mounted in a pair of sunglasses that projects an image to a computer, which then digitizes those signals and sends them to a pad on the tongue. This pad contains about 300 sensors to recreate the visual data allowing him to "see". In counseling, this can be used to assist clients in understanding that our eyes may receive input from our environment, but we actually see using our brain, and the occipital lobe in particular.

The temporal lobes are referred to in the plural form because unlike the other three lobes, these lobes are located on opposite sides of the brain. The auditory cortex is found in the temporal lobe and processes complex sounds. The parietal lobe contains the somatosensory cortex, which processes information coming in through the skin and touch, for example, pain, pressure, and temperature. It is also where language comprehension is located, also known as Wernicke's area. Speech comprehension is governed by the frontal lobe, which is where Broca's area is also located. This makes sense in that speech involves movement, and the frontal lobe contains the primary and secondary motor cortices. The prefrontal cortex is also located in the frontal lobe, and governs conscious sensations, abstract thought, reasoning, planning, and working memory (Luke, 2020). The lobes are important for a number of reasons, but perhaps the most salient and relevant for treating trauma is that sensory experience does not make meaning; the brain region that processes sensory signals does.

5. Systems for Self-Regulation

There are myriad systems in children and adolescents that could be listed, but this review focuses on five major systems that serve as a starting place for understanding the impact and clinical implications of trauma and the brain: the central nervous system, peripheral nervous system, autonomic nervous system, sympathetic nervous system, and parasympathetic nervous system. The central nervous system (CNS) includes the brain and nervous system, and directs all conscious (and non-conscious) cognitive and behavioral functioning. The peripheral nervous system, in contrast, regulates most non-conscious biological functioning. It is made up of the somatic and autonomic nervous systems. The autonomic nervous system is the focus of this review, as it is made up of the sympathetic and parasympathetic nervous systems, responsible for fight/flight/freeze and rest/digest responses, respectively.

The sympathetic nervous system (SNS) is responsible for preparing the body and mind for response to threats. It does this by increasing heart rate, dilating pupils, slowing or stopping digestion, stimulating adrenal glands, and constricting blood vessels. These processes promote survival; for example, we do not need to digest that burger from lunch if we are about to die. Likewise, adrenaline provides the burst of energy needed to take self-protective action. A key to understanding this system's function is that it takes over in the presence of a *perceived* threat, regardless of whether the threat materializes. Better a false positive that just makes us aware and afterward tired, than a false negative whereby we relax, only to be harmed unexpectedly. In other words, "perception creates real bodily experiences" (Luke, 2020, p. 48).

SAM and HPA

Two networks that are part of the autonomic nervous system make up the core of the neurobiology of trauma in children and adolescents, and have significant implications for clinical practice. The sympathetic–adrenal–medullary (SAM) axis is a stress network that drives the initiation of the sympathetic nervous system's stress response as previously described. Jones, Rybak, and Russell-Chapin (2017) summarize it best: "the hypothalamus sends messages down to the adrenal glands . . . to release epinephrine and norepinephrine" (p. 66). This leads to sympathetic system slowing non-essential system functioning (like digestion) and redirects resources (blood, oxygen, glucose) to systems essential for self-protective functions, like fight/flight/freeze responses. Life-threatening situations – real or perceived – require some action, even if that action is stillness, not contemplative responding. For this reason, instinct and reflex take over rational problem-solving.

The second step in responding involves the hypothalamic–pituitary–adrenal (HPA) axis. Jones et al. (2017) again puts it most clearly:

> [HPA] is the functional connection between three endocrine glands. The hypothalamus releases corticotropin-releasing hormone to the pituitary gland. This hormone stimulates the pituitary gland to release adrenocorticotropic hormone (ACTH). ACTH then travels down to the adrenal glands, which sit on top of the kidneys. The ACTH activates the adrenal cortex . . . to release glucocorticoids, in particular cortisol. The function of cortisol is to help restore homeostasis after stress, and is essential to life.
>
> (pp. 13–14)

But as we know, if the trauma or stressor does not abate or if the individual is incapable of tolerating or resolving the stressor, cortisol stays in the limbic region for too long. This can result in decreases in hippocampal volume, leading to disrupted memory function. Readers are directed to the practical discussion of this process in greater detail in Jones, Rybak, and Russell-Chapin (2017).

To express the process succinctly, we present the description proffered by Luke, Redekop, and Jones (2018) and paraphrased by Luke (2020):

> The HPA axis is comprised of the hypothalamus, pituitary gland, and adrenal glands. The hypothalamus is the midbrain/hindbrain border structure that controls a host of involuntary life functions, such as digestion, sleep, temperature, and perhaps most notably, "emergency responses to stressors in the environment" (Saper & Lowell, 2014, p. R1111). This means that, initiated by the role of the amygdala in threat detection (perception), the hypothalamus plays a key role in threat response through its influence on the pituitary gland (Garrett & Hough, 2018). The pituitary gland controls hormone production and release. In times of stress in particular, the pituitary gland triggers the production and secretion of adrenocorticotropic hormone and serves as the primary chemical conduit between the pituitary and the cortex (outer portion) of the adrenal glands. The adrenal cortex releases cortisol, which functions as a glucocorticoid. As such, cortisol speeds up metabolic processes related to sugar (and proteins) to provide fuel for the body to perform at peak exertion during high-stress periods and increase mental acuity, at least for short durations (LeDoux, 2012). This is also the system that releases the endogenous opioids. The SAM system engages the SNS, which triggers the interior of the adrenal glands (adrenal medulla) to release noradrenaline (norepinephrine) and adrenaline (epinephrine). Norepinephrine functions as both a hormone and a neurotransmitter, especially in response to stress, by activating attention and arousal related to the environment. Enoch (2011) identified the role of early stress-filled environments as hampering the development of stress resilience in the brains of children. This increased developmental vulnerability appears also to translate into susceptibility to addiction (Enoch, 2011).
>
> (pp. 225–226)

The critical matter for clinicians working with children and adolescents is what happens in the brain prior to trauma and stress. The larger – and quickly expanding – body of neurobiological research on both humans and non-human animals demonstrates the importance of genetic, relational, and environmental factors on the developing brain (Kindsvatter & Geroski, 2014). These early relational contexts are vital to the development of the SAM and HPA axes, and promote the resilience of the individual.

In addition to these early contexts, there are the physiological dynamics of the transition from childhood to adolescence. For example:

> There is also considerable evidence that pubertal development is a significant sensitive period in the development and functioning of the SAM and HPA (including cortisol and increased sensitivity) – making one more vulnerable to stress; so it's not just early life stress – it is definitely that – and adolescence is a period of stress sensitivity (Doom & Gunnar, 2013; Wadsworth et al., 2019). One of the interesting things about this is up until puberty we do not see any sex specific functioning in autonomic response to stress but following puberty we do. This may underlie some of the sex-differences in development of mood disorders. All of this also intersects with the development and sexual differentiation of the gut microbiome, including gonadal hormones and the associated increase in allied hormones likely lead to this differentiation as well, which then has an impact on stress responsivity, development of posttraumatic struggles, etc. (van den Bos, De Rooij, Miers, Bokhorst, & Westenberg, 2014).
>
> (Laura K. Jones, personal communication)

The Case of Jemma

Jemma is a 13-year-old female, referred by the school for verbal aggression with peers and a decline in academic performance. We examine her case through the lens of the eight-factor model and its neural correlates to better understand how trauma affects the development brain. Through the biopsychosocial intake process, we learn that Jemma was reared by her mother and hnas never know her father. Her mother had a series of live-in boyfriends from the time Jemma was 2 years old, most of whom were physically, verbally, and emotionally violent toward her mother. Two of these boyfriends had been arrested for domestic violence, when she was 4 and again when she was 10. Jemma and her mother both assert that Jemma was never physically hurt by these men. Currently, Jemma lives with her mother and two younger siblings. Her mother states that as a single mother, she has severely restricted financial resources and that Jemma is often left at home to care for her siblings while her mother works two jobs. To understand Jemma's experience better, we present eight dimensions of stress in Table 8.1.

Table 8.1 Eight Dimensions of Stress Applied to Child/Adolescent

Dimension	Description	Neuro-Correlate	Example
Relationships	Relationships – early and current – are vital to inoculating clients against the deleterious effects of stressors and what could be traumatic events; they also form the basis of resilience when stressors and or traumas occur	Relational problems early on inhibit the development of resilience through the strengthening of the stress response systems in the brain and CNS, leading to vulnerabilities to stress and trauma responses later on	Without blaming her mother or father or taking away responsibility for her choices today, counseling may focus on restorative relationships, beginning with the counselor

Dimension	Description	Neuro-Correlate	Example
Thoughts	Perception of stressor (e.g., self-talk) often determines the extent to which a stressor is experienced as stress, distress, etc.; perseveration; disrupted concentration and focus; memory problems; potential for dissociation in extreme cases	Metabolic rate in hippocampus shifts, resulting in short-term focus and disabling long-term memory temporarily; dendrite death in the hippocampus as a result of long-term or intense stress	Jemma comes to counseling focused with negative self-talk, filtering out instances of successes; because of her stage of development, and her prolonged exposure to violence, rather than helping her dispute her negative thoughts, counseling may include short-term memory training and general cognitive skills development
Feelings	Range from mild discomfort to extreme emotional dysregulation, from mild anxiety to vivid re-experiencing of an event	Harmony between left and right hemispheres, and among top-, mid-, and hindbrain, is essential for keeping the individual as regulated as possible during times of stress	Jemma has had to adapt to her early environment by living out of more primal parts of her brain (reptilian) in order to cope, so counseling may need to address her ability to attend to her body, breathing, and heart rate in order to evaluate situations differently
Behaviors	Avoidance is a hallmark of stress-based behavioral responses: avoidance of feelings associated with stress, avoidance of circumstances related to specific stressors or events	Overactive amygdala sounds alarm when in perceived proximity to reminders of stressors or events (tied to memory creation and recall in the hippocampus), bypasses higher order cognitive processes	Jemma's brain has patterned her response to problems as avoidance, so movement away is as natural to her as breathing, making avoidance automatic, almost functionally autonomic, if not technically so. While counterintuitive at first, Jemma's verbal and physical responses may be about avoidance of more primary emotions like fear and helplessness leading to acting outwardly
Environment (Past and Present)	Exposure to a stressor(s) (e.g., death, serious injury, sexual violation, domestic violence)	The pre-stress environment shapes the patterns of cognitive, affective, and behavioral responses, which then influence evaluation and interpretation of environmental stimuli	Jemma's previous environment has primed her to react to current environmental triggers, many of which are outside of her awareness, so rather than focusing on coping skills for triggers, it is vital to first identify the variety of triggers that she may not be aware of; this is done in part through breath and body awareness
Experiences	Emotional, physical, social, economic, and other factors or events are primarily external to the individual – they exist objectively and independently from the individual	The interpretation and attribution of personal meaning, causes, and likelihood of recurrence are embodied internally through neural narrative, imposing meaning and value on otherwise external events	Jemma's current experiences with parentification and financial hardship leave little time or opportunity for her brain and body to respond to developmental critical periods, instead forestalling these steps by supporting her need (imposed by previous experiences and current environment)

(Continued)

Table 8.1 (Continued)

Dimension	Description	Neuro-Correlate	Example
Biology/ Genetics	Environmental events can trigger gene expression; anxiety/stress disorders are more prevalent in women; sufferers are likely to have genetic vulnerability to overactive amygdala	Genes are not deterministic: genes, even if present, may never be expressed (turned to the "on" position), and even when in the "on" position, they can be canceled out by other "on" genes	Jemma certainly experiences stress bodily, which she then reinforces by interpreting those bodily experiences as signs of stress, thereby exacerbating her stress; she may also have had a genetic predisposition to certain emotional responses that were activated through both her experience and her behavior (i.e., experience- and activity-dependent plasticity)
Socio-cultural milieu	Both shared and unique markers for unity and distinction: race, ethnicity, gender, family rules, ability, size, etc.; it also is somewhat universal – see *DSM5* examples of cultural distress (American Psychiatric Association, pp. 833–837): Ataque de nervios, Dhat syndrome, Khyal cap, Kufungisisa, Maladi moun, Nervios, Shenjing shuairuo, Susto, Taijin kyofusho	Stress is relational, and certain social systems have their own rules for/ways of experiencing and then dealing with stress	Jemma's avoidance of stress is a learned behavior from her environment in terms of her relationships in her family – in this case the most salient, relevant cultural milieu for her presenting problem

Source: Adapted from Luke, 2020

Axioms From Neurobiology for Working With Children and Trauma

With the previous material in mind, we offer five axioms for the neurobiology of childhood trauma.

1. Children's Brains Are Highly Malleable

During development in utero and in the first 24 months following birth, neurogenesis proliferates, adding neurons and making synaptic connections rapidly. This proliferation allows for building the systems and supporting structures that enable the infant to survive and thrive. During this time, circuits or networks are strengthened or pruned away, based on the perceived need of separate systems. It is useful to think of this in terms of Erikson's psychosocial stages of development (1968). During the first 18 months, the crisis of trust versus mistrust means that the infant's brain is learning – learning whether her cries will be heard and attended to, or not. If this crisis is resolved through caregiver responsiveness then the brain's genetic preprogramming will continue to develop according to a "normal" trajectory, moving toward the next developmental crisis. If, however, the cries of the infant are ignored or met with hostility, the brain's development follows an alternate trajectory, one wherein the needs of the individual are not met, and must be met some other way. If this occurs too early in life and too severely, the infant may simply die as a form of adaptation. In the majority of cases, the infant's brain begins to organize around this reality that needs are not met by the environment. Connection circuits are pruned, in favor of resources and organization being directed toward reptilian-level survival circuits.

In neuroscience, this process is referred to as metaplasticity (Sweatt, 2016). Hebb (1949) first described neurons that fire together, wire together, as the process of neural connections strengthens as a result of paired activity, leading to more efficiency in repeating a thought or behavior. This is also known at the "use it or lose it" principle of neuroplasticity, that just as synapses are strengthened through paired activation, unused pairings can get pruned back, making adaptation more difficult.

2. Critical Periods of Development for Growth and Harm

As alluded to previously, and presaged by Erikson (1968), development occurs during critical periods that allow for optimal development. Because the stages build on one another, earlier stages of development are even more critical. This means that disruption at earlier development (e.g., trust/mistrust; autonomy/shame) have more detrimental effects with ramifications for later development. This is why pre-, post-, and peri-natal care are so crucial in the life of an infant. The synaptic growth and pruning are designed to increase efficiency of development, so circuits deemed less necessary are provided fewer resources or are pruned away altogether. In the life of an infant, if crying does not yield results (food, nurturance) or if it elicits harm (yelling, hitting) then the brain reorganizes itself around this "reality". Once the "mistrust circuits" are formed, subsequent organization is similarly, negatively affected.

When considering stages of development, it may be useful to consider the tasks associated with the steps as risers. On a set of stairs, the part your feet touches are called treads, while the part that gives the stairs its gradual elevation is called the riser. The tasks of stages involve persistence moving upward and resilience in the presence of setbacks; this is development. But it is also imperative to understand the vulnerability that is realized as one leaves one tread and steps up to the next. Any number of things can happen in that transition, leading one to stumble, and for anyone who has taken a tumble down brick or concrete steps, it makes one rethink trying it again. In working with children and adolescents from a neuro-informed perspective, and those who have experienced trauma in particular, it is not safe to assume that they are able, let alone want to ascend the next step. And a physical step takes but an instant, whereas psychosocial development takes place over years, and involves a series of trial and error attempts at conquering these steps or stages.

Let's make this a little more concrete by paralleling post-or peri-trauma development through a loose but illustrative example from our non-but-almost-human companions, dogs. If you have ever tried to assist in a puppy in climbing stairs – to use our recent analogy – you may have noted two types of approaches to, in this example, climbing down stairs: the first type is the helpless resignation of lying down at the top of the stairs, whimpering, and generally looking sad and helpless (this is no doubt a personified projection of the human experience). The pup in this case may wait to be picked up, nudged, or lie there whimpering – which is kind of heartrending to watch. The second type of "coping" with stairs is sort of a reckless diving down the stairs, either because of unintended momentum, or desperation to get down the stairs. This often results in a crash along the way with a pile of puppy parts at the bottom of the stairs. This is equally difficult to watch.

This is analogous to the child or adolescent brain with trauma: the reducing of challenging tasks (within developmental stages) to helpless withdrawal or desperate hurling into danger. This trauma-based response dichotomy presents itself – in humans – in a variety of ways that can be challenging to identify and even more challenging to treat. To return to our puppy-on-stairs analogy: there are times when no amount of coaxing, reassuring, or threatening can move them from that fear-based place, and equally, no amount of yelling, rationalizing, or warning can stop them from launching themselves into inevitable pain and potential injury just to get it over with. Many authors, most notably van der Kolk (2014) and Siegel (2015), have noted that when the brain experiences and seeks to recover from trauma, there is decreased capacity for spontaneity, creativity, and connection, and instead the individual becomes rigid in responding. Unfortunately, the client's family system may continue to engage with them as if their brain remains unchanged. Counseling, therefore, can be a place that is safe and welcoming to non-verbal, expressive engagement.

3. Child Brain Development Is Dependent on and Occurs in the Context of Relationship

Many authors have heralded the reality of brain development as a relational act. In other words, studies of the brain, and in particular brain development, which do not take into account the brain's function in relationship to another, miss a great deal of understanding. Specifically, the infant and child brain patterns its development via the modeling and even the relational resonance with the primary caregiver (henceforth, "mother"). This means that the brain of an infant/child develops according to the observations it makes of the mother. Seigel describes the process in terms of the mother loaning her prefrontal cortex (regulation and decision-making center) to the infant whose not-yet-fully-developed prefrontal is dependent upon this modeling in order to develop itself. This is a primary reason that self-help, while useful to a certain extent, is inadequate to replace the relationship context that therapy brings. This relationship with the mother provides the neurophysiological structure that underlies the infant/child's ability to manage stress and to navigate through the world. Without this regulated "other" to learn from, the infant/child's brain is unable to imprint and to lay down the neural template for growth and development.

4. The Human Brain Is Designed to Be Resilient: Beware Projective Sympathy

Projective sympathy is the process whereby we imagine how we would feel if what happened to another person happened to us. We then assume that those feelings we think we would have are also what the other person feels or experiences. Finally, we treat them according these projections, as if what we think we would need is what the other person needs. This is tied to the neuroscience concept of mirror neurons. While purported in early papers to be the neural underpinnings of empathy, mirror neurons tell only part of the story. For example, when person A observes person B scratching their nose, person A's mirror neurons – actually motor neurons – become active (i.e., "fire") in the same way as if person A had scratched their own nose. But there is a key difference: despite the same type of neural activity associated with movements around nose scratching, person A is still unaware of the actual mental state of person B as they scratch their nose. Person A can intuit, assume, or infer, but the individual experience of person B is inaccessible to person A. This is an overly simplified explanation of a basic human behavior: nose scratching. In most cases, person A can assume with relative certainty that person B is scratching their nose because it itches, just as seeing someone fall or being scared can lead to fairly reasonable assumptions about their experience. The picture changes as the observed behaviors become more ambiguous, outside of the observer's experience, and the context less clear. In children and adolescents, and the transition to adolescents in particular, sensitivity to social situations and certainly social evaluation can be more pronounced. These individuals experience a sensitive period of development wherein they are indeed resilient, but also vulnerable to the vicissitudes of their reorganization of their SAM and HPA (van den Bos et al., 2014; Wadsworth et al., 2019).

5. Trauma Is Often Verbally and Chronologically Unstable

Time and time sequencing are important factors in most therapeutic approaches. For example, psychoanalytic approaches want to understand what happened in the past, existential-humanistic approaches want to understand what is happening in the present, cognitive-behavioral approaches want to understand antecedents and consequents, and solution-focused approaches want to understand the future. These are admittedly reductive, but you get the point. Time is also an important factor in trauma, in several ways. The first is that sequences in recall are often convoluted, so recounting traumatic events in order can be extremely difficult. In addition, clients often experience past trauma in the present, while simultaneously projecting trauma into the future. As discussed in what follows, childhood maltreatment can result in decreases in nerve fibers that connect regions within the temporal lobe with the frontal cortex, which are key in human language and communication (Teicher & Samson, 2016). In other words, early neglect and later verbal abuse can limit the neural structures that give individuals the ability to put their experience into words. This has a number of implications for talk therapy with neglected and abused children and adolescents.

Neurobiology of ACEs

Several features of adverse childhood experiences (ACEs) appear to affect neurobiology: time (chronicity), timing (age and stage of individual), type, and intensity (Kirlic, Cohen, & Singh, 2020). For example, sexual abuse (high intensity) of a 3–5-year-old child (timing) that occurs once (chronicity) affects neurobiological development differently than does yelling and screaming (intense) at an 11–14-year-old (timing) that occurs regularly (chronicity) (Herzog & Schmahl, 2018). So, in general (intensity being equivalent), the younger the individual the more of an impact it has on development. For example, an 8-month-old, who may have no developed linguistic capabilities and who one would think may be more resilient because they cannot cognitively understand what is going on, actually can be impacted more than an older child in the same situation (Laura K. Jones, personal communication). Briefly, ACEs, depending on these factors, affect brain development via the amygdala, hippocampus, insula, and anterior cingulate cortex. Studies demonstrate that during an adverse childhood experience, the amygdala might increase in volume – a sign of hyperactivation – but in the time following the experience, may shrink in volume below its original density, an indication of hypoactivation. This would indicate a reduced ability to discern salient stimuli in the environment. In other words, there is increased potential for false positives and false negatives in perceived salient (i.e., threatening) stimuli in the individual's environment. So, during an adverse event, hyperactivation of the amygdala increases fight/flight/freeze responses, inhibiting the ability to make decisions and pursue purposeful action. As the volume of the amygdala shrinks in the aftermath of the adverse experience, the ability for meaningful connection and contact in relationships is diminished due to the inability to judge stimuli as salient (threatening) or not.

Teicher and Samson (2016) make a compelling case from neurobiology which serves as a complementary counterpoint to the "ACEs lead to brain damage" perspective that pervades the literature. They suggest that the brain is designed to adapt to adversity, or else survival in a threatening world would not be possible, and that the brains of children growing up in adverse environments develop along a different trajectory that promotes survival but may violate social norms or conditions. This argument, which is best understood in the context of the prevailing view of the deleterious effects of ACEs on children and adults and extending into adulthood, makes intuitive sense. In fact, psychopathology itself is based more on normative (average) responses, meaning that adaptation in one context (e.g., home environment) is tantamount to maladaptation in another (e.g., school, work, society in general).

There is also a sense that the critical periods of ACEs may also carry delayed onset of symptoms. Counselors and mental health providers may readily recount cases of later adolescent and adult clients who describe ACEs but neither were treated for those nor recognize the connection between those earlier ACEs and their current distress or maladaptive behaviors. Fortunately, the neuroplastic properties of the human brain allow for growth and recovery, making children and adolescents highly resilient. Understanding the interplay between the adverse and resiliency factors can not only instill hope but also explain why some youth may have more severe outcomes than others, given the same timing and severity (Laura K. Jones, personal communication).

Multicultural Implications and Advocacy

We know from much of the information presented in this text so far that it is imperative for counselors to consider culture in all they do. In terms of trauma, specifically ACEs, counselors must be aware that children and adolescents of culturally diverse backgrounds experience ACEs at a greater rate than that of white children. Specifically, in the United States, 61% of Black children and 51% of Latinx children, as opposed to 40% of white children, have experienced at least one adverse childhood experience (Jamieson, 2018). Further, when noting the impact of trauma, especially for African Americans, Native Americans, and other cultures, we must seek to understand historical trauma as a major component deeply impacting whole communities of individuals (SAMHSA, n.d.). Historical trauma notes the cumulative, collective, and growing psychological and emotional impact of trauma that is passed down through generations and in communities (SAMHSA, n.d.). Counselors need to understand this as it plays a role in the lives of the children, adolescents, and parent/caregivers we serve (see McEwen, 2017 on "Neurobiological and Systemic Effects of Chronic Stress").

Summary

This chapter discussed the general structure, systems, and functions of the human brain as a whole unit. Counselors were given information to assist in differentiating stress from trauma and to understand how it applies to children and adolescents in counseling. We explained and discussed application of the eight-factor model of human phenomena to stress and trauma and identified five neuroscience axioms for working with trauma in children and adolescents. We discussed the importance of counselors becoming familiar with ACEs and noted multicultural implications for this, as well.

Clinician's Corner

In my work, as both a clinician and supervisor, with survivors of interpersonal violence, I have witnessed the impact of trauma on adults and adolescents alike. I also have seen the remarkable and inspirational resilience of both populations. One adolescent will always stand out to me in this regard. The 11-year-old had just escaped a domestic violence situation with their mother and sibling. Having been witness and victim to that violence from a young age, the client had experienced numerous adverse childhood experiences. Furthermore, given the fear of partner retaliation, the family was in hiding, which included homeschooling. As such, the young client had no social interaction outside of their newly modified family unit and family pets. This client reportedly had begun experiencing escalating difficulty with self-regulation, which had led to unintentional self-injury, yet appeared to be of above average intelligence for their age.

Several physiological considerations immediately became salient to me in this case. First, the early and ongoing life adversity this child faced may have impacted their physiological development in such a way as to make self-regulation, a proxy to autonomic regulation, and stress tolerance more challenging. Second, given the age of the client, 11 years, gonadal development also had likely recently commenced, such that emotion regulation may have been further complicated. As such, some of what the client was experiencing may have been developmental in nature and not solely a result of the early life trauma. The client also possessed several resiliency factors and strengths, including a very caring and close relationship with both their mother and sibling, and their notable empathy for others, individuals, and pets, as well as their own marked intelligence and desire to seek out knowledge and understanding. All of these factors are important in conceptualizing the intrapersonal, interpersonal, situational, and systemic contexts of the individual.

However, what was especially striking about this individual and case was the client's use of verbal metaphor in understanding and processing their traumatic experiences. It is not uncommon for metaphorical approaches, particularly non-verbal, to be used in trauma work with children and adolescents (e.g., play therapy, bibliotherapy, etc.). This approach allows children and adolescents a way of expressing the at times inexpressible (physiologically and figuratively) events they have experienced and titrating the exposure in a manner in which they physiologically still feel safe (i.e., they still have the ability to regulate their autonomic nervous system during expression). Although some equate it to narrative work in adults, it is not quite equivalent, as telling the direct story of the trauma is often significantly more physiologically arousing and difficult, even for adults. However, young adolescents at 11 years of age at times still have difficulty, developmentally, understanding and using abstract verbal metaphors. Nevertheless, this client created abstract and intricate verbal metaphors in understanding their experiences and building a sense of agency in relation to those. Their stories related to themes of their ability to protect others and self, forgiveness, resilience, and love. The client was expressing their experiences through stories both outside and inside of the counseling space. Furthermore, they found mastery in their environment by becoming a seeming expert in certain advanced content areas. Had any of these stories or experiences been interpreted concretely, which they could have been given their realistic nature, a therapeutic opportunity could have easily been missed. Furthermore, having rushed the client to express their story directly may have only exacerbated their difficulty with self (autonomic)-regulation by creating further stress in their intrapersonal environment. Self-regulation skills could have been taught, and yet, this client was already employing their own, and those need to be honored. As such, in allowing for the client to stay with those stories and using those extended metaphors as a part of therapy and in the home environment, the client was able to maintain self-regulation and concurrently have a space in which they were able to interpersonally process their experiences. This case was a remarkable illustration of one way adolescents, an oft-overlooked population, not only can respond and work through traumatic events, but also how their natural abilities (i.e., strengths) serve as points of resiliency that are essential to recognize within counseling. It also illustrated the importance, when working with adolescent trauma survivors, of considering both developmental and trauma-related origins of symptomatology. This was an incredible young person, and it was an honor to bear witness to what pieces of their story they were willing to share.

Laura K. Jones, PhD, MS, NCC, ACS
University of North Carolina at Asheville

References

American Psychiatric Association. (2013). *DSM5 diagnostic and statistical manual of mental disorders*. APA.

Doom, J. R., & Gunnar, M. R. (2013). Stress physiology and developmental psychopathology: Past, present, and future. *Development and psychopathology*, 25(4pt2), 1359–1373.

Enoch, M. A. (2011). The role of early life stress as a predictor for alcohol and drug dependence. *Psychopharmacology*, 214(1), 17–31. https://doi.org/10.1007/s00213-010-19166

Erikson, E. H. (1968). *Identity: Youth and crisis*. W.W. Norton & Company.

Field, T. A., Jones, L. K., & Russell-Chapin, L. A. (2017). *Neurocounseling: Brain-based clinical approaches*. American Counseling Association.

Garrett, B., & Hough, G. (2018). *Brain and behavior: An introduction to biological psychology* (5th ed.). Thousand Oaks, CA: Sage.

Hebb, D. O. (1949). *The organization of behavior: A neuropsychological theory*. Wiley.

Herzog, J. I., & Schmahl, C. (2018). Adverse childhood experiences and the consequences on neurobiological, psychosocial, and somatic conditions across the lifespan. *Frontiers in Psychiatry*, 9, 420–420.

Jamieson, K. (2018). *ACEs and minorities*. Center for Child Counseling. Retrieved from www.centerforchildcounseling.org/aces-and-minorities/

Jones, L. K., Rybak, C., & Russell-Chapin, L. A. (2017). Neurophysiology of traumatic stress. In T. A. Field, L. K. Jones, & L. A. Russell-Chapin (Eds.), *Neurocounseling: Brain-based clinical approaches* (pp. 61–80). American Counseling Association.

Kindsvatter, A., & Geroski, A. (2014). The impact of early life stress on the neurodevelopment of the stress response system. *Journal of Counseling and Development*, 92(4), 472–480.

Kirlic, N., Cohen, Z. P., & Singh, M. K. (2020). Is there an ACE up our sleeve? A review of interventions and strategies for addressing behavioral and neurobiological effects of adverse childhood experiences in youth. *Adversity and Resilience Science*, 1, 5–24. https://doi.org/10.1007/s42844-020-00001-x

LeDoux, J. (2012). Rethinking the emotional brain. *Neuron*, 73(4), 653–676. https://doi.org/10.1016/j.neuron.2012.02.004

Luke, C. (2020). *Neuroscience for counselors and therapists: Integrating the sciences of the mind and brain*. Cognella.

Luke, C., Redekop, F., & Jones, L. K. (2018). Addiction, stress, and relational disorder: A neuro-informed approach to intervention. *Journal of Mental Health Counseling*, 40(2), 172–186. https://doi.org/10.17744/mehc.40.2.06

MacLean, P. D. (1990). *The triune brain in evolution: Role of paleocerebral functions*. Plenum.

McEwen, B. S. (2017). Neurobiological and systemic effects of Chronic Stress. *Chronic Stress*, 1, 1–11. https://doi.org/10.1177/2470547017692328

Purves, D., Augustine, G. J., Fitzpatrick, D., Hall, W. C., LaMantia, A. S., Mooney, R. D., . . . White, L. (2018). *Neuroscience*. Sinauer Associates.

SAMHSA. (n.d.). *Trauma: SAMHSA-HRSA center for integrated health solution*. Retrieved from www.integration.samhsa.gov/clinical-practice/trauma-informed

Saper, C. B., & Lowell, B. B. (2014). The hypothalamus. *Current Biology, 24*, R1111–R1116. https://doi.org/10.1016/j.cub.2014.10.023

Siegel, D. J. (2012). *Pocket guide to interpersonal neurobiology: An integrative handbook of the mind*. WW Norton & Company.

Siegel, D. J. (2015). *The developing mind: How relationships and the brain interact to shape who we are*. Guilford Publications.

Sweatt, J. D. (2016). Neural plasticity and behavior – Sixty years of conceptual advances. *Journal of Neurochemistry, 139*, 179–199. https://doi.org/10.1111/jnc.13580

Teicher, M. H., & Samson, J. A. (2016). Annual research review: Enduring neurobiological effects of childhood abuse and neglect. *Journal of Child Psychology and Psychiatry, 57*(3), 241–266. https://doi.org/10.1111/jcpp.12507

van den Bos, E., De Rooij, M., Miers, A. C., Bokhorst, C. L., & Westenberg, P. M. (2014). Adolescents' increasing stress response to social evaluation: Pubertal effects on cortisol and alpha-amylase during public speaking. *Child Development, 85*(1), 220–236.

van der Kolk, B. A. (2014). *The body keeps the score: Brain, mind and body in the healing of trauma*. New York: Viking.

Wadsworth, M. E., Broderick, A. V., Loughlin-Presnal, J. E., Bendezu, J. J., Joos, C. M., Ahlkvist, J. A., . . . McDonald, A. (2019). Co-activation of SAM and HPA responses to acute stress: A review of the literature and test of differential associations with preadolescents' internalizing and externalizing. *Developmental Psychobiology, 61*(3).

9 At-Promise Children and Adolescents

*Charmayne Adams, Jillian Blueford,
Chad Luke, and Rebekah Byrd*

Charmayne Adams and Jillian Blueford
as guest contributors

Objectives

- Recognize the ways in which a child's or adolescent's referral behavior may be reflective of disruptions in the family system.
- For each form of disruption, identify resources and resilience for use in counseling.
- Define child maltreatment and its many facets.
- Identify the ways maltreatment affects clients and ways to address it in counseling.
- Describe the effects of divorce on children and adolescents.
- Identify the complications associated with parental/caregiver substance misuse.
- Recognize the strengths and needs of children and adolescents displaced from their homes and into foster care/adoption scenarios.
- Address the risk and protective factors in working with children and adolescents with incarcerated parents/caregivers.

Reflective Questions

- What is my understanding of the "identified client" in the context of working with children and adolescents from disrupted family systems?
- How would I approach viewing clients as at-promise and not just at-risk? How would this affect my counseling?
- What are my own biases about who gets abused or neglected and who does not?
- To what extent has the prevalence of divorce in modern society blunted my appreciation for how difficult it is for children and adolescents?
- What have been my experiences with substance misuse and how might that affect my ability to assess and treat clients?
- What are my opinions about the role of foster care in supporting the well-being of children?
- Do I have un-reflected biases toward children and adolescents whose parents are or have been incarcerated?

You may have noted that this chapter is entitled "At-Promise" rather than "At-Risk". Children and adolescents face a variety of challenges growing up, many that exist outside of themselves, that indeed pose risks to their well-being. But this ignores the innate strengths that hold the promise of resilience despite these risks. Many of our younger clients will present to counseling due to disruptions in their family system, even if the referral behavior seems focused on them alone. This chapter addresses specific challenges that may lead to children or adolescents seeking services from a community mental health or school counselor. It examines a variety of family system disruptions including child maltreatment, children and adolescents impacted by divorce, children and adolescents of parents with substance use issues, children and adolescents in adoptive and foster families, and children and adolescents with incarcerated parents/caregivers (grief is addressed in a separate chapter). Each section provides foundational knowledge on the topic, risk and protective factors for children and families, and intervention suggestions, while working with children and adolescents impacted by these specific circumstances.

Child Maltreatment

Counselors working with children and families have the responsibility and legal obligation to understand and report child maltreatment. Depending on your setting, this can present various challenges. Examples of the questions that arise from these challenges include the following. What do we do when we have a parent or child vaguely mention the use of physical discipline in the household? How do we keep children and families engaged in treatment as we collect information that we know we will be reporting to child protective services? What does it look like to foster a relationship based on collaborative strengths with a parent who you will be reporting to the department of child services? How do we keep children safe when we have reported an allegation, but we know that at the end of the school day, they will be going home to the same situation? What does it look like to maintain the therapeutic relationship with a child or adolescent who may be losing their primary caretaker due to your report? The answers to all of these questions begin with an understanding of what child maltreatment is, and how it impacts the children and adolescents we are working with.

Defining Maltreatment

Each state defines child maltreatment in a different way and requires professionals, including professional counselors in schools and agencies, to be familiar with these definitions and report any known or suspected abuse. The federal government in the Federal Child Abuse Prevention and Treatment Act [CAPTA] (1974/2010) provides the minimum standards for child maltreatment. These behaviors include:

- Any act or failure to act which presents an imminent risk of serious harm
- Any recent act or failure to act on the part of a parent or caregiver which results in death, serious physical or emotional harm, sexual abuse or exploitation

It is a counselor's responsibility to understand the reporting laws and definitions of child maltreatment in their specific state.

In the United States, the National Child Abuse and Neglect Data System (NCANDS) is a federally sponsored program that collects and analyzes data on child maltreatment, specially abuse and neglect. NCANDS receives data from state-level child protective services (CPS) agencies on all cases in which the agency has an investigative or alternative response. All 50 states, the Commonwealth of Puerto Rico, and the District of Columbia voluntarily submit the CPS cases that are screened and deemed substantial enough to need a report and intervention. They refer to these cases as "screened-in". Among those states, 46 also report all referrals that were "screened-out", which means that there was a response to the referral but no report was made and often no investigation was deemed necessary (USDHHS, 2020).

In data from 2018 and published in 2020, which is the latest NCANDS Child Maltreatment Report at the time of writing, CPS received an estimated 4.3 million referrals alleging maltreatment involving approximately 7.8 million children. Of those 4.3 million referrals, 2.4 million were evaluated and a report was created (USDHHS, 2020). Of the 46 states that reported data on both screened-in and screened-out referrals, 56% of referrals were screened-in and 44% of referrals were screened-out. The estimated national rate of how many referrals end in a report being made is 32.5 for every 1,000 children in the national population. Professionals reported almost 70% of the allegations of child abuse or neglect in 2018. The majority of these allegations (21%) were reported by educational personnel which included teachers, school counselors, and school administrators. Social service personnel, which included mental health counselors, were responsible for reporting approximately 11% of the allegations (USDHHS, 2020). These percentages make sense when you take into account that children spend the majority of their time in school and may only be seeing their outpatient counselor for an hour or so each week. They also further drive home the importance of both school and clinical mental health counselors being adequately trained in identifying and addressing child maltreatment.

Types of Child and Adolescent Maltreatment

Understanding what types of behavior fall under the umbrella of child maltreatment is the first step in being able to implement preventative interventions or report suspected/known cases to law enforcement or child protective services. The NCANDS report (USDHHS, 2020) describes four distinct types of maltreatment: neglect, physical abuse, psychological maltreatment, and sexual abuse.

Neglect is a type of maltreatment that refers to the failure by the caregiver to provide needed, age-appropriate care although financially able to do so or offered financial or other means to do so. An example of neglect is withholding food, shelter, clothing, or other essentials from children as a form of punishment. There are two subset types of neglect: (a) *medical neglect*; and (b) *educational neglect*. Medical neglect is caused by a failure of the caregiver to provide for appropriate healthcare of the child although financially able to do so or offered financial or other resources to do so. An example of this may be a caregiver withholding insulin from their child as punishment for a poor grade. *Educational neglect* is not included in the NCANDS report (USDHHS, 2020), but is included in the definition of neglect in some states. States including Connecticut, Illinois, and Utah have laws stating that this form of neglect includes caregivers allowing excessive and chronic truancy, withholding children from attending school or refusing to allow children to attend school, purposefully failing to attend to children's special education needs, or refusing to ensure appropriate education after being provided with a notice of violating one of the state educational acts (Child Welfare Information Gateway, 2019).

Physical abuse refers to physical acts such as hitting, pushing, or kicking that cause or could have caused physical injury to a child (USDHHS, 2020). Some states include the language that the act must be "non-accidental". In most states (42), "the definition of abuse includes acts or circumstances that threaten the child with harm or create a substantial risk of harm to the child's health or welfare". In some states, this definition also includes human trafficking for the purposes of "labor trafficking, involuntary servitude" in their definitions (Child Welfare Information Gateway, 2019).

Psychological maltreatment, sometimes referred to as emotional abuse, is any act or omission that would not be considered physical or sexual abuse that causes or could have caused conduct, cognitive, emotional, behavioral, or mental disorders. This often includes verbal abuse or excessive demands on a child's performance and can be evidenced by emotional distress such as depression, anxiety, aggression, and/or isolation (Child Welfare Information Gateway, 2019; USDHHS, 2020).

Every state includes a definition for *sexual abuse* in its child maltreatment definitions. *Sexual abuse* is any act that involves children in sexual activity to provide sexual gratification or financial benefit to the perpetrator. This can include molestation, rape, pornography, incest, or any other exploitative sexual activities. Thirty-three states include a definition for sexual trafficking in their definition for child maltreat, and states have the option to report any sex trafficking victim under the age of 24 to the NCANDS to be tracked separately from sexual abuse. *Sexual trafficking* includes children who are recruited, harbored, transported, or engaged in prostitution, marriage, and involuntary servitude for sexual gratification (TVPA, 2000).

Who Is Most at Risk?

The youngest children are the most vulnerable to maltreatment, with over 15.3% of the victims reported under 1 year old. That is almost double the rate per 1,000 children who are more than 1 year old (USDHHS, 2020). This statistic is especially important for counselors working with families with newborn children, working with couples or families expecting a newborn child, or working with children who recently had a new child born into their family. The implications for treatment include psychoeducation, wellness assessments, stress reduction interventions, and brainstorming plans for respite and overall mental health. Introducing a newborn baby into the family system can cause tremendous stress (in addition to tremendous joy!). Counselors have the skills to help families navigate this challenge. Additionally, with an understanding of the national statistics, professional counselors should understand the importance of assessing for the safety of this very vulnerable subset of children. Even though children under 1 year old are rarely our clients, it is our obligation to report any form of maltreatment we may hear from siblings, adults, and caretakers. We also should not underestimate the ripple effect that supporting our clients may have for the entire family system.

Who Are the Perpetrators?

Understanding who may be at risk to harm children helps professional counselors ask children and adolescents the right questions to assess if maltreatment is happening in the household. It also helps us better understand how to support families as a whole. We are able to build on strengths, provide psychoeducation, and implement preventative programming. Based on the USDHHS (2020):

- 40% of reported cases were perpetrated by the victim's mother
- 22% of reported cases were perpetrated by the victim's father
- 21% of reported cases were perpetrated by the victim's mother and father
- 7% of reported cases were perpetrated by the victim's mother and a nonparent
- 5% of reported cases were perpetrated by a relative of the victim
- 3% of reported cases were perpetrated by an unmarried partner of the child's parent
- 1% of reported cases were perpetrated by the victim's father and a nonparent
- 1% of reported cases were perpetrated by more than one nonparental perpetrator
- Less than 2% of reported cases were perpetrated by a daycare provider, foster parent, friend and neighbor, group home and residential staff, or other professional

These percentages are rounded up and based on information submitted from 51 U.S. states and territories. These statistics further reinforce information that professional counselors should already be familiar with: in the majority of maltreatment cases, the perpetrator is someone the child or adolescent already knows. Additionally, the child or adolescent is most likely related and living with the perpetrator.

Working With Children and Adolescents Who Are Survivors of Maltreatment

When counselors are working with children and adolescents who are survivors of maltreatment or are currently experiencing maltreatment, there are three primary areas for treatment: (a) the children's needs; (b) the families' needs; and (c) the parents' needs.

By attending to the entire family system, the child, and the parent, counselors can ensure that they are connecting everyone to the needed services. This may include individual counseling, family counseling, housing stability information, access to food stability programs such as food banks or federally funded programming, parent support groups, anger management, or child protective services. Counselors should be creative and flexible as they work to assess for safety and stabilization along with helping children, families, and parents plan for long-term wellness and recovery.

Child Advocacy Centers

Many communities have child advocacy centers (CACs) which can be a great resource and referral option for counselors working with children they suspect are being maltreated. CACs are centers dedicated to developmentally appropriate physical and mental health services for children. They often have specially trained multidisciplinary response teams that consist of forensic interviewers, law enforcement, nurses, doctors, social workers, and counselors. *Forensic interviewers* are sometimes requested by law enforcement or attorneys in cases of abuse. In CACs, forensic interviewers are used to reduce the chances of re-traumatization of children. They are trained professionals who conduct developmentally appropriate taped interviews, with one of the primary goals being to reduce the number of times a child needs to recount their story of abuse. These individuals know the correct questions to ask to get all of the information that police, attorneys, child protective services, or medical staff may need to make an informed decision. Medical examinations are also often requested in cases of physical or sexual maltreatment to document the physical impacts of the traumatic experience. Housing these services within the same organization reduces anxiety for children, allows for better tracking, and increases the ability for caregivers to access all of the services they may need to support a child who has been maltreated. Counselors should be aware of these organizations in their community and familiar with the services they offer. We are able to advocate for access to services for the children and families we work with when we are aware of the support services in our communities. Additional information about child advocacy centers can be found at the National Children's Advocacy Center website, www.nationalcac.org/.

Trauma-Informed Care

Trauma-informed care is the act of treating every child and adolescent that you work with as if they had a history of trauma. This is a holistic approach that begins the moment they contact you and extends through every aspect of treatment. The Substance Abuse and Mental Health Services Administration (SAMHSA) summarized the trauma-informed care approach as having four main components:

1. Understand the widespread impact of trauma and understand the potential treatment options for recovery

2. Recognize signs and symptoms associated with trauma responses in clients, families, colleagues, and staff members involved in the treatment system
3. Integrate knowledge of trauma response and the needs of trauma survivors into system policies, procedures, and clinical/administrative practice
4. Examine and amend any policy, procedures, or practices that may re-traumatize clients

(Substance Abuse and Mental Health Services Administration, 2014)

By understanding these components and integrating them into every aspect of their work, counselors can ensure that they are approaching every child and adolescent that they work with through a systematic framework that empowers and minimizes re-victimization.

Strengths-Based Strategies for Counselors

When working with children who have been maltreated, it is helpful to start by gaining an understanding of how the child or adolescent is making meaning out of the situation, and what they understand about the situation. Often children blame themselves for the maltreatment or may not even understand that the maltreatment was wrong. One of the primary treatment goals in strengths-based counseling for this population is providing education and reducing isolation. There are many books that can help a child untangle the complicated feelings they are having and provide the vocabulary to better understand the situation: *A Terrible Thing Happened* (Holmes, 2000); *Help Your Dragon Cope with Trauma* (Herman, 2019); and *Healing Days: A Guide for Kids Who Have Experienced Trauma* (Straus & Bogade, 2013). Counselors should focus on strengths, resilience, and resources rather than deficits, especially when working with children who have experienced maltreatment (Hunter, 2006).

Counseling Treatment Modalities

Trauma-Focused Cognitive Behavioral Therapy (TF-CBT) and Eye Movement Desensitization and Reprocessing (EMDR) are evidenced-based, trauma-specific treatments to help children recover from traumatic experiences (Karadag, Gokcen, & Sarp, 2019; Nixon, Sterk, & Pearce, 2012; Rudd et al., 2019). Randomized control trials, which are the gold standard in treatment efficacy research, show no effect size difference between these two treatment modalities, and a large effect size compared to wait-list control groups (de Arellano et al., 2014; Diehle, Opmeer, Boer, Mannarino, & Lindauer, 2015). Both of these treatment modalities require specific training to be able to implement them with children and adolescents.

Counselors can receive certification for TF-CBT through the Trauma-Focused Cognitive Behavioral Therapy National Therapist Certification Program (https://tfcbt.org/). The average number of sessions in TF-CBT is 12–20 and has been shown to be effective for children from 3–18 years old (there is also research to show its efficacy with adults). It is appropriate for children who have a known history of trauma and are experiencing post-traumatic stress symptoms as a result of the trauma exposure. This form of treatment is not appropriate for children with intellectual developmental disabilities. It is most effective when there is active caregiver participation. TF-CBT works in three phases: (1) stabilization; (2) trauma narrative phase; and (3) integration/consolidation phase. In addition to those three phases, throughout the entire treatment, exposure therapy and parent skills training are integrated. For counselors working with many children who have been exposed to maltreatment, this form of therapy is typically recommended as the first line of treatment for children and adolescents with post-traumatic stress disorder (PTSD) (Blankenship, 2017).

EMDR is a form of therapy that utilizes bilateral stimulation – clients moving their eyes side to side, alternating buzzers in the client's hands, knee tapping, alternating tones, or alternating hand claps – to aid in the reprocessing of a traumatic memory. Even though EMDR has been heavily researched and proven to be effective in reducing symptoms of post-traumatic stress (Karadag, Gokcen, & Sarp, 2019), there still is not a consensus on how the bilateral stimulation works (Logie, 2014). Like TF-CBT, EMDR trained therapists go through extensive training online and face-to-face. The EMDR Institute (www.emdr.com) manages the certification process. Additionally, there are the auxiliary trainings such as EMDR with sand tray, EMDR with pre-teens & adolescents, and EMDR with children. EMDR works in phases also: (1) history of the client and the distressing event; (2) teaching imagery and stress reduction techniques to use in session and between sessions; (3–6) identifying the target memory, processing the experience, and using bilateral simulation to reduce the emotional experience attached to the memory; (7) closure and documentation of distress outside of the counseling session; and (8) review of progress. EMDR therapy can be completed in conjunction with traditional talk therapy or in lieu of traditional talk therapy.

Multisystemic Therapy for Child Abuse and Neglect is not a trauma-specific treatment modality but builds off of traditional multisystemic therapy models. This treatment model is protocol-driven like TF-CBT and EMDR and should be delivered in the manner in which the protocol describes to ensure treatment efficacy (Henggeler, Schoenwald, Borduin, Rowland, & Cunningham, 2009). The sessions are generally conducted in the family's home, but can be done in the school or the community. Through this system, the counselor carries a maximum of four families on their caseload and the counselors work with the family around their schedule. The team working with the family is on-call 24 hours a day, seven days a week to help families work through any crisis that may arise. For the most part, treatment focuses on the adults in the family to help support them in managing situations and consistently using healthy coping strategies to manage conflict in the household (Rubin, 2012). Counselors are encouraged to always take a strengths-based perspective and default to the family as the expert. It is important to listen to the family members' past experiences and help them problem-solve and draw on the way problems were solved in the past to help build healthy relationships and communication patterns for the future. The interventions used by counselors rely on the strengths of the family and should be tailored to fit the needs of each family. For all families, the initial session consists of creating a safety plan to understand the risk associated with their specific family needs (Rubin, 2012). Training for this type of therapy is typically facilitated by a community mental health organization or a contracted organization working with child protective services due to the intensive delivery method. More information on training can be found at the Multisystemic Therapy Services website: www.mstservices.com/mst-can-child-welfare-program.

The recovery outlook for children and adolescents who have experienced maltreatment is dependent on the support of caring adults and communities. Children are incredibly resilient, but that resilience is taught through intentionally caring interactions and healthy relationships. Healthy attachment with a teacher, counselor, coach, or mentor can change the life of a child. Counselors have a pivotal role to play in supporting children and families who are at risk. We have the ability to support these families and implement preventative strategies. Counselors can support by understanding prevalence rates, knowing which local organizations can help in cases of maltreatment, and having developmentally appropriate resources for both prevention and support in recovery. It is our ethical duty to talk about reporting standards in the first session, but our obligation does not end there; we must be vigilant in monitoring for signs of maltreatment and empowering others to report any abuse they may suspect. We can display the phone numbers and locations for local organizations and educate parents and caregivers on resources in the community. We are trained to facilitate hard conversations in a wellness-oriented, developmentally appropriate way. We have a skill set that can help disseminate challenging information in a way that educates communities about risk and protective factors while also connecting clients to resources that support lifelong family and community wellness.

Children and Adolescents Impacted by Divorce

Parental divorce can be a significant stressor and life-altering event for children and adolescents (Stadelmann, Perren, Groeben, & von Klitzing, 2010; Brand, Howcroft, & Norman Hoelson, 2017). The separation of two influential figures is an experience that often requires children and adolescents to quickly adapt to new environments and routines, and continue to adjust to this momentous change over time. With the prevalence of divorce steadily high in the United States, counselors can expect to encounter children and adolescents impacted by parental divorce. Further, the finality proceedings of a divorce are not the only source of tension and adjustment for children and adolescents. Parental figures who have chosen to separate or are estranged from one other can result in children and adolescents experiencing emotional and behavioral responses similar to a divorce as they navigate this loss and transition. And, just like adults, a rift in the family unit will create challenges for children and adolescents to maintain their social and emotional well-being, as well as their academic achievement. As school and agency mental health counselors, it is crucial to acknowledge the areas where children and adolescents of divorced parents are most affected, and to integrate developmentally appropriate approaches and interventions.

Statistics

In 2018, 782,038 divorces and annulments were reported in the United States alone (Centers for Disease Control and Prevention [CDC], 2019). Although there are many influences in couples' decision to divorce, the effects of the separation impact more than the immediate parties involved (Emery, 2012; Krumrei, Coit, Martin, Fogo, & Mahoney, 2007). Boelen and van den Hout (2010) state that the number of individuals experiencing a marital dissolution is increasing and that this type of loss will impact all those involved, including extended family members, peers, and children and adolescents. Although divorces are common experiences, the negative long-term effects and healing process can be as severe, if not worse, than grieving the death of a loved one (Papa, Lancaster, & Kahler, 2014). Those similar thoughts, emotions, and behaviors associated with grieving a death can manifest before, during, and after divorce proceedings. While children and adolescents are likely to be thought of and supported when their parental figures are proceeding with a divorce, over time, that same attention and intentional conversations can decrease, leading to ongoing stress and interference with daily functioning (Boring, Sandler, Tein, & Horan, 2015).

Risk and Resilience

While children and adolescents attempt to adjust to their parental figures' divorce, their reactions to this change can be fluid and unanticipated. Conceptualizing an end of a marriage/partnership can be difficult for many, but children and adolescents of the divorced parental figures often have additional barriers to overcome that could interfere with adaptive coping. This can include having to transition to living in multiple homes, learning new routines, reconciling with the idea of their parental figures no longer having a romantic relationship, and forming new relationships with new step-parents or parental figures. Although each response to parental divorce is unique (Amato, 2012), children and adolescents may display their internalized thoughts and feelings of their parental figures' divorce through a variety of behaviors. Counselors can help support the child/adolescent by empathizing with them and being flexible with expectations, yet maintaining consistency. Even though the legal conclusion of a marriage may be a one-time event, counselors would do well to recognize that children and adolescents may have encountered months or years of parental conflict prior to the separation and may have to continue managing this tension after the divorce is finalized. We also want to make sure that we include parents/caregivers who may have split up and not been recorded in statistics about formal divorce – as this can have just the same impact on children and adolescents in households where their caregivers may not have been legally married, but were together nonetheless, and they find themselves in a situation where parents/caregivers are separating.

Emotional Impact

While parental figures may have the intention to minimize the negative effects on children and adolescents throughout the divorce process, there are often significant emotions held by children and adolescents that can carry on after the divorce has been finalized; these can impact their daily functioning (Basson, 2013). These emotions can include guilt, abandonment, loneliness, confusion, and anger. For some children and adolescents, they could have witnessed parental conflicts leading up to and throughout the divorce and may have internalized perceived responsibility for their parental figures separating (Papilia, Feldman, & Martorell, 2014). Further, younger children may have a more difficult time verbalizing their emotions (McFarland & Tollerud, 2009), and express their emotions through behavioral responses. As a counselor, you will want to talk to children and adolescents about their perceptions of the divorce and determine whether or not there is guilt or beliefs that they caused the divorce, in order to effectively dispel those misconceptions. In addition, it is important to support parents/caregivers in empathizing with the child's or adolescent's emotional and behavioral responses to this significant, ongoing stressor.

Social Impact

Developmentally, children and adolescents are focused on forming friendships and connecting with peers of similar interests (Feldman, 2016). Children and adolescents of divorced caregivers often feel isolated and believe that they are the only individuals with a similar experience, making it challenging to identify commonalities with peers. Further, children and adolescents may have had swift transitions to new communities and schools, leaving them without proper goodbyes to their friends and classmates, and forcing them to develop new relationships during a stressful time. Further, results of a divorce may mean limited interactions with one or both parental figures, as well as extended family. Children and adolescents' social networks are valuable and may be a source of tension as they learn how to continue to have these relationships under different circumstances.

Academic Impact

Although experiencing the divorce of parental figures can be painful and time-consuming, children and adolescents are often still expected to maintain their academics. However, this process can distract children and adolescents from their schoolwork and cause them to withdraw from teachers and friends both within the classroom and with sports and extracurricular activities. In addition, children and adolescents may be required to change schools during the academic year, which can entail prolonged absences and adjusting to a new setting and curriculum quickly. While all children and adolescents may not experience a drop in grades or academic achievement, it is important to expect a significant life stressor, such as experiencing a divorce, can impact academic performance and school involvement.

Counseling Interventions

As a counselor, you have the opportunity to normalize and validate the chaos and helplessness that children and adolescents may be feeling, as well as implement strategies and clinical approaches to help them adjust to their new reality. Remember that this child and/or adolescent is experiencing significant grief and loss (see Chapter 11 in this volume). While individual counseling may be the appropriate counseling modality in some cases, consider facilitating small counseling groups. This approach can help children and adolescents meet others impacted by a divorce and address their emotional, social, and academic concerns with support and structure (Pugliese, 2018). The following are potential interventions:

- *Responsibility pie chart:* Often children and adolescents will blame themselves for the divorce. By having them create a responsibility pie chart, you can have a clearer idea of the severity of the perceived responsibility of the divorce and determine appropriate interventions to reframe any cognitive distortions.
- *Bibliotherapy:* This tool can be most effective for younger children who may not have the vocabulary to describe their feelings, but can relate to book characters. Examples of appropriate books are *Dinosaurs Divorce: A Guide for Changing Families* (Brown & Brown, 1986), *The D Word: Divorce* (Cook, 2011), and *Two Homes* (Masurel, 2003).
- *Mindfulness and relaxation:* It will be essential for children and adolescents impacted by divorce to implement healthy strategies to mitigate their stress as much as possible. Model mindfulness and relaxation techniques in the session, and encourage children and adolescents to practice these techniques when they notice their anxiety and stress rising and interfering with their daily activities. These do not have to be overly complex or sophisticated. Remembering that that is a lot of stress and distraction can help you select simple, easy-to-implement mindfulness activities for children/adolescents and their parents/caregivers. See Chapter 17 of this volume on mindfulness techniques.

Children and Adolescents of Parents/Caregivers With Substance Misuse

Children and adolescents living in a home with a parent struggling with substance misuse display incredible amounts of resilience, but without adequate support, they may be at risk for long-term psychological distress. Parents with substance misuse not only struggle to manage their own personal lives, but also struggle to meet family obligations – in particular, attending to the emotional and relational needs of their child/adolescent. Depending on the type of treatment the caregiver seeks out, or if they seek out treatment at all, the child or adolescent may not be involved in the recovery process even though their lives have been impacted by the addiction. One thing is for certain: caregiver substance misuse has negative effects on children (SAMHSA, 2017). It is important that school- and community-based counselors are aware of how to support these children and their families to advocate for entire family system support as parents seek to not only move themselves toward wellness, but also toward mending the family unit as a whole.

Statistics

In the United States, 20.2 million adults struggle with drug and/or alcohol dependency; more specifically, 16.3 million with alcohol use disorder and 6.2 million with illicit drug use disorder. Out of those 20.2 million adults, SAMHSA reports that only 7.6% receive treatment for their addiction, citing cost and access to services as the primary barriers (Park-Lee, Lipari, Hedden, Copello, & Kroutil, 2016; SAMHSA, 2017). Based on combined data collected between 2009 and 2014 by the National Surveys on Drug Use and Health, 8.7 million children lived in households in the United States with at least one parent who was struggling with a substance use disorder. In the United States, 1 out of every 10 children has lived in a household where at least one parent has struggled with alcohol use disorder (SAMHSA, 2017). Combining both illicit drug use disorders and alcohol use disorders, 1 in every 8 children lives in a home with at least one caregiver impacted by dependency issues. Even prior to birth, children can be impacted by drug and alcohol use in the home. SAMHSA (2017) reported that every year, approximately 15% of infants are prenatally exposed to drugs or alcohol. Furthermore, between 2000 and 2009, there was a significant increase in the number of infants exposed to opioids prior to birth. This type of exposure leads to neonatal opioid withdrawal, which can cause difficulties with feeding, seizures, struggles to breathe, and distress from increased irritability (Forray & Foster, 2015). It is imperative that all counselors, regardless of setting, have an understanding of how to assess and effectively intervene with this population.

How Substance Misuse Impacts the Family Unit

Children of a caregiver substance misuser are more likely to live in poverty and have increased difficulties in multiple aspects of their lives, including school, social settings, and within the family (SAMHSA, 2017). Additionally, children living in this situation are at a higher risk for mental health and behavioral distress, including depression, anxiety, problems with cognitive or verbal skills, and parental abuse or neglect (Peleg-Oren & Teichman, 2006; Lipari & Van Horn, 2017). In families where a member has a substance use disorder, the homeostasis of the unit is disrupted or alters to form around the misuse, and family members attempt to shift boundaries and roles to create balance in the family system. Families often put a significant amount of effort into hiding or covering up what is happening within the household, which perpetuates a culture of shame and secrecy (Hawkins & Hawkins, 2012).

Boundaries within the family are impacted due to inconsistent communication, hiding or secrecy, inability to problem-solve and collaborate within the family unit, and higher levels of conflict within the household. This combination of behaviors within the household creates isolation among the family members, which compounds the isolation the family members feel from the community due to perpetuating secrecy around the family dynamics. In contrast to isolation, some family members may also become enmeshed with the caregiver struggling with substance misuse and assume responsibility for their actions. Of all of the family members involved in this system, children have the least control and are often unable to remove themselves from the situation.

Children growing up in these family systems are impacted by inconsistent caregiving and are always adapting to the ever-changing family dynamics characterized by uncertainty. This lack of structure, strict or laissez-faire household rules, parentification, and triangulation can have significant impacts on child development. When children are focusing on understanding and managing family dynamics, they are taking time away from being creative, learning healthy ways of relating to the world and themselves, and engaging in play which are all crucial for healthy development (Capuzzi & Stauffer, 2020).

The Adult Children of Alcoholics (ACOA) movement has advocated to understand outcomes and interventions to support children living with caregivers struggling with dependency issues. The National Association for Children of Addiction (https://nacoa.org) offers a variety of resources and training for interdisciplinary support. These resources are for professional counselors and for families to get assistance inside the home, in the counseling office, or in a school setting.

Counseling Treatment Modalities

Multidimensional family therapy (MDFT) is a manualized six-month outpatient therapy originally started to support adolescents and their families struggling with substance use disorders. This is a family-based approach that integrates multiple forms of therapy including individual counseling, family therapy, drug and alcohol specific counseling, and systemic interventions (Greenbaum et al., 2015). This form of therapy focuses on four areas: (a) the individual's substance dependency issues; (b) parenting skills and personal functioning; (c) developing healthy communication and relationships between the caregiver and adolescent; and (d) interactions between family members and social systems. The counselor's approach is strengths-based, with a focus on the possibility of change and protective factors within the family (Liddle, Rowe, Dakof, Henderson, & Greenbaum, 2009). This form of therapy has been consistently shown to be effective across cultures and in brief formats.

Celebrating Families! (http://celebratingfamilies.nacoa.org/) is a 16-session evidence-based curriculum that uses the principles of Cognitive Behavioral Therapy. This support group is for families where one or both caregivers is struggling with substance misuse and there is a high risk for violence in the home including domestic violence or child abuse. Skills such as anger management, communication, healthy expression of feelings, boundaries, problem-solving, relaxation, and identification of safe people are integrated in this intervention. Additionally, there is a psychoeducation component that teaches facts about alcohol and tobacco addiction, and brain chemistry; domestic violence; and the impact of drugs and alcohol on the family. This therapy is listed on both the SAMHSA registry and the National Registry of Effective Programs and Practices.

SAMHSA published the Children's Program Kit and the National Association for Children of Addiction published the Kit for Parents, both of which are available for free through their respective websites. The Children's Program Kit is a comprehensive resource guide to support children who have caregivers with dependency issues. The curriculum has video tapes, in addition to the program guide. The kit is divided into five sections: (1) introduction; (2) program in-services; (3) interventions for therapists to use with clients; (4) program curriculum; and (5) additional resources. The Kit for Parents has a lot of resources to help caregivers communicate with their children in developmentally appropriate ways about their addiction. This kit includes a message to parents, tips and suggestions, a letter to children to help them understand what may be happening to their caregiver, facts about drugs and alcohol that are developmentally appropriate to share with children, a list of books that may be useful for children or adolescents, and a color infographic explaining the seven C's (I didn't cause it. I can't cure it. I can't control it. I can help take care of myself by communicating my feelings, making healthy choices, and celebrating me).

Drug and alcohol use disorders impact not only the caregiver with the disorder, but the entire family. Since children and adolescents often have the least amount of power and are unable to escape the situation, they can experience lasting distress or disruptions in development. In order to support children in these homes, counselors must not only attend to the individual needs of the child, but also advocate for family services. By working from a strengths-based perspective that encourages families to examine the resilience they have displayed in often chaotic and uncertain family situations, counselors can help them move toward a healthier way of relating to each other and the outside world.

Children and Adolescents in Adoptive and Foster Families

Even though children can be taught to be incredibly resilient, change in the primary caregiver can be extremely disorienting. Any disruption in a formative family unit can have harmful and long-term ramifications for children and adolescents if it is not done with care. The losses involved in separating from one familial unit and attempting to adjust to another are significant and include cognitive, affective, and behavioral changes, in addition to that child or adolescent adjusting to a new physical environment (Sun & Li, 2014). Further, transitions to a new school, community, and potentially new peers and friends are additional burdens and challenges to endure. If a child or adolescent has had to be part of the foster care system for a prolonged period of time, then there could be a history of trauma, ruptured attachments, and a sense of identity confusion as children and adolescents make sense of their circumstances and need for belonging (Miranda, Molla, & Tadros, 2019).

Foster Care System

There can be several reasons why children and adolescents are removed from their families of origin and placed under welfare protective services and in the foster care system. However, it ultimately comes down to safety, and with over 430,000 children placed in foster care per year (U.S. Department of Health and Human Services, Administration for Children and Families, Children's Bureau, 2018), this system is set in place to ensure children's safety is warranted. Reunification, or the process of returning the child or adolescent to their home, continues to be debated as an appropriate approach. Concerns surrounding reunification include extreme stress for both the minor and the family, lack of education and resources set in place prior to the return, and the potential for further harm and safety concerns (Miranda et al., 2019).

In the event that the child or adolescent is not reunified with their biological family, then they are placed into the foster care system until they are either adopted or reach an age of independence, often 18 years of age, and are emancipated from government "parental" protections (Cunningham & Diversi, 2012). Before then, children and adolescents are often shuffled between several foster families or group homes, potentially disrupting their development and attachment to caregivers. Further, children and adolescents – especially those with a history of trauma – may lack trust for their foster families. This disconnection can lead to disruptive behaviors, poor academic performance, interactions with law enforcement, and negative interpersonal development (Miranda et al., 2019; Siegel & Hartzell, 2004). Further, depending on the age the child or adolescent becomes part of the foster care system, they may not be able to have the experience of a stable, safe home environment prior to exiting the foster care system and having developed intrapersonal and interpersonal skills engaged in secure attachments. It is important for counselors to recognize that no matter how dysfunctional the system is or appears to be to outsiders, this was their family or origins, and those roots of connections and loyalty run deep. Therefore, while it may seem like a relief for the child/adolescent to be out of a neglectful or abusive home, they may view it as forced abandonment.

Adoption

The adoption process can be arduous and emotional for both the child or adolescent and the families involved. There can be significant connections formed between the adoptee and the family, in addition to the losses and transitions (Barroso & Barbosa-Ducharne, 2019). Along with the joys that can occur after the adoption process has ended, for that child or adolescent, understanding their identity formation can just begin and take place over several developmental stages. Children and adolescents becoming part of a new family unit mean determining their role in that unit and their attachment to their caregivers, siblings, and extended family members, as well as reflecting back on the torn relationships with their family of origin. Oftentimes, children and adolescents can be adopted by families they had no former relationship with, or into families that have a biological connection. Either way, the acceptance of coming into a new system while reconciling with the losses of their family of origin can be a constant tension point for the adoptee.

In addition to the process of adjusting to a different family, children and adolescents may find themselves yearning to learn more about their family of origin. This can be particularly true for children and adolescents who were adopted at birth and do not have any type of relationship with their families of origin. The curiosity they may have could lead to a desire to reconnect and learn more about the decision to place them for adoption (Brodzinsky, 2011). Further, adoptees of all developmental stages may carry perceived blame or responsibility for their circumstances. Thoughts such as "maybe my parents did not love me" or "I did something wrong for them to get rid of me" may be occurring often and become disruptive to the adoptee's daily functioning and adjustment. There also may be instances when there is limited information available regarding biological families, adding a layer of complexity to their grief and loss, as there may be questions and insights the adoptee will never receive answers to.

Implications and Interventions

As counselors, you can engage with children and adolescents with a wide spectrum of experiences with the foster care system and adoption processes. It will be imperative that you understand the experiences through the lens of that child or adolescent while considering the systemic impacts of their situational factors. Further, you will want to take into consideration the family dynamics, culture, and potential history of trauma in your clinical approaches and identified interventions. Building a strong relationship and genuineness and trust may take time, as this population may have experienced abuse, neglect, and abandonment from others. Finally, take time to reflect on your idea of a family and notice any biases or assumptions that could interfere with your engagement with this population.

Consider the following when engaging with children and adolescents:

- Presenting mental health concerns and diagnoses is more likely as a result of trauma, swift and abrupt transition, and attachment concerns. While you may want to address the mental health concerns first, remember there may be underlying causes and historical events that you may need to address prior to engaging with the presenting concerns.
- If there are supportive and safe adults involved, include them in the treatment process. Provide education on the developmental considerations and needs this population will have, and therapeutic responses. This may include ongoing conversations with biological foster and adoptive parents. Each unit can benefit from gaining

insight and understanding of the experiences their child or adolescent is having and how to engage in safe and restorative parenting practices.
- Consider incorporating Filial Therapy into your approach (Capps, 2012). This type of therapy can connect family members together and enhance the relationship among all involved.
- Utilize creative expressive and experiential techniques (see associated Chapter 18 of this volume) to help children and adolescents express their thoughts and feelings. Further, encourage creating a personalized definition of family and explore how this belief of what makes a family unit has changed for them.
- Connect with school counselors and school-based counselors to discuss the idea of facilitating small groups. This can provide another level of support by connecting peers with similar experiences.

Children and Adolescents With Incarcerated Parents/Caregivers

Children and adolescents with incarcerated caregivers can feel incredible shame and face social stigma. Mass incarceration has had an enormous impact on families and communities, which results in risks for the healthy development of children and adolescents living within these systems. There is a need for clinical mental health and school counselors to understand the unique risk and resilience factors associated with this population to effectively support the children and families impacted by the criminal justice system.

Statistics

Over the past three decades, the number of individuals incarcerated in state and federal prisons has increased significantly. In 2015, the United States had 2.2 million people incarcerated, according to the U.S. Justice Department, and more than half of those individuals were parents (United States Department of Justice, 2016). From 1991–2007, there was a 79% increase in the number of parents who were incarcerated. The Pew Charitable Trust (2010) estimated that 2.7 million children grow up with a mother or a father behind bars. Currently, approximately 1 in every 14 children in the United States is impacted by incarceration. Children in marginalized communities are disproportionately impacted by the mass incarceration policies, with Murphy and Cooper's (2015) study finding 12.5% of children in poverty, 11.5% of Black children, 10.7% of children in rural communities, and 6.4% of Hispanic children as experiencing parental incarceration.

Caregiver Attachment Disruption

Separation from a primary caregiver can have a significant impact on children. Research has shown that children of incarcerated parents may show early signs of anti-social behavior; increased risk of externalizing behaviors; behavioral health issues including depression and anxiety, aggressive behavior, and delinquent or criminal activity; and school-related problems (Warren, Coker, & Collins, 2019). Attachment theory (Bowlby, 1958) suggests that children who have a healthy relationship with their primary caregiver have an increased ability to regulate their emotions and engage in healthy relationships across their lifespan. Disruptions in their early child and caregiver relationship can have impacts on children's ability to trust in themselves and others throughout their lifetime (Kobak, Zajac, & Madsen, 2016).

Social Stigma and Educational Consequences

Beyond the impact on the family unit, children of incarcerated parents can face social stigma and academic challenges. These children may be viewed negatively by their peers and teachers (Skinner-Osei & Levenson, 2018). This negativity can lead to excessive truancy, decrease in academic performance, and school disciplinary issues, and may potentially lead children to drop out of school. In response, children and parents may hide the fact that a caregiver or a family member is incarcerated. This secrecy can cause significant stress for children and families that increases feelings of isolation, in addition to the challenges of trying to keep information secret in the age of social media (Morsy & Rothstein, 2016). An important aspect for school counselors is the need to advocate for these students and support healthy school relationships in their peer interactions and their interactions with teachers. Research has shown that when teachers have knowledge of a student whose parent is incarcerated, it plays a role in how they treat that student. Additionally, students whose mother was incarcerated were viewed as less competent in comparison with students who had parents absent for other reasons such as work or military service (Dallaire, Ciccone, & Wilson, 2010).

As mentioned in the previous section on working with children who have experienced maltreatment, trauma-informed care can be a powerful tool when supporting children whose parents are incarcerated. This type of conceptualization allows the counselor to take into consideration the contextual elements that may be risk and resilience factors for these children. It allows the counselor to come from a strengths-based and empowerment perspective, which allows children to see their responses as adaptive and resilient. When practitioners work with a trauma-informed lens, they conceptualize the presenting problem from a perspective of coping responses and skills that the child is using to survive the present circumstances instead of a deficit. This in combination with the basic tenets of attachment theory can help counselors support clients in understanding that they are doing the best they can to adapt to a situation wherein their primary caregiver may not be meeting their needs. This allows for interventions that help support family engagement, healthy development, and attachment.

Advocacy

The American Counseling Association (ACA) has an endorsed model to support counselors as they advocate in various ways for their clients (Toporek & Daniels, 2018). These advocacy competencies outline the skills, knowledge, and behavior that counselors can use to address systemic barriers and issues facing their clients. This model describes various domains whereby the counselor can advocate with the client or on behalf of the client in individual, group, or public settings. These competencies can be found on the ACA website (www.counseling.org/docs/default-source/competencies/aca-2018-advocacy-competencies.pdf?sfvrsn=1dca552c_6). It is important that counselors understand the complex nature of working with children whose parents are incarcerated and see advocacy as one of the primary ways that we can support this population.

In-school services are essential to support children whose parents are incarcerated. School counselors have a variety of services that could be implemented in their school programs that could help support students with an incarcerated caregiver (Warren et al., 2019). The first thing school counselors must do is find a way to identify which students in their schools may be in need of support due to an caregiver being incarcerated. By building healthy relationships with families and community parents who may be helping these students through community-based services, they may understand important information and needs of their students. After students have been identified, school counselors can assess the strengths and risk factors associated with that individual student to better understand how to tailor support for both the student and their family. Throughout this process, it is important for counselors to reflect on their own thoughts, beliefs, bias, and privilege concerning incarceration. If necessary, consulting with other school counselors may be helpful in reflecting on how our personal experiences may be impacting our work with this population. Additionally, discreetly starting a group for students may be helpful. It is important to empower students to tell their own stories, so providing a safe space and then letting students guide how much they want to disclose to peers is the most appropriate way to approach this population. There are great books to help children understand their experience that may be appropriate to integrate into individual or group counseling in a school setting: *Far Apart, Close in Heart* (Birtha, 2017); *Coping When a Parent is Incarcerated* (DeCarlo, 2018); *Visiting Day* (Woodson, 2015); and *Jakeman* (Ellis, 2007).

There are a variety of protective and resilience factors that counselors can support in clients with incarcerated parents. Frequent visitation, quality communication by phone or video chat, increasing social and emotional coping skills, supporting academic achievement, engagement in school and community leadership positions, and support from a faith community can all help support children who may have a caregiver who is incarcerated. Counselors have the opportunity to empower this population in both schools and the community through advocacy and counseling services. We have the knowledge and skills to support healthy attachment relationships and support families as they try to navigate this challenging situation.

Achievement Gap

Even with education reform set in place to promote academic achievement for all students, there continues to be a gap preventing equity in education. The outcomes of this substantial gap have the most impact on children and adolescents with marginalized identities who have a history of oppression and limited access to educational resources (Darling-Hammond, 2007). The disparity of academic success between students of several marginalized racial and ethnic identities, as well as students from low-income families and communities, is apparent and growing (Strand, 2014; Annie E. Casey Foundation, 2017). In addition, the relationship between the widening academic achievement gap and the discipline gap often negatively affects the same groups of children and adolescents, in addition to students with neurobiological diversity, while hindering retention, persistence, and graduation (Bryan, Day-Vines, Griffin, & Moore-Thomas, 2012). Although much of the attention to address these gaps are centered around education, as counselors, there is an opportunity to approach this inequity with a holistic lens. It will be imperative to consider and reflect on a student's academic performance and barriers set in place preventing academic success.

Closing the gap will require help from counselors to address the social and emotional well-being and development of children and adolescents (Barna & Brott, 2011). While many may look to educators and administrators as leading agents in academic achievement, counselors can contribute significantly to children and adolescents adapting to environmental and systemic circumstances. In working with this younger population, counselors have to acknowledge the significant amount of time their clients spend in schools and systems that are reinforcing the inequity in education. Further, counselors can be a source of support and validation for their younger clients, in addition to working alongside them as they learn to adjust, cope, and navigate the educational system. In fostering the social and emotional development of children and adolescents, it is important to consider what external factors may be impeding their development.

Culturally Responsive Education, Practices, and Advocacy

The first approach to empowering children and adolescents and addressing the achievement gap begins with the counselor. Enhancing your cultural competency and self-awareness will be crucial to ensure that you do not further perpetuate the achievement gap. It is the counselor's ethical responsibility to reflect and identify potential biases and assumptions placed on the educational system overall, in addition to the marginalized communities most affected by educational injustices (Farinde-Wu, Glover, & Williams, 2017). This reflection must be intentional and authentic to ourselves and to others, as this process can be ongoing and, at times, difficult. However, the power held by counselors can be a significant asset to clients of all ages; it can also hinder the counseling relationship and trust with your younger clients if you are not willing to recognize the disparities in the educational systems and the role you have as a counselor to be a social justice advocate.

As counselors reflect on their personal experiences and insight in order to grow into culturally competent counselors, clinical approaches and interventions can be facilitated with cultural humility and sensitivity. Culturally responsive practices depict that as counselors we see children and adolescents as evolving with ideals, values, beliefs, and behaviors influenced by their culture and societal norms. Therefore, engaging in conversations regarding culture with a mindset of openness and acceptance will be an essential component of the counseling relationship (Goodman-Scott, Betters-Bubon, & Donohue, 2019). You will want to keep the following in mind when approaching children and adolescents with cultural humility:

- *Accept that you may be wrong at times:* It is not your job to assume, but rather listen to the experiences children and adolescents share with you.
- *Educate yourself:* One class, training, or text will not provide a comprehensive view of any cultural identity that is applicable to all children and adolescents. Continue to push yourself out of your comfort zone.
- *Be a* source *of support and education for children, adolescents, and their families:* Often, children and adolescents can place blame on themselves for not succeeding in their academics, when in fact it can be the barriers that reinforce the achievement gap and lack of resources that could be contributing factors to their academic success.

Working to end the achievement gap will require collaboration among counselors, educators, helping professionals, and legislators to acknowledge and begin to repair the current attitudes, policies, and procedures set to keep this gap in place. While counselors have the competence to address the mental well-being concerns of children and adolescents, the efforts to do so can be in conjunction with collaborating with others. Further, by working together with other professionals, a stronger advocacy approach can result in more positive outcomes and effectively addressing the diverse needs of closing the achievement gap.

Multicultural Implications and Advocacy

The content in this chapter presents a glimpse into the various ways that disruptions in the family systems of children and adolescents can affect their sense of well-being and their behavior. In thinking about the Multicultural and Social Justice Counseling Competencies (MSJCC) (Ratts, Singh, Nassar-McMillan, Butler, & McCullough, 2015), it is important to recognize the areas of our development that may be lacking, which may limit our ability to work productively with these individuals. It is incumbent upon the counselor to explore attitudes and beliefs about (a) parents/caregivers who neglect or abuse their children, misuse substances, divorce or separate and thus create hardships for their children, are or have been incarcerated, and/or lose custody of their children; and (b) the condition of children and adolescents living in or coming out of these family systems. For example, it may happen that a counselor views these parents as wantonly destructive and degenerate, and that the children do not stand a chance in the world. It may be challenging to view these clients as anything more than damaged, much less look for the promise that each holds.

At the same time, counselors may need to enhance their knowledge and skills in ascertaining the full extent of the impact these disruptions in the family system have on their young clients, and how to tailor a course of treatment that is both realistic and hopeful. Client factors can be misleading, as children and adolescents living in or coming from these disrupted family systems are living both their genetic and environmental inheritances. Therefore, it is vital that their presenting concerns be understood both in terms of being a casualty of these systems and in terms of them being capable of taking responsibility to use the supports available to them. Finally, the contextual factors of the client played heavily into their referral behaviors, so it will be necessary to draw upon contextual supports in order to facilitate these individuals living at-promise rather than only at-risk.

Summary

This chapter covers various forms of family system disruption including child maltreatment, children and adolescents impacted by divorce and caregivers struggling with substance misuse, children and adolescents growing up in adoptive families or with foster families, children and adolescents with a caregiver or parent who is incarcerated, and how all of this impacts academic achievement. This chapter ended by addressing multicultural concerns and advocacy. Throughout the chapter, many examples of strengths-based interventions and techniques that can be used in various settings were described. Additionally, resources such as websites and supporting organizations were provided for further reading on these topics. Children and adolescents growing up in family systems may experience disruptions, but we hope you take away from this chapter that these families also display incredible amounts of resiliency. With support from professional counselors in both community mental health and school settings, they can overcome many of these adverse experiences.

Clinician's Corner

Although it makes sense intuitively (and is also supported in numerous research results), working with the families of children and adolescents we counsel is often afforded less time and effort than might be optimal. Specifically, in schools, it is regrettable how little consideration this potentially beneficial collaboration sometimes receives. When the relationship with the young person's family is given attention, often it's negative. It's not unusual for school personnel to harbor assumptions that the family isn't supportive or doesn't care. Once early in my career, while interviewing for a PK–12 job, I asked the principal how involved families were in their children's education at the school. To my dismay, she responded "not much, thank God".

When I would start in a new school as a counselor, I often received warnings about certain families on my caseload (accompanied by lurid tales of tempest and terror). To be honest, I can't recall any families who weren't willing to work with me as an active ally on their child's "success team". Sometimes this was the fruit of a fair amount of patience and persistence. Other times, it was surprisingly simple. In one such case, having heard about the tirades and tense encounters with one parent the previous school year, I sought out this parent early in the fall at a school sporting event in which their child was participating. After introductions, we chatted amiably on and off for the first half of the game. I then moved on to meet some other folks.

Not long after that, the first scheduled IEP (individualized education program) meeting was held for the student. Previously, the parent had been accompanied at these meetings by an advocate with a reputation for being very assertive and appearing to have an adversarial agenda. The meetings apparently lasted longer than the time allotted, shouting was sometimes involved, and agreement was often not secured until multiple meetings were held. This year, the parent came alone. I would be lying to call it a lovefest, but we endeavored to keep it positive by acknowledging the importance of working together while respecting and accessing everyone's expertise. Subsequent meetings built on this foundation. As you likely guessed, the student's interactions with teachers and staff grew to have a more hopeful and helpful hue, too. As counselors, it's easy to become preoccupied with the young person in front of you (and all of the paperwork, policies, and procedures), yet building culturally responsive connections with families (and the communities in which they live) can provide rich resources that foster success.

Tim Grothaus, Ph.D.
Old Dominion University

References

Amato, P. R. (2012). The consequences of divorce for adults and children: An update. *Drustvena Istrazivanja*, 23(1), 5–24. https://doi.org/10.5559/di.23.1.01

Annie E. Casey Foundation. (2017). *Race for results: Building a path to opportunity for all children*. Retrieved from www.aecf.org/resources/2017-race-for-results/

Barna, J. S., & Brott, P. E. (2011). How important is personal/social development to academic achievement? The elementary school counselor's perspective. *Professional School Counseling*, 14(3), 242–249. https://doi.org/10.1177/2156759X1101400308

Barroso, R., & Barbosa-Ducharne, M. (2019). Adoption-related feelings, loss, and curiosity about origins in adopted adolescents. *Clinical Child Psychology and Psychiatry*, 24(4), 876–891. https://doi.org/10.1177/1359104519858117

Basson, W. J. (2013). Helping divorced parents to benefit adolescent children: A prospective enrichment programme. *Journal of Psychology in Africa*, 23(4), 675–678. https://doi.org/10.1080/14330237.2013.10820687

Birtha, B. (2017). *Far apart, close in heart: Being a family when a loved one is incarcerated*. Albert Whitman & Company.

Blankenship, D. M. (2017). Five efficacious treatments for posttraumatic stress disorder: An empirical review. *Journal of Mental Health Counseling*, 39(4), 275–288. https://doi.org/10.17744/mehc.39.4.01

Boelen, P. A., & van den Hout, M. A. (2010). Inclusion of other in the self and breakup-related grief following relationship dissolution. *Journal of Loss and Trauma*, 15(6), 534–547. https://doi.org/10.1080/15325024.2010.519274

Boring, J. L., Sandler, I. N., Tein, J.-Y., & Horan, J. J. (2015). Children of divorce – Coping with divorce: A randomized control trial of an online prevention program for youth experiencing parental divorce. *Journal of Consulting and Clinical Psychology*, 83(5), 999–1005. http://doi.org/10.1037/a0039567

Bowlby, J. (1958). The nature of children's tie to his mother. *International Journal of Psychoanalysis*, 39, 350–373.

Brand, C., Howcroft, G., & Norman Hoelson, C. (2017). The voice of the child in parental divorce: Implications for clinical practice and mental health practitioners. *Journal of Child & Adolescent Mental Health*, 29(2), 169–178. https://doi.org/10.2989/17280583.2017.1345746

Brodzinsky, D. M. (2011). Children's understanding of adoption: Developmental and clinical implications. *Professional Psychology: Research and Practice*, 42(2), 200–207. https://doi.org/10.1037/a0022415

Brown, L. K., & Brown, M. (1986). *Dinosaurs divorce: A guide for changing families*. Little, Brown Books for Young Readers.

Bryan, J., Day-Vines, N. L., Griffin, D., & Moore-Thomas, C. (2012). The disproportionality dilemma: Patterns of teacher referrals to school counselors for disruptive behavior. *Journal of Counseling & Development*, 90(2), 177–190. https://doi.org/10.1111/j.1556-6676.2012.00023.x

Capps, J. E. (2012). Strengthening foster parent – Adolescent relationships through filial therapy. *The Family Journal: Counseling and Therapy for Couples and Families*, 20(4), 427–432. https://doi.org/10.1177/1066480712451245

Capuzzi, D., & Stauffer, M. (2020). *Foundations of addictions counseling* (4th ed.). Hoboken, NJ: Pearson Education.

Centers for Disease Control and Prevention. (2019). *Marriage and divorce*. Retrieved from www.cdc.gov/nchs/data/dvs/national-marriage-divorce-rates-00-18.pdf

Child Abuse Prevention and Treatment Act of 1974, 42 U.S.C.A. § 5106g. (1974) [amended in 2010 by CAPTA Reauthorization Act]. Retrieved from www.congress.gov/bill/93rd-congress/senate-bill/1191

Child Welfare Information Gateway. (2019). *Definitions of child abuse and neglect*. Washington, DC: U.S. Department of Health and Human Services, Children's Bureau.

Cook, J. (2011). *The D word (divorce)*. National Center for Youth Issues.

Cunningham, M. J., & Diversi, M. (2012). Aging out: Youths' perspectives on foster care and the transition to independence. *Qualitative Social Work*, 12(5), 587–602. https://doi.org/10.1177/1473325012445833

Dallaire, D. H., Ciccone, A., & Wilson, L. C. (2010). Teachers' experiences with and expectations of children with incarcerated parents. *Journal of Applied Developmental Psychology*, 31(4), 281–290. https://doi.org/10.1016/j.appdev.2010.04.011

Darling-Hammond, L. (2007). Race, inequality, and educational accountability: The irony of "no child left behind". *Race Ethnicity and Education*, 10(3), 245–260.

de Arellano, M. A., Lyman, D. R., Jobe-Shields, L., George, P., Dougherty, R. H., Daniels, A. S., . . . Delphin-Rittmon, M. E. (2014). Trauma-focused cognitive-behavioral therapy for children and adolescents: assessing the evidence. *Psychiatric Services (Washington, D.C.)*, 65(5), 591–602. https://doi.org/10.1176/appi.ps.201300255

DeCarlo, C. (2018). *Coping when a parent is incarcerated*. Rosen Young Adult.

Diehle, J., Opmeer, B. C., Boer, F., Mannarino, A. P., & Lindauer, R. J. (2015). Trauma-focused cognitive behavioral therapy or eye movement desensitization and reprocessing: What works in children with posttraumatic stress symptoms? A randomized controlled trial. *European Child & Adolescent Psychiatry*, 24(2), 227–236. https://doi.org/10.1007/s00787-014-0572-5

Ellis, D. (2007). *Jakeman*. Fitzhenry and Whiteside.

Emery, R. E. (2012). Grieving divorce: The leaver and the left. In R. Emery (Ed.), *Renegotiating family relationships: Divorce, child custody, and mediation* (2nd ed., pp. 39–61). New York: Guilford Press.

Farinde-Wu, A., Glover, C., & Williams, N. (2017). "It's not hard work; it's heart work": Strategies of effective, award-winning culturally responsive teachers. *The Urban Review*, 49(2), 279–299.

Feldman, R. S. (2016). *Development across the life span*. Pearson.

Forray, A., & Foster, D. (2015). Substance use in the perinatal period. *Current Psychiatry Reports*, 17(11), 1–19. https://doi.org/10.1007/s11920-015-0626-5

Greenbaum, P. E., Wang, W., Hall, K., Henderson, C. E., Kan, L., Dakof, G. A., & Liddle, H. A. (2015). Gender and ethnicity as moderators: Integrative data analysis of multidimensional family therapy randomized clinical trials. *Journal of Family Psychology, 29*(6), 919–930. https://doi.org/10.1037/fam0000127

Goodman-Scott, E., Betters-Bubon, J., & Donohue, P. (Eds.). (2019). *The school counselor's guide to multi-tiered systems of support.* Routledge.

Hawkins, C. A., & Hawkins, R. C. (2012). Family systems and chemical dependency. In C. A. McNeece & D. M. DiNitto (Eds.), *Chemical dependency: A systems approach* (4th ed., pp. 256–284). Boston, MA: Pearson.

Henggeler, S. W., Schoenwald, S. K., Borduin, C. M., Rowland, M. D. & Cunningham, P. B. (2009). *Multisystemic therapy for antisocial behavior in children and adolescents* (2nd ed.). Guilford.

Herman, S. (2019). *Help your dragon cope with trauma.* Digital Golden Solutions, LLC.

Holmes, M. M. (2000). *A terrible thing happened* (C. Pillo, Illustrator). American Psychological Association.

Hunter, S. V. (2006). Understanding the complexity of child sexual abuse: A review of the literature with implications for family counseling. *The Family Journal, 14*(4), 349–358. https://doi.org/10.1177/1066480706291092

Karadag, M., Gokcen, C., & Sarp, A. (2019). EMDR therapy in children and adolescents who have post-traumatic stress disorder: A six-week follow-up study. *International Journal of Psychiatry in Clinical Practice*, 1–6. https://doi.org/10.1080/13651501.2019.1682171

Kobak, R., Zajac, K., & Madsen, S. D. (2016). Attachment disruptions, reparative processes, and psychopathology: Theoretical and clinical implications. In J. Cassidy & P. R. Shaver (Eds.), *Handbook of attachment: Theory, research, and clinical applications* (3rd ed., pp. 25–39). New York: Guilford Press.

Krumrei, E., Coit, C., Martin, S., Fogo, W., & Mahoney, A. (2007). Post-divorce adjustment and social relationships: A meta-analytic review. *Journal of Divorce & Remarriage, 46*(3/4), 145–166. https://doi.org/10.1300/J087v46n03_09

Liddle, H. A., Rowe, C. L., Dakof, G. A., Henderson, C. E., & Greenbaum, P. E. (2009). Multidimensional family therapy for young adolescent substance abuse: Twelve-month outcomes of a randomized controlled trial. *Journal of Consulting and Clinical Psychology, 77*(1), 12–25.

Lipari, R. N., & Van Horn, S. L. C. (2017). *Children living with parents who have a substance use disorder.* The CBHSQ Report: August 24, 2017. Center for Behavioral Health Statistics and Quality, Substance Abuse and Mental Health Services Administration, Rockville, MD.

Logie, R. (2014). EMDR – more than just a therapy for PTSD? *The Psychologist, 27*(7), 512–516.

Masurel, C. (2003). *Two homes.* Candlewick.

McFarland, W., & Tollerud, T. (2009). Counseling children and adolescents with special needs. In A. Vernon (Ed.), *Counseling children and adolescents* (pp. 257–310). Love.

Miranda, M., Molla, E., & Tadros, E. (2019). Implications of foster care on attachment: A literature review. *The Family Journal, 27*(4), 394–403. https://doi.org/10.1177/1066480719833407

Morsy, L., & Rothstein, R. (2016). *Mass incarceration and children's outcomes.* Washington, DC: Economic Policy Institute.

Murphy, D., & Cooper, P. M. (2015). *Parents behind bars: What happens to their children?* Retrieved from www.childtrends.org/publications/parents-behind-bars-what-happens-to-their-children

Nixon, R., Sterk, J., & Pearce, A. (2012). A randomized trial of cognitive behaviour therapy and cognitive therapy for children with posttraumatic stress disorder following single-incident trauma. *Journal of Abnormal Child Psychology, 40*(3), 327–337. https://doi.org/10.1007/s10802-011-9566-7

Papa, A., Lancaster, N. G., & Kahler, J. (2014). Commonalities in grief responding across bereavement and non-bereavement losses. *Journal of Affective Disorder, 16*(1), 136–143. http://doi.org/10.1016/j.jad.2014.03.018

Papilia, D., Feldman, R., & Martorell, G. (2014). *Experience human development* (13th ed.). McGraw-Hill.

Park-Lee, E., Lipari, R. N., Hedden, S. L., Copello, E. A. P., & Kroutil, L. A. (2016). *Receipt of services for substance use and mental health issues among adults: Results from the 2015 National Survey on Drug Use and Health.* NSDUH Data Review. Retrieved from http://samhsa.gov/data/

Peleg-Oren, N., & Teichman, M. (2006). Young children of parents with substance use disorders (SUD): A review of the literature and implications for social work practice. *Journal of Social Work Practice in the Addictions*, 6(1–2), 49–61.

Pew Charitable Trust. (2010). *Collateral costs: Incarceration's effects on economic mobility*. Washington, DC: Author.

Pugliese, A. (2018). Grief. In S. I. Springer, L. Moss, N. Manavizadeh, & A. Pugliese (Eds.), *A school counselor's guide to small groups: Coordination, leadership, and assessment* (pp. 283–333). Association for Specialists in Group Work.

Ratts, M. M., Singh, A. A., Nassar-McMillan, S., Butler, S. K., & McCullough, J. R. (2015). *Multicultural and social justice counseling competencies*. Retrieved from www.counseling.org/docs/default-source/competencies/multicultural-and-social-justice-counseling-competencies.pdf?sfvrsn=20

Rubin, A. (2012). *Programs and interventions for maltreated children and families at risk*. Hoboken, NJ: John Wiley & Sons.

Rudd, B., Last, B., Gregor, C., Jackson, K., Berkowitz, S., Zinny, A., . . . Beidas, R. (2019). Benchmarking treatment effectiveness of community-delivered trauma-focused cognitive behavioral therapy. *American Journal of Community Psychology*, 64(3–4), 438–450. https://doi.org/10.1002/ajcp.12370

Siegel, D. J., & Hartzell, M. (2004). *Parenting from the inside out: How a deeper self-understanding can help you raise children who thrive*. J. P. Tarcher/Putnam.

Skinner-Osei, P., & Levenson, J. (2018). Trauma-informed services for children with incarcerated parents. *Journal of Family Social Work*, 21(4–5), 421–437. https://doi.org/10.1080/10522158.2018.1499064

Stadelmann, S., Perren, S., Groeben, M., & von Klitzing, K. (2010). Parental separation and children's behavioral/emotional problems: The impact of parental representations and family conflict. *Family Process*, 49(1), 92–108. https://doi.org/10.1111/j.1545-5300.2010.01310.x

Strand, S. (2014). School effects and ethnic, gender and socioeconomic gaps in educational achievement at age 11. *Oxford Review of Education*, 40(2), 1–29. http://doi.org/10.1080/03054985.2014.891980

Straus, S. F., & Bogade, M. (2013). *Healing days: A guide for kids who have experienced trauma*. Magination Press.

Substance Abuse and Mental Health Services Administration. (2014). *SAMHSA's concept of trauma and guidance for a trauma-informed approach*. (HHS Publication No. SMA14–4884). Rockville, MD: Substance Abuse and Mental Health Services Administration. Retrieved from http://store.samhsa.gov/shin/content//SMA14-4884/SMA14-4884.pdf

Substance Abuse and Mental Health Services Administration. (2017). *Key substance use and mental health indicators in the United States: Results from the 2016 National Survey on Drug Use and Health* (HHS Publication No. [SMA] 17–5044, NSDUH Series H-52). Rockville, MD: Center for Behavioral Health Statistics and Quality, Substance Abuse and Mental Health Administration. Retrieved from www.samhsa.gov/data/sites/default/files/NSDUH-FFR1-2016/NSDUH-FFR1-2016.htm

Sun, Y., & Li, Y. (2014). Alternative households, structural changes, and cognitive development of infants and toddlers. *Journal of Family Issues*, 35(11), 1440–1472. https://doi.org/10.1177/0192513X13495399

Trafficking Victims Protection Act (TVPA). (2000). Pub. L. No. 106–386, § 102(b) (14–15) (2000).

Toporek, R. L., & Daniels, J. (2018). *2018 update and expansion of the 2003 ACA advocacy competencies: Honoring the work of the past and contextualizing the present*. Retrieved from www.counseling.org

U.S. Department of Health & Human Services, Administration for Children and Families, Administration on Children, Youth and Families, Children's Bureau (USDHHS). (2020). *Child maltreatment 2018*. Retrieved from www.acf.hhs.gov/cb/research-data-technology/statistics-research/child-maltreatment

U.S. Department of Health & Human Services, Administration for Children and Families, Children's Bureau. (2018). *Adoption and foster care analysis and reporting system report*. Retrieved from www.acf.hhs.gov/sites/default/files/cb/afcarsreport26.pdf

U.S. Department of Justice. (2016). *Prisoners in 2015*. Retrieved from www.bjs.gov/content/pub/pdf/p15.pdf.

Warren, J., Coker, G., & Collins, M. (2019). Children of incarcerated parents: Considerations for professional school counselors. *The Professional Counselor*, 9(3), 185–199. https://doi.org/10.15241/jmw.9.3.185

Woodson, J. (2015). *Visiting day*. Puffin Books.

Part III

Specific Skills, Theories, and Techniques

10 Children and Adolescents With Myriad Presenting Concerns

Rebekah Byrd, Amanda LaGuardia, and Chad Luke
Amanda LaGuardia as guest contributor

Objectives

- Understand many specific concerns that children and adolescents may encounter.
- Describe ways in which counselors can be aware of strengths-based perspectives when working with youth dealing with myriad presenting concerns.
- Examine different types of assessments and interventions that can be useful with specific concerns.
- Analyze ways in which understanding multiple intelligences can assist counselors in a strengths-based approach.
- Understand multicultural implications of diagnosis and treatment.

Reflective Questions

- What behaviors do I expect to notice in relation to each topic area discussed (i.e., what do I think I will notice if I am interacting with a child who self-injures)?
- How would I build rapport with a child who expresses suicidal ideation within the context of each topic and involve caregivers when fulfilling my duty to warn?
- How might understanding multiple intelligences help me encourage and empower children and adolescents with whom I work?
- How can I increase competency for working with exceptional children and adolescents?
- What is my current understanding of effective ways to work with gifted children and adolescents?
- Reflecting on my own cultural context (i.e., family and community values you adhere to), what values or beliefs outside of my own could present barriers in developing rapport given each topic? For instance, often individuals who have beliefs that individuals should not engage in sexual activity before marriage have difficulty addressing risky sexual behavior when an adolescent or adolescent's family does not hold that belief.

This chapter focuses on many presenting issues and concerns for children and adolescents. It includes areas of particular interest and issues that children and adolescents encounter. Many of these issues are difficult to conceptualize, thus knowledge of up-to-date research and treatment techniques can be practically helpful. Counselors must first understand the presenting issue, and how it manifests within the unique biopsychosocial context of each young person, in order to identify appropriate treatments. Knowledge and awareness as to how these concerns influence the development and daily functioning of the children and adolescents experiencing them serves as an essential foundation for professional counselors seeking to learn effective counseling skills and strategies. The content of this chapter will elucidate many of these issues.

We will not have space to focus on in-depth diagnostic criteria or assessment procedures, but we will reference resources for further exploration in these areas. This chapter is not meant to replace or expand upon your training in psychopathology, diagnosis, and treatment planning with regard to deficits in youth; a deficit perspective has been normalized with regard to treatment approaches, and thus resources specific to this perspective are plentiful. A strengths-based, wellness-oriented approach to these issues concerning children and adolescents is emphasized. Professional counselors are invited to consider environmental context and strengths in relation to each concern rather than overly attending to deficit oriented pathological procedure.

We would like to express a word of caution to mental health counselors working with children and adolescents: *be careful with your power to diagnose*. While it is important to help clients get the support and services they need, it is also crucial to advocate in a way that empowers both individual and systems changes. Often children and adolescents need a supportive adult, a listening ear, help in working through trauma, grief and loss, or help with anxiety influenced by a normal developmental process or transitional life event. This book discusses many techniques for working with children and adolescents to address change within and around a young person to exhaust behavioral and process options prior to moving to biological intervention (e.g., use of medication). Even when medication is used in treatment, it has been shown to be most effective in conjunction with counseling. "We know that the number of children and adolescents diagnosed with and treated for mental disorders has skyrocketed over the past decades" (Merten, Cwik, Margraf, & Schneider, 2017, p. 2). In his book *Saving Normal: An Insider's Revolt Against Out-Of-Control Psychiatric Diagnosis, DSM-5, Big Pharma, and the Medicalization of Ordinary Life*, Allen Frances (2013), chair of the DSM-IV task force, stated "because of diagnosis inflation, there are far too many" (p. 25) diagnoses. Please be diligent in your duties and make sure you are carefully working with the person (child, adolescent, or family) in front of you instead of looking for or focusing on a set of symptoms as a sole determinant of your approach. Approximately 10% of children and youth experience serious emotional disturbance that results from a number of factors, and 80% of those children fail to receive necessary services; thus, it is important we meet the mental health needs of our youth in an appropriate and evidenced-based manner (SAMHSA, 2019) that is informed by context.

Anxiety

Some of the most common diagnoses in early childhood are anxiety-related disorders (CDC, 2020). Links exist between anxiety symptoms and intolerance of uncertainty, and when tolerance is improved, anxiety symptoms are likely to decrease in response (Boswell, Thompson-Hollands, Farchione, & Barlow, 2013). Generally, younger children can experience anxiety as it relates to caregiver attachment and separation anxiety. It can look like a number of behaviors sometimes conflated with oppositional defiance or difficulty managing anger, especially in children younger than 10. When children become anxious, they can have difficulty recognizing, verbalizing, and managing their emotions as emotional experiences of fear commonly intersect with feelings of anxiety. Thus, children can attempt to deflect through inattention to their surroundings, angry outbursts and tantrums, or retreat and isolation from others. It is imperative that anxiety issues be recognized for what they are, as approaches to anxiety intervention in the moment are different from interventions for behavioral defiance (e.g., emotional labeling and guided calming versus punishment). Children need help verbalizing and learning to self-soothe if experiencing anxiety rather than immediacy in ignoring or instituting logical and natural consequences, which are common responses to management of defiance or conduct problems.

Evidence exists to indicate Acceptance and Commitment Therapies (ACT) are highly effective in addressing symptoms of anxiety for adults and children (Arch et al., 2012; Livheim et al., 2015), and thus translate as an approach that would be useful throughout the lifespan. Any techniques designed to assist in identification and communication of emotional experience in the moment and skills training to build efficacy for self-soothing are helpful in addressing symptoms of anxiety in children and youth in addition to recognizing behavioral reinforcers. Anxiety has been linked to perfectionistic beliefs and attitudes, which are in turn linked to risk for suicide (Burgess & DiBartolo, 2016). Thus, early identification and treatment of anxiety is imperative to prevent potential escalation and development of more severe symptomology or destructive coping strategies. Anxiety and perfectionism are common for high-achieving and gifted youth, but are not limited to that group. Anxiety can be exacerbated by a number of factors, including parenting strategies that utilize criticism, lack a structure for behavioral expectations and patterns of living, are overprotective or controlling (fail to foster independence and self-efficacy of the child), and lack warmth (support, affection, and statements of approval). Involvement of parents when working with youth experiencing anxiety is useful in ensuring long-term prevention and improvement of symptoms. A focus on improving self-concept and resilience has been shown to reduce risks associated with childhood anxiety (Mammarella, Donolato, Caviola, & Giofre, 2018).

Depression

Depression is often first diagnosed either in young adulthood or in older adult populations (CDC, 2020). Occasional feelings of sadness or experiences of hopelessness are common and normal for youth to experience as they grow. When these symptoms persist and interfere with functioning, this could indicate a problem in need of professional intervention. The U.S. Preventive Services Taskforce (2019) recommends early screening for children and adolescents with persistent symptoms associated with Major Depressive Disorder to prevent long-term academic impairment and relational problems, which may serve to exacerbate problematic symptom experience. If persistent and intrusive depression is assessed to be an issue in need of treatment, common interventions involve both counseling and psychopharmacological treatment. There are known risks to the use of serotonin re-uptake inhibitors (SSRIs) in the treatment of youth depression specific to exacerbation or development of suicidal ideation. If use of medication is closely monitored by a medical professional, these risks may be manageable to ensure positive outcomes. Collaborative care models have also been shown to be more effective in treating youth depression than typical approaches to care, especially when symptoms co-occur with anxiety (Choi et al., 2019). Parent, community mental health, primary care, and school involvement in treatment can be essential components in ensuring symptom improvement for children and adolescents as long as professional communication is focused on clear role differentiation with an integrated approach to treatment planning for a youth's mental healthcare.

Screenings for depression that have shown usefulness in identifying the need for treatment are the Center for Epidemiologic Studies Depression Scale (CES-D) for children older than 11; the Patient Health Questionnaire for Adolescents (PHQ-A), which shows high predictive ability for identifying depression for adolescents; and the Beck Depression Inventory (BDI) for its level of sensitivity in identifying major depression, especially for males. The BDI also has a youth version available (BYI) for children as young as 7. Risk factors for childhood depression include overprotective parenting (lack of child autonomy), low level of overall life satisfaction, hopelessness (belief that life cannot get better), and trauma exposure (specifically the loss of a caregiver or experiences of abuse). For more on assessment, see the SAMHSA-HRSA Center for Integrated Health Solutions. Healthy peer and family relationships, access to community mental healthcare resources, and coping resiliency (ability to manage distress) are protective factors; thus, similarly to anxiety, parental involvement in treatment and a focus on distress management in counseling are essential to improving depressive symptoms (Cairns, Yap, Pilkington, & Jorm, 2014). Depression has been linked to substance abusing behaviors, risky sexual behavior, and suicide for children and youth, thus early identification and improvement of symptoms may be important for prevention of potentially detrimental coping behaviors or the development of factors associated with suicide.

Substance Abuse

According to the National Institute on Drug Abuse (2019), misuse and abuse of substances – legal or illegal – are on the rise in the United States, particularly among youth. Misuse of substances have been linked to a number of environmental and mental health concerns, including attention deficit/hyperactivity disorder (ADHD), childhood mistreatment and abuse, childhood trauma, youth homelessness, and suicide attempts (Slesnick, 2008; De Sanctis, 2011). The general perception of youth substance misuse and abuse relates to a need for education, access, peer use, and a youth's ability to cope with developmental and environmental difficulties. According to SAMHSA (2012): "Families with alcohol and drug problems usually have high levels of stress and confusion. High stress family environments are a risk factor for early and dangerous substance use, as well as mental and physical health problems" (para. 3). If parents are struggling with substance abuse issues, it can have a profound effect on children in the home and presents a risk that youth may begin misusing substances, including alcohol, cigarettes, marijuana, illegal drugs and prescribed medications. According to SAMHSA (2019), schools play a critical role in identifying and preventing substance abuse and misuse for youth. Youth substance use typically begins between ages of 12 and 17, with approximately 16% using illicit drugs and 31% endorsing use of alcohol or tobacco and 4% of those meet criteria for diagnosis of a substance use disorder (SAMHSA, 2019).

In order for schools and communities to best address this growing problem in youth, a multi-tiered system of supports (MTSS) is needed to include programs that model and teach appropriate social skills, prosocial behavior, youth mental health literacy (e.g., Youth Mental Health First Aid), and emotional awareness, and improve student-teacher relationships (PBIS, 2019). Ultimately, fact-based education about substance use (excluding scare tactics and focusing on healthy coping and physiological effects of substances), early screening, and parental involvement are important components for prevention of substance misuse and abuse. SAMHSA's Bringing Recovery Supports to Scale Technical Assistance Center Strategy (BRSS TACS) provides many resources to community providers, schools, and parents in addressing youth substance abuse issues. For instance, it recommends a program from The Center for Motivation and Change that assists caregivers and loved ones in approaching and supporting youth with potential substance use problems. The Parent's Guide (The Center for Motivation and Change, 2016) is available for purchase, but a number of resources are also available free on the center's website at https://the20minuteguide.com/parents/introduction-guide. This guide includes information about screening and finding treatment for youth engaging in substance abuse.

A common screening tool used to assess youth risk for substance abuse and misuse is the CRAFFT, designed for children younger than 21 (Knight, Sherritt, Shrier, Harris, & Chang, 2002). This screener consists of two parts. Part A assesses for any use of alcohol, marijuana, or other drugs. If there is a positive response to any of the three items in part A, part B is completed and includes six CRAFFT items. CRAFFT stands for Car, Relax, Alone, Forget, Family and Friends, and Trouble, relating to the content of each item. This screener assists in identifying criteria for substance abuse and dependence and takes about 5–10 minutes to administer. This screening is linked to the SBIRT program (Screening, Brief Intervention, and Referral for Treatment). A free app, developed by Baylor College of Medicine, is available for use by healthcare and mental health professionals trained in SBIRT. To find screeners and other resources related to substance abuse and to access a free online SBIRT training, go to www.integration.samhsa.gov/clinical-practice/sbirt.

Risky Sexual Behavior

Sexual behavior and exploration is a normal part of human development. Defining risky sexual behavior can be somewhat difficult, given that risk associated with sex is largely understood within cultural norms and expectations. However, within the healthcare literature, risky sexual behavior is often perceived as behaviors with potentially harmful health outcomes (e.g., unsafe sex) or sexual behaviors that result in negative outcomes on families and relationships and have been linked to substance abuse (CDC, 2019). The association between high-risk sexual behaviors and substance abuse has been well established in the research literature (Ritchwood, Ford, DeCoster, Sutton, & Lochman, 2015), and thus if one concern is present, the other should also been screened for. Accurate sex education has been shown to mitigate a number of issues associated with risky sex, such as adolescent pregnancy and sexually transmitted infections (STIs) (Breuner & Mattson, 2016). The need for youth sex education becomes increasingly pertinent when one considers CDC (2017b) estimates of youth and young adults ages 15–24 as making up over "one quarter of the sexually active population, but account for half of the 20 million new sexually transmitted infections that occur in the United States each year" (para. 1).

With regard to assessment for high-risk sexual behavior, a number of subjective and objective measures exist, but these measures reflect numerous definitions of what constitutes high-risk sex. Chawla and Sarkar (2019) provide a review of these assessments and offer a somewhat central definition of high-risk sex, which includes STIs, unwanted pregnancy, legal and family conflict, HIV, a partner who is an injecting drug user, irregular, and incentive driven, and sexual activity that begins early in the lifespan, is unprotected, paid for, or done under the influence of a substance. One such brief screening tool is the Risky Sex Scale (RSS; O'Hare, 2001) and has demonstrated efficacy when screening youth with substance use problems (Tubman, Des Rosiers, Schwartz, & O'Hare, 2012). This screener includes 14 items and includes subscales for risky sex expectancies, risky sex behaviors, and gender-based sexual risk perceptions. Ultimately, if a youth is suspected of engaging in risky sexual behavior, a non-judgmental approach to discussing sexual activity will be vitally important to building trust and determining the level of risk posed to the youth in order to determine and engage in approach psychoeducation. The influence of family values (stigmatizing or otherwise) and cultural expectations related to sexual activity and their differential influences based on gender norms are essential considerations when developing prevention programming or engaging in mental healthcare that includes treatment goals specific to sexual behaviors.

Self-Injury

According to the International Society for the Study of Self-injury (2018), non-suicidal self-injury (NSSI) is a self-inflicted behavior intended to produce bodily harm or damage, which excludes suicide-related behaviors (intent to die) and socially sanctioned behaviors (like tattoos or piercings). NSSI can present differently based on a youth's gender identity and performance; for instance, males engage in more self-burning whereas females engage in more self-scratching, both presenting with equal severity (Victor et al., 2018). NSSI includes cutting, burning, and bruising of the skin and can include embedding of objects under the skin for the purpose of producing pain. NSSI is different from self-mutilation in that mutilation results in severe or permanent injury beyond scarring (i.e., cutting off limbs, breaking bones, etc.). NSSI is linked to suicidal ideation in youth and is indicated to be the number one risk factor for youth who make eventual suicide attempts (i.e., Chesin et al., 2017; Whitlock et al., 2013). In a study on adolescent perceptions of self-injury, 10% reported engaging in NSSI at some point in their life and most often told friends about their self-injury, more often than informing adults such as caregivers, counselors, or educators (Berger, Hasking, & Martin, 2017). Recognition of the onset of NSSI is common at the beginning of puberty, between ages 12–14, and thus coincides with a number of cognitive and social-emotional developmental changes (Emelianchik-Key & La Guardia, 2019). A developmental perspective of self-injury can assist in the development of contextually appropriate approaches to prevention and intervention.

Central to a developmental understanding is the perspective that NSSI is an attempt to cope with emotionally overwhelming or confusing life experiences. Youth using self-injury to cope are typically attempting to manage both external and internal triggers that exacerbate feelings of anxiety and depression, and sometimes to manage suicidal thoughts and urges. NSSI is a survival technique and effective coping skill (see the Cornell Research Program for Self-Injury and Recovery). While NSSI is destructive, one uses it with the purpose of facilitating life by regulating emotions. Emotional dysregulation is a strong risk factor in youth who engage in self-injury, including emotional awareness, lack of emotional clarity, difficulty controlling impulses, and non-acceptance of emotional responses (You et al., 2018). Often, adolescents and young adults who engage in self-injury over an extended period find a sense of identity and community in the behavior, as the internet and peer relationships facilitate connections between people who are struggling with both NSSI and associated emotional issues. Youth who engage in self-injurious behaviors tend to have at least one friend who also uses NSSI to cope (Jarvi, Jackson, Swenson, & Crawford, 2013). Thus, relational components are an important part of any treatment. For more on the issues related to NSSI, assessment, and treatment visit Cornell's "Self-Injury and Recovery Resources (SIRR)" page at www.selfinjury.bctr.cornell.edu.

When working with individuals who self-injure (Table 10.1), it is important to know about the psychological benefit of the behavior (e.g., management of anxiety), other co-occurring and potentially harmful coping behaviors (e.g., substance abuse and eating disordered behavior), and presence of suicidal ideation. Co-occurring harmful coping and suicidal ideation increases risk for suicide for youth engaging in self-injury. It is important to note that engagement in NSSI has been linked to experiencing of anxiety, and thus, treatment of anxiety may be a central component to working with those engaging in self-injury. Often, when youth experience suicidal ideation and NSSI, depression becomes a component of their emotional experience, most often tied to thoughts of suicide. Thus, addressing symptoms of depression and anxiety are central for both the cessation of NSSI and treatment of suicidal ideation, when present.

Table 10.1 Assessments for Screening and Treatment of Non-Suicidal Self-Injury

Assessment/Intervention	Overview
NSSI Assessment Tool (NSSI-AT) (Whitlock, Exner-Cortens, & Purington, 2014)	Available in full (27 items) and brief (12 items) versions used to assess the characteristics, frequency, and function of NSSI and primarily designed for research purposes, but could be useful in practice.
Deliberate Self-Harm Inventory (DSHI) (Gratz, 2001)	A self-report questionnaire designed to assess deliberate self-harm frequency and type. This self-report inventory consists of 17 items.
Suicide Attempt Self-Injury Interview (SASII) (Linehan, Comtois, Brown, Heard, & Wagner, 2006)	This interview protocol was designed to assess both suicide attempts and deliberate self-injury through scoring of seven scales (22 items) including suicide intent, lethality, rescue likelihood, risk/rescue ratio, suicide communications, interpersonal influence, and emotion relief. The scale also includes nine open-ended questions.
Self-Harm Behavior Questionnaire (SHBQ) (Gutierrez, Osman, Barrios, & Kopper, 2001)	This questionnaire (22 items) includes four sections that measure non-suicidal self-harm, suicide attempts, suicide threats, and suicidal ideation.
Emotional Regulation Individual Therapy for Adolescents (ERITA) (Bjureberg et al., 2017)	A manualized treatment that integrates components of cognitive behavioral, acceptance, dialectical, mindfulness-based, and experiential, emotion-focused treatments to assist in identifying, differentiating, describing, and accepting emotions.
SIRR (Bubrick, Goodman, & Whitlock, 2010)	A protocol for school counselors for response to and management of self-injurious students in primary and secondary school settings.
CBT (Weinberg, Gunderson, Hennen, & Cutter, 2006)	A brief manual-assisted Cognitive Behavioral Therapy (MACT) extending for 6–8 sessions including optional parent sessions and incorporating problem-solving elements of CBT, bibliotherapy, and emotionally focused elements of Dialectical Behavior Therapy (DBT).
DBT-A (Fleischhaker, Böhme, Sixt, & Brück, 2011)	A manualized Dialectical Behavioral Therapy program extending for 16–24 weeks. DBT is a behavioral, problem-solving focused approach blended with acceptance-based strategies, and an emphasis on skills training and motivational enhancement.
Treatment for Self-Injurious Behaviors (T-SIB) (Andover, Schatten, Morris, & Miller, 2015)	A brief nine-session approach specifically designed to treat young people engaging in NSSI through identification of behavioral functions and reinforcers, as well as the development of adaptive coping strategies.
Acceptance and Commitment Therapy (ACT) for Emotional Regulation (Blackledge & Hayes, 2001)	ACT's premise is that cognitive processes distort and enhance experiencing of unpleasant emotion, leading to engagement in problematic behaviors to avoid or attenuate unpleasant emotions. ACT works to guide clients in experiencing problematic emotions and understanding their function in a useful way, rather than working to change cognitions or reduce problematic emotional experiences.

Suicidal Ideation

For youth, suicide is the second leading cause of death for those aged 10–35 (CDC, 2017a). Between 2007 and 2017, significant climbs in suicide were evident among both male and female youth (Hedegaard, Curtin, & Warner, 2018). Suicide is linked to a number of co-occurring risk factors, including mental health diagnoses, childhood maltreatment, harsh parenting, and experiences with oppression and severe or terminal illness. However, a recent meta-analysis of all suicide research over the last several decades conducted by Franklin et al. (2017) highlights an issue with our current understanding of risk and protective factors. Ultimately, conclusions indicated that assessment of suicidal ideation and behaviors must be contextual to determine accurately if a suicide attempt is imminent. Franklin postulates that suicide may follow with scientific theories of indeterminacy, which is described philosophically in ideas related to deconstructionism (a construct, such as suicide, cannot be understood divorced from context). This means that the clinician, a peer, and/or family member would likely be the best person to determine if someone is likely to attempt suicide if these individuals understand the context of the person at risk (i.e., their needs, beliefs, and barriers). Following Franklin's logic, anyone could engage in suicidal behavior given certain circumstances. Thus, your relationship with the youth would be critical in determining need related to suicide risk.

Suicidal ideation, attempts, and death by suicide are serious concerns for youth, and thoughts of suicide are not an uncommon occurrence during adolescent development. Counselors need to be able to discuss thoughts of suicide openly and without judgment. There are a number of training programs available for youth and those working with youth to assist in the open communication of suicidal thoughts and behaviors. Some of these programs and interventions are briefly reviewed in Table 10.2. As youth often share their struggles with peers, as is developmentally appropriate, peer-to-peer programs designed to prevent suicide may be a valuable resource in schools (e.g., Hope Squads and Signs of Suicide). Hope Squads focus on training students to be appropriate resources for their peers and to recognize when a peer is suicidal and have conversations about suicide in an open, caring way. School staff are trained to serve as support and a point of contact for trained peer participants. Staff and students are educated about suicide in a non-stigmatizing way to prevent perceptions of shame often associated with thoughts and feelings of suicide. Signs of Suicide takes a different approach in that all students are trained to communicate with one another about suicide prevention. Programming is designed to empower schools to collaborate with community stakeholders in the training, and provides materials for school administrators to set up prevention programming. Implementation of an evidence-based suicide prevention program with schools is an effective and important way for counselors to address multiple issues related to suicide, such as those discussed in this chapter (e.g., depression), and provide a support atmosphere wherein youth feel comfortable addressing their struggles.

Safety Planning

Safety or stabilization planning requires involvement, investment, and agreement from a youth and a caregiver when a concern for self-harm (e.g., NSSI, substance abuse) or suicidal behaviors is evident. Many versions of safety plans are available from a variety of sources and examples are provided by the Suicide Prevention Resource Center (www.sprc.org). When writing a safety plan, it is useful to include both risk factors for suicide or harm as well as resources and strengths that may improve someone's emotional experience. Listing strengths and assets, useful and effective coping strategies for distress, and people who might be helpful to contact when the client is feeling isolated or having suicidal thoughts are important for prevention. One method for safety planning was developed as

Table 10.2 Approaches to Suicide Prevention in Youth

Approach	Overview
Hope Squad https://hopesquad.com/	A peer-to-peer prevention program in which adolescents are nominated by their peers to be Hope Squad representatives and serve as a resource to their peers who are struggling. Faculty and staff are trained to provide support and assistance to Hope Squad volunteers.
Signs of Suicide www.sprc.org/resources-programs/sos-signs-suicide	S.O.S. is a universal, school-based depression awareness and suicide prevention program designed for students in middle school (ages 11–13) or high school (ages 13–17). The goal is to decrease suicide through education, encourage help seeking, reduce stigma, and engage parents and caregivers.
ASIST www.livingworks.net/	ASIST is a two-day, two-trainer workshop for family, friends, and other community members that may be the first to talk with a person at risk. ASIST can also provide those in formal helping roles with professional development to ensure that they are prepared to provide suicide first aid.
CAMS https://cams-care.com/	Collaborative Assessment and Management of Suicidality is a therapeutic framework for suicide-specific assessment and treatment of suicidal risk. It includes screening, safety planning, and an intervention protocol for reducing suicidal ideation. Research indicates that it is as effective as DBT (Andreasson et al., 2016).
CT-SP and Brief CBT (Stanley et al., 2009)	Cognitive Behavior Therapy (CBT): Suicide Prevention (CT-SP) and Brief CBT is a 10-session protocol and an evidence-based, manualized cognitive behavioral treatment for adults with suicidal ideation and behaviors, and has shown effectiveness for work with adolescents.
DBT (CADTH, 2010)	Dialectical Behavior Therapy (DBT) was initially developed as an intervention for parasuicidal individuals. It consists of mindfulness training, distress tolerance and acceptance, interpersonal effectiveness, and emotional regulation. It has shown to be effective with suicidal youth specific to decreasing instances of suicidal ideation.

part of the Collaborative Assessment and Management of Suicide protocol (CAMS) which highlights the importance of discussing reduction of access to lethal means and including emergency contact numbers (including the national suicide hotline, 1-800-273-TALK) in safety plans, as well as potential barriers and solutions to attending scheduled mental healthcare appointments. The FCC recently approved the use of a three-digit number for suicide emergencies, similar to 911. That number has been proposed to be 988 (as of December 2019). Busby et al. (2019) highlighted the potential importance of crisis hotline availability, particularly for youth, finding willingness to engage and actual use to be high among adolescent participants who had visited an emergency department due to suicidal ideation or attempt. In safety planning, it may also be important to attend to aspects of Joiner's Interpersonal Theory of Suicide (IPTS). This highly researched perspective states that an individual is at highest risk for attempt if three concerns are present: (a) a feeling and belief that they do not belong; (b) a feeling and belief that they are a burden on those they love; and (c) they have access to a means for suicide, in conjunction with capability of acquiring such means. Talking to youth about concerns related to each of these areas may help counselors in making decisions about care.

ADHD

ADHD stands for attention deficit/hyperactivity disorder. Diagnosis of this disorder can sometimes elicit controversy. According to the CDC (2020), ADHD is the most commonly diagnosed childhood disorder in the United States since the 1960s, and highlights how cultural, social, and environmental factors often play a role in diagnosis (Smith, 2017). Regardless of your personal beliefs about ADHD, we will examine some information to assist you in understanding this prevalent issue. It is also imperative for counselors to advocate on behalf of children and adolescents when it comes to inaccurate diagnosis and labeling of children and adolescents presenting with normal developmental responses to multiple stimuli. Professionals warn about the difficulty of diagnosing ADHD due to the symptoms resembling normal child and adolescent behaviors (Rowland, Lesesne, & Abramowitz, 2002), a concern evident at the initial conception of ADHD in the 1950s (Smith, 2017). Further, the diagnosis often results from caregiver and teacher reports of symptomatic behavior as, according to Rowland et al. (2002), "no laboratory tests reliably predict ADHD", and prevalence rates are "sensitive to who is asked what and how information is combined" (p. 162).

Although the overdiagnosis and overmedication of ADHD has been well researched and largely noted (Merten et al., 2017), rates of ADHD continue to dramatically increase across groups, including those defined by race and ethnicity (CHADD, 2016). An estimated 6.1 million (9.4%) children and adolescents in the United States ages 2–17 had been diagnosed with ADHD at some point in their development (Danielson et al., 2018). The *Diagnostic and Statistical Manual of Mental Disorders* (*DSM-5*) revised criteria for diagnosis to now include six of the nine symptoms related to inattention such as "fails to give close attention to details" and/or "often avoids, dislikes, or is reluctant to engage in tasks that require sustained mental effort" (p. 59) (American Psychiatric Association, 2013). The individual may also meet six of nine symptoms related to hyperactivity/impulsivity such as "often fidgets with or taps hands or feet or squirms in seat" or "often has difficulty waiting his or her turn" (p. 60) to be identified with ADHD. According to the *DSM-5*, symptoms must be present for at least six months "to a degree that is inconsistent with developmental level" (p. 59), have been present before the individual was 12 years old, and are present in at least two settings and are not better described by another disorder, which is why knowledge relating to diagnosis of childhood anxiety is important as often symptoms of anxiety, hyperactivity, and inattention can be conflated. When diagnosing older adolescents and adults (17 and older), the number of symptoms needed is five of nine.

Although this text will not go into detail about diagnostic criteria, we encourage counselors to be very aware of the impact of diagnosis on children and youth, especially those impacting them at disproportionate rates. Counselors need to be very familiar with criteria in order to prevent overdiagnosis and know when it may be appropriate to advocate for children and adolescents experiencing a normal range of developmental reaction to their context of living. Many educators and researchers believe ADHD to be a sham. Corrigan (2014) writes:

> The time has come for debunking ADHD and exposing how this invented disorder created to drug children does not exist. Despite unanimous agreement that no test exists to identify ADHD, 6.4 million American children are labeled with ADHD. To make matters worse, approximately two-thirds of those children diagnosed with ADHD are prescribed drugs with many dangerous side effects, which include more serious mental disorders and death. After six decades of marketing stimulants and scaring parents

into thinking something is seriously wrong with their highly creative, energetic, and communicative child, ADHD drug manufacturers still claim they have no idea what ADHD drugs actually do to children's' brains. They make such claims when research shows ADHD drugs cause permanent brain damage in lab animals.

(back cover)

It is important to understand the biopsychosocial context of symptoms consistent with an ADD (attention deficit disorder)/ADHD diagnosis, as well as the cultural context of such behaviors. Recent studies indicate genetic markers associated with symptoms of inattention and hyperactivity, which could indicate some biological basis supporting the diagnosis (Demontis et al., 2019). Explore this topic while thoughtfully examining your beliefs and perspectives on such controversial topics.

Treatment decisions should be based on research evidence, not opinion; however, we know that counselors carry biased perspectives even when not meaning to, due to our own responses to cultural messaging. It is critical that those who experience symptoms of ADHD not be stigmatized (e.g., engaging in conversations regarding the existence of their experience), as their treatment is imperative and should be the focus of clinical work. We simply want to highlight the need for counselors to understand diagnostic procedures, treatment, and effective approaches to working with individuals. We need to be able to assist clients and provide support for children, adolescents, and families, while meeting clients where they are and advocating for them in a way that is useful for their long-term wellness and functioning. It is also important for counselors to understand that receiving a diagnosis of ADHD can lead to stigma, lower behavioral self-concept, lower self-esteem (Cook, Knight, Hume, & Qureshi, 2014; Wiener et al., 2012), stereotyping (Walker-Noack, Corkum, Elik, & Fearon, 2013), and decreased career and educational achievement (Kuriyan et al., 2013). This is not an uncommon outcome for those diagnosed with significant mental health issues in youth, highlighting the need to address mental health stigma to improve the lives of our clients. Further, Kemper et al. (2018) discussed:

> Misdiagnosis can lead to overdiagnosis or underdiagnosis and can also miss conditions that can be similar in appearance to ADHD (e.g., anxiety, conduct disorders, speech or language delay, other medical disorders/diseases, or other developmental disorders) that may warrant a different course of treatment.
>
> (p. 2)

As previously noted, symptoms associated with various diagnoses may be associated with challenges consistent with normal development, response to trauma, or anxiety resulting from a developmental struggle or life event. It is imperative to focus on the child instead of a collection of symptoms. A recent study elucidates the following specific to ADHD: higher incidences of physician-diagnosed ADHD occur in high-income household areas, males are more likely to be diagnosed than females at a ratio of 3:1, and from 2001–2010, researchers noted a 95% increase of ADHD diagnosis among Black females (Getahun et al., 2013). Multicultural competency and awareness as they relate to contextual factors influencing diagnostic criteria are important aspects of assessment and treatment. Additionally, if diagnosing is a must, counselors must work to ensure an accurate diagnosis, as ADHD can often overlap and/or mimic symptoms of anxiety, depression (Segenreich et al., 2015), and/or PTSD (Weinstein, Staffelbach, & Biaggio, 2000). Further, researchers Brown et al., caution "if clinicians are not routinely identifying ACEs [adverse childhood experiences; see Chapter 8 of this volume], particularly among children with behavioral concerns such as ADHD, there might be a heightened risk of missing an underlying trauma history or misattributing some of the symptoms of traumatic stress as solely those of ADHD" (2014, p. 350). It is also imperative for counselors to keep in mind that child maltreatment (Stern et al., 2018), physical abuse, sexual abuse, and female children's exposure to parental domestic violence are significantly associated with ADHD (Fuller-Thomas & Lewis, 2015), which may indicate a trauma-linked process consistent with PTSD.

We have worked with multiple children and families who discussed feeling pressured by their school or preschool to get a diagnosis for their child and put them on medication. We recall countless counseling and caregiver sessions where caregivers expressed feeling as if they had no choice as to how to advocate for and help their child. Often, trauma or a life event such a divorce or a death in the family was noted, caregivers were in touch with the school, and they were still feeling intimidated. We certainly understand that schools have a job to do, as well. Teachers have an impossible task of caring for their students while teaching in underfunded, overcrowded classrooms (our highest respect toward teachers is impossible to convey). We just want to highlight the role of advocacy and alternatives to psychopharmacological interventions when other approaches have yet to be attempted. Counselors can offer to come observe the student in the classroom, work with the school counselor and other members of the school team and caregivers, develop a treatment team approach, and discuss and design techniques and interventions that work for this specific child and the specific needs discovered, so all feel included, heard, and valued. Often this approach is beneficial for many presenting issues. As counselors who have worked in multiple settings with children and adolescents, these are approaches we have seen work firsthand while strengthening relationships and supporting both the families and the school. Counselors are encouraged to work with youth and their families in multiple settings while collaborating with other professionals involved in the child's life.

Exceptional Children and Adolescents

Counselors must also learn to work with, advocate for, and support exceptional children and adolescents. Exceptional children and adolescents are often misunderstood and frequently receive less services from counselors (Tarver-Behring & Spagna, 2004). The term exceptional refers to any child or adolescent "who may be an 'exception' to the rule" (Hunt & Marshall, 2012, p. 3). This can include students who receive special education services, students who use a wheelchair, students who are blind, students who are gifted, and students who have a cognitive or physical disability that influences the way in which they learn or interact with others (Hunt & Marshall, 2012, p. 3).

Ability Status

Ability status is a term referring to whether or not a person experiences privilege in relation to their physical or mental needs. We are aware that terms such as abled, disabled, able-bodied, etc., are used to describe individuals; however, it is important to refer to individuals as someone "having a disability" or "not having a disability" as opposed to defining them by their ability status (Hixson & Lorah, 2006). In other words, person-first language demonstrates an interest in honoring a person as they are rather than through a potentially biased perception of their identity. For example, you may be working with a child *with* autism, not an autistic child. You may work with someone who uses a wheelchair, not a handicapped or wheelchair-bound person. You may have a client with epilepsy, not a client who is an epileptic.

The U.S. Census Bureau reports that approximately 56.7 million people (around 19%) reported a disability (Brault, 2012). The Census Bureau also indicated that 5.2 million children under the age of 15 reported some kind of disability (Brault, 2012). According to the *Health Disparities Chart Book on Disability and Racial and Ethnic Status in the United States* report, "if people with disabilities were a formally recognized minority group, at 19% of the population, they would be the largest minority group in the United States" (Drum, McClain, Horner-Johnson, & Taitano, 2011).

Categories of Disabilities

Every year, millions of children and adolescents with disabilities are able to obtain services intended to meet their individual and unique needs under federal law through the Individuals with Disabilities Education Act (IDEA) (National Dissemination Center for Children with Disabilities [NICHCY], 2012). These services are important to the success, development, and achievement of many (NICHCY, 2012). NICHCY has defined 13 categories of disabilities under IDEA, as a result of which individuals aged 3–21 years old may qualify for services:

1. *Autism* means a developmental disability significantly affecting verbal and nonverbal communication and social interaction (generally evident before age three) that adversely affects a child's educational performance. Other characteristics often associated with autism are engaging in repetitive activities and stereotyped movements, resistance to environmental change or change in daily routines, and unusual responses to sensory experiences. The term *autism* does not apply if the child's educational performance is adversely affected primarily because the child has an emotional disturbance, as defined in #4 below. A child who shows the characteristics of autism after age 3 could be diagnosed as having autism if the criteria above are satisfied.
2. *Deaf-Blindness* means concomitant [simultaneous] hearing and visual impairments, the combination of which causes severe communication and other developmental and educational needs that cannot be accommodated in special education programs solely for children with deafness or children with blindness.
3. *Deafness* means a hearing impairment so severe that a child is unable or has extreme difficulty processing linguistic information through hearing, with or without amplification, which adversely affects a child's educational performance.
4. *Emotional Disturbance* means a condition exhibiting one or more of the following characteristics over a long period of time and to a marked degree that adversely affects a child's educational performance:
    a) An inability to learn that cannot be explained by intellectual, sensory, or health factors.
    b) An inability to build or maintain satisfactory interpersonal relationships with peers and teachers.
    c) Inappropriate types of behavior or feelings under normal circumstances.
    d) A general pervasive mood of unhappiness or depression.
    e) A tendency to develop physical symptoms or fears associated with personal or school problems.

The term includes schizophrenia. The term does not apply to children who are socially maladjusted, unless it is determined that they have an emotional disturbance.

5. *Hearing Impairment* means an impairment in hearing, whether permanent or fluctuating, that adversely affects a child's educational performance but is not included under the definition of "deafness".
6. *Intellectual Disability* means significantly sub-average general intellectual functioning, existing concurrently [at the same time] with deficits in adaptive behavior and manifested during the developmental period, that adversely affects a child's educational performance.
7. *Multiple Disabilities* means concomitant [simultaneous] impairments (such as intellectual disability-orthopedic impairment), the combination of which causes such severe educational needs that they cannot be accommodated in special education programs solely for one of the impairments. The term does not include deaf-blindness.
8. *Orthopedic Impairment* means a severe orthopedic impairment that adversely affects a child's educational performance. The term includes impairments caused by a congenital anomaly, impairments caused by a disease (e.g., poliomyelitis, bone tuberculosis), and impairments from other causes (e.g., cerebral palsy, amputations, and fractures or burns that cause contractures).
9. *Other Health Impairment* means having limited strength, vitality, or alertness, including a heightened alertness to environmental stimuli, that results in limited alertness with respect to the educational environment, that

    a) Is due to chronic or acute health problems such as asthma, attention deficit disorder or attention deficit hyperactivity disorder, diabetes, epilepsy, a heart condition, hemophilia, lead poisoning, leukemia, nephritis, rheumatic fever, sickle cell anemia, and Tourette syndrome; and
    b) Adversely affects a child's educational performance.

10. *Specific Learning Disability* means a disorder in one or more of the basic psychological processes involved in understanding or in using language, spoken or written, that may manifest itself in the imperfect ability to listen, think, speak, read, write, spell, or to do mathematical calculations. The term includes such conditions as perceptual disabilities, brain injury, minimal brain dysfunction, dyslexia, and developmental aphasia. The term does not include learning problems that are primarily the result of visual, hearing, or motor disabilities; of emotional disturbance; or of environmental, cultural, or economic disadvantage.
11. *Speech or Language Impairment* means a communication disorder such as stuttering, impaired articulation, a language impairment, or a voice impairment that adversely affects a child's educational performance.
12. *Traumatic Brain Injury* means an acquired injury to the brain caused by an external physical force, resulting in total or partial functional disability or psychosocial impairment, or both, that adversely affects a child's educational performance. The term applies to open or closed head injuries resulting in impairments in one or more areas, such as cognition; language; memory; attention; reasoning; abstract thinking; judgment; problem-solving; sensory, perceptual, and motor abilities; psychosocial behavior; physical functions; information processing; and speech. The term does not apply to brain injuries that are congenital or degenerative, or to brain injuries induced by birth trauma.

13. *Visual Impairment Including Blindness* means an impairment in vision that, even with correction, adversely affects a child's educational performance. The term includes both partial sight and blindness.

(NICHCY, 2012, pp. 3–4).

Intellectual and Developmental Disabilities

The American Association on Health and Disability (AAHD, 2014) reported that there are more than seven million people in the United States with intellectual disability. The Individuals with Disabilities Education Act (IDEA) is a federal statute protecting the rights of children and adolescents with disabilities to access a free appropriate public education (FAPE). The IDEA also assists at the state and local level with funding for additional costs accrued to educate children and adolescents with disabilities (Dragoo, 2017). "In 2015–16, the number of students ages 3–21 receiving special education services was 6.7 million, or 13 percent of all public school students. Among students receiving special education services, 34 percent had specific learning disabilities" (McFarland et al., 2018, p. 74). The National Institutes of Health (2010) defines intellectual and developmental disabilities as follows.

> *Intellectual disability* refers to a group of disorders characterized by a limited mental capacity and difficulty with adaptive behaviors such as managing money, schedules and routines, or social interactions. Intellectual disability originates before the age of 18 and may result from physical causes, such as autism or cerebral palsy, or from nonphysical causes, such as lack of stimulation and adult responsiveness.
>
> *Developmental disability* is a severe, long term disability that can affect cognitive ability, physical functioning, or both. These disabilities appear before age 22 and are likely to be life-long. The term "developmental disability" encompasses intellectual disability but also includes physical disabilities. Some developmental disabilities may be solely physical, such as blindness from birth. Others involve both physical and intellectual disabilities stemming from genetic or other causes, such as Down syndrome and fetal alcohol syndrome.
>
> (p. 1)

According to the American Association of Intellectual and Developmental Disabilities (AAIDD, 2019), the three main criteria for intellectual disability are: substantial limitations in intellectual functioning, substantial limitations in adaptive behavior, and onset before 18 years of age. AAIDD also notes that IQ tests are used to measure mental capacity for reasoning, problem-solving, and learning. An IQ test score below or close to 70, or even up to 75, suggests a limitation in intellectual functioning. AAIDD discussed that other tests are used to determine limitations in adaptive behavior, which contains three types of skills:

- *Conceptual skills:* linguistic and verbal understanding; currency, time, number concepts; and self-initiation
- *Social skills:* relational skills, social responsibility, self-esteem, self-compassion, naïveté, community problem-solving, and the capacity to follow rules and laws, and avoid maltreatment
- *Practical skills:* activities of daily life (personal care), job-related skills, healthcare, wellness, travel/transportation, schedules/routines, safety/protection, use of money, use of technology

Additionally, in the 11th edition of *Intellectual Disability: Definition, Classification, and Systems of Supports* (Schalock, Borthwick-Duffy, Buntinx, Coulter, & Craig, 2010), authors noted the following five assumptions to applying a definition of intellectual disability:

1. Limitations in present functioning must be considered within the context of community environments typical of the individual's age peers and culture.
2. Valid assessment considers cultural and linguistic diversity as well as differences in communication, sensory, motor, and behavioral factors.
3. Within an individual, limitations often coexist with strengths.
4. An important purpose of describing limitations is to develop a profile of needed supports.
5. With appropriate personalized supports over a sustained period, the life functioning of the person with intellectual disability generally will improve.

(p. 1)

Physical Disabilities

Counselors should be aware of two other federal laws that protect the educational rights of children and adolescents. As noted, IDEA serves as a federal statute for children with disabilities and provides funding, and

> section 504 of the Rehabilitation Act of 1973 and the Americans with Disabilities Act (ADA) of 1990 (as amended by the ADA Amendments Act in 2008) address civil rights broadly, prohibiting discrimination against any individual with disabilities, and do not provide any federal funds to assist with implementation.
> (Lipkin & Okamoto, 2015, p. 1651)

IDEA discusses physical disabilities in terms of an *orthopedic impairment* that unfavorably impacts an individual's academic and educational performance severely. Counselors should refer to the definitions listed in this chapter and note how the IDEA defines this in terms of congenital/inherited anomaly, by disease/illness, and in terms of other causes.

In Table 10.3, Lipkin and Okamoto (2015, p. 1653) discuss examples of accommodations and support in school settings for children and/or adolescents who may qualify.

Gifted Children and Adolescents

This section is tricky to write because we believe that all children are in some ways gifted. It is one of our many jobs as counselors to find this gift, talent, or characteristic within this child and build upon it. However, we recognize that there is a more formal understanding of gifted, especially in the academic realm, and we felt it necessary to include these children and adolescents in our conversation as they may often go unnoticed, unsupported, and misdiagnosed or overdiagnosed.

The U.S. Department of Education Office for Civil Rights (2016) notes that:

> Gifted and talented education (GATE) programs are programs during regular school hours that provide special educational opportunities including accelerated promotion through grades and classes and an enriched curriculum for students who are endowed with a high degree of mental ability or who demonstrate unusual physical coordination, creativity, interest, or talent.
> (p. 11)

Table 10.3 Examples of Children or Teenagers Who May Qualify for Special Health and/or Behavioral Accommodations and Support in a School Setting

- Child with intellectual or developmental disability, including the following:
  - Autism spectrum disorder
  - Cerebral palsy
- Child with learning disabilities:
  - Oral expression
  - Listening comprehension
  - Written expression
  - Basic reading skills
  - Reading fluency skills
  - Reading comprehension
  - Mathematics calculation
  - Mathematics problem-solving
- Child with condition affecting behavior in school, including those with a mental health condition, including the following:
  - Teen who is suicidal
  - A child aggressive to others
  - Child shortly after injury, with residual issues, including the following:
    - Child postconcussion and other traumatic brain injury
    - After automobile or other injury
- Child with chronic condition affecting performance, including those with episodic or occasional issues, including the following:
  - Child with asthma or diabetes
  - Child with seizure disorder
  - Child with allergy to food
  - Child with physical disabilities such as juvenile arthritis and muscular dystrophy/neuromuscular disorder
- Child with chronic infection, either on treatment or noncompliant, including the following:
  - Child with HIV/AIDS
  - Child with multidrug-resistant tuberculosis
- Child requiring technological supports, such as
  - Tube feeding or special modified diet (ie, textured or pureed foods or low salt)
  - Ventilator or oxygen

These students may be served by IDEA law, section 504, or the ADA depending on the child's needs in a school setting.

The National Association for Gifted Children (NAGC) notes that the current federal definition of gifted was developed in 1972 but has been modified many times to its current form, which is in the Elementary and Secondary Education Act:

> Students, children, or youth who give evidence of high achievement capability in areas such as intellectual, creative, artistic, or leadership capacity, or in specific academic fields, and who need services and activities not ordinarily provided by the school in order to fully develop those capabilities.
>
> (NAGC, n.d.)

Medical and mental health professionals receive little to no training about the needs and characteristics of gifted individuals (Amend & Beljan, 2009). Gifted students have a variety of needs, ranging from mental health needs to normal developmental concerns that merit immediate consideration and care (Wood & Peterson, 2018). "While gifted students are no more or less likely to experience concerns tied to mental health, they do experience the world differently because they are gifted" (Wood & Peterson, 2018, p. 10). Researchers have also noted that among gifted children and adolescents, intensity is a common experience. Daniels and Piechowski (2009) noted that gifted children often possess a high level of energy and emotional intensity as they react and respond quicker and more intensely than others:

> Because they can be so greatly stimulated, and because they perceive and process things differently, gifted children are often misunderstood. Their excitement is viewed as excessive, their high energy as hyperactivity, their persistence as nagging, their questioning as undermining authority, their imagination as not paying attention, their passion as being disruptive, their strong emotions and sensitivity as immaturity, their creativity and self-directedness as oppositional. They stand out from the norm. But then, what is normal?
>
> (p. 4)

"School counselors who recognize that gifted students may struggle with intensity can normalize strong feelings and dramatic behaviors for these students, who may actually fear they are 'crazy', and help them develop coping strategies" (Wood & Peterson, 2018, p. 35). It is imperative that all counselors understand the characteristics of gifted children. As you read the preceding quote, what other characteristics could be mistaken for those of gifted children? Gifted children are often misdiagnosed with ADD/ADHD, anxiety, bipolar disorder, obsessive-compulsive disorder, Asperger's syndrome (Amend & Beljan, 2009), oppositional defiant disorder, conduct disorder, intermittent explosive disorder, and other mental health diagnoses (Webb et al., 2016). Remember how important advocacy skills are in working with children and adolescents as gifted children are widely and commonly misdiagnosed.

Gifted children and adolescents may be both gifted and also have a mental health diagnosis and/or a learning issue, and are then referred to as twice- or multi-exceptional (Amend & Beljan, 2009). As a child and adolescent counselor, you should also be aware that often an individual's "disability" may hide their "giftedness" and "giftedness" may often hide a "disability" (Foley-Nicpon & Candler, 2018). When both giftedness and another diagnosis is present, interventions must address both areas to see improvement, optimal functioning, and positive results (Amend & Beljan, 2009).

Counselors need to be aware of unique needs for working with gifted students of color. Kitano (2012) discusses the importance of counselors and school counselors advocating for gifted students of color and being in a unique position to address needs, especially counselors working in the school setting who interact with stakeholders and are also involved in student development aspects. Counselors must work to support social and emotional development of gifted students of color. Kitano (2012) notes that these goals may be fitting for all students, but there are problems inherent in achieving these goals which make them particularly unique to students of color and include:

- Having access to appropriate programming and services.
  Establishing a coherent identity that embraces achievement and high aspirations.
- Developing resilience and persistence needed to achieve personal goals.
- Managing intergenerational and other issues associated with immigration.

(p. 210)

According to the U.S. Department of Education Office for Civil Rights' *Civil Rights Data Collection: Data Snapshot on College and Career Readiness* (2014), the opportunity gap in gifted and talented programs is growing. "Black and Latino students represent 26% of the students enrolled in gifted and talented education programs, compared to black and Latino students' 40% enrollment in schools offering gifted and talented programs" (p. 1). This report also noted that:

> White and Asian-American students make up 70% of the students enrolled in gifted and talented education programs, compared to 55% of white and Asian-American enrollment in schools offering gifted and talented programs. Latino and black students represent 26% of the students enrolled in gifted and talented programs, compared to 40% of Latino and black student enrollment in schools offering gifted and talented programs.
>
> (p. 3)

Perhaps this is a good time to remind you of Gardner's theory of multiple intelligences. In the 1980s, Gardner introduced the theory of multiple intelligence because he believed that intelligence was not defined accurately and included a much more limited view than what correctly describes intelligence and what it entails (Gardner, 2006). This information included seven types of intelligence that went beyond traditional testing and IQ measurements. He has since updated his original work to include an eighth and potentially a ninth (Gardner, 1999). Armstrong (2017) describes these nine intelligences in Table 10.4. Counselors are advised to learn more about multiple intelligence and how Gardner

> seriously questioned the validity of determining intelligence through the practice of taking individuals out of their natural learning environment and asking them to do isolated tasks they'd never done before – and probably would never choose to do again. Instead, Gardner suggested that intelligence has more to do with the capacity for (1) solving problems and (2) fashioning products in a context-rich and naturalistic setting.
>
> (Armstrong, 2017, p. 2)

By looking for strengths and building on multiple intelligences, we can assist children and adolescents in believing in self and building self-compassion.

Multicultural Implications and Advocacy

Multicultural sensitivity is imperative when discussing presenting concerns, diagnosis, and advocacy. Counselors must be curious and think critically about statistics that note disproportionate rates of diagnosis in minority and marginalized groups. Counselors must also be aware of the gaps in opportunities, environmental factors, and cultural implications which exist for each client, and how these play a role in presenting concerns.

What does this mean for counselors specifically? Does this mean that certain diagnoses exist at disproportionate rates among certain groups of individuals? "Researchers highlighting the disproportionate prevalence of particular diagnosis among individuals for diverse identities argue that these rates result from individuals belonging to typically oppressed groups (e.g., racial/ethnic minorities, women, sexual minorities) being diagnosed with more severe diagnosis" (Hays, Prosek, & McLeod, 2010, p. 114), meaning that individuals from diverse backgrounds are receiving different diagnoses than they would if they were of the dominant group/culture. Over time and across mental health professionals, racial

Table 10.4 MI Theory Summary Chart

Intelligence	Core Components	Symbol Systems	High End-States	Neurological Systems (Primary Areas)	Developmental Factors	Ways That Cultures Value	Evolutionary Origins	Presence in Other Species	Historical Factors (Relative to Current U.S. Status)
Linguistic	Sensitivity to the sounds, structure, meanings, and functions of words and languages	Phonetic languages (e.g., English)	Writer, orator (e.g., Virginia Woolf, Martin Luther King Jr.)	Left temporal and frontal lobes (e.g., Broca's/Wernicke's areas)	"Explodes" in early childhood; remains robust until old age	Oral histories, storytelling, literature	Written notations found dating to 30,000 years ago	Apes' ability to name	Oral transmission more important before printing press
Logical-Mathematical	Sensitivity to, and capacity to discern, logical or numerical patterns; ability to handle long chains of reasoning	Computer languages (e.g., BASIC)	Scientist, mathematician (e.g., Madame Curie, Blaise Pascal)	Left frontal and right parietal lobes	Peaks in adolescence and early adulthood; higher math insights decline after age 40	Scientific discoveries, mathematical theories, counting and classification systems	Early number systems and calendars found	Bees calculate distances through their dances	More important with influence of computers
Spatial	Capacity to perceive the visual-spatial world accurately and to perform transformations on one's initial perceptions	Ideographic languages (e.g., Chinese [Cantonese and Mandarin])	Artist, architect (e.g., Frida Kahlo, I.M. Pei)	Posterior regions of right hemisphere	Topological thinking in early childhood gives way to Euclidean paradigm around age 9–10; artistic eye stays robust into old age	Artistic works, navigational systems, architectural designs, inventions	Cave drawings	Territorial instinct of several species	More important with advent of video and other visual technologies

Bodily-Kinesthetic	Ability to control one's body movements and to handle objects skillfully	Sign languages, Braille	Athlete, dancer, sculptor (e.g., Martha Graham, Auguste Rodin)	Cerebellum, basal ganglia, motor cortex	Varies depending upon component (strength, flexibility) or domain (gymnastics, baseball, mime)	Crafts, athletic performances, dramatic works, dance forms, sculpture	Evidence of early tool use	Tool use of primates, anteaters, and other species	Was more important in agrarian period
Musical	Ability to produce and appreciate rhythm, pitch, and timbre; appreciation of the forms of musical expressiveness	Musical notational systems, Morse code	Composer, performer (e.g., Stevie Wonder, Midori)	Right temporal lobe	Earliest intelligence to develop; prodigies often go through developmental crisis	Musical compositions, performances, recordings	Evidence of musical instruments back to Stone Age	Bird song	Was more important during oral culture, when communication was more musical in nature
Interpersonal	Capacity to discern and respond appropriately to the moods, temperaments, motivations, and desires of other people	Social cues (e.g., gestures and facial expressions)	Counselor, political leader (e.g., Carl Rogers, Nelson Mandela)	Frontal lobes, temporal lobe (especially right hemisphere), limbic system	Attachment/bonding during first three years critical	Political documents, social institutions	Communal living groups required for hunting/gathering	Maternal bonding observed in primates and other species	More important with increase in service economy
Intrapersonal	Access to one's own "feeling" life and the ability to discriminate among one's emotions; knowledge of one's own strengths and weaknesses	Symbols of the self (e.g., in dreams and artwork)	Psychotherapist, religious leader (e.g., Sigmund Freud, the Buddha)	Frontal lobes, parietal lobes, limbic system	Formation of boundary between "self" and "other" during first three years critical	Religious systems, psychological theories, rites of passage	Early evidence of religious life	Chimpanzees can locate self in mirror; apes experience fear	Continues to be important with increasingly complex society requiring choice-making

(*Continued*)

Table 10.4 (Continued)

Intelligence	Core Components	Symbol Systems	High End-States	Neurological Systems (Primary Areas)	Developmental Factors	Ways That Cultures Value	Evolutionary Origins	Presence in Other Species	Historical Factors (Relative to Current U.S. Status)
Naturalist	Expertise in distinguishing among members of a species, recognizing the existence of other neighboring species, and charting out the relations, formal or informal, among several species	Species classification systems (e.g., Linnaeus), habitat maps	Naturalist, biologist, animal activist (e.g., Charles Darwin, E.O. Wilson, Jane Goodall)	Areas of left parietal lobe important for discriminating "living" from "nonliving" things	Shows up dramatically in some young children; schooling or experience increases formal or informal expertise	Folk taxonomies, herbal lore, hunting rituals, animal spirit mythologies	Early hunting tools reveal understanding of other species	Hunting instinct in innumerable species to discriminate between prey and non-prey	Was more important during agrarian period, then fell out of favor during industrial expansion; now "earth-smarts" are more important than ever to preserve endangered ecosystems

Source: Armstrong, 2017, pp. 6–7

inequalities in regard to mental health diagnoses have been documented and described (Schwartz & Blankenship, 2014). Many examples of this exist within the literature. One study found that of individuals admitted to a state psychiatric hospital, African American individuals were four times more likely than white individuals to be diagnosed with schizophrenia (specifically, paranoid subtype) as opposed to other mood disorders such as bipolar disorder and major depressive disorder (Barnes, 2008). Schwartz and Blankenship (2014) reviewed empirical literature conducted over the last 24 years examining racial disparities in diagnosing and found that:

- African American rates of Schizophrenia are often 3–4 times higher when compared to Euro Americans, and the literature continued to exhibit a long-term increased rate of the schizophrenia diagnosis.
- Latinx Americans were diagnosed with schizophrenia at rates more than 3 times higher than Euro-Americans.
- In general, African Americans were more likely to be diagnosed with a psychotic disorder than Euro Americans
- Latinx Americans and African Americans were found to have an amplified lifetime prevalence rate of psychotic symptoms as compared to Euro Americans and Asians, as reported by clinicians.
- African American and Latinx Americans under the age of 18 were also twice as likely to be diagnosed with a psychotic disorder as Euro American youth.

As noted, diagnostic differences can occur in relation to gender and affectional/sexual orientation as well (Hays et al., 2010, p. 114). One example of this is the diagnosis of borderline personality disorder primarily in women (APA, 2013). However, researchers note that this may not actually be the case and may have to do with limited research, diagnostic bias toward women, and a misdiagnosis of anti-social personality disorder in men (Bayes & Parker, 2017). Additionally, a recent study conducted on a large group of helping professionals (mental health providers, medical doctors, nurses, and other service providers) found that "moderate to strong implicit preferences for straight people over lesbian women or, in particular, gay men, are widespread among heterosexual providers" (Sabin, Riskind, & Nosek, 2015, p. 1836). Sabin et al.'s research highlights how affectional/sexual orientation biases can contribute to healthcare disparities among LGBTGEQIAP+ individuals.

Specific to counselors, a 2010 study analyzing the role of culture on a counselor's clinical decision making indicated that not only were counselors disregarding, overlooking, or minimizing cultural factors, counselors were also diagnosing at disproportionate frequency rates more severe diagnoses for clients belonging to oppressed cultural groups such as race, ethnicity, and gender. Counselors need to be aware of the research around diagnosing and culture. Counselors are encouraged to consider the following questions suggested by Hays et al. (2010):

1. What cultural characteristics define the client?
2. What symptoms does the client present with?
3. How could the symptoms be caused or perpetuated by cultural characteristics?
4. How might symptom expression be related to environmental factors and situational factors?
5. What diagnosis or diagnoses fit this client?

6. To what degree does the client's cultural characteristics – of the interface between these characteristics and environmental factors – influence my diagnosis or diagnoses?
7. Would I give the same diagnosis or diagnoses to a client with different cultural characteristics?

(p. 119)

As discussed, all counseling is multicultural. Counselors need to be well versed in broaching culture in session, and certainly in paying close attention to biases as they arise.

Summary

In this chapter, we discussed common developmental issues of childhood within the context of atypical behaviors, cognitive difficulties, and differences in ability. This information informs counselors of approaches to assessment, intervention, and prevention, and serves to facilitate insightful development of setting/client/student specific programming. It is important to keep in mind that mental health experience intersects within a variety of cultural perspectives and identities, which influences observed behaviors and interactions of the child with others, as well as a child's perception of self. We hope that after reading this chapter, you now have a better idea of what children encountering issues like non-suicidal self-injury and hyperactivity need from the adults in their lives, including school counselors, mental health providers, educators, and caregivers.

Clinician's Corner

In May of 1989, I graduated from the University of Mississippi's School of Pharmacy. I had completed all of my practice hours; so, in June, I took and passed my national licensure exam. Within a month, I was licensed as a pharmacist. I quickly realized I had not learned enough in pharmacy school. I was managing a small, independent pharmacy in my hometown, and I began to see children, who were not that different than me when I was a child, being medicated. My first year of practice was the beginning of an uptick in the number of children and adolescents being diagnosed with ADHD. The more I saw, the more I thought that there had to be a better way. It was then that I said to myself that one day I would return to school and learn another way to help children.

In 1997, the opportunity came, and I returned to university learning. In 2000, I completed my undergraduate in psychology, in 2002 a master's in counseling, and finally in 2009 a doctorate in counselor education in supervision. My original goal of learning more in order to help children had become a lot more. Over my second education, I was introduced to attachment theory, play therapy, and the quickly expanding field of neuroscience. After this, there was no looking back, and my lens for viewing everything changed.

Now, for more than 10 years, I have written about, presented on, and advocated for the developmentally appropriate treatment of children and adolescents. I'm still a pharmacist and have been licensed for nearly 31 years, so much of what I do now relates to working with traumatized children who are medicated. Trauma is enough to have to conceptualize and treat. Add medication to the equation, and watch things change. Sometimes the medication-counseling synergy is beneficial. However, all too often, little time is given to getting the balance correct. In the process of finding regulation for the dysregulated, over medication and side effects occur. Children and adolescents, who have experienced maltreatment, are among the most dysregulated that we see in counseling. These individuals are also more likely to be prescribed multiple medications to moderate mood and behavior. Much is known about developing brains and – to a lesser extent – medicated, developing brains. However, few have attempted to understand medicated, dysregulated, developing brains.

My challenge to everyone is to learn more and find a good set of resources that help increase your understanding of development, the developing brain, and medication.

In what follows, I have included some resources for caregivers and professionals connected to children with myriad issues

Medication Resources

RxList (www.rxlist.com)

This website was created over 25 years by pharmacists. It is focused on detailed and current pharmaceutical information on brand and generic drugs. The staff of RxList routinely and systematically review and update the site based on articles written by pharmacists, physicians, and data sources like the U.S. Food and Drug Administration (FDA). The site is searchable through an A-Z list and includes a symptoms checker. It also includes images of medications that may bed for identification.

Drugs.com (www.drugs.com)

This website provides objective, comprehensive, and up-to-date information about medication. It is written in clear terms so that it may be used by the public, as well those in healthcare. The site is searchable through an A-Z list and includes a side effects checker.

Recommended Textbooks about Medications

Sinacola, R. S., Peters-Strickland, P., & Wyner, J. D. (2020). *Basic psychopharmacology for mental health professionals* (3rd ed.). Pearson Education, Inc.

Preston, J. D., O'Neal, J. H., Talaga, M. C., & Moore, B. A. (2021). *Child and adolescent clinical psychopharmacology made simple* (4th ed.). New Harbinger Publications.

Resources for Caregivers and Professionals about Developmental and Mental Health Illness in Children

Center on the Developing Child (https://developingchild.harvard.edu)

This website, from Harvard University, provides up to date information on the developmental needs of children and families.

Child Mind Institute (www.childmind.org)

This website provides information about children with mental health and learning disorders. It presents information about the developing brain to educate parents, professionals, and policy makers.

National Institute of Mental Health, Child and Adolescent Mental Health (www.nimh.nih.gov/health/topics/child-and-adolescent-mental-health/index.shtml)

This website provides comprehensive information about research on mental disorders. It is searchable by mental disorder.

Conveying Complex Information in Simple and Understandable Terms

Plain Language Action and Information Network (PLAIN) (www.plainlanguage.gov)

This website is focused on providing guidelines and training to help individuals and agencies communicate clearly. The website links to online trainings from the National Institutes of Health, the

Centers for Disease Control and Prevention, the Center for Medicare and Medicaid Services, and others.

Food and Drug Administration (FDA) (www.fda.gov/about-fda/plain-writing-its-law/plain-language-principles)

This website provides suggestions for communicating clearly without unnecessary or overly technical terms.

Edward F. Hudspeth, PhD, NCC,
LPC-S, ACS, RPT-S, RPh, CPC
Sacred Heart University

References

Amend, E. R., & Beljan, P. (2009). The antecedents of misdiagnosis: When normal behaviors of gifted children are misinterpreted as pathological. *Gifted Education International, 25*, 131–143.

American Association of Intellectual and Developmental Disabilities (AAIDD). (2019). *Frequently asked questions on intellectual disability*. Retrieved from https://aaidd.org/intellectual-disability/definition/faqs-on-intellectual-disability.

American Association on Health and Disability (AAHD). (2014). *Population specific fact sheet: What to know when assisting a consumer with intellectual disability*. Retrieved from https://nationaldisabilitynavigator.org/wp-content/uploads/Materials/Population-Specific-Fact-Sheet-ID.pdf.

American Psychiatric Association. (2013). *Diagnostic and statistical manual of mental disorders* (5th ed.). Arlington, VA: Author.

Americans with Disabilities Act. Pub L No. 101–336, 104 Stat 328 (1990), amended Pub L 110-325 (2008).

Andover, M. S., Schatten, H. T., Morris, B. W., & Miller, I. W. (2015). Development of an intervention for nonsuicidal self-injury in young adults: An open pilot trial. *Cognitive and Behavioral Practice, 22*(4), 491–503. https://doi.org/10.1016/j.cbpra.2014.05.003

Andreasson, K., Krogh, J., Wenneberg, C., Jessen, H. K. L., Krakauer, K., Gluud, C., . . . Nordentoft, M. (2016). Effectiveness of dialectical Behavioral Therapy versus Collaborative Assessment and Management of Suicidality treatment for reduction of self-harm in adults with borderline personality traits and disorder: A randomized observer–blinded clinical trial. *Depression and Anxiety, 33*, 520–530. https://doi.org/10.1002/da.22472

Arch, J. J., Eifert, G. H., Davies, C., Vilardaga, J. C. P., Rose, R. D., & Craske, M. G. (2012). Randomized clinical trial of cognitive behavioral therapy (CBT) versus acceptance and commitment therapy (ACT) for mixed anxiety disorders. *Journal of Consulting and Clinical Psychology, 80*(5), 750–765. https://doi.org/10.1037/a0028310

Armstrong, T. (2017). *Multiple intelligences in the classroom* (4th ed.). Alexandria, VA: ASCD.

Barnes, A. (2008). Race, schizophrenia, and admission to state psychiatric hospitals. *Social Work, 53*(1), 78–83. https://doi.org/10.1093/sw/53.1.77

Bayes, A., & Parker, G. (2017). Borderline personality disorder in men: A literature review and illustrative case vignettes. *Psychiatry Research, 257*, 197–202. https://doi.org/10.1016/j.psychres.2017.07.047

Berger, E., Hasking, P., & Martin, G. (2017). Adolescents' perspectives of youth non-suicidal self-injury prevention. *Youth & Society, 49*(1), 3–22. https://doi.org/10.1177/0044118X13520561

Bjureberg, J., Sahlin, H., Hellner, C., Hedman-Lagerlöf, E., Gratz, K. L., Bjärehed, J., . . . Umeå Universitet. (2017). Emotion regulation individual therapy for adolescents with nonsuicidal self-injury disorder: A feasibility study. *BMC Psychiatry, 17*(1), 411–411. https://doi.org/10.1186/s12888-017-1527-4

Blackledge, J. T., & Hayes, S. C. (2001). Emotion regulation in acceptance and commitment therapy. *Journal of Clinical Psychology, 57*(2), 243–255. https://doi.org/10.1002/1097-4679

Boswell, J. F., Thompson-Hollands, J., Farchione, T. J., & Barlow, D. H. (2013). Intolerance of uncertainty: A common factor in the treatment of emotional disorders. *Journal of Clinical Psychology*, 69(6), 630–645.

Brault, M. W. (2012). Americans with disabilities: 2010. *Current Population Reports*, 70–131, U.S. Census Bureau, Washington, DC.

Breuner, C. C., & Mattson, G. (2016). Sexuality education for children and adolescents. *Pediatrics*, 138(2). https://doi.org/10.1542/peds.2016-1348

Brown, N. M., Brown, S. N., Briggs, R. D., German, M., Belamarich, P. F., & Oyeku, S. O. (2014). Associations between adverse childhood experiences and ADHD diagnosis and severity. *Academic Pediatrics*, 17(4), 349–355. https://doi.org/10.1016/j.acap.2016.08.013

Bubrick, K., Goodman, J., & Whitlock, J. (2010). *Non-suicidal self-injury in schools: Developing and implementing school protocol. [Fact sheet] Cornell Research Program on Self-Injurious Behavior in Adolescents and Young Adults*. Retrieved from http://crpsib.com/userfiles/NSSI-schools.pdf

Burgess, A., & DiBartolo, P. (2016). Anxiety and perfectionism: Relationships, mechanisms, and conditions. In F. Sirois & D. Molnar (Eds.), *Perfectionism, health, and well-being*. Switzerland: Springer. https://doi.org/10.1007/978-3-319-18582-8_8

Busby, D. R., King, C. A., Brent, D., Grupp-Phelan, J., Gould, M., Page, K., . . . The Pediatric Emergency Care Applied Research Network (PECARN). (2019). Adolescents' engagement with crisis hotline risk-management services: A report from the emergency department screen for teen suicide risk (ED-STARS) study. *Suicide & Life-Threatening Behavior*, 50(1), 72–82. https://doi.org/10.1111/sltb.12558

Cairns, K. E., Yap, M. B., Pilkington, P. D., & Jorm, A. F. (2014). Risk and protective factors for depression that adolescents can modify: A systematic review and meta-analysis of longitudinal studies. *Journal of Affective Disorders*, 169, 61–75.

Canadian Agency for Drugs and Technologies in Health (CADTH). (2010). Dialectical behaviour therapy in adolescents for suicide prevention: Systematic review of clinical-effectiveness. *CADTH Technology Overviews*, 1(1).

CDC. (2017a). *10 Leading causes of death by age group, United States – 2017*. Retrieved from www.cdc.gov/nchs/data/databriefs/db330-h.pdf

CDC. (2017b). *Sexually transmitted diseases*. Retrieved from www.cdc.gov/std/life-stages-populations/adolescents-youngadults.htm

CDC. (2019). *Substance use and sexual risk behaviors among youth*. Retrieved from www.cdc.gov/healthyyouth/substance-use/dash-substance-use-fact-sheet.htm

CDC. (2020). *Data and statistics on children's mental health*. Retrieved from www.cdc.gov/childrensmentalhealth/data.html

The Center for Motivation and Change. (2016). *The parent's 20-minute guide* (2nd ed). Lulu.com

CHADD. (2016). *General prevalence of ADHD*. Retrieved from https://chadd.org/about-adhd/general-prevalence/

Chawla, N., & Sarkar, S. (2019). Defining "high risk sexual behavior" in the context of substance use. *Journal of Psychosexual Health*, 1(1), 26–31. https://doi.org/10.1177/2631831818822015

Chesin, M. S., Galfavy, H., Sonmez, C. C., Wong, A., Oquendo, M. A., Mann, J., & Stanley, B. (2017). Non-suicidal self-injury is predictive of suicide attempts among individuals with mood disorders. *Suicide and Life Threatening Behavior*, 47(5), 567–579. Retrieved from www.ncbi.nlm.nih.gov/pmc/articles/PMC5724372/

Choi, K. R., Sherbourne, C., Tang, L., Castillo, E., Dixon, E., Jones, A., . . . Wells, K. (2019). A comparative effectiveness trial of depression collaborative care: Subanalysis of comorbid anxiety. *Western Journal of Nursing Research*, 41(7), 1009–1031. https://doi.org/10.1177/0193945918800333

Cook, J., Knight, E., Hume, I., & Qureshi, A. (2014). The self-esteem of adults diagnosed with Attention-Deficit/Hyperactivity Disorder (ADHD): A systematic review of the literature. *ADHD Attention Deficit and Hyperactivity Disorders*, 6(4), 249–268. https://doi.org/10.1007/s12402-014-0133-2

Corrigan, M. W. (2014). *Debunking ADHD: 10 reasons to stop drugging kids for acting like kids*. Lanham, MD: Rowman & Littlefield.

Daniels, S., & Piechowski, M. M. (2009). *Living with intensity: Understanding the sensitivity, excitability and emotional development of gifted children, adolescents and adults*. Scottsdale, AZ: Great Potential Press.

Danielson, M. L., Bitsko, R. H., Ghandour, R. M., Holbrook, J. R., Kogan, M. D., & Blumberg, S. J. (2018). Prevalence of parent-reported ADHD diagnosis and associated treatment among U.S. children and adolescents, 2016. *Journal of Clinical Child & Adolescent Psychology, 47*(2), 199–212. https://doi.org/10.1080/15374416.2017.1417860

Demontis, D., Walters, R. K., Martin, J., Mattheisen, M., Als, T.D., Agerboet, E., . . . Neale, B.M. (2019). Discovery of the first genome-wide significant risk loci for attention deficit/hyperactivity disorder. *Nat Genet, 51*, 63–75. https://doi.org/10.1038/s41588-018-0269-7

De Sanctis, V. A. (2011). *The effects of childhood maltreatment on criminal and substance abuse outcomes in urban youth diagnosed with ADHD*. ProQuest 9781124707624.

Dragoo, K. E. (2017). The individuals with disabilities education act (IDEA), part B: Key statutory and regulatory provisions. *Congressional Research Service*. Retrieved from https://fas.org/sgp/crs/misc/R41833.pdf

Drum, C., McClain, M. R., Horner-Johnson, W., & Taitano, G. (2011). *Health disparities chart book on disability and racial and ethnic status in the United States*. Institute on Disability: University of New Hampshire. Retrieved from https://iod.unh.edu/sites/default/files/media/Project_Page_Resources/HealthDisparities/health_disparities_chart_book_080411.pdf

Emelianchik-Key, K., & La Guardia, A. (2019). *Non-suicidal self-injury throughout the lifespan*. Routledge.

Fleischhaker, C., Böhme, R., Sixt, B., & Brück, C. (2011). Dialectical behavioral therapy for adolescents (DBT-A): A clinical trial for patients with suicidal and self-injurious behavior and borderline symptoms with a one-year follow-up. *Child and Adolescent Psychiatry and Mental Health, 5*(3).

Foley-Nicpon, M., & Candler, M. M. (2018). Psychological interventions for twice-exceptional youth. In S. I. Pfeiffer, E. Shaunessy-Dedrick, & M. Foley-Nicpon (Eds.), *APA handbook of giftedness and talent* (pp. 545–558). Washington, DC: American Psychological Association.

Frances, A. (2013). *Saving normal: An insider's revolt against out-of-control psychiatric diagnosis, DSM-5, big pharma, and the medicalization of ordinary life*. New York: HarperCollins Publishers.

Franklin, J. C., Ribeiro, J. D., Fox, K. R., Bentley, K. H., Kleiman, E. M., Huang, X., . . . Nock, M. K. (2017). Risk factors for suicidal thoughts and behaviors: A meta-analysis of 50 years of research. *Psychological Bulletin, 143*(2), 187–232. https://doi.org/10.1037/bul0000084

Fuller-Thomas, E., & Lewis, D. A. (2015). The relationship between early adversities and attention-deficit/hyperactivity disorder. *Child Abuse & Neglect, 47*, 94–101. https://doi.org/10.1016/j.chiabu.2015.03.005

Gardner, H. (1999). *Intelligence reframed: Multiple intelligences for the 21st century*. New York: Basic Books.

Gardner, H. (2006). *Multiple intelligences: New horizons*. New York: Basic Books.

Getahun, D., Jacobsen, S. J., Fassett, M. J., Chen, W., Demissie, K., & Rhoads, G. G. (2013). Recent trends in childhood attention-deficit/hyperactivity disorder. *JAMA Pediatric, 167*(3), 282–288. https://doi.org/10.1001/2013.jamapediatrics.401

Gratz, K. L. (2001). Measurement of deliberate self-harm: Preliminary data on the deliberate self-harm inventory. *Journal of Psychopathology and Behavioral Assessment, 23*, 253–263. https://doi.org/10.1023/A:1012779403943

Gutierrez, P. M., Osman, A., Barrios, F. X., & Kopper, B. A. (2001). Development and initial validation of the self-harm behavior questionnaire. *Journal of Personality Assessment, 77*(3), 475–490. https://doi.org/10.1207/S15327752JPA7703_08

Hays, D. G., Prosek, E. A., & McLeod, A. L. (2010). A mixed methodological analysis of the role of culture in the clinical decision-making process. *Journal of Counseling and Development, 88*(1), 114–121. https://doi.org/10.1002/j.1556-6678.2010.tb00158.x

Hedegaard, H., Curtin, S. C., & Warner, M. (2018). *Suicide mortality in the United States: 1999–2017*. Retrieved from www.cdc.gov/nchs/data/databriefs/db330-h.pdf

Hixson, A., & Lorah, P. (2006). *Introduction to power and privilege*. Retrieved from https://edge.psu.edu/workshops/mc/power/definitions.shtml

Hunt, N., & Marshall, K. (2012). *Exceptional children and youth* (5th ed.). Belmont, CA: Wadsworth Cengage Learning.

International Society for the Study of Self-injury. (2018). *What is self-injury?* Retrieved from https://itriples.org/about-self-injury/what-is-self-injury/

Jarvi, S., Jackson, B., Swenson, L., & Crawford, H. (2013). The impact of social contagion on nonsuicidal self-injury: A review of the literature. *Archives of Suicide Research*, 17(1), 1–19. https://doi.org/10.1080/13811118.2013.748404

Kemper, A. R., Maslow, G. R., Hill, S., Namdari, B., Allen LaPointe, N. M., Goode, A. P., . . . Sanders, G. D. (2018). Attention deficit hyperactivity disorder: Diagnosis and treatment in children and adolescents. *Comparative Effectiveness Review*, 203. Rockville, MD: Agency for Healthcare Research and Quality. https://doi.org/10.23970/AHRQEPCCER203

Kitano, M. (2012). Social-emotional needs of gifted students of color. In T. L. Cross & J. R. Cross (Eds.), *Handbook for counselors serving students with gifts and talents: Development, relationships, school issues, and counseling needs/interventions* (pp. 209–226). Waco, TX: Prufrock Press.

Knight, J. R., Sherritt, L., Shrier, L. A., Harris, S. K., & Chang, G. (2002). Validity of the CRAFFT substance abuse screening test among adolescent clinic patients. *Archives of Pediatrics & Adolescent Medicine*, 156(6), 607–614.

Kuriyan, A. B., Pelham, W. E., Molina, B. S. G., Waschbusch, D. A., Ghaggy, E. M., Sibley, M. H., . . . Kent, K. M. (2013). Young adult educational and vocational outcomes of children diagnosed with ADHD. *Journal of Abnormal Child Psychology*, 41(1), 27–41. https://doi.org/10.1007/s10802-012-9658-z

Linehan, M. M., Comtois, K. A., Brown, M. Z., Heard, H. L., & Wagner, A. (2006). Suicide Attempt Self-Injury Interview (SASII): Development, reliability, and validity of a scale to assess suicide attempts and intentional self-injury. *Psychological Assessment*, 18(3), 303–312. https://doi.org/10.1037/1040-3590.18.3.303

Lipkin, P. H., & Okamoto, J. (2015). The individuals with disabilities education act (IDEA) for children with special educational needs. *Pediatrics*, 136(6), 1650–1662, https://doi.org/10.1542/peds.2015-3409

Livheim, F., Hayes, L., Ghaderi, A., Magnusdottir, T., Högfeldt, A., Rowse, J., . . . Samhällsvetenskapliga Fakulteten. (2015). The effectiveness of acceptance and commitment therapy for adolescent mental health: Swedish and Australian pilot outcomes. *Journal of Child and Family Studies*, 24(4), 1016–1030. https://doi.org/10.1007/s10826-014-9912-9

Mammarella, I. C., Donolato, E., Caviola, S., & Giofre, D. (2018). Anxiety profiles and protective factors: A latent profile analysis in children. *Personality and Individual Differences*, 124, 201–208. https://doi.org/10.1016/j.paid.2017.12.017

McFarland, J., Hussar, B., Wang, X., Zhang, J., Wang, K., Rathbun, A., . . . Bullock Mann, F. (2018). *The condition of education 2018 (NCES 2018–144). U.S. department of education.* Washington, DC: National Center for Education Statistics. Retrieved from https://nces.ed.gov/pubsearch/pubsinfo.asp?pubid=2018144

Merten, E. C., Cwik, J. C., Margraf, J., & Schneider, S. (2017). Overdiagnosis of mental disorders in children and adolescents (in developed countries). *Child and Adolescent Psychiatry and Mental Health*, 11(5), 1–11. https://doi.org/10.1186/s13034-016-0140-5

National Association for Gifted Children. (n.d.). *Frequently asked questions about gifted education.* Retrieved from www.nagc.org/resources-publications/resources/frequently-asked-questions-about-gifted-education

National Dissemination Center for Children with Disabilities (NICHCY). (2012). *Categories of disability under IDEA.* Retrieved from www.parentcenterhub.org/wp-content/uploads/repo_items/gr3.pdf

National Institutes of Health. (2010). *Fact sheet: Intellectual and developmental disabilities.* Retrieved from https://report.nih.gov/NIHfactsheets/Pdfs/IntellectualandDevelopmentalDisabilities(NICHD).pdf

National Institute on Drug Abuse. (2019). *Monitoring the future survey: High school and youth trends.* Retrieved from www.drugabuse.gov/publications/drugfacts/monitoring-future-survey-high-school-youth-trends

O'Hare, T. (2001). Substance abuse and risky sex in young people: The development and validation of the Risky Sex Scale. *Journal of Primary Prevention*, 22, 89–101. https://doi.org/10.1023/A:1012653717412

PBIS. (2019, August 8). *When school mental health is integrated within a MTSS: What's different?* Retrieved from www.pbis.org/resource/fact-sheet-isf-201-when-school-mental-health-is-integrated-within-a-mtss-whats-different

Ritchwood, T. D., Ford, H., DeCoster, J., Sutton, M., & Lochman, J. E. (2015). Risky sexual behavior and substance use among adolescents: A meta-analysis. *Children and Youth Services Review*, 52, 74–88. https://doi.org/10.1016/j.childyouth.2015.03.005

Rowland, A. S., Lesesne, C. A., & Abramowitz, A. J. (2002). The epidemiology of attention-deficit/hyperactivity disorder (ADHD): A public health view. *Mental Retardation and Developmental Disabilities Research Review*, 8(3), 162–170. https://doi.org/10.1002/mrdd.10036

Sabin, J. A., Riskind, F. G., & Nosek, B. A. (2015). Health care providers' implicit and explicit attitudes toward lesbian women and gay men. *American Journal of Public Health*, 105(9), 1831–1841. https://doi.org/10.2105/AJPH.2015.302631

SAMHSA. (2012). *Alcohol and drug addiction happens in the best of families*. Retrieved from https://store.samhsa.gov/system/files/phd1112.pdf

SAMHSA. (2019). *Guidance to states and school systems on addressing mental health and substance use issues in schools*. Retrieved from https://store.samhsa.gov/system/files/joint_info_bulletin_school_based_services_final_508_6.28.19.pdf

Schalock, R. L., Borthwick-Duffy, S. A., Buntinx, W. H., Coulter, D. L., & Craig, E. M. (2010). *Intellectual disability: Definition, classification, and systems of supports*. American Association on Intellectual and Developmental Disabilities.

Schwartz, R. C., & Blankenship, D. M. (2014). Racial disparities in psychotic disorder diagnosis: A review of empirical literature. *World Journal of Psychiatry*, 4(4), 133–140. https://doi.org/10.5498/wjp.v4.i4.133

Section 504 of the Rehabilitation Act of 1973. 29USC §701 et seq (1973).

Segenreich, D., Paez, M. S., Regalla, M. A., Fortes, D., Faraone, S. V., Sergeant, J., & Mattos, P. (2015). Multilevel analysis of ADHD, anxiety and depression symptoms aggregation in families. *European Child & Adolescent Psychiatry*, 24(5), 525–536. https://doi.org/10.1007/s00787-014-0604-1

Slesnick, N. (2008). Treatment attendance among homeless youth: The impact of childhood abuse and prior suicide attempts. *Substance Abuse*, 29(2), 43–52. https://doi.org/10.1080//08897070802093056

Smith, M. (2017). Hyperactive around the world? The history of ADHD in global perspective. *Social History of Medicine*, 30(4), 767–787. https://doi.org/10.1093/shm/hkw127

Stanley, B., Brown, G., Brent, D. A., Wells, K., Poling, K., Curry, J., . . . Hughes, J. (2009). Cognitive-behavioral therapy for suicide prevention (CBT-SP): Treatment model, feasibility, and acceptability. *Journal of the American Academy of Child and Adolescent Psychiatry*, 48(10), 1005–1013. https://doi.org/10.1097/CHI.0b013e3181b5dbfe

Stern, A., Agnew-Blais, J., Danese, A., Fisher, H. L., Jaffee, S. R., Matthews, T., . . . Arseneault, V. (2018). Associations between abuse/neglect and ADHD from childhood to young adulthood: A prospective nationally-representative twin study. *Child Abuse and Neglect*, 81, 274–285. https://doi.org/10.1016.j.chiabu.2018.04.025

Tarver-Behring, S., & Spagna, M. E. (2004). Counseling with exceptional children. *Focus on Exceptional Children*, 36(8), 1–12.

Tubman, J. G., Des Rosiers, S. E., Schwartz, S. J., & O'Hare, T. (2012). The use of the risky sex scale among adolescents receiving treatment services for substance use problems: Factor structure and predictive validity. *Journal of Substance Abuse Treatment*, 43(3), 359–365. https://doi.org/10.1016/j.jsat.2012.01.002

U.S. Department of Education Office for Civil Rights. (2014). *Civil rights data collection: Data snapshot on college and career readiness*. Retrieved from www.uncf.org/wp-content/uploads/PDFs/CRDC-College-and-Career-Readiness-Snapshot-2.pdf

U.S. Department of Education Office for Civil Rights. (2016). *2013–2014 Civil rights data collection "A first look"*. Retrieved from www2.ed.gov/about/offices/list/ocr/docs/2013-14-first-look.pdf

U.S. Preventive Services Task Force. (2019, May). *Final recommendation statement: Depression in children and adolescents: Screening*. Retrieved from www.uspreventiveservicestaskforce.org/Page/Document/RecommendationStatementFinal/depression-in-children-and-adolescents-screening1

Victor, S. E., Muehlenkamp, J. J., Hayes, N. A., Lengel, G. J., Styer, D. M., & Washburn, J. J. (2018). Characterizing gender differences in non-suicidal self-injury: Evidence from a large clinical sample of adolescents and adults. *Comprehensive Psychiatry*, 82, 53–60. Retrieved from www.ncbi.nlm.nih.gov/pmc/articles/PMC5845831/#__ffn_sectitle

Walker-Noack, L., Corkum, P., Elik, N., & Fearon, I. (2013). Youth perceptions of attention deficit/hyperactivity disorder and barriers to treatment. *Canadian Journal of School Psychology*, 28(2), 193–218. https://doi.org/10.1177/0829573513491232

Webb, J. T., Amend, E. R., Beljan, P., Webb, N. E., Kuzujanakis, M., Olenchak, F. R., & Goerss, J. (2016). *Misdiagnosis and dual diagnosis of gifted children and adults*. Scottsdale, AZ: Great Potential Press.

Weinberg, I., Gunderson, J. G., Hennen, J., & Cutter, C. J., Jr. (2006). Manual assisted cognitive treatment for deliberate self-harm in borderline personality disorder patients. *Journal of Personality Disorders*, 20(5), 482–492. https://doi.org/10.1521/pedi.2006.20.5.482

Weinstein, D., Staffelbach, D., & Biaggio, M. (2000). Attention-deficit hyperactivity disorder and posttraumatic stress disorder: Differential diagnosis in childhood sexual abuse. *Clinical Psychology Review*, 20(3), 359–378. https://doi.org/10.1016/S0272-7358(98)00107-X

Whitlock, J. L., Exner-Cortens, D., & Purington, A. (2014). Validity and reliability of the non-suicidal self-injury assessment test (NSSI-AT). *Psychological Assessment*, 26(3), 935–946.

Whitlock, J. L., Muehlenkamp, J., Eckenrode, J., Purington, A., Abrams, G. B., Barreira, P., & Kress, V. (2013). Nonsuicidal self-injury as a gateway to suicide in young adults. *Journal of Adolescent Health*, 52, 486–492.

Wiener, J., Malone, M., Varma, A., Markel, C., Biondic, D., Tannock, R., & Humphries, T. (2012). Children's perceptions of their ADHD symptoms: Positive illusions, attributions and stigma. *Canadian Journal of School Psychology*, 27(3), 217–242. https://doi.org/10.1177/0829573512451972

Wood, S. M., & Peterson, J. S. (2018). *Counseling gifted students: A guide for school counselors*. New York: Springer Publishing Company.

You, J., Ren, Y., Zhang, X., Wu, Z., Xu, S., & Lin, M. (2018). Emotional dysregulation and nonsuicidal self-injury: A meta-analytic review. *Neuropsychiatry*, 8(2), 733–748. https://doi.org/10.4172/Neuropsychiatry.1000399

11 Grief and Loss Issues in Children and Adolescents

Rebekah Byrd and Chad Luke

Objectives

- Describe and define many key terms from this chapter as associated with grief and loss.
- Understand the difference between primary and secondary loss – and how to identify and recognize secondary loss.
- Identify ways in which grief and loss manifest for children and adolescents.
- Compare and contrast types of grief and loss.
- Examine appropriate techniques for working with children and adolescents with grief and loss concerns.
- Evaluate multicultural aspects to one's grief and loss.

Reflective Questions

- What are my current ideas about how individuals grieve?
- What are my current conceptualizations about how many children and adolescents deal with grief and loss issues?
- How might grief and loss be different for children and adolescents?
- How do I understand my own grief, and how is understanding my own process essential for understanding others?
- What are cultural implications for grief and loss that I am currently aware of?

Grief is not just a concept you read about in a textbook. Grief is real and it is beyond painful and debilitating for many individuals. It has many faces and many names. We think back over the years and remember so many amazing children and adolescents with whom we have worked who have been courageous and strong enough to share their grief. We do not take that honor lightly. We feel incredible amounts of gratitude to these individuals for teaching us about their unique process of grief and loss through their pain, confusion, anger, and despair.

I (Rebekah) think about Jordan, an 11-year-old who suddenly lost his mother. I remember brothers Aiden (2.5 years old) and Cameron (4 years old), who were taken from their mother and father due to severe sexual abuse. I recall Greta, whose father committed suicide when she was 10. Twelve-year-old Keisha, who was displaced and lost loved ones in Hurricane Katrina. Anthony, a 7-year-old, whose father was arrested, in his presence, and taken to prison. Miguel (6-year-old), who moved to a new home and school. John (14 years old), whose father was killed in front of him. Laney, a 13-year-old who continually struggled with the divorce of her parents, the coming out of her father, and feeling torn between two families. Brittany (12 years old), who was shot in a drive-by while holding her newborn baby sister – the shot missed her sister's head by a few inches. Ava, a 7-year-old who lost her very best friend – her dog – in a car accident. Unfortunately, the list goes on and on. The grief and loss that children and adolescents deal with on a daily basis tears at our core – and we imagine it does yours, too.

Definitions

Grief is a normal and natural reaction to loss. When understanding issues of grief and loss, it is important to first understand that grief can manifest differently for everyone. Every individual grieves in her/his own unique way. "The way grief is experienced can be influenced by many different factors: Who or what was lost; how a loss occurred; how it was experienced; and personal characteristics such as the griever's age, culture, gender, and temperament" (Pataky & Parent, 2018, p. 2). Further, what adults may think is grief and loss may look very different for children and adolescents (Malone, 2007). Counselors need to remember that "children and adolescents are not always cognizant of the impact of death as it relates to their own fears, suppression of feelings, and finality" (Dickens, 2014, p. 119).

Grief also knows no age limit. Everyone can experience grief and loss – even very young children. One does not have to understand grief and loss to be able to feel the impact. Dyregrov (2008) notes:

> Even though smaller children's concept of death is not fully developed, there is no reason to doubt that they react strongly to loss at this age. Even children less than two years old are able to express their understanding that someone is not present any more, and remember this for a long time afterwards.
>
> (p. 11)

While is it accurate to understand grief as a natural and normal reaction, it is also important to understand that the mental suffering can lead to mental health issues and physical health issues if ignored and unrecognized (Archer, 1999). "The feelings and emotions experienced from these losses can be intense and frightening, frequently resulting in depression, destructive behaviors, drug and alcohol use, self-mutilation, and eating disorders" (Walker & Shaffer, 2007, p. 67).

While many resources exist for grieving adults, little is available for children and adolescents. Further, children and adolescents often find themselves grieving alone and with minimal support (Walker & Shaffer, 2007). Grieving adolescents often keep their suffering to themselves, due to factors such as peer pressure and also the desire to not further hurt or upset parents and caregivers in situations when the parents and caregivers are also grieving (Dickens, 2014). Additionally, adolescents may postpone, suppress, or repress their grieving in an attempt to appear independent and not in need of help or support (Malone, 2016).

The definition of *grief* may depend on the individual who is grieving. Many feel and understand grief in different ways. Generally speaking, the "usual reaction to bereavement [i.e., intense distress] is termed grief, defined as a primarily emotional (affective) reaction to the loss of a loved one through death. It incorporates diverse psychological (cognitive, social-behavioral) and physical (physiological-somatic) manifestations" (Stroebe, Hansson, Stroebe, & Schut, 2001, p. 6). Loss can refer to many experiences, such as the ones previously noted (e.g., loss of a pet, parents or caregiver separation or divorce, moving, incarceration of a friend or family member, or sickness of a friend or family member). Many children and adolescents are experiencing loss not associated with a death, and

Primary and Secondary Loss

Primary loss refers to a substantial loss – in many cases, a death of a loved one (Humphrey, 2009). The phrase *secondary loss* refers to all of the losses associated with or consequences of the primary loss and can vary based on the person experiencing the loss and depending on the loss itself (Humphrey, 2009). For example, if a child experiences the loss of a sibling, the secondary losses may include loss of a companion, loss of connectedness, loss of family role, loss of feelings of safety, etc. If a person loses their job, the loss of the job would be primary, and secondary losses could include loss of financial security, loss of independence, loss of identity, loss of self-confidence/self-esteem, loss of future dreams/goals, and much more, depending on the individual experience. It is important to understand the impact of secondary losses, as they are often unnoticed (Humphrey, 2009). Recognizing the many facets of grief and loss and the impact on children and adolescents can assist in the healing process. "Healing a child's grief cannot be rushed, dismissed, or ignored. The belief that you can stop support at any point is false. The child negotiates this difficult process until maturity" (Di Ciacco, 2008, p. 81).

Statistics

- Nearly 8% of the population may experience the death of a sibling before the age of 25 (Fletcher, Mailick, Song, & Wolfe, 2013).
- Over two million children in the United States are impacted directly by a parent's service in the military during deployment to both Afghanistan and Iraq, with 40% being younger than the age of 5 (Office of the Deputy Under Secretary of Defense [Military Community and Family Policy], 2005).
- 2.3% of the estimated 74 million U.S. children younger than 18 had a parent in prison (Glaze & Maruschak, 2008).
- 3.1 million children lived with no parent in 2009. This includes children living with foster parents (274,000) and those living with grandparents (59%) (Kreider & Ellis, 2011).
- According to the U.S. Census Bureau, approximately 1.5 million children live in a single-parent home due to the death of one parent (as cited in Owens, 2008).
- Astoundingly, 2.5 million children are homeless every year in the United States – 1 out of every 30 children, a historical high. (Bassuk, DeCandia, Beach, & Berman, 2014).
- A study conducted in Britain found that 5% of children and adolescents had experienced the death of a mother or a father by the time they turned 16 (Parsons, 2011).
- Out of a sample of 11–16-year-old adolescents in England, 77.6% indicated that they had recently lost a close relative or a close friend (Harrison & Harrington, 2001).

Recognizing Grief and Loss

As noted, grief and loss look different for everyone. What adults may understand as grief and loss may not look the same for children and adolescents, and vice versa. Table 11.1 outlines the many different grief, loss, and trauma responses for children and adolescents.

Table 11.1 Adolescent Loss, Grief, and Trauma Responses

Physical	Social	Emotional	Cognitive
Headaches	Feeling different from peers	Dazed	Decline in school performance
Sleep disturbances	Perception of peers being intolerant of their grief	Numb	Paranormal (hallucinatory) experiences
Muscle pain and tension	Social isolation	Shocked	Preoccupation
Stomachaches	Isolation from family	Afraid	Thoughts of own death
Eating disturbances; trouble eating	Risk-taking behavior	Frustrated	Sense of presence of the deceased
Joint pain	Increased sense of maturity	Depressed	Realization of the permanency of death
Being ill more often	Experience of unkind remarks from peers	Alone	Disbelief
Lump in throat	Avoidance of reminders	Anxious	Confusion
Tightness in chest	Antisocial	Guilty	Distracted
Aching and heavy arms and legs	Withdrawal from normal activities	Uncomfortable when happy	Difficulty with concentration
Muscle weakness	Change in peer group	Sad	Intrusive thoughts
Dry mouth	Self-destructive behavior	Irritable	Lowered self-esteem
Lack of energy	Vulnerable	Memory problems	
Eating disturbances		Angry, aggressive	

Source: Malone, 2007, p. 16

Having counselors who understand the many facets of responses for children and adolescents is imperative. Ignoring or not recognizing needs associated with grief and loss can be problematic. Counselors must carefully listen for and acknowledge the losses that occur for clients so that we are aware of the grieving taking place (Humphrey, 2009). "Children are vulnerable to the neglect of their needs, especially if the adults are overwhelmed and unavailable to support them through the grief process" (Di Ciacco, 2008, p. 36).

When individuals are not free or able to express their pain and other emotions associated with grief and loss issues, this can lead to depression and other problematic behaviors (Dickens, 2014). Further, Figure 11.1 from Oltjenbruns (2001, p. 177) describes grief and loss responses by categories including somatic, intrapsychic, and behavioral responses. Somatic responses typically describe reactions or symptoms felt in the body (e.g., stomach discomfort, headaches, wetting the bed). Intrapsychic responses refer to those responses or reactions of the mind (e.g., depression, anxiety, fear, phobia). Behavioral responses are described as responses or reactions that manifest in activity (e.g., regression, temper tantrums, diminished activity). This chart noted that factors listed are found more among clinical samples than in a sample that is community based (Oltjenbruns, 2001).

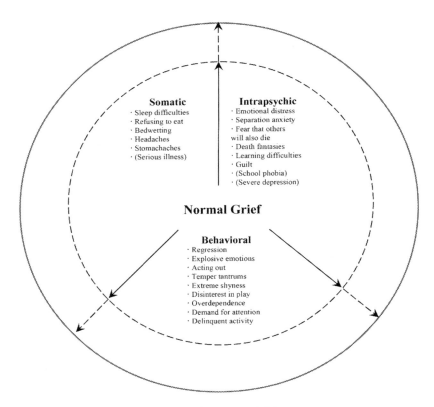

Figure 11.1 Common Manifestations of Grief Among Children
Source: Oltjenbruns, 2001, p. 177

Counselors need to be prepared to recognize grief and loss symptoms and the ways in which they manifest for children. Adults and counselors alike cannot rely on the child or adolescent to verbally describe feelings associated with grief and loss. Understanding this is imperative to the healing process. Sorensen (2008) warns:

> Children often don't know what they are feeling except a vague sense of confusion and discomfort which is more likely to be expressed through play, or through behavioral difficulties. To help these children move closer to expressing their feelings and resolving those feelings means that we need to equip them with the words and materials to process their endings.
>
> (p. 11)

Types of Grief and Loss

This chapter will cover a few different types of grief and loss. This is not a complete list. Therefore, counselors should be equipped to do their own work in this area to prepare for the different types of grief our clients experience. Many types and definitions exist and may present in unique ways for each individual.

Ambiguous Loss

Ambiguous loss has impacted many children and adolescents. This type of loss can be especially detrimental and in need of attention and consideration. "Of all the losses experienced in personal relationships, ambiguous loss is the most devastating because it remains unclear, indeterminate" (Boss, 1999, pp. 5–6). Boss describes ambiguous loss in two types (1999). She notes that the first type of ambiguous loss occurs when a person is physically absent but psychologically present. In these types of situations, it is often unclear if the individual is still alive or if they are in fact dead. Examples include individuals missing in natural disasters, individuals missing in war, kidnapping, and family displacement. For children and adolescents, ambiguous loss can often occur during situations of divorce, blended and adoptive families, or in any situation when a family member or significant other is viewed as absent or lost.

The second type of ambiguous loss is characterized by the person being perceived as physically present but psychologically absent (Boss, 1999). Examples of this type of loss include a person experiencing some sort of coma, someone with Alzheimer's disease, chronic mental illness, and situations of addiction. For children and adolescents, ambiguous loss can often occur in situations when a parent or caregiver is constantly consumed with work or other interests and are therefore unavailable to their child. When dealing with issues of grief and loss, Boss (1999) suggests clinicians ask the question "is the patient experiencing any ambiguous losses that might account for his or her immobilization?" (p. 10) in order to best assist and seek to understand presenting issues, concerns, and grief and loss behaviors.

Anticipatory Grief

Anticipatory grief describes the loss before it happens. Anticipatory grief refers to a death that one is expecting and in many ways preparing for but the death has not yet occurred (Hogan, 2009). The most common example of anticipatory grief is when a loved one has a severe sickness or some form of terminal illness. However, other examples can include persistent suicidality, situations of war, gang involvement, and high-risk drug and alcohol use/abuse. Divorce can also be included in anticipatory grief and can especially impact children and adolescents. "The experience of expected grief forces us to constantly and simultaneously juggle the past, present and future" (Hogan, 2009, para 6). The following is from the children's book *Cinnamon Roll Sunday: A Child's Story of Anticipated Grief* (Allen, 2016).

> Noah imagined shrinking himself down and riding Daddy's cinnamon roll down into his belly where he'd join the battle. He was so angry at the cancer for making Daddy sick.
> (back cover)

Complicated Grief

Complicated grief includes persistent or unsuccessful grieving, and may also include similar symptoms such as anticipation, avoidance, and/or disturbance (Allen, Oseni, & Allen, 2011). Other aspects may include denial, a seeming powerlessness to accept the death, an unreasonable desire to be with the deceased, and persistent and invasive thoughts about the departed (Dickens, 2014). Unresolved complicated grief can lead to traumatic grief in children and adolescents (Dickens, 2014).

Delayed Grief

Delayed grief describes grief and loss feelings that occur later than one might expect. Many believe that if individuals are not able or allowed to grieve openly, they can suffer delayed grief responses (Bonanno & Field, 2001). Additionally, individuals who display few or no signs of grief or aspects of working through grief and loss issues may also inevitably suffer delayed grief responses (Bonanno & Field, 2001).

Disenfranchised Grief

Doka first introduced the concept of *disenfranchised grief* in 1985. He defines this as "grief that results when a person experiences a significant loss and the resultant grief is not openly acknowledged, socially validated, or publicly mourned" (Doka, 2008, p. 224). Often times, society and the given culture determine what is socially acceptable to grieve. For example, the relationship may not be socially acceptable or recognized (Humphrey, 2009) (e.g., loss of an individual in an affair, loss of partner in cohabitating relationship, same-sex relationships, multiple partner relationships). Disenfranchised loss can also include a loss that is not deemed legitimate by the culture or society therein (e.g., loss of a companion animal, loss of one's culture, loss of family heirlooms, miscarriage, loss of one's identity) (Humphrey, 2009). In brief, disenfranchised grief is when an individual is experiencing deep, valid, and very real grief and loss responses, but "there is no social recognition that the person has a right to grieve or a claim for social sympathy or support" (Doka, 2008, p. 224). Pataky and Parent (2018) note that grief can become disenfranchised based on whether or not it is recognized and acknowledged by others.

Traumatic Grief

According to Cohen, Mannarino, and Deblinger, the term *traumatic grief* refers to "a condition in which both unresolved grief and PTSD symptoms are present, often accompanied by depressive symptoms as well" (2006, p. 17). As trained counselors, we can assist children and adolescents in acknowledging and eventually confronting the painful feelings, thoughts, and memories associated with the traumatic loss (Dickens, 2014). By modeling appropriate coping skills and acknowledging grief and loss, as opposed to ignoring issues that are difficult to discuss, counselors can guide children and adolescents in managing detrimental reactions and/or ineffective coping behaviors (Malone, 2016). These responses have significant emotional and neurological effects on how children and adolescents cope with loss and grief well into adulthood (Malone, 2016). Counselors assist children and adolescents in seeking to understand the impact of the loss and discover meaning therein in an attempt to "make some sense from the senseless" (Dickens, 2014, p. 120).

Adaptive Grieving Style

Martin and Doka (2000) conceptualize *adaptive grieving* strategies that assist individuals in dealing with, adapting to, and managing loss. These can include: (a) cognitive strategies (e.g., reframing, denial, avoidance); (b) affective strategies (e.g., emotional regulation or acceptance); (c) spiritual strategies (e.g., prayer, redefinition of event, submission to higher power); and (d) behavioral strategies (e.g., seeking support, acting out behaviors, physical activity). Recent research supports the concept that individuals grieve in their own unique way and that most people utilize a combination of both affective and cognitive behavioral

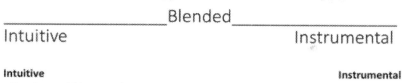

Figure 11.2 Continuum of Three Primary Styles of Grieving

strategies (Doughty, 2009). The strategies that individuals use reflect the individual and unique process of inward and outward expressions of grief and how those differ for everyone (Humphrey, 2009). Figure 11.2 describes three primary styles. These styles are understood on a continuum. You will notice that the left side outlines characteristics of an intuitive grieving style, and the right side notes those of an instrumental grieving style. The middle describes a blended grieving style that combines characteristics from both. Most people fall somewhere in the middle and tend to draw from both styles in an individualized way (Martin & Doka, 2000).

Dual Process Model

Stroebe and Schut (1999) discuss a model of grieving called the *dual process model*. This model is a classification describing the ways in which people come to terms with, cope with, and process grief and loss. In this model, there are two groupings: *loss-oriented coping* and *restoration-oriented coping*. *Loss-oriented coping* refers to the stressors related to the particular loss (Humphrey, 2009). This includes rumination specifically about the deceased, the situation and context surrounding the death, and a deep longing for the deceased (Stroebe & Schut, 1999). This also includes a varied range of emotions and reactions that can include pleasant memories and painful loneliness; and relief that the deceased is at peace and despair for the significant feelings of loss (Stroebe & Schut, 1999). The second grouping described in this model is restoration-oriented coping. *Restoration-oriented coping* refers to the stressors associated with the changes that are associated with the loss. This can include having to take over tasks the deceased would normally take care of and/or having to develop a new sense of self apart from the deceased (e.g., widow, parent, etc.).

Many emotions are present with this type of coping, and they can range from feelings of accomplishment that one was able to successfully take over new skills to feelings of defeat and desolation that one will not succeed. The researchers note that these extra stressors exacerbate the feelings of loss and can cause increased anxiety and distressing emotions. *Oscillation* between loss-oriented coping and restoration-oriented coping can be seen when an individual will at times seem to avoid discussing or thinking about the deceased and other times confront their loss. Oscillation between these two groupings is normal, natural, and important for the individual and can be seen as critical to healing. Figure 11.3 describes the dual process model.

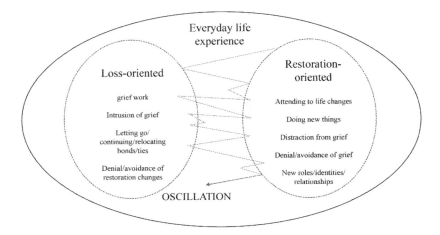

Figure 11.3 Stroebe and Schut Dual Process Model (1999)

Techniques

"Children naturally identify with, and express feelings through their play, art, or metaphorical stories. Language and recognition of more subtle emotions does not occur until much later" (Sorensen, 2008, p. 17). This text will discuss many techniques that are appropriate to use when children and adolescents experience grief and loss. Since children and adolescents (and adults!) are not able to name, understand, and verbally process feelings, expressive arts are imperative to assist in coping and healing. The following quote from Di Ciacco (2008) is a significant reminder that speaks to the need for counselors who understand how children and adolescents communicate – instead of requiring children to communicate in the ways adults desire.

> Children do not have the capacity to separate, classify, or organize their losses into their larger world. When in distress, they cannot talk about it. They have not acquired the ability to express their deep feelings, thoughts, and emotions in words. Rather, they act out their fear, anger, sadness, emptiness, confusion, and loneliness. Their behavior is immediate and shows in their facial expressions. This is how they work out their grief. They are showing us (i.e. telling us) by their behavior.
>
> (p. 50)

In this text, you will find many chapters dedicated to play therapy, Sandtray Therapy, mindfulness practices, and expressive and experiential techniques including yoga, art, drama, music, and wilderness/outdoor/adventure therapy. These techniques seek to encourage and empower the child and adolescent by assisting in self-expression to promote healing. "Play and expressive art work can be beneficial in enabling the child to express their pain and, ultimately, to transform it" (Sorensen, 2008, p. 13).

Working With Parents/Caregivers

The following are tips to share with parents and caregivers (adapted from Dyregrov, 2008, p. 35–36).

- Give children an immediate sense of being taken care of.
- Use physical closeness to provide security.
- Take the child onto your lap and relate what has happened, listen to the child's understanding of what you have said to make sure that they have grasped this, encourage them to express their thoughts and questions, and accept their reactions or lack of reaction.
- Place importance on giving the child information and facts about the loss which will contribute to a concrete understanding of the situation.
- Be careful to trace misunderstandings, misconceptions, and magical thinking. Help the child find the personal meaning the events have for them.
- Set the scene so that the child can express what has happened in different ways; in other words, let the child talk, play, or re-enact the events.
- Emphasize openness and honesty in the home.
- Return quickly to normal routines at home and at school.
- As parents/caregivers, you will find advice about children's reactions and needs very helpful. Inform the school staff at an early stage so that they can give the child the best possible support.

Multicultural Implications and Advocacy

Understanding the importance of multicultural competency is an ethical obligation. Knowledge and awareness of cultural differences in grieving is essential to supporting our clients and assisting them in moving through the grief and loss process. Counselors understand that culture, tradition, religious/spiritual beliefs, and community impact the ways in which individuals grieve. This section offers limited information on cultural differences. It is up to the counselor to seek more education and training in this area and to continually further knowledge and awareness of cultural implications and differences related to how individuals grieve and experience loss. By doing this, counselors seek to assist each client individually and strive to supportively encourage the unique ways in which individuals cope – with culture specifically in mind. Without this information, counselors may miss symptoms of grief and loss.

A handful of cultural differences will be discussed. In Latinx cultures, death is valued and accepted. An example of this is the Mexican celebration of All Souls Day and All Saints Day that takes place in November (Di Giorgio, 2014). Additionally, in Latinx culture, grieving is portrayed – if the family is Catholic – by gathering the family together to pray for nine days with the rosary (Di Giorgio, 2014). Another example of cultural diversity can be observed in Cambodian culture. In this culture, it is often thought that if certain burial and post-burial rituals are not carried out, then the deceased may not be able to move into the next spiritual level to become a spiritual healer (Hinton, Peou, Joshi, Nickerson, & Simon, 2013). It is important to note that some cultures, including Cambodians, are not able to carry out all of their cultural rituals and ceremonies in the United States (Di Giorgio, 2014). This can also be another form of grief, loss, and distress. An important exercise for counselors would be to contact local funeral homes and speak with the directors about the services they provide. Often, funeral homes have been supportive establishments in the community for some time. Directors can discuss the many cultures present in the local community, specific cultural practices, services they are able to carry out, and services they cannot accommodate due to state regulations and their infrastructures or abilities.

Traditional Chinese culture has important rituals, as do many cultures. Walsh and McGoldrick (2004) discuss that when individuals leave a traditional Chinese funeral in Hong Kong, they receive an envelope including three items:

> A white washcloth to wipe away tears, candy to remind the bereaved of the sweetness of life, and a coin, as a symbolic token of the ancient custom of reimbursing mourners for travel to the funeral so that they wouldn't suffer further loss.
>
> (p. 4)

Traditionally, the mourning period for Chinese families is most commonly 49 days (Lee & Chan, 2004), and discussing dying and death is not typically seen as acceptable (Di Giorgio, 2014). Counselors need to understand and respect cultural ideas that may prevent children and adolescents from freely discussing their feelings of grief and loss. Expressive and experiential techniques are vital in working with grief and loss. Counselors also need to recognize and respect such attributes of one's grieving process, such as specific mourning periods. Counselors can advocate for children and adolescents within schools and agencies to establish communities that are supportive of cultural grieving practices.

Individuals who are Hindu may see death as a circular cycle in which a person dies only to be reborn with a new identity (Gire, 2014). The dominant U.S. culture of Christianity typically understands physical death as happening one time. In other cultures, such as Native American and Cambodian, the deceased reside amid the living and can impact the living in different ways (Gire, 2014). Native Hawaiians are positively impacted by the belief that deceased individuals communicate with them (Pentaris, 2011).

Tribal differences exist in terms of how Native Americans express and cope with grief and loss. Each tribe will be unique and have its own associated values, practices, and rituals. It is important for counselors to seek information to the specific tribe. Cacciatore (2009) outlines some general factors for working with Native Americans, who value listening and extended moments of silence. They possess a more indirect style of communication that may include avoiding eye contact and flat affect – even during a traumatic event, death, or crisis situation. It is important for the counselor to understand these differences as a part of culture and not mistake this as resistance (Sutton & Nose, 1996).

Summary

It is important for counselors to remember that there is no right or wrong way to express emotions associated with grief and loss. Children and adolescents need to be encouraged and supported so that they can express their feelings in their own way, accept their feelings, and acknowledge what they are feeling and expressing at the moment (Sorensen, 2008). Well-trained counselors are imperative to assisting children and adolescents in dealing with grief and loss. With all of the intense situations our children and adolescents are faced with, it is essential that counselors develop the tools needed to promote child and adolescent well-being. Children and adolescents need constant care, attention, insight, and love so that they can feel safe to express themselves and grow in a holistic manner (Di Ciacco, 2008). Counselors may be the only adult to provide such necessary conditions – especially when dealing with grief and loss. "Thus, this gentle reminder: Fragile. Handle with Care" (Di Ciacco, 2008, p. 81).

Clinician's Corner

Our school has suffered some terrible losses over the last two years. We have had five students die, two by suicide. Needless to say, our students have been struggling this year to deal with all of this. As our department saw many students having similar issues dealing with grief and depression, we decided to try a different approach to handle it. We decided to try having groups – I say this is new because groups have never been run at my school. Finding time for groups in a high school schedule is always difficult. The schedule and the teacher's reluctance to give up instructional time are the usual culprits. Fortunately, our schedule changed this year and we now have an extra period in the day that is purely used for electives and response to intervention (RTI). It's a shorter period, 45 minutes, and lasts the entire year. This is a great period to have groups, since the classes are supposed to be all project based and are non-tested.

We made a short survey that asked the students to check if they were interested in groups in any of the areas – grief, anxiety, and depression. Anxiety was added because of the sheer number of clients seen at our school with this issue. We had great response to the surveys, which were given in homeroom. We decided to begin with the grief group. We had 50 students say they might be interested. It divided evenly into 25 for ninth and 10th grade and 25 for 11th and 12th. We held our first group meeting this week. The students that attended had varied grief experiences from death of friends and families, to many moves, to different foster families, to breakup of first love relationships, and even change in family's financial status due to job loss. It was neat to see that they understood that grief presents in many different ways throughout their lives.

We are excited to begin this new part of our program and will continue to run groups throughout the year. I hope it helps us to serve even more students in our school and address their needs.

Lori McCorkle
High school counselor

References

Allen, B., Oseni, A., & Allen, K. E. (2011). The evidenced-based treatment of chronic posttraumatic stress disorder and traumatic grief in an adolescent: A case study. *Psychological Trauma: Therapy, Research, Practice and Policy*, 4(6), 631–639. https://doi.org/10.1037/a0024930

Allen, J. L. (2016). *Cinnamon roll Sunday: A child's story of anticipatory grief*. CreateSpace Independent Publishing Platform.

Archer, J. (1999). *The nature of grief: The evolution and psychology of reactions to loss.* New York: Routledge.

Bassuk, E. L., DeCandia, C. J., Beach, C. A., & Berman, F. (2014). *America's youngest outcasts: A report card on child homelessness.* Waltham, MA: The National Center on Family Homelessness at American Institutes for Research.

Bonanno, G. A., & Field, N. P. (2001). Examining the delayed grief hypothesis across 5 years of bereavement. *The American Behavioral Scientist*, 44(5), 798–816.

Boss, P. (1999). *Ambiguous loss: Learning to live with unresolved grief.* Cambridge, MA: Harvard University Press.

Cacciatore, J. (2009). Appropriate bereavement practice after the death of a Native American child. *Families in Society: The Journal of Contemporary Social Science*, 90(1), 46–50. https://doi.org/10.1606/1044-3894.3844

Cohen, J. A., Mannarino, A. P., & Deblinger, E. (2006). *Treating trauma and traumatic grief in children and adolescents.* New York: Guilford Press.

Di Ciacco, J. A. (2008). *The colors of grief: Understanding a child's journey through loss from birth to adulthood.* London: Jessica Kingsley Publishers.

Dickens, N. (2014). Prevalence of complicated grief and posttraumatic stress disorder in children and adolescents following sibling death. *The Family Journal: Counseling and Therapy for Couples and Families*, 22(1), 119–126. https://doi.org/10.1177/1066480713505066

Di Giorgio, C. M. (2014). *Cultural differences in grieving: Curriculum development for helping professionals*, ProQuest Dissertations & Theses Global. (1552740270). Retrieved from https://

login.iris.etsu.edu:3443/login?url=http://search.proquest.com.iris.etsu.edu:2048/docview/1552740270?accountid=10771

Doka, K. J. (1985). *Disenfranchised grief*. Death Education, Symposium Conducted at the Foundation of Thanatology, New York.

Doka, K. J. (2008). Disenfranchised grief in historical and cultural perspective. In M. S. Stroebe, R. O. Hansson, H. Schut, & W. Stroebe (Eds.), *Handbook of bereavement research and practice: Advances in theory and intervention* (pp. 223–240). Washington, DC: American Psychological Association. http://doi.org.iris.etsu.edu:2048/10.1037/14498-011

Doughty, E. A. (2009). Investigating adaptive grieving styles: A Delphi study. *Death Studies*, *33*, 462–280. https://doi.org/10.1080/07481180902805715

Dyregrov, A. (2008). *Grief in children: A handbook for adults* (2nd ed.). London: Jessica Kingsley Publishers.

Fletcher, J., Mailick, M., Song, J., & Wolfe, B. (2013). A sibling death in the family: Common and consequential. *Demography*, *50*, 803–826. https://doi.org/10.1007/s13524-012-0162-4

Gire, J. (2014). How death imitates life: Cultural influences on conceptions of death and dying. *Online Readings in Psychology and Culture*, *6*(2). http://doi.org/10.9707/2307-0919.1120

Glaze, L. E., & Maruschak, L. M. (2008). *Parents in prison and their minor children*. Bureau of Justice Statistics Special Report. U.S. Department of Justice Office of Justice Programs.

Harrison, L., & Harrington, R. (2001). Adolescents' bereavement experiences. Prevalence, associated with depressive symptoms, and use of services. *Journal of Adolescents*, *24*, 159–169. https://doi.org/10.1006/jado.2001.0379

Hinton, D. E., Peou, S., Joshi, S., Nickerson, A., & Simon, N. M. (2013). Normal grief and complicated bereavement among traumatized Cambodian refugees: Cultural context and the central role of dreams of the dead. *Culture, Medicine and Psychiatry*, *37*(3), 427–464. https://doi.org/10.1007/s11013-013-9324-0

Hogan, M. (2009). *Anticipatory grief: Expecting the loss, feeling the pain*. Sacred Vigil Press.

Humphrey, K. M. (2009). *Counseling strategies for loss and grief*. Alexandria, VA: American Counseling Association.

Kreider, R. M., & Ellis, R. (2011). Living arrangements of children: 2009. *Current Population Reports*, 70–126. U.S. Census Bureau, Washington, DC. Retrieved from www.census.gov/prod/2011pubs/p70-126.pdf

Lee, E., & Chan, J. (2004). Mourning in the Chinese culture. In F. Walsh & M. McGoldrick (Eds.), *Living beyond loss: Death in the family* (2nd ed., pp. 131–126). New York: W.W. Norton & Company.

Malone, P. A. (2007). The impact of peer death on adolescent girls: A task-oriented group intervention. *Journal of Social Work in End-of-Life & Palliative Care*, *3*(3), 23–37.

Malone, P. A. (2016). *Counseling adolescents through loss, grief and trauma*. New York: Routledge.

Martin, T. L., & Doka, K. J. (2000). *Men don't cry . . . women do: Transcending gender stereotypes of grief*. Philadelphia: Brunner/Mazel.

Office of the Deputy Under Secretary of Defense (Military Community and Family Policy). (2005). *Demographics profile of the military community*. Washington, DC: Office of the Deputy Under Secretary of Defense. Retrieved from http://download.militaryonesource.mil/12038/MOS/Reports/2005%20Demographics%20Report.pdf

Oltjenbruns, K. A. (2001). Developmental context of childhood: Grief and regrief phenomena. In M. S. Stroebe, R. O. Hansson, W. Stroebe, & H. Schut (Eds.), *Handbook of bereavement research: Consequences, coping and care* (pp. 169–197). Washington, DC: American Psychological Association.

Owens, D. A. (2008). Recognizing the needs of bereaved children in palliative care. *Journal of Hospice and Palliative Nursing*, *10*(1), 14–16.

Parsons, S. (2011). *Long-term impact of childhood bereavement: Preliminary analysis of the 1970 British Cohort Study (BCS70)*. Retrieved from https://assets.publishing.service.gov.uk/government/uploads/system/uploads/attachment_data/file/181353/CWRC-00081-2011.pdf

Pataky, M. G., & Parent, K. T. (2018). Ambiguous loss in schools: Guidelines for practitioners. *School Social Work Journal*, *43*(1), 1–19.

Pentaris, P. (2011). Culture and death: A multicultural perspective. *Hawaii Pacific Journal of Social Work Practice*, 4(1), 45–84.

Sorensen, J. (2008). *Overcoming loss: Activities and stories to help transform children's grief and loss*. London: Jessica Kingsley Publishers.

Stroebe, M. S., Hansson, R. O., Stroebe, W., & Schut, H. (2001). Introduction: Concepts and issues in contemporary research on bereavement. In M. S. Stroebe, R. O. Hansson, W. Stroebe, & H. Schut (Eds.), *Handbook of bereavement research: Consequences, coping and care* (pp. 3–22). Washington, DC: American Psychological Association.

Stroebe, M. S., & Schut, H. (1999). The dual process model of coping with bereavement: Rationale and description. *Death Studies*, 23(3), 197–224.

Sutton, C. T., & Nose, M. A. (1996). American Indian families. In M. McGoldrick, J. Giordano, & J. K. Pearce (Eds.), *Ethnicity and family therapy* (pp. 31–41). New York: Guilford Press.

Walker, P., & Shaffer, M. (2007). Reducing depression among adolescents dealing with grief and loss: A program evaluation report. *Health and Social Work*, 32(1). 67–68.

Walsh, F., & McGoldrick, M. (2004). Loss and the family: A systemic perspective. In F. Walsh & M. McGoldrick (Eds.), *Living beyond loss: Death in the family* (2nd ed., pp. 3–26). New York: W.W. Norton & Company.

12 Working With Transgender and Gender-Expansive Children and Adolescents

Rebekah Byrd, Mickey White, and Chad Luke
Mickey White as guest contributor

Objectives

- Describe and define many key terms from this chapter associated with TGE children and adolescents.
- Understand the many alarming statistics associated with TGE individuals.
- Examine appropriate principles for affirming care.
- Understand legal and ethical issues that apply to TGE children and adolescents.
- Evaluate ways counselors can work with schools and community settings to make spaces more affirming and supportive.

Reflective Questions

- What are my current beliefs about TGE children and adolescents? Are there beliefs I may need to undo?
- What is my current understanding of concepts and terms? Do I understand the importance of language as it applies to TGE children and adolescents?
- What are ways I can work to make my office space and work setting safe and affirming for TGE clients?
- What are legal and ethical issues I need to be aware of for advocating for and with TGE children and adolescents?
- What ways can counselors work to advocate for TGE clients?

Transgender and gender-expansive (TGE) children and adolescents need knowledgeable, aware, and skilled clinicians for the many facets of societal issues they will inevitably face. This chapter discusses important concepts and terms, introduces crucial statistics, discusses experiences at home and at school, and other important considerations for TGE individuals. Counseling implications and legal and ethical considerations are also presented.

Concepts and Terms

In an effort to introduce some definitions and terms we will use in this chapter and in the next, we think it is important to get on the same page with language usage. Language is ever evolving, especially as it relates to TGE youth and adolescents. With the understanding that language and understanding changes rapidly (as we will note in the current definitions) for individuals and society, we believe it is important to introduce the expanded acronym used by the Society for Sexual, Affectional, Intersex, and Gender Expansive Identities (SAIGE), formerly the Association for LGBT Issues in Counseling (ALGBTIC): LGBTGEQIAP+. LGBTGEQIAP+ includes terms associated with clients identifying as lesbian; gay; bisexual;

trans*, transgender and Two-Spirit (2S; Native Identity); gender expansive; queer and questioning; intersex; agender, asexual and aromantic; pansexual, pan/polygender and poly relationship systems; and other related identities. While at first glance this acronym may seem clunky, it is one that is most representative of the wide variety of TGE identities throughout history and the world.

According to the ALGBTIC *Competencies for Counseling Transgender Clients* (2009), counselors will

> understand the importance of using appropriate language (e.g., correct name and pronouns) with transgender clients; be aware that language in the transgender community is constantly evolving and varies from person to person; seek to be aware of new terms and definitions within the transgender community; honor client's definitions of their own gender; seek to use language that is the least restrictive in terms of gender (e.g., using client's name as opposed to assuming what pronouns the clients assert are gender affirming); recognize that language has historically been used to oppress and discriminate against transgender people; understand that the counselor is in a position of power and should model respect for the client's declared vocabulary.
>
> (p. 8)

In order to clarify and guide the discussion that follows, following are some general definitions offered by the Gay, Lesbian, and Straight Education Network (GLSEN, 2020) in its document on key concepts and terms.

> *Ableism:* A system of oppression that benefits able-bodied people at the expense of people with disabilities.
>
> *Asexual:* A person who does not experience sexual attraction, but may experience other forms of attraction (e.g., intellectual, emotional). Asexual people may also identify as "bisexual," "gay," "lesbian," "pansexual," "queer," "straight," and many more.
>
> *Bisexual:* A person who is emotionally and/or physically attracted to two or more genders, often used to describe people attracted to "genders like theirs" and "other genders."
>
> *Bodily Characteristics:* Physical traits that compose one's body; primary characteristics such as chromosomes, genitals, internal reproductive organs, hormone levels, and secondary characteristics such as facial hair, chest development, etc.
>
> *Cisgender:* A person whose gender identity and expression are aligned with the gender they were assigned at birth or by society.
>
> *Classism:* A system of oppression that benefits people with high and middle socioeconomic status at the expense of people with lower socioeconomic status.
>
> *Coming Out:* The ongoing process that an LGBTQ person goes through, to recognize their own identities pertaining to sexual orientation and/or gender identity and gender expression, and to be open about them with others.
>
> *Dyke:* A derogatory term directed at a person perceived as a lesbian. It is oftentimes used against women who are gender nonconforming, with the assumption being that their gender nonconformity implies a sexual attraction to women. Some lesbians (of all gender-expressions) have reclaimed the term and use it as an affirming label with which to identify.

Fag/Faggot: A derogatory term directed at a person perceived as a gay man. It is oftentimes used against men who are gender nonconforming, with the assumption being that their gender nonconformity implies a sexual attraction to men. Some gay men (of all gender-expressions) have reclaimed the term and use it as an affirming label with which to identify.

Gay: Someone, who can be transgender or cisgender, who is attracted to someone of the same gender.

Gender: A set of cultural identities, expressions and roles – codified as feminine or masculine – that are assigned to people, based upon the interpretation of their bodies, and more specifically, their sexual and reproductive anatomy. Since gender is a social construction, it is possible to reject or modify the assignment made, and develop something that feels truer and just to oneself.

Gender Binary: A socially constructed system of viewing gender as consisting solely of two categories, "male" and "female", in which no other possibilities for gender are believed to exist. The gender binary is inaccurate because it does not take into account the diversity of gender identities and gender expressions among all people. The gender binary is oppressive to anyone that does not conform to dominant societal gender norms.

Gender Expression: The multiple ways (e.g., behaviors, dress) in which a person may choose to communicate gender to oneself and/or to others.

Gender Identity: How an individual identifies in terms of their gender. Gender identities may include, "male," "female," "androgynous," "transgender," "genderqueer" and many others, or a combination thereof.

Genderism: A system of oppression that benefits cisgender people at the expense of transgender and gender nonconforming people. Genderism may take the form of Transphobia, bias and discrimination towards transgender and gender nonconforming people.

Gender Nonconforming or Gender Variant: A person whose gender identity and/or gender expression does not conform to the gender they were assigned at birth or by society. People who identify as "gender nonconforming" may or may not also identify as "transgender".

Heterosexism: A system of oppression that benefits straight/heterosexual people at the expense of lesbian, gay and bisexual people. Heterosexism may take the form of Homophobia or Biphobia, bias and discrimination towards lesbian, gay and bisexual people.

Homosexual: A person who is emotionally and/or physically attracted to some members of the same gender. Many people prefer the terms "lesbian" or "gay" instead.

Identity: Identity is how we understand ourselves, what we call ourselves and often who we connect to and associate with. Each of us has a unique diversity of social identities based on our sexual orientation, gender identity, race/ethnicity, socioeconomic status, religion and other important parts of who we are. Those identities develop over time, intersect with one another and help give meaning to our lives. Below, you'll find many common terms that people use to identify themselves, especially in relation to their sexual orientation, gender identity and gender expression. It's important to remember that these terms are about self-identification; no one can tell anyone else how to identify or what terms to use.

Intersex: People who have any range of bodily characteristics that may not fit typical expectations for "male" or "female" development. Some intersex traits are identified at birth, while others may not be discovered until puberty or later in life. There are over thirty specific medical terms for intersex variations and each intersex person is different. Experts estimate that as many as 1.7% of people are born intersex.

Lesbian: Someone, who can be transgender or cisgender, who generally considers themselves a woman or femme who is attracted to other women and/or femmes.

LGBTQ: An umbrella term referring to people who identify as lesbian, gay, bisexual and/or transgender. The acronym can also include additional letters, in reference to other identities that do not conform to dominant societal norms.

Nonbinary: An umbrella term for people who do not identify with the binary of man/woman or masculine/feminine. Nonbinary people are often included under the trans umbrella, but not all may identify as transgender. Other genders that may be included under the nonbinary umbrella are genderqueer, genderfluid, and agender.

Oppression: Systems of power and privilege, based on bias, which benefit some social groups over others. Oppression can 1) take many forms, including ideological, institutional, structural, interpersonal and internalized; 2) be intentional and unintentional; 3) be conscious and unconscious; and 4) be visible and invisible. Oppression prevents the oppressed groups and individuals from being free and equal. Many people face oppression based on more than one of their identities, creating a unique complexity of challenges and resilience.

Pansexual: A person who is emotionally and/or physically attracted to some people, regardless of their gender identity.

Person of Color: A person who identifies as African-American/Black, Latinx/Hispanic, Native American/First Nation, Asian and Pacific Islander, Middle Easter, and/or having mixed ancestry may also identify as a "Person of Color."

Pronouns: The pronoun or set of pronouns that a person identifies with and would like to be called when their proper name is not being used. Examples include "she/her/hers," "he/him/his," "ze/hir/hirs," and "they/them/theirs." Some people prefer no pronouns at all. For more information, refer to GLSEN's Educator Resource on Pronouns at www.glsen.org/trans

Queer: An umbrella term used to describe a sexual orientation, gender identity or gender expression that does not conform to dominant societal norms. While it is used as a neutral, or even a positive term among many LGBTQ people today, historically "queer" was used as a derogatory slur.

Questioning: A person who is in the process of understanding and exploring what their sexual orientation and/or gender identity and gender expression might be.

Racism: A system of oppression that benefits white people at the expense of people of color.

Reclaimed Words: As language evolves, some individuals and communities choose to identify with terms that had previously been used as slurs against them. The words are "reclaimed" and given new meaning, often imbued with a sense of pride and resilience. Examples include, "queer," "dyke," and "tranny," among others. It's important to remember that identity is unique to each individual; not all members of a community readily accept the use of reclaimed words, as they may still find them offensive and hurtful.

Sexism: A system of oppression that benefits male-identified people at the expense of anyone who is not a cis-male.

Sexual Orientation: The inner feelings of who a person is attracted to emotionally and/or physically, in relation to their own gender identity. Some people may identify as "asexual," "bisexual," "gay," "lesbian," "pansexual," "queer," "straight," and many more.

Straight or Heterosexual: A person who is emotionally and/or physically attracted to some members of another gender (specifically, a male-identified person who is attracted to some females or a female-identified person who is attracted to some males).

Tranny: A derogatory term directed at a transgender person, most typically used towards trans women. Some transgender people have reclaimed the term and use it as an affirming label with which to identify.

Transgender: An umbrella term describing people whose gender identity does not match the gender they were assigned at birth or by society.

(pp. 1–4)

Another acronym to be familiar with is SOGIE, which stands for sexual orientation and gender identity and expression. For the purposes of this chapter, we will be using the acronym TGE (transgender and gender expansive), as this feels more positive and inclusive than the term gender non-conforming, which implies the individual is going against the norm. Gender Spectrum (2019a) defines gender expansive as:

An umbrella term used for individuals that broaden their own culture's commonly held definitions of gender, including expectations for its expression, identities, roles, and/or other perceived gender norms. Gender-expansive individuals include those with transgender and non-binary identities, as well as those whose gender in some way is seen to be stretching society's notions of gender.

(para 1)

All in all, proper language use is imperative, particularly for LGBTGEQIAP+ individuals. Counselors have a duty to create the conditions in which each and every client has the space and freedom to define self, as opposed to being defined by others around them.

TGE Children and Adolescents in the United States

According to a recent report, there are an estimated 150,000 TGE youth ages 13–17, and over 1.4 million TGE adults, in the United States (Herman, Flores, Brown, Wilson, & Conron, 2017). This data, however, is incomplete, as there have not been any dedicated population surveys and individuals may come to accept a TGE identity later in life or be unable to be "out" as TGE for fear of persecution or rejection. It is likely that the true number of TGE individuals in the United States is higher (Herman et al., 2017).

To understand the gravity and necessity of recommendations made in this chapter, it is necessary to discuss the effects of gender-related discrimination (e.g., heterosexism, cissexism, genderism) and how it impacts TGE individuals. Throughout the next few sections, we will discuss the experiences of TGE youth as reported by researchers and scholars in the fields of counseling, education, psychology, and law. Until recently, scholars have primarily explored the negative effects of discrimination, but we want to stress that, while still at risk, TGE youth demonstrate incredible resilience to oppression (Grossman, D'Augelli, & Frank, 2011; Singh, 2013; Singh, Hays, & Watson, 2011). As counselors, we want to use a strengths-base approach to working with TGE individuals, empower TGE children and adolescents, and build upon their remarkable resilience.

Experiences in School

Our schools have a long way to go to be safe spaces for TGE students. Although there are some schools making strides in this area, on a whole there is much work to be done. The *U.S. Transgender Survey* (USTS; James et al., 2016) discussed:

> The majority of respondents who were out or perceived as transgender while in school (K–12) experienced some form of mistreatment, including being verbally harassed (54%), physically attacked (24%), and sexually assaulted (13%) because they were transgender. Further, 17% experienced such severe mistreatment that they left a school as a result.
>
> (p. 4)

The *2017 National School Climate Survey* (Kosciw, Greytak, Zongrone, Clark, & Truong, 2018) found an increase in verbal harassment based on gender in schools, as well as numerous reports of gender-based discrimination. For instance, almost half of respondents were prevented from using locker rooms or bathrooms according to gender identity, and 42.1% of those surveyed stated that school administrators actively prevented or did not support the use of chosen names and correct pronouns for students (Kosciw et al., 2018).

With regard to TGE athletes, there have been ongoing debates about inclusion or exclusion based on gender identity. Sports are traditionally sex-segregated, and the back and forth of gender identity inclusion in Title IX protections has created many confusing situations for TGE athletes (Lucas-Carr & Krane, 2011). Such was the case for a Texas transgender boy in 2017 who, although identifying as male and undergoing hormone replacement therapy (HRT), was denied his request to wrestle on the boys' team and was forced to wrestle on the girls team. At the collegiate level, the National Collegiate Athletic Association (NCAA) allows TGE athletes to compete, but there are stringent requirements related to which teams TGE athletes can compete on based on whether the individual is undergoing HRT (NCAA, 2011). Ultimately, TGE students have often been forced to choose whether to transition and be unable to compete, delay transitioning to compete, or compete on teams according to their sex assigned at birth, regardless of medical transitioning (Skinner-Thompson & Turner, 2013).

TGE students in higher education face similar barriers. Discriminatory policies, such as refusal to change a student's gender marker or name in systems without court orders (which are often difficult or costly to obtain) and sex-segregated facilities with no gender-neutral options available are common (Beemyn & Brauer, 2015; Linley & Kilgo, 2018), which often disproportionately affect transgender women and nonbinary or genderqueer individuals (Seelman, 2016). Student-accessible healthcare is often found to have trans-exclusionary policies that do not cover HRT or counseling for gender-related concerns (Singh, Meng, & Hansen, 2013). Further, acts of discrimination (e.g., misgendering, harassment) by students, faculty, and staff are common across college campuses (Goldberg, Kuvalanka, & Dickey, 2019; James et al., 2016).

Unsurprisingly, based on these findings, many TGE students may feel unsafe at school. Thankfully, many school districts have implemented policies and procedures that support TGE students, and students with supportive schools and positive educational experiences experience greater academic gains and more positive emotional functioning (Kosciw et al., 2018). Organizations such as GLSEN and the National Center for Transgender Equality have published recommendations for schools, as well as for TGE individuals and families to self-advocate. Their websites are helpful roadmaps, and may be especially useful for school counselors (www.glsen.org/and https://transequality.org/school-action-center).

Experiences at Home

The USTS surveyed the experiences of close to 28,000 TGE individuals (ages 18 and older) living in the United States and is to date the largest collected dataset of TGE experiences (James et al., 2016). This report included important information regarding the home experiences of TGE individuals, and found a wide variety of discrepant experiences between those with family support and those with unsupportive families, with family support being associated with a reduced likelihood of negative experiences. Respondents with family support were:

- More likely to be employed (65%) than those with unsupportive families (52%).
- Less likely to have ever done sex work (11%) than those with unsupportive families (16%).
- Less likely to have experienced homelessness (27%) than those with unsupportive families (45%).
- Less likely to report currently experiencing serious psychological distress (31%), in contrast to those with unsupportive families (50%).
- Less likely to have attempted suicide (37%) than those with unsupportive families (54%).

(p. 70)

These findings highlight the necessity of supportive home environments for TGE individuals. In fact, having access to just one supportive adult can substantially mitigate suicide risk (The Trevor Project, 2019), though the greater the number of supportive adults, the better.

Unfortunately, TGE youth represent a disproportionate number of unstably housed youth (Quintana, Rosenthal, & Krehely, 2010; Whitbeck, Lazoritz, Crawford, & Hautala, 2014). TGE youth may face housing insecurity and homelessness due to rejection or to escape abuse by family of origin. Many youth-serving organizations have limited or no policies which include TGE youth, making it difficult for them to access safe and affirming services (Shelton, 2015). Further, housing insecurity often coincides and exacerbates other concerns such as food insecurity, economic stability, and educational retention.

Other Concerns

TGE youth are at significant risk of being forced to undergo conversion therapy. Conversion therapy refers to the practice of attempting to change an individual's sexual orientation or gender identity, often by using methods of punishment and aversive tactics. The practice may also be referred to as reparative therapy. One report (Mallory, Brown, & Conron, 2018) estimated that 20,000 LGBTQQIA youth will receive conversion therapy from licensed mental healthcare professionals before the age of 18, often at the request of caregivers. While at the time of this writing, 18 states and a number of cities and municipalities have implemented bans on conversion therapy for minors, other states have begun proposing regulations to criminalize providers for offering transgender-related healthcare to minors, even with parental consent, despite research demonstrating the use of puberty blockers and gender-affirming treatments in adolescence helps to reduce suicide risk and increase psychological well-being into adulthood (Turban, King, Carswell, & Keuroghlian, 2020).

For TGE individuals, negative effects of oppression such as psychological distress, substance abuse, and suicidality are serious concerns. Depending on the substance, TGE youth are up to four times as likely to use substances, and often engage in use at earlier ages (Day, Fish, Perez-Brumer, Hatzenbuehler, & Russell, 2017). Depression, eating disorders, and self-harm are present at higher rates for TGE individuals than cisgender peers (Connolly, Zervos, Barone, Johnson, & Joseph, 2016). Researchers in one study found TGE youth had double to triple the risk of psychological distress and suicidality than cisgender peers (Reisner et al., 2015).

In a recent survey that discussed suicide attempts, "among the starkest findings is that 40% of respondents have attempted suicide in their lifetime, nearly nine times the attempted suicide rate in the U.S. population (4.6%)" (James et al., 2016, p. 114), while 7% of respondents (many of them young) reported attempting suicide within the past year. Another extremely disturbing statistic noted in this survey was specific to suicidal thoughts and ideation. Eighty-two percent of participants had seriously considered killing themselves at some point during their lives. This rate among TGE individuals is about nine times higher than the annual prevalence rate of suicidal ideation among the U.S. population (Piscopo, Lipari, Cooney, & Glasheen, 2016). Further, for TGE youth, how one identifies is often a significant risk factor for suicidality, with TGE youth identifying outside of the gender binary at higher risk (Grossman & D'Augelli, 2007).

TGE youth are resilient, despite the challenges presented by oppressive systems. Particularly today, TGE youth can be seen advocating and engaging in work dismantling hegemonic systems of power and privilege. TGE youth are often supportive of one another, and social support is a large factor of resilience for TGE youth (Grossman et al., 2011; Stieglitz, 2010), particularly for TGE youth of Color (Singh, 2013).

Counseling Implications

Literature has noted a deficit in knowledge about TGE individuals and affirming practices leading to substantial mental health ramifications (APA, 2015). A first step for counselors is to understand and reflect on personal knowledge, awareness, and skill level for working with TGE individuals. When providing services to children, adolescents, caregivers, and families being impacted by stress and discrimination associated with a sexual minority status, SAMHSA (2015) suggests the following as a scientific foundation of treatment based on the APA's (2015) guidelines:

- Same-gender sexual identity, behavior, and attraction do not constitute a mental disorder;
- Transgender identities and diverse gender expressions do not constitute a mental disorder;
- Same-gender sexual attractions are part of the normal spectrum of sexual orientation and occur in the context of a variety of sexual orientations and gender identities;
- Variations in gender identity and expression are normal aspects of human diversity, and binary definitions of gender may not reflect emerging gender identities;
- Gay men, lesbians, bisexual, and transgender individuals can lead satisfying lives as well as form stable, committed relationships and families.

(p. 24)

Further, Gender Spectrum (2019b) notes how mental health professionals play an integral role in either the affirmation or, sadly, the denial of a child's or adolescent's gender diversity. Many in the helping profession have discussed what affirming support and care looks like and have noted the presence of some core principles. Gender Spectrum (2019b) outlines principles of gender affirming care to include the understanding that:

- There exist naturally occurring variations in gender, and these variations are not inherently negative and should not be categorized as disordered;
- Gender roles and presentations are diverse and varied across societies and over time, and any attempt to analyze them must account for various cultural and historical factors;
- One's authentic gender emerges from the complex interaction of biology, gender expression and gender identity;
- Gender is not binary, but rather fluid, both at a particular time and sometimes within an individual across time; and,
- Pathologies associated with a child's gender diversity most often result from the negative reactions of those surrounding, rather than from within, the child.

(para 5)

Additionally, counselors must understand that possessing binary concepts of gender identity and affectional orientation have frequently served as a way to further oppress the LGBTGEQIAP+ community (Farmer & Byrd, 2015). Understanding and exploring how gender identity intersects with one's experience through the context of other aspects of identity (e.g., race, disability) is also crucial. Counselors must be aware of and address intersectionality with clients.

Specifically, the following is APA's *Guidelines for Psychological Practice with Transgender and Gender Nonconforming People* (2015, located in Appendix B).

Foundational Knowledge and Awareness

Guideline 1. Psychologists understand that gender is a nonbinary construct that allows for a range of gender identities and that a person's gender identity may not align with sex assigned at birth.

Guideline 2. Psychologists understand that gender identity and sexual orientation are distinct but interrelated constructs.

Guideline 3. Psychologists seek to understand how gender identity intersects with the other cultural identities of TGNC people.

Guideline 4. Psychologists are aware of how their attitudes about and knowledge of gender identity and gender expression may affect the quality of care they provide to TGNC people and their families.

Stigma, Discrimination, and Barriers to Care

Guideline 5. Psychologists recognize how stigma, prejudice, discrimination, and violence affect the health and well-being of TGNC people.

Guideline 6. Psychologists strive to recognize the influence of institutional barriers on the lives of TGNC people and to assist in developing TGNC-affirmative environments.

Guideline 7. Psychologists understand the need to promote social change that reduces the negative effects of stigma on the health and well-being of TGNC people.

Life Span Development

Guideline 8. Psychologists working with gender-questioning and TGNC youth understand the different developmental needs of children and adolescents and that not all youth will persist in a TGNC identity into adulthood.

Guideline 9. Psychologists strive to understand both the particular challenges that TGNC elders experience and the resilience they can develop.

Assessment, Therapy, and Intervention

Guideline 10. Psychologists strive to understand how mental health concerns may or may not be related to a TGNC person's gender identity and the psychological effects of minority stress.

Guideline 11. Psychologists recognize that TGNC people are more likely to experience positive life outcomes when they receive social support or trans-affirmative care.

Guideline 12. Psychologists strive to understand the effects that changes in gender identity and gender expression have on the romantic and sexual relationships of TGNC people.

Guideline 13. Psychologists seek to understand how parenting and family formation among TGNC people take a variety of forms.

Guideline 14. Psychologists recognize the potential benefits of an interdisciplinary approach when providing care to TGNC people and strive to work collaboratively with other providers.

Research, Education, and Training

Guideline 15. Psychologists respect the welfare and rights of TGNC participants in research and strive to represent results accurately and avoid misuse or misrepresentation of findings.

Guideline 16. Psychologists seek to prepare trainees in psychology to work competently with TGNC people.

Copyright 2015 by the American Psychological Association. Reproduced with permission. The official citation that should be used in referencing this material is American Psychological Association (2015). No further reproduction or distribution is permitted without written permission from the American Psychological Association.

Legal and Ethical Implications

The 2014 American Counseling Association *Code of Ethics* (2014) states that counselors do not discriminate "against prospective or current clients, students, employees, supervisees, or research participants based on . . . gender, gender identity, sexual orientation . . . or any basis proscribed by law" (p. 9). The code also states that our principal responsibility as counselors is to uphold, support, respect, and "promote the welfare of clients" (p. 4). Additionally, the American School Counselors Association (ASCA, 2016) ethical standards emphasize that all students have the right to:

> Be respected, be treated with dignity and have access to a comprehensive school counseling program that advocates for and affirms all students from diverse populations including but not limited to: ethnic/racial identity, nationality, age, social class,

economic status, abilities/disabilities, language, immigration status, sexual orientation, gender, gender identity/expression, family type, religious/spiritual identity, emancipated minors, wards of the state, homeless youth and incarcerated youth. School counselors as social-justice advocates support students from all backgrounds and circumstances and consult when their competence level requires additional supports.

(p. 1)

Counselors need to be up to date on ethical codes, competencies, and information for advocacy for TGE youth.

Legal protections for TGE children and adolescents exist. Counselors need to be aware of such protections so as to advocate effectively and appropriately for clients and to provide resources and supports for caregivers who are also advocating. The National Center for Transgender Equality (NCTE, 2020) notes that "the First Amendment of the U.S. Constitution protects students' freedom of speech and freedom of expression. That includes the right to dress according to your gender identity, talk about being transgender openly, and express your gender in other ways" (para 9). Two federal laws protecting TGE students are Title IX and FERPA. Title IX (Education Amendments Act of 1972) is a federal law that bans discrimination in schools based on sex. The U.S. Department of Justice and the U.S. Department of Education (2016) stated that Title IX does encompass gender identity, though this continues to be hotly debated. The National Center for Transgender Equality (NCTE, 2020) further explains that "Courts have made it clear that that includes discrimination against someone because they are transgender or don't meet gender stereotypes or expectations" and that "Title IX applies to all schools (including both K–12 schools and colleges) that get federal money, including nearly all public schools" (p. 9).

At the time this chapter was written, only 20 states (and the District of Columbia) address bullying and harassment of students based on gender identity and affectional orientation (Arkansas, California, Colorado, Connecticut, Delaware, D.C., Illinois, Iowa, Maine, Maryland, Massachusetts, Minnesota, Nevada, New Hampshire, New Jersey, New York, North Carolina, Oregon, Rhode Island, Vermont, and Washington) (HRC, 2019b). Further, the quality of these anti-bullying laws can be drastically different depending on the state (HRC, 2019a). To date, 15 states (and D.C.) have state laws specific to gender identity and sexual orientation that prohibit discrimination against students receiving public education (HRC, 2019a). These states include California, Colorado, Connecticut, D.C., Hawaii, Illinois, Iowa, Maine, Massachusetts, Minnesota, Nevada, New Jersey, New York, Oregon, Vermont, and Washington (HRC, 2019a). Counselors need to be aware of laws in their state applying to TGE children and adolescents and to also be aware of policies and ethical codes in respective work environments. If such protections are not in existence, counselors can work to advocate for them.

Working With Parents/Caregivers of TGE Children and Adolescents

Counselors are often tasked with supporting the entire family system when working with TGE children and adolescents. One important aspect to consider is the pervasiveness of caregiver (and youth) beliefs surrounding gender expansiveness and transgender identity. For instance, Indigenous cultures have historically had reverence for Two-Spirit identities, though the effects of colonization have resulted in the loss of much of that reverence. Alternatively, cultures with traditional strict gender roles and boundaries and deference to age-related authority, such as African American and Latinx cultures, may experience more difficulty affirming TGE identities. Thus, familiarity with activities to encourage dialogue and healthy communication between children and caregivers is essential (Keo-Meier & Ehrensaft, 2018).

Baum et al. (2015) reported that for TGE youth to increase levels of self-esteem, develop a positive self-concept, and promote growth and development, support from parents and caregivers is essential. However, only 43% of TGE youth report that they have a supportive adult present in their family (Baum et al., 2015). Counselors, it is absolutely imperative that we are that supportive adult – especially when we work with so many children and adolescents who would not otherwise have one. For a review on the impact of one supportive adult, please refer back to Chapter 1 of this volume. Further, it is imperative that we support parents and caregivers so that they may support their child and/or adolescent.

Working With Schools

Counselors can advocate, affirm, and support TGE youth in many ways. In addition to the resources referenced earlier by GLSEN and NCTE, Sylvia Rivera Law Project (2019) outlines the following recommendations for schools:

- Arrange for transgender awareness training for faculty, staff, and administrators from a qualified community-based trainer.
- Incorporate positive information about transgender issues into curricula.
- Create gender-neutral restrooms.
- If a student talks to you about their gender identity, listen in a respectful and non-judgmental way.
- Avoid perpetuating gender stereotypes.
- Intervene and take action when students use gender-specific terminology to make fun of each other.
- Create gender-neutral and/or mixed gender spaces.
- Always refer to transgender and gender-nonconforming students appropriately.
- Ensure that employment opportunities at your school are open to transgender and gender-nonconforming people.
- Listen to criticism from transgender, gender nonconforming, and questioning students.

(p. 3–4)

Each of these recommendations can be implemented in a variety of ways. For instance, school counselors can serve as liaisons between TGE students and other faculty, staff, and administrators to act as advocates. School counselors should also strive to develop and implement a variety of diverse programming for students, which could include TGE-identified guest speakers, TGE-inclusive sex education, and including intersectionality into sexual and gender diversity programming. Counselors in the community might consider partnering with school counselors and schools to provide TGE-focused support groups and activities.

Community Considerations

Counselors working in community settings can work to make environments more affirming and supportive. Some recommendations include:

- Review, develop, and enforce workplace policies and ethical guidelines based on non-discrimination and anti-bullying/harassment that explicitly protect TGE individuals.

- Examine forms and paperwork to ensure that they are inclusive of all identities.
- Have gender-neutral restrooms.
- Include resources that display and are inclusive of TGE individuals (books, movies, articles, pamphlets, etc.).
- Conduct events, presentations, and programming that are safe for TGE individuals.
- Disseminate newsletters that include TGE issues.
- Continually educate yourself and others.
- Be supportive of employees in their stages of development while working to protect clients.

Additionally, as previously noted, counselors can partner with other organizations to provide services.

Most importantly, counselors must *listen* and continue to educate themselves and others. This includes acknowledging and addressing biases, including our own beliefs regarding sex, gender identity, and gender expression. Counselors, particularly those who are cisgender, must also be able and willing to broach the topics of gender identity with TGE youth. It can be difficult to build rapport with youth (as anyone who has worked with adolescents can attest!), and TGE youth are likely to be especially wary – and especially in need of connection. Addressing identities through a lens of privilege and oppression (see the MSJCC) is especially relevant. Finally, as we noted at the beginning of this chapter, language changes rapidly, and counselors need to stay up to date.

Summary

Transgender and gender-expansive youth need skilled clinicians who understand how to advocate and promote well-being for all children and adolescents. This chapter addressed the importance of language in an ever growing and changing landscape. Essential statistics were discussed to assist counselors in understanding the many factors impacting these individuals. Concerns such as experiences in school and experiences at home were offered for perspective on this issue. We understand that this chapter could have been a book in and of itself (as every chapter in this text could be). We have provided information for counselors to build their knowledge base, grow in their awareness, and start to increase skills for working with TGE children and adolescents. There are many wonderful resources out there to grow in this area, as you will need to continue to do. Thank you for empowering and encouraging our TGE children and adolescents through informed and affirming practice.

Clinician's Corner

Working with transgender youth is like a "create your own adventure" of gender expression. As a transgender-identified individual working with LGBTQ youth, specifically T, it is a natural discussion for me. The caveat is the big C: countertransference. How can I advocate for a youth in a system that does not think outside the binary? I knew that going into this client's world was going to be beautiful, painful, enlightening, and frustrating. My small view into their world was during a meeting where key stakeholders blamed me for "making their kid trans". First off, I will admit, I was absolutely terrified. I then thought of how my client must feel being even less in control of their life. They live with that guillotine over their head because adults still had rights to their body. That meant that they still had a say in their life pertaining to medical and legal transition. I sat and pondered for hours on end how to advocate and assist the youth in moving forward with their transition socially, medically, and emotionally in an environment that puts every barrier before them. Then I hit my counselor's funny bone and realized this is countertransference. I don't have the power here, nor should I. I can provide them the tools, but only they can choose how to use them. They simply need a safe space to work.

Ajay Rashe, Foster Care Counselor
Youth Villages

References

American Counseling Association (ACA). (2014). *Code of ethics and standards of practice*. Alexandria, VA: Author.

American Psychological Association (APA). (2015). Guidelines for psychological practice with transgender and gender nonconforming people. *American Psychologist, 70*, 832–864. https://doi.org/10.1037/a0039906

American School Counselor Association (ASCA). (2016). *Ethical standards for school counselors*. Retrieved from www.schoolcounselor.org/asca/media/asca/Ethics/EthicalStandards2016.pdf

Association of Lesbian, Gay, Bisexual, and Transgender Issues in Counseling (ALGBTIC). (2009). *Competencies for counseling with transgender clients*. Alexandria, VA: Author.

Baum, J., Brill, S., Brown, J., Delpercio, A., Kahn, E., Kenney, L., & Nicoll, A. (2015). *Supporting and caring for our gender expansive youth*. Retrieved from www.hrc.org/youth-report/supporting-and-caring-for-our-gender-expansive-youth

Beemyn, G., & Brauer, D. (2015). Trans-inclusive college records: Meeting the needs of an increasingly diverse US student population. *TSQ: Transgender Studies Quarterly, 2*, 478–487. https://doi.org/10.1215/23289252-2926455

Connolly, M. D., Zervos, M. J., Barone, C. J., Johnson, C. J., & Joseph, C. L. M. (2016). The mental health of transgender youth: Advances in understanding. *Journal of Adolescent Health, 59*, 489–495. https://doi.org/10.1016/j.jadohealth.2016.06.012

Day, J. K., Fish, J. N., Perez-Brumer, A., Hatzenbuehler, M. L., & Russell, S. T. (2017). Transgender youth substance use disparities: Results from a population-based sample. *Journal of Adolescent Health, 61*, 729–735. https://doi.org/10.1016/j.jadohealth.2017.06.024

Education Amendments Act of 1972, 20 U.S.C. §§1681–1688 (2018).

Farmer, L. B., & Byrd, R. (2015). Genderism in the LGBTQQIA community: An interpretative phenomenological analysis. *Journal of Lesbian, Gay, Bisexual, and Transgender Issues in Counseling, 9*(4), 288–310. https://doi.org/10.1080/15538605.2015.1103679

Gay, Lesbian, and Straight Education Network. (2020). *Key concepts and terms*. Retrieved from www.glsen.org/activity/glsen-safe-space-kit-be-ally-lgbtq-youth

Gender Spectrum. (2019a). *Glossary: Gender expansive*. Retrieved from www.genderspectrum.org/glossary/gender-expansive/

Gender Spectrum. (2019b). *Mental health*. Retrieved from www.genderspectrum.org/explore-topics/mental-health/

Goldberg, A., Kuvalanka, K., & Dickey, L. M. (2019). Transgender graduate students' experiences in higher education: A mixed-methods exploratory study. *Journal of Diversity in Higher Education, 12*(1), 38–51. http://doi.org/10.1037/dhe0000074

Grossman, A. H., & D'Augelli, A. R. (2007). Transgender youth and life-threatening behaviors. *Suicide and Life-Threatening Behavior, 37*(5), 527–527. doi:10.1521/suli.2007.37.5.527

Grossman, A. H., D'Augelli, A. R., & Frank, J. A. (2011). Aspects of psychological resilience among transgender youth. *Journal of LGBT Youth, 8*, 103–115. https://doi.org/10.1080/19361653.2011.541347

Herman, J. L., Flores, A. R., Brown, T. N. T., Wilson, B. D. M., & Conron, K. J. (2017). *Age of individuals who identify as transgender in the United States*. Los Angeles, CA: The Williams Institute.

Human Rights Campaign (HRC). (2019a). *State laws: Education*. Retrieved from www.hrc.org/state-maps/education

Human Rights Campaign (HRC). (2019b). *State laws: School anti-bullying*. Retrieved from www.hrc.org/state-maps/anti-bullying/pdf

James, S. E., Herman, J. L., Rankin, S., Keisling, M., Mottet, L., & Anafi, M. (2016). *The report of the 2015 U.S. transgender survey*. Washington, DC: National Center for Transgender Equality.

Keo-Meier, C., & Ehrensaft, D. (Eds.). (2018). *The gender affirmative model: An interdisciplinary approach to supporting transgender and gender expansive children*. Washington, DC: American Psychological Association.

Kosciw, J. G., Greytak, E. A., Zongrone, A. D., Clark, C. M., & Truong, N. L. (2018). *The 2017 National School climate survey: The experiences of lesbian, gay, bisexual, transgender, and queer youth in our nation's schools*. New York: GLSEN.

Linley, J. L., & Kilgo, C. A. (2018). Expanding agency: Centering gender identity in college and university student record systems. *Journal of College Student Development, 59*, 359–365. https://doi.org/10.1353/csd.2018.0032

Lucas-Carr, C. B., & Krane, V. (2011). What is the T in LGBT? Supporting transgender athletes through sports psychology. *The Sport Psychologist, 25*, 532–548. https://doi.org/10.1123/tsp.25.4.532

Mallory, C., Brown, T. N. T., & Conron, K. J. (2018, January). *Conversion therapy and LGBT youth*. Retrieved from https://williamsinstitute.law.ucla.edu/publications/conversion-therapy-and-lgbt-youth/

National Center for Transgender Equality (NCTE). (2020). *Know your rights: Schools*. Retrieved from https://transequality.org/know-your-rights/schools

National Collegiate Athletics Association. (2011). *NCAA inclusion of transgender student athletes*. Retrieved from www.ncaapublications.com/p-4335-ncaa-inclusion-of-transgender-student-athletes.aspx

Piscopo, K., Lipari, R. N., Cooney, J., & Glasheen, C. (2016). *Suicidal thoughts and behavior among adults: Results from the 2015 national survey on drug use and health*. NSDUH Data Review. Retrieved from www.samhsa.gov/data/sites/default/files/NSDUH-DR-FFR3-2015/NSDUH-DR-FFR3-2015.pdf

Quintana, N., Rosenthal, J., & Krehely, J. (2010). *On the streets: The federal response to gay and transgender homeless youth*. Retrieved from www.americanprogress.org/issues/2010/06/on_the_streets.html

Reisner, S. L., Vetters, R., Leclerc, M., Zaslow, S., Wolfrum, S., Shumer, D., & Mimiaga, M. J. (2015). Mental health of transgender youth in care at an adolescent urban community health center: A matched retrospective cohort study. *Journal of Adolescent Health, 56*, 274–279. https://doi.org/10.1016/j.jadohealth.2014.10.264

Seelman, K. L. (2016). Transgender adults' access to college bathrooms and housing and the relationship to suicidality. *Journal of Homosexuality, 63*, 1378–1399. https://doi.org/10.1080/00918369.2016.1157998

Shelton, J. (2015). Transgender youth homelessness: Understanding programmatic barriers through the lens of cisgenderism. *Children and Youth Services Review, 59*, 10–18. https://doi.org/10.1016/j.childyouth.2015.10.006

Singh, A. A. (2013). Transgender youth of color and resilience: Negotiating oppression and finding support. *Sex Roles, 68*, 690–702. https://doi.org/10.1007/s11199-012-0149-z

Singh, A. A., Hays, D. G., & Watson, L. S. (2011). Strength in the face of adversity: Resilience strategies of transgender individuals. *Journal of Counseling and Development, 89*, 20–27. https://doi.org/10.1002/j.1556-6678.2011.tb00057.x

Singh, A. A., Meng, S., & Hansen, A. (2013). "It's already hard enough being a student": Developing affirming college environments for trans youth. *Journal of LGBT Youth, 10*, 208–223. https://doi.org/10.1080/19361653.2013.800770

Skinner-Thompson, S., & Turner, I. M. (2013). Title IX's protections for transgender student athletes. *Wisconsin Journal of Law, Gender & Society, 28*, 271–300. Retrieved from https://scholar.law.

colorado.edu/articles/739/?utm_source=scholar.law.colorado.edu%2Farticles%2F739&utm_medium=PDF&utm_campaign=PDFCoverPages

Stieglitz, K. A. (2010). Development, risk, and resilience of transgender youth. *Journal of the Association of Nurses in AIDS Care, 21*, 192–206. https://doi.org/10.1016/j.jana.2009.08.004

Substance Abuse and Mental Health Services Administration (SAMHSA). (2015). Ending conversion therapy: Supporting and affirming LGBTQ youth. *HHS Publication No. (SMA)* 15–4928. Retrieved Working from https://store.samhsa.gov/product/Ending-Conversion-Therapy-Supporting-and-Affirming-LGBTQ-Youth/SMA15-4928

Sylvia Rivera Law Project. (2019). *Fact sheet: Transgender and gender nonconforming youth in schools*. Retrieved from https://srlp.org/wp-content/uploads/2012/08/youth-rights-bw.pdf

The Trevor Project. (2019). *Research brief: Accepting adults reduce suicide attempts among LGBTQ youth*. Retrieved from www.thetrevorproject.org/2019/06/27/research-brief-accepting-adults-reduce-suicide-attempts-among-lgbtq-youth/

Turban, J. L., King, D., Carswell, J. M., & Keuroghlian, A. S. (2020). Pubertal suppression for transgender youth and risk of suicidal ideation. *Pediatrics, 145*. https://doi.org/10.1542/peds.2019-1725

U.S. Department of Justice and the U.S. Department of Education. (2016). *Dear colleague: Letter on transgender students*. Retrieved from www2.ed.gov/about/offices/list/ocr/letters/colleague-201605-title-ix-transgender.pdf

Whitbeck, L., Lazoritz, M., Crawford, D., & Hautala, D. (2014). *Street outreach program data collection project executive summary*. Retrieved from www.acf.hhs.gov/programs/fysb/resource/sop-executive-summary

13 LGB Children and Adolescents

Rebekah Byrd, Christian Chan, and Chad Luke
Christian Chan as guest contributor

Objectives
- Describe and define many key terms from this chapter associated with LGB children and adolescents.
- Understand the many alarming statistics associated with LGB individuals.
- Examine appropriate principles for creating and supporting safe spaces.
- Understand legal and ethical issues that apply to LGB children and adolescents.
- Evaluate ways counselors can work with schools and community settings to make spaces more affirming and supportive.
- Examine ways to empower and encourage LGB children and adolescents.

Reflective Questions
- What are my own experiences surrounding sexual, affectional, and gender diversity?
- In what ways will I work to understand the importance of language?
- Throughout my life, what messages did I receive from family, school, work, and society about LGB communities and sexual, affectional, and gender diversity?
- How can I continue to work on my biases and gaps in culturally responsive practices toward LGB children and adolescents?
- How can I advocate for our LGB children and adolescents in varying settings?
- What ways can I work to empower and encourage LGB children and adolescents?

Concepts and Terms

Chapter 12 of this volume included many terms associated with LGBTGEQIAP+ individuals and discussed the importance of language. Counselors should understand that affectional/sexual identity and orientation does not just exist on a binary; LGB individuals need skilled clinicians who understand how to advocate and promote health for all children and adolescents. You will notice the term used previously, affectional/sexual orientation. This term is used to underscore the meaningful relationship that exists between people instead of focusing on the term "sexual" which often diminishes, minimizes, and "others" the relationship to something less than that of heteronormative relationships. If we must use a term, we prefer to use affectional orientation. Reiterated below are a few terms we will discuss most in this chapter. Taken from GLSEN (2020) the following are definitions:

> *Bisexual:* A person who is emotionally and/or physically attracted to two or more genders, often used to describe people attracted to "genders like theirs" and "other genders."

Gay: Someone, who can be transgender or cisgender, who is attracted to someone of the same gender.

Lesbian: Someone, who can be transgender or cisgender, who generally considers themselves a woman or femme who is attracted to other women and/or femmes.

LGBTQ: An umbrella term referring to people who identify as lesbian, gay, bisexual and/or transgender. The acronym can also include additional letters, in reference to other identities that do not conform to dominant societal norms.

As previously mentioned, language is important. Counselors should be comfortable using appropriate language and terms with clients (Ginicola, Smith, & Rhoades, 2016; Ginicola, Smith, & Filmore, 2017). This creates a safe atmosphere for the client. To also broaden the counselors' vocabulary with LGBTGEQIAP+-affirming interventions, we recommend reviewing several guiding documents, such as the ALGBTIC Competencies for Counseling Transgender Clients (ALGBTIC, 2009); ALGBTIC Competencies for Counseling with Lesbian, Gay, Bisexual, Queer, Questioning, Intersex, and Ally Individuals (Harper et al., 2012); ALGBTIC Standards of Care in Assessment of Lesbian, Gay, Bisexual, Transgender, Gender Expansive, and Queer/Questioning (LGBTGEQ+) Persons (Goodrich et al., 2017); and ALGBTIC Standards of Care for Research with Participants Who Identify as LGBTQ+ (Griffith et al., 2017).

LGB Youth and Adolescents in the United States

It is beyond troubling that a 2019 national survey reported that nearly 7 in 10 (69.8%) school mental health professionals (this includes school counselors, school-based counselors, social workers, and psychologists) reported that they received little to no graduate training in working with LGB individuals (GLSEN, ASCA, ACSSW, & SSWAA, 2019). In this same national survey, 64.3% of school mental health professionals gave their graduate training programs a score of fair or poor in preparing them for working with LGB students in the school setting. We know that not all readers will work in a school setting, but it is important to understand how to work with this system, as most all of the children and adolescents you will work with will likely be in a school somewhere. Working with the school is important in providing best practice for clients, even if you are in an agency, private practice, or other setting, since children and adolescents spend most of their time in schools. This chapter provides an essential place to start when learning how to advocate, support, and affirm LGB children and adolescents in many settings.

Important to understand is that LGB children and adolescents do not face these concerns as a result of their identity status. The concerns they deal with have to do directly with how society accepts them, issues they deal with at home and at school, and these concerns are a result of living in a heterosexist society. It is important to understand that LGB individuals are not just inherently at risk; their risk is from having to navigate unsupportive and unsafe spaces often on a daily basis. Providing support early and often is crucial to aid in the prevention of the development of health disparities later in the life of an LGB person (Calzo et al., 2017; Luke, Harper, Goodrich, & Singh, 2017).

In 2017, suicide was the second leading cause of death among children and youth ages 10–14 and also the second leading cause of death among youth and adults ages 15–34, according to the Centers for Disease Control and Prevention *WISQARS Leading Cause of Death Reports* (CDC 2017). In the 2016 CDC report on *Sexual Identity, Sex of Sexual Contacts, and Health-Risk Behaviors Among Students in Grades 9–12* (YRBS), LGB youth reported attempting suicide one or more times during last 12 months at a rate almost 5 times higher than their heterosexual peers (CDC 2016). LGB youth were also 5 times more likely to need medical treatment after a suicide attempt. This same report also noted that LGB youth are also 3 times as likely to seriously consider suicide and 3 times as likely to make a suicide plan as heterosexual youth.

This CDC report in 2016 was the agency's first national study of health of LGB students in grades 9–12. In this study, the following were also noted:

- 17.8% of LGB students were physically forced to have sexual intercourse. That is a rate more than 3 times higher than heterosexual students.
- 22.7% of LGB students experienced dating violence of a sexual nature. That is a rate more than 2 times higher than heterosexual students.
- 17.5% of LGB students experienced dating violence of a physical nature. That is a rate more than 2 times higher than heterosexual students.
- 34.2% of LGB students experienced being bullied on school property. This rate is 2 times higher than heterosexual students.
- 28% of LGB students experienced being bullied electronically. This rate is 2 times higher than heterosexual students.
- 12.5% of LGB students did not attend school due to feeling unsafe at school or on their travels to and from school. This rate is more than 2 times higher than heterosexual students.
- 60.4% of LGB students reported feeling hopeless or sad. This rate is more than 2 times higher than heterosexual students.
- 42.8% of LGB students reported suicidal ideation. This rate is 3 times higher than heterosexual students.
- 29.4% reported attempting suicide. This rate is more than 4 times higher than heterosexual students.

Other statistics from this CDC report (2016) were also alarming.

- 11.5% of LGB students reported having ever used hallucinogenic drugs. This is a rate more than 2 times higher than heterosexual students.
- 10.1% of LGB students reported having ever used ecstasy. This is a rate more than 2 times higher than heterosexual students.
- 6% of LGB students reported ever having used heroin. This is a rate more than 4 times higher than heterosexual students.
- 8.2% of LGB students reported having ever used methamphetamines. This rate is 4 times higher than heterosexual students.
- 9.7% of LGB students reported having taken steroids without a prescription. This is a rate more than 3 times higher than heterosexual students.
- 17.3% of LGB students reported having ever used inhalants. This is a rate more than 3 times higher than heterosexual students.
- 5.4% of LGB students reported having ever injected an illegal drug. This rate is 5 times higher than heterosexual students.

Counselors should be aware that the chief reason an LGB child or adolescent is kicked out or removed from home is due to conflict related to an adolescent's sexual or gender identity (Ryan, Huebner, Diaz, & Sanchez, 2009). Berberet (2006) conducted a needs assessment of LGBTQ youth living in out-of-home care in San Diego and found that of the youth surveyed, 65% had been in either foster care or a residential group home facility and 39%

reported being "kicked out" of their own home due to their gender identity or their sexual orientation. Further, Berberet noted that 90% of the LGTBQ youth in this assessment reported surviving on the streets by dealing drugs; "trading drugs for money, food, and a place to sleep" (p. 374). Additionally, LGBTQ-identifying youth are overrepresented in the child welfare system and experience poor educational outcomes, probation, and homelessness at higher rates than peers (Martain, Down, & Earney, 2016). Martain et al. further posited that these disparities are even worse for LGBTQ youth of color and represent alarming and bleak outcomes about their experiences.

Many county and state estimates in the child welfare system note that the proportion of gender and sexual minority youth are much higher than the general youth statistics (Detlaff, Washburn, Carr, & Vogel, 2018). Some evidence suggest that this rate is about 15.5% – or 146,000 youth in the welfare system identify specifically as LGB (Detlaff et al., 2018). This estimate does not take into account those youth who are not openly out or who may be questioning. Further, Detlaff et al. also found that LGB youth of color are overrepresented in the welfare systems and that LGB youth were much more likely to meet criteria for adverse mental health concerns. This study found substantial differences between LGB youth and heterosexual youth in regard to diagnostic criteria for trauma, depression, and substance abuse, and also in overall mental health and behavioral issues. Prevention and early intervention efforts aimed at teaching parents, caregivers, and families about the deleterious effects of rejecting behaviors is imperative to assist with keeping these LGB youth in their homes (Ryan et al., 2009).

Experiences in School

One study found that higher levels of school connectedness predicted less suicidal ideation among LGB youth supporting evidence that school connectedness (factors included safety concerns, school relationships, and school bonding/belongingness) may in fact serve as a protective factor against suicide for LGB individuals (Whitaker, Shapiro, & Shields, 2016). In the most recent *National School Climate Survey* conducted by GLSEN (Gay, Lesbian, and Straight Educators Network), researchers confirmed that schools are still very hostile places for LGBTQ children and adolescents (Kosciw, Greytak, Zongrone, Clark, & Truong, 2018). Researchers found that:

- Almost every LGBTQ person (98.5%) surveyed reported hearing discriminatory and anti-LGBTQ language at school.
- 56.6% of students surveyed reported hearing discriminatory and/or anti-LGBTQ language from teachers and school staff.
- 59.5% of LGBTQ students in the schools reported feeling unsafe at school due to their affectional/sexual orientation.
- 34.8% missed an entire day of school in the past month due to feeling uncomfortable or unsafe in school while 10.5% of LGBTQ students miss four or more days due to feeling uncomfortable or unsafe – in the last month.
- 75.4% of LGBTQ students reported that they avoided school functions due to feeling uncomfortable or unsafe.
- 70.5% of LGBTQ students reported that they avoided extracurricular activities due to feeling unsafe or uncomfortable.
- Almost a fifth of LGBTQ students surveyed reported having had to change schools due to feeling unsafe or uncomfortable.
- 70.1% of LGBTQ students were verbally harassed at school based on affectional/sexual orientation.

- 28.9% of LGBTQ students experienced being physically harassed based on affectional/sexual orientation – in the past year.
- 48.7% of LGBTQ students reported being harassed electronically (social media or text messaging) in the past year.
- 57.3% of LGBTQ students reported being sexually harassed at school in the past year.
- 55.3% of the LGBTQ students who experienced assault or harassment did not report it to school staff or administration due to fearing the situation would get worse or due to having little faith that an intervention would occur.
- 60.4% of the students who reported that they did notify school staff or administration about an incident stated that school staff did not respond to said reported incident or told the student to ignore the situation.

Though the statistics are alarming, they are important for understanding how to create a safe school environment. Advocating for all students is both an ethical and legal obligation for counselors (ACA, 2014, ASCA, 2012). Specifically, the ASCA's *The Professional Counselor and LGBTQ Youth* (2016b) position statement advocated:

> School counselors promote equal opportunity and respect for all individuals regardless of sexual orientation, gender identity or gender expression. School counselors recognize the school experience can be significantly more difficult for students with marginalized identities. School counselors work to eliminate barriers impeding LGBTQ student development and achievement.
>
> (p. 1)

This position statement has also been updated to include specific areas in which school counselors provide support and advocacy in school from working in individual sessions to advocating for equitable extracurricular and educational opportunities. This position statement also addressed the need for counselors to advocate for gender-neutral facilities in the school, supporting an inclusive curriculum at every grade level, advocating and adopting policies at school that directly address discrimination prevention, encouraging staff training, and supporting families and communities to be affirming and inclusive. These are not merely suggestions. These are ethical imperatives and necessary safety measures for all of our LGBTGEQIAP+ children and adolescents. Both ACA (2014) and ASCA (2016a) ethical codes outline the importance of social justice, multicultural competency, and advocacy efforts specific to LGBTGEQIAP+ individuals.

It has also been noted in this text multiple times the role that supportive adults play in the lives of children and adolescents. LGBTQ students who report feeling supported and safe at school report better experiences in school and increased academic success (Kosciw et al., 2018). Kosciw et al. (2018) also "found that LGBTQ students whose parents engaged in advocacy with their school, overall, had better well-being, including higher levels of self-esteem and lower levels of depression" (p. 25).

It is clear that there still exists great need for creating affirming, supportive, and caring schools for all students. Counselors working with children and adolescents should be at the forefront of this movement as we seek to advocate for all of our students. This essential work from GLSEN regarding school climate makes excellent recommendations and suggestions that still need attention. GLSEN suggests the following recommendations (Kosciw et al., 2018):

- Increasing student access to appropriate and accurate information regarding LGBTQ people, history, and events through inclusive curricula, and library and internet resources;

- Supporting student clubs, such as GSAs, that provide support for LGBTQ students and address LGBTQ issues in education;
- Providing professional development for school staff to improve rates of intervention and increase the number of supportive teachers and other staff available to students;
- Ensuring that school policies and practices, such as those related to dress codes and school dances, do not discriminate against LGBTQ students;
- Enacting school policies that provide transgender and gender-nonconforming students equal access to school facilities and activities and specify appropriate educational practices to support these students; and
- Adopting and implementing comprehensive anti-bullying/harassment policies that specifically enumerate sexual orientation, gender identity, and gender expression in individual schools and districts, with clear and effective systems for reporting and addressing incidents that students experience.

(xxviii)

School counselors, school-based counselors, and anyone working with children and adolescents can also take part in, promote, and even provide safe space trainings, as research has shown that safe space training specific to counselors increased counselor levels of knowledge, awareness, and skills related to the LGBTGEQIAP+ competency (Byrd & Hays, 2013).

Experience at Home

Familial rejection of LGB children and adolescents can lead to many negative outcomes. Ryan et al. (2009) noted that LGB young adults who indicated higher levels of familial rejection during their adolescence were 8.4 times more likely to have attempted suicide, 3.4 times more likely to have used substances, 5.9 times more likely to experience higher levels of depression, and 3.4 times more likely to disclose having unprotected sex compared to LGB peers reporting no familiar rejection or low levels of familial rejection related to sexual orientation or identity when an adolescent. Additionally, "negative parental responses to sexual orientation or gender are associated with young people's psychological distress; however, parent-child relationships characterized by closeness and support, however, are an important correlate of mental well-being" (SAMHSA, 2015, p. 21). The Trevor Project (2019a) research brief on accepting adults report noted that LGBTQ youth who had at least one accepting and supportive adult were 40% less likely to attempt suicide in the last year.

Ryan et al. have provided research that clearly shows a link between parental/caregiver rejection and rejective behaviors when children and adolescents were growing up and adverse health outcomes in LGB individuals into young adulthood. When working with LGB children and adolescents, counselors must evaluate, assess, and educate parents, caregivers, and families about the negative and far-reaching impact of rejecting behaviors (Chan, 2018; Estrada, Singh, & Harper, 2017; Ryan et al., 2009). Counseling families can provide the needed support, safe space, and help necessary to increase well-being of LGB children and adolescents (Harper et al., 2012; Mills-Koonce, Rehder, & McCurdy, 2018; Ryan et al., 2009). Ryan and colleagues (2009), in particular, further recommended that those working with children and adolescents can start increasing support for LGB and decrease family rejection by doing the following:

1. Ask LGB adolescents about family reactions to their sexual orientation and gender expression and refer to LGB community support programs and for supportive counseling as needed.

2. Identify LGB support programs in the community and online resources to educate parents about how to help their LGB children. Parents need access to positive parental role models to help decrease rejection and increase family support for their LGB children.
3. Advise parents that negative reactions to their adolescent's LGB identity may negatively influence their child's health and mental health.
4. Recommend that parents and caregivers modify highly rejecting behaviors that have the most negative influence on health concerns, such as suicidality.
5. Expand anticipatory guidance to include information on the need for support and the link between family rejection and negative health problems in LGB young people.

(p. 351)

Creating Safe Spaces

Counselors must advocate for safe spaces for all. Due to discrimination, harassment, prejudice, and lack of legal protections, many LGBTGEQIAP+ individuals feel unsafe in many environments. Unfortunately, our schools and counseling offices are often no different. We must make our environments safe spaces. Many resources and ideas exist for how to create safe spaces for all. This section discusses some ideas.

Safe Schools

GLSEN's most recent *National School Climate Survey* (Kosciw et al., 2018) provided helpful information for making schools safer for all of our LGBTGEQIAP+ youth. These recommendations are specific to school systems yet should also include such general ideas as making paperwork inclusive, providing examples of LGBTGEQIAP+ individuals on bulletin boards and historical celebrations/holidays, rules against bullying and heterosexist speak, and challenging heterosexist biases on a daily basis. GLSEN's recommendations for schools specifically are:

- Faculty and staff need to support clubs such as Gay-Straight Alliances or Gender and Sexuality Alliances (GSAs). These student clubs are supportive for LGBTGEQIAP+ students and help to address LGBTGEQIAP+ issues in education.
- Trainings for school staff are necessary. These trainings help educate all and have been shown to improve rates of knowledge, awareness, and interventions, while increasing the number of supportive teachers and staff accessible to students.
- Provide and have available appropriate and accurate information and resources concerning LGBTGEQIAP+ individuals, history, and occurrences through curricula that are inclusive and updated library and internet resources.
- Confirm that school protection policies and practices exist and are followed. These can include dress code policies and/or school dance policies that do not discriminate against LGBTGEQIAP+ students.
- Endorse and implement policies and practices that do not discriminate against transgender and gender-expansive students and their equal access to education.
- Approve and implement comprehensive and inclusive school and district anti-bullying/harassment policies that specifically discuss affectional/sexual orientation, gender identity, and gender expression as protected categories along with race, ability status, and religion. These policies need to include definitive and operative procedures for reporting and addressing occurrences that students experience.

Safe Community Agencies

While the previous information focused on the school setting specifically, counselors in a variety of settings across communities and agencies must also advocate for creating safe spaces. Counselors are housed in hospitals, mental health clinics, government buildings, private practices, substance abuse facilities, outpatient counseling agencies, prison systems, and assisted living facilities. The following recommendations can be essential places to start in making all of our spaces more supportive and affirming.

- Review, develop, and enforce workplace policies based on non-discrimination and anti-bullying/harassment that explicitly protect LGBTGEQIAP+ individuals.
- Examine forms to ensure that they are inclusive of all identities (e.g., intake forms could include multiple options for gender or a blank to fill in, instead of a forced choice male/female option).
- Conduct and provide continuing education on LGBTGEQIAP+-relevant information.
- Have gender-neutral restrooms.
- Include resources, references, and community supports that display and are inclusive of LGBTGEQIAP+ individuals (books, brochures, movies, articles, pictures, magazines, community resources, etc.).
- Conduct events, presentations, and programming that are supportive, safe, and affirming for LGBTGEQIAP+ individuals.
- Disseminate newsletters that include LGBTGEQIAP+ concerns and are inclusive of all clients.
- *Listen!*
- Educate yourself and others.
- *Advocate!*
- Be supportive of employees in their various stages of development while challenging heterosexist and heteronormative ideas and concepts.

Legal and Ethical Implications

Counselors should also be aware that most LGB individuals reside in states with no legal protection against discrimination based on sexual orientation, gender identity, and expression (SOGIE) (Detlaff et al., 2018). Further, Detlaff et al. state:

> because no overarching federal protections exist to protect LGBTQ+ individuals from discrimination, system involved youth in these states are left vulnerable to inequitable treatment in schools or within human services agencies, and also in public spaces related to housing and placement.
>
> (p. 192)

There has been recent discriminatory legislation passed allowing those in the helping profession to refuse services to individuals that would go against the provider's religious beliefs (Tennessee being one of them). Tennessee state House Bill (HB 1840, 2016), also referred to as the Counselor's Bill, states:

> Mental Health & Substance Abuse Services, Dept. of – As enacted, declares that no person providing counseling or therapy services will be required to counsel or serve a client as to goals, outcomes, or behaviors that conflict with the sincerely held principles

of the counselor or therapist; requires such counselor or therapist to refer the client to another counselor or therapist; creates immunity for such action; maintains liability for counselors who will not counsel a client based on the counselor's religious beliefs when the individual seeking or undergoing the counseling is in imminent danger of harming themselves or others.

Amends TCA Title 4; Title 49 and Title 63

Although some of this legislation is vague, the origin was specifically discriminating against LGBTGEQIAP+ individuals. The Family Action Council of Tennessee, Inc. (2019) stated that the bill provides both criminal and civil protections to Tennessee counselors (in private practice) who decide to refer clients if the client's goals are in conflict with the counselor's "sincerely held principles or religious beliefs" (para 1) and that this bill "deletes the new provision of the ACA code of ethics that prohibits referrals in such instances" (para 3). This provision they are referring to was added and clarified to the newest version of the ACA *Code of Ethics* (ACA 2014) and states:

> A.11.b. Values Within Termination and Referral: Counselors refrain from referring prospective and current clients based solely on the counselor's personally held values, attitudes, beliefs and behaviors. Counselors respect the diversity of clients and seek training in areas in which they are at risk of imposing their values onto clients, especially when the counselor's values are inconsistent with the client's goals or are discriminatory in nature.

The Mississippi state Religious Liberty Accommodations Act (HB 1523), also called the Protecting Freedom of Conscience from Government Discrimination Act, is another similar law. CNN Wire stated that

> under the law, religious organizations will be able to deny LGBT people marriage, adoption and foster care services; fire or refuse to employ them; and decline to rent or sell them property. Medical professionals will be permitted to refuse to participate in treatments, counseling and surgery related to "sex reassignment or gender identity transitioning".
>
> (2016, para 9)

These types of legislation will lead to further limiting access to services for LGB individuals, limiting placement options or those in the welfare system, and will also perpetuate the harmful and damaging belief that these individuals do not deserve, need, or require affirming, loving, supportive, and safe households (Detlaff et al., 2018). Under such bills, members of the LGBT community could also be denied counseling, medical treatment, suicide hotline services, and could even be forced into "conversion therapy" (Bolles, 2016).

"Conversion Therapy"

It is also important for us to say a bit about what is known as "conversion therapy". We have put this phrase in quotation marks because this is actually not therapy at all. This practice is extremely dangerous and has long lasting harmful and damaging outcomes. "Conversion therapy refers to attempts to change a person's sexual orientation or gender identity through a variety of methods, including induced vomiting and electric shock" (Equality Federation, n.d.). The Trevor Project (2019b) *National Survey on LGBTQ Mental Health* reported that youth who had been subjected to conversion therapy were more than twice as likely to attempt suicide as LGBTGEQIAP+ youth who were not subjected to conversion therapy. This is on top of their already increased levels of suicide. Mallory, Brown, and Conron (2018) estimate that:

- 20,000 LGBT youth (ages 13–17) will receive conversion therapy from a licensed healthcare professional before they reach the age of 18 in the 41 states that currently do not ban the practice.
- 6,000 LGBT youth (ages 13–17) who live in states that ban conversion therapy would have received such therapy from a licensed healthcare professional before age 18 if their state had not banned the practice.
- 57,000 youth (ages 13–17) across all states will receive conversion therapy from religious or spiritual advisors before they reach the age of 18.
- 698,000 LGBT adults (ages 18–59) in the United States have received conversion therapy, including about 350,000 LGBT adults who received treatment as adolescents.

(p. 1)

The Substance Abuse and Mental Health Services Administration (2015) notes that conversion therapy "is a practice that is not supported by credible evidence and has been disavowed by behavioral health experts and associations" (p. 1). Equality Federation (n.d.) further emphasizes that "all of the nation's leading professional medical and mental health associations condemn conversion therapy as unnecessary, ineffective, and dangerous". Take a moment to think about that. *All* of the leading professional mental health organizations in the United States not only oppose this despicable practice, but believe it to be dangerous. So why then is this still being not only practiced, but mental health professionals are actually still referring individuals to this perilous practice?! Additionally, if helping professionals are ethically obligated to adhere to best practice procedures and utilize empirically based strategies (ACA, 2014), how could an ethical counselor ever refer for "conversion therapy" when "none of the existing research supports the premise that mental or behavioral health interventions can alter gender identity or sexual orientation" (SAMHSA, 2015, p. 1), and why would ethical counselors want to? With the previously stated estimations indicating that this is still happening at alarming rates, counselors have an ethical and legal obligation to not only refrain from such referrals, but to actively advocate against such practices.

Working With Family Members of LGB Children and Adolescents

In addition to several of the contextual, social, and political factors to consider for LGB children and adolescents, professional counselors can strongly consider partnerships and collaboration with family members and parents/caregivers to sustain allyship (Estrada et al., 2017; Harper et al., 2012). According to Chan (2018), families can serve as meaningful and transformative allies for LGB children and adolescents, given the lack of legal and environmental support for children and adolescents within several community systems. Vital to a comprehensive set of supports, parents/caregivers and family members can often use their own privileges and safety to advocate in collaboration with LGB children and adolescents (Chan, 2017, 2018). Since numerous LGB children and adolescents spend the majority of their time at home and in schools, it would be pertinent for counselors to consider how they might leverage school/community/family partnerships to facilitate potential forms of advocacy. Additionally, stronger relationships with parents/caregivers for LGB children can decrease interpersonal and systemic forms of minority stress and discrimination (Meyer, 2010, 2014; Ryan et al., 2009). In particular, Magette, Durtschi, and Love (2018) noted that adolescents and emerging adults with strong relationships with parents/caregivers can reduce substance use and improve coping strategies. Watson, Rose, Doull, Adjei, and Saewyc (2019) supported this notion by highlighting the vital role of fathers in support and connectedness of LGB adolescents. Substantiating the relationship of families to LGB children and adolescents, LGB children and adolescents are primarily exposed to the family system as an immediate source of support and can transfer this experience to other systems (e.g., community supports, school, church; Chan, 2017, 2018; Estrada et al., 2017; Mills-Koonce et al., 2018).

Counselors in a diversity of work settings (e.g., community agencies, schools) play a pivotal role in connecting with children and adolescent clients, particularly school counselors (Byrd & Hays, 2013). In the context of LGB children and adolescents, school counselors can have a profound impact on their academic achievement, climate of safety, and social and emotional well-being (Byrd & Hays, 2013; Luke et al., 2017). This point operates in tandem with the findings developed by several researchers to augment an understanding of affirmative practices (see Farmer, 2017; Farmer, Welfare, & Burge, 2013). To bolster the inclusion and collaboration of families in developing more affirming environments for LGB children and adolescents, counselors can use a variety of considerations and tools to initiate interpersonal and systemic changes (Luke et al., 2017).

When counselors provide their services in multiple work settings, they have an opportunity to develop a number of tools for assisting families with connecting to experiences of an LGB child or adolescent. Namely, counselors assess for affirmative knowledge and environments within families, where families may have misconceptions or underlying ideologies about sexual and affectional diversity. In assessing for knowledge, it is important for counselors to capitalize on the strengths of family members who may already carry significant empathy with LGBTGEQIAP+ communities; participate in community and legislative advocacy for LGBTGEQIAP+ communities; or hold extensive knowledge about LGBTGEQIAP+ affirming practices. Given these possibilities, counselors cannot necessarily assume that families of LGB adolescents are not affirming. Rather, counselors can more so consider the level of development and knowledge of family members to enhance their support, allyship, and solidarity with another LGB family member.

In working with family members, counselors can also draw from broaching behaviors in their counseling practice (see Day-Vines et al., 2007; Day-Vines, Ammah, Steen, & Arnold, 2018). As a vital component of culturally responsive practices, broaching behaviors alludes to explicit discussions of cultural factors in counseling practice, where counselors thereby validate discussions of culture and provide a safer space for clients and students (Day-Vines et al., 2007). With the intention to enhance the counseling relationship and to empower the client or student, initiating broaching behaviors requires key ingredients from the Multicultural and Social Justice Counseling Competencies (MSJCC) along the domains of knowledge, attitudes and beliefs, skills, and advocacy (Ratts, Singh, Nassar-McMillan, Butler, & McCullough, 2015). A distinct connection between the model of broaching and the MSJCC entails increased attention to the attitudes and beliefs, which would ultimately bolster a counselor's awareness of their own relationships, power, and privilege with clients. For instance, a counselor using the infusing behavior on the continuum of broaching would incorporate culturally sensitive interpersonal responses with family members of LGB children and adolescents while infusing discussions on systems and power (Day-Vines et al., 2018). Moving intentionally toward the infusing behavior can serve as a meaningful experience for working with families of LGB children and adolescents to transfer the relationship as a teachable moment, where family members can feel empowered to examine their own privilege, systemic factors, and cultural sensitivity to an LGB child or adolescent.

Adding to the practice of broaching, counselors can primarily build the knowledge of parents/caregivers and family members to form affirming spaces and environments for their LGB children and adolescents (Harper et al., 2012). Several key aspects can inform the learning process for family members and strengthen their relationships with LGB children and adolescents. An explicit example involves counselors teaching family members foundational language about LGBTGEQIAP+ communities, particularly surrounding sexual and affectional diversity (Goodrich et al., 2017). It would be helpful for a counselor to provide family members language to maintain curiosity and ask questions about sexuality and diversity in a supportive manner. For instance, a family member can explicitly state, "In our house and our society, people can choose to love anyone of any gender. If you feel comfortable sharing with us, how would you describe who you love and how you might identify your affectional or sexual identity? We want to make sure we use the language that supports you". Another example might involve explicitly discussing forms of oppression, where a parent might share, "It is possible that you have been hurt or might get hurt because people have failed to understand how you feel attracted to or love someone else. It does not mean there is an issue with you. It is more of an issue with that person or with society". In this instance, family members and parents/caregivers can characterize a supportive response and environment while socializing their LGB children and adolescents for the potential harm they might face in society. Teaching parents/caregivers and family members about these examples can also illustrate a method to socialize LGB children and adolescents for the grief process when society fails to affirm them (Luke et al., 2017).

Empowerment and Encouragement

Counseling with LGB children and their family members entails an explicit approach on language, knowledge of key issues, and recognition of cultural and environmental contexts. Several of these areas revolve around the tools of affirmation, but can be broadened even further through empowerment and encouragement. A prominent tool of social justice for LGB children stems from the skill of empowerment in interpersonal relationships – concepts upon which this book is based. From this experience, LGB children can apply such empowerment to their own personal lives and feel validated in a multitude of their experiences. Additionally, counselors can collaborate with LGB children to build upon experiences of empowerment to ultimately culminate in systemic interventions, programming at school or the community, and advocacy-based initiatives.

For LGB children, cultivating a safer space for students to name their experiences and their social identities with sexuality and affection can be widely impactful. Throughout time and history, children navigating their sexual and affectional identities have often been positioned within the boundaries of several identity categories, primarily gay and lesbian. However, the history and context surrounding affectional/sexual minority categories create barriers for children to understand and feel more congruent in their affectional and sexual identities. This issue can instill an experience of exclusion for children who identify outside of affectional/sexual binaries, such as pansexual, demisexual, omnisexual, bisexual, and queer (Cor & Chan, 2017; Moe, Bower, & Clark, 2017). Even for children identifying as gay and lesbian, barriers surrounding sexuality and affection can deter them from naming and disclosing their sexual and affectional identities in order to fit assumptions within the identity categories. Operating from this perspective, counselors can encourage LGB children to recognize an anti-essentialist viewpoint, which means that their affectional or sexual identity may not appear the same as everyone else (Lugg, 2003; Lugg & Murphy, 2014). Additionally, anti-essentialism includes a viewpoint that illustrates sexuality and affection as unique experiences, despite sharing identities (Misgav, 2016). For instance, two children may identify as gay, but carry a variety of differing experiences and socializations. They do not automatically face or hold the same experiences simply as a result of their identity, which realizes the uniqueness of each individual (Chan, 2018; Chan, Erby, Farmer, & Friday, 2017a; Cor & Chan, 2017; Goodrich et al., 2017).

To continue empowering LGB children, counselors can also highlight negative cultural messages (Singh, 2019), notably to locate external forces affecting their well-being. Specifically with the advances in microaggression literature, LGB children internalize experiences associated with discrimination on interpersonal and systemic levels (see Gartner & Sterzing, 2018; Harkness & Israel, 2018; Nadal, Whitman, Davis, Erazo, & Davidoff, 2016). Counselors can increase critical consciousness around the effects of microaggressions and how they communicate problematic messages for LGB children and adolescents (Singh, 2013). In doing so, they are raising awareness for children and adolescents as clients and students to recognize they are not the root of their problems (Ratts & Greenleaf, 2018). Oppressive experiences can result in a multitude of mental health disparities, health disparities, and lowered outcomes of wellness (Harper et al., 2012; Mustanski, Birkett, Greene, Hatzenbuehler, & Newcomb, 2014). In fact, Boyas, Villarreal-Otálora, Alvarez-Hernandez, and Fatehi (2019) identified an increasing prevalence among Latinx LGB youth regarding suicidal ideation, planning, and lethal attempts. Within the Boyas et al. (2019) study, factors contributing to suicidal ideation illustrated a connection with substance use and experiences of oppression and bullying. More critical to the Boyas et al. (2019) study, practitioners and communities could more adequately address this issue by eliciting interventions at multiple systemic levels (e.g., micro, meso, macro, chrono) while targeting harmful messages diminishing a climate of safety.

Similarly, counselors can use a myriad of strategies to highlight the practice of resilience among LGB children (Singh, 2013, 2019). One way to assist LGB children in discovering their own practices of resilience emanates from the emphasis on curating materials on LGB heroes into their personal libraries, curricula, and collections of resources (Simons, Beck, Asplund, Chan, & Byrd, 2018; Simons, Chan, Beck, & Asplund, 2019), which would allow children to see a positive representation of their own identities. Another characteristic aspect to resilience is drawing from intersectional resilience (Chan, 2018; Singh, 2013) by (a) using experiences from another marginalized identity to detail how they might have bounced back or (b) understanding the uniqueness of their intersecting identities. Similarly, recognizing the intersections among multiple marginalized identities and the ability to navigate these identities can elicit moments of resilience for LGB children since they were able to build on their tools, resources, and coping (Singh, 2013). To further increase encouragement about sexual and affectional identity, counselors can ask children and adolescents to (a) discuss their identities when they feel safe and (b) use stories to elaborate on the meaning of their sexual and affectional identity (Chan et al., 2017a; Simons et al., 2019).

Intersecting Identities for Consideration

LGB children and adolescents consist not only of one singular identity. Rather, they function in a multitude of systems and social contexts that shed light on numerous social identities (e.g., race, ethnicity, sexual identity, gender identity, gender expression, social class), their linkages, and their overlapping forms of oppression (see Bowleg, 2012, 2013; Chan, 2018; Singh, 2013; Singh & McKleroy, 2011). Of visible importance, researchers have postulated the importance of examining LGB communities and the intersection of race and ethnicity to identify complex connections between racism and heterosexism (e.g., Bowleg, 2013; Chan et al., 2017a; Chan, Erby, & Ford, 2017b; Mosley, Gonzalez, Abreu, &

Kaivan, 2019; Singh, 2013). This prominent aspect is especially important to consider, given that LGBTGEQIAP+ communities are subject to oppression internally within communities. LGBTGEQIAP+ communities can maintain oppressive dynamics, such as racism, ableism, and genderism, within communities (Chan et al., 2017a, 2017b; Farmer & Byrd, 2015). It is also important for counselors to broach these linkages while foreseeing potential intersections that might influence another identity (Chan, 2017, 2018). Additionally, counselors must take social context (e.g., school, church, policies) into account (Collins & Bilge, 2016), which might exacerbate the prevalence and manifestation of certain forms of oppression. For example, LGB children and adolescents of color may face more racism in certain environments while experiencing more heterosexism in other environments. Supportive adults, specifically parents and family members, can reduce the likelihood of suicidal ideation and the effects of heterosexism (Abreu, Black, Mosley, & Fedewa, 2016; Boyas et al., 2019; Chan, 2018; Levy, Russon, & Diamond, 2016).

Advocacy

Important to the discussion on extending affirmative practices, resilience, and empowerment for LGB children and adolescents, counselors can benefit primarily from the Multicultural and Social Justice Counseling Competencies (MSJCC) endorsed by the ACA (Ratts et al., 2015; Ratts, Singh, Nassar-McMillan, Butler, & McCullough, 2016). Ratts and colleagues (2016) constructed the MSJCC on the basis of meeting the current state of multicultural research and reinforcing the urgency to move toward a fifth force of social justice. With the inclusion of social justice in the most recent document, counselors were encouraged to realize their responsibilities in advocating for historically marginalized communities (Ratts, 2017; Ratts & Greenleaf, 2017). As a result, counselors are required to reconceptualize their professional development of multiculturalism and social justice as integral factors within their practice while meeting ethical standards to view these aspirational goals as a lifelong developmental process (Ratts et al., 2016). Crucial to the development of the MSJCC, counselors attend to knowledge, attitudes, beliefs, and skills both for clients/students and themselves, but more importantly, they must attend to action and advocacy (Ratts & Greenleaf, 2017).

Applied to LGB adolescents, the MSJCC position on advocacy intertwines with the previous development of the ALGBTIC guiding documents over the past decade (e.g., ALGBTIC, 2009; Goodrich et al., 2017; Griffith et al., 2017; Harper et al., 2012). It is crucial for counselors to constantly enhance their knowledge, address their biases, and conduct further research to integrate more cultural empathy for LGB children and adolescents (Singh, 2019). In certain circumstances, counselors potentially rely on the strategy of asking LGB children and adolescents to teach them knowledge about sexual and affectional diversity, which creates an antithetical approach to the MSJCC (Guth et al., 2019). Additionally, this strategy positions clients and students uncomfortably in the role of teaching the counselor and reinforces the power and privilege of the counselor (Ratts, 2017; Ratts & Greenleaf, 2018).

Counselors also primarily need to dismantle internalized binaries about sexuality by expanding sexual and affectional identity categories (Lugg & Murphy, 2014). Additionally, counselors can enhance their knowledge on affirmative and updated language to recognize the identities and lived experiences of LGB children and adolescents (ALGBTIC, 2009; Harper et al., 2012). It is vital for counselors to increase their knowledge and attitudes and beliefs specifically about their own biases (Abreu et al., 2016; Simons et al., 2018, 2019). Increasing knowledge about LGB-affirmative practices can also provide opportunities to sustain efforts surrounding LGBTGEQIAP+ advocacy, resources, supports, and community partners (Beck, Maier, Means, & Isaacson, 2018a). Education about personal biases can assist counselors with effectively planning interventions and reducing the likelihood of discriminatory behaviors in counseling (Day-Vines et al., 2018). Examples of advocacy can involve interpersonal forms of advocacy, such as educating other paraprofessionals, teachers, family members, and counselors about different forms of language (Abreu et al., 2016; Beck et al., 2018a; Beck, Rausch, Wikoff, & Gallo, 2018b). Other examples of advocacy can result in more systemic changes, such as examining community agency and school efforts and policies to support the climate of safety for LGBTGEQIAP+ students (Astramovich, Chan, & Marasco, 2017; Chan, 2018).

Summary

The importance of language usage was reiterated for the LGBTGEQIAP+ community and in this chapter specifically, our LGB children and adolescents. We outlined many troubling statistics for LGB children and adolescents, including information on suicide statistics, dating violence, harassment, experiences at home and school, drug use, and homelessness. Legal and ethical considerations were addressed, while emphasizing that counselors must understand that advocating for LGB children and adolescents is both an ethical and a legal obligation. Counselors were provided with information for working with family members of LGB children and adolescents. Many recommendations were made for creating and supporting safe spaces in multiple settings while seeking to also support intersecting identities. Strategies and techniques for empowering and encouraging our LGB children and adolescents were also emphasized.

Clinician's Corner

Years ago, when working in an inpatient psychiatric setting, many patients stood out to me and still come to mind today. One in particular was a young woman who ended up in the unit multiple times for suicide attempts and ideation. Approximately two years later, at around the age of 16 with a diagnosis of borderline personality disorder, she was once again on my caseload at an outpatient day crisis treatment facility. She noticed me and remembered me and said she felt more comfortable with a familiar face. Still struggling with suicidal ideation, it was a few months before she came out – in a session with me and her mother. Mom was supportive but noted family and school were not, and that these were exceptionally hard times. We continued to work together and I watched the young woman grow in self-acceptance, confidence, and self-compassion. She had a wonderful team of professionals advocating for her in the community, in-home, and school settings. School ended up being supportive and she was out and proud and helped to advocate for others. Many youth have very different outcomes once coming out to family, friends, and classmates – to whom this likely sounds like a fairy tale. I couldn't help but wonder how many of our LGB children and youth frequent both inpatient and outpatient centers with suicidal ideation (among other presenting issues) and are diagnosed with axis II disorders who are really struggling with society's acceptance of them. How many counselors question (often) rapidly made diagnoses? How many clients question these diagnoses, as well? This is one of many stories, and we know from our suicide statistics that many aren't as fortunate. How will you stand up and advocate for LGB children and adolescents?

Rebekah Byrd Ph.D., LPC, (TN), LCMHC (NC), NCC, RPT-S
Sacred Heart University

References

Abreu, R. L., Black, W. W., Mosley, D. V., & Fedewa, A. L. (2016). LGBTQ youth bullying experiences in schools: The role of school counselors within a system of oppression. *Journal of Creativity in Mental Health*, 11(3–4), 325–342. https://doi.org/10.1080/15401383.2016.1214092

American Counseling Association (ACA). (2014). *ACA code of ethics*. Alexandria, VA: Author.

American School Counseling Association (ASCA). (2012). *The ASCA national model: A framework for school counseling programs* (3rd ed.). Alexandria, VA: Author.

American School Counseling Association (ASCA). (2016a). *ASCA ethical standards for school counselors*. Alexandria, VA: Author. Retrieved from www.schoolcounselor.org/asca/media/asca/Ethics/EthicalStandards2016.pdf

American School Counseling Association (ASCA). (2016b). *The professional school counselor and LGBTQ youth (ASCA position statement)*. Retrieved from www.schoolcounselor.org/asca/media/asca/PositionStatements/PS_LGBTQ.pdf

Association of Lesbian, Gay, Bisexual, and Transgender Issues in Counseling (ALGBTIC). (2009). *Competencies for counseling with transgender clients*. Alexandria, VA: Author.

Astramovich, R. L., Chan, C. D., & Marasco, V. M. (2017). Advocacy evaluation for counselors serving LGBTQ populations. *Journal of LGBT Issues in Counseling*, 11(4), 319–329. https://doi.org/10.1080/15538605.2017.1380553

Beck, M. J., Maier, C. A., Means, A., & Isaacson, L. A. (2018a). Interdisciplinary collaboration for LGBTQ students in foster care: Strategies for school counselors. *Journal of LGBT Issues in Counseling*, 12(4), 248–264.

Beck, M. J., Rausch, M. A., Wikoff, H. D., & Gallo, L. L. (2018b). Ecological considerations and school counselor advocacy with LGBT students. *Journal of Counselor Leadership & Advocacy*, 5(1), 45–55. https://doi.org/10.1080/2326716X.2017.1402393

Berberet, H. M. (2006). Putting the pieces together for queer youth: A model of integrated assessment of need and program planning. *Child Welfare*, 85, 361–384.

Bolles, A. (2016). *How 6 LGBT Mississippians would be harmed by HB 1523*. Retrieved from www.glaad.org/blog/how-6-lgbt-mississippians-would-be-harmed-hb-1523

Bowleg, L. (2012). The problem with the phrase *women and minorities:* Intersectionality – An important theoretical framework for public health. *American Journal of Public Health*, 102(7), 1267–1273. https://doi.org/10.2105/AJPH.2012.300750

Bowleg, L. (2013). "Once you've blended the cake, you can't take the parts back to the main ingredients": Black gay and bisexual men's descriptions and experiences of intersectionality. *Sex Roles*, 68(11–12), 754–767. https://doi.org/10.1007/s11199-012-0152-4

Boyas, J. F., Villarreal-Otálora, T., Alvarez-Hernandez, L. R., & Fatehi, M. (2019). Suicide ideation, planning, and attempts: The case of the Latinx LGB youth. *Health Promotion Perspectives*, 9(3), 198–206. https://doi.org/10.15171/hpp.2019.28

Byrd, R., & Hays, D. G. (2013). Evaluating a safe space training for professional school counselors and trainees using a randomized control group design. *Professional School Counseling*, 17(1), 20–31. https://doi.org/10.5330/PSC.n.2013-17.20

Calzo, J. P., Melchiono, M., Richmond, T. K., Leibowitz, S. F., Argenal, R. L., Goncalves, A., . . . Burke, P. (2017). Lesbian, gay, bisexual, and transgender adolescent health: An interprofessional case discussion. *MedEdPORTAL: The Journal of Teaching and Learning Resources*, 13, 1–11. https://doi.org/10.15766/mep_2374-8265.10615

Centers for Disease Control and Prevention. (2016). Sexual identity, sex of sexual contacts, and health-related behaviors among students in grades 9–12, 2015. *Morbidity and Mortality Weekly Report*. Retrieved from www.cdc.gov/nchhstp/newsroom/docs/2016/LGB-Media-Data-Summary.pdf

Centers for Disease Control and Prevention (CDC). (2017). *WISQARS leading cause of death reports*. Retrieved from https://webappa.cdc.gov/sasweb/ncipc/leadcause.html

Chan, C. D. (2017). A critical analysis of systemic influences on spiritual development for LGBTQ+ youth. *Journal of Child and Adolescent Counseling*, 3(3), 146–163. https://doi.org/10.1080/23727810.2017.1341795

Chan, C. D. (2018). Families as transformative allies to trans youth of color: Positioning intersectionality as analysis to demarginalize political systems of oppression. *Journal of GLBT Family Studies, 14*(1–2), 43–60. https://doi.org/10.1080/1550428X.2017.1421336

Chan, C. D., Erby, A. N., Farmer, L. B., & Friday, A. R. (2017a). LGBTQ identity development. In W. K. Killam & S. E. Degges-White (Eds.), *College student development: Applying theory to practice on the diverse campus* (pp. 149–160). New York: Springer Publishing.

Chan, C. D., Erby, A. N., & Ford, D. J. (2017b). Intersectionality in practice: Moving a social justice paradigm to action in higher education. In J. M. Johnson & G. C. Javier (Eds.), *Queer people of color in higher education* (pp. 9–29). Charlotte, NC: Information Age Publishing.

CNN Wire. (2016). *Mississippi passes religious freedom bill that LGBT groups call discriminatory*. Retrieved from https://www.wtkr.com/2016/04/06/mississippi-passes-religious-freedom-bill-that-lgbt-groups-call-discriminatory-2

Collins, P. H., & Bilge, S. (2016). *Intersectionality*. Malden, MA: Polity Press.

Cor, D. N., & Chan, C. D. (2017). Intersectionality feminism and LGBTIQQA+ psychology: Understanding our present by exploring our past. In R. Ruth & E. Santacruz (Eds.), *LGBT psychology and mental health: Emerging research and advances* (pp. 109–132). Santa Barbara, CA: Praeger/ABC-CLIO.

Day-Vines, N. L., Ammah, B. B., Steen, S., & Arnold, K. M. (2018). Getting comfortable with discomfort: Preparing counselor trainees to broach racial, ethnic, and cultural factors with clients during counseling. *International Journal for the Advancement of Counselling, 40*(2), 89–104. https://doi.org/10.1007/s10447-017-9308-9

Day-Vines, N. L., Wood, S. M., Grothaus, T., Craigen, L., Holman, A., Dotson-Blake, K., & Douglass, M. J. (2007). Broaching the subjects of race, ethnicity, and culture during the counseling process. *Journal of Counseling & Development, 85*, 401–409. https://doi.org/10.1002/j.1556-6678.2007.tb00608.x

Detlaff, A. J., Washburn, M., Carr, L. C., & Vogel, A. N. (2018). Lesbian, gay and bisexual (LGB) youth within welfare: Prevalence, risk and outcomes. *Child Abuse and Neglect, 80*, 183–193. https://doi.org/10.1016/j.chiabu.2018.03.009

Equality Federation. (n.d.). *Legislation action center: Conversion therapy bans*. Retrieved from www.equalityfederation.org/lac/conversiontherapy/

Estrada, D., Singh, A. A., & Harper, A. J. (2017). Becoming an ally: Personal, clinical, and school-based social justice interventions. In M. M. Ginicola, C. Smith, & J. M. Filmore (Eds.), *Affirmative counseling with LGBTQI+ people* (pp. 343–358). American Counseling Association.

Family Action Council of Tennessee, Inc. (2019). *Counselors' bill (HB 1840) fact sheet*. Retrieved from http://factn.org/legislation-bill-tracking-state-legislature/counselors-bill-hb-1840-fact-sheet/

Farmer, L. B. (2017). An examination of counselors' religiosity, spirituality, and lesbian-, gay-, and bisexual-affirmative counselor competence. *The Professional Counselor, 7*(2), 114–128. https://doi.org/10.15241/lbf.7.2.114

Farmer, L. B., & Byrd, R. B. (2015). Genderism in the LGBTQQIA community: An interpretative phenomenological analysis. *Journal of LGBT Issues in Counseling, 9*(4), 288–310. https://doi.org/10.1080/15538605.2015.1103679

Farmer, L. B., Welfare, L. E., & Burge, P. L. (2013). Counselor competence with lesbian, gay, and bisexual clients: Differences among practice settings. *Journal of Multicultural Counseling and Development, 41*(4), 194–209. https://doi.org/10.1002/j.2161-1912.2013.00036.x

Gartner, R. E., & Sterzing, P. R. (2018). Social ecological correlates of family-level interpersonal and environmental microaggressions toward sexual and gender minority adolescents. *Journal of Family Violence, 33*(1), 1–16. https://doi.org/10.1007/s10896-017-9937-0

Gay, Lesbian, and Straight Education Network (GLSEN). (2020). *Key concepts and terms*. Retrieved from www.glsen.org/activity/glsen-safe-space-kit-be-ally-lgbtq-youth

Ginicola, M. M., Smith, C., & Filmore, J. M. (2017). Developing competence in working with LGBTQI+ communities: Awareness, knowledge, skills, and action. In M. M. Ginicola, C. Smith, & J. M. Filmore (Eds.), *Affirmative counseling with LGBTQI+ people* (pp. 1–20). American Counseling Association.

Ginicola, M. M., Smith, C., & Rhoades, E. (2016). Love thy neighbor: A guide for implementing safe school initiatives for LGBTQ students in nonaffirming religious communities. *Journal of LGBT Issues in Counseling*, 10(3), 159–173. https://doi.org/10.1080/15538605.2016.1199992

GLSEN, ASCA, ACSSW, & SSWAA. (2019). *Supporting safe and healthy schools for lesbian, gay, bisexual, transgender, and queer students: A national survey of school counselors, social workers, and psychologists.* GLSEN.

Goodrich, K. M., Farmer, L. B., Watson, J. C., Davis, R. J., Luke, M., Dispenza, F., . . . Griffith, C. (2017). Standards of care in assessment of lesbian, gay, bisexual, transgender, gender expansive, and queer/questioning (LGBTGEQ+) persons. *Journal of LGBT Issues in Counseling*, 11(4), 203–211. https://doi.org/10.1080/15538605.2017.1380548

Griffith, C., Akers, W., Dispenza, F., Luke, M., Farmer, L. B., Watson, J. C., . . . Goodrich, K. M. (2017). Standards of care for research with participants who identify as LGBTQ. *Journal of LGBT Issues in Counseling*, 11(4), 212–229. https://doi.org/10.1080/15538605.2017.1380549

Guth, L. J., Nitza, A., Pollard, B., Puig, A., Chan, C. D., Singh, A., & Bailey, H. (2019). Ten strategies to intentionally use group work to transform hate, facilitate courageous conversations, and enhance community building. *The Journal for Specialists in Group Work*, 44(1), 3–24. https://doi.org/10.1080/01933922.2018.1561778

Harkness, A., & Israel, T. (2018). A thematic framework of observed mothers' socialization messages regarding sexual orientation. *Psychology of Sexual Orientation and Gender Diversity*, 5(2), 260–272. https://doi.org/10.1037/sgd0000268

Harper, A., Finnerty, P., Martinez, M., Brace, A., Crethar, H., Loos, B., . . . Lambert, S. (2012). *Association for Lesbian, Gay, Bisexual, and Transgender Issues in Counseling (ALGBTIC) competencies for counseling with lesbian, gay, bisexual, queer, questioning, intersex and ally individuals.* Retrieved from www.counseling.org/docs/ethics/algbtic-2012-07

HB 1840 (2016). Amends TCA Title 4; Title 49 and Title 63.

Kosciw, J. G., Greytak, E. A., Zongrone, A. D., Clark, C. M., & Truong, N. L. (2018). *The 2017 National School Climate Survey: The experiences of lesbian, gay, bisexual, transgender, and queer youth in our nation's schools.* GLSEN.

Luke, C. (2017). Learner-centered counseling theory: An innovative perspective. *Journal of Creativity in Mental Health*, 12(3), 305–319. https://doi.org/10.1080/15401383.2016.1249445

Levy, S. A., Russon, J., & Diamond, G. M. (2016). Attachment-based family therapy for suicidal lesbian, gay, and bisexual adolescents: A case study. *Australian & New Zealand Journal of Family Therapy*, 37(2), 190–206. https://doi.org/10.1002/anzf.1151

Lugg, C. A. (2003). Sissies, faggots, lezzies, and dykes: Gender, sexual orientation and new politics of education? *Educational Administration Quarterly*, 39(1), 95–134.

Lugg, C. A., & Murphy, J. P. (2014). Thinking whimsically: Queering the study of educational policy-making and politics. *International Journal of Qualitative Studies in Education*, 27(9), 1183–1204. https://doi.org/10.1080/09518398.2014.916009

Luke, M., Harper, A. J., Goodrich, K. M., & Singh, A. A. (2017). LGBTQI+ youth development. In M. M. Ginicola, C. Smith, & J. M. Filmore (Eds.), *Affirmative counseling with LGBTQI+ people* (pp. 41–48). American Counseling Association.

Magette, A. L., Durtschi, J. A., & Love, H. A. (2018). Lesbian, gay, and bisexual substance use in emerging adulthood moderated by parent-child relationships in adolescence. *The American Journal of Family Therapy*, 46(3), 272–286. https://doi.org/10.1080/01926187.2018.1493958

Mallory, C., Brown, T. N. T., & Conron, K. J. (2018). *Conversion therapy and LGBT youth.* The Williams Institute. Retrieved from https://williamsinstitute.law.ucla.edu/wp-content/uploads/Conversion-Therapy-LGBT-Youth-Jan-2018.pdf

Martain, M., Down, I., & Earney, R. (2016). *Out of the shadows: Supporting LGBTQ youth in child welfare through cross system collaboration.* Center for the Study of Social Policy. Retrieved from https://cssp.org/resource/out-of-the-shadows/

Meyer, I. H. (2010). Identity, stress, and resilience in lesbians, gay men, and bisexuals of color. *The Counseling Psychologist*, 38(3), 442–454. https://doi.org/10.1177/0011000009351601

Meyer, I. H. (2014). Minority stress and positive psychology: Convergences and divergences to understanding LGBT health. *Psychology of Sexual Orientation and Gender Diversity*, *1*(4), 348–349. https://doi.org/10.1037/sgd0000070

Mills-Koonce, W. R., Rehder, P. D., & McCurdy, A. L. (2018). The significance of parenting and parent-child relationships for sexual and gender minority adolescents. *Journal of Research on Adolescence*, *28*(3), 637–649. https://doi.org/10.1111/jora.12404

Misgav, C. (2016). Some spatial politics of queer-feminist research: Personal reflections from the field. *Journal of Homosexuality*, *63*(5), 719–721. https://doi.org/10.1080/00918369.2015.1112191

Moe, J., Bower, J., & Clark, M. (2017). Counseling queer and genderqueer clients. In M. M. Ginicola, C. Smith, & J. M. Filmore (Eds.), *Affirmative counseling with LGBTQI+ people* (pp. 213–226). Alexandria, VA: American Counseling Association.

Mosley, D. V., Gonzalez, K. A., Abreu, R. L., & Kaivan, N. C. (2019). Unseen and underserved: A content analysis of wellness support services for bi + people of color and indigenous people on U.S. campuses. *Journal of Bisexuality*, *19*(2), 276–304. https://doi.org/10.1080/15299716.2019.1617552

Mustanski, B., Birkett, M., Greene, G. J., Hatzenbuehler, M. L., & Newcomb, M. E. (2014). Envisioning an America without sexual orientation inequities in adolescent health. *American Journal of Public Health*, *104*(2), 218–225. https://doi.org/10.2105/AJPH.2013.301625

Nadal, K. L., Whitman, C. N., Davis, L. S., Erazo, T., & Davidoff, K. C. (2016). Microaggressions toward lesbian, gay, bisexual, transgender, queer, and genderqueer people: A review of the literature. *Journal of Sex Research*, *53*(4/5), 488–508. https://doi.org/10.1080/00224499.2016.1142495

Ratts, M. J. (2017). Charting the center and the margins: Addressing identity, marginalization, and privilege in counseling. *Journal of Mental Health Counseling*, *39*(2), 87–103. https://doi.org/10.17744/mehc.39.2.01

Ratts, M. J., & Greenleaf, A. T. (2017). Multicultural and social justice counseling competencies: A leadership framework for professional school counselors. *Professional School Counseling*, *21*(1b), 1–9. https://doi.org/10.1177/2156759X18773582

Ratts, M. J., & Greenleaf, A. T. (2018). Counselor – Advocate – Scholar model: Changing the dominant discourse in counseling. *Journal of Multicultural Counseling and Development*, *46*(2), 78–96. https://doi.org/10.1002/jmcd.12094

Ratts, M. J., Singh, A. A., Nassar-McMillan, S., Butler, S. K., & McCullough, J. R. (2015). *Multicultural and social justice counseling competencies*. Retrieved from www.counseling.org/docs/default-source/competencies/multicultural-and-social-justice-counseling-competencies.pdf?sfvrsn=14

Ratts, M. J., Singh, A. A., Nassar-McMillan, S., Butler, S. K., & McCullough, J. R. (2016). Multicultural and social justice counseling competencies: Guidelines for the counseling profession. *Journal of Multicultural Counseling and Development*, *44*(1), 28–48. https://doi.org/10.1002/jmcd.12035

Ryan, C., Huebner, D., Diaz, R. M., & Sanchez, J. (2009). Family rejection as a predictor of negative health outcomes in white and Latino lesbian, gay, and bisexual adults. *Pediatrics*, *123*, 346–352.

Simons, J. D., Beck, M., Asplund, N., Chan, C. D., & Byrd, R. (2018). Advocacy for gender minority students: Recommendations for school counsellors. *Sex Education: Sexuality, Society and Learning*, *18*(4), 464–478. https://doi.org/10.1080/14681811.2017.1421531

Simons, J. D., Chan, C., Beck, M. J., & Asplund, N. (2019). Using the emancipatory communitarian approach to increase LGBTQI advocacy. *Journal of Gay & Lesbian Social Services*, *31*(4), 458–475. https://doi.org/10.1080/10538720.2019.1642279

Singh, A. A. (2013). Transgender youth of color and resilience: Negotiating oppression and finding support. *Sex Roles*, *68*, 690–702. https://doi.org/10.1007/s11199-012-0149-z

Singh, A. A. (2019). *The racial healing handbook: Practical activities to help you challenge privilege, confront systemic racism, and engage in collective healing*. New Harbinger Publications.

Singh, A. A., & McKleroy, V. S. (2011). "Just getting out of bed is a revolutionary act": The resilience of transgender people of color who have survived traumatic life events. *Traumatology*, *17*(2), 34–44. https://doi.org/10.1177/1534765610369261

Substance Abuse and Mental Health Services Administration (SAMHSA). (2015). *Ending conversion therapy: Supporting and affirming LGBTQ youth*. HHS Publication No. (SMA) 15–4928. Author.

The Trevor Project. (2019a). *The trevor project research brief: Accepting adults reduce suicide attempts among LGBTQ youth*. Retrieved from www.thetrevorproject.org/wp-content/uploads/2019/06/Trevor-Project-Accepting-Adult-Research-Brief_June-2019.pdf

The Trevor Project. (2019b). *National survey on LGBTQ mental health*. Author.

Watson, R. J., Rose, H. A., Doull, M., Adjei, J., & Saewyc, E. (2019). Worsening perceptions of family connectedness and parent support for lesbian, gay, and bisexual adolescents. *Journal of Child and Family Studies, 28*(11), 3121–3131. https://doi.org/10.1007/s10826-019-01489-3

Whitaker, K., Shapiro, V. B., & Shields, J. P. (2016). School-based protective factors related to suicide for lesbian, gay, and bisexual adolescents. *Society for Adolescent Health and Medicine, 58*, 63–68.

Woodside, M., & Luke, C. (2018). *Practicum in counseling: A developmental guide*. Cognella Academic Press.

14 Celebrating Diversity

Chad Luke and Rebekah Byrd

Objectives

- Increase understanding of and appreciation for childhood and adolescence as their own culture.
- Explore the concept of intersectionality as it relates to child and adolescent culture.
- Identify signs of culture shock when working with children and adolescents.
- Increase appreciation for how adult privilege manifests in counseling relationships.
- Develop awareness of microaggressions in the context of adult-child relationships.
- Differentiate sympathy, empathy, and projective sympathy in working with children and adolescents.
- Identify the relevance of the MSJCC in working with children and adolescents.

Reflective Questions

- What are the defining characteristics about me?
- What do I recall about my experience as a child and adolescent?
- What benefits and limitations were present during those periods of my life?
- What do I recall about my relationships with adults during those periods? How do I think adults viewed and treated me?
- In what ways did my cultural characteristics (race, ethnicity, gender, affectional/sexual orientation, spirituality, etc.) intersect with my identity as a child and then as an adolescent?

Before we dive into the content of this chapter, we invite you to reflect on the 10 characteristics or traits about yourself. Take a moment to list those. Now, rank order them, more important or salient, to less important. What do you notice about your list? Did "adult" or "emerging adult" make it onto the list? How about race? With 10 years of running this type of activity in a multicultural counseling course, we have observed several trends. This first is that no one records adulthood in their list. Second, only individuals of color list race as salient. Third, heterosexual, cisgender students do not list affectional/sexual identity or orientation in their top 10. Fourth, women and transgender students are the only ones who include their gender in the list; male students do not. What do you make of these observations? How does it correlate with your list and self-identity? We find that the more majority-status characteristics one has, the less likely they are to make the list, or if they do, they are rarely in the top five. In contrast, minority or underrepresented statuses typically make it into the top three, and often in this order: race, gender, and affectional/sexual orientation. Throughout this chapter, we will examine what this means, especially in the context of counseling children and adolescents.

Much of this chapter is informed by two sources: *Practicum in Counseling: A Developmental Guide* (Woodside & Luke, 2018) and *Empathic Counseling: Building Skills to Empower Change* (Slattery & Park, 2020). The approaches of these texts align with our values related to working with all individuals. For example, both texts address diversity through a lens of empathic responding to the culture of the individual. Woodside and Luke describe this as experiencing the client as a "culture of one", stating, "*Counselors can never presume to 'know' the client in front of them based on any single characteristic or group membership*" (p. 99, italics in original). In a complementary way, Slattery and Park describe the value of understanding the client through multiple group memberships and tailoring treatment accordingly; however, even from a multiple group memberships perspective, the counselor must learn about the individual and their preferred interaction style and response to intervention. We think this can be best expressed with the hashtag #learnthelanguage.

Freedman and Combs (1996) suggest four premises of narrative therapy – just one approach for working with children, adolescents, and their caregivers – that bear special relevance here: realities are socially constructed; realities are constituted through language; realities are organized and maintained through narrative (e.g., dominant stories); and truth is unknowable. We can best illustrate this through the case of Royal.

Royal is a male; this has implications for Royal's experience of and in the world. If we add that Royal is an African American male, the meaning of Royal's gender and race changes as a result of their intersection with one another. To illustrate, Royal is actually an African American female, so given the role of Black women in U.S. society, each of those characteristics takes on different meaning together. Royal is also 13 years old. As you think about this, how might the stage of life that 13 represents intersect with Royal's gender and race? What if we added that Royal lives in poverty? Now Royal is referred to you for counseling for "attitude problems". As you can see, the complexities of these characteristics expand exponentially, not just in an additive way.

Realities are socially constructed in that groups agree together on what reality is and then act in accordance. In the case of slavery, white Europeans determined that light skin was superior and acted on that by oppressing, subjugating, and ultimately enslaving Africans (and many others, as well). This, of course, is a necessarily reductive analysis, but illustrates two things: first, white-skinned Europeans agreed that dark-skinned Africans were inferior and therefore less than human, and second, Africans and then African Americans started to accept and internalize this oppression.

A second example is that of the view of women in societies. It can be seen in a creation myth: Adam, the first man, was headstrong and punished accordingly, whereas Eve, the first woman, was weak minded (easily deceived), and was punished accordingly. This socially constructed dichotomy has even infiltrated science. The popular notion of moral reasoning, advanced by Kohlberg (1969), was influenced by this social construction of female inferiority leading to the conclusion that women are less moral than men. That is, however, until Carole Gilligan (1977) challenged this perspective and demonstrated that women make moral judgments using different processes, but were certainly no less moral than men.

In the lab, this socially constructed bias against women showed itself in the studies of stress responses in mice. The narrative that emerged became known as *fight or flight*. That is, until Taylor et al. (2000) demonstrated that female mice had a very different stress response that has come to be known as *tend and befriend*. Taylor and colleagues found that in the earlier studies of mice, female mice were excluded from the trials because their menstrual cycles made their inclusion difficult by interfering with measurement of hormones. Taylor et al. were able to control for this variable and found a very different coping mechanism that challenged the socially constructed narrative. Consider the following intuition gleaned from these studies: in hunter-gather societies, females stayed close to home and cared for their offspring and managed home-related tasks. If a threat emerged (e.g., wild animal), to fight was to risk injury or to flee would both leave offspring vulnerable. However, if, in preparation for such eventualities, females formed social bonds with (befriended) other females in the community, they would be in stronger position to work together to tend to the needs of one another in case of threat. Males, in contrast, during hunting or battles, would need to assess the situation to determine whether fighting would lead to success, or, if facing insurmountable odds, fleeing to fight another day was the better option.

Research into fight-or-flight and tend-and-befriend responses have illuminated what may be biologically preprogrammed gender differences in response to threats. The bigger point, however, is that in the larger socio-cultural milieu, these responses have been viewed as gender-related values, wherein males' responses are seen as strong (fight) or strategic (flee and live to fight another day), whereas females' responses were viewed as weak. These two brief examples highlight the social construction of reality in two groups, African Americans and females, and this is the environment that clients may be brought up in. As such, these sociohistorical realities shape their view of themselves and the world around them and it is incumbent upon counselors to recognize this. One way is through the next level of social constructionism: language.

Freedman and Combs (1996) assert that realities are constituted through language. So, if we want to understand Royal's reality within the broader constructed social reality, we have to listen closely to the language she uses. If, for example, she describes feeling powerless in a situation at school, it is important to tune in to her feelings and language, rather than assuming she is externalizing or trying to avoid taking responsibility for herself. She might say, "I cannot help but curse at those bullies during gym class". In that statement, she is expressing her view of reality that she feels attacked, helpless to defend herself, and unable to find alternatives in the moment. This is not the time to remind her of the consequences if she does not change her behavior; instead, it is an opportunity to move more deeply into her lived experience. It is also time to explore her reality against the backdrop of wider social reality. For instance, African Americans are (viewed as) being more emotionally expressive, which is often taken to be aggressive, overly assertive, oppositional, etc., so it may be that Royal is being treated unfairly because of negative stereotypes. It may also be that she has sought other means for dealing with conflict at school, only to be met with recommendations for personal responsibility, rather than advocacy (e.g., "you cannot control others; you can only control yourself"). In working with a client such as Royal, listening to and seeking understanding of her experience through her language will help her feel heard, but also provide insight into her dominant narratives.

The third component of Freedman and Combs' discussion of narrative approaches, is realities are organized and maintained through narrative. This may not be the first time that Royal has experienced powerlessness in her environment. In fact, this situation may be more the rule of her experience than the exception. To explore this, the counselor might ask, "Have there been other times you have felt this way? Can you tell me about that?" What is likely to emerge is a narrative related to the three-fold nature of the characteristics we know about Royal: female, adolescent, African American. Each will contribute to her narrative, as we learn from her language, as long as *we* #learnthelanguage.

Slattery and Park (2011) describe the multiple identities perspective that complements the concept of intersectionality (discussed later in this chapter). The multiple identities perspective highlights the overlaps of various categories of differences to create the unique individual. Slattery and Park illustrate this with a Venn diagram of intersections with socio-economic status, race, gender, affectional/sexual orientation, and religion. At the nexus of these five dimensions resides the unique self, that is, a blend of these categories of diversity. This, of course, is an oversimplification that omits any number of other factors such as age, trauma, ableness, ethnicity, etc. In addition, while the multiple identities view is related to intersectionality, it does not capture the rich complexity of the interactions between and among these multiple factors of identity. Slattery and Park address this by describing the addition of characteristics to a person, one at a time. We adapt that for work with children and adolescents.

To add one additional complication, assume that you have completed a course on multicultural counseling, where you encountered statistics on African Americans and other cultural characteristics. You may learn that African Americans, statistically speaking, tend to rely more on extended family relationships, referred to by some as "fictive kin" (Sue, Sue, Neville, & Smith, 2019), or that African American youth are more "expressive" and "confrontational" than their white peers (Slattery & Park, 2020). What does this say about Royal and your work with her (personal pronoun)? We submit that it *does not* mean that it is safe to assume that Royal was raised by a grandmother or family friend, nor does it mean that she will be confrontational with you in session. Further, it does not mean that "confrontational" means the same thing to a white counselor as it does to an African American. In fact, having learned these things, we believe you know nothing additional about Royal until you talk with her.

On the contrary, there are things you can learn in advance that may make you more effective in working with Royal. The experience of 13-year-old females in middle school settings can be very difficult on the fragile self-image of these individuals, wherein bullying, relational aggression, and female objectification collide with the biological maelstrom that is occurring for these young members of society. You may also learn that as an African American, Royal is statistically more likely to have her behavior scrutinized (e.g., is she being aggressive, stealing, etc.), her emotions invalidated (e.g., is she angry, overly emotional), and her family members – even herself – racially profiled. These are statistics that can be used to more fully understand the referral behaviors that led Royal to talk with you, and also have implications for your work with her. Yet, her individual experience (phenomenologically speaking) is her own, and must be approached with openness and respect.

To express this differently, we turn to Luke's (2016, 2020) model of understanding the human experience described in Chapter 3 of this volume. Since these have been discussed in general, we offer specific application to a client like Royal, in an emergent model of the individual client experience (Table 14.1).

As you can see, the picture becomes quite complex, especially in terms of Royal's perception of the situation at school compared with her parents and the school. You may also notice that these eight domains are separate from but interact with the major categories of diversity discussed previously: race, ethnicity, religion, gender, and affectional/sexual orientation.

Counseling Children and Adolescents as a Cross-Cultural Enterprise

A theme that runs throughout this text is that working with children and adolescents is a cross-cultural enterprise. Children are not miniature adults and adolescents are not older children. Each has their own characteristics that distinguish them from one another and from adults. At the same time, they are not less than human, despite how they are often portrayed in American media and legislation. As we will see, an example, as of this writing, children have more rights and protections while still in the womb than they do once in the outer world. Culturally, as a society, there is a strong vacillation between the two poles of experience and understanding of children and adolescents: miniature humans, with all the expectations that come with it, and less-than-fully-human beings. Therefore, it is vital that counselors working with children and adolescents understand this background tension, which will aid in conceptualizing work with these two populations as cross-cultural.

Table 14.1 Emergent Model of the Individual Client Experience

Eight-Factor Model Component	Royal's Characteristics
Socio-Cultural Milieu	Suburban, two-parent family, third child of four, African American, conservative Christian, primarily white neighborhood
Relationships	Close with father and paternal grandmother; conflictual with mother; stable sibling relations; two close friends at school – one African American and one white; feels lonely at times
Biology/Genetics	Mother has history of depression; brother diagnosed with ADHD; heart disease on father's side; puberty has been difficult as with many middle-schoolers: internal and external changes create attention from others and makes her unsure how to respond
Experiences	Past: supportive family but has witnessed verbal abuse and myriad microaggressions toward family members, herself, and her friends of color Present: picked on at school by some white students for living in the suburbs, while alienated by some Black students for the same reason
Environments	While very successful in elementary school (K–5), sixth and now seventh grade (middle school) is a difficult place for her to be; at home, she has trouble describing her school difficulties and is given advice that worked for her parents (perhaps) but does not resonate with her experience
Thinking	Due in part to her developmental changes, she believes others are evaluating her and judging her harshly; she takes this to mean that something is wrong with her
Feeling	She feels alone in her experience and at times unworthy of love
Behavior	She "stands up for herself" by cursing and once shoving one of the bullies at school (the school does not believe that she is being bullied)

Cross-cultural, in this context, means that children experience the world very differently from adolescents and adults. Slattery and Park (2011) discuss features of culture that include "shared identity, with similar values, beliefs, assumptions, goals, patterns of behavior, preferences, and norms" (p. 66). As you think about what defines culture, consider these factors related to childhood and adolescence. Children have their own language, based on their age and level of development. This can make communication an unexpected challenge. Likewise, adolescents have their own language, even between early and late adolescents. Children use play and fantasy language (Landreth, 2012), while many adolescents may favor paraverbals (e.g., "mmhh", "uh-huh") over verbalizations. Play itself looks very different across the developmental range from infancy to early childhood, to pre-adolescence to later adolescence. Adolescents have a completely personal inner experience, described by Elkind (1967): the personal fable, egocentrism, and personal invulnerability. These are not developmental flaws to be endured until age and maturity remedy them; they are cultural characteristics and should be appreciated and harnessed.

Culture Shock: "Why Won't They Talk?"

The cross-cultural dimensions for working with children and adolescents reveal themselves through a form of culture shock. A common issue we hear from our students and supervisees is the struggle to get young clients to talk to them. Graduate students in particular have been trained to communicate in precise verbalizations and in writing; in essence, to be eloquent in adult-like communication patterns. This training, through reading, writing, and presentation, translates poorly to communicating with children and adolescents, resulting in a type of culture shock. We encourage you to set aside the linguistics of adulthood and enter the world of the child or adolescent through their language, that of play.

MSJCC

The Multicultural and Social Justice Counseling Competencies (MSJCC) (Ratts, Singh, Nassar-McMillan, Butler, & McCullough, 2015) represent the next iteration of the Multicultural Counseling Competencies (Sue et al., 2019) and provide general guidelines for counselors to be able to increase their ability to work with a variety of clients. The competencies are presented in four overarching domains: self-awareness, client worldview, counseling relationship, and advocacy and interventions. For each domain, there is a set of dispositions or relative domains: attitudes and beliefs, knowledge, skills, and action. To understand this better, Table 14.2 presents the competencies in a grid format. Each

Table 14.2 Considerations for Multicultural Competency Domains

	Self-Awareness	*Client Worldview*	*Counseling Relationship*	*Advocacy and Interventions*
Attitudes and Beliefs	What attitudes and beliefs do I hold toward a client who is a child or adolescent that I need to become more aware of?	What are the unique and shared attitudes and beliefs of my client who is a child or adolescent that may affect our working relationship?	What is or might be the nature of the interaction between me and my client – who is a child or adolescent – and their attitudes and beliefs as they relate to the therapeutic relationship?	a. What are the individual characteristics and related interventions needed to work effectively with my client who is a child or adolescent? b. What are the interpersonal dynamics (family, friends, peers) and related interventions needed to work effectively with my client who is a child or adolescent? c. What are the institutional entities (e.g., schools, churches) through which to address inequities for my client who is a child or adolescent? d. What are the community dynamics (e.g., norms, values, regulations) that either promote or impede success for my client who is a child or adolescent?
Knowledge	What knowledge do I need to be aware of that is needed in order to work effectively with a client who is a child or adolescent?	What are areas of knowledge that I can develop related to the experiences of my client, who is a child or adolescent?	What do I need to learn about my client – who is a child or adolescent – and their experiences to work effectively through the counseling relationship?	
Skills	What skills do I need in order to be able to work more effectively with a client – who is a child or adolescent – that I am currently unaware of?	Based on the attitudes and beliefs of my client – who is a child or adolescent – and the knowledge I have or need to obtain, how can I act skillfully in addressing their presenting concerns?	What assessment, analytical, application, evaluation, and communication skills are necessary for me to work effectively with my client – who is a child or adolescent?	

(Continued)

Table 14.2 (Continued)

	Self-Awareness	Client Worldview	Counseling Relationship	Advocacy and Interventions
Action	What action do I need to take in order to increase my self-awareness in the previous areas that will assist me in working more effectively with a client who is a child or adolescent?	What action do I now need to take in light of the knowledge and skills needed to work with my client – who is a child or adolescent – based on their individual worldview (attitudes and beliefs)?	What action must I take both inside and out of the session to strengthen the therapeutic relationship with my client, who is a child or adolescent?	e. How might I address public policy that impedes my client – who is a child or adolescent – and their success? f. Are there global issues that affect the well-being of my client who is a child or adolescent?

quadrant contains a reflection question that illustrates the intersection of domains for working with children and adolescents.

As you can see from Table 14.2, gaining competence is a complex task, but it is intended to take a lifetime of exploring and refining one's attitudes, knowledge, skills, and behaviors.

Understanding Culture

In writing about culture and ethics in career counseling, Fouad and Kantamneni (2008) illustrate the multiple dimensions of intersection when seeking to understand the experience of individuals (Figure 14.1). Woodside and Luke (2018) applied this model to counseling

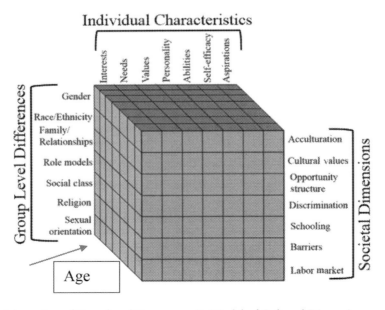

Figure 14.1 Adaptation of Fouad and Kantamneni's Model of Cultural Dimensions

Celebrating Diversity 253

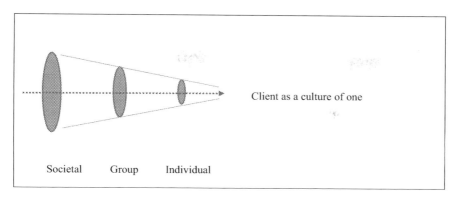

Figure 14.2 Client-Related Dimensions

in general, particularly in the context of counseling practicum. A cursory glance of the models reveals what is, in terms of this text, a glaring omission, which is childhood and adolescence as key cultural dimensions. As a group, children's individual characteristics, group differences, and societal dimensions affect and are affected by both chronological and developmental ages. It is, of course, impossible to account for all characteristics, differences, and dimensions and fit them into one model, but we invite you to take a moment to reflect on why age is not included here, and where you might place it. To aid you in this reflection, Figure 14.2 is provided (Woodside & Luke, 2018). Beginning with the societal dimension as a lens through which children and adolescents are viewed, consider first how children and adolescents are viewed in society, and second, what each of these societal dimensions might look like for these populations. "One point is critical when considering various client-related dimensions: Counselors can never presume to 'know' the client in front of them based on any single characteristic or group membership" (Woodside & Luke, 2018, p. 99).

Empathy is one of those concepts that most people think they understand and use in common parlance, but whose meaning can be elusive when used in a clinical context. Empathy, according to Rogers (1959), is

> to perceive the internal frame of reference of another with accuracy and with the emotional components and meanings which pertain thereto as if one were the person, but without ever losing the "as if" condition. Thus it means to sense the hurt or the pleasure of another as he senses it and to perceive the causes thereof as he perceives them, but without ever losing the recognition that it is as if I were hurt or pleased and so forth. It this "as if" quality is lost, then the state is one of identification.
>
> (pp. 210–221)

Too often in counseling with children and adolescents, counselors – who are, of course, adults – may believe that since they went through childhood and adolescence, they have a natural understanding of their client. Sommers-Flanagan and Sommers-Flanagan (2007) caution that adults may not recall their own childhood and adolescence very accurately at all. In fact, children and adolescents may be the most likely population to evoke countertransference and projective identification. As noted previously, empathy – despite its essential nature in counseling – is subject to being mistaken and even misused. Further, counselors don't base clinical skills and insights on their own personal experiences, but on those of the client.

Luke, Redekop, and Moralejo (2020) discuss the neurobiology of empathy and its counterparts with which it is often confused: sympathy, neural empathy, and projective sympathy. Sympathy is contrasted with empathy, as it is feeling the same feelings of another person. This is often effective in our close personal relationships, wherein it is safe for both parties to open themselves to the emotion of the other. Neural empathy is the experience most often referenced in counseling texts as mirror neurons. Another misunderstood concept, mirror neurons are neurons in the premotor cortex of the parietal lobe in the cerebral cortex. The function of these neurons, at least in part, is to anticipate and interpret the *movements* of another person. This is a crucial distinction from viewing mirror neurons for aiding in reading emotions, as the premotor cortex prepares the motor cortex to take some action, not to feel an emotion. In other words, mirror neurons help humans interpret behavior of others. Separate systems are used for mental simulations of the emotions of others. Finally, projective sympathy is the most insidious of the phenomena confused with empathy. Luke et al. (2020) define it as, "'I feel what I would feel if it were mine, then assume that's what you feel as well'. . . . When we respond to a person in pain or in need in ways that we ourselves would prefer, we risk imposing what may work for us rather than what may work for others". Woodside and Luke (2018) describe this in the context of training practicum students. Projective sympathy is almost instantly invalidating to the individual. This is a high risk in working with children and adolescents who may regularly experience devaluation and personalization, often under the guise of training and education. The opposite extreme can also be problematic.

Consider a practical clinical example: A 14-year-old male has gotten caught possessing a joint. In an effort to head off a problem before it gets bad, the judge makes participation in an intensive outpatient program (IOP) a condition of the adolescent's probation. What this means is that after seven or eight hours of school, primarily sitting, he now has to attend counseling sessions for three hours each evening, three to four days per week. These sessions take place immediately following school, so he is whisked from school to the treatment center. During the second hour of group therapy, he falls asleep or is distractible and distracting to others. If he doesn't comply with the behavioral expectations of therapy, he may get reported for noncompliance, which may result in a violation of probation, which brings with it additional consequences. We are not saying the IOP interventions are not helpful, but we wonder if this approach is developmentally responsive. We further wonder how many adults would be able to sustain their attention and comportment for three straight hours following a full day's work. Another limitation of empathy is once it is experienced, how we effectively express it. Slattery and Park (2020) offer guidance in communicating empathy to our clients, and we have adapted it for working with children and adolescents.

Summary

In this chapter, we hope you found yourself asking, *"What attitudes and beliefs do I hold toward a client who is a child or adolescent that I need to become more aware of?"*, and using this time as a graduate student to really examine your beliefs, where they originated, and if they are worth holding on to, and if you should be making space for other beliefs that may benefit your clients and yourself in myriad ways. Our hope is that you are able to apply Multicultural and Social Justice Counseling Competencies (MSJCC) (Ratts et al., 2015) in all counseling scenarios and model this for others. As counselors, we must seek to apply the eight-factor model (Luke, 2016, 2017, 2020) for deeply understanding our child and adolescent clients, helping them feel heard, and inevitably assisting in a healing and empowering counseling experience. As counselors, we understand that this complex and lifelong process of multiculturally sensitive work starts with us.

Clinician's Corner

I was a school counselor in elementary schools and high schools in Taiwan before I came to the United States. A common goal that brought elementary school students to counseling was for them to overcome learning difficulties and emotional and behavioral problems. Most students I worked with had immigrant parents and they were referred to counseling by school teachers. Due to language barriers, play therapy activities were used as a tool to communicate with those students. For high school students, I provided individual and group counseling. A common goal that brought high school students to counseling was the sincere wish to find them career interests and develop interpersonal skills. I enjoyed working with children and teenagers because I could foster a development of career interests and social skills in their early life stages. Even if I were not able to see them thrive during the period of time we crossed, I would hold onto hope that with early intervention they would blossom like flowers one day.

Hsin-Ya Tang, Ph.D., NCC
Assistant Professor, Louisiana State University in Shreveport

References

Elkind, D. (1967). Egocentrism in adolescence. *Child Development, 38*(4), 1025–1034.

Fouad, N. A., & Kantamneni, N. (2008). Contextual factors in vocational psychology: Intersections of individual, group, and societal dimensions. In S. D. Brown & R. W. Lent (Eds.), *Handbook of counseling psychology* (Vol. 4, pp. 408–425). Wiley.

Freedman, J., & Combs, G. (1996). *Narrative therapy: The social construction of preferred realities.* W.W. Norton & Company.

Gilligan, C. (1977). In a different voice: Women's conceptions of self and of morality. *Harvard Educational Review, 47*(4), 481–517. https://doi.org/10.17763/haer.47.4.g6167429416hg5l0

Kohlberg, L. (1969). Stage and sequence: The cognitive – Developmental approach to socialization. In D. A. Goslin (Ed.), *Handbook of socialization theory and research* (pp. 347–480). Rand McNally.

Landreth, G. L. (2012). *Play therapy: The art of the relationship* (3rd ed.). Routledge.

Luke, C. (2016). *Neuroscience for counselors and therapists: Integrating the sciences of mind and brain.* Sage.

Luke, C. (2020). *Neuroscience for counselors and therapists: Integrating the sciences of the mind and brain.* Cognella.

Luke, C., Redekop, F., & Moralejo, J. (2020). From microaggressions to neural aggressions: A neuroinformed counseling perspective. *Journal of Multicultural Counseling and Development, 48*(2), 120–129. https://doi.org/10.1002/jmcd.12170

Ratts, M. J., Singh, A. A., Nassar-McMillan, S., Butler, S. K., & McCullough, J. R. (2015). Multicultural and social justice counseling competencies: Guidelines for the counseling profession. *Journal of Multicultural Counseling and Development, 44*(1), 28–48. https://doi.org/10.1002/jmcd.12035

Rogers, C. R. (1959). A theory of therapy, personality and interpersonal relationships as developed in the client-centered framework. In S. Koch (Ed.), *Psychology: A study of a science, vol. III. Formulations of the person and the social context* (pp. 184–256). McGraw Hill.

Slattery, J. M., & Park, C. L. (2011). *Empathic counseling: Meaning, context, ethics, and skill.* Brooks/Cole.

Slattery, J. M., & Park, C. L. (2020). *Empathic counseling*. American Psychological Association.
Sommers-Flanagan, J., & Sommers-Flanagan, R. (2007). *Tough kids, cool counseling* (2nd ed.). American Counseling Association.
Sue, D. W., Sue, D., Neville, H. A., & Smith, L. (2019). *Counseling the culturally diverse: Theory and practice* (8th ed.). John Wiley & Sons.
Taylor, S. E., Klein, L. C., Lewis, B. P., Gruenewald, T. L., Gurung, R. A., & Updegraff, J. A. (2000). Biobehavioral responses to stress in females: Tend-and-befriend, not fight-or-flight. *Psychological Review*, *107*(3), 411–429. https://psycnet.apa.org/doi/10.1037/0033-295X.107.3.411
Woodside, M., & Luke, C. (2018). *Practicum in counseling: A developmental guide*. Cognella.

15 Play Therapy

Rebekah Byrd, Teresa Christensen, and Chad Luke
Teresa Christensen as guest contributor

Objectives

- Describe key terms from this chapter associated with play therapy and the practice of play therapy in counseling.
- Examine the many benefits of play therapy and its application to working with children and adolescents.
- Understand the therapeutic powers of play therapy.
- Examine different theories of play therapy.
- Understand basic play therapy skills.

Reflective Questions

- What are my current thoughts on why play therapy is appropriate for work with children and adolescents?
- How might play therapy benefit clients, as opposed to talk therapy techniques?
- How can I incorporate the powers of play in work I do with clients?
- How does play facilitate brain development?
- What are some of the different uses for play therapy that I think are particularly significant?
- What are my thoughts and reactions to the eight basic principles of play therapy?

Play is the highest form of research.
– Albert Einstein

What Is Play and Play Therapy?

In understanding play therapy, we must first understand play. What is play specifically? Burghardt, in his book on animal play, discussed an understanding of play based on psychology, ethology, ecology, evolution, physiology, and neuroscience. Burghardt offers an in-depth understanding of play (2005) that was summarized by Gaskin and Perry (2014) this way: "first, play mimics or approximates a common or important purposeful behavior; second, play is voluntary, is pleasurable, and has no immediate survival role or obvious 'purpose'; and, finally, play takes place in a nonthreatening, low-duress context" (p. 179). These authors emphasize that these vital aspects to play are quite regularly at odds with numerous well-intentioned, yet mostly unsuccessful, therapeutic experiences (Gaskin & Perry, 2014).

Play therapy is a type of counseling in which play is used to communicate instead of relying on talk as in traditional therapy modalities. The Association for Play Therapy (n.d.) defines play therapy as "the systematic use of a theoretical model to establish an interpersonal process wherein trained play therapists use the therapeutic powers of play to help clients prevent or resolve psychosocial difficulties and achieve optimal growth and development". Play therapy is an evidenced-based practice and is shown to be effective with children with varying presenting problems and concerns, and also as a tool for wellness and prevention (Ray & McCullough, 2016). In play therapy, there is a playroom where the child is able to play out their thoughts, feelings, and situations by using toys, art, and other play media tools. Using a child's language of play is important since children younger than the age of 12 generally have limited ability to discuss their thoughts and feelings, and also lack the ability to use abstract verbal reasoning (Kottman, 2011).

We believe wholeheartedly in the therapeutic powers of play therapy and have seen the change this has made in the lives of many children, adults, and families throughout our years as play therapists and play therapy supervisors. Play is a child's natural form of communication. Instead of adults trying to get kids to talk, play therapy lets the child communicate through play. We firmly believe that children are *always* communicating with us. They may not always be talking, but they are always communicating. It is our job as counselors to learn and respect their form of communication and to pay attention. As Landreth (2012) noted, play is the child's language and toys are, in a sense, their words. We hope that by introducing you to this amazing type of counseling, you will seek out further training as this requires specialized training, education, and supervised experience to become a registered play therapist. "It is in playing and only in playing that the individual child or adult is able to be creative and to use the whole personality, and it is only in being creative that the individual discovers self" (Winnicott, 1971, pp. 72–73).

We believe that the play therapist is so very important to the therapeutic relationship. In understanding what play therapy is, it is imperative to think critically about the role of the play therapist. We encourage you to take time to process the eight basic principles which follow. Do these principles describe you? Are there aspects you could strengthen? Are there concepts on this list you feel very grounded in? Do you believe these principles to be true? The following are the eight basic principles of play therapy that Landreth (2012) borrows and extends on what Axline clarified in 1969 discussing the communication between the child and the therapist in the child-centered approach that serve as an outline for beneficial contact with children.

- The therapist is genuinely interested in the child and develops a warm, caring relationship.
- The therapist experiences unqualified acceptance of the child and does not wish that the child were different in some way.
- The therapist creates a feeling of safety and permissiveness in the relationship, so the child feels free to explore and express herself completely.
- The therapist is always sensitive to the child's feelings and gently reflects those feelings in such a manner that the child develops self-understanding.
- The therapist believes deeply in the child's capacity to act responsibly, unwaveringly respects the child's ability to solve personal problems, and allows the child to do so.
- The therapist trusts the child's inner direction, allows the child to lead in all areas of the relationship, and resists any urge to direct the child's play or conversation.
- The therapist appreciates the gradual nature of the therapeutic process and does not attempt to hurry the process.
- The therapist establishes only those therapeutic limits necessary to anchor the session to reality and which help the child accept personal and appropriate relationship responsibility.

(p. 80)

Neuroscience and Play

Understanding the structure of the nervous system and the brain is important for those working with children and adolescents. Chapter 8 of this volume is dedicated to just this, and we hope that you will seek out additional training, resources, and information in this area. This short section will outline information regarding neuroscience and play, specifically. This information certainly isn't comprehensive, but our hope is that you will be able to understand the importance of play and its impact on the brain, and be able to back up the necessity play has on the developing child.

Continued research supports evidence that the brain processes experiences, affect, and emotions into meaningful material (Mellenthin, 2018). In an article discussing neuroscience and play therapy, Stewart, Field, and Echterling (2016) stated:

> Play is an emotionally engaging and creative experience that increases levels of oxytocin. As noted earlier, this hormone enhances feelings of emotional wellbeing and trust, thus supporting the creation of a therapeutic relationship between the child and play therapist. Mirror neurons are also activated in play, helping the therapist accurately read and connect with the child's emotional state.
>
> (p. 5)

As discussed in what follows, play allows an access to the unconscious. The part of the mind we may not be cognizant of, but that certainly influences behavior and emotions, is the unconscious. Through play, individuals are able to access this part of their mind. Levy (2011) discussed:

> In contrast to the dynamic unconscious, where unconscious material is actively kept out of awareness, one cannot directly become aware of implicit thought because of its essential nature. This form of cognition is thought to operate in parallel to the dynamic unconscious. Although implicit and explicit thought are distinct, they may be integrated to some extent. Play appears to promote such integration and it appears to foster reorganization of neural structures to form more complex, integrated systems.
>
> (p. 50)

Whole parts of the brain are involved when a child is playing which develops critical connections leading to positive development and growth of the child (Mellenthin, 2018).

What follows is a brief explanation of play therapy concepts and terms. We believe there to be many concepts important to the practice of play therapy, and we encourage counselors to seek additional training in order to provide these services.

Therapeutic Powers of Play

Play therapy literature has discussed the curative factors or what produces change in the child during treatment (Schaefer, 1993). Schaefer (1993) originally identified 14 primary therapeutic powers of play therapy based on play therapists' clinical experiences and research that had been conducted at that time. Schaefer and Drewes (2009, 2010, 2014) and Drewes and Schaefer (2016) later expanded this list to *20 therapeutic powers* that were classified into *four categories*: facilitates communication, fosters emotional wellness, enhances social relationships, and increases personal strengths (Peabody & Schaefer, 2019).

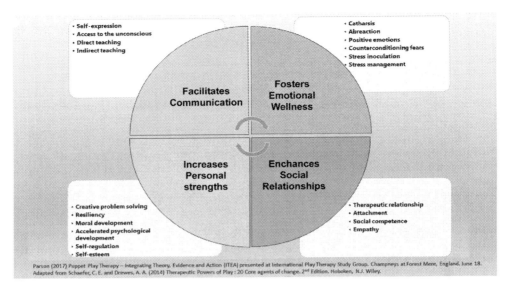

Figure 15.1 Therapeutic Powers of Play

Many of these therapeutic factors (Figure 15.1) are listed and discussed in the following subsections (Schaefer & Drewes, 2009, 2010).

Category One: Facilitates Communication

Category One: Facilitates Communication includes self-expression, access to the unconscious, and direct and indirect teaching (Drewes & Schaefer, 2016; Peabody & Schaefer, 2019).

Self-Expression

Children do not communicate in the same way as adults. They also do not think in the same abstract and critical ways. This is also true for adolescents. By using play, children are able to communicate and express their feelings and thoughts. Further, by using toys to communicate, children are able to distance themselves from difficult and strong emotions and begin healing.

Access to the Unconscious

The unconscious refers to the part of the mind we may not be aware of, but that impacts behavior and certainly emotions. Play allows access to this part of the mind. By playing, children can become aware of behavior and emotions they were not previously aware of.

Direct and Indirect Teaching

Play therapy provides opportunities for direct and indirect instruction, allowing assistance in overcoming knowledge and skills discrepancies in clients. Play therapists are able to teach or provide alternative responses to toys, puppets, dolls, etc., in a non-threatening and non-judgmental way. This can result in the child learning a possible solution or alternative response to a problem or troubling situation. Through directly teaching concepts and healthy coping mechanisms, children are able to rehearse and practice being assertive versus being aggressive, for example. In the playroom, new adaptive behaviors can be modeled by the play therapist and tried out by the child (Schaefer, 1999).

Category Two: Fosters Emotional Wellness

Category Two, Fosters Emotional Wellness includes catharsis, abreaction, positive emotions, counterconditioning fears, stress inoculation, and stress management (Drewes & Schaefer, 2016; Peabody & Schaefer, 2019).

Catharsis

Play therapy allows for the release of and relief from strong emotions. Play can facilitate this relief by providing a safe space for emotional release such as crying. Play can also facilitate release via an activity by providing a safe space for approved emotional releases such as stomping egg cartons, ripping a phone book, or pounding playdough (Schaefer, 1999).

Abreaction

In play, children are able to recreate, re-enact, and re-experience problematic and traumatic circumstances while gaining a sense of power and control over those experiences (Schaefer, 1999). A natural way of coping or trying to figure something out to a child is to play out the situation or circumstance. "Adults tend to 'talk out' unpleasant experiences, such as an operation, while children play them out" (Schaefer, 1999). Through play, children learn coping skills for life events and problematic situations by playing out these events, changing the outcomes, and trying out new ways of being in response to that event.

Positive Emotions

Children tend to be less anxious and/or depressed while involved in play. Children and adults alike are able to feel better, have a more positive outlook, and a sense of well-being through play (Schaefer, 1999). Play, enjoyment, and therefore laughter become an important remedy to negative affects such as anxiety and depression (Schaefer, 1999).

Counterconditioning Fears

Drewes and Schaefer (2016) discussed that it is not possible for two equally exclusive internal positions to exist at the same time. For example, one cannot be both anxious and relaxed. In the playroom, playing out our fears can help reduce these fears (for example, playing with hospital-related toys and assisting in reducing fears related to hospitals). This type of play also allows the child to be in the active role (pretending to take a doll's temperature) instead of being in a passive role. Shaeffer (1999) also discussed that fantasy play facilitates projection, repetition, and identification, which can be helpful in changing a negative affect.

Stress Inoculation

Stress inoculation refers to the child's ability to play out possibly stressful events that have not yet occurred. Think back to when you were a child – was there anything that you were stressed or apprehensive about before it even happened? We can certainly experience anxiety around moving, starting new schools, and making new friends. By playing out these situations and scenarios, it provides an opportunity to lessen the anxiety association with it.

Stress Management

Play therapists teach and help children practice stress management skills. In other words, play therapists work to redirect inappropriate, problematic, or unacceptable behaviors. This allows the child to test limits in a safe environment and to also learn boundaries and appropriate behavior through play. Play therapists assist clients by providing alternative solutions for problematic behaviors (e.g., hitting, punching, screaming, etc.) without judgment, blame, or shame, and allows practice for these solutions to be integrated into the child's behavior (Drewes & Schaefer, 2016; Peabody & Schaefer, 2019).

Category Three: Enhances Social Relationships

Category Three: Enhances Social Relationships includes therapeutic relationships, attachment, social competence, and empathy (Drewes & Schaefer, 2016; Peabody & Schaefer, 2019).

Therapeutic Relationships

Play strengthens and promotes the positive emotional bond between child and caregiver. Because play therapists use unconditional positive regard and foster the development of the therapeutic relationship, children learn vicariously how to be in relation with another person. Play therapists work to create a safe, comforting environment, while also setting limits to protect the integrity of the relationship and to teach children. By playing, children are able to practice reading social cues and are able to test situations, coping strategies, and outcomes to understand the difference between fantasy play and real-life scenarios. Schaefer (1999) discusses that in play, children are able to switch back and forth between pretend roles and their real selves. Practice in this switch is helpful for children.

Attachment

Models of play therapy have demonstrated improvements that increase attachment and bonding between child and caregiver. Some of these models utilize live-coaching and a step-by-step process that can result in beneficial and positive experiences, safe experience, and a nurturing bond through the child and caregiver playing together – thus promoting healthy attachment.

Social Competence

By playing, children are able to practice reading social cues and are able to test situations, coping strategies, and outcomes to understand the difference between fantasy play and real-life scenarios. Other aspects of social competence pertain to teaching and role-playing appropriate social relationship skills and boundaries (Drewes & Schaefer, 2016; Peabody & Schaefer, 2019).

Empathy

Children are able to develop their ability to understand what someone else might be experiencing or feeling (empathy) and to understand things from multiple perspectives.

In play, children often role-play characters, animals, situations, and stories allowing them the opportunity to play out different perspectives while experimenting with how that feels.

Category Four: Increases Personal Strengths

Category Four: Increases Personal Strengths includes creative problem-solving, resiliency, moral development, accelerated psychological development, self-regulation, and self-esteem (Drewes & Schaefer, 2016; Peabody & Schaefer, 2019).

Creative Problem-Solving

Children are able to experience feelings of both power and control while in the playroom, thus promoting their ability to create their own and model problem-solving skills. As a child-led experience, the play therapist allows the child to take the play where they need it to go and to recreate experiences in order to practice mastery. Children often feel out of control in the world around them while adults, parents/caregivers, and teachers make decisions with which children must try to comply. Further, children often have experienced traumatic events in which they were not in control and were powerless over what occurred. In the playroom, children get to determine what it is that they will do with the toys during the session. This can assist children in conquering feelings of uncertainty, insecurity, and helplessness.

Resiliency

Studies show that play and playfulness in children have been associated with increased levels of creativity, imagination, divergent thinking, and resiliency (Schaefer, 1999). Play therapy focuses on the process of play instead of the product of that play which promotes creativity, exploration, discovery, and problem-solving (Schaefer, 1999), thus empowering children to learn how resilient they are in a variety of ways. Further, Russ (2007) discussed the idea that a child engaged in pretend play is actively involved in divergent thinking, which can also be linked to coping strategies. Russ (2007) stated:

> When one speculates as to why pretend play is related to the ability to think of coping strategies, divergent thinking appears to be the common link between play ability and a child's ability to think of a number of coping strategies under stress. A major component of creative problem solving is the ability to generate a variety of ideas, the definition of divergent thinking.
>
> (pp. 13–14)

Moral Development

Through the therapeutic relationship, clients are allowed an opportunity to explore their own values, while play therapists foster, exhibit, and promote moral development (Drewes & Schaefer, 2016). Schaefer (1999) discusses that in play children are able to switch back and forth between pretend roles and their real selves. Practice in this switch is helpful for children. Schaefer and Drewes (2009) stated:

> Game play experiences help children move beyond the early stage of moral realism, in which rules are seen as external restrictions arbitrarily imposed by adults in authority,

to the concept of morality that is based on the principles of cooperation and consent among equals.

(p. 8)

Games provide children with opportunities to practice rule-governed behavior such as rule-making and rule-enforcing (Kottman, 2011).

Accelerated Psychological Development

Scheafer (1999) noted that a child's developmental level can advance beyond the normal level for their age through play. He further noted that this may not become evident until later on, but the child's level of thinking will also advance. Vygotsky (1967) detected that during play, children are constantly above their average age and behavior.

Self-Regulation

By engaging in play, children are able to learn competence through creativity, trial and error, and mastery. The play therapist is also able to empower and encourage children by returning responsibility to build competence and self-control. Play therapists also allow children the space to practice self-control through play by providing limits when necessary and creating a space where they are allowed to test in a safe environment. Play can assist in self-control through thought and behavior stopping in that children can start to formulate ideas, think critically, and plan ahead for good decision making. These skills are practiced in the play setting and can be generalized to many other areas of a child's life, such as home and school.

Self-Esteem

Play therapy promotes self-discovery by allowing a child to experience self in a non-judgmental, safe, and non-evaluative environment. This promotes the client's ability to learn about their self and develop healthy self-esteem. The play therapist does not attach judgment or evaluation to the child's play, but instead tracks the child's play as a way of attending, being with, and noting what the child is doing. This provides a mirror, in a sense, for the child to understand feelings and thoughts, and start to develop self-awareness (Schaefer, 1999).

Types of Play Therapy

According to the Association for Play Therapy magazine *Play Therapy* (APT, 2019), seminally significant theories in play therapy include: (a) Adlerian; (b) attachment through Theraplay and Filial Therapy; (c) Child-Centered; (d) Cognitive Behavioral; (e) Ecosystemic; (f) Gestalt; (g) Jungian Analytical; and (h) Psychoanalytic, as these theories have been substantiated. Our purpose in this section is not to offer a comprehensive approach but to briefly introduce a few different types of play therapy for you to consider. Unfortunately, we are not able to cover them all, but we hope you do further reading in this area because your process for play therapy will often depend on the type of theory you use.

Adlerian Play Therapy

Adlerian play therapy is defined as "an integrated approach that combines both non-directive and directive play to encourage, teach, and partner with the child and parents to foster egalitarian relations, social interest, explore lifestyles, gain insight, and teach new skills" (Schaefer & Peabody, 2016, p. 23). Kottman and Ashby (2015) discussed:

> The theoretical [tenets] of individual psychology offer a guide to aid the therapist in the conceptualization of client issues and subsequent treatment planning. The process of AdPT unfolds in four phases: (1) an initial relationship building phase, (2) a phase devoted to an exploration of client lifestyles, (3) a phase designed to help clients develop insight into their lifestyles, and (4) a final phase in which the play therapist facilitates client reorientation and reeducation.
>
> (p. 32)

Adlerian play therapy utilizes assets, life tasks, goals of misbehavior, mistaken beliefs, crucial c's, personality priorities, and other Adlerian constructs to work with children through play (Kottman & Ashby, 2015). The major concepts of Adlerian play therapy are (Kottman & Ashby, 2015):

- People are creative and desire the liberty to control their own lives.
- People observe and notice reality individually and subjectively.
- Behavior is goal-directed and serves a purpose.
- People are striving for belongingness and meaningful connection with others.
- People have an inclination for inferior feelings to others.
- Understanding lifestyle is important.
- Maladjustment can best be understood in terms of discouragement.

Attachment Through Theraplay and Filial Therapy

Theraplay is based on face-to-face, reciprocal play with another individual, ideally the caregiver. According to Booth and Lindaman (2019), "Theraplay is an evidenced-based, relationship-focused play therapy that integrates current theories of attachment, physiological state, affect regulation, and interpersonal neurobioloby" (p. 14). While the focus of treatment is on the relationship between caregiver and child and the stimulation of healthy development of the emotional brain from the bottom up, Theraplay focuses on strengths and challenges in four dimensions of the caregiver-child interaction: (a) structure; (b) engagement; (c) nurture; and (d) challenge (Booth & Jernberg, 2010; Booth & Lindaman, 2019).

Landreth noted "the nature of parent-child relationships is of primary importance to the present and future mental health of children" (2012). Therefore, it is important to train parents in how to work with their children and connect with them in meaningful ways. Louise and Bernard G. Guerney developed Filial Therapy. In 1964, Bernard G. Guerney published the first definition and description of Filial Therapy, which is rooted in Child-Centered Play Therapy (CCPT) and involves a psychoeducational approach focused on teaching parents/caregivers the basic concepts and techniques of CCPT (Scuka & Guerney, 2019). Consequently, Filial Therapy is sometimes also referred to as Child-Parent Relationship Therapy (CPRT). This therapy can take place in the playroom as the play therapist assists the parent/caregiver. Glazer (2010) discusses:

> Filial therapy provides the opportunity for the parent to become the child's primary therapist under the guidance of the play therapist. Although still child centered, the intervention uses the attachment bond between parent and child to facilitate change and provide the context for processing.
>
> (p. 90)

In Filial Therapy or CPRT, the parent/caregiver maintains the safety and permissiveness of the playroom while also nurturing a growth-oriented atmosphere where the child is able to strive toward reaching his or her full potential (Landreth & Bratton, 2006). CPRT is usually a 10-session training that teaches parents how to use play skills, techniques, and activities to strengthen the parent-child bond and grow their relationship (Landreth & Bratton, 2006).

Child-Centered Play Therapy

CCPT was developed by Virginia Axline before 1947 (VanFleet, Sywulak, & Sniscak, 2010). Axline was a student of Carl Rogers, the developer of the theoretical orientation of client-centered therapy (Rogers, 1951). In her pivotal work, Axline (1969) discussed that this theoretical approach is based on a belief and acceptance of the child, the desire for growth, and the ability to solve problems. This approach is founded on the "belief that children will heal, grow, and change if they are provided with an atmosphere where the prosocial aspects of self can flourish" (Mullin & Rickli, 2014, p. 5). CCPT, which focuses on the child rather than the problem, has 10 broad objectives for helping children. Landreth (2012) listed these goals for child-centered play therapy, which can be applied to other types of play therapy as well. These objectives provide an outline to understanding play therapy goals, benefits, and processes of the approach.

1. Develop a more positive self-concept.
2. Assume greater self-responsibility.
3. Become more self-directing.
4. Become more self-accepting.
5. Become more self-reliant.
6. Engage in self-determined decision making.
7. Experience a feeling of control.
8. Become sensitive to the process of coping.
9. Develop an internal source of evaluation.
10. Become more trusting of self.

(p. 85)

Cognitive Behavioral Play Therapy

Cognitive Behavioral Therapy (CBT) expands upon cognitive therapy philosophies and comprises additional techniques concentrating on altering behavior by using techniques such as reinforcement, modeling, and role-playing (Knell & Dasari, 2010). Established as a focused and structured counseling approach, CBT was geared toward helping individuals change their thoughts and perceptions thus changing the associated behavior (Knell & Dasari, 2010). Cognitive Behavioral Play Therapy is based on the incorporation of theories associated with cognitive therapy, emotional development, behavioral modification, and psychopathology (Knell & Dasari, 2010). Cognitive Behavioral Play Therapy also includes interventions derived from these theories mentioned (Knell & Dasari, 2010). This type of play therapy is more directive in nature.

Ecosystemic Play Therapy

Ecosystemic Play Therapy is described as a theory that places importance on understanding and improving the roles of the numerous systems in which the child is rooted and in ensuring the child's needs are being met effectively within these multiple systems (O'Connor, 2016). The notion of ecosystems is multifaceted, and consists of intrapsychic systems (e.g., self, others, world, developmental systems), interpersonal systems (e.g., family and friends), social systems (e.g., school systems, mental health systems, medical systems), and also metasystems (e.g., cultural and political systems) (O'Connor & Ammen, 2013). In this type of play therapy, the responsibility for direction and content of the sessions is up to the play therapist (O'Connor & Ammen, 2013).

Gestalt Play Therapy

Based on Perls' (1973) Gestalt therapy, Oaklander (2007) presented a book discussing the application of Gestalt techniques for working with children and adolescents. Gestalt play therapy can be thought of as a psychotherapeutic method that utilizes the techniques and philosophies of Gestalt therapy in play therapy (Blom, 2006). "Gestalt therapy is a humanistic and process-oriented form of therapy" (Blom, 2006, p. 17) that focuses on the present. Gestalt Play Therapy is focused on the relationship between the therapist and the child/adolescent (Oaklander, 2001). Another main concept is referred to as organismic self-regulation, which can be understood as one's need and search for homeostasis (Oaklander, 2001). Another important factor of Gestalt Play Therapy is the process of assisting children and adolescents in discovering a strong sense of self, as this is imperative for healing.

Jungian Analytical Play Therapy

The basis for Jungian Analytical Play Therapy (JAPT) starts with the construction of the psyche – which includes and incorporates both the conscious and the unconscious constructs (Lilly, 2015). "Jung believed that children's psyches contain a transcendent function – an innate striving for personality integration – occurring by symbolic identification. Children's symbols of archetypes are understood only in concepts of macrosystem in which they are contained, typically from their own phenomenological viewpoint" (Green, 2009, p. 83). Archetypes are essential elements of the psyche (Lilly, 2015) and contain both spiritual energy and feelings related to cultural metaphors and/or imagery (Green, 2009). In JAPT, the clinician views the collective unconscious as a fundamental emphasis and the playroom itself is viewed as an assortment of archetypal possibilities (Lilly, 2015).

Psychoanalytic Play Therapy

Psychoanalytic therapy originated with Freud and views the development of one's personality as a multilayered, dynamic, and complex process of development "based on the concept of infantile sexuality, with its sequence of libidinal phases characterized by distinct instinctual drives and their related energies" (Mordock, 2015, p. 67). Psychoanalysts believe that all behavior is then driven and motivated by the expression of these drives/energies and their object cathexes (Lee, 2009), which is "the investment of mental and/or emotional energy in a person, object, or idea" (Mordock, 2015, p. 68). Psychoanalysis works to assist the child or adolescent in reorganizing and reforming the personality by reconceptualizing experiences, memories, desires, and wishes that are repressed (Lee, 2009).

Uses for Play Therapy

Myriad research supports the notion that play therapy is appropriate and effective treatment for children with varying presenting concerns. Kottman (2011) notes these as follows:

- anxiety
- depression

- developmental delays
- fetal alcohol syndrome
- selective mutism
- aggression and acting out behavior
- withdrawal/anxious behavior
- grief and loss
- maladaptive perfectionism
- social problems
- other behavioral problems

Play therapy can also be appropriate for children who have experienced:

- abuse/neglect
- chronic or terminal illness
- divorce
- family violence
- family problems
- foster care/adoption
- homelessness
- hospitalization
- natural disasters
- parental alcoholism
- parental military deployment
- sexual abuse
- trauma

Further, play therapy can assist other treatment modalities for children who have been diagnosed with:

- attachment disorders
- ADHD
- autism spectrum
- mood disorders
- learning disabilities
- speech difficulties
- children in residential treatment facilities

Meta-analytic articles examining over 100 play therapy outcome studies (Bratton, Ray, Rhine, & Jones, 2005; LeBlanc & Ritchie, 2001; Lin & Bratton, 2015; Ray, Armstrong, Balkin, & Jayne, 2015) found that play therapy results in positive overall treatment effects ranging from moderate to high (Lilly et al., n.d.).

Play Therapy Clients

While play therapy is often associated with younger children (ages 3–12), many practitioners have implemented play therapy techniques and interventions with *all* ages (birth–death). A variety of play therapists have written about their utilization of play therapy with clients across the lifespan and in a variety of therapeutic modalities (i.e., individual, group, couples, and family counseling). For example, Gil (2015) wrote a book about implementing play therapy in family counseling. In 2004, Packman and Solt wrote about how to use

Filial Therapy for preadolescents, and Charles Schaefer (2003, 2019) has written about how to use play therapy with adults.

Basic Play Therapy Skills

In addition to traditional counseling/clinical skills – feeling reflections, summarizing content, using open-ended probing questions, immediacy (processing what is happening in the here and now), and confrontation (when appropriate) – there are other skills that are specific to play therapy. The following subsections outline the basic play therapy skills that are consistent across theoretical orientations. Note that specific theories may use different terminology to describe the same or similar skills, and/or have additional skills.

Structuring Skills

Structuring skills involve the counselor maintaining and managing the organization of the actual session. This can include setting up the playroom and managing the beginning, middle, and end of the session. It may also pertain to play therapists' decisions about the use of a non-directive, directive, or integrated approach. Structuring skills also pertain to the setup of the playroom or specific activity. Finally, structuring skills also involve how the counselor sets up a system and boundaries for entering and exiting the playroom, giving time cues, how to deal with interruptions/bathroom breaks, etc.

Tracking Behaviors

This involves narrating or summarizing (literally and metaphorically) what is happening in the room and what the client is doing, feeling, thinking – in an age-appropriate way.

Limit Setting

Limit setting was developed by Virginia Axline (1969), later developed and expanded by Gary Landreth (2012), and is the cornerstone of how play therapists set boundaries and teach children self-regulation skills related to the safety of the child, the counselor, the playroom/materials, and the therapeutic relationship. Landreth (2012) developed a system for how to set limits that involved the following acronym (ACT).

- A = Accept and Acknowledge the child's feeling or intent. For example: "I can see you are feeling angry".
- C = Communicate the limit or boundary. For example: "People are *not* for hitting" or "I am *not* for hitting".
- T = Target an alternative behavior or prosocial response. For example, "You can use the sandtray or toys to show me how you feel" or "You can use your words or draw a picture about your anger".

Returning Responsibility

This concept pertains to allowing space for the client's own feelings, behaviors, themes, and metaphors to emerge in the playroom. In order to do this, the counselor returns the responsibility for making choices and even naming toys/items in the playroom with clients' own words and symbolism. In non-directive sessions, a counselor uses a lot of "this" and "that" until the client names the toy or object. Then the counselor will call it what the client wants from then on. In addition, counselors are encouraged to refrain from doing things for the child in the playroom – instead, we encourage them to try by saying something like, "In here, you get to decide what that is called" or "I know you can open that if you want to".

Fantasy/Pretend Play

It is crucial for counselors to be able and willing to engage in pretend or fantasy play with children, as this is how they act out and work through a variety of emotions and experiences. This skill involves allowing the child to use their imagination to create a role and then direct the counselor to act out the role, *or* this can also come in the form of the counselor taking the lead and saying something like, "Let's pretend that you have magic and you can change anything about your life . . . ," etc.

Esteem Building/Pointing Out Strengths

Counselors are encouraged to make notice of, point out, or summarize clients' choices, noting their creativity, resourcefulness, and tenacity in an age-appropriate way. This does not involve giving trite and externally based compliments like "Good job", or "That is a pretty picture you drew". Instead, we want to focus on internal locus of control and encourage the client's effort and creativity, rather than the outcome/product. An example would be to tell a client, "I can see how hard you worked at solving this problem. What a different and unique idea to try" rather than, "Good job". From our perspective, this is the way to build positive self-esteem and resiliency.

Playroom Design

In 2018, O'Connor indicated that the perception of what is "an ideal playroom" will depend heavily on: (a) the counselors' theoretical orientation; (b) the developmental factors posed by presenting clients; (c) the therapeutic needs of the client population; and (d) "the cultural context in which the play therapy is being provided" (p. 5). In addition to prioritizing safety, size of the space, and setting (i.e., school, agency, private practice, hospital), counselors are encouraged to consider their own theoretical orientation and approach (non-directive, directive, or integrative) to play therapy.

Room Characteristics and Furniture

In terms of size, it is advised that playrooms are small enough to facilitate connection with the counselor and large enough to allow for some gross motor skills and physical movement. Ideally, counselors also have enough space to facilitate sessions with more than two or three people; this allows for group, family, and parent sessions. In terms of arrangement of the playroom, the key is to avoid clutter and create an organized and consistent way of presenting the toys and materials. Developmental considerations should be taken into account, and we recommend having materials for a variety of developmental phases (i.e., blocks and larger animals for young children or lava lamps and more sophisticated crafts/supplies and materials for pre-teens and teens). If counselors have the luxury of having more than one room, they can designate one room for younger children and preteens and then one for teens and parent/family sessions. It is also recommended to use quality equipment and furniture that is durable, and keep this in mind:

Unless one's practice is devoted exclusively to working with very young children, it is best to get furniture that is full-size or close to it. Small children readily adapt to larger tables and chairs, but older children may feel infantilized when asked to use preschool-sized furniture.

(O'Connor, 2018, p. 6)

Play Materials: What, Where, and How?

Once again, theoretical orientation will influence counselors as they make selections about what toys, art materials, sandtray miniatures, etc., they will place in the playroom and where. As Landreth (2012) instructs, it is important for play therapists to select – *not* collect – materials for the playroom. With the general goal of providing opportunities for clients to express themselves and interact with the counselor in a multitude of ways, we encourage counselors to be purposeful and thoughtful when selecting items for the playroom. In general terms, think of items that provide symbolism or metaphor for real-life themes and aspects of what it means to be human and alive in our world.

What?

Following is a list of specific toys, materials, and supplies that we recommend: animal family dynamic (i.e., small, medium, large), puppets, nurturing items (food, bottles, blankets, etc.), dress-up materials (costumes, cloths, scarves, hats), magic wand, dart gun (maybe), medical equipment, sandtray (you could use rice or beans) and miniatures, therapeutic board games and books, regular games (cards, checkers, Candy Land, tic-tac-toe, Monopoly), art supplies (a variety of mediums), play money, cash register, took kit, comfortable rug or mat and a couple of pillows for meditation and yoga, anger release activities (phone book, bubbles, bobo or Nerf guns, pillows to punch), crafts and invention materials. The materials listed here are in addition to those listed in Table 15.1.

Where?

Organization and consistency are extremely important aspects of where to place toys and materials. Use shelves and furniture that is bolted to the wall or safe and that can easily be reached by clients. Keep toys clean and at eye level for clients' appropriate developmental phases, and organize art supplies so that materials are appealing and ready for each client.

How?

It is also important to consider the clients' presenting issue when considering how to arrange the playroom – and in some cases, what materials or medium to select on a case-by-case basis. For example, a counselor may choose to have a book about grief and loss sitting on the table at the beginning of a session when working with a young client whose mother recently died. Furthermore, if counselors work with groups or families, they may need to rearrange furniture or take something out of the room when getting ready to have more than two people in the playroom.

Working With Parents/Caregivers in Play Therapy

The approach and manner with which counselors work with parents depends on various factors including culture, presenting issue, setting, and counselors' theoretical orientation.

As already introduced in this chapter, some counselors include parents/caregivers directly in the play therapy relationship and sessions; in essence: Theraplay (Booth & Jernberg, 2010), Play in Family Therapy (Gil, 2015), Filial Therapy (Scuka & Guerney, 2019), and Child-Parent Relationship Therapy (CPRT) (Bratton, Landreth, Kellam, & Blackard, 2006). Other approaches to involving parents and caregivers pertain to psychoeducational programs wherein counselors teach specific skills from a set curriculum. Then parents/caregivers go home and attempt to apply the skills.

Yet another approach that counselors often use is to offer parent consultation and family counseling simultaneous to individual counseling. Parent consultation involves holding regularly scheduled meetings (i.e., after every three individual sessions or every other session) wherein the counselor and the parent meet to discuss what is happening, what is being done to address the issue, what might need adjustment and what is working, and what the plan is for moving forward. During these meetings, counselors might even teach specific skills such as limit setting or help brainstorm discipline strategies. In closing, our most poignant message is that it is important to involve parents/caregivers in any way possible (Gil, 2015).

Play Therapy in the School Setting

Play therapy is appropriate for use in multiple settings. "Schools are important settings for implementing preventative interventions" (Peabody, Johnson, & Hightower, 2010, p. 164). We would like to address how play therapy can also be used in the school setting. We certainly understand the time constraints, space issues, and demanding caseloads of school counselors, and believe that play therapy can be an essential part of a school counselor's responsive services (ASCA, 2012). It can be helpful to do a short in-service training on play therapy for the teachers and staff, as we often heard teachers (and caregivers) wanting to take away play therapy as a consequence for a child's unfavorable actions. Providing information about what play therapy is and is not (just a child coming to play for free time) can help alleviate these issues and ideas. Play is a child's work. Remember, we would not tell a depressed adult that they were too depressed to go to counseling. Play therapy is neither a reward nor a punishment – play is hard work, and play therapy is a needed therapeutic intervention. With the number of children with noteworthy emotional and behavioral concerns growing at a disturbing rate in the United States (Lin & Bratton, 2015), counselors need to offer evidence-based practices in all settings where children and adolescents have access. Since school is where most children and adolescents spend the majority of their lives, it makes sense that this amazing therapeutic tool is offered.

School counselors and school-based therapists may also have space constraints. Many school counselors (the author included) found it useful to have a travel play therapy kit. Table 15.1 presents some suggested items (Landreth, 2012, pp. 166–67) that may be useful to have in your travel kit.

You can also set up a small corner of your office to use for play therapy if you have space. A kit can be helpful if you are able to move from a small office to a larger room when available. Table 15.1 is a general list of items to include in a travel kit, not one specific to use in a school setting. In a school setting, guns and other violent-type toys should be excluded. Counselors are encouraged to discuss this with their supervisors and administrators. School counselors and school-based counselors may decide to add other aggressive toys to their kits such as puppets, blocks, or a bop bag (Perryman & Doran, 2010). Understanding that children will do what is necessary to create the toy they need (using their fingers as guns, creating one out of playdough or paper, etc.) is important because it lets the counselor set a limit that "people are not for shooting".

Table 15.1 Travel Play Therapy Kit Supplies

Aggressive hand puppet (alligator, wolf, or dragon)	Newsprint
Band-aids	Nursing bottle (plastic)
Bendable doll family	Pipe cleaners
Bendable Gumby (nondescript figure)	Playdough
Blunt scissors	Popsicle sticks
Costume jewelry	Rubber knife
Cotton rope	Small airplane
Crayons (eight-count box)	Small car
Dart gun	Spoons (avoid forks because of sharp points)
Dollhouse (use box that holds reams of paper, box lid serves as dollhouse, draw lines on inside of lid to mark rooms, box doubles as storage for toys)	Telephone (two)
Dollhouse furniture	Toy soldiers (20-count size is sufficient)
Handcuffs	Transparent tape
Lone Ranger-type mask	Two play dishes or cups (plastic or tin)
Medical mask (white dust mask will suffice)	Nerf ball (rubber ball bounces too much)

Multicultural Implications and Advocacy

Play therapy is multiculturally sensitive in that it does not rely on language development or acquisition as the main form of communication. Further, play is multicultural in that all children play – inherently and intrinsically. Play is not a taught skill. "Play therapy provides a culturally sensitive approach because students of diverse cultures, socio-economic status, and varying academic and language abilities can communicate through the vehicle of play" (Trice-Black, Bailey, & Riechel, 2013, p. 304). Since play does not rely on verbal communication, cultural experiences can be conveyed through play. Sweeney and Landreth note that play therapy is culturally appropriate because "the child is free to communicate through play in a manner that is comfortable and typical for the child, including cultural adaptations of lay and expression" (2009, p. 135).

Summary

Play therapy is a specific type of counseling in which play is used to communicate instead of relying on talk as in traditional therapy modalities. In play therapy, there is a playroom where the child is able to play out their thoughts, feelings, and situations by using toys, art, and other play media tools. Play is a child's natural form of communication. Instead of adults trying to get kids to talk, play therapy lets the child communicate through play. We firmly believe that children are *always* communicating with us. It is our job as counselors to learn and respect their form of communication and to pay attention. We believe that the play therapist is so very important to the therapeutic relationship. Whole parts of the brain are involved during play, thus making play a critical factor in growth and development. Play therapy is multiculturally sensitive in that it does not rely on language development or acquisition as the main form of communication.

Clinician's Corner

I had the opportunity to train under a skilled play therapist during my internship. During that time, I worked with a little girl who had been abused by her biological father. She was so confused by what happened to her and tried to understand why it happened. As her counselor, I tried to help her learn how to deal with the traumatic experiences. We used a shark as an example of a scary event, instead of trying to find the right words. I showed her how she could escape or deal with the emergency/dangers by preparing a safe place in the playroom where she could hide if needed. Over time, she learned to stand up for herself. For instance, she often expressed "I am strong" and "Stop!" to the shark in the play therapy room. She loved playing with superhero capes and made a song "We Are the Heroes". As we played, I highlighted how strong and brave she was and is.

I also met a girl who is very shy and quiet. Initially, it was so hard for me to build a relationship with her. She also had difficulty talking about her feelings with her caregiver, so I often followed what she did and imitated her play style. Instead of just trying to talk about feelings, I used feeling cards with faces on them. We guessed the feelings of each one and she shared when she had those feelings. I strongly believe that play therapy helped me to interact with her more effectively. As I continued sessions with her, she became slightly more talkative and shared her struggles with me.

Through cases like these, I learned how important play is. I also learned that it is valuable to explain to parents/caregivers that play therapy is not just playing with children, but a tool for communication they could use at home. One 45-minute session in a week is not enough, but if I can communicate well and discuss the strategy with the parents, I can make a difference in the child's life.

Ryoko Tsukada
Clinical Mental Health Counseling Student

References

American School Counselor Association (ASCA). (2012). *The ASCA national model: A framework for school counseling programs* (3rd ed.). Alexandria, VA: Author.

Association for Play Therapy. (2019). Back to basics. *Play Therapy, 14*(3), 12–46.

The Association for Play Therapy. (n.d.). Retrieved from www.a4pt.org/page/AboutAPT

Axline, V. (1969). *Play therapy*. New York: Ballantine Books.

Blom, R. (2006). *The handbook of gestalt play therapy: Practical guidelines for child therapists*. London: Jessica Kingsley Publishers.

Booth, P. B., & Jernberg, A. M. (2010). *Theraplay: Helping parents and children build better relationships through attachment-based play* (3rd ed.). San Francisco, CA: Jossey-Bass.

Booth, P. B., & Lindaman, S. (2019). Attachment theory and theraplay ®. *PlayTherapy, 14*(3), 14–16.

Bratton, S., Landreth, G. L., Kellam, T., & Blackard, S. R. (2006). *Child parent relationship therapy (CPTR) treatment manual: A 10-Session filial therapy model for training parents*. New York: Routledge.

Bratton, S., Ray, D., Rhine, T., & Jones, L. (2005). The efficacy of play therapy with children: A meta-analytic review of treatment outcomes. *Professional Psychology: Research and Practice, 36*(4), 376–390. https://doi.org/10.1037/0735-7028.36.4.376

Burghardt, G. M. (2005). *The genesis of animal play: Testing the limits*. Cambridge, MA: MIT Press.

Drewes, A. A., & Schaefer, C. E. (2016). The therapeutic powers of play. In K. J. O'Connor, C. E. Schaefer, & L. D. Braverman (Eds.), *Handbook of play therapy* (2nd ed., pp. 35–62). Hoboken, NJ: Wiley.

Gaskin, R. L., & Perry, B. D. (2014). The neurobiological power of play: Using the neurosequential model of therapeutics to guide play in the healing process. In C. A. Malchiodi & D. A. Crenshaw

(Eds.), *Creative arts and play therapy for attachment problems* (pp. 178–194). New York: The Guilford Press.

Gil, E. (2015). *Play in family therapy* (2nd ed.). New York: The Guilford Press.

Glazer, H. R. (2010). Filial play therapy for grieving preschool children. In C. E. Schaefer (Ed.), *Play therapy for preschool children* (pp. 89–105). Washington, DC: American Psychological Association.

Green, E. J. (2009). Jungian analytical play therapy. In K. J. O'Connor & L. D. Braverman (Eds.), *Play therapy theory and practice: Comparing theories and techniques* (2nd ed., pp. 83–122). John Wiley & Sons.

Knell, S. M., & Dasari, M. (2010). Cognitive-behavioral play therapy for preschoolers: Integrating play and cognitive-behavioral interventions. In C. E. Schaefer (Ed.), *Play therapy for preschool children* (pp. 157–178). Washington, DC: American Psychological Association.

Kottman, T. (2011). *Play therapy: Basics and beyond* (2nd ed.). Alexandria, VA: American Counseling Association.

Kottman, T., & Ashby, J. S. (2015). Adlerian play therapy. In D. A. Crenshaw & A. L. Stewart (Eds.), *Play therapy: A comprehensive guide to theory and practice* (pp. 32–47). New York: The Guilford Press.

Landreth, G. (2012). *Play therapy: The art of the relationship* (3rd ed.). New York: Brunner-Routledge.

Landreth, G., & Bratton, S. (2006). *Child-parent relationship therapy (CPRT): A 10-session filial therapy model*. New York: Routledge.

LeBlanc, M., & Ritchie, M. (2001). A meta-analysis of play therapy outcomes. *Counseling Psychology Quarterly, 14*, 149–163.

Lee, A. (2009). Psychoanalytic play therapy. In K. J. O'Connor & L. D. Braverman (Eds.), *Play therapy theory and practice: Comparing theories and techniques* (2nd ed., pp. 25–82). John Wiley & Sons.

Levy, A. J. (2011). Neurobiology and the therapeutic action of psychoanalytic play therapy with children. *Clinical Social Work Journal, 39*(1), 50–60. https://doi.org/10.1007/s10615-009-0229-x

Lilly, J. P. (2015). Jungian analytical play therapy. In D. A. Crenshaw & A. L. Stewart (Eds.), *Play therapy: A comprehensive guide to theory and practice* (pp. 48–65). Guilford Press.

Lilly, J. P., O'Connor, K. J., Krull, T., Schaefer, C. E., Landreth, G., & Pehrsson, E. D. E. (n.d.). *Play therapy makes a difference*. Retrieved from www.a4pt.org/page/PTMakesADifference

Lin, Y., & Bratton, S. C. (2015). A meta-analytic review of child-centered play therapy approaches. *Journal of Counseling and Development, 93*(1), 45–58. https://doi.org/10.1002/j.1556-6676.2015.00180.x

Mellenthin, C. (2018). *Play therapy: Engaging and powerful techniques for the treatment of childhood disorders*. Eau Claire, WI: PESI Publishing & Media.

Mordock, J. B. (2015). Psychodynamic play therapy. In D. A. Crenshaw & A. L. Stewart (Eds.), *Play therapy: A comprehensive guide to theory and practice* (pp. 66–82). Guilford Press.

Mullin, J. A., & Rickli, J. M. (2014). *Child-centered play therapy workbook: A self-directed guide for professionals*. Champaign, IL: Research Press Publishers.

Oaklander, V. (2001). Gestalt play therapy. *International Journal of Play Therapy, 10*(2), 45–55. http://dx.doi.org/10.1037/h0089479

Oaklander, V. (2007). *Windows to our children: A Gestalt approach to children and adolescents*. The Gestalt Journal Press.

O'Connor, K. J. (2016). Ecosystemic play therapy. In K. J. O'Connor, C. E. Schaeger, & L. D. Braverman (Eds.), *Handbook of play therapy* (2nd ed., pp. 195–226). John Wiley & Sons.

O'Connor, K. J. (2018). Playroom design. *Play Therapy, 13*(1), 4–7.

O'Connor, K. J., & Ammen, S. (2013). *Play therapy treatment planning and interventions: The ecosystemic model and workbook*. Waltman, MA: Academic Press.

Packman, J., & Solt, M. D. (2004). Filial therapy modifications for preadolescents. *Journal of Play Therapy, 13*(1), 57–77.

Parson, J. (2017). Puppet play therapy – Integrating Theory, Evidence and Action (ITEA) presented at international play therapy study group. Champneys at Forest Mere, England. June 18. Adapted from Shaefer, C. E. and Drewes, A. A. (2014) *Therapeutic powers of play: 20 Core agents of change* (2nd ed.). Wiley.

Peabody, M. A., Johnson, D., & Hightower, A. D. (2010). Primary project: An evidence-based approach. In A. Drewes & C. Schaefer (Eds.), *School based play therapy* (2nd ed., pp. 163–180). Hoboken, NJ: Wiley.

Peabody, M. A., & Schaefer, C. E. (2019, September). The therapeutic powers of play: The heart and soul of play therapy. *Play Therapy, 14*(3), 4–6.

Perls, F. (1973). *The Gestalt approach and eyewitness to therapy*. Science and Behavior Books.

Perryman, K., & Doran, J. (2010). Guidelines for incorporating play therapy in the schools. In A. Drewes & C. Schaefer (Eds.), *School based play therapy* (2nd ed., pp. 61–86). Hoboken, NJ: Wiley.

Ray, D. C., Armstrong, S. A., Balkin, R. S., & Jayne, K. M. (2015). Child-centered play therapy in the schools: Review and meta-analysis. *Psychology in the Schools, 52*(2), 107–123. https://doi.org/10.1002/pits.21798

Ray, D. C., & McCullough, R. (2015; revised 2016). *Evidence-based practice statement: Play therapy* (Research report). Retrieved from Association for Play Therapy website: www.a4pt.org/?page=EvidenceBased

Rogers, C. R. (1951). *Client-centered therapy*. Boston, MA: Houghton Mifflin.

Russ, S. W. (2007). Pretend play: A resource for children who are coping with stress and managing anxiety. *NYS Psychologist, IX*(4), 13–17.

Schaefer, C. E. (1993). *The therapeutic powers of play therapy*. Northvale, NJ: Jason Aronson.

Schaefer, C. E. (1999). Curative factors in play therapy. *The Journal for the Professional Counseling, 14*(1), 7–16.

Schaefer, C. E. (Ed.). (2003). *Play therapy with adults*. Hoboken, NJ: John Wiley and Sons.

Schaefer, C. E. (2019). Top stress-release toys for adults. *Play Therapy, 14*(4), 28–30.

Schaefer, C. E., & Drewes, A. A. (2009). The therapeutic powers of play and play therapy. In A. Drewes (Ed.), *Blending play therapy with cognitive behavioral therapy: Evidence-based and other effective treatment and techniques* (pp. 3–15). Hoboken, NJ: Wiley.

Schaefer, C. E., & Drewse, A. A. (2010). The therapeutic powers of play and play therapy. In A. Drewes & C. Schaefer (Eds.), *School based play therapy* (2nd ed., pp. 3–16). Hoboken, NJ: Wiley.

Schaefer, C. E., & Drewes, A. A. (Eds.). (2014). *The therapeutic powers of play: 20 core agents of change* (2nd ed.). Hoboken, NJ: Wiley.

Schaefer, C. E., & Peabody, M. A. (2016, June). Glossary of play therapy terms. *Play Therapy*, 20–24.

Scuka, R. F., & Guerney, L. (2019). Filial therapy. *PlayTherapy, 14*(3), 20–22.

Stewart, A. L., Field, T. A., & Echterling, L. G. (2016). Neuroscience and the magic of play therapy. *International Journal of Play Therapy, 25*(1), 4–12. https://doi.org/10.1037/pla0000016

Sweeney, D., & Landreth, G. (2009). Child-centered play therapy. In K. O'Connor & L. Braverman (Eds.), *Play therapy theory and practice: Comparing theories and techniques* (2nd ed., pp. 123–162). Wiley.

Trice-Black, S., Bailey, C. L., & Riechel, M. E. K. (2013). Play therapy in school counseling. *Professional School Counseling, 16*(5), 303–312.

VanFleet, R., Sywulak, A. E., & Sniscak, C. C. (2010). *Child-centered play therapy*. New York: The Guilford Press.

Vygotsky, L. S. (1967). Play and its role in the mental development of the child. *Soviet Psychology, 5*(3), 6–16. https://doi.org/10.2753/RPO1061-040505036

Winnicott, D. W. (1971). *Playing and reality*. Oxford: Penguin.

16 Sandtray Therapy

Sonya Lorelle, Rebekah Byrd, and Chad Luke
Sonya Lorelle as guest author

Objectives

- Describe key terms from this chapter associated with sandtray and the practice of sandtray in counseling.
- Examine the many benefits of sandtray and its application to working with children and adolescents.
- Understand the different ways in which sandtray can be used in counseling.
- Examine different types of sandtray.
- Understand the sandtray process.

Reflective Questions

- What are my current beliefs about sandtray?
- How do I currently rely on traditional talk therapy means for counseling children and adolescents?
- How might sandtray benefit children and adolescents in my current setting?
- How might children and adolescents benefit from sandtray work?
- How might I incorporate more play media, expressive, and creative techniques for counseling children and adolescents?
- What connections are there between sandtray and multicultural counseling competence?

What Is Sandtray Therapy?

Children think *and* understand the world differently than adults, and therefore when counseling children, it is important to consider their developmental level and best ways of communicating. Play is the natural language children use to express their inner worlds (Landreth, 2012). It is important to consider the methods and means made available to children in counseling, as the toys become the vocabulary with which children can express themselves. The sandtray is a counseling intervention that provides a confined space of a tray filled with sand where children can use a vast array of miniatures that represent many aspects of the world and imagination (Homeyer & Sweeney, 2011). These miniatures enter the sand tray and become both literal and metaphorical representations of children's internal processes.

While Sandtray Therapy is supported as an effective intervention for children and adolescents with varying presenting issues, it is important to note that as with any skill or technique, counselors need to be appropriately trained. This chapter can provide information and resources useful to your work with children and adolescents; however, it cannot delve into each topic in depth. Additional training and supervision is necessary for best ethical practices for any counselor using Sandtray Therapy (Homeyer & Sweeney, 2011).

Introduction to Concepts and Terms

Margaret Lowenfeld was one of the first to realize the benefits of using symbolic objects to allow children to express themselves (Lowenfeld, 1979). Given that children do not think linearly, these figures allowed them to more fully convey their internal worlds. She developed the World Technique, in which she asked children to build their world in the sand. She saw the value in these materials because the trays and figures were multidimensional, which allowed children to represent multiple parts of themselves that can be taken in by the child and the counselor as a whole (Lowenfeld, 1991).

Prior to language skills developing, children think in images constructed from sensory experience, and therefore the images that are able to be recreated in the sand tray align with children's developmental capacity (Rae, 2013). Language is linked to the left hemisphere, and images are associated with the right hemisphere (Rae, 2013). The figure and imaged focused aspect of sandtray stimulates the right-brain emotional processes that can't be accessed through verbal methods and provides the whole brain an opportunity to be engaged in the process (Badenoch, 2008, Rae, 2013). Homeyer and Sweeney (2011) describe the sand tray as a non-verbal method of communicating that provides a level of safety that provides children the opportunity to address "emotionally charged issues" (p. 4) and allows for repressed emotions to emerge.

Sandtray is useful because it facilitates expression beyond that of which the client is consciously aware (Monakes, Garza, Wiesner, & Watts, 2011; Turner, 2005). This ability to move beyond conscious awareness is especially important for children and adolescents who have not yet developed the language skills or ability to convey their thoughts, feelings, and experiences. The tray itself also provides benefits by serving as a contained, controlled, and protected space where children and adolescents are able to express aspects of their experiences as they choose (Labovitz & Goodwin, 2000). The container of the tray, and the metaphorical communication, provides therapeutic distance and has inherent boundaries, which creates safety (Homeyer & Sweeney, 2011). In this safe space, children are able to develop creativity where they try new behaviors and solutions (Tornero & Capella, 2017).

Sandtray provides clients with therapeutic means to use their senses in a way that encourages release, healing, and relaxation (Oaklander, 2007; Gil, 2006). There is a tactile and sensory quality in the sand that children resonate with (Homeyer & Sweeney, 2011). The sensory experience in sandtray offers "a contrasting tactile experience where they may reconnect with their own body and experience positive and pleasurable sensations that promote physical and psychological wellbeing" (Tornero & Capella, 2017, p. 10). This physical aspect helps children who have been abused and traumatized reconnect with their bodies in a new way rather than remaining in a dissociated or compartmentalized state (Zappacosta, 2013).

Materials

There are many aspects to consider when setting up the equipment and preparing for implementing Sandtray Therapy. The tray, the sand, and the types of miniatures all should be selected thoughtfully and with the type of intervention and clients it will be used with in mind.

Sand tray

A sand tray is a container holding sand that the child or adolescent places selected items into. These trays can be of varying shapes and sizes, and can be made out of wood or plastic. There are a variety of types and shapes and sizes that can be used. A standard size is a rectangular tray measuring 20 × 30 × 3 inches (Homeyer & Sweeney, 2011). Wood trays painted blue on the inside can represent sky or water. There are other options to consider when choosing trays. A circle tray could create an alternative space. De Demenico found that smaller trays helped to focus the children and allowed them to play longer and process the contents more clearly (as cited in Boik & Goodwin, 2000). Whatever the size or shape, the purpose of the tray is to serve as a regulating factor that allows the client to take in the whole scene and issue presented all at once (Homeyer, 2020).

The tray can be adjusted for the child or the setting. For example, in large group settings when teaching sandtray to students or clinicians, we often use aluminum trays to provide a cheap and easily transportable means for carrying supplies. A school counselor could bring these small portable trays into classroom interventions. When counseling or training overseas, we have used a circular aluminum cookie tin to be the container. When we have needed to be more portable as counselors, we have used the brand "Really Useful Box" which was a blue plastic tub with a lid and handle for easy transportation.

Sand

The type of sand used in the tray is also something to be chosen thoughtfully. A fine-grain sand can be soothing to run fingers through, but does not hold shape when building a mountain or carving out a river. Cheap playground sand may be dirty and have large stones or pebbles. It is important to look for a medium-grain sand that can be manipulated and formed. You may consider having a wet sand tray and a dry sand tray, as wet sand can be molded even more precisely and provides an even broader range of expression for children (Homeyer & Sweeney, 2011).

Miniatures

Miniature items are placed in the trays according to the creator's preferences. Many items can be used as sandtray miniatures. There are sandtray rooms with shelves upon shelves of miniatures, and there are portable sand trays with a few available. While not every single item listed in Table 16.1 is required to make a usable sand tray, there should be a wide variety of the world represented since there should be a range of symbols available for children to use to express themselves. For example, there should be animals, people, scary objects, magical objects, vulnerable objects, buildings, trees, rocks and fences, and a variety of small versions of day-to-day objects in the world. The quality of the variance of the miniatures is more important than the quantity. It is important to consider a diverse range of stories that children may want to tell in the tray, so the counselor needs to provide enough tools for the child to express. Table 16.1 of possible items to include follows.

It is also important to think about how these will be displayed and organized. It is ideal that the miniatures are displayed in a way that all of them are easily seen (Boik & Goodwin, 2000). If space is limited, baskets or a portable set in plastic bins could be used. Similar items should be grouped together, meaning there could be a shelf for transportation including cars, trains, planes, and boats. There could be another section of people, another section for mythical figures, one for scary animals, another one for gentle animals, and a separate section for buildings, trees, rocks, and fences.

Table 16.1 Categories and Example Figures

Category and Subcategory	Example
People	
Diverse ethnic and cultural groups	People with diverse skin colors
Diverse ages	Infants, children, adolescents, adults
Diverse workers	Mechanics, soldiers, firefighters, doctors, teachers
Diverse work environments	Farms, factories, schools, hospitals
Animals	
Domestic animals	Dogs, cats, camels
Farm animals	Cows, horses, pigs
Wild animals	Tigers, lions, bears, zebras
Prehistoric animals	Tyrannosaurus rex, triceratops
Birds	Pigeons, eagles, penguins
Sea creatures	Starfish, sea horses, whales, seals, dolphins, sea turtles
Insects	Spiders, grasshoppers, ladybugs
Reptiles	Frogs, cobras, garden snakes, lizards
Buildings	
Ruins	Houses, barns
Architectural	Lighthouses, jails
Fences and bridges	Wood fences, stone bridges
Landforms and nature	Rocks, mountains, rainbows
Conflict figures	Guns and swords, knights, Hulks
Spiritual figures	Crosses, priests and nuns, Buddha and God figures
Mythical and whimsical figures	Pegasus, unicorns, wizards, tricksters, clowns
Symbolic figures	Coffins, skeletons, knights, treasure chests
Vehicles	Airplanes, cars, ambulances, school buses, motorcycles, boats
Vegetation	Deciduous trees, evergreens, shrubs, tropical trees, flowers
Household items	Kitchenware, hourglass timers, rocking chairs, beds

Source: Sangganjanavanich & Magnuson, 2011, p. 267

Sandtray Therapy Clients

Even though this is a text dedicated to working with children and adolescents, it is important to note that sandtray is not just for children and adolescents. Sandtray has been shown to be beneficial with individuals of varying ages, cultural backgrounds, and presenting issues. Sandtray has been used with adult males in substance abuse treatment (Monakes et al., 2011), elderly clients (Baker, 2004; Pappas, 2015), career decision making (Sangganjanavanich & Magnuson, 2011; Swank & Jahn, 2017), and group therapy with parents (James & Martin, 2002).

Sandtray has also been useful in counselor training and professional identity. Using sandtray assisted in skill integration, attitudes, and self-perceptions of counselors in training in understanding their values and their views of becoming a counselor educator (Felton, 2016). After completing a sand tray, one graduate student remarked: "This was the most meaningful thing I have done all year!" That was a powerful statement to hear about sandtray. It was an honor to witness such power!

Basic Skills

Basic sandtray skills are very similar to basic play therapy skills found in the previous chapter. You can hone your play therapy skills to use in sandtray sessions with individuals, groups, couples, etc. Webber and Mascari (2008) suggest some basic guidelines for counselors when utilizing sandtray in the therapeutic process:

- Provide a deeply safe and protected healing environment.
- Avoid speaking until the client completes the sand tray creation.
- Stand or sit so that the entire building process and tray can be viewed.
- Notice the client's development of the sand tray. Which figure is placed first? What items are moved? Does the creator engage the figures in action? Does the creator narrate the action or speak for the figures?
- Observe the client's contact with the sandbox and self-soothing with sand. Does the creator move the sand with his/her hands or a tool? Moisten the sand? Place figures under the sand? Work outside the tray?
- Hold back from giving interpretation, meaning, or names to the client's sand tray.
- Respect the pace of sand tray construction and the client's need for repetition in reconstructing the trauma story. Do not rush the process.
- Recognize, with the client's stories, the potential personal impact of vicarious trauma.

(p. 7)

The Sandtray Process

There are both directive and non-directive ways of using the sand tray. A non-directive approach allows for the client to lead fully and enables them to make anything in the tray they need or want. The entire time it is a collaborative process, with the client leading by expressing themselves through the sand tray and the miniature figures and the counselor intuitively following to help understand their internal process that becomes a three-dimensional scene in the counseling room.

The first step is to invite the client to build the tray. In this approach the counselor begins by saying something like, "create or build a world in the sand" (Homeyer & Sweeney, 2011). The counselor can invite the client to use as many or as few miniatures and as much time as they would like.

The next step involves the client building the tray. The child has the opportunity to explore the miniatures and begin creating the world in the sand. The counselor should stay quiet and engagingly observe the process (Rae, 2013). How are the miniatures selected? Is the client cautious or confident? Is the client quiet or talkative? Which miniatures are selected? How are they arranged? What is placed in the middle? What items are grouped? Are there boundaries? What items are buried? Each of these observations give clues to the metaphors and internal process of the client. The counselor should remain quiet and not interfere in the process.

After the client has completed their world, the counselor can begin to engage and process it. The counselor can prompt, "Tell me about your world". The child may describe the scene or tell a story, or say what is happening (Oaklander, 2007). Each part of the world and the characters in the world are explored. Non-directive skills are the foundation for responding. If the child continues to move and manipulate the miniatures, counselors can track the story, while reflecting feelings of the characters and the client. Open questions that help to understand the world can also be asked. What is happening in the world? What is it like for the characters to be in the world? What happens next in the world? The counselor should avoid using *why* questions such as, "Why did you put the tree in the center?" that require the client to justify their decisions. Rather there should be an approach made with curiosity to seek understanding and what it means to the client. The counselor should also avoid making assumptions about the interpretation of what it means to the client such as, "Is the tree in the center there for the little boy to hide when the monster comes?" Rather, counselors can openly explore, "what is it like for the animals to have a tree in the center of this world?" or "How does the little boy feel about having that tree there?" The counselor can notice parts of the world: "I notice there is a buried treasure under the tree". Clients will often fill in the story if it is an important part of the world. Counselors can also facilitate conversations between characters in the sand tray (Oaklander, 2007). What would the tree say to the little boy sitting underneath it? What would the wizard say to the rabbit who is scared? What would the mom say to the baby? What would the little girl say to the dad? Finally, to continue to explore the tray, the counselor can ask children to describe their feelings about the world they created (Bainum, 2004).

The counselor can also look at the organization of the tray in order to make guesses about what the client may be experiencing (Homeyer & Sweeney, 2011). From the Jungian perspective, there are typical organizations of sandtray that the clinician can internally interpret:

1. An empty world could represent an unhappy place or a lack of resources.
2. A world without people could represent a child's anger or hostility towards people or their desire to escape from people.
3. A fenced world could represent the client's need for protection, compartmentalization, keeping out danger, or need for external control.
4. A rigid world with systemic arrangements could represent a desire for order or control.
5. A chaotic world with no organization could represent inner confusion or chaos in their world.
6. An aggressive world with a battle or fighting or crashes could represent anger, and the tray is a safe way to express it.

However, these insights should remain hunches for counselors to attempt to understand the clients rather than interpreting this for them. It is less important what the conceptualization of the counselor is, and more important what the sand tray means to the child (Rae, 2013).

Therapeutic metaphors can emerge from the client's sandtray play (Homeyer & Sweeney, 2011). These metaphors can be powerful and allow for the internal issues to be accessed more thoroughly and more rapidly. Because people inherently make meaning out of their experiences and world, Sandtray Therapy is an opportunity to externalize these internal processes (Rae, 2013). The counselor can facilitate these new perceptions and connections as part of this process. The counselor should help the client to "discover and explore their own inherent layers and meanings in the sand world" (Rae, 2013, p. 63) and clarify what it means to them. Counselors then can magnify the themes of the tray or story told about the tray.

Often, there are predictable themes that show up in the trays about such topics as power and control or fear and helplessness. In one qualitative study with children who had been sexually abused and experienced Sandtray Therapy, the researchers found consistent themes in the play, including themes of violence and aggression between people, the need for care and protection, and stories about resolving conflicts (Tornero & Capella, 2017).

By enlarging the meaning, the counselor verbally reflects the meaning of the information tentatively to the child so that this interpretation can be accepted or rejected (Homeyer & Sweeney, 2011). Reflecting the feelings of the characters helps to validate the experience and perceptions that are true for the client in the metaphors represented in the tray, bringing insight and awareness of beliefs and desires. While there may be similar themes in the client's life to the metaphor played out in the sand tray, the reflections and comments should most often be kept in the metaphor so it can remain the safe distance for the client to process.

Depending on the stage of therapy and the readiness of the client, the counselor can consider restorying, which can be understood as exploring alternative solutions and perspectives (Ivey, Ivey, & Zalaquett, 2017). While there is value in externally expressing the internal world, the sand tray also gives an opportunity to be able to recreate and assimilate new meaning (Rae, 2013). In this process, the counselor may ask the client if there is anything they would want to change about the world. Together, the counselor and client can imagine solutions, reflect on resources, and explore new perspectives. If there was a battle or a character was sick or injured, the counselor can wonder if there was anything or anyone that could be added to help the good characters win or assist the character to recover. Are there any resources they can add to make the world safer? Are there fences that help keep them protected? Oaklander (2007) stated that she sometimes encourages a child to carry out actions, such as if an animal is going to attack everyone, she will encourage the child to make that happen in the sand tray. This new action can lead to something new in the tray or perspective. When working through trauma, by playing in the sand tray, children are able to ascribe new meanings to their traumatic experiences (Tornero & Capella, 2017).

Clients can also try new behaviors, as the sandtray can be very experiential. While the puppy in the story may be the one being cared for and nurtured, it can be a part of the child that experiences care and nurturing. To facilitate this connection, the counselor can ask: "What is it like for the puppy to be hugged? What is it like for you to see the puppy hugged?" This process may not happen in the initial stand tray, as in the beginning the clients may need to tell their story and are not ready to reimagine or may not have the internal resources to imagine solutions right away.

Ending the sand tray is another process that should be implemented thoughtfully. Prior to dismantling the tray, the counselor can document the tray. If the client gives permission, photos can be taken and placed in the file. The progression of photos can be reviewed when preparing for termination to reflect on the process of their time together (Homeyer & Sweeney, 2011). After taking time to document the tray, the process of dismantling can begin. There is a variety of options for this process. Homeyer and Sweeney (2011) suggest leaving the tray intact until the client leaves in order to honor the work the child did in the tray. Rae (2013), conversely, suggests allowing the child to clear the tray in order to have more time to reflect on the work. Following Adlerian theory, the child is asked to put away the most important miniature first (Bainum, 2004). Whichever method is followed, the sand should be smoothed between sessions so the next child has a blank slate from which to work (Bainum, 2004).

Directive sandtrays have a specific direction or topic that focuses the client. The counselor can choose the theme for the world the child creates or create games. Examples of directed sandtrays include drawing a line down the middle of the sand tray and asking the child to do comparing scenes, such as mom's house/dad's house or my world before the divorce and after divorce for children experiencing their parents' divorce. The child could be asked to create a sand world about a person that has a problem similar to what the child is experiencing or select objects that represent their family members and discuss ways the family resembles the miniatures chosen (Labovitz & Goodwin, 2000). The counselor can play hide and seek by hiding relevant miniatures in the sand and asking the child to find one and tell a story about the object they find (Labovitz & Goodwin). Garrett (2015) developed 100 directive sand tray prompts for a variety of types of clients. For children, the author recommended topics such as, "Build a tray that depicts your (average) day at school. What would your life look like if you didn't have to follow your parents' rules? Make a picture of the future. Make a picture of yesterday" (p. 47).

Oaklander (2007) developed directive sand trays unique to the child. For example, she may ask a child to "play out" a particular experience such as a home visit in the sand tray in order to gain insight about the child's perspective of the experience. She might also select figurines that relate to the child and ask them to make a tray with the pieces based on a specific session. She also asks how the tray relates to the children in order to make connections to the themes and their life.

Gomez (2019) creates safe spaces with clients. She encourages children to add items to the sand tray that would create a safe space for a miniature that represents them. If the children get stuck, especially because they don't have a concept of safety, she provides menu items as examples to help children think of what they may want. Do they want food, shelter, someone to hug, a barrier, fun, etc.? As with the non-directive methods, these directive techniques would include giving time and space for the child to complete the task and open-ended processing to explore the meaning with the child.

While these directive models can be followed for guidelines, it is important to note that it should be adapted for the specific client process and responses and developmental level. For example, some sand trays are not static and instead take on an ongoing shifting story and a compilation of scenes like the play of non-directive play therapy. These active sand trays give the child the ability to enact "their image-thinking as they experiment, explore, form, destroy, and form anew" (Rae, 2013, p. 141). This type of play is more likely to be seen with younger children who don't have the abstract thinking abilities to analyze the tray in a verbal way. In this case, the counselor can follow the ongoing story and play with the tracking skills and enhance the meaning. Likewise, not all sand trays require verbal processing. There can be silent sessions that are just as meaningful, as the power is in the images, not the words (Rae, 2013).

Types of Sandtray Therapy

Sandtray can be useful in many types of clinical work, with multiple populations and ages of individuals. Sandtray has been useful in individual work, group processes, family therapy, and couples counseling, and has been used in clinical supervision. We will briefly explore some uses for sandtray.

Group Sandtray

We all know how important peer groups are to adolescents, and we hopefully understand the importance of friendships with younger children. Using sandtray in group counseling as an activity-based intervention can provide participants a means for addressing intrapersonal issues, learning socialization skills, and developing a caring community within the context of the group and beyond (Draper, Ritter, & Willingham, 2003). In a group, each child can be given a small portable sand tray and then the group is given a directive prompt that aligns with the theme of the group. After time for building the tray, each group member can share about the meaning of the tray they built as a way to begin sharing and connecting in the group (Homeyer, 2020). As an alternate method, a large sand tray could be the space that everyone in the group collaborates on and contributes to the same scene.

Groups can serve as important learning experiences and provide many positive benefits to children and adolescents. The following are Yalom and Leszca's (2005) primary therapeutic factors or benefits to participating in group therapy:

1. Instillation of hope
2. Universality
3. Imparting information
4. Altruism
5. The corrective recapitulation of the primary family group
6. Development of socialization techniques
7. Intimate behavior
8. Interpersonal learning
9. Group cohesiveness
10. Catharsis
11. Existential factors

(p. 1–2)

Sandtray in the group setting has the ability to promote many of these factors. By building and sharing the tray, there is the opportunity for catharsis, increased insights, and self-disclosure. But processing the tray, whether individual or in a large tray format, provides the opportunity for acceptance, interpersonal interaction, and universality. The non-verbal, creative, and metaphoric nature of sandtray allows a different type of communication, and some experiences may be better accessed this way for child group members (Draper et al., 2003).

Just as you would with any group, understanding the purpose or identifying the group's goals will direct your work together. When leading a group using sandtray, it is important to remember the developmental age of the group members and that if working with very young children, a group of only two or three is appropriate (Homeyer & Sweeney, 2011). Also, it is developmentally appropriate and expected that children in group sandtray will alternate back and forth between individual play and cooperative play within the group setting (Homeyer & Sweeney, 2011).

Couples Sandtray

Sandtray can be used in couples work. The couple can be directed to create their world in the sand together using one tray; the sandtray could have a line drawn down the middle to separate the tray and have the couple create their worlds individually in the same tray, or each person could have their own tray to work with and explore while in counseling. Using sandtray in couples work can provide "a method that can facilitate transformation in the couple dynamics, revealing unconscious conflicts symbolically, thus providing the couple with the possibility of reflection and the opportunity to reorganize their psychological contents in a healthy manner" (Albert, 2015, p. 32). Sandtray can also be used as a means to applying traditional couple and family techniques and skills inside the framework of the sandtray process (Homeyer & Sweeney, 2011). The counselor can direct the couple to explore different parts of their relationship including: "Create a scene about how you met. Create a scene about your strongest memory as a couple. Create a scene about how you see this relationship in 5 or 10 years" (Garrett, 2015, p. 47).

Supervision Sandtray

Many supervisors and counselor educators are using sandtray as a form of supervision. Using sandtray in supervision can assist counselors in processing their roles as counselors

286 *Sonya Lorelle et al.*

in a different way. Markos, Coker, and Jones (2008) note the "use of expressive arts in counseling has been shown to be effective in creating a deeper level and meaning to counselor and client interactions" (p 3). Some directives these authors have used specifically in supervision with counselors in training and with professionals are:

- Create a world in the sand that depicts your relationship with your client.
- Create a world in the sand in which you feel confident in your counseling skills.
- Create a world in the sand that describes your growth as a counselor in training.
- Create a world in the sand that depicts your greatest fear in counseling.
- Create a world in the sand that reflects how you view counseling success with your clients.
- Create a world in the sand in which you are able to let go of a client you are holding on to.

In response to this last directive, when conducting a presentation on sandtray and supervision, a professional came up at the end of an extensive experiential session and said through the sand tray she created she had finally been able to let go of a client she had been worried and anxious about for the last 25 years. She said she just couldn't seem to let him go, and this was still very distressing to her. She discussed her self-awareness of this and how she had had supervision on this, but for whatever reason, thoughts of this client lingered and she would worry about him still to this day. The sandtray experience brought insight and closure for her. In tears and visibly lighter, she was beyond thankful for this experience and discussed how powerful this sandtray was for her.

Markos et al. (2008) found that counselors in training rated the use of sandtray positively compared to traditional approaches to supervision. McCurdy and Owen (2008) discussed sandtray as effective as traditional supervision in building working alliance. Important to note is that sandtray can be used within different models of supervision and can be used at different developmental stages with the counselor in training or the supervisee.

Sandtray Therapy in the School Setting

One quick Google image search will reveal entire rooms and practices dedicated to just Sandtray Therapy. Other counseling and therapy rooms have a sand tray and miniatures in the room available for use, among other play media and art items. Some playrooms have a single large sand tray with many miniatures, while others may not have a sand tray at all. In some places we have worked, we created a portable sand tray on a movable cart with multiple drawers for categories of miniatures along with smaller sand trays (clear storage containers) and other small storage containers with a select group of miniatures to move from room to room or have many available in each room if needed. In the school setting, space, time, and resources are often extremely limited, and one could get discouraged by seeing the beautiful rooms dedicated to sandtray. While these are wonderful and useful, this is not necessary to still engage in this powerful technique. Counselors working in settings with small rooms, rooms unable to be dedicated to sandtray alone, and small funds can make small, portable sand trays for use. In the school setting, we have used small sand trays and children and adolescents were drawn to them – as many are – for the soothing feeling of the sand. School counselors and school-based counselors can use sandtray in the same ways and capacities as described in this chapter. Goss and Campbell (2004) suggest that school counselors could use sandtray more effectively than typical talk therapies specifically with children and adolescents struggling with specific socioemotional and/or cognitive issues.

Research also discusses the use of group sandtray in the school setting. One study found significant differences as rated by both parents and teachers of preadolescents participating in a 10-week sandtray group as opposed to those not receiving the treatment (Flahive & Ray, 2007). Another study (Draper et al., 2003) on the use of group sandtray in an alternative school setting discussed that "sand tray group counseling is one way of circumventing initial resistance and getting to work in a way that provides engaging activity for the group" (p. 258). Groupwork in the school setting offers school counselors a way to reach more students and sandtray could be an important part of the comprehensive school counseling program.

Working With Parents and Caregivers in Sandtray Therapy

Play therapy has been shown to be especially effective when parents are involved in the process (Bratton, Ray, Rhine, & Jones, 2005). Counselors who see families but do not use play are at risk of not engaging the children and losing a valuable voice and contributor in the family (Sori, Maucieri, Bregar, & Kendrick, 2015). "Family sandtray therapy groups provide the opportunity for all members of the family to be fully involved with the wide variety of developmental ages. The family sessions become truly inclusive" (Homeyer & Sweeney, 2011, p. 63). These authors also point out that family or origin issues can be explored and exposed during a family sandtray because of its metaphorical nature. By allowing less guarded communication in this more playful and symbolic way, the family can connect and express emotions in a new way (Pettigrew, Raimondi, & Mcwey, 2016). Playful interventions provide an opportunity to observe important structural dynamics and interactional patterns of the family (Gil, 2015). It also provides an opportunity to build family cohesion.

Using sandtray and family work can:

- Provide a nonverbal means of expression when individuals are not able to verbally express themselves
- Provide counselors the opportunity to observe nonverbal communication and relationship dynamics
- Assist in helping mitigate the effects of focusing on one person as the identified client

(Homeyer & Sweeney, 2011)

When including parents and caregivers in a sandtray play session with a child or adolescent, the family can be asked to build worlds that represent their current experiences or their idealized vision (Pettigrew et al., 2016). Counselors can ask parents/caregivers and the child to make a standtray together. The tray could be divided into sections and each person gets a part to build their scene, or the family can also work together to build a scene in the sand together using prompts like: "Build a scene how your family is like now" or "Create a scene that represents the child's world". The benefits of creating separate scenes is the family can see the differences in perspective between family members. If one family member creates a nurturing environment, and another creates a disconnected stark environment, a conversation could be had to discuss what each scene is like and how these different perspectives have developed. It can be very impactful for parents and caregivers to observe a scene built by their child. This can assist parents and caregivers in gaining insight into their child's inner world.

If the family builds a tray together, the counselor can see how the family collaborates together as the family dynamics are acted out in session (Gil, 2015). When the scene is complete, ask processing questions such as: "Tell me about the scene. What is happening? What will happen next? What is it like to be in this world? How does it feel for this character to be here? What is the title of this scene?" When giving these instructions, let the family know they will have a certain amount of time to build the tray and step back and watch the family in their process, noting who takes the lead, who has and doesn't have a voice, what are the types of figures that are chosen by each family member, and how in tune emotionally are the parents with the child in the process. When the tray is complete, the counselor can re-engage with the family and process bringing attention to the family dynamics and the emotional impact of these patterns (Daley, Miller, Bean, & Oka, 2018).

Case Study

Elliot, 7 years old, was brought to counseling by his parents. They were concerned because his school performance had dropped, he had lost interest in his friends, and he rarely spoke at home anymore, always expressing a flat affect. Through the initial interview with the parents, it was discovered that he had been experiencing bullying in school. The shift in his behavior aligned in the timing with this experience at school. His parents described him as bright, having done well in school, curious and open to new experiences, and sensitive in a way that if corrected he would become sad and worked hard to not get in trouble again. When working with Elliot for the first time individually, he was withdrawn, did not speak, and kept eyes lowered toward the floor. Rather than pushing him to verbally communicate, he was invited to use the sand tray and to make a world in the sand (Figure 16.1). He was hesitant at first, visually inspecting the sand and the miniatures near him. Using basic attending skills, he was given distance to engage in the process in the way he preferred, and reflected back the interest and curiosity he was expressing: "I see you are checking out some of the toys". This space and acceptance seemed to give him permission to explore further.

He began to pick up a dragon figure and set it in the tray. He added a few people figures, and his world began to form. In this particular sandtray intervention, he did not build a static world that was processed after it was complete, but rather he developed an ongoing scene which included a battle. He played out an uneven battle where one side had big soldiers, dragons, and monsters, and the other side had people and kid figurines. It was clear that one boy figurine was under attack the most, and perhaps represented him in the scene. The battle would conclude, and all the people would end up dead. Tracking the play, reflecting feelings about helplessness and fear, and enhancing themes of having no one to turn to, this likely mirrored his experience with the bullies at his school. He replayed this scene over and over and each time, all the people ended up dead, though as the battle continued, there were also strengths and areas of resilience that were reflected in the play. The little boy would fight back. He would be able to kill a monster. He also was able to ask for help from others. All of this was reflected to him and was evidence of his creativity and of him trying on new roles. Even though the strength was there, the battle continued, and the people died again. He continued to lead and again he picked up the battle, and the epic fight started again. As the session was coming to a close, one by one, the monsters and soldiers were killed and buried until only a few people remained standing, including the boy figure (Figure 16.2). While sessions continued to address his anxiety and experiences with bullying at school, this first session with the sand tray provided an opportunity to understand the battle he had in his life, and for the counselor to express that understanding and accept him. He was also able to process tough emotions of anger, helplessness, and fear, and tried on new roles of using his power, all through the safe distance of the metaphor. This expression was not possible prior to this sand tray, as he had withdrawn and did not

Sandtray Therapy 289

Figure 16.1 Elliot's Initial Sand Tray

Figure 16.2 Elliot's Final Sand Tray

seem to have the words to communicate this to his parents or teachers. It provided a good start for building a relationship and trust in continuing that communication.

Multicultural Implications and Advocacy

The language of play is universal, so play therapy and sandtray can work with every culture; however, it is important to be thoughtful about how culture may impact the dynamics and experience. First, the images and symbols that are represented in the sand tray are multilayered in both personal experiences and cultural meanings. This context should be considered when interpreting and understanding the child, the dynamics, and messages within the tray. For example, in traditional Chinese homes, children are raised to be obedient and accommodating, and therefore in counseling children may present as quieter and have more anxiety if pressured to talk (Kao & Landreth, 2001). Given that sandtray does not require verbal communication, it could be a benefit for working with children of this nature. I (Sonya) saw this when I counseled children in the Asian country of Bhutan which had similar values. I had to adjust my approach, given the language barriers and children who presented with more silence. For example, I asked more closed questions so that it was easier for them to nod yes or no. Other times, when a child was timid to engage with the figurines, I asked them to point and direct what they wanted to happen in the world. I began by asking which figures they wanted in the world, and slowly asked where each one should go. We collaborated in this way until clear themes emerged about vulnerability and protection. I didn't need verbal language to understand the child's inner world.

It is also important to consider culture when selecting the miniatures. These miniatures need to represent the world the child lives in. This representation is accomplished by having people of all races and ages. Consider integrating religious symbols that represent a wide variety of traditions, as well. An example of this is that when I (Sonya) was working in Bhutan, I was sure to include mini prayer wheels and Buddhas, as the country is primarily Buddhist.

Summary

Ongoing research supports the benefits of play-based techniques such as sandtray. In this chapter, we examined the many uses of sandtray and discussed some of the benefits. In addition to being beneficial for children and adolescents, sandtray has also been shown to be effective for counselors in training, counselors, and supervisees. You do not need a large sand tray setup for this intervention to be beneficial, and sandtray can be used in many different work settings with clients of varying developmental stages and cultural backgrounds. We hope that you will learn more about sandtray and seek additional training to utilize this beneficial technique in counseling.

Clinician's Corner

I remember the first time I discovered the power of the sand tray and the feeling of total awe witnessing something so simple as sand serving as such a powerful modality: breaking down barriers of unspoken pain and opening pathways to healing.

Chloe was a 12-year-old girl who, along with her siblings, had been sexually abused by a much older family member and came to therapy to prepare for the trial in which they would testify. Chloe knew she would have to face her perpetrator, a close family member, and she was terrified. Any time the mention of court would arise, Chloe would become tense, silent, and tearful.

She couldn't describe to me the pain and anguish she was experiencing. One day in the sandtray room, Chloe picked up a block and placed it in the tray. Then she placed a female figure on the block. Facing the figure on the block, she began lining up multiple figures in the sand until a large crowd consumed the rest of the sand tray. She then carefully scanned the shelves of miniatures until she found a Dracula figure which she placed directly in between the crowd and in front of the elevated girl. She moved the girl's arm forward in a pointing motion.

She pondered the tray for a long time without saying a word. Then, as if something shifted and her brain knew what she needed in order to heal, she gathered up flower petals and heart-shaped beads and started scattering them all around the girl. Finally, she placed three smaller female figures behind the girl on the platform. She took a step back, and looking at her sand tray, took a deep breath before whispering, "I can do this". It was in that moment I became an avid believer of the healing powers of the sandtray.

Laura Martorano-Boring, LPC/MHSP, RPT
Sunny Path Counseling, PLLC

References

Albert, S. C. (2015). Sandplay therapy with couples within the framework of analytical psychology. *The Society of Analytical Psychology*, 60(1), 32–53.

Badenoch, B. (2008). *Being a brain-wise therapist: A practical guide to interpersonal neurobiology*. New York: W.W. Norton & Company.

Bainum, C. R. (2004). *An Adlerian model for sand tray therapy*, Doctoral Dissertation. ProQuest Dissertations & Theses Global (305040896). Retrieved from https://search.proquest.com/openview/010fd795e3b002fbebdc78a332f7d04b/1?pq-origsite=gscholar&cbl=18750&diss=y

Baker, A. (2004). The use of sandtray with older adult clients. In R. C. P. Magniant (Ed.), *Art therapy with older adults: A sourcebook* (pp. 35–52). Springfield, IL: Charles C. Thomas.

Boik, B. L., & Goodwin, E. A. (2000). *Sandplay therapy: A step-by-step manual for psychotherapists of diverse orientations*. New York: W.W. Norton & Company.

Bratton, S. C., Ray, D., Rhine, T., & Jones, L. (2005). The efficacy of play therapy with children: A meta-analytic review of treatment outcomes. *Professional Psychology: Research and Practice*, 36(4), 376–390. https://doi.org/10.1037/0735-7028.36.4.376

Daley, L., Miller, R., Bean, R., & Oka, M. (2018). Family systems play therapy: An integrated approach. *The American Journal of Family Therapy*, 46(5), 1–16. https://doi.org/10.1080/01926187.2019.1570386

Draper, K., Ritter, K. B., & Willingham, E. U. (2003). Sand tray group counseling with adolescents. *Journal for Specialists in Group Work*, 28(3), 244–260. https://doi.org/10.1177/0193392203252030

Felton, A. (2016). *Identity in the sand: The exploration of counselor educators'-in-training professional identity development through sandtray*, ProQuest Dissertations and Theses. Retrieved from https://books.google.com/books/about/Identity_in_the_Sand.html?id=51C9nQAACAAJ

Flahive, M. W., & Ray, D. (2007). Effect of group sandtray therapy with preadolescents. *The Journal for Specialists in Group Work*, 32(4), 362–382. https://doi.org/10.1080/01933920701476706

Garrett, M. (2015). 100+ ideas for directed sandtrays in counseling. *Journal of Education and Human Development*, 4(1), 45–50. https://doi.org/10.15640/jehd.v4n1a6

Gil, E. (2006). *Helping abused and traumatized children: Integrating directive and nondirective approaches*. New York: The Guilford Press.

Gil, E. (2015). *Play in family therapy* (2nd ed.). New York: Guilford.

Gomez, A. (2019). *The world of stories and symbols: EMDR, sandtray and play therapy*. Presented at the Illinois Association for Play Therapy Conference, Itasca, IL.

Goss, S., & Campbell, M. (2004). The value of sandplay as the therapeutic tool for school guidance counsellors. *Australian Journal of Guidance and Counselling*, 14(2), 211–220. https://doi.org/10.1017/S103729110000251x

Homeyer, L. E (2020). *Trauma-informed sandtray therapy for the play therapist*. Presented at the Illinois Association for Play Therapy Conference, Oak Park, IL.

Homeyer, L. E., & Sweeney, D. S. (2011). *Sandtray therapy: A practical manual* (2nd ed.). New York: Routledge.

Ivey, A. E., Ivey, M. B., & Zalaquett, C. P. (2017). *Intentional interviewing and counseling: Facilitating client development in a multicultural society* (9th ed.). Belmont, CA: Brooks/Cole.

James, L., & Martin, D. (2002). Sand tray and group therapy: Helping parents cope. *Journal for Specialists in Group Work, 27*(4), 390–405. https://doi.org/10.1080/714860201

Kao, S. C., & Landreth, G. L. (2001). Play therapy with Chinese children: Needed modifications. In G. L. Landreth (Ed.), *Innovations in play therapy: Issues, process, and special populations* (pp. 43–49). Brunner-Routledge.

Labovitz, B., & Goodwin, E. (2000). *Sandplay therapy: A step-by-step manual for psychotherapists of diverse orientations.* New York: W.W. Norton & Company.

Landreth, G. L. (2012). *Play therapy: The art of the relationship* (3rd ed.). Oxford: Routledge.

Lowenfeld, M. (1979). *Understanding children's sandplay: Lowenfeld's world technique.* London: Allen and Unwin.

Lowenfeld, M. (1991). *Play in childhood.* New York: Cambridge University Press.

Markos, P. A., Coker, J. K., & Jones, W. P. (2008). Play in supervision: Exploring the sandtray with beginning practicum students. *Journal of Creativity in Mental Health, 2*(3), 3–15.

McCurdy, K. G., & Owen, J. J. (2008). Using sandtray in Adlerian-based clinical supervision: An initial empirical analysis. *Journal of Individual Psychology, 64*(1).

Monakes, S., Garza, Y., Wiesner, V., & Watts, R. (2011). Implementing Alderian sand tray therapy with adult male substance abuse offenders: A phenomenological inquiry. *Journal of Addictions and Offender Counseling, 31*, 94–107. https://doi.org/10.1002/j.2161-1874.2011.tb00070.x

Oaklander, V. (2007). *Windows to our children: A gestalt therapy approach to children and adolescents.* Gouldsboro, ME: The Gestalt Journal Press.

Pappas, S. W. (2015). *A grounded theory study of expressive arts therapy used with elderly clients*, Unpublished doctoral dissertation. California Institute of Integral Studies.

Pettigrew, H. V., Raimondi, N., & McWey, L. M. (2016). Family sandplay: Strengthening the parent-child relationship. In C. F. Sori, L. L. Hecker, & M. E. Bachenberg (Eds.), *The therapist's notebook for children and adolescents: Homework, handouts, and activities for use in psychotherapy* (pp. 88–91). Routledge/Taylor & Francis Group.

Rae, R. (2013). *Sandtray: Playing to heal, recover, and grow.* Lanham, MA: Rowmand and Littlefield Publishing.

Sangganjanavanich, V. F., & Magnuson, S. (2011). Using sand trays and miniature figures to facilitate career decision making. *The Career Development Quarterly, 59*, 264–273. https://doi.org/10.1002/j.2161-0045.2011.tb00068.x

Sori, C. F., Maucieri, L., Bregar, C., & Kendrick, A. (2015). Training graduate students to work with children and families: A content analysis of students' perceptions of a child-focused course. *The Family Journal, 23*(4), 427–434.

Swank. J. M., & Jahn, S. A. B. (2017). Using sand tray to facilitate college students' career decision-making: A qualitative inquiry. *The Career Development Quarterly, 66*, 269–278. https://doi.org/10.1002/cdq.12148

Tornero, M. D. L. A., & Capella, C. (2017). Change during psychotherapy through sand play tray in children that have been sexually abused. *Frontiers in Psychology, 8*, 1–12. https://doi.org/10.3389/fpsyg.2017.00617

Turner, B. (2005). *The handbook of sandplay therapy.* Cloverdale, CA: Temenos Press.

Webber, J. M., & Mascari, J. B. (2008, March). Sand tray therapy and the healing process in trauma and grief counseling. Based on a program presented at the ACA Annual Conference & Exhibition, Honolulu, HI. Retrieved December 31, 2019, from http://counselingoutfitters.com/vistas/vistas08/Webber.htm

Yalom, I., & Leszca, M. (2005). *The theory and practice of group psychotherapy* (5th ed.). New York: Basic Books.

Zappacosta, J. D. (2013). Sandplay therapy: A way of rediscovering inner wisdom in the body and psyche. In S. Loue (Ed.), *Expressive therapies for sexual issues* (pp. 181–199). New York: Springer.

17 Mindfulness Techniques for Working With Children and Adolescents

Rebekah Byrd, Rebecca Milner, and Chad Luke
Rebecca Milner as guest contributor

Objectives

- Describe key terms from this chapter associated with mindfulness and its practice in counseling.
- Examine the many benefits of mindfulness and its application to working with children and adolescents.
- Understand the different ways in which mindfulness has been used in counseling.
- Examine different types of mindfulness practices.
- Understand multicultural implications of mindfulness.

Reflective Questions

- What are my current beliefs about mindfulness or being mindful?
- What does it mean to "be mindful" versus to "practice mindfulness"?
- How much is mindfulness currently a part of my personal life and my professional life?
- How might mindfulness be an important intervention to implement at my work setting?
- How can children and adolescents benefit from practicing mindfulness?
- How might I start to incorporate mindfulness in my own life?
- How might mindfulness benefit me as a counselor?
- What connections are there between mindfulness practice and multicultural counseling competence?

Self-Evaluation of Mindfulness

Before we get started discussing what mindfulness is, how to use it in counseling, and research supporting its use, let's see where you are personally in terms of mindfulness. The following is a common primary instrument for assessing mindfulness (Brown, Marquis, & Guiffrida, 2013). Take about 10 minutes to complete the questionnaire developed by Baer, Smith, Hopkins, Krietemeyer, and Toney (2006). Please answer honestly about your current level of mindfulness. This questionnaire is just for you.

Five Facet Mindfulness Questionnaire

Description

> This instrument is based on a factor analytic study of five independently developed mindfulness questionnaires. The analysis yielded five factors that appear to

represent elements of mindfulness as it is currently conceptualized. The five facets are observing, describing, acting with awareness, non-judging of inner experience, and non-reactivity to inner experience.

Please rate each of the following statements using the scale provided. Write the number in the blank that best describes your own opinion of what is generally true for you.

1	2	3	4	5
never or very rarely true	rarely true	sometimes true	often true	very often or always true

_____ 1. When I'm walking, I deliberately notice the sensations of my body moving.
_____ 2. I'm good at finding words to describe my feelings.
_____ 3. I criticize myself for having irrational or inappropriate emotions.
_____ 4. I perceive my feelings and emotions without having to react to them.
_____ 5. When I do things, my mind wanders off and I'm easily distracted.
_____ 6. When I take a shower or bath, I stay alert to the sensations of water on my body.
_____ 7. I can easily put my beliefs, opinions, and expectations into words.
_____ 8. I don't pay attention to what I'm doing because I'm daydreaming, worrying, or otherwise distracted.
_____ 9. I watch my feelings without getting lost in them.
_____ 10. I tell myself I shouldn't be feeling the way I'm feeling.
_____ 11. I notice how foods and drinks affect my thoughts, bodily sensations, and emotions.
_____ 12. It's hard for me to find the words to describe what I'm thinking.
_____ 13. I am easily distracted.
_____ 14. I believe some of my thoughts are abnormal or bad and I shouldn't think that way.
_____ 15. I pay attention to sensations, such as the wind in my hair or sun on my face.
_____ 16. I have trouble thinking of the right words to express how I feel about things.
_____ 17. I make judgments about whether my thoughts are good or bad.
_____ 18. I find it difficult to stay focused on what's happening in the present.
_____ 19. When I have distressing thoughts or images, I "step back" and am aware of the thought or image without getting taken over by it.
_____ 20. I pay attention to sounds, such as clocks ticking, birds chirping, or cars passing.
_____ 21. In difficult situations, I can pause without immediately reacting.
_____ 22. When I have a sensation in my body, it's difficult for me to describe it because I can't find the right words.
_____ 23. It seems I am "running on automatic" without much awareness of what I'm doing.
_____ 24. When I have distressing thoughts or images, I feel calm soon after.
_____ 25. I tell myself that I shouldn't be thinking the way I'm thinking.
_____ 26. I notice the smells and aromas of things.
_____ 27. Even when I'm feeling terribly upset, I can find a way to put it into words.
_____ 28. I rush through activities without being really attentive to them.

_____ 29. When I have distressing thoughts or images, I am able just to notice them without reacting.
_____ 30. I think some of my emotions are bad or inappropriate and I shouldn't feel them.
_____ 31. I notice visual elements in art or nature, such as colors, shapes, textures, or patterns of light and shadow.
_____ 32. My natural tendency is to put my experiences into words.
_____ 33. When I have distressing thoughts or images, I just notice them and let them go.
_____ 34. I do jobs or tasks automatically without being aware of what I'm doing.
_____ 35. When I have distressing thoughts or images, I judge myself as good or bad, depending what the thought/image is about.
_____ 36. I pay attention to how my emotions affect my thoughts and behavior.
_____ 37. I can usually describe how I feel at the moment in considerable detail.
_____ 38. I find myself doing things without paying attention.
_____ 39. I disapprove of myself when I have irrational ideas.

Scoring Information

Observe items: 1, 6, 11, 15, 20, 26, 31, 36
Describe items: 2, 7, 12R, 16R, 22R, 27, 32, 37
Act with awareness items: 5R, 8R, 13R, 18R, 23R, 28R, 34R, 38R
Nonjudge items: 3R, 10R, 14R, 17R, 25R, 30R, 35R, 39R
Nonreact items: 4, 9, 19, 21, 24, 29, 33

How did you do on the questionnaire? The higher your scores, the more mindful you are. This questionnaire is broken down into five subscales – were you higher on some than others? Can you identify some areas in which you could be more mindful? As you continue reading this chapter, think about how you may benefit from incorporating a mindfulness practice into your life.

What Is Mindfulness?

Mindfulness continues to gain momentum in counseling as an effective intervention for a variety of mental health concerns (Rasmussen & Pidgeon, 2010). Mindfulness can be understood as paying total attention to the present moment, with a non-judgmental awareness of the inner and outer experience as it changes from moment to moment (Kabat-Zinn, 2003). In short, it can be described as "paying attention in a particular way: on purpose, in the present moment, and nonjudgmentally" (Kabat-Zinn, 1994, p. 4). Mindfulness is a form of meditation, and meditation is

> any way in which we engage in (1) systemically regulating our attention and energy (2) thereby influencing and possibly transforming the quality of our experience (3) in the service of realizing the full range of our humanity and of (4) our relationships to others and the world.
>
> (Kabat-Zinn, 2016, p. 1).

Mindfulness can be a way of *being with* ourselves, much as we can *be with* clients. Mindfulness encourages the counselor to attend to the entirety of one's experience, as it unfolds, with acceptance, just as the counselor seeks to attend to, understand, and validate the unfolding experience of the client. This mindful attention creates potential for uncovering thoughts, affective responses, physiological reactions, and the meanings that we assign to these experiences that were previously out of awareness. This includes painful, difficult, embarrassing, or threatening feelings and thoughts. Rather than ignore or suppress distressing aspects of the self-experience, a mindful approach encourages the gentle opening to full, non-judgmental self-awareness, ultimately to relieve the distress and suffering (McCarney, Schulz, & Grey, 2012). Further, mindfulness is not focused on pathology and is instead a strengths-based intervention (Remple, 2012). In this chapter, we will review the current literature on mindfulness, beginning with an overview of mindfulness traditions in the counseling and psychological literature.

Introduction to Concepts and Terms

Known as "the heart" of Buddhist meditation, mindfulness is foundational to dharma teaching (Kabat-Zinn, 2003) and was made more accessible to Westerners by Vietnamese Zen master Thich Nhat Hanh (Brazier, 2013). The work of Thich Nhat Hanh inspired Jon Kabat-Zinn, a North American psychologist, who further secularized mindfulness, removed religious references, and applied mindfulness to everyday interactions and tasks (Brazier, 2013). In 1979, Kabat-Zinn developed Mindfulness-Based Stress Reduction (MBSR), a clinical intervention that uses daily meditation practice toward the development of self-regulatory skills and the treatment of physical and psychological disorders (Hart, Ivtzan, & Hart, 2013). MBSR has been the focus of numerous studies presenting evidence of its efficacy in promoting well-being and improving physical and mental health problems (Hart et al., 2013). In the decades following the introduction of MBSR, mindfulness principles have been integrated into several psychological interventions, including Mindfulness-Based Cognitive Therapy (MBCT), a form of MBSR; a Mindfulness-based Sex and Intimate Relationship (MSIR) protocol (Kocsis & Newbury-Helps, 2016); Dialectical Behavior Therapy (DBT); and Acceptance and Commitment Therapy (ACT) (Chiesa, Calati, & Serretti, 2011). The extent to which mindful meditation is incorporated into these and other mindful mediation practices varies significantly. Despite the differences in definitions and applications, mindfulness is "positively associated with numerous aspects of well-being, including happiness, positive emotions, life satisfaction, vitality, sense of autonomy, optimism, self-regulation, and several aspects of cognitive performance" (Hart et al., 2013, p. 453).

It is important to distinguish the concepts of trait versus state mindfulness. Research studies have investigated mindfulness as both a state and trait, with questionnaires developed to assess both concepts (Hart et al., 2013). Practice inducing and maintaining a mindful state has been shown to enhance trait mindfulness. Twelve qualities of consciousness have been identified as comprising the cognitive mode and practice of mindfulness:

> (a) nonjudging – neutral observation of the present, moment by moment; (b) nonstriving – not forcing things and not aiming to achieve an end; (c) acceptance – recognizing and embracing things as they are; (d) patience – letting things progress in their time and pace; (e) trust – having confidence in oneself and in the processes unfolding in life; (f) letting go – not holding on to thoughts, feelings, or experiences; (g) gentleness – a soft, considerate, and tender outlook; (h) generosity – giving without expecting returns; (i) empathy – understanding another person's state of mind; (j) gratitude – being thankful; (k) loving-kindness – caring for others, forgiving and loving unconditionally; and (l) openness – considering things anew, creating new possibilities.
>
> (Hart et al., 2013, p. 455)

Techniques and Practices

The practice of mindfulness meditation is centered on the monitoring and regulation of self-awareness by noticing all internal and external experiences with an interested, open, accepting attitude (Hart et al., 2013). Negative, painful, and depleting experiences are also observed with the mindset of curiosity and non-judgment, in contrast to avoidance, criticism, alteration, or evaluation (Hart et al., 2013). By becoming a detached observer, psychological space is created between the practitioner and the focus of attention (Brazier, 2013). Again, the attitude of warmth, curiosity, and openness frames this "dispassionate engagement" (Brazier, 2013, p. 134). Mindfulness practices may be unguided or guided. For example, Maex (2013) shared a brief guided mindfulness meditation used as part of MBSR. His example used his verbal instructions and the participants' focus on their breathing as "guides" during the activity. In this chapter, we will share some guided techniques for use with children and adolescents.

Sears, Tirch, and Denton (2011) distinguished mindfulness from hypnosis, relaxation techniques, and other forms of meditation, acknowledging similarities and noting important differences. Hypnosis aims to enact change by inducing a trance state and prompting the subconscious mind. While both hypnosis and mindfulness may result in relaxation, the practice of mindfulness involves intentional focus and presence without intention to alter or change one's perspective. Sears et al. summarized most relaxation and visualization techniques as being implemented toward the goal of stress reduction, noting the potential paradoxical effect of increasing stress and anxiety. They differentiated mindfulness from these techniques by highlighting that relaxation and visualization may offer "mini-vacations" from stressors, whereas mindfulness changes one's relationship to stressors. Using a mindfulness approach, you are not trying to clear your mind; rather, you are simply noticing what comes up, without judgment or attachment, and then watching it "float by" in your awareness without trying to change it. Hilt and Pollak (2012) explain that "mindfulness involves purposely focusing on mental events in a non-judgmental manner. It allows individuals to acknowledge negative emotions without pushing them away or becoming overwhelmed; rather, view them as passing mental events" (p. 1158). Further, increased awareness of thoughts and instincts through mindfulness practice "should result in decreased emotional reactivity and vulnerability" (Thomas & Gauntlet-Gilbert, 2008, p. 396). A proposed benefit of intentionally engaging in mindfulness practices can increase overall trait mindfulness; in other words, the more someone practices mindfulness skills, the more they can utilize these skills in their day-to-day life outside of an intentional meditation. Mindfulness is really about the totality of the inner and outer experience and not just managing negative emotions – it is about objective, non-judgmental awareness of all internal and external sensations, as well as affects and cognitions.

Mindfulness meditation is one of many forms of meditative practices, including absorption, loving-kindness, and goal-directed meditations (Sears et al., 2011). Similar to the body awareness techniques introduced later in this chapter, mindfulness can be used in conjunction with other meditative practices. These practices have different goals, such as the goal in loving-kindness to foster an ever-expanding sense of compassion and empathy for the self and all sentient beings (Sears et al., 2011). The goal of mindfulness meditation remains an intentional, open, curious observation of the mind as experiences emerge and disperse.

Those who practice mindfulness can cultivate moment-to-moment body awareness via an assortment of meditative venues including breathing, sitting, walking, standing, lying (Brazier, 2013), eating (Sears et al., 2011), and yoga (Douglass, 2011). Progressive muscle relaxation, despite its roots as a behavioral technique, is now sometimes presented as a body awareness mindfulness activity (Sears et al., 2011). During a progressive muscle relaxation, participants are instructed to hold and then release tension in muscle groups, usually working systematically up or down the body. Body scan is another body awareness technique that, similar to progressive muscle relaxation, utilizes systematic attentiveness to the body (an example exercise is outlined later in the chapter). Rather than tensing muscles, during a body scan, the practitioner notices "physical sensations until arriving at a unified awareness of the whole body" (Brown et al., 2013, p. 98). As with any of these body awareness techniques, the practice of mindfulness is ultimately about paying attention to all internal and external experiences as they unfold during the activity. Additional outcomes can include relaxation and consequences of heightened body awareness, such as reduced long-term muscle tension or food consumption.

Uses for Mindfulness in Counseling

Mindfulness practices and techniques have been integrated into counseling practice, counselor supervision, and counselor education. The following subsections provide an overview of the ways mindfulness has been implemented in each of these facets of professional counseling, and mention some of the early research findings that demonstrate this as a promising addition to the profession.

Clinical Practice

Mindfulness techniques are used to target a very diverse range of client populations by counselors from various theoretical orientations. Brown et al. (2013) suggested that counselors begin by providing clients with psychoeducation about the fundamentals of mindfulness, followed by the introduction of basic mindfulness practices, and leading to encouragement of integrating mindfulness in clients' daily lives. This can include both formal techniques, such as those previously described, and informal implementation into a variety of mundane, daily tasks like washing your hands or making the bed. The broad application of mindfulness techniques in clinical practice "has created a number of distinct therapies with considerable commonality" (McCarney et al., 2012, p. 281). As previously stated, the extent to which mindfulness is incorporated into clinical practices varies greatly, from infrequent, less structured interventions to formal clinical interventions such as MBSR, MBCT, MSIR, DBT, and ACT. The current literature explores the use of mindfulness in clinical practice and shows a trend of very positive treatment outcomes.

Mindfulness practices have been adapted for use in inpatient and outpatient settings with individuals, groups, intimate partners, parents, children, adolescents, and the elderly (Sears et al., 2011). There is an abundance of mindfulness studies in the literature examining the impact of mindfulness on a variety of mental health-related issues. "Research has consistently demonstrated that counseling interventions using mindfulness improve well-being and reduce psychopathology" (Brown et al., 2013, p. 96). Mindfulness has shown promise as an effective treatment for several clinical issues, including but not limited to depression and anxiety (Hofmann, Sawyer, Witt, & Oh, 2010; Khoury et al., 2013; Lo, Ng, & Chan, 2015; McCarney et al., 2012), stress reduction (Kabat-Zinn, 2003), trauma (Bernstein, Tanay, & Vujanovic, 2011), enhanced cognitive abilities (Chiesa et al., 2011), substance use disorders (Chiesa & Serretti, 2014), PTSD (Polusny et al., 2015), and chronic pain and opioid misuse (Garland & Black, 2014). The relaxation response elicited by mindfulness practices has been related to significant physical health benefits (Bhasin et al., 2013; Young, 2011), and brain imaging studies have provided fascinating evidence of changes in the brain after engaging in mindfulness practices (Bhasin et al., 2013; Brown & Jones, 2010; Hölzel et al., 2011; Kilpatrick et al., 2011; Laneri et al., 2016). Further, a perusal of the literature reveals an ever-expanding research base investigating new applications of mindfulness with variety of mental health problems and physical health problems. A few of the many topics under study include disordered eating (Douglass, 2011; Sears et al., 2011), psychosis (Khoury, Lecomte, Gaudiano, & Paquin, 2013), dissociation (Zerubavel & Messman-Moore, 2013), temporal brain injury (McHugh & Wood, 2013), memory care in older adults (Hyer, Scott, Lyles, Dhabliwala, & McKenzie, 2014), cancer (Zainal, Booth, & Huppert, 2013), Tourette syndrome and chronic tic disorder (Reese et al., 2015), HIV treatment side effects (Duncan et al., 2012), and fibromyalgia (Lauche, Cramer, Dobos, Langhorst, & Schmidt, 2013). With many additional topics already under study, there exists an ever-expanding swath of literature available for those interested.

The research on mindfulness covers a wide range of clinical applications; however, the field of mindfulness in mental health has substantial room to grow. This is especially true for research focused on the child and adolescent population. Researchers agree that mindfulness can be effectively integrated into widely used and supported counseling interventions, but they are not proposing that mindfulness procedures completely replace other counseling techniques (Brown et al., 2013). Mindfulness has also been found to be helpful when practiced by the counselors. One study investigated the predictive relationship between mindfulness and counseling, and found that mindfulness may be significant in the growth and development of essential counselor preparation outcomes such as empathy and attention (Greason & Cashwell, 2009). Another study found that mindfulness practice contributed growth and development in global counseling skills such as building rapport and accepting affect, as well as other more specific counseling skills such as paraphrasing, summarizing, and skillful questioning (Buser, Buser, Peterson, & Seraydarian, 2012). Further, a study evaluating the impact of mindfulness on client perceptions found a positive correlation between the counselor's personal mindfulness practice and "client perceptions of counselors' level of regard, unconditionality, and congruence as well as all aspects of the working alliance" (Greason & Welfare, 2013, p. 247).

Supervision

Mindfulness has been proposed as a useful technique to use in counselor supervision. Daniel, Borders, and Willse (2015) noted:

> For supervisees, mindfulness training is valuable in managing the stress and anxiety of their counseling programs, developing greater empathy and compassion, enhancing their therapeutic presence with clients, and increasing their counselor self-efficacy. For supervisors, more mindful supervisors form stronger supervisory relationships and achieve greater depth in their supervision sessions, at least from their perspective.
> (p. 229)

The capacity of mindfulness to promote compassion, empathy, attunement, and connectedness in relationships (Brown, Ryan, & Creswell, 2007) is posited to benefit the supervisee-supervisor relationship as it does the client-supervisee relationship (Sturm, Presbury, & Echterling, 2012). Increased awareness is also a proposed benefit, both for supervisees' understanding of clients (Safran, Muran, Stevens, & Rothman, 2008) and illuminating dynamics between the supervisor and supervisee (Sturm et al., 2012).

Drawing on work by Safran et al. (2008), Sears et al. (2011) suggested beginning supervision sessions with a brief mindfulness exercise "to clear away the mental distractions and get in touch with present-moment experience" (p. 141). This can help supervisees access and identify subtle reactions they may be having to clients which can then be used to inform the counseling relationship. Sturm et al. (2012) also emphasized the importance of here-and-now awareness, so that significant immediate information in the supervision room is not overlooked. This also creates the foundation for the beginner's mind approach (Safran et al., 2008; Sturm et al., 2012), a way of perception that is open to learning and discovery instead of being constricted by "known" and inflexible expertise. Sturm et al. (2012) posited that "in a truly mindful, and respectful, and intentional supervisory relationship, we too are using the relationship to nurture the never-ending beginner's mind of wonder, curiosity, and openness" (p. 10).

Sturm et al. (2012) suggested using mindfulness in triadic supervision, during which an observer brings to attention dynamics in the room that may otherwise go unnoticed or unacknowledged. One level of mindfulness involves the use of process comments, so that the supervisor and supervisee are working in the here and now, which can enhance the supervisee's ability to be mindful of present-moment experiences. The observer in the triadic model can add to the here-and-now dialogue, contributing process comments about dynamics that may be happening out of the awareness of the supervisor. This collaborative format invites both the supervisor and supervisee to bring their experiences in the relationship into awareness and speak about them, unlike models that do not require that level of mindfulness of the supervisor. Unlike Sears et al., this application requires both the supervisee and supervisor to utilize mindfulness strategies in the encounter. The use of creative and play-based supervision techniques can also invite learning about and from parallel processes taking place through the use of creative and play-based interventions used by the counselor with child and adolescent clients. Sturm et al. (2012) also suggested merging mindfulness into creative and play-based supervision techniques, adding intentional awareness and self-reflection during the session. Finally, Sturm et al. (2012) proposed a model of mindful supervision based on the ancient practice of mindfulness and metaphorically framed by the five elements of earth, wind, fire, air, and space, concepts used in Buddhism and Hinduism for a wide range of philosophies and learning. In the model, these elements serve as metaphors for guiding principles for the supervisory encounter framed by curiosity, openness, and wonder.

Andersson, King, and Lalande (2010) also presented a playful and explorative approach to supervision via mindfulness-based role-play (MBRP). This technique uses role-play of the client by supervisees with the supervisor initiating "dialogical mindfulness". Dialogical mindfulness "refers to the application of mindfulness in a dialogue between two people, either when they are both present or when one of them is only imagined to be present, as in a role-play" (Andersson et al., 2010, p. 288). All multisensory observations, cognitions, and movements that occurred during the session are invited into awareness during the MBRP supervision session. The aim of MBRP was to enhance awareness and supervisee empathic understanding of clients and, in this very small, exploratory pilot study, the results offered preliminary support for its effectiveness. Participants also reported a sense of safety and feeling less judged than in other supervisory experiences.

In a preceding work, Safran et al. (2008) offered awareness-oriented role-plays as a supervision technique to address relationship ruptures and impasses. During these role-plays, the counselor enacts a problematic part of a session, using what they remember from the impasse as a starting point and letting the reenactment creatively flow. The counselor may play both roles, or in group sessions, other members can take on the client and/or therapist roles. Deviation from the original session content is common and unimportant; the exploration and identification of "feelings that are unconsciously influencing the interaction with the client" (p. 147) are the goals. The supervision session concludes with group discussion to share final impressions and check in with the supervisee who presented the case. This technique engages all supervisees in the experiential learning process while reducing the "one-upmanship common to group supervision settings and case conferences" (p. 147). Additionally, it proposes to increase empathy for the counselor's dilemma, create a collaborative and trusting group environment, illuminate counseling dynamics previously operating out of the counselor's awareness, and facilitate the genuine self-exploration needed when feeling stuck. Present in each of the techniques described is the use of experiential methods to raise awareness.

Counselor Education

Once again congruent with the relative newness of mindfulness applications in the counseling research, there is limited research on mindfulness in counselor education. Unlike the broad uses of mindfulness in clinical settings previously described, the literature on applications of mindfulness in counselor education (and related fields) primarily focuses on self-care and self-compassion, which then leads to greater self-efficacy. As previously discussed briefly, mindfulness courses and interventions have been shown to enhance the overall well-being of counselors and therapists in training, and also positively impact their work with clients (Boellinghaus, Jones, & Hutton, 2014; Christopher & Maris, 2010; Schure, Christopher, & Christopher, 2008; Shin & Jin, 2010; Stafford-Brown & Pakenham, 2012). Specific outcomes included increased awareness, greater insight into counseling dynamics and process, greater acceptance, increased mental flexibility, improvement in interpersonal functioning, increased comfort with silence, increased empathy, and improved ability to tolerate and manage strong and threatening emotions (Christopher & Maris, 2010; Schure et al., 2008).

As the literature base for the benefits of mindfulness in clinical practice with clients grew, so did the notion that clinicians could also benefit from adoption of mindfulness practices for personal use (Rothaupt & Morgan, 2007). The emerging research noted previously offered early support for the potential benefits in counselor self-care and client focus. Further, Kabat-Zinn (2003) asserted that "some degree of understanding . . . through exposure and personal engagement in practice" (p. 149) is required for authentic teaching of mindfulness practices. In order to teach the clinical use of mindfulness, Rothaupt and Morgan (2007) suggested that counselor educators and supervisors also engage in the practice. In addition to the potential benefits of increased self-care and self-compassion, "mindfulness practice by counselors, supervisors, and counselor educators is both a prerequisite for incorporating mindfulness into clinical practice, as well as a good match for meeting clinicians' need for ongoing self-awareness" (Rothaupt & Morgan, 2007, p. 41).

Langer (1997) advocated for a mindful approach to learning, which is inherently characterized by "the continuous creation of new categories; openness to new information; and an implicit awareness of more than one perspective" (p. 4). The Langer school of thought on mindfulness has run parallel to Kabat-Zinn for more than 30 years and can be conceptualized as "creative mindfulness" (Hart et al., 2013, p. 461). Langer's approach to mindfulness typically involves focus on external stimuli and induction of a state of mindfulness for short, instructional interventions for use by healthy people in everyday settings (Hart et al., 2013). Langer (1997) challenged traditional instructional methods and described how to take a mindful perspective in teaching and learning, concepts that can certainly be applied to counselor training and preparation.

Additional noted characteristics of teaching mindfully include student empowerment, dynamic engagement via active experiential learning, attentiveness to student uniqueness including acknowledgment of abilities and differences, non-judgmental acceptance of student level of development, and using flexible teaching styles (Napoli & Bonifas, 2013). Similar themes are found in Langer, who also promoted the use of creativity and play. Of significant importance for counselors and the long-term impact of mindfulness is that when counselors in training learn mindfulness strategies, these can "help prevent burnout, compassion fatigue, and vicarious traumatization" (Christopher & Maris, 2010, p. 114).

Benefits of Mindfulness With Children and Adolescents

Current research on the benefits of mindfulness with children and adolescents is growing. Researchers have noted that mindfulness increases consideration for others and also increases levels of empathy (Abid, Irfan, & Naeem, 2017). Researchers suggest that mindfulness teaches children a way in which to manage or cope with stress, and that "mindfulness training may also change brain structure and function in a manner that helps to buffer against dysregulated stress reactivity" (Brown, 2015, p. 302). Hilt and Pollak (2012) discussed how mindfulness training can help children and adolescents out of a ruminative state. Mindfulness is also noted to have a negative association with bullying behaviors (Abid et al., 2017). Further,

> the currently available studies support the conclusion that mindfulness training is efficacious for some neurocognitive, psychosocial, and psychobiological outcomes, and that this training approach is feasible and acceptable for diverse groups of youth, with no published reports of treatment contraindications.
>
> (Brown, 2015, p. 303)

Counselors working with children and adolescents can use mindfulness techniques to increase impulse control and self-awareness and to reduce emotional reactivity to problematic and stressful events (Thomas & Gauntlet-Gilbert, 2008).

A recent systematic review of mindfulness-based interventions in schools with participants ranging from 11–14 years of age (including both qualitative and quantitative data) discussed many benefits from mindfulness-base interventions (McKeering & Hwang, 2018). These benefits include (Table 17.1):

Table 17.1 Benefits From Mindfulness-Based Interventions

Increased improvements in psychological well-being	Decrease in suicidal ideation
Increased improvements in cognitive well-being	Decrease in affective disturbances
Increased improvements in emotional well-being	Decrease in depression
Increase in working memory capacity	Decrease in negative coping
Increase in optimism	Decrease in negative affect
Increase in positive affect	Decrease in self-hostility
Increase in awareness	Decrease in rumination
Increase in prosocial functioning	Decrease in anxiety
Increase in attention	Decrease in reactivity
Increase in social and emotional competence	Decrease in stress
Increase in social and emotional regulation	Decrease in disruptive behaviors
Increase in positive classroom behavior	Decrease in worry
Increase in positive coping strategies	
Increase in concentration	
Increase in behavioral regulation	
Increase in on-task behavior (in classroom)	
Increase in positive classroom climate (positive classroom behavior)	

As you can see, mindfulness interventions are beneficial for children and adolescents in multiple settings. While we need continued research in the area of counseling, there is much research in existence supporting the efficacy of this important intervention. "The continuing adaptation of acceptance- and mindfulness-based interventions for child and adolescent populations presents a critical need for self-report and more objective methodologies to assess mindfulness skills and related processes such as psychological acceptance and self-compassion" (Greco, Baer, & Smith, 2011, p. 612).

Presented at the beginning of the chapter was a questionnaire for adults. Mindfulness assessments for children and adolescents also exist. Greco et al. (2011) developed the Child and Adolescent Mindfulness Measure (CAMM). This is a short, 10-item questionnaire on a five-point Likert scale that is useful in understanding an individual's level of mindfulness. This is a self-report measure and the child or adolescent (over the age of 9) reflects on how accurate and true the statement is for their life. Lower overall scores note lower levels of mindfulness and higher scores reflect higher mindfulness levels. This assessment can provide counselors with a valuable way to evaluate an individual's baseline levels or starting levels of mindfulness, and also can allow counselors to evaluate the effectiveness of mindfulness interventions and techniques used (Brown et al., 2013). Take a look at the CAMM in Table 17.2:

Table 17.2 Child and Adolescent Mindfulness Measure (CAMM)

	Never True	Rarely True	Sometimes True	Often True	Always True
1. I get upset with myself for having feelings that don't make sense.	0	1	2	3	4
2. At school, I walk from class to class without noticing what I'm doing.	0	1	2	3	4
3. I keep myself busy so I don't notice my thoughts or feelings.	0	1	2	3	4
4. I tell myself that I shouldn't feel the way I'm feeling.	0	1	2	3	4
5. I push away thoughts that I don't like.	0	1	2	3	4
6. It's hard for me to pay attention to only one thing at a time.	0	1	2	3	4
7. I get upset with myself for having certain thoughts.	0	1	2	3	4
8. I think about things that have happened in the past instead of thinking about things that are happening right now.	0	1	2	3	4
9. I think that some of my feelings are bad and that I shouldn't have them.	0	1	2	3	4
10. I stop myself from having feelings that I don't like.	0	1	2	3	4

We want to know more about what you think, how you feel, and what you do. **Read each sentence. Then, circle the number that reflects *how often* each sentence is true for you.**

CAMM: Scoring Instructions

First reverse all scores by changing 0 to 4, 1 to 3, 3 to 1, and 4 to 0 (2 stays unchanged). Then sum all items. Higher scores correspond to higher levels of mindfulness.

You've now read about the benefits of mindfulness practices for adults and children, and in the next section, we provide sample activities. Keep in mind that these activities can be modified for use with people of all ages, and can be done alone, with groups, and with families. All people can benefit from the stress reduction, physical and mental well-being, emotion regulation, focus, and psychological flexibility that regular mindfulness practice can foster. There has been increasing research in support of the relevance and benefit of mindfulness in parenting (see Corthorn & Milicic, 2016). This means that as counselors, teachers, parents, and other caregivers engage in mindfulness activities with young persons, they will increase their skills in facilitating the activities, as well as their personal mindfulness skills, while reaping the rewards of sustained mindfulness practice.

Types of Practice With Children and Adolescents

Many techniques and activities for practicing mindfulness with children and adolescents are readily available in books and on the internet. In the following subsections, we have listed a few for you to review. Please know that if the ones listed do not appeal to you, there are many more. Also keep in mind that what works for you and what works for others will differ, so we suggest utilizing a variety of types of activities and interventions to match the variety of learning needs and styles of young people.

Mindful Breathing

Mindful breathing is one of the most widely used mindfulness techniques. There are many ways to teach and practice this with children and adolescents. Some creative ways to teach kids about breathing can include blowing balloons, feathers, soap bubbles, or air bubbles in a drink with a straw, and other means for teaching about short breaths, long breaths, and deep belly breathing. Other activities for kids can include lying down to notice the stomach rising and even blowing a feather above while watching it float around as they practice different types of breathing. Following are two examples. The first example is adapted from Stewart and Braun's (2017) activity pack for teaching kids mindfulness strategies. These can be used for ages four and up. If using for older adolescents (and even adults) you may want to alter the language to reflect older ages.

Practice: Mindful Breathing – Waking Up Your Mind and Your Body

> Begin by sitting up mindfully with your back comfortably straight and the rest of your body in a relaxed position.
> When you wake up every morning, first notice your breath. Begin each day by taking three slow, gentle, and mindful breaths. Notice these breaths in your body and how they feel.
> Take a few breaths in and notice the air coming in your nose. How does it feel? Does that air feel soft? Breathe out and count to one.
> Take another breath in, and be aware of the air coming into your lungs. How does this feel? How do your lungs feel? How does your ribcage feel? Breathe out again and count to two.
> Take another breath in and feel the air growing and increasing in your body. Notice how your tummy moves. Breathe out and count to three.
> You are invited to repeat this twice. Notice the breath in your nose, lungs, and in your tummy. Continue to breath mindfully to wake up and prepare for the day ahead.

The following activity can be used to both teach about different types of breathing and as a mindful exercise. The activity was presented in a book written for caregivers in teaching their children mindfulness techniques (Roberts, 2018). This can be a helpful way to provide a visual and a playful way of learning about mindfulness. The following activity was modified from the original and can be used for a variety of ages.

Practice: Bubble Breathing

What Is Bubble Breathing?

Bubble breathing is a fun and different activity to use to help children and adolescents examine the breath and how it can help us feel good, calm, and relaxed.

How Does Bubble Breathing Help?

Bubble breathing provides children and adolescents (and adults) with a visual representation of different types of breath. It allows us to explore what it looks like to breath in different ways (deep, light, short, etc.). As you play together, you can learn about different types of breathing techniques and discover which ones help you feel calm, centered, and more relaxed.

What Do You Need for This Activity?

Bubble wands (you can use different ones with varying sizes, or just one will work to do this activity)
Liquid soap

Tips

For additional fun, you can try different colors or even use the hard-to-pop bubbles.
Anyone who has played with bubbles recently knows that they leave behind an often sticky and even slippery residue. This could be dangerous, depending on your location. This could also be very messy. Please keep this in mind when doing this so that all involved are safe. Adult supervision is suggested.

Simple Steps for Kids

Begin by swirling your wand around in the soap. Next, hold the wand close to your lips (but not too close – bubbles taste yucky!).
Next, blow air gently out as your notice your bubble getting bigger.
Try experimenting with different techniques – blowing a hard, sharp burst of air and blowing a slow, gentle, long, deep breath.
Which is better for making a bubble? Which doesn't work so well for the bubble to form?
Notice in your body how different breaths feel. What happens to your belly and your lungs when you make different types of breaths?
Notice what feels better, harder, easier. Do some breathing techniques feel different than others?
Notice which breath makes the biggest bubbles. Which make the smallest bubbles? Which don't make any bubbles?
Be sure to have fun doing this! Make as many bubbles as you would like.
Use this activity to feel good and relax. Become aware of how breathing can help you feel relaxed when you are angry, upset, frustrated, anxious, or mad. What

other times might you benefit from breathing exercises? You can do this technique any time you need to (and you don't need bubbles to do it!).

Body Scan

Body scan is another popular method of practicing mindfulness and is another technique that you can do anywhere with the time you have. Available online and in books are short body scans (anywhere from three minutes) all the way to long body scans (up to 60 minutes). These can be guided by listening to an audio recording or by reading a prepared script. The script listed below is taken from a book teaching caregivers mindful practices for working with ADHD. Bertin (2015) provided the following easy-to-follow version of a body scan.

Practice: Body Scan Meditation

> The instructions below are intended for your own use. When doing this meditation, remember that, as always, there's no need to strive to make anything happen. Simply observe what you find and practice letting things be for a while. When something uncomfortable grabs your attention, like pain or an itch, observe it first and see if it changes. If you find you need to address it, that's fine. Noticing that, pause and make an adjustment. In this way, the body scan provides an opportunity to practice responsiveness.
>
> Begin by lying down or sitting in a comfortable chair. If lying down, let your arms and legs relax and fall to the sides; if seated, find a balanced and stable position.
>
> Take a few moments to notice sensations of breathing.
>
> Draw your attention to your feet. Notice the pressure of your feet against the floor or bed, the temperature, comfort or discomfort, itches, or anything else. Expect your mind to wander, and when it does, return your attention to your feet without judging yourself or giving yourself a hard time. Let your attention rest with your feet in this way for a few minutes.
>
> Move attention to your lower legs. You might feel the touch of clothing or a blanket, and you might feel nothing at all. Sustain your attention without rigidly exhausting yourself. Whatever you experience, that's what you're supposed to feel right now.
>
> After a few minutes, shift attention to your upper legs, observing them in the same way. Pacing yourself, turn this same kind of attention to your abdomen and then your chest. Notice physical sensations, such as breathing, internal feelings, like hunger or fullness, and the resonance of any emotions – physical manifestations of happiness, sadness, tension, anger, feeling open or closed, and so on.
>
> Continue turning attention to the rest of your body in the same way, spending several minutes each on your back, then your hands, then your arms. Then bring attention to your neck and shoulders, releasing tension when you're able without fighting what remains.
>
> Finally, bring your attention to your face and head, noticing expressions and reflections of emotions that occur around your mouth and eyes in particular.
>
> Whether you feel relaxed or tense, restless or invigorated, pause before concluding. Take a moment of stillness, and then, with intention, chose when to move on with your day.
>
> (p. 189–190)

Mindful Eating

Another popular activity to practice mindfulness can be an activity involving mindful eating. We have done these with oranges, raisins, or by asking participants to bring a small snack food of their choice. Depending on food preferences and allergies, having options can be helpful. Depending on your food choice, you may need paper towels and a trashcan.

In this activity, mindfulness is practiced because you are paying attention to the present moment. During this mindful eating activity, either hand out the food and place it on the individual's (group, class, etc.) paper towel, or ask them to retrieve their selected food item, then go through the following directions in a slow, calm, and relaxed manner, allowing the child or adolescent time to be thoughtful about this process.

Practice: Mindful Eating Meditation

> We will practice being fully present in this current moment. Get comfortable in your chair and take a few deep breaths – feeling the breath go in and out of your nose, mouth, and body. Relax into your chair while you bring your attention to your _____ (food item).
> Begin by using your senses to notice the food in front of you. Use your eyes to examine the appearance. What does this item look like? Is it smooth? Rough? What shape is it? Does it look like something you want to eat?
> Next use your nose to examine this food. What does this smell like? Does it smell sweet? Sour?
> As you use your sense of smell and sight to examine this, notice your sense of touch. What does this food item fell like? It is soft? Hard? Squishy? Bumpy? Smooth? What do you notice about the shape?
> Does this food item make a sound?
> Next place the food item in your mouth – do not chew yet. Notice what happens when you begin to taste the food. How does it feel on your tongue? Does it feel rough? Smooth?
> Begin to chew the food and notice your taste buds. What does this taste like? Sweet? Salty? Sour? When you feel the urge, swallow the food. When doing so, notice how it feels on your throat. Are their sounds being made by your body during this time? How does your stomach feel?
> When you are finished, return your focus to your breathing and sit relaxed in your chair.
> The counselor can discuss what this activity was like with the child or adolescent. What was it like to pay such close attention to this particular food? What was it like to examine it and use all your senses, then place it in your mouth but not yet eat? Did distractions come up? How did you manage those?

Mindful Walking

Mindful walking is another way in which we can practice mindfulness in our everyday lives. This is a technique that can easily be used in multiple settings whether indoor or outdoor, and larger or more confined spaces. The adapted example as follows is based on Harper's Walking Meditation activity (2013) and can incorporate yoga mats for this practice. If using in an inpatient or school setting, you can also mark spaces or outlines on the floor with tape for children and adolescents to use instead of a mat.

Practice: Mindful Walking Meditation

When your child is able to practice walking meditation, this activity helps to ground and steady their beings. This activity is also one that your child can do at most any time and most any place when needed. This walking meditation allows the participant an opportunity to pay attention and tune in to his/her own mind, body, and spirit. This is a not a complex activity, and it provides much support and calming for the participant. Practicing in this way is important. The repetition involved in walking mindfully is soothing for many children and this also helps to quiet their bodies and their minds. It is suggested to do this with bare feet when possible.

> First, begin by noticing, connecting with, and becoming grounded to your feet in mountain pose. Stand up tall and proud, but in a comfortable manner, while focusing on being relaxed with your feet about hip-width apart.
> Check in with your shoulders to ensure that they are calm and relaxed. Take a few breaths in and out calmly.
> Begin to bring your attention to your feet and how they feel touching the ground (or mat). Shift or move your weight around just a bit to notice how it feels and see the difference when you move one way or another. Start to bend forward and now backward, and then move side to side with feet still on the ground. Now think about your balance – find the center where you feel balanced, comfortable, and strong.
> You will now begin to walk slowly. If using a mat, you can start to walk from one end to the other end and then turn around and walk back and forth. You can also do this outside on the grass somewhere quiet, comfortable, and safe. If not using a mat, you may walk a short way in the grass, dirt, or room you are in and then turn around and go back to where you began.
> Begin to notice what your feet feel when you walk. What sensations are you aware of? How do your heels feel? The arches of your feet? What sensations do you notice in all of your toes?
> Next, begin to become aware of what walking feels like to not just your feet, but to your whole body. What do you notice your legs doing when you walk? What about your knees and hips? What do you notice about your arms when walking? Your neck and head?
> Practice your walking for an amount of time that lets you become aware of your own unique walking pace, beat, and rhythm.
> While walking, if you notice that your mind starts to drift off, do not worry. Take notice of this and softly bring your attention back to your walking being.
> Nearing the end of your mindful walk, find the place you began and return to mountain pose. Deep breathe into this experience and mindful activity while thanking your body for supporting you in this way.

Follow-Up

> Children can use mindful walking as a technique for tuning in and bringing attention and awareness to the many sensations and feelings in their whole body. Walking is not the only activity that this mindful awareness can be used with – some examples include mindful biking, mindful swinging, and mindful swimming. Many children may be motivated by knowing that learning to pay attention to their body could strengthen their skills in sports and athletics, as well.

Challenges

Mindfulness is a skill – and like any skill, this can take time to achieve. When your child is struggling with this, it can help to invite them to walk in playful ways. Some examples include: How does it feel to walk on your heels? What does it feel like to walk in the grass on just your toes? Notice how different it can feel to walk using only the outside edges of your feet. By altering the activity and experience, we can enhance and increase the child's level of engagement and comfort of focusing in this new and different way. As the child develops and becomes more skilled and comfortable with this activity and with mindfulness in general, reduce the time spent on playful prompts and return to the focused mindful walking activity.

Daily Practice

When incorporated into a daily activity, mindful walking can help us stay grounded and in the present moment. This experience also helps us notice and connect with our bodies and sensations within. It can be helpful to give children a tangible goal such as using mindful walking when you first leave your home daily or setting a time aside where you walk mindfully to the car, the bus, or to your destination. This can have a positive impact on the remainder of your day.

Pebble Meditation

There are numerous benefits to spending time in nature (Sturm, Metz, & Oxford, 2013) and research on practicing mindfulness in nature has also been shown to be beneficial (Unsworth, Palicki, & Lustig, 2016). The following pebble meditation is adapted from Thich Nhat Hanh's (2010) work. For this activity, you can either have a container of pebbles already, or you can practice mindful walking and have children or adolescents walk outside to select four pebbles or rocks for this exercise. By using pebbles in this activity, it can provide a tangible element to mindfulness that can be grounding for many children and adolescents. They can also keep their pebbles in their pockets to have and remind them of mindfulness and self-compassion.

Practice: Pebble Meditation

In a circle on the floor with others, or seated by yourself, focus on your breathing as you take out your four pebbles and place them in front of you. Select one that represents a flower. Hold the pebble and repeat (out loud or in your mind):

(Breathing in) I envision myself as a flower.
(Breathing out) I feel renewed.

Repeat this three times and then return the pebble to the pile. Select another pebble to represent a mountain. Hold the pebble and repeat (out loud or in your mind):

(Breathing in) I envision myself as a mountain.
(Breathing out) I feel solid and strong.

Repeat this three times and then return the pebble to the pile. Select another pebble to represent still water. Hold the pebble and repeat (out loud or in your mind):

(Breathing in) I envision myself as still, calm water.
(Breathing out) I mirror things as are they actually are.

Repeat this three times and then return the pebble to the pile. Select the last pebble to represent space and freedom. Hold the pebble and repeat (out loud or in your mind):

(Breathing in) I envision myself as space.
(Breathing out) I feel light and free.

Repeat this also three times and then return the pebble to the pile.

You can also modify the words to fit the needs of the particular young persons with whom you are working. For example, additional versions could include:

I see myself as a tree. I feel firmly rooted and also flexible with the breeze.
I see myself as the sun. I feel energetic and give warmth to others.
I see myself as the rain. I feel cleansed and renewed.

Mindfulness Techniques in the School Setting

Mindfulness practices have been implemented in school settings with children and youth, and are gaining momentum. Table 17.1 notes many benefits for children and adolescents in the school setting. A study utilizing mindfulness interventions with teachers in a classroom setting "confirmed existing literature that training in mindfulness practice may be beneficial in strengthening relationships, reducing stress and anxiety and promoting inner well-being and social-emotional learning in youth" (Smith-Carrier et al., 2015, p. 376). A recent study examined mindfulness techniques such as mindful breathing and mindful walking on high school students enrolled in an alternative school setting (Wisner & Starzec, 2015). The study noted:

Intrapersonal benefits included themes of self-awareness and self-regulation (including cognition, emotions, and behavior). Interpersonal benefits included themes of building relationships (with peers, family members, and teachers) and learning to trust.

(p. 245)

Additionally, Carsley, Khoury, and Heath (2018) completed a recent meta-analysis that examined the effectiveness of mindfulness interventions and concluded that overall mindfulness techniques were beneficial. They also noted that interventions during late adolescence (ages 15–18), with a variety of mindfulness techniques and activities, had the largest effects on both the well-being and mental health of the participants. Even CNN has reported benefits to mindfulness in schools when a Baltimore elementary school decided to use meditation instead of traditional disciplinary referrals such as suspension and detention (Bloom, 2016). In addition to switching the detention room to a "Mindful Moment Room", the school starts and ends each school day with 15 minutes of guided meditation delivered via the school intercom and provides opportunities for students to practice yoga during and after school (Bloom, 2016).

Many of these school-based programs are creatively using interventions like the ones we have included in this chapter in individual, small group, and classroom settings. Other research conducted by Anand and Sharma (2014) found that a mindfulness-based stress reduction program significantly reduced both emotional and physiological indications of stress, stress from peer interactions, and academic stress while strengthening personal well-being and academic self-concept. "Mindful Schools (Fernando, 2013) is an innovative program that offers training to teachers, school counselors, and school psychologists to educate elementary, middle, and secondary school students in the practice of mindfulness techniques" (Echterling et al., 2016). Multiple programs teaching mindfulness to teachers – for personal use in addition to teaching to students – have also been developed and implemented (Frank, Reibel, Broderick, Cantrell, & Metz, 2013). Mindfulness practices in the schools have also benefited teachers in increased levels of compassion, enhancements in classroom organization, reduction of fatigue, and improvements on interactions with students (López-Hernáez, 2016). There are many research-based mindfulness programs that can be implemented in the schools. Of course, we understand that time is an issue in many settings, especially the school setting. It is important to note that many of these programs and practices with mindfulness do not take up much time at all to train, teach, or implement – but offer clear benefits that are long withstanding. Researchers Bostic et al. (2015) discussed many key points to implementing mindfulness in the school setting: "practicing mindfulness frequently, even for short intervals, results in positive health benefits and neurobiologic changes in reactivity to stress" (p. 245).

Multicultural Implications and Advocacy

Christopher and Maris (2010) noted that "the experience of mindfulness is universal and found in virtually all cultural, spiritual, and religious traditions" (p. 115). A recent meta-analysis examining studies specific to mindfulness-based interventions with youth with an anxiety disorder in five different countries (United States, Sri Lanka, Australia, Canada, and Kosovo) revealed that mindfulness interventions confirmed significant and positive effects on anxiety (Borquist-Conlon, Maynard, Brendel, & Farina, 2019). However, there remains a limitation in the current research related to mindfulness in clinical practice in the relative lack of studies that include ethnically diverse participants (Brown et al., 2013).

Fuchs, Lee, Roemer, and Orsillo (2013) conducted a meta-analysis of published and unpublished empirical studies that used mindfulness and acceptance-based treatments with individuals from non-dominant and/or marginalized backgrounds. Thirty-two studies met selection criteria and, although overall findings demonstrated support of these interventions with these populations, there is a need for continued and more rigorous research (Fuchs et al., 2013). Only one study in their meta-analysis included participants with a disability (intellectual disability). In a study on adolescents with autism that included a three-year follow-up, Singh et al. (2011a) described the benefits of using a mindfulness technique to self-manage their physical aggression. A similar study, including a four-year follow-up, also noted benefits of teaching a mindfulness technique to control aggressive behavior to adolescents with Asperger's (Singh et al., 2011b).

In spring 2013, the journal *Mindfulness* published a special issue that highlighted current innovative research on applications of mindfulness in the field of developmental disabilities. The 11 studies included in the special issue indicated positive results in a variety of applications – for example, improvements in stress reduction and psychological health in care providers for people with disabilities, significant aiding of smoking cessation for men with mild intellectual disabilities, decreased cortisol and anxiety levels in people with Williams Syndrome, and significant reductions in verbal and physical aggression by adults with developmental disabilities (Hastings & Manikam, 2013). These promising early results clearly warrant continued research on the diverse applications of mindfulness in the treatment, care, and interventions for people with developmental disabilities (Hastings & Manikam, 2013).

Napoli and Bonifas (2013) advocated for the use of mindfulness for clinicians to provide culturally competent services to Native Americans. They suggested that the mindful stance of openness and curiosity "contributes to greater cultural awareness and understanding"

(p. 200). In the article, the authors highlighted the congruence of mindfulness principles with Native American cultural values and practices. Examples include comfort with silence, respect for a different experience of time, acceptance without judgment (with a specific example about the use of humor), and attentiveness with interruption. This parallel of principles and concepts was presented in support for clinicians who work with Native Americans to develop a mindfulness practice in order to promote cultural competence with the population they serve. The authors also included a framework for teaching mindfulness practice that has four components:

1. empathically *acknowledging* what is occurring,
2. intentionally paying *attention* to one's physical and emotional reactions to what is occurring,
3. *accepting* one's reactions without judgment, and
4. taking *action* toward *change* based on associated insights.

(p. 204, italics in original)

Summary

Ongoing research continues to show the many benefits to mindfulness-based practices. We examined some of these benefits and discussed how mindfulness is an effective intervention for a variety of mental health concerns (Rasmussen & Pidgeon, 2010). Mindfulness has been shown to provide countless benefits to those who practice it, and has even shown to be beneficial for counselors in training, counselors, teachers, supervisors, and caregivers. You can practice mindfulness anywhere, at any time, and free of charge! We can also help children and adolescents do this. With many books, articles, programs, and open-access resources available, we hope you will try many different techniques and avenues to mindfulness. You are now more aware of your own levels of mindfulness, and we hope that you will cultivate your own personal mindfulness practice for yourself and for the benefit of the clients you serve.

Clinician's Corner

In my experience as a still green therapist, I have and am still discovering that mindfulness is much more than a coping skill that is facilitated or practiced during a counseling session in order to offer a client symptomatic relief. Mindfulness is a way of being, on par with Carl Rogers' philosophy. This is the art form I practice and try my best to emulate whatever counseling or life setting I am in, mobile crisis, individual counseling or youth center. One example is the youth program I work in, where I am the "just in case" counselor. It would be rare that I would whip out a prescribed meditation or mindfulness worksheet with these youth. Instead, you will find me playing Yu-Gi-Oh!, drinking strawberry milkshakes and shredding the guitar (horribly) with the kids who ask me to engage with them and spend time with them (except the milkshake is more for me than them). And I still consider this a form of mindfulness. My favorite definition of mindfulness is by Jon Kabat-Zinn (1994) and that is: "paying attention in a particular way: On purpose, in the present moment, and nonjudgementally to something in a particular way without judgment" (p. 4). I find that this is easier done with a partner by building on trust, hope, empathy, and belief. I am invited in to engage with them and help them attune to their present experience, as well as my own, and it is practiced very casually and naturally over a game of Scrabble or during a check-in after a skateboard session. I know this is not the standard form practiced in a traditional setting where you can facilitate a quiet, still space where this form of mindfulness can be achieved. I'm offering a way of being for these youth by modeling and offering up my own experience and engaging with them on their level. I am a catalyst of mindfulness that offers nonjudgment toward self and reminds them of their humanity, which is a great defender against shame, guilt, and low self-esteem.

Samantha Bishop, LPC/MHSP
Franklin, Tennessee

References

Abid, M., Irfan, M., & Naeem, F. (2017). Relationship between mindfulness and bullying behavior among school children: An exploratory study from Pakistan. *Journal of Postgraduate Medical Institute, 31*(1), 256–259.

Anand, U., & Sharma, M. P. (2014). Effectiveness of a mindfulness-based stress reduction program on stress and well-being in adolescents in a school setting. *Indian Journal of Positive Psychology, 5*(1), 17–22.

Andersson, L., King, R., & Lalande, L. (2010). Dialogical mindfulness in supervision role-play. *Counselling & Psychotherapy Research, 10*(4), 287–294. https://doi.org/10.1080/1433141003599500

Baer, R. A., Smith, G. T., Hopkins, J., Krietemeyer, J., & Toney, L. (2006). Using self-report assessment methods to explore facets of mindfulness. *Assessment, 13*, 27–45. https://doi.org/10.1177/1073191105283504

Bernstein, A., Tanay, G., & Vujanovic, A. A. (2011). Concurrent relations between mindful attention and awareness and psychopathology among trauma-exposed adults: Preliminary evidence of transdiagnostic resilience. *Journal of Cognitive Psychotherapy: An International Quarterly, 25*(2), 99–113. https://doi.org/10.1891/0889-8391.25.2.99

Bertin, M. (2015). *Mindful parenting for ADHD*. Oakland, CA: New Harbinger Publications, Inc.

Bhasin, M. K., Dusek, J. A., Chang, B.-H., Joseph, M. G., Denninger, J. W., Fricchione, G. L., Benson, H., & Libermann, T. A. (2013). Relaxation response induces temporal transcriptome changes in energy metabolism, insulin secretion and inflammatory pathways. *PLoS One, 8*(5), e62817. https://doi.org/10.1371/journal.pone.0062817

Bloom, D. (2016, November 8). *Instead of detention, these students get meditation*. Retrieved from www.cnn.com/2016/11/04/health/meditation-in-schools-baltimore/index.html

Boellinghaus, I., Jones, F. W., & Hutton, J. (2014). The role of mindfulness and loving-kindness meditation in cultivating self-compassion and other-focused concern in health care professionals. *Mindfulness, 5*(2), 129–138. https://doi.org/10.1007/s12671-012-0158-6

Borquist-Conlon, D. S., Maynard, B. R., Brendel, K. E., & Farina, A. S. J. (2019). Mindfulness-based interventions for youth with anxiety: A systematic review and meta-analysis. *Research on Social Work Practice, 29*(2), 195–205. https://doi.org/10.1177/1049731516684961

Bostic, J. Q., Nevarez, M. D., Potter, M. P., Prince, J. B., Benningfield, M. M., & Aguirre, B. A. (2015). Being present at school: Implementing mindfulness in schools. *Child and Adolescent Psychiatric Clinics of North America, 24*(2), 245–259. https://doi.org/10.1016/j.chc.2014.11.010

Brazier, C. (2013). Roots of mindfulness. *European Journal of Psychotherapy and Counselling, 15*(2), 127–138. https://doi.org/10.1080/13642537.2013.795336

Brown, A. P., Marquis, A., & Guiffrida, D. A. (2013). Mindfulness-based interventions in counseling. *Journal of Counseling and Development, 91*, 96–104. https://doi.org/10.1002/j.1556-6676.2013.00077.x

Brown, C. A., & Jones, A. K. (2010). Meditation experience predicts less negative appraisal of pain: Electrophysiological evidence for the involvement of anticipatory neural responses. *Pain, 150*, 428–438. https://doi.org/10.1016/j.pain.2010.04.017

Brown, D. S. (2015). Mindfulness training for children and adolescents: A state-of-the-science review. In K. W. Brown, J. D. Creswell, & R. M. Ryan (Eds.), *Handbook of mindfulness: Theory, research and practice*. New York: Guilford Press.

Brown, K. W., Ryan, R. M., & Creswell, J. D. (2007). Mindfulness: Theoretical foundations and evidence for its salutary effects. *Psychological Inquiry*, 18(4), 211–237. https://doi.org/10.1080/10478400701598298

Buser, T. J., Buser, J. K., Peterson, C. H., & Seraydarian, D. G. (2012). Influence of mindfulness practice on counseling skills development. *Journal of Counselor Preparation and Supervision*, 4(1), 20–26. https://doi.org/10.7729/41.0019

Carsley, D., Khoury, B., & Heath, N. L. (2018). Effectiveness of mindfulness interventions for mental health in schools: A comprehensive meta-analysis. *Mindfulness*, 9(3), 693–707. https://doi.org/10.1007/s12671-017-0839-2

Chiesa, A., Calati, R., & Serretti, A. (2011). Does mindfulness training improve cognitive abilities? A systematic review of neuropsychological findings. *Clinical Psychology Review*, 31(3), 449–464. https://doi.org/10.1016/j.cpr.2010.11.003

Chiesa, A., & Serretti, A. (2014). Are mindfulness-based interventions effective for substance use disorders? A systematic review of the evidence. *Substance Use & Misuse*, 49(5):492–512. doi:10.3109/10826084.2013.770027

Christopher, J. C., & Maris, J. A. (2010). Integrating mindfulness as self-care into counseling and psychotherapy training. *Counselling and Psychotherapy Research*, 10, 114–125. https://doi.org/10.1080/14733141003750285

Corthorn, C., & Milicic, N. (2016). Mindfulness and parenting: A correlational study of nonmeditating mothers of preschool children. *Journal of Child and Family Studies*, 25, 1672–1683. https://doi.org/10.1007/s10826-015-0319-z

Daniel, L., Borders, L. D., & Willse, J. (2015). The role of supervisors' and supervisees' mindfulness in clinical supervision. *Counselor Education and Supervision*, 54(3), 221–232. https://doi.org/10.1002/ceas.12015

Douglass, L. (2011). Thinking through the body: The conceptualization of yoga as therapy for individuals with eating disorders. *Eating Disorders*, 19, 83–96. https://doi.org/10.1080/10640266.2011.533607

Duncan, L. G., Moskowitz, J. T., Neilands, T. B., Dilworth, S. E., Hecht, F. M., & Johnson, M. O. (2012). Mindfulness-based stress reduction for HIV treatment side effects: A randomized, wait-list controlled trial. *Journal of Pain and Symptom Management*, 43(2), 161–171. https://doi.org/10.1016/j.jpainsymman.2011.04.007

Echterling, L. G., Presbury, J., Cowan, E., Staton, A. R., Sturm, D. C., Kielty, M., . . . Evans, W. F. (2016). *Thriving!: A manual for students in the helping professions*. Sage.

Fernando, R. (2013). *Sustainability of a mindfulness-based in-class intervention*. Retrieved from www.mindfulschools.org/pdf/Mindful-Schools-Study-Highlights.pdf

Frank, J. L., Reibel, D., Broderick, P., Cantrell, T., & Metz, S. (2013). The effectiveness of mindfulness-based stress reduction on educator stress and well-being: Results from a pilot study. *Mindfulness*, 4, https://doi.org/10.1007/s126710-013-0246-2

Fuchs, C., Lee, J. K., Roemer, L., & Orsillo, S. M. (2013). Using mindfulness- and acceptance-based treatments with clients from nondominant cultural and/or marginalized backgrounds: Clinical considerations, meta-analysis findings, and introduction to the special series: Clinical considerations in using acceptance- and mindfulness-based treatments with diverse populations. *Cognitive and Behavioral Practice*, 20(1), 1–12. https://doi.org/10.1016/j.cbpra.2011.12.004

Garland, E. L., & Black, D. S. (2014). Mindfulness for chronic pain and prescription opioid misuse: Novel mechanisms and unresolved issues. *Substance Use & Misuse*, 49(5), 608–611. https://doi.org/10.3109/10826084.2014.852801

Greason, P. B., & Cashwell, C. S. (2009). Mindfulness and counseling self-efficacy: The mediating role of attention and empathy. *Counselor Education and Supervision*, 49, 2–19. https://doi.org/10.1002/j.1556-6978.2009.tb00083.x

Greason, P. B., & Welfare, L. E. (2013). The impact of mindfulness and medication practice on client perceptions of common therapeutic factors. *Journal of Humanistic Counseling*, 52, 235–253. https://doi.org/10.1002/j.2161-1939.2013.00045.x

Greco, L. A., Baer, R. A., & Smith, G. T. (2011). Assessing mindfulness in children and adolescents: Development and validation of the child and adolescent mindfulness measure (CAMM). *Psychological Assessment*, 23(3), 606–614. https://doi.org/10.1037/a0022819

Hanh, T. N. (2010). *A pebble for your pocket: Mindful stories for children and grown-ups*. Berkeley, CA: Plum Blossom Books.

Harper, J. C. (2013). *Little flower yoga for kids: A yoga and mindfulness program to help your child improve attention and emotional balance*. Oakland, CA: New Harbinger Publications, Inc.

Hart, R., Ivtzan, I., & Hart, D. (2013). Mind the gap in mindfulness research: A comparative account of the leading schools of thought. *Review of General Psychology*, 17(4), 453–466. https://doi.org/10.1037/a0035212

Hastings, R. P., & Manikam, R. (2013). Mindfulness and acceptance in developmental disabilities: Introduction to the special issue. *Mindfulness*, 4, 85–88. https://doi.org/10.1007/s12671-013-0207-9

Hilt, L. M., & Pollak, S. D. (2012). Getting out of rumination: Comparison of three brief interventions in a sample of youth. *Journal of Abnormal Child Psychology*, 40(7), 1157–1165. https://doi.org/10.1007/s10802-012-9638-3

Hofmann, S. G., Sawyer, A. T., Witt, A. A., & Oh, D. (2010). The effect of mindfulness-based therapy on anxiety and depression: A meta-analytic review. *Journal of Consulting and Clinical Psychology*, 78(2), 169–183. https://doi.org/10.1037/a0018555

Hölzel, B. K., Carmody, J., Vangel, M., Congleton, C., Yerramsetti, S. M., Gard, T., & Lazar, S. W. (2011). Mindfulness practice leads to increases in regional brain gray matter density. *Psychiatry Research: Neuroimaging*, 191, 36–43. https://doi.org/10.1016/j.pscychresns.2010.08.006

Hyer, L., Scott, C., Lyles, J., Dhabliwala, J., & McKenzie, L. (2014). Memory intervention: The value of a clinical holistic program for older adults with memory impairments. *Aging & Mental Health*, 18(2), 169–178. https://doi.org/10.1080/13607863.2013.819832

Kabat-Zinn, J. (1994). *Wherever you go, there you are: Mindfulness meditation in everyday life*. New York: Hyperion.

Kabat-Zinn, J. (2003). Mindfulness-based interventions in context: Past, present, and future. *Clinical Psychology: Science and Practice*, 10(2), 144–156. https://doi.org/10.1093/clipsy/bpg016

Kabat-Zinn, J. (2016). *Mindfulness for beginners: Reclaiming the present moment-and your life*. Boulder, CO: Sounds True, Inc.

Khoury, B., Lecomte, T., Fortin, G., Masse, M., Therien, P., Bouchard, V., . . . Hofmann, S. G. (2013). Mindfulness-based therapy: A comprehensive meta-analysis. *Clinical Psychology Review*, 33(6), 763–771. https://doi.org/10.1016/j.cpr.2013.05.005

Khoury, B., Lecomte, T., Gaudiano, B. A., & Paquin, K. (2013). Mindfulness interventions for psychosis: A meta-analysis. *Schizophrenia Research*, 150(1), 176–184. https://doi.org/10.1016/j.schres.2013.07.055

Kilpatrick, L. A., Suyenobu, B. Y., Smith, S. R., Bueller, J. A., Goodman, T., Creswell, J. D., . . . Naliboff, B. D. (2011). Impact of mindfulness-based stress reduction training on intrinsic brain connectivity. *NeuroImage*, 56, 290–298. https://doi.org/10.1016/j.neuroimage.2011.02.034

Kocsis, A., & Newbury-Helps, J. (2016). Mindfulness in sex therapy and intimate relationships (MSIR): Clinical protocol and theory development. *Mindfulness*, 7, 690–699. https://doi.org/10.1007/s12671-016-0506-z

Laneri, D., Schuster, V., Dietsche1, B., Jansen, A., Ott, U., & Sommer, J. (2016). Effects of long-term mindfulness meditation on brain's white matter microstructure and its aging. *Frontiers in Aging Neuroscience*, 7(254), 1–12. https://doi.org/10.3389/fnagi.2015.00254

Langer, E. (1997). *The power of mindful learning*. Reading, MA: Addison-Wesley.

Lauche, R., Cramer, H., Dobos, G., Langhorst, J., & Schmidt, S. (2013). A systematic review and meta-analysis of mindfulness-based stress reduction for the fibromyalgia syndrome. *Journal of Psychosomatic Research*, 75(6), 500–510. https://doi.org/10.1016/j.jpsychores.2013.10.010

Lo, H. H. M., Ng, S. M., & Chan, C. L. W. (2015). Evaluating compassion-mindfulness therapy for recurrent anxiety and depression: A randomized control trial. *Research on Social Work Practice*, 25(6), 715–725. https://doi.org/10.1177/1049731514537686

López-Hernáez, L. (2016). Mindfulness techniques in the schools: Academic and personal development of is participants. *Revista Española De Orientación y Psicopedagogia*, 27(1), 134–146.

Maex, E. (2013). Therapeutic applications of mindfulness: Mindfulness-based stress reduction. In A. Fraser (Ed.), *The healing power of meditation: Leading experts on Buddhism, psychology, and* medicine explore the health benefits of contemplative practice. Boston, MA: Shambhala Publications.

McCarney, R., Schulz, J., & Grey, A. (2012). Effectiveness of mindfulness-based therapies in reducing symptoms of depression: A meta-analysis. *European Journal of Psychotherapy and Counselling*, *14*(3), 279–299. Retrieved from www.tandfonline.com/doi/pdf/10.1080/13642537.2012.713186

McHugh, L., & Wood, R. (2013). Stimulus over-selectivity in temporal brain injury: Mindfulness as a potential intervention. *Brain Injury*, *27*(13–14), 1595–1599. https://doi.org/10.3109/02699052.2013.834379

McKeering, P., & Hwang, Y. S. (2018). A systematic review of mindfulness-based school interventions with early adolescents. *Mindfulness*, *10*(4), 593–610. https://doi.org/10.1007/s12671-018-0998-9

Napoli, M., & Bonifas, R. (2013). Becoming culturally competent: Mindful engagement with American Indian clients. *Journal of Ethnic & Cultural Diversity in Social Work: Innovation in Theory, Research & Practice*, *22*(3–4), 198–212. https://doi.org/10.1080/15313204.2013.843121

Polusny, M. A., Erbes, C. R., Thuras, P., Moran, A., Lamberty, G. J., Collines, R. C., . . . Lim, K. O. (2015). Mindfulness-based stress reduction for posttraumatic stress disorder among veterans: A randomized clinical trial. *JAMA*, *314*(5), 456–465. https://doi.org/10.1001/jama.2015.8361

Rasmussen, M. K., & Pidgeon, A. M. (2010). The direct and indirect benefits of dispositional mindfulness on self-esteem and anxiety. *Anxiety, Stress, & Coping*, *24*(2), 227–233. https://doi.org/10.1080/10615806.2010.515681

Reese, H. E., Vallejo, Z., Rasmussen, J., Crowe, K., Rosenfield, E., & Wilhelm, S. (2015). Mindfulness-based stress reduction for Tourette syndrome and chronic tic disorder: A pilot study. *Journal of Psychosomatic Research*, *78*(3), 293–298. https://doi.org/10.1016/j.jpsychores.2014.08.001

Remple, K. D. (2012). Mindfulness for children and youth: A review of the literature with an argument for school-based implementation. *Canadian Journal of Counselling and Psychotherapy*, *46*(3), 201–220.

Roberts, L. (2018). *Teach your child meditation: 70 fun and easy ways to help kids de-stress and chill out*. Toronto, Ontario: Sterling Publishing Co., Inc.

Rothaupt, J. W., & Morgan, M. M. (2007). Counselors' and counselor educators' practice of mindfulness: A qualitative inquiry. *Counseling and Values*, *52*(1), 40–54. https://doi.org/10.1002/j.2161-007X.2007.tb00086.x

Safran, J. D., Muran, J. C., Stevens, C., & Rothman, M. (2008). A relational approach to supervision: Addressing ruptures in the alliance. In C. A. Falender & E. P. Shafranske (Eds.), *Casebook for clinical supervision: A competency-based approach* (pp. 137–157). Washington, DC: American Psychological Association. https://doi.org/10.1037/11792-007

Schure, M. B., Christopher, J., & Christopher, S. (2008). Mind-body medicine and the art of self-care: Teaching mindfulness to counseling students through yoga, meditation, and Qigong. *Journal of Counseling & Development*, *86*(1), 47–56. https://doi.org/10.1002/j.1556-6678.2008.tb00625.x

Sears, R. W., Tirch, D. D., & Denton, R. B. (2011). *Mindfulness in clinical practice*. Sarasota, FL: Professional Resource Press/Professional Resource Exchange.

Shin, T.-B., & Jin, S.-R. (2010). The qualitative study of "mindfulness group" toward the self-care and counseling practice of counselor interns. *Bulletin of Educational Psychology*, *42*(1), 163–184.

Singh, N. N., Lancioni, G. E., Manikam, R., Winton, A. S. W., Singh, A. N. A., Singh, J., & Singh, A. D. A. (2011a). A mindfulness-based strategy for self-management of aggressive behavior in adolescents with autism. *Research in Autism Spectrum Disorders*, *5*, 1153–1158. https://doi.org/10.1016/j.rasd.2010.12.012

Singh, N. N., Lancioni, G. E., Singh, A. D. A., Winton, A. S. W., Sing, A. N. A., & Singh, J. (2011b). Adolescents with Asperger syndrome can use mindfulness-based strategies to control their aggressive behavior. *Research in Autism Spectrum Disorders*, *5*, 1103–1109. https://doi.org/10.1016/j.rasd.2010.12.006

Smith-Carrier, T., Koffler, T., Mishna, F., Wallwork, A., Daciuk, J., & Zeger, J. (2015). Putting your mind at ease: Findings from the mindfulness ambassador council programme in Toronto area schools. *Journal of Children's Services*, 10(4), 376–392. https://doi.org/10.1108/JCS-10-2014-0046

Stafford-Brown, J., & Pakenham, K. I. (2012). The effectiveness of an ACT informed intervention for managing stress and improving therapist qualities in clinical psychology trainees. *Journal of Clinical Psychology*, 68(6), 592–613. https://doi.org/10.1002/jclp.21844

Stewart, W., & Braun, M. (2017). *Mindful kids: 50 mindfulness activities for kindness, focus and calm.* Cambridge, MA: Barefoot Books.

Sturm, D. C., Metz, A., & Oxford, R. L. (2013). Toward an ecological self amid an empathy deficit. In J. Lin, R. L. Oxford, & E. J. Brantmeier (Eds.), *ReEnvisioning higher education: Embodied pathways to wisdom and social transformation* (pp. 231–248). Charlotte, NC: Information Age Publishing, Inc.

Sturm, D. C., Presbury, J., & Echterling, L. G. (2012). The elements: A model of mindful supervision. *Journal of Creativity in Mental Health*, 7(3), 222–232. https://doi.org/10.1080/15401383.2012.711718

Thomas, M., & Gauntlet-Gilbert, J. (2008). Mindfulness with children and adolescents: Effective clinical application. *Clinical Child Psychology and Psychiatry*, 13(3), 395–407. https://doi.org/10.1177/1359104508090603

Unsworth, S., Palicki, S.-K., & Lustig, J. (2016). The impact of mindful meditation in nature on self-nature interconnectedness. *Mindfulness*, 7(5), 1052–1061. https://doi.org/10.1007/s12671-016-0542-8

Wisner, B. L., & Starzec, J. J. (2015). The process of personal transformation for adolescents practicing mindfulness skills in an alternative school setting. *Child and Adolescent Social Work Journal*, 33(3), 245–257. https://doi.org/10.1007/s10560-015-0418-0

Young, S. N. (2011). Biologic effects of mindfulness meditation: Growing insights into neurobiologic aspects of the prevention of depression. *Journal of Psychiatry and Neuroscience*, 36(2), 75–77. doi:10.1503/jpn.110010

Zainal, N. Z., Booth, S., & Huppert, F. A. (2013). The efficacy of mindfulness-based stress reduction on mental health of breast cancer patients: A meta-analysis. *Psycho-Oncology*, 22(7), 1457–1465. https://doi.org/10/1002/pon.3171

Zerubavel, N., & Messman-Moore, T. L. (2013). Staying present: Incorporating mindfulness into therapy for dissociation. *Mindfulness*, No Pagination Specified. https://doi.org/10.1007/s12671-013-0261-3

18 Expressive and Experiential Techniques

Rebekah Byrd, Sybil Smith, and Chad Luke
Sybil Smith as guest contributor

Objectives

- Describe key methods from this chapter associated with expressive and experiential techniques in counseling.
- Examine the many benefits of using expressive and experiential techniques with children and adolescents.
- Understand the different clients and settings for which expressive and experiential techniques can be utilized.
- Examine how different types of alternative and complementary modalities can be used with children and adolescents in counseling.
- Understand a few of the many creative approaches for reaching children and adolescents.

Reflective Questions

- What is my current knowledge level about expressive and experiential techniques in counseling?
- What are the many benefits of using expressive and experiential techniques in counseling?
- How will I use expressive and experiential techniques in counseling?
- What are the many benefits to using alternative and complementary modalities in counseling?
- What are my current beliefs about using expressive and experiential techniques and alternative and complementary modalities in counseling?
- What can I do to further my knowledge, awareness, and skills in these important areas of both expressive and experiential techniques, and alternative and complementary modalities?

The goal of this chapter is to provide you with many therapeutic techniques to use with children and adolescents. We hope that by giving you some information on many different modalities, you will look further into techniques that can be successful with children and adolescents. We understand that entire books are written on each of these topics, and hope you do much more reading and training beyond this text. As with any therapeutic approach, there is much training in the history, foundations, and theory involved. Most of these therapeutic approaches require specific and rigorous training to become registered or certified in an area. Perhaps you will become interested in some areas to further your training. We also want to balance the specific distinctions of therapy with using aspects for working with children and adolescents. One does not need to have a degree in art therapy to use art media in counseling. However, you are not an art therapist without this degree. We hope that this makes sense and that this chapter provides you with both areas for further training and offers ideas for incorporating aspects of art, play, drama, etc., into creative work with children and adolescents. The purpose of this chapter is not to chronologically explore the history of the discipline, although we believe understanding origins are important. We want to help you find your niche and understand the many approaches that exist to working with children and adolescents so as to fit the approach with the child, and not vice versa.

Adventure/Wilderness/Outdoor Therapy

Adventure/wilderness/outdoor therapy is defined as "the prescriptive use of Adventure experiences provided by mental health professionals, often conducted in natural settings that kinesthetically engage clients on cognitive, affective, and behavioral levels" (Gass, Russell, & Gillis, 2012, p. 1). Gass et al. discuss the many aspects of adventure therapy and note the evolution of the field. Its roots are found in the Outward Bound model and therapeutic camping methods which use wilderness to challenge individuals to build self-esteem, a stronger sense of self, and self-compassion. The field strives for a unified approach, but you may see it written in many ways. If an author specifically delineates, we will use the term provided by that author; if not, we will use the terms combined.

Gass (1993) discussed key elements that provide the foundation for adventure therapy: (a) action-centered therapy; (b) unfamiliar environment; (c) climate of change; (d) assessment capabilities; (e) small group development and caring community; (f) focus of successful behaviors (strengths) rather than dysfunctional behaviors (deficits); and (g) altered role of the therapist (as cited in Gass et al., 2012). Aspiro (2020), a wilderness therapy provider, discussed that the goals of wilderness therapy as being: "1. Therapeutic assessment, 2. Intervention and treatment of problem behaviors, 3. Safety [and] stabilization, and 4. Lasting change" (para 6). Further, they noted that wilderness-based approaches characteristically involve the following:

1. A Radical Change of Environment – Wilderness therapy immerses participants in the natural environment as part of the therapeutic process to evoke introspection and facilitate change.
2. Challenge Experiences – facilitate self-discovery and personal growth by means of challenging experiences. These experiences teach psychological concepts like flow, grit, growth mindset, and self-efficacy (more on these below).
3. Healthy Relationship Development – living in peer groups provides opportunities for clients to practice healthy relationships.
4. Therapy – individual and group therapy sessions facilitate clients' individual improvements and use group dynamics as a foundation to improve interpersonal effectiveness in families & relationships.
5. Teaching Healthy Coping Strategies – programming and educational curricula focused on developing mastery & skills. The wilderness staff guide and model the application of skills and introspection for students.

(para 6)

Types of Adventure/Wilderness/Outdoor Therapy

As noted, adventure therapy has roots in Outward Bound and other therapeutic camping approaches (summer camps, etc.). Outward Bound, adventure-based therapeutic approaches, wilderness therapy camps, ropes courses, outdoor therapy day treatment facilities, and more are all different types of adventure/wilderness/outdoor therapy programs. These programs can be day treatment, set times weekly, or intensive treatment programs (ranging from days to many weeks), and can be used for individual, group, and family work, depending on the setting.

Uses for Adventure/Wilderness/Outdoor Therapy

Research supports the use of wilderness therapy in improving "overall functioning of adolescent clients, as well as specifically reducing symptoms of distress related to interpersonal and mental health challenges" (Norton et al., 2014, p. 48). Lewis (2013) noted a decrease in disruptive behavior disorders and improvement with substance use, which were maintained over a 12-month period. Russell (2008) also presented a case study that noted reduced substance use. Clem, Smith, and Richards (2012) found improved group unity, group cohesion, increased self-confidence, and interpersonal growth as a result of wilderness/adventure programming. Further, Tucker, Javorski, Tracy, and Beale (2013) studied 1,135 youth and found that participants in adventure therapy had significant reductions in problem severity, with larger reductions found among the female and African American client populations. A recent meta-analysis found medium effect sizes for characteristics such as self-esteem, personal effectiveness, behavioral observations, locus of control, clinical measures, and interpersonal measures for adolescents receiving wilderness therapy (Bettmann, Gillis, Speelman, Parry, & Case, 2016). Additionally, a qualitative study conducted in 2018 found that adolescents who participated in wilderness therapy reported experiencing increases in self-worth, self-efficacy, self-confidence, social skills, and coping skills (Conlon, Wilson, Gaffney, & Stoker, 2018).

Further, Aspiro (2020) listed many challenges that wilderness therapy has been successful in treating (Table 18.1). The following list appears on their website (https://aspiroadventure.com/wilderness-therapy-programs/).

Table 18.1 Challenges That Wilderness Therapy Is Successful in Treating

ADD/ADHD	Failing college
Addiction	Lack of motivation
Adoption issues	Learning disabilities
Anger issues	Mood disorders
Anxiety	Nonverbal Learning Disorder (NLD)
Asperger's syndrome	Oppositional Defendant Disorder (ODD)
At-risk youth/risky behaviors	Personality disorders
Autism	Post-Traumatic Stress Disorder (PTSD)
Behavior issues	Relational issues
Body image issues	Risky/harmful sexual behaviors
Cutting and self-harm	School avoidance of failure
Divorce conflict	Self-esteem issues
Depression	Traumatic brain injuries (TBI)
Substance abuse	Troubled youth
Eating disorders that don't require medical intervention	Gender identity struggles
Female identity empowerment	Suicidal ideation

Music Therapy

As defined by the American Music Therapy Association (AMTA, 2020), "music therapy is the clinical and evidence-based use of music interventions to accomplish individualized goals within a therapeutic relationship by a credentialed professional who has completed an approved music therapy program" (para 1). The earliest known reference to the term "music therapy" appeared in the late 1700s, and the first recorded music therapy intervention was in the 1800s. It became a fully accepted model of therapy and healing in the 1940s with the formation of the profession as an organization (AMTA, 2020).

Music therapy uses specific music interventions, both instrumental and vocal, to facilitate changes that are non-musical in nature. The triad of the client, music therapist, and music creates a unique therapeutic environment for healing. With music's ability to activate the nervous system, both hemispheres of the brain, and the sensory system so fully, it becomes an adaptable medium for a variety of struggles each client faces. These therapeutic music experiences help the client transfer their healing from the session into their daily life (AMTA, 2020).

The aim of music therapy is to heal or develop the emotional, physical, cognitive, and social needs of the individual, through individual or group music interventions. When words are not sufficient, music helps to bypass the verbal barrier, fills in the gap, and provides a soundscape for the client to work on developing communication, self-regulation, coping skills, emotional expression, social interactions, attention and focus, self-esteem, anxiety, increased motivation, and safe release of emotional material (Bodner et al., 2007).

The transformational elements of music therapy are: self-reflection, self-regulation, play, socialization, intrinsic motivation, and multimodal delivery.

- Music helps clients self-reflect on their thoughts, feelings, and values to develop a clearer sense of self-mastery and opportunity for self-expression (Montello & Coons, 1998).
- Self-regulation happens as a result of the intrinsic nature of music engaging the whole brain and nervous system. This sensory engagement releases muscle tension and naturally decreases activation in the nervous system (Field et al., 1998).
- Play is a necessary part of the developing nervous system, and music creates the experience of play for both children and adults, which helps grow developmental tasks and skill building (AMTA, 2006).
- Socialization naturally occurs with group music making or through collective listening experiences and gives the opportunity for self-expression, reduced social isolation, differentiation, and cohesion (Tang, Yao, & Zheng, 1994).
- Motivation for sustained attention and participation can be a barrier for many clients. Music transcends this barrier, helping clients stay engaged longer and more fully through their healing process (Ross et al., 2008).
- Music provides for a multimodal delivery, using instruments, the voice, the physical body, and/or receptive skills, making music therapy an adaptive model for implementation (AMTA, 2006).

Each element can be layered for a more simple or complex experience for the client, meeting their individual emotional, developmental, kinesthetic, sensory, or physical needs.

Types of Music Therapy

There are two main types of music therapy: expressive and receptive. Expressive music therapy involves active music making. Interventions include songwriting, improvisation, music re-creation, drum circles, entrainment, and motor movement work for communication and skill building. Receptive music therapy is the passive form of receiving, but not creating, sound. These interventions include lyric analysis, music listening, guided imagery, music for relaxation, emotion matching and storytelling, and music autobiography.

Using a combination of expressive and receptive music therapy categories, there are six defined theoretical branches within the music therapy field. Each of these branches are empirically proven as evidence-based practices. Music therapists who use these methodologies go through additional training to become specialists. The six branches are:

1. *The Bonny Method of Guided Imagery and Music:* music and imagery used to explore and heal the inner psychological world of the client
2. *Dalcroze Eurhythmics:* skill building through rhythmic movement and sound
3. *Kodály:* use of a base rhythm and sound to improve perceptual function, conceptual formation, and motor skills
4. *Neurologic Music Therapy:* uses music to create positive neurologic changes in the brain
5. *Nordoff-Robbins:* spontaneous music creation to create meaning and connection in children with disabilities
6. *Orf-Schulwerk:* uses music to improve learning ability and communication skills in children of all abilities

Uses for Music Therapy

Music therapists adapt to a wide variety of settings, and are self-employed or facility-employed to provide assessment, consultation, or treatment services from prenatal through the end of life. The individual and group settings include inpatient and outpatient treatment centers, juvenile detention facilities, early intervention programs, schools, mental health clinics, rehabilitation facilities, wellness programs, nursing homes, senior centers, group homes, day care treatment centers, medical and psychiatric hospitals, substance abuse programs, hospice and bereavement programs, and forensic facilities.

Of note, music therapy is also used as a social intervention and crisis support service. In one example described by Loewy and Frisch-Hara (2007), the AMTA sponsored the NYC 9/11 Music Therapy Relief Project, composed of 20 community programs and 33 music therapists throughout the city to provide mental health support to the residents, workers, nurses, and teachers for nine months after the tragedy.

Yoga Therapy

Yoga as a spiritual practice has been around for thousands of years in India. It made an appearance in the United States in the early 1800s as a spiritual practice, and then began to be recognized as a tool for healing and therapy in the 1980s. The first mention of yoga as therapy was in an article written by Dr. Dean Ornish, who showed that a healthy lifestyle, including a yoga practice, could reverse heart disease. The medical field's acceptance of this practice as therapy came in 1990, with the acceptance of yoga therapy on insurance coverage (GoodTherapy, 2017).

According to the International Association of Yoga Therapists (IAYT), yoga therapy is defined as "the specific application of yogic tools to address the individual physical, mental, and emotional needs" (n.d.). Because of the wide range of treatment options, a yoga therapist's training includes nutrition, anatomy and physiology, psychology, and a strong base in yoga philosophy. While yoga therapy originated as a treatment for physical issues and pain, it is widely accepted as a method for treating mental health issues. There is strong evidence of yoga therapy's ability to help decrease depression (Prathikanti et al., 2017); decrease parent-reported ADHD symptoms (Jensen & Kenny, 2004); improve attention, memory, and concentration (Ferreria-Vorkapic et al., 2015); increase self-esteem and empathy; inspire communication and socialization building (Goldberg, 2013); and act as self-regulation for the treatment of PTSD (Gard, Noggle, Park, Vago, & Wilson, 2014).

Yoga therapy is less about teaching and more about adapting yoga to help the client meet their needs and reach their goals. The aim is to fit the yoga process tools (described following) to the client, rather than fitting the client to the yoga philosophy, as is done in a yoga practice. In a yoga therapy session, there is a formal assessment of the client's inner and outer experience and needs, which guides the goals for yoga therapy treatment (Kepner et al., 2014). Goldberg (2013) describes that the process tools are adapted to fit the client's needs, using all of the senses as well as kinesthetic, visual, auditory, and tactile modes of implementation, which are then adapted to fit those goals (p. 16).

Types of Yoga Therapy

Two of the key components of the yoga philosophy are self-regulation and reappraisal. The simultaneous top-down and bottom-up processes of yoga therapy allow the client to process the changes in a more complete manner than linear talk therapy models. This is especially helpful for children's continually developing neurology. Participating in yoga therapy organically provides the supportive environment children need to heal.

The eight limbs of traditional yoga philosophy have been condensed down into four specific process tools used in therapy (Goldberg, 2013, p. 16). They are:

1. *Ethics:* the practice of self-reflection, self-discipline, nonviolence, truthfulness, and devotion
2. *Postures:* connecting the mind-body interface, building proprioception and interoception
3. *Breath regulation:* building down regulation and increased awareness skills
4. *Meditation:* practicing concentration, holding attention, and mental stillness

Uses for Yoga Therapy

Yoga therapy can be used in individual, small group, or school settings. Each of these methods of treatment allows for the therapist to assess and create a specific treatment plan for the goals set by the client. Goals for individual sessions include self-regulation, self-esteem, and the previously mentioned mental health issues. Breathing and meditation techniques taught and practiced here should be adapted to the child's developmental stage, accounting for attention and concentration tolerance. Goals for group settings include communication skills, socialization, and implementing self-regulation within the support system (i.e., school or family or peer groups) so that the skills learned in the session are more easily transferred out of the session (Goldberg, 2013, pp. 3–16). Yoga therapy can also be implemented during school or in physical education classes. These sessions may improve emotional regulation and empathy on the whole, teaching students to rely on their peer network for support and healthy connection (Noggle, Braun, & Khalsa, 2013).

When children learn to self-regulate through movement, meditation and breathing, they are empowered to moderate their own mood state, allowing them to build more stable connections and continue their development in healthy adaptive ways. When delivered in a therapeutic setting, children learn how to reframe their experiences without self-judgment and develop skills to more rapidly regulate from an activated state. These skills translate directly from the yoga therapy session into their daily life.

Dance/Movement Therapy

Dance and movement are natural actions to individuals and are used to express many functions and emotions. All around the world, dance and movement are used in our heritages, rituals, traditions, and celebrations (Payne, 2020). Dance/movement therapy is "a profession based upon the art of dance and augmented by psychological and physiological theories involving core human processes" (Chaiklin & Wengrower, 2016, p. 3). Levy (1988) discussed dance therapy as

> the use of dance/movement as a psychotherapeutic or healing tool, is rooted in the idea that the body and the mind are inseparable. Its basic premise is that body movement reflects inner emotional states and that changes in movement behavior can lead to changes in the psyche, thus promoting health and growth. Helping those individuals who are generally healthy as well as those who are emotionally or mentally disturbed, physically or mentally disabled to regain a sense of wholeness by experiencing the fundamental unity of body, mind, and spirit is the ultimate goal of dance therapy.
>
> (p. 1)

The American Dance Therapy Association (ADTA) defines dance/movement therapy as a therapeutic approach for promoting and encouraging social, emotional, cognitive, and physical incorporation and integration of the person (n.d.). Further, ADTA states that dance/movement therapy is

> focused on movement behavior as it emerges in the therapeutic relationship. Expressive, communicative, and adaptive behaviors are all considered for group and individual treatment. Body movement, as the core component of dance, simultaneously provides the means of assessment and the mode of intervention for dance/movement therapy.
>
> (para 2)

Dance/movement therapy's foundation is in the following four constructs: (a) movement is language; (b) mind, body, and spirit are interconnected; (c) movement can be functional, communicative, developmental, and expressive; and (d) movement is both an assessment tool and a primary mode of intervention (Welling, 2014, para 3). Gladding (2011) noted that movement and dance are important parts of counseling because they give individuals a chance to physically experience something as opposed to only discussing it, they involve the total person in counseling, and they can assist clients in understanding and processing what has been experienced in a more impactful way than they could with words alone.

Types of Dance/Movement Therapy

Interested counselors may look into training to become a Registered Dance/Movement Therapist (R-DMT) or a Board-Certified Dance/Movement Therapist (BC-DMT). The ADTA can guide you in the direction that is best for you. We also want to note that all counselors can use dance and movement techniques in counseling to assist growth and development of clients. Many dance/movement activities exist. We specifically like the ones outlined by Shaw and Benzio (2019) and think these can be helpful to use in counseling, as most don't require special athletic ability, they are free, and are easily accessible to clients depending on their ability status:

- *Travel:* In this dance/movement activity, individuals are asked to move around a room in any way that they choose based on a given prompt. Examples of prompts could include "Move around the room as if you were happy" or "Move around the room as if you were excited". Other prompts could explore deeper inner feelings such as "Move around the room as if you loved yourself" or "Move around the room as if you respected the person you are". Other prompts could be "Move around the room as if you just won a prize" or "Move around the room as if you feel bad about something you did".
- *Mirror:* This dance/movement activity offers individuals the chance to be observant of their own movements in large mirrors. As movement prompts are given, individuals can watch the responses from their own bodies in these large mirrors.
- *Mirroring:* In this dance/movement activity, individuals can mirror the responses of others, others can mirror or match the response of an individual (if in group setting or with more than one participant), or the clinician/leader can echo movements of the individual and vice versa. This can often allow a different reflection from another person who isn't the same as the mirror activity.
- *Life's journey:* In this dance/movement activity, the individual is asked to dance/move out their life's journey illustrating from the time they were born to their future. By using different movements, the individual paints this picture physically. Prompts could include "Dance or move in a way the illustrates your childhood" or "Dance or move in a way that portrays a picture of your adolescence" – moving to young adulthood, middle adulthood, today, tomorrow, the future; these prompts should be developmentally appropriate based on the age of the individual.
- *Simon says:* In this dance/movement activity, like the childhood game, by saying "Simon says", the individual copies movement of another participant or of the clinician/leader. This can allow an opportunity to focus on one brief simple movement at a time.
- *Movement metaphors:* In this dance/movement activity, metaphors or props are used to assist an individual in expressing a specific challenge, accomplishment, or issue. The individual can decide their own metaphor, or the clinician/leader can provide the individual with a specific metaphor to illustrate.

Uses for Dance/Movement Therapy

ADTA (n.d.) notes that dance/movement therapy is utilized in many settings such as mental health facilities, medical centers, educational settings, nursing homes and assisted living facilities, forensic settings, childcare centers, health and wellness programs, private practices and more. A recent meta-analysis reported results that propose that dance/movement therapy increases cognitive skills, increases interpersonal skills, increases quality of life, decreases anxiety, and decreases depression (Koch et al., 2019). Further, follow-up information reported that these factors remained the same or even slightly elevated 22 weeks after the intervention (Koch et al., 2019). Additionally, researchers Tarr, Launay, and Dunbar (2016) note that dance leads to increased pain thresholds and promotes social bonding and social closeness. Dance/movement therapy is useful for people of all ages and cultural backgrounds, and can be used in formats involving individuals, couples, groups, and family work (ADTA, n.d.).

Art Therapy

Art therapy developed at the junction of visual symbolism and psychotherapy. The earliest art was a healing agent in ancient society, and included carved idols, as well as sacred paintings and symbols. As psychotherapy developed, art was incorporated first as an activity and later as its own therapeutic intervention. It was recognized in the 1940s as a stand-alone therapeutic model (Edwards, 2014, p. 24).

Art therapy is defined by the American Art Therapy Association (AATA, 2017) as "an integrative mental health and human services profession that enriches the lives of individuals, families, and communities through active art-making, creative process, applied psychological theory, and human experience within a psychotherapeutic relationship" (para 1). It is facilitated by a trained art therapist, and supports both individuals and collective community goals.

Types of Art Therapy

Art therapy is easily adapted to fit within broader frameworks of psychotherapy, such as feminist theory, CBT, Jungian psychoanalysis, Gestalt, etc. (Hogan, 2016). In both of these methodologies, the same three elements are used: the art, the client, and the art therapist. This differentiates art therapy from general uses of art that may feel therapeutic (Edwards, 2014, p. 2). No matter the methodology, there are four elements of change unique to art therapy: materials, process, session structure, and power dynamics (Potash, 2019). Each are described as follows.

Materials can include any combination of books, boxes, clay, collage, craft, design, drawing, fiber arts, glass, masks and body casting, found objects and nature elements, paint, performance art, photography, stamping, puppets, video, and film. Some materials are experienced as easy or hard to control, hard or soft, malleable or permanent, shades or thickness of color, and small versus large motor movement. Different materials are used depending on the needs and goals of the client (Moon, 2010).

The process element of change describes the way the art is used in session, as a finished product, or the process as the therapeutic intervention. Depending on the theoretical background of the art therapist, the art is used as a different part of the intervention. These differences divide art therapy into two schools of practice: art as therapy or art psychotherapy (Moon, 2010). When art as therapy is used, the art therapist is focusing more on the final product, which is then processed, often verbally. For one client, the goal may be creating a work of art, a final piece, which expresses emotions that have been hard to express in words. In art psychotherapy, the art process of creating art is the focal point of the therapy setting. For example, an art therapist may have a client create a drawing with the non-dominant hand to explore the emotions and thoughts that arise as the challenge is experienced.

Session structure can vary, depending on the theoretical framework of the art therapist. On one end of the spectrum is a high level of structure and instruction, which can be helpful when working with groups or a community art product focus. This might include specific materials, timing, images, and processes to create together. The other end of the spectrum is very fluid and organic, allowing the client full choice over materials and outcome, with very little prompting by the art therapist.

Power dynamics, as described by Moon (2010), can be explored using different materials in several ways. The art therapist may encourage the client to learn mastery over materials or intentionally challenge the client to use unfamiliar materials. Other considerations for working through power dynamics include freedom of expression, sensory stimulation, and decision making during the art creation process. Each of these can support or challenge the client in different ways. (p. 7).

Kapitan (2012) talks about an additional change agent during art therapy: meditative and flow states. These naturally occur when we engage in any type of art making, and both have been linked to lower blood pressure, pulse rates, and respiration. She goes on to talk about the bottom-up processing that is natural to art therapy, where the experience, either product-oriented or process-oriented, makes way for meaning-making and change to happen internally, before the cognitive process happens.

For example, a client who struggles with initiation may need materials that give immediate results and are easy to control (pencil, crayon, marker). The process of creating art, not the product itself, is the therapeutic intervention, focusing on the client's beginning movements and choices. A high level of structure to begin with may feel supportive and encouraging to the client, so they feel safe enough to begin. Working the power dynamic could be done through having a freedom of expression through the end of the art process, once initiation has been achieved and a flow state has emerged. In simplistic terms, the session could look like a client drawing an image of a tree with a pencil. This becomes art therapy because of the interplay of the client's needs, the materials for creation, and the expertise of the art therapist in choosing the best materials, process, structure, and power dynamic for the client's therapeutic goals.

Uses for Art Therapy

The senses are fully engaged in art therapy, making it an ideal medium for working with children, adolescents, and especially those with developmental issues, particularly when verbal language is a barrier to healing. In analysis of outcome data, there is significant growth in the areas of self-concept, community collaboration, insight development, creative thinking, reading comprehension, social skills, anxiety, and depression (Reynolds, Nabors, & Quinlan, 2000). The AATA names hospitals, schools, veterans' clinics, private practice, rehabilitation facilities, community clinics, crisis centers, forensic institutions, and senior communities among the settings where art therapy is practiced. It is easily adapted to individuals, groups, or most notably, social change in communities.

Hogan (2016) talks specifically about art therapy's multifaceted nature. As it is able to hold multiple meanings at once, it allows the paradoxical nature of life to be fully expressed, examined, and interpreted, making art a flexible and fluid medium to explore the psyche. She emphasizes how important it is to create and manipulate images as well as destruct them, as that mimics human nature. This ability makes art a helpful window through which to see the self.

Drama Therapy

The North American Drama Therapy Association (NADTA, 2020a) defines drama therapy as:

> an active, experiential approach to facilitating change. Through storytelling, projective play, purposeful improvisation and performance, participants are invited to rehearse desired behaviors, practice being in a relationship, expand and find flexibility between life roles, and perform the change they wish to be an see in the world.
>
> (para 1)

Many factors exist to understanding drama therapy and the importance of this work with clients of all ages. Jones (1996) describes nine major factors that are integral to the therapeutic work in drama therapy. What follows is a much abbreviated description of those nine core processes used in drama therapy:

Dramatic projection: When individuals project characteristics of their experiences or themselves into acting or theatrical processes and are able to express inner struggles.

Therapeutic performance process: This refers to the process or structure of identifying a need to express a particular troubling issue or inner struggle.

Dramatheraputic empathy and distancing: The development of empathy and empathic responses to a particular situation or dramatic activity may be the essence of therapeutic work itself. Understanding and further developing empathy is important, and also being able to distance oneself so that critical thinking, reflection, and perspective taking can take place is also necessary.

Personification and impersonation: Through impersonation, an individual represents a person, issue, or feeling.

Interactive audience and witnessing: This act of witnessing, observing, or being the audience to self or to others is an important aspect of drama therapy.

Embodiment – dramatizing the body: This is understanding the ways in which the body itself relates to an individual and their identity.

Playing: A playful state is part of how an individual encounters and explores dramatic material.

Life-drama connection: This is the process describing how an individual role-plays or works through a specific inner struggle or life experience through drama.

Transformation: This refers to how real-life events and struggles are transformed into dramatic symbols or depictions of real events. Individuals are also transformed into different characteristics or roles.

Types of Drama Therapy

Many types of drama therapy exist. Snow (2009) discussed the two essential types of drama therapy as "(1) process oriented and (2) performance-based or focused" (p. 117). Further, Johnson and Emunah (2009) edited a text that has noted the many approaches to drama therapy (e.g., developmental transformation, narradrama, psychodrama) and have even detailed many types and companies providing drama therapy services and trainings (e.g., ENACT used in schools, STOP-GAP company that delivers programs to at-promise communities, and the Bergman Drama Therapy approach that has been used in prisons). GoodTherapy (2017) also notes that role-playing, puppetry, games, scripts, storytelling, and improvisation can be used in drama therapy.

Uses for Drama Therapy

According to the NADTA (2020b), many can benefit from drama therapy. This therapy is not just for children and adolescents but useful for individuals, groups, and couples across the lifespan. NADTA (2020b) notes that at-promise youth, individuals dealing with addiction, those with intellectual and developmental disabilities, those who are homeless, survivors of abuse and family issues, individuals serving time in prison, those with behavioral health concerns, individuals with autism, those struggling with disordered eating, individuals in foster care, and the general population can all benefit from drama therapy. Drama therapy can be used in individual work, couples work, group work, private practice, schools, mental health agencies and much more. NADTA notes the many community and mental health settings where drama therapists may work (Table 18.2):

Table 18.2 Community and Mental Health Settings Where Drama Therapists Work

Mental health clinics	Programs for refugees and immigrants
Schools	Shelters
Hospital medical units	Residential facilities
Hospital mental health units	Nursing homes
Substance abuse treatment centers	Private practice settings
Adult day treatment facilities	Corporations
Correctional facilities	Theaters
Community centers	Housing projects
Programs for persons with disabilities	Medical schools
Businesses	Training organizations

Complementary, Alternative, and Other Healing Modalities

Many complementary and alternative techniques exist for working with individuals in meaningful ways. As mentioned, there are entire books written on these topics. We have discussed a few in what follows, but please know that there are many more for you to become familiar with – this is not a comprehensive list.

Guided Imagery

Many different counseling theories use imagery (Gladding, 2011). Imagery can be a very powerful and effective technique for working with many populations including children and adolescents (Gladding, 2011). Hall, Hall, Stradling, and Young (2006) describe the experience of using guided imagery this way:

> Working with guided imagery, the counselor acts as a facilitator or guide and provides the client with an imagery theme to work with, for example, a journey up a mountain. The client describes aloud the internal images that spontaneously emerge. In the guiding role, the counselor may invite the client to imagine that they are elements in the imagery journey and even set up conversations between them.
>
> (p. 9)

Myrick and Myrick (1993, pp. 63–65) originally introduced five guidelines to consider when using guided imagery with children in a school setting. Gladding (2011) summarized these in his book on creative counseling. We have further adapted these as follows for use with children and adolescents (all-aged clients really) in multiple settings:

1. *Create a scripted story:* A script helps the counselor to select the right and developmentally appropriate words for an activity, depending on the age of the client, as well as to concentrate on creating a relaxed and safe mood.
2. *Set the mood:* Setting a mood consists of two parts. First is introducing the activity to the client. Second is helping clients find a comfortable and relaxed position for participating in the imagery activity.

3. *Speak softly and smoothly:* When the counselor speaks in a relaxed and calming manner, clients are able to concentrate on the imagery, not the counselor.
4. *Bring closure to the guided imagery experience:* This can be accomplished in a number of ways, such as posing a final question or simply informing students that the imagery activity is about to come to a close. It is a good idea to give clients an opportunity to end their process and not end abruptly.
5. *Discuss the experience:* If clients are to benefit from an imagery activity, they need to be able to share their experiences with others. A discussion of what occurred may be directed by the counseling asking specific questions, or it may take a more open-ended format by allowing the client to discuss the experience. The important point is that clients get to process and voice their thoughts and feelings.

Sample Activity

What follows is an example of a scripted guided imagery activity by Hall et al. (2006). This particular script could be used with clients of varying ages – making sure to shorten length if needed for younger children or larger groups – and to also chose developmentally appropriate words for your particular client or setting. The following is called "A walk along the seashore":

> Take two deep breaths and allow your body to relax. . . . Just let the tension go. . . . And now I want you to imagine you are on the seashore. . . . It doesn't have to be a place you know or have visited. It can be an imaginary place. . . . Take a look around you. . . . What can you see? . . . Is it a rocky beach or a sandy shoreline? . . . What is the sea like? . . . Is it rough or calm? . . . Are there other people around? . . . Become aware of the weather, hot or cold, rainy or dry. . . . Feel the temperature on your skin. . . . Is there any wind? . . . Now listen to the sound of the sea. . . . Are there any other sounds you can hear around you? . . . Notice the scents and smells of the sea. . . . Feel the surface you are sitting or standing on. . . . How do you feel about being here by the sea? . . . Now, in imagination, set off to look for a special shell. . . . Look along the shore or in rock pools. . . . As you look, none of the shells seem quite right . . . perhaps broken or dull. . . . Can you see other things in the pools? . . . Now, just along the shore you can see the sun glinting in a pool. . . . In the pool you will find your special shell. . . . Make your way toward it. . . . Pick it up and take a good look at it. . . . What is the shape like? . . . Is it colored or plain? . . . Feel the texture of the shell and inhale its aroma. How do you feel about holding your special shell? . . . [longer pause] Now put your shell somewhere safe and slowly walk away from the seashore. . . . Remember your shell will always be in that safe place if you want to go back and look at it again. . . . Now build up the sense that you are letting the images go and when it is right for you, breathe a little deeper and begin to come back to the room. . . . But don't rush from the sense of being relaxed.
>
> (p. 53–54)

This script is meant to be relaxing and bring forth feelings of calm. As with any guided imagery technique, there is a chance the script or focus could bring up undesirable feelings and this is, of course, important to process in a safe space.

There are many different scripts, videos, and audio recordings of guided imageries that can be used with children and adolescents. This is also a readily available resource that can be practiced for the client to use on their own and doesn't cost any money. This technique can incite relaxation and can also be used with mindfulness techniques (Chapter 17 of this volume).

Aromatherapy

Aromatherapy is defined as "the art and science of using plant oils for health, well-being, and medical treatment" (d'Angelo, 2002, p. 72). As with many complementary and alternative techniques, aromatherapy is often used in conjunction with another type of treatment. D'Angelo discussed that aromatherapy has been used with individuals experiencing ADHD symptoms and individuals with addictions, depression, and anxiety. Aromatherapy is used by either diffusing the essential oil or by placing a few drops on a cotton ball. It is important to get further training in the use of essential oils and aromatherapy to make sure you have all the necessary information for using such an approach. It is also important to check the safety of specific essential oils with every client. We recommend consulting with a certified aromatherapist, as some essential oils are toxic. We do not want to discourage use of complementary and alternative modalities, but we do want to highly recommend looking further into such complementary and alternative treatments.

Biofeedback

Biofeedback is said to be a holistic approach (including body and mind) and often assists the biological, genetic, and biochemical components to a client's concerns or issues (Moss, 2002). Studies have supported the therapeutic benefit for a range of both mental health and medical issues (Moss & Shaffer, 2017). The Mayo Clinic (2020) provides this definition:

> Biofeedback is a technique you can use to learn to control some of your body's functions, such as your heart rate. During biofeedback, you're connected to electrical sensors that help you receive information about your body. This feedback helps you make subtle changes in your body, such as relaxing certain muscles, to achieve the results you want, such as reducing pain. In essence, biofeedback gives you the ability to practice new ways to control your body, often to improve a health condition or physical performance.
>
> (para 1–2)

Biofeedback is used to help depression, anxiety disorders, issues with alcoholism and drug use (Moss, 2002), stress, ADHD (The Mayo Clinic, 2020), and more. For information on becoming certified, visit www. bcia.org.

EMDR

EMDR stands for eye movement desensitization and reprocessing therapy. EMDR is "a psychotherapy that enables people to heal from the symptoms and emotional distress that are the result of disturbing life experiences" (EMDR Institute, Inc., 2020, para 2). EMDR is an evidenced-based approach for working with children and adolescents (Gomez, 2013). In short, EMDR is an eight-phase psychotherapy treatment approach that originated in design to lessen the signs and symptoms present from trauma (CEBC, 2019). This treatment has been used with children, adolescents, and adults. The goals of EMDR are: (a) identify the previous events that caused the disturbance; (b) identify the present or existing situations that cause disturbance; (c) decide upon the instruction and skills necessary for upcoming functioning; (d) decrease individual distress; (e) increase and support positive beliefs; (f) discard negative physical responses; and (g) endorse and encourage knowledge and integration in order for trauma memory to become a basis of resilience (CEBC, 2019).

Summary

It is important to remember that many of these distinctions have their own education, training, certification, and registration processes (e.g., yoga therapist, registered drama therapist, licensed professional art therapist). If a practitioner is going to call themselves licensed or certified, one must go through proper training and credentialing. We do want to note that while this chapter was meant to give you a bit of information about certain distinctions, there is a difference between becoming a music therapist and using music as a creative technique in counseling. There is a difference between becoming a yoga therapist and using movement to enhance your work and counseling techniques, just as one does not need to be in a wilderness-based treatment program to use the outdoors in working with children and adolescents. Please keep in mind the distinctions in these relevant areas and also be flexible and creative in the work you do with children and adolescents. While many counselors will decide to go into further training areas and specific therapy distinctions, it is also necessary to learn that you can use techniques from adventure/wilderness/outdoor therapy, music work, yoga and movement, dance, art, drama, guided imagery, and many other complementary and alternative healing modalities to help children and adolescents in meaningful ways that move far beyond just talk therapy approaches.

This chapter presents some techniques that are not likely covered in other classes and are imperative to working with children and adolescents. Adventure/wilderness/outdoor therapy, music therapy, yoga therapy, dance/movement therapy, art therapy, and drama therapy were each discussed in a similar format. Each of those sections addressed an introduction to the specific type of therapy. The subsections noted different types of the respective therapy and multiple uses. Clients appropriate for this technique were mentioned. The final section in this chapter introduced some of the many complementary and alternative healing modalities. This subsection was a brief introduction of such modalities such as guided imagery, aromatherapy, biofeedback, and EMDR. We hope you look into more as there are wonderful techniques for using expressive and experiential techniques with children and adolescents.

Resources

American Music Therapy Association – www.musictherapy.org/
The International Association of Yoga Therapists – www.iayt.org/
American Dance Therapy Association – https://adta.org/how-to-become-a-dmt/
American Art Therapy Association – https://arttherapy.org/
Biofeedback Certification International Alliance – www. bcia.org
EMDR – www.emdr.com/

Clinician's Corner

How do you wrap up all the complexities of our emotional experience into the limitations of broad emotion words like sad, happy, angry, etc.? Conversational words can be limiting for all of us, especially in times where our emotions are high. Art opens wide the possibilities of authentic expression, and it happens at every stage of the process. From art material and color use selection . . . to the act of creating . . . to the reflections happening throughout the creation . . . to sharing of the product, every stage of art making creates opportunities for self-expression and exploration.

Art making in and of itself is therapeutic and supports an individual's well-being, healing, and growth. Making art within the context of art therapy, where an art therapist is present, creates opportunities to dive in deeper within the security and safety of a therapeutic safe space.

As an art therapist, my extensive training has provided me intuitive skills to witness the art-making process through the lens of mental health and also as a deep interpersonal journey, where the art making process and the art product becomes a third participant in the therapeutic relationship. The way that I approach it differs with each individual. With children, I find myself engaging play techniques to help support their imagination, where I can find myself being guided by the child to co-act out their artwork to explore beyond the two-dimensional or sometimes three-dimensional product. With adolescents, I find myself using art as a bridge to connect us when conversation feels too vulnerable or overwhelming. With adults, I find that art acts as a catalyst to re-engaging a sense of creativity that might have been pushed down many years before. Each art therapy session is unique and exciting to be a part of. The possibilities always seem endless and within reach when creativity is invited into the therapeutic space.

C. Alexis Decosimo, DrPH, ATR, LCMHCA
Executive Director and Founder of Playing to Live

References

American Art Therapy Association (AATA). (2017). *About art therapy*. Retrieved from https://art-therapy.org/about-art-therapy/

American Dance Therapy Association (ADTA). (n.d.). *General questions: What is dance/movement therapy?* Retrieved from https://adta.org/faqs/

American Music Therapy Association (AMTA). (2006). *Music therapy and young children*. Retrieved from www.musictherapy.org/assets/1/7/MT_Young_Children_2006.pdf

American Music Therapy Association. (2020). Retrieved from www.musictherapy.org/about/musictherapy/

Aspiro. (2020). *Wilderness therapy programs: A comprehensive guide for parents*. Retrieved from https://aspiroadventure.com/wilderness-therapy-programs/

Bettmann, J. E., Gillis, H. L., Speelman, E. A., Parry, K. J., & Case, J. M. (2016). A meta-analysis of wilderness therapy outcomes for private pay clients. *Journal of Child and Family Studies, 25*(9), 2659–2673. https://doi.org/10.1007/s10826-016-0439-0

Bodner, E., Iancu, J., Gilboa, A., Sarel, A., Mazor, A., & Amir, D. (2007). Finding words for emotions: The reactions of patients with major depressive disorder towards various musical excerpts. *Arts in Psychotherapy, 34*(2), 142–150. http://doi.org/10.1016/j.aip.2006.12.002

California Evidence-Based Clearinghouse for Child Welfare (CEBC). (2019). *Eye movement desensitization and reprocessing (EMDR) Trauma treatment – client-level interventions (child & adolescent)*. Retrieved from www.cebc4cw.org/program/eye-movement-desensitization-and-reprocessing/

Chaiklin, S., & Wengrower, H. (2016). *The art and science of dance/movement therapy: Life is dance*. Routledge.

Clem, J. M., Smith, T. E., & Richards, K. V. (2012). Effects of low-element challenge course on abstinence, self-efficacy and group cohesion. *Research on Social Work Practice, 22*(2), 151–158.

Conlon, C. M., Wilson, C. E., Gaffney, P., & Stoker, M. (2018). Wilderness therapy intervention with adolescents: Exploring the process of change. *Journal of Adventure Education and Outdoor Learning, 18*(4), 353–366. https://doi.org/10.1080/14729679.2018.1474118

d'Angelo, R. (2002). Aromatherapy. In S. Scott (Ed.), *Handbook of complementary and alternative therapies in mental health* (pp. 71–92). Academic Press.

Edwards, D. (2014). *Art therapy: Creative therapies in practice*. Sage.

EMDR Institute, Inc. (2020). *What is EMDR?* Retrieved from www.emdr.com/what-is-emdr/

Ferreira-Vorkapic, C., Feitoza, J. M., Marchioro, M., Simões, J., Kozasa, E., & Telles, S. (2015). Are there benefits from teaching yoga at schools? A systematic review of randomized control trials of yoga-based interventions. *Evidence-Based Complementary and Alternative Medicine, 2015*, 1–17. https://doi.org/10.1155/2015/345835

Field, T., Martinez, A., Nawrocki, T., Pickens, J., Fox, N. A., & Schanberg, S. (1998). Music shifts frontal EEG in depressed adolescents. *Adolescence, 33*(129), 109–116.

Gard, T., Noggle, J. J., Park, C. L., Vago, D. R., & Wilson, A. (2014). Potential self-regulatory mechanisms of yoga for psychological health. *Frontiers in Human Neuroscience, 8*. https://doi.org/10.3389/fnhum.2014.00770

Gass, M. A. (1993). *Adventure therapy: Therapeutic applications of adventure programming*. Dubuque, IA: Kendal/Hunt Publishing.

Gass, M. A., Russell, K. C., & Gillis, H. L. (2012). *Adventure therapy: Theory, research, and practice*. Retrieved from https://ebookcentral.proquest.com

Gladding, S. (2011). *The creative arts in counseling* (5th ed.). American Counseling Association.

Goldberg, L. (2013). *Yoga therapy for children with autism and special needs*. W.W. Norton & Company.

Gomez, A. M. (2013). *EMDR therapy and adjunct approaches with children: Complex Trauma, attachment, and dissociation*. Springer.

GoodTherapy. (2017). *Drama therapy*. Retrieved from www.goodtherapy.org/learn-about-therapy/types/drama-therapy

Hall, E., Hall, C., Stradling, P., & Young, D. (2006). *Guided imagery: Creative interventions in counselling and psychotherapy*. Sage.

Hogan, S. (2016). *Art therapy theories: A critical introduction*. Routledge.

International Association of Yoga Therapists. (n.d.). *What is Yoga Therapy?* Retrieved from https://yogatherapy.health/what-is-yoga-therapy/

Jensen, P. S., & Kenny, D. T. (2004). The effects of yoga on the attention and behavior of boys with attention-deficit/hyperactivity disorder (ADHD). *Journal of Attention Disorders, 7*(4), 205–216. http://doi.org/10.1177/108705470400700403

Johnson, D. R., & Emunah, R. (2009). *Current approaches in drama therapy* (2nd ed.). Charles C. Thomas, Publisher, Ltd.

Jones, P. (1996). *Drama as therapy: Theatre as living*. Routledge.

Kapitan, L. (2012). Does art therapy work? Identifying the active ingredients of art therapy efficacy. *Art Therapy, 29*(2), 48–49. http://doi.org/10.1080/07421656.2012.684292

Kepner, J., Devi, N. J., Le Page, J., Le Page, L., Kraftsow, G., & Lee, M. (2014). The differences between yoga teacher training and yoga therapist training and the distinction between yoga teaching and yoga therapy. *International Journal of Yoga Therapy, 24*(1), 7–21. https://doi.org/10.17761/ijyt.24.1.j763817j752215mj

Koch, S. C., Riege, R. F. F., Tisborn, K., Biondo, J., Martin, L., & Beelman, A. (2019). Effects of dance movement therapy and dance on health-related psychological outcomes. A Meta-analysis update. *Frontiers in Psychology*, 1–28.

Levy, F. (1988). *Dance movement therapy: a healing art*. VA: National Dance Association.

Lewis, S. F. (2013). Examining changes in substance use and conduct problems among treatment-seeking adolescents. *Child and Adolescent Mental Health, 18*(1), 33–38. https://doi.org/10.1111/j.1475-3588.2012.00657.x

Loewy, J., & Frisch-Hara, A. (2007, 2002). *Caring for the caregiver: The use of music and music therapy in grief and trauma*. Silver Spring, MD: American Music Therapy Association.

The Mayo Clinic. (2020). *Biofeedback*. Retrieved from www.mayoclinic.org/tests-procedures/biofeedback/about/pac-20384664

Montello, L. M., & Coons, E. E. (1998). Effect of active versus passive group music therapy on preadolescents with emotional, learning, and behavioral disorders. *Journal of Music Therapy, 35*, 49–67. http://doi.org/10.1093/jmt/35.1.49

Moon, C. H. (2010). *Materials and media in art therapy: Critical understandings of diverse artistic vocabularies*. Routledge.

Moss, D. (2002). Biofeedback. In S. Scott (Ed.), *Handbook of complementary and alternative therapies in mental health* (pp. 71–92). Academic Press.

Moss, D., & Shaffer, F. (2017). The application of heart rate variability biofeedback to medical and mental health disorders. *Biofeedback*, 45(1), 2–8. https://doi.org/10.5298/1081-5937-45.1.03

Myrick, R. D., & Myrick, L. S. (1993). Guided imagery: From mystical to practical. *Elementary School Guidance and Counseling*, 28, 62–70.

Noggle, J. J., Braun, T. D., & Khalsa, S. B. S. (2013). *Yoga during school may promote emotion regulation capacity in adolescents: a group randomized, controlled study.* Proceedings of the 3rd Symposium on Yoga Research of the International Association of Yoga Therapists. Newton, MA.

North American Drama Therapy Association (NADTA). (2020a). *What is drama therapy?* Retrieved from www.nadta.org/

North American Drama Therapy Association (NADTA). (2020b). *Who can benefit from drama therapy?* Retrieved from www.nadta.org/what-is-drama-therapy.html

Norton, C. L., Tucker, A., Russell, K. C., Bettmann, J. E., Gass, M. A., Gillis, H. L. "Lee," & Behrens, E. (2014). Adventure therapy with youth. *Journal of Experiential Education*, 37(1), 46–59. https://doi.org/10.1177/1053825913518895

Payne, H. (2020). *Creative dance and movement in groupwork* (2nd ed.). Routledge.

Potash, J. S. (Editor in Chief). (2019). Continuous acts of creativity: Art therapy principles of therapeutic change. *Art Therapy*, 36(4), 173–174. http://doi.org/10.1080/07421656.2019.1684159

Prathikanti, S., Rivera, R., Cochran, A., Tungol, J. G., Fayazmanesh, N., & Weinmann, E. (2017). Treating major depression with yoga: A prospective, randomized, controlled pilot trial. *Plos One*, 12(3). https://doi.org/10.1371/journal.pone.0173869

Reynolds, M. W., Nabors, L., & Quinlan, A. (2000). The effectiveness of art therapy: Does it work? *Art Therapy*, 17(3), 207–213. http://doi.org/10.1080/07421656.2000.10129706

Ross, S., Cidambi, I., Dermatis, H., Weinstein, J., Ziedonis, D., Roth, S., & Galanter, M. (2008). Music therapy: A novel motivational approach for dually diagnosed patients. *Journal of Addictive Diseases*, 27(1), 41–53. http://doi.org/10.1300/j069v27n01_05

Russell, K. C. (2008). Adolescent substance-use treatment: Service delivery, research on effectiveness, and emerging treatment alternatives. *Journal of Groups in Addiction & Recovery*, 2(2/4), 68–96.

Shaw, D., & Benzio, K. (2019). *Types of dance therapy.* Retrieved from www.honeylake.clinic/types-of-dance-therapy/

Snow, S. (2009). Ritual/theatre/therapy. In D. R. Johnson & R. Emunah (Eds.), *Current approaches in drama therapy* (2nd ed., pp. 115–144). Charles C. Thomas, Publisher, Ltd.

Tang, W., Yao, X., & Zheng, Z. (1994). Rehabilitative effect of music therapy for residual schizophrenia: A one-month randomised controlled trial in Shanghai. *British Journal of Psychiatry*, 165(24), 38–44. http://doi.org/10.1192/s0007125000292969

Tarr, B., Launay, J., & Dunbar, R. I. M. (2016). Silent disco: Dancing in synchrony leads to elevated pain thresholds and social closeness. *Evolution and human behavior*, 37(5), 343–349. https://doi.org/10.1016/j.evolhumbehav.2016.02.004

Therapy. (2017). *Yoga therapy.* Retrieved from www.goodtherapy.org/learn-about-therapy/types/yoga-therapy

Tucker, A. R., Javorski, S., Tracy, J., & Beale, B. (2013). The use of adventure therapy in community-based mental health: Decreases in problem severity among youth clients. *Child Youth Care Forum*, 42, 155–179.

Welling, A. (2014). *What is dance/movement therapy?* Retrieved from https://adta.org/2014/11/08/what-is-dancemovement-therapy/

Appendix
Empowering Our Youth Resource Guide

Counselors working with children and adolescents seek to empower and advocate for their clients in many ways. One way is by understanding that gender and gender identity is on a continuum. The following list of resources is dedicated to individuals who identify as girls or boys, and specific issues faced by these individuals. The list is broken down into issues facing boys and those facing girls. Statistically speaking, social construction on boys asks them to be tough and hide their feelings (which leads to multiple mental health concerns), and promotes violence. These issues contribute to many unpleasant feelings and can lead our boys in feeling invisible, devalued, and ignored if they don't succumb to these pressures telling them how to act, behave, and believe. Race and discrimination are also other issues facing boys today.

Statistically speaking, girls seem to struggle with pressures related to appearance, relational aggression, feelings of low self-worth, and also race discrimination. Girls are held to impossible standards which can lead to risky behaviors (eating disorders, self-injury) and/or suicidal ideation. Healthy eating and body image are struggles for both boys and girls. Research has supported an emphasis on girls, but we are starting to see a rise in how boys are impacted by this, as well. Counselors need to heed these implications in the work they do with boys, as well as with girls. Harassment is discussed, as well as the school-to-prison pipeline, examining what constitutes healthy relationships (romantic and friendships), violence, rape culture, and teaching of consent and respect. The following resources are intended to provide strengths-based perspectives and resilience, as protective factors are also addressed in detail. Counselors are a part of – or maybe the only protective factor for – children and adolescents.

Boys

Pressure to Be Tough and Not Acknowledge Feelings

The Miseducation of the American Boy www.theatlantic.com/magazine/archive/2020/01/the-miseducation-of-the-american-boy/603046/

How Boys Suffer: The Boy Code and Toxic Masculinity www.parentmap.com/article/how-boys-suffer-the-boy-code-and-toxic-masculinity

Randell, E., Jerdén, L., Öhman, A., Starrin, B., & Flacking, R. (2016). Tough, sensitive and sincere: how adolescent boys manage masculinities and emotions. *International Journal of Adolescence and Youth*, 21(4), 486–498. https://doi.org/10.1080/02673843.2015.1106414

Tough Guys Have Feelings Too www.amazon.com/Tough-Guys-Have-Feelings-Too/dp/1909263664 – children's book

Boys Do Cry: By 12 Men Who Did. Woke Up. And Redefined What It Means to Be a Man www.amazon.com/Boys-Do-Cry-Redefined-Means-ebook/dp/B07KHP84ZW

Act Tough and Hide Weakness: research reveals pressure young men are under https://theconversation.com/act-tough-and-hide-weakness-research-reveals-pressure-young-men-are-under-74898

Why We Should Help Boys Embrace All Their Feelings https://greatergood.berkeley.edu/article/item/why_we_should_help_boys_to_embrace_all_their_feelings

Violence

Harmful Masculinity and Violence: Understanding the Connection and Approaches to Prevention www.apa.org/pi/about/newsletter/2018/09/harmful-masculinity – includes a long list of additional resources at the end of the article

Boys and Girls Are Taught Different Things About Violence www.weforum.org/agenda/2018/01/boys-and-girls-are-taught-different-things-about-violence

Progressive Gender Beliefs, Teen Boys and Violence www.chp.edu/news/122719-miller-gender-attitude

Girls

Pressure on Appearance

Girls Feeling Pressure to Be "Sexy, Famous and Perfect" https://ct.counseling.org/2016/04/girls-feeling-pressure-to-be-sexy-famous-and-perfect/

Relentless Cultural Pressures for Today's Girls www.psychologytoday.com/us/blog/girls-women-and-wellness/201507/relentless-cultural-pressures-todays-girls

Relational Aggression

The Development of Relational Aggression: The Role of Media Exposure www.apa.org/science/about/psa/2013/07-08/relational-aggression

Boys and Girls

Race and Discrimination

The Impact of Racism on Child and Adolescent Health https://pediatrics.aappublications.org/content/144/2/e20191765

Talking to Kids About Discrimination www.apa.org/helpcenter/kids-discrimination

How Racism Harms Children www.health.harvard.edu/blog/how-racism-harms-children-2019091417788

Becoming Upended: Teaching and Learning about Race and Racism with Young Children and Their Families www.naeyc.org/resources/pubs/yc/may2018/teaching-learning-race-and-racism

60+ Resources for Talking to Kids About Racism https://bouncebackparenting.com/resources-for-talking-to-kids-about-race-and-racism/

How to Talk to Kids About Race: Books and Resources That Can Help www.readbrightly.com/how-to-talk-to-kids-about-race-books-and-resources-that-can-help/

Addressing Race and Trauma in the Classroom: A Resource for Educators www.schoolcounselor.org/asca/media/PDFs/FINAL-Race-and-Trauma-in-the-Classroom-Factsheet.pdf

338 *Appendix*

Healthy Eating

Healthy Eating: Centers for Disease Control and Prevention: Childhood Nutrition Facts www.cdc.gov/healthyschools/nutrition/facts.htm
Healthy Eating During Adolescence www.hopkinsmedicine.org/health/wellness-and-prevention/healthy-eating-during-adolescence

Body Image

Encouraging a Healthy Body Image https://kidshealth.org/en/parents/body-image.html
Body Image and Children www.webmd.com/parenting/building-healthy-body-image-for-children#1
How to Teach Children to Love Their Bodies https://health.usnews.com/wellness/for-parents/articles/2019-02-12/body-image-issues-affect-kids-too

Harassment

Talking to Our Children about Sexual Harassment and Consent www.plannedparenthood.org/planned-parenthood-massachusetts/local-training-education/parent-buzz-newsletter/parent-buzz-e-newsletters/talking-our-children-about-sexual-harassment-and-consent
Multiple Types of Harassment: Associations With Emotional Well-Being and Unhealthy Behaviors in Adolescents www.jahonline.org/article/S1054-139X(13)00742-8/pdf

School-to-Prison Pipeline

The School-to-Prison Pipeline, Explained www.justicepolicy.org/news/8775
School-to-Prison Pipeline www.aclu.org/issues/juvenile-justice/school-prison-pipeline
The School-to-Prison Pipeline www.tolerance.org/magazine/spring-2013/the-school-to-prison-pipeline
School-to-Prison Pipeline: A Curated Collection Of Links www.themarshallproject.org/records/67-school-to-prison-pipeline

Healthy Relationships

Healthy Relationships in Adolescence www.hhs.gov/ash/oah/adolescent-development/healthy-relationships/index.html

Violence

Children Exposed to Violence https://nij.ojp.gov/topics/articles/children-exposed-violence
Impact on Children and Youth www.childwelfare.gov/topics/systemwide/domviolence/impact/children-youth/
World Health Organization – *Violence against children* www.who.int/news-room/fact-sheets/detail/violence-against-children

Rape Culture

RAINN (Rape, Abuse and Incest National Network): Victims of Sexual Violence: Statistics www.rainn.org/statistics/victims-sexual-violence

NSRVC (National Sexual Violence Resource Center): Preventing Child Sexual Abuse Resources www.nsvrc.org/preventing-child-sexual-abuse-resources

Disrupting Rape Culture Through Education www.tolerance.org/magazine/disrupting-rape-culture-through-education

Teaching Consent and Respect

Consent at Every Age www.gse.harvard.edu/news/uk/18/12/consent-every-age

Let's Talk About Body Boundaries, Consent and Respect: Teach Children About Body Ownership, Respect, Feelings, Choices and Recognizing Bullying Behaviors www.amazon.com/Lets-About-Boundaries-Consent-Respect/dp/1925089185

6 Resources to Help Parents Talk to Kids About Consent www.nsvrc.org/blogs/how-parents-can-talk-their-kids-about-consent – resources for parents

Teaching Sexual Consent https://search.proquest.com/docview/2023683256?pq-origsite=gscholar

Teaching Consent to Elementary Students www.edutopia.org/article/teaching-consent-elementary-students

Index

Note: Page numbers in *italic* indicate a figure and page numbers in **bold** indicate a table on the corresponding page.

2017 National School Climate Survey 215

AAI *see* Adult Attachment Interview (AAI)
ability status 176–177
ableism 211
abreaction 261
accelerated psychological development 264
Acceptance and Commitment Therapy (ACT) 167, **171**, 296
access to unconscious 260
accommodation 55, **181**
achievement gap 154; closing 154–155; culturally responsive education, practices, and advocacy 155; and discipline gap 154
ACS (Approved Clinical Supervisor) 73
adaptive grieving 202–203; primary styles of *203*; strategies 202
ADHD *see* attention deficit/hyperactivity disorder (ADHD)
Adler, A. 94
Adlerian family therapy 94
Adlerian play therapy 264–265
Adlerian theory 44
Administration for Children and Families, Children's Bureau 150
adoptive and foster families, children and adolescents in 150; adoption 151; foster care system 150; implications and interventions 151–152
adrenal gland 127
adrenocorticotropic hormone (ACTH) 127
Adult Attachment Interview (AAI) 54
Adult Children of Alcoholics (ACOA) movement 149
adventure/wilderness/outdoor therapy 319; challenges of wilderness therapy **320**; defined 319; key elements 319; types of 319–320; uses for 320
adverse childhood experiences (ACEs): neurobiology of 133–134; serve and return 63–64
agencies and private practices, issues in 83

Ainsworth, M. D. S. 52–54
ALGBTIC Competencies for Counseling Transgender Clients 211, 227
ALGBTIC Competencies for Counseling with Lesbian, Gay, Bisexual, Queer, Questioning, Intersex, and Ally Individuals 227
ALGBTIC Standards of Care for Research with Participants Who Identify as LGBTQ+ 227
ALGBTIC Standards of Care in Assessment of Lesbian, Gay, Bisexual, Transgender, Gender Expansive, and Queer/Questioning (LGBTGEQ+) Persons 227
Allen, J. P., 60
ambiguous loss 201
American Academy of Child and Adolescent Psychiatry ((AACAP) 120
American Art Therapy Association (AATA) 326
American Association for Marriage and Family Therapy 74
American Association of Intellectual and Developmental Disabilities (AAIDD) 179; conceptual skills 179; IQ tests 179; practical skills 179; social skills 179
American Association on Health and Disability (AAHD) 179
American Counseling Association (ACA) 153; Code of Ethics 7, 70, 72–74, 76, 83, 219, 234; ethical codes 230
American Dance Therapy Association (ADTA) 324
American Music Therapy Association (AMTA) 321
American School Counseling Association (ASCA) 5, 73, 219, 230; Code of Ethics 76; ethical codes 230; ethical standards 219; Ethical Standards for School Counselors 106; *The Professional Counselor and LGBTQ Youth* 230; School Counselor Professional Standards and Competencies 106
Anderson, S. K. 70, 72
anticipatory grief 201

anxiety 166–167; ACT for 167; insecure attachment and 60
Armstrong, T. 183
aromatherapy 331
art therapy 326; art as therapy 326; art psychotherapy 326; defined 326; power dynamics 326–327; types of 326–327; uses for 327
asexual 211
Ashby, J. S. 265, 267
ASIST 173
assent 78
assimilation 55
Association for LGBT Issues in Counseling (ALGBTIC) 210–211
Association for Play Therapy 74, 257, 264
attachment 52, 262; during adolescence 59–60; avoidant infant 54; behavioral system 53; caregivers and 60–62; child development and 54–56; counseling interventions 62; developmental progression of 56–60; disorganized infant 54; during infancy and early childhood 57–58; during middle childhood 58–59; multicultural implications and advocacy 63; in parent-child relationship 61–62; resistant infant 54; secure infant 54
Attachment and Biobehavioral Catch-up (ABC) 62
attachment insecurity: adolescents 60; behaviors associated with 61; in parenting relationship 61
Attachment Parenting 119
attachment theory 52–54; attachment behavioral system 53; Bowlby's 57; caregiver attachment disruption 152; caregiving system 53; exploratory behavioral system 53; fear/wariness system 53; infant mental health 58; internal working models 53–54; measurement and classification of style or category 54; prototype *versus* revisionist models 53–54; sociable system 53; stability over time 53–54
attention deficit/hyperactivity disorder (ADHD) 174–176
auditory cortex 125–126
authoritarian parenting/caregiving 112
authoritative parenting/caregiving 112
autism 177
autonomic nervous system 126
autonomy 72
avoidant infant attachment 54
Axline, V. 266, 269

Baum, J. 221
Beauchamp, T. 70
Beck Depression Inventory (BDI) 167
behavioral grief responses 199
behavioral systems of attachment 53
beneficence 70–71; ABCDE guide 70–71; and non-maleficence 71–72

Berberet, H. M. 228–229
bibliotherapy 147
biofeedback 331
bisexual 211, 226
Blankenship, D. M. 187
blindness 179
Board-Certified Dance/Movement Therapist (BC-DMT) 324
bodily characteristics 211
body scan meditation 306
Boelen, P. A. 145
Bonifas, R. 311
Bonny Method of Guided Imagery and Music, The 322
Booth, P. B. 265
Boss, P. 201
Bowlby, J. 52–53, 57, 61–62
Bowlby's attachment theory 57
brain 123–124; cortical lobes 125–126; hemispheres 124–125; levels of functional governance 125; structure, systems, and functions of 123–126; systems for self-regulation 126
Broca's area 126
bubble breathing 305–306
Burghardt, G. M. 257
Byrd, R. 3, 16, 34, 52, 69, 93, 110, 123, 138, 165, 196, 210, 218, 226, 231, 236, 246, 257, 277, 293, 318

caregiving: attachment and 60–62; sensitive and responsive 60; system 53
catharsis 261
CDC *see* Centers for Disease Control and Prevention (CDC)
Center for Epidemiologic Studies Depression Scale (CES-D) 167
Centers for Disease Control and Prevention (CDC) 113–114, 227–228
central nervous system (CNS) 126
Chan, C. D. 235
Chawla, N. 169
child abuse, reporting 80–81
child advocacy centers (CACs) 142
Child and Adolescent Mindfulness Measure (CAMM) 303–304
Child-Centered Play Therapy (CCPT) 265–266
childhood trauma, axioms for neurobiology of: brain development, dependent 132; children's brains, malleable 130–131; critical periods of development for growth and harm 131–132; projective sympathy 132–133; trauma, verbally and chronological unstable 133
Child-Parent Relationship Therapy (CPRT) 62, 265, 272
children and adolescents, strategies for working with 20–25
Children's Program Kit 149
Childress, J. F. 70

Cinnamon Roll Sunday: A Childs Story of Anticipated Grief (Allen) 201
Circle of Security intervention (COS) 62
cisgender 211
Civil Rights Data Collection: Data Snapshot on College and Career Readiness 183
classism 211
Coaston, S. C. 10
codes of ethics 73–74; ACA 7, 70, 72–74, 219, 234; certification codes 74; specialization codes 73; state licensure codes 73–74
cognitive- and behavior-based perspectives 45
Cognitive Behavioral Therapy (CBT) 36, 149, **171**, **173**, 266
Cognitive Therapy (CT) 45
Collaborative Assessment and Management of Suicide protocol (CAMS) 173
Combs, G. 247–248, 248
coming out 211
common factors (CF) approach 35–36
complementary, alternative, and other healing modalities 329; aromatherapy 331; biofeedback 331; EMDR 331; guided imagery 329–330
complicated grief 201
confidentiality: importance of 76–77; maintaining 116–117; and privileged communication 77
consciousness 44
constructivist/postmodern perspectives 45–47
conversion therapy 216, 234–235
Coping When a Parent is Incarcerated (DeCarlo) 154
Corrigan, M. W. 174
cortisol 127
Council for Accreditation of Counseling and Related Education Programs (CACREP) 34
counseling: children and adolescents 5–6; interventions 62–63; minors 74; multicultural 20; relationship, benefits of 6; whole child 28
Counseling the Culturally Diverse (CCD) 30
counterconditioning fears 261
couples sandtray 285
CRAFFT 169
creative mindfulness 301
creative problem-solving 263
cross-cultural enterprise 249–250
cultural competency 30, 84, 120, 155
cultural dimensions 252–253
cultural humility 155
culture 252–254; on clinical decision making 187–188; shock 250–251
custody disputes, managing 79–80

Dalcroze Eurhythmics 322
dance/movement therapy 324; constructs 324; types of 324–325; uses for 325
Daniels, S. 182

Davidson, K. 6
Davis, T. E. 72
deaf-blindness 177
deafness 177
decision making: ethical 83; model for 83–86
delayed grief 202
Deliberate Self-Harm Inventory (DSHI) **171**
depression 167–168; risk factors for 167–168; screenings for 167; use of serotonin re-uptake inhibitors 167
Detlaff, A. J. 229, 233, 234
developmental disability 179
developmental progression of attachment 56–57; adolescence 59–60; infancy and early childhood 57–58; middle childhood 58–59
Dialectical Behavior Therapy (DBT) **171**, **173**, 296
dialogical mindfulness 300
Di Ciacco, J. A. 204, 206
dimensions of human experience 37–40; biology/genetics 38; cognition, affect, and behavior 38–39; environment 38; experience 38; relationships 37; socio-cultural milieu 37–38, *39*
Dinosaurs Divorce: A Guide for Changing Families (Brown & Brown) 147
direct and indirect teaching 260–261
directive sandtrays 283–284
disabilities: categories of 177–179; developmental 179–180; intellectual 179–180; physical 180
disenfranchised grief 202
disenfranchised loss 202
disorganized infant attachment 54
diversity 247, 249
divorce, parental 145; academic impact 146–147; counseling interventions 147; emotional impact 146; risk and resilience 145–146; social impact 146; statistics 145
Dozier, M. 62
drama therapy 327–328; core processes 328; defined 327; types of 328; uses for 328–329
Dreikurs, R. 96–97, 99
Drewes, A. A. 259–263
DSM (Diagnostic and Statistical Manual of Mental Disorders) diagnosis 45, 174
dual process model 203, *204*; loss-oriented coping 203; restoration-oriented coping 203
Dubois-Comtois, K. 60
duty to protect and warn 81–82
D Word: Divorce, The (Cook) 147
dyke 211
Dyregrov, A. 197
dysfunctional stances 98

Ecosystemic Play Therapy 266–267
educational neglect 140
Elementary and Secondary Education Act 181

emotional abuse *see* psychological maltreatment
emotional attunement . 95, 100
emotional disturbance 177–178
emotional dysregulation 170
Emotional Regulation Individual Therapy for Adolescents (ERITA) **171**
Empathic Counseling: Building Skills to Empower Change (Slattery & Park) 247
empathy 61, 253, 262–263; in attachment and caregiving 61; humanistic-existential perspectives 40–41; motivational interviewing 42; neural 254; neurobiology of 254; as play therapy 262–263
empowering children and adolescents 5
encouragement *vs.* praise 24–25
Enoch, M. A. 127
epinephrine 127
Epstein, J. L. 114
Erikson, E. H. 131
Erikson psychosocial developmental model 55–56, 130; Autonomy/Shame and Doubt stage 56; Ego Integrity/Despair stage 56; Generativity/Stagnation stage 56; Identity/Role Confusion stage 56; Industry/Inferiority stage 56; Initiative/Guilt stage 56; Intimacy/Isolation stage 56; Trust/Mistrust stage 55–56
ethical decision making 83
ethics 70
exceptional children and adolescents 176; ability status 176–177; categories of disabilities 177–179; intellectual and developmental disabilities 179–180; physical disabilities 180
experience-dependent plasticity 38
Experiences in Close Relationships Scale (ECR) 54
exploratory behavioral system 53
expressive and experiential techniques 27–28
Eye Movement Desensitization and Reprocessing (EMDR) 143–144, 331; auxiliary trainings 144; bilateral stimulation 144; goals of 331; phases 144; post-traumatic stress 144

fag/faggot 212
Family Action Council of Tennessee, Inc. 234
family counseling 25–26, 93–95; conducting assessment 96; counseling session using a genogram 100–106; home-based 106–107; implementing change 100; multicultural implications and advocacy 107; relationship forming 95; in school setting 106; shared meaning and goal setting 99; six lenses 96–98; stages 95–100
Family Educational Rights and Privacy Act (FERPA) 78, 83, 220
Far Apart, Close in Heart (Birtha) 154

fear/wariness system 53–54, 56, 58
Federal Child Abuse Prevention and Treatment Act (CAPTA) 139
Fetherling, D. 112
fidelity 72
fight or flight response 7, 133, 247, 248
Filial Therapy 62, 152, 265–266
First Amendment of the U.S. Constitution 220
forensic interviewers 142
Forester-Miller, H. 72
Fouad, N. A. 252
Franklin, J. C. 172
Freedman, J. 247, 248

Garcia, J. G. 84–86
Gardner's theory of multiple intelligences 183, **184–186**
Gaskin, R. L. 257
Gass, M. A. 319
gay 212, 227
Gay, Lesbian, and Straight Education Network (GLSEN) 211, 226; National School Climate Survey 232; recommendations for schools 216, 221, 230–232
Gay-Straight Alliances 232
gender 212
Gender and Sexuality Alliances (GSAs) 232
gender binary 212
gender expansive 214
gender expression 212
gender identity 212, 218–222
genderism 212
gender nonconforming or gender variant 212
Gender Spectrum 214, 218
genograms (McGoldrick) 95–96, 97, 100–106
Gestalt Play Therapy 267
gifted and talented education (GATE) programs 180
gifted children and adolescents 180–183
Gil, E. 268, 272
Gilligan, C. 247
grief 196, 197
grief and loss: adaptive grieving 202–203; ambiguous loss 201; anticipatory grief 201; complicated grief 201; definition of 197–198; delayed grief 202; disenfranchised grief 202; dual process model 203–204; multicultural implications and advocacy 205–206; primary loss 198; recognizing 198–200; secondary loss 198; somatic, intrapsychic, and behavioral responses 200; statistics 198; techniques 204; and trauma responses **199**; traumatic grief 202; types of 200–202; working with parents/caregivers 204–205
group counseling 154
group sandtray 284–285
guided imagery 329–330; guidelines 329–330; scripted 330

Guidelines for Psychological Practice with Transgender and Gender Nonconforming People 218–219
guiding principles 70–73

Hays, D. G. 187
Healing Days: A Guide for Kids Who Have Experienced Trauma (Straus & Bogade) 143
health impairment 178
Health Insurance Portability and Accountability Act (HIPAA) 78
hearing impairment 178
Help Your Dragon Cope with Trauma (Herman) 143
Herlihy, B. 69, 77, 81, 84–85
heterosexism 212
Hilt, L. M., 297, 302
Hogan, S. 327
home-based family counseling (HBFC) 106–107
homosexual 212
Hope Squad 172, **173**
hormone replacement therapy (HRT) 215
Hout, M. A. van den 145
humanistic-existential perspectives 40–42
human nature, beliefs about 17–20
human validation process model (Satir) 94–95
hypnosis 297
hypothalamic-pituitary-adrenal (HPA) axis 126–128; adrenal gland 127; hypothalamus 127; pituitary gland 127
hypothalamus 127

identity 212
IMH *see* infant mental health (IMH)
incarcerated parents/caregivers, children and adolescents with 152; advocacy 153–154; caregiver attachment disruption 152; social stigma and educational consequences 153; statistics 152
Index Person (IP) 96
individuals change 17–19; personal factors **19**; stages of change 17–18; therapist behaviors 18–19
Individuals with Disabilities Education Act (IDEA) 177, 179
infant mental health (IMH) 58
informed consent and assent 77–78
informed decisions 83–86
intellectual disability 178–180; criteria for 179; definition of 179
Intellectual Disability: Definition, Classification, and Systems of Supports 180
intelligence 55
internal working models (IWMs) 53–54, 53–56, 59
International Association of Yoga Therapists (IAYT) 322

International Society for the Study of Self-injury 170
intersectionality 248–249
intersex 213
interventions and techniques 25–28; expressive and experiential techniques 27–28; family counseling 25–26; mindfulness techniques 27; play therapy 26; sandtray therapy 26–27
intrapsychic grief responses 199
IWMs *see* internal working models (IWMs)

Jakeman (Ellis) 154
Joiner's Interpersonal Theory of Suicide (IPTS) 173
Jones, E. 61
Jones, P. 327
Jungian Analytical Play Therapy (JAPT) 267
justice 72

Kabat-Zinn, J. 296, 301
Kantamneni, N. 252
Kapitan, L. 327
Keller, H. 63
Kitano, M. 182
Kitchener, K. S. 70, 72
Kit for Parents 149
Kohlberg, L. 247
Kosciw, J. G. 230, 232
Kottman, T. 265, 267

Landreth, G. 258, 265–266, 269, 271, 273
Langer, E. 301
learning 55
legal advice, obtaining 74–76
legal and ethical implications: agencies and private practices, issues in 83; beneficence 70–71; child abuse, reporting 80–81; codes of ethics 73–74; confidentiality, importance of 76–77; confidentiality and privileged communication 77; counseling minors 74; custody disputes 79–80; duty to protect and warn 81–82; fidelity 72; informed consent and assent 77–78; informed decisions 83–86; justice 72; LGB children and adolescents 233–235; multicultural implications and advocacy 86; non-maleficence 71–72; obtaining legal advice 74–75; record keeping 78–79; rights of parents and guardians 75–76; school, issues in 82–83; subpoenas, responding to 80
Leilani 21
lens model: developmental lens 98; gender lens 98; internal family systems 96; multicultural lens 98; organizational lens 98; sequence lens 96
lesbian 213, 227
Levy, A. J. 259
LGB children and adolescents: advocacy 239–240; conversion therapy 234–235;

empowerment and encouragement 237–238; experience at home 231–232; experiences in school 229–231; intersecting identities 238–240; legal and ethical implications 233–235; safe community agencies 233; safe schools 232; in the United States 227–231; working with family members of 235–237
LGBTGEQIAP+ 12, 210, 214, 218, 226, 230–237
LGBTQ 213, 227
Lindaman, S. 265
linguistic therapy 94
loss-oriented coping 203
Lowenfeld, M. 278
Luke, C. 3, 16, 34, 36–37, 39–47, 52, 69, 93, 110, 123, 125–127, 138, 165, 196, 210, 226, 236–237, 246–247, 249, 252–254, 257, 277, 293, 318

MacLean, P. 125
Main, M. 54
Major Depressive Disorder 187
maltreatment: child 139; child advocacy centers 142; definition of 139–140; EMDR 143–145; NCANDS report 139–140; neglect 140; perpetrators 141–142; physical abuse 140; psychological 140; at risk 141; sexual abuse 141; strengths-based strategies for counselors 143; survivors of 142; TF-CBT 143–145; trauma-informed care 142–143; treatment modalities 143–145; types of child and adolescent 140–141
Marvin, R. S. 58, 62
Mascari, J. B. 281
McGoldrick, M. 98
medical neglect 140
meditation 295; *see also* body scan meditation; mindful eating meditation; mindful walking meditation; pebble meditation
memory systems 44
Mental Health & Substance Abuse Services, Dept 233
metaplasticity 131
mindful breathing 304–305
mindful eating meditation 307
mindfulness 295–296; benefits of 302–304; body scan meditation 306; bubble breathing 305–306; clinical applications 299; clinical practice 298–299; components 312; in counseling 298–302; counselor education 301–302; dialogical 300; five facet questionnaire 293–295; hypnosis and 297; Langer's approach to 301; mindful breathing 304–305; mindful eating meditation 307; mindful walking meditation 307–309; multicultural implications and advocacy 311–312; pebble meditation 309–310; self-evaluation of 293; supervision 299–301; techniques and practices 297–298; techniques in school setting 310–311; trait *versus* state mindfulness 296; types of practice 304–310
Mindfulness 311
mindfulness and relaxation techniques 147
Mindfulness-Based Cognitive Therapy (MBCT) 296
mindfulness-based role-play (MBRP) 300
Mindfulness-based Sex and Intimate Relationship (MSIR) protocol 296
Mindfulness-Based Stress Reduction (MBSR) 10, 296
mindfulness techniques 27
Mindful Schools 310–311
mindful walking meditation 307–309
mirror neurons 132, 254
Mississippi state Religious Liberty Accommodations Act (HB 1523) 234
moral development 263–264
moral reasoning 247
Morelli, G. 63
motivational interviewing 42–43; ambivalence and discrepancy 42; communicating empathy 42; evoking self-efficacy 43; rolling with resistance 42–43
MSJCC *see* Multicultural and Social Justice Counseling Competencies (MSJCC)
Multicultural and Social Justice Counseling Competencies (MSJCC) 155, 236, 239, 251–252, 254
multidimensional family therapy (MDFT) 149
multiple disabilities 178
Multisystemic Therapy for Child Abuse and Neglect 144
multi-tiered system of supports (MTSS) 168
music therapy 321; theoretical branches 322; transformational elements of 321; types of 321–322; uses for 322

Napoli, M. 311
narrative therapy 94
National Association for Children of Addiction 149
National Association for College Admission Counseling (NACAC) 5
National Association for Gifted Children (NAGC) 181
National Board for Certified Counselors (NBCC) 74
National Center for Transgender Equality (NCTE) 216, 220
National Child Abuse and Neglect Data System (NCANDS) 139–140
National Collegiate Athletic Association (NCAA) 215
National Dissemination Center for Children with Disabilities (NICHCY) 177
National Institute on Drug Abuse 168
National Institutes of Health 179

National School Climate Survey 229, 232
National Survey on LGBTQ Mental Health 234
NCC (National Certified Counselor) 73
Neff, K. D. 10
neglect 140; see also educational neglect; medical neglect
neural empathy 254
Neurologic Music Therapy 322
Neuroscience for Counselors and Therapists (Luke) 123
nonbinary 213
non-maleficence 71–72
non-suicidal self-injury (NSSI) 170, **171**
Nordoff-Robbins 322
norepinephrine 127
North American Drama Therapy Association (NADTA) 327
NSSI Assessment Tool (NSSI-AT) **171**
NTU psychotherapy 94

Oaklander, V. 267
object-relations family therapy 94
oppression 213
Orf-Schulwerk 322
organismic self-regulation 267
orthopedic impairment 178, 180

Packman, J. 268
pansexual 213
Parent, K. T. 202
parent-adolescent therapy 60
parent/caregiver relationship: in counseling 115–116; empowering and encouraging 117–119; engagement in agencies 115; engagement in schools 113–115; importance of 110–111; maintaining confidentiality 116–117; multicultural implications and advocacy 119–120; parenting styles 111–113
parent-child relationship 61, 265
parents and guardians, rights of 75–76
Parent's Guide (The Center for Motivation and Change) 168
parietal lobe 126
Park, C. L. 247–250, 254
Pataky, M. G. 202
Patient Health Questionnaire for Adolescents (PHQ-A) 167
pebble meditation 309–310
peripheral nervous system 126
permissive parents/caregivers 112
Perry, B. D. 257
person of color 213
person of counselor 20
physical abuse 140
physical disabilities 180, **181**
Piaget, J. 55
Piaget's cognitive developmental theory 55; concrete operational stage 55; formal operational stage 55; pre-operational stage 55; sensorimotor stage 55
Piechowski, M. M. 182
pituitary gland 127
Play in Family Therapy 272
playroom design 270; play materials 271; room characteristics and furniture 270–271
play therapy 26; Adlerian 264–265; child-centered 266; clients 268–269; cognitive behavioral 266; ecosystemic 266–267; filial therapy 265–266; Gestalt 267; Jungian Analytical 267; multicultural implications and advocacy 273; neuroscience and 259; play and 257–258; principles of 258; psychoanalytic 267; in school setting 272; therapeutic powers of 259–264; Theraplay® 265–266; travel kit supplies **273**; uses for 267–268; working with parents/caregivers in 271–272
Play Therapy Best Practices: Clinical, Professional, and Ethical Issues 74
play therapy skills 269; esteem building/pointing out strengths 270; fantasy/pretend play 270; limit setting 269; returning responsibility 269–270; structuring skills 269; tracking behaviors 269
Pollak, S. D. 297, 302
positive emotions 261
power of one 11–13
power struggles 23–24
Practicum in Counseling: A Developmental Guide (Woodside & Luke) 247
prefrontal cortex 126
primary loss 198
privileged communication 77
Professional Counselor and LGBTQ Youth, The 230
projective sympathy 132–133, 254
pronouns 213
Protecting Freedom of Conscience from Government Discrimination Act 234
prototype model 54
Psychoanalytic Play Therapy 267
psychoanalytic/psychodynamic perspectives 43–45
psychological maltreatment 140
psychotherapy 94

queer 213
questioning 213

racial disparities in schizophrenia 187
racism 213
Rational Emotive Behavior Therapy (REBT) 34, 45
reappraisal, as yoga therapy 323
Reardon, T. 115
reclaimed words 213–214
recognition reflex 99

record keeping 78–79
Registered Dance/Movement Therapist (R-DMT) 324
relapse 18
Relational Family Therapy 93
relaxation techniques 297
Remley, T. P. 69, 77, 81, 84–85
reparative therapy 216
Research Program for Self-Injury and Recovery 170
resiliency 263
resistant infant attachment 54
responsibility pie chart 147
restoration-oriented coping 203
revisionist model 53–54
Risky Sex Scale (RSS) 169
Roben, C. K. P. 62
Rogers, C. R. 253, 266
Rosenthal, M. 112
Rowland, A. S., 174
RPT-S (Registered Play Therapist Supervisor) 73
Ryan, C. 231, 235

Safran, J. D. 299–300
SAMHSA *see* Substance Abuse and Mental Health Services Administration (SAMHSA)
SAMHSA-HRSA Center for Integrated Health Solutions 168
SAMHSA's Bringing Recovery Supports to Scale Technical Assistance Center Strategy (BRSS TACS) 168
Samson, J. A. 134
sandtrays 278, 279; couples 285; directive 283–284; group 284–285; group counseling 287; supervision 285–286
sandtray therapy 26–27, 277–278; basic skills 281; case study 288–290; clients 280; couples 285; family 287; group 284–285; materials 278–279, **280**; multicultural implications and advocacy 290; process 284; in school setting 286–287; supervision 285–286; working with parents and caregivers in 287–288
Sarkar, S. 169
Satir, V. 94–95, 98, 107
Saving Normal: An Insider's Revolt Against Out-Of-Control Psychiatric Diagnosis, DSM-5, Big Pharma, and the Medicalization of Ordinary Life (Frances) 166
SBIRT program (Screening, Brief Intervention, and Referral for Treatment) 169
Schaefer, C. E. 259–265, 269
school, issues in 82–83
Schut, H. 203–204
Schwartz, R. C. 187
Scott, J. 6
Sears, R. W. 297–300
secondary loss 198
secure attachment and empathy 61
secure infant attachment 54

self-care 7–11
self-care assessment 8–10
self-compassion 7–11
self-esteem 264
self-expression 260
Self-Harm Behavior Questionnaire (SHBQ) **171**
self-injury 170; *see also* non-suicidal self-injury
Self-Injury and Recovery Resources (SIRR) 170, **171**
self-regulation 264; increases personal strengths 264; as music therapy 321; systems for 126; yoga therapy 323; *see also* organismic self-regulation
serotonin re-uptake Inhibitors (SSRIs) 167
sexism 214
sexual abuse 141
sexual behavior 169; assessment for 169; and substance abuse 169
Sexual Identity, Sex of Sexual Contacts, and Health-Risk Behaviors Among Students in Grades 9–12 227
sexual orientation 214
sexual orientation, gender identity and expression (SOGIE) 214, 233
sexual trafficking 141
Siegel, D. J. 124, 132
Signs of Suicide 172, **173**
Skovholt, T. M. 10
Slattery, J. M. 247–250, 254
Smith, E. J. 5
sociable system 53
social competence 262
Society for Sexual, Affectional, Intersex, and Gender Expansive Identities (SAIGE) 210
SOGIE *see* sexual orientation, gender identity and expression (SOGIE)
Solomon, J. 54
Solt, M. D. 268
solution-focused/solution-oriented brief therapy 94
solution-focused therapy (SFT)/counseling 47
somatic grief responses 199
Sommers-Flanagan, J. 116, 253
Sommers-Flanagan, R. 116, 253
Sorensen, J. 200, 204, 206
specific learning disability 178
speech or language impairment 178
SSP *see* Strange Situation Procedure (SSP)
stages of change *see* Transtheoretical Model
straight or heterosexual 214
Strange Situation Procedure (SSP) 54
strategic therapy 94
strengths-base counseling theory 4–5
strengths-based approach 4–5
stress: definition of 6–7; dimensions of *128–130*; distress and burnout 6–7; inoculation 261–262; management 262
Stroebe, M. S. 203–204
structural family therapy 94

Sturm, D. C. 300
subpoenas, responding to 80
Substance Abuse and Mental Health Services Administration (SAMHSA) 134, 142–143, 147–149, 168, 217, 231, 235
substance abuse and misuse 168–169; role of schools in preventing 168; screening 169
substance misuse, parents/caregivers with 147; counseling treatment modalities 149–150; impact on family unit 148–149; statistics 148
suicidal ideation 172; approaches to suicide prevention **173**; risk factors 172; safety planning 172–173
Suicide Attempt Self-Injury Interview (SASII) **171**
Suicide Prevention (CT-SP) **173**
Suicide Prevention Resource Center 172
supervision sandtray 285–286
survival: in community 125; and connection 125; of individual 125
Sylvia Rivera Law Project 221
symbolic-experiential therapy (Whitaker) 94
sympathetic-adrenal-medullary (SAM) axis 126–128
sympathetic nervous system (SNS) 126
sympathy 254

Tan, J. S. 60
Tarasoff v. Regents of University of California 82
Tarvydas, V. M. 84
Taylor, S. E. 247
Teicher, M. H. 134
temporal lobes 125
tend-and-befriend response 7, 247, 248
Tennessee state House Bill 233
Terrible Thing Happened, A (Holmes) 143
Thapar v. Zezulka 82
theories 34, 36–37; applications of 47, 48; common factors approach 35–36; dimensions of human experience 37–40; multicultural implications and advocacy 47; *see also* Adlerian theory; Cognitive Behavioral Therapy (CBT); Gestalt play therapy; Rational Emotive Behavior Therapy (REBT); solution-focused therapy (SFT)/counseling
therapeutic powers of play 259–260; enhances social relationships 262–263; facilitates communication 260–261; fosters emotional wellness 261–262; increases personal strengths 263–264
therapeutic relationships 262
therapeutic silence 23
Theraplay® 265–266, 272
Title IX (Education Amendments Act of 1972) 220
Tough Kids, Cool Counseling (Sommers-Flanagan) 116
trait *versus* state mindfulness 296
tranny 214

transactional analysis 45
Transcultural Integrative Model 84–86
transgender 214
transgender and gender-expansive (TGE) children and adolescents 210, 214–215; athletes 215; community considerations 221–222; counseling implications 217–218; experiences at home 216; experiences in school 215–216; legal and ethical implications 219–220; other concerns 216–217; in the United States 214–217; working with parents/caregivers of 220–221; working with schools 221
Transtheoretical Model 17
Trauma-Focused Cognitive Behavioral Therapy (TF-CBT) 143–144; certification 143; phases 143
trauma in childhood and adolescence: axioms for neurobiology of 130–133; case of Jemma 128; multicultural implications and advocacy 134
trauma-informed care 142–143
traumatic brain injury 178
traumatic grief 202
Treatment for Self-Injurious Behaviors (T-SIB) **171**
Trevor Project 216, 231, 234
Twenge, J. M. 5
Two Homes (Masurel) 147

unconscious 260
uninvolved parenting/caregiving 112–113
U.S. Census Bureau 177
U.S. Department of Education 113, 220
U.S. Department of Education Office for Civil Rights 180, 183
U.S. Department of Health and Human Services 80, 150
U.S. Department of Justice 220
U.S. Transgender Survey (USTS) 215–216
"use it or lose it" principle of neuroplasticity 131

Video-based Intervention to Promote Positive Parenting (VIPP) 62
Visiting Day (Woodson) 154
visual impairment 179

Webber, J. M. 281
wellness 28
wellness-based approach 28
wellness wheel 28–30
Wernicke's area 126
Whole Family Therapy (WFT) 93
wilderness therapy 319–320
WISQARS Leading Cause of Death Reports 227
Woodside, M. 252–254

yoga therapy 322–323; defined 322; process tools 323; types of 323; uses for 323–324

Zeanah, C. H. 62